Tokyo

timeout.com/tokyo

Time Out Guides Ltd

Universal House
251 Tottenham Court Road
London W1T 7AB
United Kingdom
Tel: +44 (0)20 7813 3000
Fax: +44 (0)20 7813 6001
Email: guides@timeout.com
www.timeout.com

Published by Time Out Guides Ltd, a wholly owned subsidiary of Time Out Group Ltd.
Time Out and the Time Out logo are trademarks of Time Out Group Ltd.

10 9 8 7 6 5 4 3 2 1

This edition first published in Great Britain in 2010 by Ebury Publishing.
A Random House Group Company
20 Vauxhall Bridge Road, London SW1V 2SA

Random House Australia Pty Ltd 20 Alfred Street, Milsons Point, Sydney, New South Wales 2061, Australia

Random House New Zealand Ltd 18 Poland Road, Glenfield, Auckland 10, New Zealand

Random House South Africa (Pty) Ltd Isle of Houghton, Corner Boundary Road & Carse O'Gowrie, Houghton 2198, South Africa

Random House UK Limited Reg. No. 954009

Distributed in the US and Latin America by Publishers Group West (1-510-809-3700)
Distributed in Canada by Publishers Group Canada (1-800-747-8147)

For further distribution details, see www.timeout.com.

ISBN: 978-1-84670-121-4

A CIP catalogue record for this book is available from the British Library.

Printed and bound by Firmengruppe APPL, aprinta druck, Wemding, Germany.

The Random House Group Limited supports The Forest Stewardship Council (FSC), the leading international forest certification organisation. All our titles that are printed on Greenpeace approved FSC certified paper carry the FSC logo. Our paper procurement policy can be found at http://www.rbooks.co.uk/environment.

Time Out carbon-offsets its flights with Trees for Cities (www.treesforcities.org).

Contents

Introduction	**4**
Map: Central Tokyo	**12**

In Context **17**

History	**18**
Tokyo Today	**30**
Architecture	**34**
Otaku	**39**

Sights **43**

Asakusa	**44**
Map: Asakusa	**45**
Ebisu & Daikanyama	**52**
Map: Meguro	**53**
Ginza	**56**
Map: Ginza	**59**
Harajuku & Aoyama	**62**
Map: Harajuku & Aoyama	**65**
Ikebukuro	**68**
Map: Ikebukuro	**69**
Marunouchi	**74**
Map: Marunouchi	**77**
Odaiba	**81**
Map: Odaiba	**83**
Roppongi	**85**
Map: Roppongi	**87**
Shibuya	**91**
Map: Shibuya	**93**
Shinjuku	**98**
Map: Shinjuku	**101**
Ueno	**105**
Map: Ueno & Yanaka	**107**
Yanaka	**111**
Further Afield	**114**

Consume **121**

Hotels	**122**
Restaurants	**143**
Bars	**176**
Coffee Shops	**187**
Shops & Services	**192**

Arts & Entertainment **219**

Calendar	**220**
Children	**227**
Film	**232**
Galleries	**237**
Gay & Lesbian	**243**
Music	**250**
Nightlife	**262**
Performing Arts	**269**
Sport & Fitness	**276**

Escapes & Excursions **285**

Yokohama	**286**
Hakone	**292**
Map: Hakone	**293**
Kamakura	**295**
Nikko	**300**
Easy Day Trips	**303**

Directory **307**

Getting Around	**308**
Resources A-Z	**311**
Further Reference	**319**
Vocabulary	**321**
Index	**324**

Maps **331**

Japan	**332**
Trips Out of Town	**333**
Tokyo Subway	**334**
Yamanote Line Connections	**336**

Introduction

Tokyo bristles with superlatives. It's the most populated, most efficient and most courteous city on earth. It has the most Michelin stars and the safest streets and has regained its title as most expensive city. It is also, in many ways, the least organised, with nothing that resembles town planning, and none of the architectural coherence of Paris, Rome or New York. Ironically for a city so famous for conformity and social order, Tokyo's builders seem determined to make each structure stand out. Relaxed planning laws and a raze-and-rebuild culture help keep things visually interesting.

Socially, of course, conformity still rules, which means that the chronic congestion that can derail other cities doesn't end in crime or violence here. You can carry all the cash you like, safe in the knowledge that not only are muggings virtually unheard of, but if you drop a purse or wallet here, someone will chase after you to hand it back.

The first time you set foot in the major commercial hubs of Ginza, Roppongi, Shibuya or Shinjuku, you'll be wide-eyed and overwhelmed. Bright signs and advertisements fill your vision; huge LCD screens blast a cacophony in your ears. But there are also oases of high culture and Zen-like calm, often just a few steps from the chaos. In Shinjuku, you'll find temples, department stores and brothels as neighbours. In Roppongi, luxury hotels, strip joints and art museums are packed together. In Harajuku, the city's largest Shinto shrine is just a couple of blocks from the trendiest boutiques.

Tokyo excels in unlikely juxtapositions, and that's just part of the fun. You'd need decades to understand this city, but you'll enjoy it the minute you arrive. *Nicholas Coldicott, Editor*

Tokyo in Brief

IN CONTEXT

To understand Tokyo you have to dig a little into Japan's brutal history of warrior monks, feudal lords, samurai and shogun; we spotlight the key events that led to the rise of the megalopolis. We also consider facets of contemporary Tokyo, from the standout architecture of a city that boasts work by the likes of Ando, Tange, SANAA and Kurokawa to the curious phenomenon known as *otaku*.
▶ *For more, see pp17-42.*

SIGHTS

At first glance, there don't appear to be many sights to see in Tokyo. The city's relentless development means it is constantly erasing its past. Nevertheless, there are three giant attractions – one temple, one shrine and the world's biggest fish market – and the last decade has brought a string of contemporary art museums. The sights are indeed there – you just have to look a little harder to find them.
▶ *For more, see pp43-120.*

CONSUME

Tokyo is the dining capital of the world. Beyond the record haul of Michelin stars, this is a city in which a ramen or yakitori restaurant can draw a two-hour queue, because the obsession with quality and seasonality reaches every nook and cranny. This is also a big drinking city: beer is big favourite, but whisky and *shochu* have both been surging in recent years, and Tokyo's cocktail bars are legendary.
▶ *For more, see pp121-218.*

ARTS & ENTERTAINMENT

The classic performing arts will always be the big draw. *Kabuki, Noh, bunraku* and *takarazuka* may be linguistically impenetrable, but it doesn't matter: they're spectacles that anyone with half an interest in Japanese culture should see. For contemporary music fans, there's a strong live scene for every genre; for clubbers, there's enough to keep you occupied – and it's getting ever better.
▶ *For more, see pp219-284.*

ESCAPES & EXCURSIONS

Tokyo is surrounded by a wealth of scenic getaways. Escape the frenzied metropolis with a trip to historic Kamakura, Nikko or Kawagoe, or head to Hakone for some scenic recuperation. There's also Japan's second city, Yokohama, on your doorstep, and the nation's iconic mountain is just a short ride away, ready for intrepid climbers.
▶ *For more, see pp285-306.*

Tokyo in 48 Hours

Day 1 A Taste of Old Tokyo

8AM Start the day in old-world **Asakusa**. Pass through the **Kaminarimon** gate and dodge past Nakamise Dori's souvenir and snack stalls to reach the city's most popular temple, **Asakusa Kannon** (*see p49*). A few blocks west is **Kappabashi Dori** (*see p199*), the kitchenware wholesale street.

11AM Head back to Asakusa station, stopping at the kiosk outside **Kamiya Bar** (*see p176*) for a bottle of their famous Denki Bran. Then take the metro to **Ueno** and begin with a stroll down **Ameyoko market** (*see p199*) jammed with around 500 stalls.

NOON On the edge of Ueno Park, **Ikenohata Yabu Soba** (*see p169*) offers a quality old-school soba lunch from ¥600. Inside Ueno Park, the **Toshogu Shrine** (*see p110*) and the **Tokyo National Museum** (*see p110*) both ooze history. From there, it's just a short walk to the sedate, low-rise district of **Yanaka**, where you'll find a horde of temples and **SCAI** (*see p241*), a classic bathhouse that now operates as a contemporary art gallery.

3.30PM Take the Yamanote line from Ueno to Komagome to visit **Rikugien** (*see p120*), the city's most impressive landscape garden, built around 300 years ago.

6PM For dinner, head to **Shinjuku**. **Tsunahachi** (*see p167*) offers decent tempura in an atmospheric old-time setting. Braver diners might like to try the tiny wooden eateries of **Omoide Yokocho**, beside the station (*see p167* **Inside Track**).

7PM Wander through Shinjuku, via **Kabukicho** if you want to see the city at its seamiest, or along **Yasukuni Dori** if you don't. The alleyways of **Golden Gai** (*see p185*) began in the post-war years as a place catering to all sorts of illicit trades, but has developed into Tokyo's most enchanting drinking district. Try **Albatross G** (*see p185*) or **La Jetée** (*see p185*).

NAVIGATING THE CITY

Tokyo isn't a walking city. The city's sights are spread wide apart, with vast tracts of grey city in between. The good news is that the transport system's reputation for efficiency is well founded. Japan Railways' Yamanote line is the best way to orientate yourself. It connects many of the city's major districts, including Shinjuku, Shibuya, Ikebukuro, Harajuku and Ueno. The other areas are a quick metro ride from one of the big Yamanote line hubs.

Most stations have bilingual signs and rail maps, but the metro has also idiot-proofed its routes by colour-coding its lines and numbering stations. Hiroo station, for example, is the third stop on the Hibiya line, and thus is marked on maps as H-3. For more about public transportation, see p308.

If you're used to house numbers and street names, Tokyo's address system will seem bewildering at first, but once you understand the system, it's not hard to use. In most instances, the three hyphenated numbers and the following district name is all you'll need. The first number denotes the *chome*, a large area

Day 2 From Fish to Fashion

4.30AM With luck, jet lag will wake you up for the trip to the famous **Tsukiji Market** (*see p61* **Something Fishy**). Watch the frantic and incomprehensible tuna auction, then browse the outer market with its piles of seafood, some of it familiar, much of it not. Finish with breakfast at **Sushi Bun** (*see p153*), then head back to the hotel to catch up on some sleep.

11AM Begin the day proper at **Tokyo Midtown** (*see p86*) in **Roppongi**. Look for **21_21 Design Sight** (*see p88*) in the garden; Issey Miyake's modern design museum is always a good bet for some inspiration. There's no shortage of lunch options in Midtown, and the long queues outside some will direct you to the favourites, but if the weather is decent, head to the gourmet basement and grab a bento or burger to eat on the Midtown lawn.

2PM Time for a trip to fashion-obsessed **Harajuku**. After a quick detour to take in the awe-inspiring **Meiji Shrine** (*see p67*), walk down Omotesando, stopping at **Oriental Bazaar** (*see p214*) if you need to shop for souvenirs, or explore the side streets to your left if you're on the lookout for fashion.

7PM If your budget stretches far enough, head back to Roppongi and **Nihonryori Ryugin** (*see p162*) for Seiji Yamamoto's cutting-edge Japanese cuisine. For something a little cheaper, try **Gonpachi** (*see p161*) instead.

9PM After dinner, head to **Roppongi Hills** and the **Mori Tower**. On the 52nd floor you'll find the entrance to the **Mori Art Museum** (*see p88*). After viewing the exhibition, head to **Mado Lounge** (*see p183*) for a nightcap with a spectacular view. (Malt lovers might prefer instead to visit the nearby **Cask** (*see p181*), with its unrivalled collection of Scotches.)

---

of several blocks. The second number denotes the block, and the third number is for the building. For a more detailed explanation of Tokyo addresses, see p311.

SEEING THE SIGHTS

The general rules for visiting museums and galleries are as follows: many are closed on Monday, entrance fees are paid in cash, ID is required for discount admission, admission ends 30 minutes before the museum closes, lockers are free (with a refundable key deposit of ¥100), photography is forbidden, and there is little

disabled access. Many museums open on national holidays and close the following day. Nearly all museums close over the New Year's holiday (28 Dec-4 Jan).

PACKAGE DEALS

Museum-hoppers should purchase a **Grutt Pass** (pronounced 'gu-roo-to' in Japanese), which offers free or reduced admission to over 50 of the city's bigger attractions. Costing ¥2,000, it's valid for two months and is available from major ticket outlets, some convenience stores and participating museums.

The travel apps city lovers have been waiting for...

Apps and maps work offline with no roaming charges

Search for 'Time Out Guides' in the app store

timeout.com/iphonecityguides

Whatever your carbon footprint, we can reduce it

For over a decade we've been leading the way in carbon offsetting and carbon management.

In that time we've purchased carbon credits from over 200 projects spread across 6 continents. We work with over 300 major commercial clients and thousands of small and medium sized businesses, which rely upon our market-leading quality assurance programme, our experience and absolute commitment to deliver the right solution for each client.

Why not give us a call?

T: London (020) 7833 6000

Tokyo in Profile

ASAKUSA
This is Tokyo as it used to be – and how many wish it still was. It's low-rise, slow-paced and you'll find it easier to buy rice crackers than digital cameras here. Asakusa is where you'll find the city's favourite temple, **Asakusa Kannon**, and it's at the top of most tourist itineraries, and with good reason.
▶ *For more, see pp44-51.*

EBISU & DAIKANYAMA
Perhaps because **Ebisu** was built by a brewer, it's an area synonymous with eating and drinking: from a mock chateau housing two Joël Robuchon restaurants to simple yakitori joints. In **Ebisu Garden Place** it has one of the earliest of Tokyo's shopping, dining and entertainment complexes. **Daikanyama** is heaven for twentysomething women – spacious, slower-paced and packed with indie fashion boutiques and cafés.
▶ *For more, see pp52-55.*

GINZA
The district that became a brand name. A Ginza address says you're a big shot in shopping, dining or drinking – and have prices to match. But in recent years, more affordable brands have also set up shop here; there's now cheap and cheerful dining side-by-side with the wallet-busting restaurants.
▶ *For more, see pp56-61.*

HARAJUKU & AOYAMA
Two adjacent fashion districts: **Harajuku** is best for backstreets filled with up-and-coming brands and second-hand shops, while **Aoyama** is home to flashier flagship stores. Harajuku is home to the **Meiji Jingu Shrine** and lively **Yoyogi Park**, while Aoyama has its own cultural retreat in the form of the **Nezu Museum**.
▶ *For more, see pp62-67.*

IKEBUKURO
It's one of the capital's major transport hubs and one of its biggest sub-centres, but most Tokyoites see Ikebukuro as no more than a cut-price Shinjuku. If you're looking for superlatives, you won't find many here, but you will find a bustling district with an earthy charm and plenty of affordable eats.
▶ *For more, see pp70-73.*

MARUNOUCHI
The high-rise mini malls and big-brand boulevard of **Naka Dori** now define the city's business district as much as the banks. Marunouchi is home to the **Imperial Palace**, and an impressive selection of museums, including the **National Museum of Modern Art** and the new **Mitsubishi Ichigokan Museum**.
▶ *For more, see pp74-80.*

ODAIBA

A stub of reclaimed land in Tokyo Bay, Odaiba feels clean, spacious and artificial, but the view across the water has made it a popular dating spot for young couples. Though its future is uncertain as leases expire, the district is currently home to a towering Ferris wheel and an Italianate outlet mall.
► *For more, see pp81-84.*

ROPPONGI

You get two cities for the price of one with Roppongi. The party scene that developed in the post-war years shows no signs of slowing down, even as fancy commercial complexes and top-end hotels move in. Pick and mix to your taste from world-class art museums, raucous rock bars, fine dining and strip clubs.
► *For more, see pp85-90.*

SHIBUYA

Affordable fashion, stellar nightlife and down-to-earth dining have made Shibuya the district of choice for Tokyo youths. The world's busiest pedestrian crossing leads to blocks and blocks of low-price, low-brow retail and entertainment. It's a prime spot for people-watching, as are the **109** fashion tower and **Center Gai**, the pedestrian street that's thronged with teen trendsetters.
► *For more, see pp91-97.*

SHINJUKU

Shinjuku is technically a city in its own right, and it certainly has everything you could ask for in a municipality. The shops are many and varied; the nightlife includes the ramshackle **Golden Gai** drinking district, the seamy **Kabukicho** and the gay heartland of **Ni-chome**; the scenery ranges from boulevards of neon to picturesque **Shinjuku Gyoen** park. It's always rammed, always on and always fun.
► *For more, see pp98-104.*

UENO

Ueno Park is home to some major cultural highlights, including the photogenic **Toshogu Shrine** and the mammoth **Tokyo National Museum**, Japan's oldest and largest museum. Shinobazu Pond is especially attractive in summer when the pink lotuses form a blanket across the water. Outside the park, **Ameyoko** is a street market crammed with stalls piled high with cheap food and clothing.
► *For more, see pp105-110.*

YANAKA

Modern life seems to have completely missed **Yanaka**. The buildings are traditional in design, and the businesses haven't changed in decades. It's known as a temple district, though not of the landmark, tourist-checklist kind. Along with the neighbouring areas of **Nezu** and **Sendagi**, it's where you go when you want to escape the world's most populous metropolis.
► *For more, see pp111-113.*

Central Tokyo

ITABASHI-KU

TOSHIMA-KU

Seibu - Ikebukuro Line

Ikebukuro

See p69

BUNKYO-KU

Yanaka

Ueno Park

Ueno

See p107

Seibu Shinjuku Line

Chuo Line

NAKANO-KU

SHINJUKU-KU

See p77

Shinjuku

See p101

Shinjuku Gyoen

Yotsuya

CHIYODA-KU

Imperial Palace

Marunouchi

Yoyogi

SHIBUYA-KU

Yoyogi Park

See p65

Harajuku

Aoyama

See p87

Ginza

See p59

Shibuya

See p93

Roppongi

Tokyo Tower

MINATO-KU

Rainbow Bridge

Daikanyama

Naka-Meguro

Tokyu Toyoko Line

See p53

MEGURO-KU

Meguro

Tokaido Line

SHINAGAWA-KU

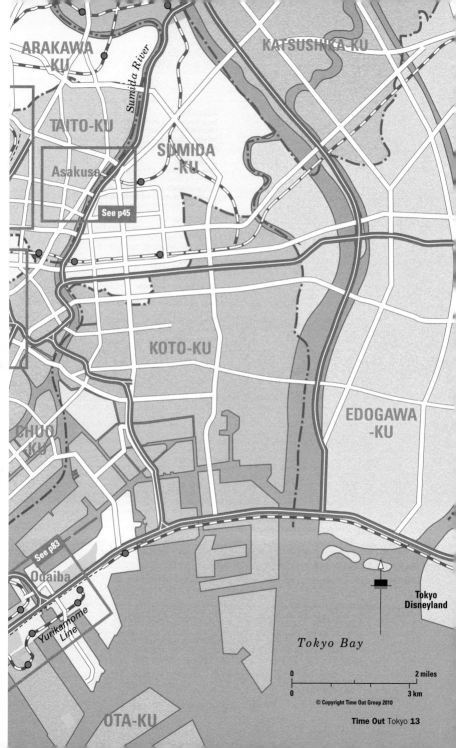

ARAKAWA
-KU

Sumida River

KATSUSHIKA-KU

TAITO-KU

SUMIDA
-KU

Asakusa

See p45

KOTO-KU

EDOGAWA
-KU

CHUO
-KU

See p83

Odaiba

Yurikamome
Line

Tokyo
Disneyland

Tokyo Bay

| 0 | | 2 miles |
| 0 | | 3 km |

© Copyright Time Out Group 2010

OTA-KU

Time Out Tokyo **13**

Tokyo

Editorial
Editor Nicholas Coldicott
Deputy Editor John Shandy Watson
Listings Editors Tomoko Kono, Maimi Kuniyoshi, Miri Shimizu, Richard Smart
Proofreader Patrick Mulkern
Indexer Jonathan Cox

Managing Director Peter Fiennes
Editorial Director Ruth Jarvis
Series Editor Will Fulford-Jones
Business Manager Dan Allen
Editorial Manager Holly Pick
Assistant Management Accountant Ija Krasnikova

Design
Art Director Scott Moore
Art Editor Pinelope Kourmouzoglou
Senior Designer Kei Ishimaru
Group Commercial Designer Jodi Sher

Picture Desk
Picture Editor Jael Marschner
Acting Deputy Picture Editor Nina Raingold
Picture Desk Assistant/Researcher Ben Rowe

Advertising
New Business & Commercial Director Mark Phillips
International Advertising Manager Kasimir Berger
International Sales Executive Charlie Sokol
Advertising Sales (Tokyo) Rumiko Ito

Marketing
Sales & Marketing Director, North America & Latin America Lisa Levinson
Senior Publishing Brand Manager Luthfa Begum
Group Commercial Art Director Anthony Huggins
Marketing Co-ordinator Alana Benton

Production
Group Production Director Mark Lamond
Production Manager Brendan McKeown
Production Assistant Katie Mulhern

Time Out Group
Director & Founder Tony Elliott
Chief Executive Officer David King
Group Financial Director Paul Rakkar
Group General Manager/Director Nichola Coulthard
Time Out Communications Ltd MD David Pepper
Time Out International Ltd MD Cathy Runciman
Time Out Magazine Ltd Publisher/MD Mark Elliott
Group Commercial Director Graeme Tottle
Group IT Director Simon Chappell

Contributors
Introduction Nicholas Coldicott. **History** Steve Walsh (*Suicidal Samurai* James Hardy). **Tokyo Today** Justin Norrie. **Architecture** Steve Walsh. **Otaku** Patrick Macias. **Asakusa** Stephen Forster (*Old Soaks* Nicholas Coldicott). **Ebisu & Daikanyama** Martin Webb. **Ginza** Nicholas Coldicott (*Something Fishy* Yukari Pratt). **Harajuku & Aoyama** Martin Webb (*Gotta Have Faith* Stephen Forster). **Ikebukuro** Tom Baker (*How to Play Pachinko* Clive France). **Marunouchi** Nicholas Coldicott (*Walk: Old Tokyo* James Hardy). **Odaiba** John Paul Catton. **Roppongi** Nicholas Coldicott. **Shibuya** Simeon Paterson (*Animania*, *Walk: People-watching* Nicholas Coldicott). **Shinjuku** Rob Schwartz (*Manga Mania* Paul Gravett; *Hey, Big Spender?* Charles Spreckley). **Ueno** Stephen Forster. **Yanaka** Stephen Forster. **Further Afield** *Naka Meguro* Martin Webb; *Shimo-Kitazawa* John Paul Catton; *The Chuo Line* James Barrett. **Hotels** Tama Miyake Lung. **Restaurants** Robbie Swinnerton (*Shojin Ryori* Nicholas Coldicott; *Super Bowls* Brian MacDuckston; *Menu Reader* Masami Hosose). **Bars** Nicholas Coldicott (*Local Potions* John Gauntner; *Japanese Whisky* Chris Bunting). **Coffee Shops** Nicholas Coldicott (*Teashops* Kobayashi Chikako). **Shops & Services** Nicholas Coldicott (*Treats Abound* Underground Yukari Pratt; *Present Perfect, Automatic for the People* John Paul Catton; *The Rag Trade* Jennifer Geacone-Cruz). **Calendar** Kodama Chie (*Superstitions* Yoko Hoshino-Krause). **Children** Mitsuru Obe, Rie Obe. **Film** Rob Schwartz. **Galleries** Jason Jenkins. **Gay & Lesbian** Ken Panadero. **Music** *Classical* Dan Grunebaum; *Jazz* James Catchpole; *Rock & pop* Rob Schwartz (*Big in Japan* Jason Jenkins). **Nightlife** Richard Smart. **Performing Arts** Dan Grunebaum (*Noh Future?* Mark Buckton). **Sport & Fitness** Fred Varcoe (*Straight outta Mongolia* Mark Buckton). **Escapes & Excursions** *Yokohama* Robbie Swinnerton; *Hakone* Tomoko Kono; *Kamakura* Robbie Swinnerton; *Nikko* Robbie Swinnerton; *Easy Day Trips* Tomoko Kono (*Climbing Mt Fuji* Nicholas Coldicott). **Getting Around, Resources A-Z** Tomoko Kono. **Vocabulary** Masami Hosose, Adam Barnes.

The Editor would like to thank Edan Corkill, Aya Hamashima, Tomoko Kono, Richard Smart, Shun Ueno, the JNTO and all contributors to previous editions of *Time Out Tokyo*, whose work forms the basis for parts of this book.

Maps john@jsgraphics.co.uk

Photography pages 4, 5 (centre), 7, 9 (top left, bottom right), 11 (bottom right), 34, 39, 40, 41, 44, 49, 52, 54, 55, 60, 63, 66, 70, 75, 81, 84, 94, 97, 99, 103, 106, 108, 109, 111, 114, 123, 126, 127, 135, 136, 139, 160, 164, 172, 177, 119, 183, 184, 187, 188, 189, 191, 194, 203, 209, 214, 217, 231, 232, 234, 239, 240, 246, 260, 263, 286, 289, 296, 298 Fumie Suzuki; pages 5 (top left, top right), 6, 9, 11, 23, 30, 33, 36, 43, 47, 48, 56, 57, 61, 62, 68, 71, 73, 82, 85, 89, 91, 98, 100, 105, 113, 115, 116, 121, 122, 125, 129, 130, 143, 149, 176, 192, 193, 210, 213, 219, 227, 228, 237, 243, 245, 247, 248, 250, 254, 259, 267 Karl Blackwell; page 9 (bottom right) Takashi Homma; pages 11 (bottom left), 74, 112, 197, 233 Nicholas Coldicott; pages 17, 37, 86, 152, 168, 169, 180, 185, 307 www.yoshidazaiphotos.com; page 18 Getty Images/Time & Life Pictures; page 21 Mary Evans Picture Library; page 26 Getty Images; pages 38, 198, 205 Kazunari Ogawa; pages 102, 133 Chester Ong; page 157 Brian MacDuckston; page 253 Yamashita Yasuhiro; page 264 Great the Kabukicho; page 269 Alamy.
The following images were provided by the featured establishments/artists: pages 163, 262, 267, 269, 275.

About the Guide

GETTING AROUND

The area chapters in our Sights section contain street maps on which are marked the locations of attractions, hotels, bars, restaurants and all other venue types. The majority of businesses listed in this guide are located in these areas; the overview map on pages 12 to 13 shows their relative locations. Maps of Japan, the greater Tokyo area and the city's transport system start on page 332.

THE ESSENTIALS

For practical information, including visas, disabled access, emergency numbers, lost property, useful websites and local transport, please see the Directory. It begins on page 307.

THE LISTINGS

Addresses, phone numbers, websites, transport information, hours and prices are all included in our listings, as are selected other facilities. All were checked and correct at press time. However, business owners can alter their arrangements at any time, and fluctuating economic conditions can cause prices to change rapidly.

The very best venues in the city, the must-sees and must-dos in every category, have been marked with a red star (★). In the Sights chapters, we've also marked venues with free admission with a FREE symbol.

PHONE NUMBERS

The area code for Tokyo is 03. You don't need to use the code when calling from a landline within Tokyo; just dial the eight-digit number as listed in this guide. If you're using a mobile phone or calling from elsewhere in Japan, you need to dial the area code first.

From outside Japan, dial your country's international access code (00 from the UK, 011 from the US) or a plus symbol, followed by the Japan country code (81), then the Tokyo code (3; the initial zero is dropped) and the eight-digit number as listed in the guide. So, to reach the Mori Art Museum, dial +81 3 6406 6100; to reach the Nezu Museum, dial +81 3 3400 2536.

For more on phones, including information on calling abroad from the UK and details of local mobile-phone access, see p316.

FEEDBACK

We welcome feedback on this guide, both on the venues we've included and on any other locations that you'd like to see featured in future editions. Please email us at guides@timeout.com.

Time Out Guides

Founded in 1968, Time Out has grown from humble beginnings into the leading resource for anyone wanting to know what's happening in the world's greatest cities. Alongside our influential weeklies in London, New York and Chicago, we publish more than 30 magazines in cities as varied as Beijing and Beirut; a range of travel books, with the City Guides now joined by the newer Shortlist series; and an information-packed website. The company remains proudly independent, still owned by Tony Elliott four decades after he launched Time Out London.

Written by local experts and illustrated with original photography, our books also retain their independence. No business has been featured because it has advertised, and all restaurants and bars are visited and reviewed anonymously.

ABOUT THE EDITOR

Nicholas Coldicott has lived in Tokyo since 1998. He works for NHK, Japan's national broadcaster, and has been involved in the Time Out Tokyo Guide since 1995. A full list of the book's contributors can be found opposite.

Discover the city from your back pocket

Essential for your weekend break, over 30 top cities available.

In Context

Shibuya Hachiko crossing.
See p91.

History   **18**
Suicidal Samurai   24
Key Events   29

Tokyo Today   **30**

Architecture   **34**

Otaku   **39**
Maid in Japan   40

History

The tempestuous path from fishing village to metropolis.

TEXT: STEVE WALSH

To look at Tokyo today, you'd think its history began some time in the 1980s. Relics of the past are few and far between, with nature, war and unsentimental developers having razed most of the evidence. But this is a city with a fascinating story.

Though it was settled as far back as the Stone Age, Tokyo spent most of its life as an unremarkable fishing village. Things began to change when a 15th-century warrior monk built a castle in the area and made it a viable power base. A century and a half later, shogun Ieyasu Tokugawa moved in and the city then known as Edo became the de facto capital.

By the time imperial rule returned in 1868, Edo was the political, economic and arguably even the cultural heart of Japan. The teenaged Emperor Meiji moved the imperial seat to what would soon become the world's most populous metropolis, the renamed 'Eastern Capital', Tokyo.

BEGINNINGS

Archaeological evidence suggests that the Tokyo metropolitan area was inhabited as long ago as the late Paleolithic period, and various stone tools belonging to the hunter-gatherers of pre-ceramic culture have been discovered at sites including Nogawa, in western Tokyo prefecture.

Pottery featuring rope-cord patterns developed in Japan during the so-called Jomon period (10,000-300 BC). Around 6,000 years ago, Tokyo Bay rose as far as the edge of the high ground that makes up the central *yamanote* area of the modern city; its retreat left behind a marshy shoreline that provided a rich food source. The late Jomon shell mounds at Omori, identified in 1877 by US zoologist ES Morse as he gazed from the window of a Shinbashi-Yokohama train, were the site of Japan's first modern archaeological dig and the forerunner to a long line of similar excavations.

The Yayoi period (300 BC-AD 300) is named after the Yayoi-cho district near Tokyo University in Hongo, where, in 1884, the Mukogaoka shell mound yielded the first evidence of a more sophisticated form of pottery. Along with other advances such as wet-rice cultivation and the use of iron, this seems to have been introduced from the Asian mainland. Only after arriving on the southern island of Kyushu did new techniques spread through to the main island of Honshu.

KYOTO: THE FIRST IMPERIAL CAPITAL

Kanto (the region in which Tokyo sits) remained a distant outpost as the early Japanese state started to form around the Yamato court, which emerged in the fourth century as a loose confederation of chieftains in what is now Nara prefecture before extending to other parts of the country. Chinese ideographs and Buddhism arrived via the Korean peninsula.

The Senso-ji temple (*see p44*) in Asakusa supposedly dates from 628, when two fishermen are said to have discovered a gold statue of the *bodhisattva* Kannon in their nets. Under Taika Reform from 645, the land on which Tokyo now stands became part of Musashi province, governed from Kokufu (modern-day Fuchu City). State administration was centralised in emulation of the Tang imperial model and China's advanced civilisation exerted a strong influence.

After the imperial capital was moved to Heian (now Kyoto) in 794, a Japanese court culture flourished. The invention of the *kana* syllabary helped the writing of classics such as Sei Shonagon's *Pillow Book* and Lady Murasaki's *Tale of Genji*. The emperors were largely figureheads, manipulated by powerful regents from the dominant Fujiwara family. But the political power of the Kyoto court nobles went into slow decline as control of the regions fell into the hands of local military aristocracy.

An early revolt against Kyoto rule was staged by Taira no Masakado, a tenth-century rebel. According to one version of the story, in 931 a quarrel over a woman among different members of the 'Eight Bands of Taira from the East' developed into full-scale military conflict, during which Masakado won control of all eight provinces of Kanto. He then declared himself emperor of a new autonomous state.

After defeat by central government forces in 940, grisly evidence of Masakado's demise was dispatched to Kyoto. Legend has it that his severed head took to the skies and flew back to be reunited with his other remains in the fishing village of Shibasaki. The site is now in the Otemachi financial district but has remained untouched by generations of city builders, perhaps fearful of Masakado's vengeful spirit.

Tokyo's original name, Edo ('Rivergate'), is thought to derive from a settlement near where the Sumida river enters Tokyo Bay. Its first-known use historically goes back to a minor member of the Taira clan, by the name of Shigenaga Edo, who is thought to have adopted it after making his home in the area. In August 1180, Shigenaga attacked the forces of Miura Yoshizumi, an ally of the rival Minamoto clan. He switched sides three months later, though, just as shogun-to-be Minamoto no Yoritomo entered Musashi province.

'In an age when London still had under one million people, Edo was probably the world's biggest metropolis.'

By the late 12th century, the rise of provincial warrior clans had developed into the struggle between the Taira and Minamoto families, later chronicled in the *Tale of Heike*. After Minamoto no Yoritomo wiped out the last of the Tairas in 1185, the emperor dubbed him Seii Tai Shogun ('Barbarian-Subduing Generalissimo'). Yoritomo shunned Kyoto, setting up his government in Kamakura (*see pp295-299*).

THE WAY OF THE WARRIOR

This inaugurated a period of military rule that was to last until the 19th century. *Bushido*, 'the way of the warrior', emphasised martial virtues, while the samurai class emerged as a powerful force in feudal society. Nevertheless, attempted Mongol invasions in 1274 and 1281 were only driven back by stormy seas off Kyushu, something attributed to the *kamikaze*, or 'wind of the gods'. Dissatisfaction grew with the Kamakura government, and in 1333 Takauji Ashikaga established a new shogunate in the Muromachi district of Kyoto.

The first castle at Edo was erected in 1457 by Dokan Ota, a *waka* poet who was known as Ota Sekenaga before taking a monk's tonsure in 1478; he is now celebrated as Tokyo's founder. Above the Hibiya inlet, Dokan Ota constructed fortifications overlooking the entrance to the Kanto plain for northbound travellers along the Pacific sea road. To improve navigation, he also diverted the Hira river east at Kandabashi to form the Nihonbashi river.

In 1486, during a military clash between branches of the locally powerful Uesugi family, Ota was falsely accused of betraying his lord, and met his end at the home of Sadamasa Uesugi in Sagami (modern-day Kanagawa).

Central government authority largely disappeared following the Onin War (1467-77), as regional lords, or *daimyo*, fought for dominance. Only after a century of on-off civil strife did the country begin to regain unity under Nobunaga Oda, although his assassination in 1582 meant that final reunification was left to Hideyoshi Toyotomi. In 1590, Hideyoshi established control of the Kanto region after successfully besieging Odawara Castle, stronghold of the powerful Go-Hojo family.

Hideyoshi ordered his ally Ieyasu Tokugawa to exchange his lands in Shizuoka and Aichi for the former Go-Hojo domains in Kanto. Rather than Odawara (which lies in present-day Kanagawa prefecture), Ieyasu chose Edo as his headquarters. A new castle was built on the site of Dokan Ota's crumbling fortifications. After Hideyoshi's death, Ieyasu was victorious in the struggle for national power at the Battle of Sekigahara in 1600, and three years later was named shogun. The emperor remained in Kyoto, but Edo became the government capital of Japan.

EDO ERA (1600-1868)

When Ieyasu arrived in 1590, Edo was little more than a few houses at the edge of the Hibiya inlet. This changed quickly. Equally divided between military and townspeople, the population grew dramatically before levelling off in the early 18th century at around 1.2 million. In an age when London still had under one million people, Edo was probably the world's biggest metropolis. Fifteen successive Tokugawa shoguns ruled for more than 250 years. All roads led to Edo: five highways radiated from the city, communications aided by regular post stations, including Shinagawa, Shinjuku, Itabashi and Senju.

Ieyasu Tokugawa.

The regional feudal lords retained local autonomy, but a system of alternate annual residence forced them to divide their time between their own lands and the capital. *Daimyo* finances were drained by the regular journeys with retinues and the need to maintain large residences in Edo. There was little chance to foment trouble in the provinces and, as a further inducement to loyalty, family members were kept in Edo as permanent hostages.

Although Ieyasu Tokugawa's advisers had included Englishman Will Adams (whose story is fictionalised in the novel *Shogun*), a policy of national seclusion was introduced in 1639. Contact with Western countries was restricted to a small Dutch trade mission on the island of Dejima, near Nagasaki in Kyushu, far from Edo. This policy didn't change for more than 200 years, resulting in Japan's culture remaining remarkably self-contained and untouched.

The layout of Edo reflected the social order, with the high ground of central Tokyo (the *yamanote*) the preserve of the military classes, and the *shitamachi* ('low city') area outside the castle walls occupied by the townspeople. There was also an attempt to conform to Chinese principles of geomancy by having the two temples that would hold the Tokugawa family tombs – Kanei-ji (*see p105*) and Zojo-ji Temple (*see p90*) – in the auspicious north-east and south-west of the city. More problematically, since Mt Fuji lay west rather than north (the traditionally favoured direction for a mountain), Edo Castle's main gate (Otemon) was placed on its east side, instead of the usual south.

Completed in 1638, Edo Castle was the world's largest. Its outer defences extended 16 kilometres (ten miles). The most important of the four sets of fortifications, the *hon-maru* or principal fortress, contained the shogun's residence, the inner chambers for his wife and concubines, and the halls of state. The keep stood on an adjacent hill, overlooking the city. Between the double set of moats, regional *daimyo* had their mansions arranged in a strict hierarchy of 'dependent' and 'outside' lords.

East of the castle walls, the low-lying *shitamachi* districts were home to merchants, craftsmen and labourers. Less than one-fifth of the land, much of it reclaimed, held around half the population. The curving wooden bridge, Nihonbashi, was the hub of the nation's highways and the spot from which all distances were measured.

Nearby were wealthy merchants' residences and grand shops such as Echigoya (forerunner of today's Mitsukoshi department store), the city's prison and the fish market. Behind grand thoroughfares, the crowded backstreet tenements of Nihonbashi and Kanda were a breeding ground for disease and in constant danger of flooding. Fires were also common in the largely wooden city.

The worst conflagration was the 'Long Sleeves Fire' of 1657, in which the original castle buildings were destroyed and more than 100,000 people died, around a quarter of Edo's total population. The flames began at a temple, Hommyo-ji in Hongo, where monks had been burning two long-sleeved kimono belonging to young women who had recently died. The fire raged for three days; by the morning of the fourth day, three-quarters of Edo had gone up in smoke.

Reconstruction work was soon under way. Roads were widened and new fire breaks introduced. Many people had perished because they couldn't escape across the Sumida river, which, for military reasons, had no bridges; opening up Fukagawa and Honjo for development, a bridge was now erected at Ryogoku. There was also a general dispersal of temples and shrines to outlying areas such as Yanaka and reclaimed land in Tsukiji. The Yoshiwara 'pleasure quarters' (licensed prostitution area) were moved out too – from Ningyocho to beyond Asakusa and the newly extended city limits.

New residences for *daimyo* were established outside the castle walls, leading to a more patchwork mix of nobles' estates and townspeoples' districts, although the basic pattern of *shitamachi* areas in the east was retained. *Daimyo* mansions inside the castle were rebuilt in a more restrained style. The innermost section of the reconstructed castle was more subdued, lacking the high tower of its predecessor.

One byproduct of the stability of the Tokugawa regime was that the large number of military personnel stationed in Edo found themselves with relatively little to do. Complex bureaucracy developed, and there were ceremonial duties, but members of the top strata of the feudal system soon found themselves outstripped economically by the city's wealthy merchants. In these circumstances, a daring vendetta attack staged by the band of masterless samurai known later as the 47 *ronin* caused a sensation (*see p24* **Suicidal Samurai**).

A vibrant new urban culture grew up in Edo's *shitamachi* districts. During the long years of peace and relative prosperity, the pursuit of pleasure provided the populace, particularly the city's wealthy merchants, with welcome relief from the feudal system's stifling social confines. Landscape artists such as Hiroshige (1797-1868) depicted a city of theatres, temples, scenic bridges, festivals and fairs. There were numerous seasonal celebrations, including big firework displays (still held) to celebrate the summer opening of the Sumida river, as well as cherry-blossom viewing along its banks in spring.

Kabuki, an Edo favourite, didn't always have the approval of the high city. In 1842, a government edict banished theatres up the Sumida river to Asakusa, where they stayed until after the fall of the shogunate. As the district already hosted the temple of Senso-ji, with its fairs and festivals, and the Yoshiwara pleasure quarters lay only a short distance away, the act merely cemented Asakusa's position as Edo's favoured relaxation centre.

THE AMERICANS ARRIVE

Notice that Japan could no longer isolate itself from the outside world arrived in Edo Bay in 1853 in the shape of four US 'black ships' under the command of Commodore Matthew Perry. Hastily prepared defences were helpless, and the Treaty of Kanagawa signed with Perry the following year proved to be the thin end of the wedge, as Western powers forced further concessions. In 1855, Edo suffered a major quake that killed over 7,000 people and destroyed large parts of the lower city. In 1859, Townsend Harris, the first US consul-general, arrived to set up a mission at Zenpuku-ji temple in Azabu.

IN CONTEXT

'Under the slogan "expel the barbarian, revere the emperor", a series of incidents took place against foreigners.'

Voices of discontent had already been raised against the government: there were increasingly frequent famines, and proponents of 'National Learning' called for a return to some purer form of Shinto (the native religion). The foreign threat now polarised opinion. In 1860, the senior councillor of the shogunate government, Naosuke Ii, was assassinated outside Edo Castle. Under the slogan 'expel the barbarian, revere the emperor', a series of incidents took place against foreigners. Power drained from Edo as the government looked to build a unified national policy by securing imperial backing in Kyoto. *Daimyo* residences in Edo were abandoned after the old alternate residence requirement was abolished in 1862.

The Tokugawa regime was finally overthrown early in 1868, when a coalition of forces from the south declared an imperial 'restoration' in Kyoto in the name of the 15-year-old emperor Meiji, and then won a military victory at Toba-Fushimi. Edo's population fell to around half its former level as remaining residents of the *yamanote* areas departed. A last stand by shogunate loyalists at the Battle of Ueno was hopeless, and left in ruins large parts of the Kanei-ji temple complex, which housed the tombs of several Tokugawa shoguns.

MEIJI ERA (1868-1912)

Following the restoration of imperial rule, the emperor's residence was swiftly transferred from Kyoto to Edo, which was renamed Tokyo ('Eastern Capital'). The city now became both the political and imperial capital, with the inner section of Edo Castle serving as the new Imperial Palace. By the mid 1880s, the population had reverted to its earlier level, but the *shitamachi* area lost much of its cultural distinctiveness as many wealthier residents moved to smarter locations. Industrialisation continued to

IN CONTEXT

Imperial Palace.

bring newcomers from the countryside. By the end of the Meiji era, in 1912, Tokyo housed a total of nearly two million people.

To the south-west of the palace, the districts of Nagatacho and Kasumigaseki became the heart of the nation's new government and bureaucratic establishment. 'Rich country, strong army' was the rallying cry, but learning from abroad was recognised to be essential: government missions were dispatched overseas, foreign experts brought in and radical reforms initiated in everything from education to land ownership.

Laying the foundations of a modern state meant sweeping away much of the old feudal structure. Government was centralised and the *daimyo* pensioned off. The introduction of conscription in 1873 ended the exclusive role of the warrior class. Disaffected elements led by Takamori Saigo rebelled in Satsuma in 1877, but were

Suicidal Samurai

Tales of honourable self-sacrifice.

IN CONTEXT

Literary celebration of suicide is not exclusively Japanese, but in a country where around 30,000 people a year take their own life, it's tackled with unique fervour. Ritualised samurai suicide was famously romanticised by novelist and nationalist revolutionary Yukio Mishima, who disembowelled himself after a failed coup in 1970.

Mishima's suicide highlights the strong literary heritage of the act. Suicides – honourable and tragic – resonate throughout the stories that make up Japan's national narrative. During the 19th-century Boshin Wars, the *Byakkotai* (White Tiger Brigade), a group of Fukushima schoolboys, killed themselves after seeing smoke rise over a hill – they mistakenly believed their lord's castle had been burned to the ground. Their errant self-sacrifice won the admiration of Mussolini, who sent a bronze eagle that still stands in the grounds of the castle in Aizu-Wakamatsu City. But these impetuous kids play second fiddle to the tale of the 47 *ronin* (masterless samurai), or *Chushingura*, as it is commonly known. Adapted, played, retold and viewable in almost every art form, it wins prize billing for its combination of honour besmirched, time bided, revenge taken and honour restored.

The tale begins with 18th-century lord Naganori Asano, who had been summoned to Edo Castle to arrange a reception for imperial envoys. According to the story, his protocol instructor, Yoshinaka Kira, called him a bumpkin and refused to teach him the rituals. Asano bore the insults until the day of the visit, when he attacked Kira in the palace grounds. For this breach of etiquette Asano was ordered to commit *seppuku*, ritual suicide.

However, 47 of Asano's samurai, shorn of their lord, their status and their means of survival, swore vengeance. On the morning of 14 December 1702, they reunited in Edo and attacked Kira's estate, eventually finding and beheading the object of their vengeance.

They then took the head to Sengaku-ji Temple (*see p120*) in Takanawa, where they placed it on Asano's tomb and turned themselves in, knowing they faced execution for their actions. In the face of public pressure, the shogun ordered 44 of them to commit *seppuku* – rather than be executed as common criminals (one had died en route, while two were not samurai rank and thus not permitted the dubious honour of committing *seppuku* – write your own 'gutted' jokes).

Those wishing to relive the experience can follow the route of the *ronin* using the map at www.tokyo-kurenaidan.com/chushingura.htm.

defeated by government forces. The following year, six former samurai from Satsuma staged a revenge attack and murdered Meiji government leader Toshimichi Okubo.

Ending old social restrictions fuelled economic development. The Bank of Japan was established in 1882, bringing greater fiscal and monetary stability. Industrialisation proceeded apace and factories sprang up near the Sumida river and in areas overlooking Tokyo Bay. After 1894, Marunouchi became the site of a business district called 'London Town' because of its blocks of Victorian-style office buildings. In 1889, a written constitution declared the emperor 'sacred and inviolable'. Real power remained with existing government leaders, but there was a nod to greater popular representation. Elections were held among the top 1.5 per cent of taxpayers, and the first session of the Imperial Diet (parliament) took place in 1890.

By the early 1890s, the government was making progress on ending the much-hated 'unequal treaties' earlier conceded to the West. Taking a leaf from the imperialists' book, Japan seized Taiwan in 1895 after a war with China. Ten years later its forces defeated the Russians in Manchuria and Korea during the Russo-Japanese War. This was the first victory over a Western power by an Asian country, but there were riots in Hibiya Park at the peace treaty's perceived leniency towards Russia. In 1910, Japan annexed Korea.

New goods and ideas from overseas started to pour into Tokyo, especially after Japan's first train line started services between Yokohama and Shinbashi station in 1872. Men abandoned their traditional topknots; married women followed the lead of the empress and stopped blackening their teeth. There were gas lights, beer halls, the first department stores and public parks, and even ballroom dancing at Hibiya's glittering Rokumeikan reception hall (designed by British architect Josiah Conder), where the elite gathered in their best foreign finery to display their mastery of the advanced new ways.

After a major fire in 1872, the former artisan district of Ginza was redeveloped with around 900 brick buildings; newspaper offices were the first to flock to what would become Tokyo's most fashionable area. Asakusa kept in touch with popular tastes through attractions such as the Ryounkaku brick tower: at 12 storeys, it was Tokyo's tallest building and contained the city's first elevator. Asakusa was also home to Japan's first permanent cinema, which opened in 1903, and the cinemas, theatres and music halls of the Rokku district remained popular throughout the early decades of the 20th century.

TAISHO ERA (1912-26)

The funeral of Emperor Meiji in 1912 was accompanied by the ritual suicide of General Nogi, a hero of the Russo-Japanese War (the house in which he killed himself can be seen at Nogi Jinja; *see p89*). The new emperor, Taisho, was in constant poor health, and his son, Hirohito, became regent in 1921.

There was a brief flowering of 'Taisho Democracy': in 1918, Takashi Hara became the first prime minister from a political party, an appointment that came after a sudden rise in rice prices prompted national disturbances, including five days of rioting in the capital. Hara was assassinated in 1921 by a right-wing extremist, but universal male suffrage was finally introduced in 1925.

Tokyo was beginning to spill over its boundaries, and part of Shinjuku was brought inside the city limits in 1920, an early indication of the capital's tendency to drift further westwards following the expansion of suburban train lines. Ginza was enjoying its heyday as a strolling spot for fashionable youth. In nearby Hibiya, the new Imperial Hotel, designed by world-famous American architect Frank Lloyd Wright, opened in 1923.

Such modernisation could not quell the forces of nature, however. Shortly before noon on 1 September 1923, the Kanto region was hit by a devastating earthquake. High winds fanned the flames of cooking fires and two days of terrible conflagrations swept through Tokyo and the surrounding area, including Yokohama, leaving more

Emperor Hirohito.

than 140,000 dead and large areas devastated. Around 63 per cent of Tokyo homes were destroyed in the Great Kanto Earthquake, with the traditional wooden buildings of the old *shitamachi* areas hardest hit. Rumours of well-poisoning and other misdeeds led vigilante groups to massacre several thousand Koreans before martial law was imposed and order restored.

Temporary structures were quickly put in place and there was a short building boom. The destruction in eastern areas accelerated the population movement to the western suburbs, but plans to remodel the city were largely laid aside because of cost.

SHOWA ERA (1926-89)

Hirohito became emperor in 1926, ushering in the Showa era. His 63-year reign – the longest of any Japanese emperor – coincided with a period of extraordinary change and turbulence. Tokyo recovered gradually from the effects of the 1923 earthquake and continued growing. Post-quake reconstruction was declared officially over in 1930.

In 1932, Tokyo's boundaries underwent major revision to take account of changing population patterns, with growing western districts such as Shibuya and Ikebukuro, and the remaining parts of Shinjuku, coming within the city limits. The total number of wards jumped from 15 to 35 (later simplified to the 23 of today), and the city's land area increased sevenfold. At a stroke, the population doubled to over five million, making Tokyo the world's second most populous city after New York.

The early 20th-century era of parliamentary government was not to last. Political stability fell victim to the economic depression that followed a domestic banking collapse in 1927 and the Wall Street crash two years later. Extremist nationalist groups saw expansion overseas as the answer to the nation's problems. In November 1930, after signing a naval disarmament treaty, prime minister Osachi Hamaguchi was killed by a right-wing extremist in Tokyo station.

In 1931, dissident army officers staged a Japanese military takeover of Manchuria, bringing conflict with world opinion. Pre-war party government ended after a short-lived rebellion of younger officers on 15 May 1932; the prime minister, Tsuyoshi Inukai, and other cabinet members were assassinated, and a series of national unity governments took over, dependent on military support. A puppet state, Manchukuo, was declared in Manchuria, and Japan left the League of Nations. On 26 February 1936, the army's First Division mutinied and attempted a coup in the name of 'Showa Restoration'. Strategic points were seized in central Tokyo, but the rebellion was put down.

'Much of Tokyo lay in ruins. As many as one in ten slept in temporary shelters during the first post-war winter.'

In an atmosphere of increasing nationalist fervour and militarism, Japan became involved in widening international conflict. Full-scale hostilities with China broke out in July 1937 (imperial troops killed 300,000 in the Chinese capital in the infamous Rape of Nanking), but Japanese forces got bogged down after early advances. In 1940, Japan signed a tripartite pact with Germany and Italy. Western powers, led by the US, declared a total embargo of Japan in summer 1941. Negotiations between the two sides reached an impasse, and on 7 December 1941 Japan attacked the US Pacific fleet at Pearl Harbor.

After a series of quick successes in the Pacific and South-east Asia, Japanese forces began to be pushed back after the Battle of Midway in June 1942. By late 1944, Tokyo lay within the range of American bombers. A series of incendiary attacks devastated the capital; the pre-dawn raid by 300 bombers on 10 March 1945 is estimated to have left 100,000 dead, a million people homeless and a quarter of the city obliterated. On 6 August, an atomic bomb was dropped on Hiroshima, followed by another on Nagasaki three days later. Cabinet deadlock left the casting vote to the emperor, whose radio broadcast to the nation on 15 August announced Japan's surrender.

Much of Tokyo lay in ruins; the lack of food and shelter posed immediate problems. As many as one in ten slept in temporary shelters during the first post-war winter.

POST-WAR PROSPERITY

Following its surrender, Japan was occupied by Allied forces under the leadership of General Douglas MacArthur, who set about demilitarising the country and promoting democratic reform. The emperor kept his throne but renounced his divine status. Article nine of the new constitution of 1946 included strict pacifist provisions, and the armed forces were disbanded. In 1948, seven 'Class A' war criminals, including wartime prime minister Hideki Tojo, were executed.

The outbreak of the Korean War in 1950 provided a tremendous boost to the Japanese economy, with large contracts to supply US forces. Under MacArthur's orders, a limited rearmament took place, leading to the eventual founding of the Self-Defence Forces (as Japan's military is called). A new security treaty with the US was signed in 1951, and the occupation ended in 1952.

With national defence left largely in US hands, economic growth was the priority under the long rule of the Liberal Democratic Party (LDP), formed in 1955. Prosperity started to manifest itself in the shape of large new office buildings in central Tokyo. In 1960, prime minister Hayato Ikeda announced a plan to double national income over a decade – a target achieved with ease in the economic miracle years that followed.

The Olympics were held in Tokyo in 1964, the same year that *shinkansen* (bullet trains) started running between the capital and Osaka. Improvements to Tokyo's infrastructure were made in preparation for the Olympics; after the Games were over, redevelopment continued apace. Frank Lloyd Wright's Imperial Hotel, amazingly a survivor of both the 1923 earthquake and the war, was demolished in 1967, the year the city's inner 23 wards achieved their peak population of almost nine million. To the west of Shinjuku station, Tokyo's first concentration of skyscrapers started to take shape during the early 1970s.

Despite the economic progress, there was an undercurrent of social discontent. Hundreds of thousands demonstrated against renewal of the US-Japan Security Treaty

IN CONTEXT

in 1960 (which allowed American military bases on Japanese soil), and the end of the decade saw students in violent revolt. In 1970, novelist Yukio Mishima dramatically ended his life after failing to spark a nationalist uprising at the city's Ichigaya barracks. In Chiba, radical groups from the other end of the political spectrum joined local farmers to battle with riot police, delaying completion of Tokyo's new international airport at Narita from 1971 to 1975, and its opening until 1978.

The post-war fixed exchange rate ended in 1971, and growth came to a temporary halt with the oil crisis of 1974, but the Japanese economy continued to outperform its Western competitors. Trade friction developed, particularly with the US. After the Plaza Accord financial agreement of 1985, the yen jumped to new highs, inflating the value of Japanese financial assets. Shoppers switched to designer labels as a building frenzy gripped Tokyo, which was deemed the world's most expensive city. Land values soared and feverish speculation fuelled a 'bubble economy'.

HEISEI ERA (1989-)

The death of Hirohito in 1989 at the age of 87 came at the beginning of the sweeping global changes marking the end of the Cold War. Hirohito's son Akihito took over, becoming Japan's 125th emperor and introducing the Heisei period.

As the 1990s wore on, the system that had served Japan so well in the post-war era stumbled. A collapse in land and stock-market prices brought the bubble economy to an end in 1990 and left Japanese banks with a mountain of bad debt. An economy that had been the envy of the world became mired in deep recession.

Tokyo ushered in a new era, in 1991, when the metropolitan government moved to a thrusting new skyscraper in Shinjuku – Tange Kenzo's twin-towered Tokyo Metropolitan Government Building No.1 (see p104) – symbolising the capital's shift away from its traditional centre. In March 1995, a sarin-gas attack on city subways by members of the Aum Shinrikyo doomsday cult provoked horror and much agonised debate.

In a new climate of job insecurity and fragile consumer confidence, the 'Heisei recession' proved resilient to the traditional stimulus of public works programmes. In April 1999, attracted by the promise of strong leadership, Tokyo elected hawkish former-LDP independent Shintaro Ishihara as its new governor. Two years later, LDP outsider Junichiro Koizumi became prime minister, boasting record popularity ratings and promising reform with 'no sacred cows'. Nevertheless, the slow pace of political and economic change in Japan continued to frustrate observers.

Tokyo sat out Japan's co-hosting of the 2002 football World Cup, with the final held in nearby Yokohama, but the event improved the nation's ties with neighbouring South Korea. Relations with China, however, stayed in the deep freeze, bedevilled by Koizumi's controversial annual visits to Yasukuni Shrine (see p80), which honours Japan's war dead, including convicted war criminals. At the same time, revelations about North Korea's nuclear arms programme and its abduction of Japanese citizens in the 1970s and '80s worsened relations between the two countries.

In contrast to the fortunes of other Iraq War allies, Koizumi voluntarily stepped down in late 2006 with his popularity intact. His successors, Shinzo Abe, followed by Taro Aso, proved more conservative and far less charismatic; in 2009, the LDP, which had ruled post-war Japan almost uninterrupted since 1954, was swept from power in a landslide election. The new government was formed by the Democratic Party of Japan, headed by Yukio Hatoyama, scion of one of Japan's most prominent political dynasties. Hatoyama promised to end the wasteful public works and misappropriations that were nicknamed the 'second budget', rein in the power of Japan's bureaucrats, and steer Japan's foreign policy toward Asia rather than the US. The first signs of US frustration with Japan's new priorities came in 2010 when Hatoyama refused to rubber stamp his predecessor's agreement to relocate a US marine base within Okinawa prefecture. Whether or not Hatoyama lasts longer than most of Japan's fleeting prime ministers, the 2009 election looks to have opened a new era in Japanese politics.

Key Events

Tokyo in brief.

c10,000-300 BC Jomon period.
c300 BC-AD 300 Yayoi period; introduction of wet-rice cultivation, bronze and ironware into Japan from continental Asia.
6th century Buddhism introduced from Korea.
710 Nara becomes imperial capital.
794 Capital moves to Heian (Kyoto).
1019 Shikibu Murasaki writes *Tale of Genji*.
1180 First recorded use of the name Edo.
1185-1333 Kamakura is site of military government.
1274, 1281 Attempted Mongol invasions.
1590 Edo becomes headquarters of Ieyasu Tokugawa; construction of Edo Castle.
1603 Ieyasu named shogun; Edo becomes seat of national government.
1639 National seclusion policy established.
1688-1704 *Genroku* period of cultural flowering.
1703 47 *ronin* vendetta carried out.
1720 Ban on import of foreign books lifted.
1787-93 Kansei reforms; rice granaries set up in Edo after famine and riots.
1804-29 Bunka-Bunsei period; peak of Edo merchant culture.
1825 Government issues 'Order for Repelling of Foreign Ships'.
1841-43 Reforms to strengthen economy.
1853 Arrival of US 'black ships' at Uraga.
1854 Treaty of Kanagawa signed with US Commodore Perry.
1860 Naosuke Ii assassinated.
1868 Tokugawa shogunate overthrown in Meiji Restoration.
1872 Shinbashi to Yokohama train service.
1874 Tokyo's first gas lights.
1889 New Meiji constitution.

1894-95 Sino-Japanese War.
1902 Anglo-Japanese alliance signed.
1904-05 Russo-Japanese war.
1912 Emperor Meiji dies; Taisho era begins.
1923 Great Kanto Earthquake; 140,000 die and Tokyo is devastated.
1925 Universal male suffrage.
1926 Hirohito becomes emperor.
1927 Asia's first subway line opens between Asakusa and Ueno.
1931 Military takeover of Manchuria.
1933 Japan leaves League of Nations.
1936 Army rebellion in central Tokyo.
1937 Hostilities in China; Rape of Nanking.
1940 Tripartite pact with Germany and Italy.
1941 Pearl Harbor attack begins Pacific War.
1945 Incendiary bombing of Tokyo. Atomic bombs dropped on Hiroshima and Nagasaki. Japan surrenders; occupation begins.
1946 Emperor renounces divinity. New constitution promulgated.
1951 Security Treaty signed with US.
1952 Occupation ends.
1954 Release of first *Godzilla* film.
1960 Demonstrations against renewal of US-Japan security treaty.
1964 Tokyo Olympic Games. First *shinkansen* bullet train runs between Tokyo and Osaka.
1989 Death of Hirohito; Heisei era begins.
1990 End of 'bubble economy'.
1993 LDP loses power after 38 years.
1995 Sarin gas attack on Tokyo subway.
1998 Asian economic crisis spreads.
2002 Japan co-hosts football World Cup. Koizumi visits North Korea.
2004 Japanese troops deployed in Iraq.
2010 Prime Minister Hatayama resigns over US base remaining in Okinawa; Naoto Kan becomes new PM.

IN CONTEXT

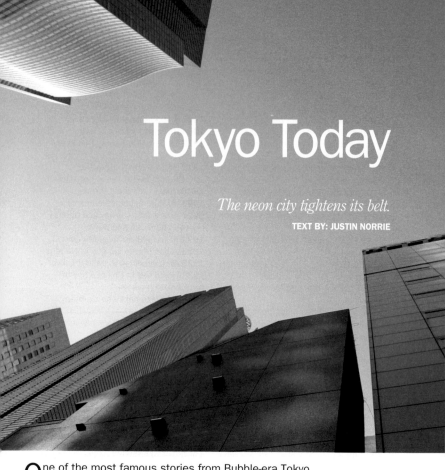

Tokyo Today

The neon city tightens its belt.

TEXT BY: JUSTIN NORRIE

One of the most famous stories from Bubble-era Tokyo was about the Imperial Residence, a 3.5-square-kilometre patch in the centre of the city that was said to be worth more than all of the land in California. It was an urban myth, but it came to be a defining feature of the Japanese capital in the late 1980s. In those days of stupendous wealth, inflation and excess, the cost of food and accommodation was enough to shock even wealthier foreign visitors and keep backpackers out almost entirely.

Twenty long years of financial hardship have redrawn the landscape. The world's most populous and pulsating megalopolis, once representative of Japan's push to overtake America as the world's largest economy, is now a city of penny-pinching and deep discounting. And while Tokyo's economic malaise continues to deepen the worry lines on the faces of its commuters, it means there's never been a better time to visit.

AUSTERITY BITES

By and large, Tokyo today is a city chastened by hard financial lessons, wary of conspicuous consumption and prepared to embrace a more sensible standard of living. Residents are more interested in saving than spending, and their employers are among the most energy-efficient companies in the world.

In recent years, the biggest success story among consumers hasn't been expensive electronics, fancy cars or Louis Vuitton accessories. Shoppers have migrated from blue-chip fashion brands to the cheap, neutral styles of Japanese 'non-label' brands MUJI and Uniqlo, as well as low-price imports H&M and Forever21. Such has been the rise and rise of Uniqlo that in 2008 it overtook the mighty Vuitton as the favourite brand for women in Japan's annual consumer preference survey.

The city's bargains aren't limited to its clothing chains. Visitors nowadays soon realise they don't have to pay a premium at one of the 197 Michelin-starred restaurants or countless world-class bars to appreciate the renowned dining culture. Excellent, cheap Japanese food – fresh sushi and sashimi, *kushiyaki* sticks of grilled meat and vegetables, hearty bowls of ramen noodles, lightly battered tempura and more – is available everywhere, from the backblocks of Shimbashi's 'salaryman town' to the boulevards of Daikanyama.

When travellers start craving the taste of home, they'll find obsessive Tokyo chefs sometimes do it just as well, and occasionally better. Western food in Japan used to be adapted to meet local tastes; the unhappy results include stodgy 'curry rice' stew, sugary spaghetti bolognese and mayonnaise pizza. But now, the same devotion to technique practised by the city's sushi masters and soba chefs is being extended to foreign cuisine. The Nakameguro district alone is home to some of the finest pizzerias on the planet, including Seirinkan, run by Susumu Kakinuma, who sensibly spent a year training for his vocation by eating pizza throughout Italy. In February, he was joined by Hisanori Yamamoto, two-time winner of the World Cup Pizza Championship in Naples, who opened Pizzeria e Trattoria da Isa a few blocks away. Best of all, much of this cuisine can be enjoyed cheaply. All but the most high-end restaurants offer lunch specials that include a meal, a drink and often a side or dessert, for around ¥1,000.

The impact of Japan's financial woes hasn't been entirely good for the national diet. Many in Tokyo's growing subset of young, struggling part-time workers have learned to get by on 100-yen curry rice and instant ramen. If they drink at all, they favour cheap *happoshu* (low-malt) beer or even cheaper, even lower malt *happosei*, a third-category quasi beer usually brewed from pea proteins or soy beans.

STILL SPECTACULAR

Fabulous extravagance can still be found in Tokyo, of course. At the Ritz-Carlton in Roppongi's opulent Tokyo Midtown tower, bartenders will whip up a Diamonds Are Forever martini (Grey Goose vodka with a twist of lime, served over a one-carat diamond) for ¥1.8 million. Across town, the world's premier designer brands still dominate the streets of Ginza – where Chanel threw down a lazy $240 million to build its ten-storey boutique – and Aoyama, home to Swiss architecture firm Herzog and de Meuron's crystalline Prada store, which features changing rooms with glass walls that turn opaque at the touch of a button. Meanwhile property tycoon Minoru Mori's lavish retail-and-residential complexes at Roppongi Hills and Omotesando Hills continue to gaze across the cityscape in defiance of the economic calamity they survey.

These and other landmarks ensure Tokyo remains a stunning spectacle to the first-time visitor. The widespread use of English-language signs only partly dampens the sense of awe most feel as they traverse greater Tokyo on one of the 101 train lines that serve the area. For those who can afford it, a nighttime backseat ride across the city's elevated expressways would be a better way to tour its landmarks: the skyscrapers of the Shiodome complex, the giant electronic billboards and

IN CONTEXT

department stores of Shibuya and Shinjuku, the hustle on Ikebukuro's gritty backstreets, and the shabby suburban sprawl that lies in between – shrouded in power lines, carved up by concreted rivers and dotted with 24-hour convenience stores.

But Tokyo isn't all crushing crowds and bright lights. Those venturing further afield may find themselves among the narrow streets of *shitamachi* (old town) districts, best explored between the *senbei* cracker stores and *wagashi* sweet shops of Yanaka, or around the azaleas and cherry-blossom trees of the 308-year-old Rikugien Park in Hon-Komagome. Unlike much of the city, the small wooden homes, shop buildings, shrines and temples that line the lanes here were largely spared during World War II bombing raids.

CARRY ON CONSTRUCTING

In Tokyo, though, the wrecking ball is never far away. Prime Minister Yukio Hatoyama has preached financial responsibility and promised to stamp out the venal relationship between politics and development. But at street level there appears to be no end to the road construction and repair work, overseen by armies of superannuated workers waving flashing red wands. Nor has there been any let up in Tokyo's other preferred pastime: knocking down bland, blocky buildings and putting up equally drab replacements.

Occasionally, architects have been permitted to indulge their sense of whimsy. The most bemusing efforts include the Reversible Destiny Lofts residential complex, a discombobulated cartoon creation at Mitaka designed by architects Arakawa and Madeline Gins to stimulate the minds of elderly residents; and Takaharu and Yui Tezuka's Fuji Kindergarten at Tachikawa, where hundreds of children play on the roof of a giant ellipse that resembles an elevated velodrome. The planners sometimes get it right on a grand scale, too, as was the case with the vast undulating glass façade of Kisho Kurokawa's **National Art Center of Tokyo** (*see p88*). The city also seems to be taken with its latest icon, the 634-metre high **Tokyo Sky Tree** (*see p38*), which was drawing crowds well before construction was complete.

Many blame the endless construction on onerous tax laws, the need to remove buildings without sufficient earthquake protection, and, most tenuously of all, the Buddhist notion that human existence is ephemeral. But money makes a more convincing explanation for most projects, such as the plan by the metropolitan government to free up a $2.1 billion site at Tsukiji by moving the world's biggest fish market to reclaimed land in Tokyo Bay – despite the fact that the proposed location is laced with toxic chemicals.

It is also the reason why so few pockets of heritage continue to defy developers. Perhaps the most poignant exception is the 108-year-old wooden home at Nogizaki where former samurai and later Japanese Imperial Army general Maresuke Nogi committed *seppuku*. The tiny, tranquil block still crouches in the shadows of the 53-storey Midtown skyscraper in Roppongi. In a rare instance of respect for earlier architectural aesthetics, the **Mitsubishi Ichigokan Museum** (*see p78*), opened in April 2010, replicated a 19th-century building knocked down almost half a century ago.

Other neighbourhoods are less fortunate. For decades, the tangle of narrow streets around Shimokitazawa train station has been home to a lively set of bars, galleries, theatres, vintage goods stores, and a young crowd of mostly earnest types. Soon, however, authorities will begin work on a 26-metre-wide expressway that will rent the counterculture centre down the middle. Many predict the weekend confluence of self-styled hipsters will be flushed elsewhere – to Koenji, Kichijoji, and regular youth beats Shibuya and Harajuku.

In the past decade, these and other young Tokyo residents have found it easier to resist the traditional pressure to find secure work in a giant corporation, get married and have children, though not always through choice. The days of stable, lifetime employment have gone. Workplace reforms introduced at the beginning of the century have made it difficult for many to break out of the cycle of part-time

IN CONTEXT

Prada. *See p31*.

work. Some resort to sleeping in cheap, 24-hour internet cafes, all the while helping to pay off the towering public debt (as a percentage of GDP, second only to the amount owed by Zimbabwe) racked up by a generation of baby-boomers now enjoying retirement in sunny Okinawa.

Recent changes to divorce laws have given more power to miserable housewives, but for young working women the path ahead remains as challenging as ever. Among the 54 candidates chosen by online magazine *Nikkei Business* for its Changemakers of the Year 2010 awards, there wasn't a single female. The selection was notable for the omission of Kazuyo Sejima, a woman who won the world's pre-eminent architecture prize – the Pritzker – a week earlier, but wasn't among the eight architects preferred by Nikkei for the shortlist.

A FRAGILE FUTURE

Some Tokyoites escape the struggle to overcome institutional impediments by immersing themselves in *otaku* ('nerd') subcultures, particularly the syrupy make-believe world of cosplay dress-ups, manga comics and anime videos that flourishes along the streets of Akihabara, Ikebukuro's Otome Road and Nakano Broadway.

But the challenges for young people will only intensify in the years ahead. Japan's rapidly ageing population has fewer children and a higher proportion of elderly citizens than any country in recorded history. Unless the fertile residents of greater Tokyo and beyond dramatically increase their rate of reproduction, the country is headed for trouble. Tokyo's population of over-65s is already at 2.55 million, or one-fifth of the total. Fifty years from now, every three workers in Japan will have two retirees to support – a ratio that could strain pension and health-care systems to breaking point.

The government is attempting to get young couples in the mood with a new child allowance that will eventually rise to ¥26,000 a month. But it pointedly refuses to address the other solution: immigration. Japanese are almost universally welcoming and hospitable to tourists, but remain wary of the idea of drastically increasing the population of foreigner residents. The enduring but false belief that outsiders are disproportionately responsible for the country's (very low) rate of crime was one unspoken factor in the decision to start photographing and fingerprinting all visitors on arrival.

Such is the sense of uncertainty about the future that few residents seemed to care when Tokyo lost the bid to host the 2016 Olympics. A campaign by nationalistic governor Shintaro Ishihara to stir support never gained traction with residents preoccupied with more immediate concerns. Still, all the anxiety has done nothing to temper the city's relentless energy and pace, nor has it dulled its personality. The vastness and vitality of Tokyo are just as fascinating as ever – only now at a more affordable price.

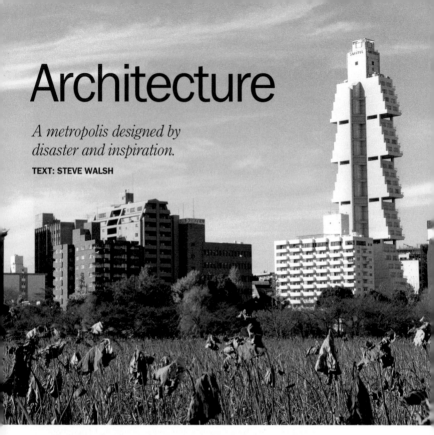

Architecture

A metropolis designed by disaster and inspiration.

TEXT: STEVE WALSH

Architecturally, the jumbled cityscape of Tokyo isn't as immediately striking as that of New York, Paris or London. It lacks grand boulevards, historic monuments and a sense of ordered urban planning. Instead, the initial impression is of a very contemporary kind of confusion, with nondescript high-rises jostling against gleaming space-age designs, one-storey dwellings overshadowed by looming skyscrapers, giant video screens and banks of neon.

The capital's traditional-style buildings are relatively few. This is partly a result of nature – a history of fires and terrible arthquakes – and partly a consequence of man-made forces: wartime bombing, compounded by breakneck post-war economic development and an unsentimental lack of attachment to the old. The metropolis is in a constant state of reinvention.

Tokyo has been a laboratory for the meeting and synthesis of local and Western styles since it first flung its doors open to the wider world, back in 1868. This drive to embrace the future continues to inform the development of the city's architecture today.

'Demands for a distinctive national look led to the so-called Imperial Crown style.'

TRADITIONAL STYLES

Japanese architecture has traditionally been based on the use of wooden materials. Very few original structures remain from the city's former incarnation as Edo, capital of the Tokugawa shoguns, although parts of the imposing pre-modern fortifications of the 17th-century Edo Castle can still be seen when walking around the moat and gardens of the Imperial Palace, built on part of the castle site.

The original wooden houses and shops of Edo-era *shitamachi* ('low city') districts have now almost completely disappeared. Outside the very heart of the city, some recognisably traditional features, such as eaves and tiled roofs, are still widely used on modern suburban housing, while tatami mats and sliding doors are common inside even more Western-style apartment blocks.

The city's shrines and temples are overwhelmingly traditional in form, though not often old. The **Meiji Shrine** (*see p67*) is an impressive example of the austere style and restrained colours typical of Shinto architecture, which is quite distinctive from that of Buddhist temples, where the greater influence of Chinese and Korean styles is usually apparent. Many present-day buildings of older religious institutions are reconstructions of earlier incarnations; the well-known temples of **Senso-ji** and **Zojo-ji** are both examples, although in these cases some remnants of earlier structures also survive. The Sanmon Gate of Zojo-ji, which dates from 1605, and **Gokoku-ji**, which dates from 1681, are rare, unreconstructed survivors.

In contrast, when the wooden building of **Hongan-ji** temple in Tsukiji burned down for the ninth time in the temple's long history after the 1923 earthquake, it was rebuilt in sturdier stone. The design by architect Chuta Ito, also responsible for the earlier Meiji Shrine, was also quite different: an eye-catching affair recalling Buddhism's roots in ancient India.

WESTERNISATION AND REACTION

After the Meiji Restoration of 1868, the twin influences of Westernisation and modernisation quickly made an impact on Tokyo, the new capital. Early attempts to combine Western and traditional elements by local architects resulted in extraordinary hybrids featuring Japanese-style sloping roofs rising above wooden constructions, with ornate front façades of a distinctly Western style. Kisuke Shimizu's **Hoterukan** (1868) at the Foreign Settlement in Tsukiji and his **First National Bank** (1872) in Nihonbashi were two notable Tokyo examples. Neither survives today.

Tokyo's earliest buildings of a purely Western design were chiefly the work of overseas architects brought to Japan by the new Meiji government. Englishman Thomas Waters oversaw the post-1872 redevelopment of Ginza with around 900 red-brick buildings, thought to be more resilient than wooden Japanese houses. Ironically, none of them made it through the 1923 earthquake.

Waters' fellow countryman, Josiah Conder, who taught at Tokyo Imperial University, was the most influential Western architect of the early Meiji period, with key projects in the capital including ministry buildings, the original **Imperial Museum** (1881) at Ueno and Hibiya's **Rokumeikan** reception hall (1883). His **Furukawa Mansion** (1914) in Komagome and **Nikolai Cathedral** (1891) in Ochanomizu still exist, although the latter was badly damaged in the 1923 earthquake.

Later Meiji official architecture was often a close reflection of Western styles, although it was Japanese architects who increasingly handled the prestige projects. Remaining red-brick structures of the period include the **Ministry of Justice** (1895),

IN CONTEXT

constructed in Kasumigaseki by the German firm of Ende & Bockman, and the **Crafts Gallery** of the National Museum of Modern Art (1910), which once housed the administrative headquarters of the Imperial Guard. The imposing **Bank of Japan** building (1896) was designed by one of Conder's former students, Kingo Tatsuno, who was also responsible for the Marunouchi wing of **Tokyo Station** (1914), modelled on Centraal Station in Amsterdam. A far more grandiose overseas inspiration, that of Versailles, is said to have been used for the **Akasaka Detached Palace** (1909), created by Tokuma Katayama, whose other work includes the **Hyokeikan** building (1909) of the Tokyo National Museum in Ueno Park.

The era after World War I saw the completion of Frank Lloyd Wright's highly distinctive **Imperial Hotel** (1922), which famously survived the Tokyo earthquake shortly after its opening, but was demolished in the 1960s. The period after the earthquake saw the spread of social housing, and a prominent example, finally knocked down in 2003, was the Dojunkai Aoyama tenement apartment blocks (1926) on Omotesando. Another post-quake innovation was the *kanban* (signboard) style, designed to protect buildings against fire by a cloaking of sheet copper, and often still seen today in the heavily oxidised green mantles of pre-war shops.

The influence of overseas trends can be discerned in the modernism of Tetsuro Yoshida's **Tokyo Central Post Office** (1931) and the art deco of the **Tokyo Metropolitan Teien Art Museum** (1933), built originally as a mansion for Prince Asaka and planned mainly by French designer Henri Rapin. The present-day **Diet Building** (1936) also shows a strong art deco influence, but its design became a source of heated debate in the increasingly nationalist climate of the period when it was completed.

A reaction against Westernisation had already been apparent in the work of Chuta Ito, who had looked towards Asian models. Demands for a distinctive national look led to the so-called 'Imperial Crown' style, exemplified by the main building of the **Tokyo National Museum** (1938) in Ueno. This was the design of Hitoshi Watanabe, an architect of unusual versatility whose other works include the **Hattori Building** (1932) of Wako department store at Ginza Yon-chome crossing, and the **Daiichi Insurance Building** (1938). The latter was used by General MacArthur as his Tokyo headquarters after the war, and is now the shorter, older part of the DN Tower 21 complex in Hibiya.

IN CONTEXT

Hongan-ji. *See p35.*

Tokyo International Forum.

POST-WAR TOKYO

The priority in the early post-war period was often to provide either extra office space for companies trying to cope with the demands of an economy hurtling along at double-digit growth rates, or a rapid answer to the housing needs of the city's growing population. Seismic instability meant that tall buildings were not initially an option, and anonymous, box-like structures proliferated.

Even as architects gained confidence in new construction techniques designed to provide greater protection against earthquakes, many of the initial results were strangely undistinguished. The city's first cluster of skyscrapers, built in West Shinjuku from the early 1970s, has been described as resembling a set of urban tombstones. Even so, a later addition, the imposing, twin-towered **Tokyo Metropolitan Government Building** (1991) by Kenzo Tange, is now among the capital's best-known landmarks.

The dominant figure of post-war Japanese architecture, Tange has combined Western and traditional Japanese elements in an astonishing variety of Tokyo projects, which stretch right back to the now-demolished metropolitan offices of Yurakucho (1957). Well-known works include **St Mary's Cathedral** (1963) in Edogawabashi, **Yoyogi National Stadium** (1964), the **Hanae Mori Building** (1978) on Omotesando, the **Akasaka Prince Hotel** (1983) and the **UN University** (1992) in Aoyama.

Tange's long career connects generations of Japanese architects. One collaborator was Kunio Maekawa, a pre-war student of Le Corbusier in Europe, who became one of Japan's foremost modern architects, with works such as the **Tokyo Metropolitan Festival Hall** (1961) and the **Tokyo Metropolitan Art Museum** (1975). Another was postmodernist Arata Isozaki, the man responsible for the **Ochanomizu Square Building** (1987), as well as the Museum of Contemporary Art (1986) in Los Angeles.

Tokyo ordered itself a postmodernist makeover as the Bubble economy took hold in the 1980s, and the resultant splurge of 'trophy architecture' left the city with a string of enjoyably arresting landmarks, including the **Spiral Building** (1985) in Aoyama, the strange, low-level **Tokyo Metropolitan Gymnasium** (1990) in Sendagaya, Philippe Starck's **Super Dry Hall** in Asakusa, and Rafael Vinoly's mid-'90s **Tokyo International Forum** (*see p253*) on the site of the old Tokyo government building in Yurakucho.

The reclamation of Tokyo Bay also opened up land for a wide range of projects. On Odaiba, designated as a futuristic showcase back in the Bubble era, Tange's **Fuji TV**

'Even when only half complete, the Tokyo Sky Tree was already the tallest structure in Japan.'

Building (1996), Sei Watanabe's **K-Museum** (1996) and Sogokeikau Sato's **Tokyo Big Sight** (1994) all vie for attention. Nearby, on the city side of Rainbow Bridge, a new generation of high-rise offices in Odaiba thrusts upwards on the waterfront skyline.

The 21st century brought a series of towering, multi-purpose complexes. First to arrive, in 2002, was the **Marunouchi Building** (*see p197*), on the site of the city's first modern office block, which cheerfully cast aside an old taboo prohibiting buildings from looking onto the emperor's residence. The following year brought lifestyle super-complex **Roppongi Hills**. Tadao Ando brought his concrete visions to fashion boulevard Omotesando in 2005, with low-rise retail and restaurant complex **Omotesando Hills** replacing a much-loved set of ivy-covered, Bauhaus-inspired apartments that had stood there since 1927. Roppongi's **Tokyo Midtown** (*see p198*), is an example of a multi-purpose complex done right, with a Japanese-themed interior and Tadao Ando's **21_21 Design Sight** (*see p88*) in the manicured garden. Joining them is the late Kisho Kurokawa's **National Art Center Tokyo** (*see p88*), with its undulating glass façade.

The skyline has been creeping up as developers chase superlative titles for their investments, but the colossal **Tokyo Sky Tree**, near Asakusa, looks set to make everything else seem nanoscale. Even when only half complete, the tower was already the tallest structure in Japan; when it opens in early 2012, it will be 634 metres (2,080 feet) tall. Though its primary purpose is as a communications tower for the digital age, it will have an observation deck three-quarters of the way up, plus yet another retail and office complex.

Tokyo continues to reinvent, rebuild and redesign itself, and the recovering economy, combined with the city's laissez-faire planning regulations, means a fast-changing, eye-popping cityscape. If the buildings today aren't to your taste, come back in ten years, and there'll be a whole new set to enjoy.

IN CONTEXT

National Art Center Tokyo.

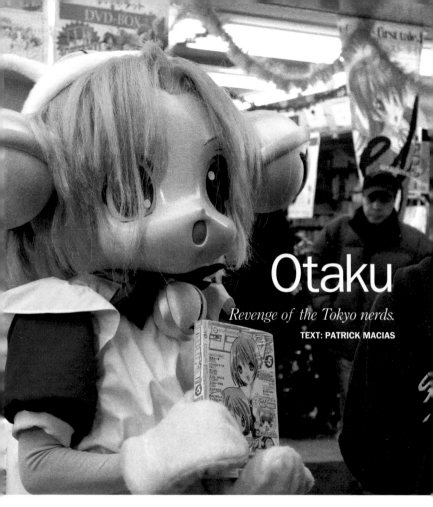

Otaku

Revenge of the Tokyo nerds.

TEXT: PATRICK MACIAS

Japan has a centuries-long history of visual culture and, more recently, a globally respected pop culture that thrives on animation and comics. At the very centre of this *anime*, manga and video-game boom are *otaku*, Japan's obsessive nerds who have colonised Tokyo's Akihabara district and parts of Ikebukuro and Nakano. This breed of obsessives derives its name from a peculiarly polite use of the Japanese language. The word '*otaku*' (literally, 'your house' or 'household') is used as an exceptionally formal second-person pronoun. Tokyo's obsessive collector types began using the word to refer to each other as it enabled them – linguistically at least – to maintain a certain level of privacy and distance. Despite their overt passions for manga, *anime* and all manner of obscure fetishes, *otaku* tend to be painfully shy about their personal lives.

Maid in Japan

The cafés of Akihabara have rather a different approach to service.

Call it geisha culture for the *otaku* age. Maid cafés far outnumber standard cafés on the streets of Akihabara, such is the demand for coffee and cakes presented by costumed young ladies who shriek 'Welcome home, master!' as you enter. Whether it's your idea of heaven or hell, the maid café is now an essential stop on any Tokyo itinerary. With around 50 such establishments in this small patch of the city, finding a café is a breeze, but the most memorable maid action awaits you at one of these two scene veterans:

Café Mai:lish
FH Kyowa Square Bldg 2F, 3-6-2 Soto-Kanda, Chiyoda-ku (5289 7310, www.mailish.jp). Akihabara station (Yamanote, Sobu lines), Electric Town exit; (Hibiya line), exit 3. **Open** 11am-10pm daily. **Credit** AmEx, JCB, MC, V.
One of Akihabara's oldest maid cafés, this is the genre's archetype. Although it is pricier than some of the newer maid establishments (¥1,000 will get you a glass of Coke and a blob of ice-cream), your investment pays off in the details. The Victorian maid uniform is a faultless re-creation, and the soda fountain looks

like something straight out of the '50s. The mood between the maids and their masters (that is, the customers) can be a bit chilly, but that's part of the appeal for the regulars who are big on 'unfulfilled longing'. Check the website for special events, such as 'Glasses Day'. Foreign nerds are welcome – there's even an English menu.

@Home Café
Mitsuwa Bldg 7F, 1-11-4 Soto-Kanda, Chiyoda-ku (5294 7707, www.cafe-athome.com). Akihabara station (Yamanote, Sobu lines), Electric Town exit; (Hibiya line), exit 3. **Open** 11.30am-10pm daily. **No credit cards**.
Here's a maid café that offers an over-the-top experience worthy of Las Vegas. The girls here aren't so much maids as performers in a kind of Hooters-style theme restaurant. Along with serving cute little bunny-wunny ice-cream cakes and heart-shaped hamburgers, the squeaky maids will (for an additional fee) play games like Rock, Paper, Scissors with the customers.
Other locations Don Quixote Akihabara 5F, 4-3-3 Soto-Kanda, Chiyoda-ku (3254 7878).

Today's male *otaku* have made the back alleys of Akihabara (Akiba to the locals) their home. Here they prowl for local delicacies, including *anime*, manga, girlfriend-simulator video games and 'idol goods' (products devoted to cutesy, nubile young girls).

When they're not devouring manga or perfecting their gaming skills, what geeks like most are maids. The maid phenomenon began with a café (*see p40* **Maid in Japan**) where boys were served by costumed young ladies with extra-squeaky voices. The concept took off and spawned not just dozens of imitators, but oddball variations, including samurai-maid hybrids (**Mononopu Café & Bar**, 4-6-2 Soto-Kanda, Chiyoda-ku, 5296 9199, www.mononopu.com) and butler cafés (**Swallowtail**, 3-12-12 Higashi-Ikebukuro, Toshima-ku, www.butlers-cafe.jp), but also a whole world of maid-related services, including maid reflexology (**Melty Cure**, 4-6-2 Soto-Kanda, Chiyoda-ku, 3254 7557, www.melcure.jp), or a maid who will clean your ears (**Tenshi no Tobira**, Hashizume Bldg 3F, 3-2-13 Soto-Kanda, Chiyoda-ku, 6206 9610, http://tenshinotobira.chicappa.jp). There are maid tour guides to help you navigate the whole Akiba fantasy land (www.akiba-guide.com). Even **Candy Fruit Optical** (3-16-3 Soto-Kanda, 3252 4902), an optician that's been supplying specs to Akihabara for over five decades, now requires its staff to dress as maids.

Elsewhere, there are silicone-doll rental stores, costume shops selling schoolgirls' uniforms in sizes up to 'Male XL', arcades devoted entirely to *gashapon* – the gumball machines that dispense plastic toys ranging from the saccharine to the sickening – and for the more committed figurine fan, there are life-size characters costing up to ¥600,000 that you can purchase in 60 easy instalments.

More fleshy fantasies used to be prevalent too, but a citywide ordinance enacted in 2009 to restrict street performance was blamed on one particular performer whose trademark was to expose her underwear in the street for eager fans to photograph. Following her arrest, things have become a little tamer. **Tora no Ana** (*see p201*) sells a massive range of *dojinshi* – small-run underground comics penned by fans.

Akiba is full to bursting with geek goods, and many elements of the *otaku*'s obsessive collector culture have crossed over to the mainstream. Even the government-sponsored Japanese National Tourist Organization (*see p318*) now offers free tours of Akihabara.

GENERATION GEEK

The first real generation of *otaku* came of age during the 1960s, nursed by early *anime* hits such as *Astro Boy* and superhero shows such as *Ultraman*. By the early '70s, there were millions of young adults in Japan reading comics, watching animation and dedicating themselves to what many in the West would write off as kids' stuff. The arrival of *Star Wars*, the robot *anime* TV series *Gundam*, and the first video games later in the decade added fuel to the fire.

IN CONTEXT

There are also butler cafés, staffed by women cross-dressing as impossibly beautiful men.

By the 1980s, it was clear that a new kind of culture was evolving out of *anime*, manga, games and science fiction. In 1983, Akio Nakamori wrote an essay entitled *A Study of Otaku*, which sought to make sense of it all. He is credited with coining the name '*otaku*' after observing the unusual usage of the word among this group.

In 1989, however, the word took on sinister overtones that still linger today. A 27-year-old man named Tsutomu Miyazaki kidnapped and murdered three young girls. When the police stormed his home, they found it full of *anime* and manga. The only term available on hand to describe such a person was *otaku,* and a full-scale backlash ensued. It was then that *otaku* really needed a haven to call their own, where they could be safe from the suspicious eyes of the public at large. They found it in Akihabara.

The area had long been Tokyo's designated hub for discount consumer electronics. But by the 1980s, there were plenty of chain stores offering such fare throughout the city. However, Akihabara's stores were still often the first to offer new releases of hardware, software and peripherals. *Otaku*, lured in by all this tech, slowly began to take over the area. And they brought with them their ravenous hunger for *anime*, manga, action figures, video games and pornography.

In the late '90s, the science fiction *anime* series *Neon Genesis Evangelion* became a massive hit in Japan, playing to mainstream and *otaku* audiences alike. Suddenly it was almost fashionable to have a vast knowledge of *anime* and manga. And, more importantly, the huge sums of money the series generated showed that there was profit in geeks. The spending habits and psychology of the *otaku* came under the scrutiny of leading academics, the media and even the government. Together they wondered if the cure to Japan's economic woes could be found within the hyper-consumerist lifestyle of the *otaku*. (Current estimates of the *otaku* industry value it at around $3 billion.)

The next big turning point for *otaku* came in 2004 with the arrival of the book *Densha Otoko* (Train Man). It concerned a typical Akihabara dweller who finds love after rescuing a beautiful woman from harassment on a commuter train. Allegedly based on real events chronicled on an internet thread (a claim now largely believed to be false), the tale was embellished with much comedy and drama, becoming a hit TV series and then a feature film. All eyes began to peer once again at Akihabara and its nerd culture.

A TOURIST ATTRACTION

With the buzz about Akihabara and *otaku* at fever pitch, the area has seen plenty of redevelopment. Among the several glitzy new skyscrapers is the UDX Center, which houses the **Tokyo Anime Center** (4-14-1 Soto-Kanda, 5298 1188). There's also been a massive influx of tourists, both domestic and foreign. Needless to say, not all *otaku* are delighted with the attention being lavished upon their once-private clubhouse.

Luckily for them, there are plenty of other geek retreats in the city. Foremost is the **Nakano Broadway** (*see p200*) shopping arcade. Located in the rear of this otherwise unspectacular mall is a maze of collector stores. The numerous rare goods all command huge prices, but some good deals can be found.

And lest it seem that cultural obsessions are the preserve of Tokyo's male population, there's also Ikebukuro's **Otome Road** – a small strip of comic shops and *anime* stores frequented by female *otaku*. The big draw is the *anime* and manga genre known as 'boys' love', which depicts same-sex liaisons between gorgeous guys. There are also butler cafés, staffed by women cross-dressing as impossibly beautiful men.

In Tokyo, anyone with even the slightest interest in *anime*, manga, maids, or even just the obscure, is sure to have their fantasies met.

IN CONTEXT

Sights

Meiji Shrine. *See p67.*

Asakusa	**44**
Map Asakusa	45
Old Soaks	50
Ebisu & Daikanyama	**52**
Map Meguro	53
Ginza	**56**
Map Ginza	59
Something Fishy	61
Harajuku & Aoyama	**62**
Map Harajuku & Aoyama	65
Gotta Have Faith	66
Ikebukuro	**68**
Map Ikebukuro	69
How to Play Pachinko	73
Marunouchi	**74**
Map Marunouchi	77
Walk Old Tokyo	79
Odaiba	**81**
Map Odaiba	83

Roppongi	**85**
Map Roppongi	87
Local View Joi Ito	90
Shibuya	**91**
Map Shibuya	93
Walk People-watching	95
Animania	96
Shinjuku	**98**
Manga Mania	99
Map Shinjuku	101
Hey, Big Spender?	102
Ueno	**105**
Map Ueno & Yanaka	107
Yanaka	**111**
Further Afield	**114**

Asakusa

Tokyo as it used to be.

Long before Roppongi or Shibuya figured on anybody's radar, Asakusa (pronounced 'a-sak-sa') was *the* place for entertainment in Tokyo. For a couple of centuries, until around 1940, this area adjacent to the eastern bank of the Sumida river was far and away the most exciting and dynamic part of town.

It's a fine example of *shitamachi*, the low-lying districts of the city where the commoners lived cheek by jowl until Tokyo's population began drifting westwards in the aftermath of the Great Earthquake of 1923 and fire bombing in World War II.

Map p45	**Restaurants** p147
Hotels p122	**Bars** p176

Today, it's a beacon for the nostalgic, oozing history from every shop front, and the contrast with the rest of the city is more apparent than ever with the 634-metre (2,080-foot) Tokyo Sky Tree rising just across the river.

INTRODUCTION TO ASAKUSA

Getting there: Asakusa is on the Ginza and Asakusa subway lines and the Tobu Isesaki railway line. Water buses arrive at/depart from the pier next to Azumabashi.

For the visitor, the greatest appeal here lies in the **Asakusa Kannon** temple. It is this temple complex and its environs that have helped make Asakusa into one of Tokyo's prime tourist attractions. Also known as

INSIDE TRACK PANDA BUS

Tourist information group Asakusa Kanko Emaki operates a free bus service (www.sg-elem.co.jp/esta/pandabus.html), taking tourists on a 40-minute tour of the Asakusa area. The bus makes eight stops, including **Hanayashiki** (*see p50*), Senso-ji's **Kaminarimon** (Thunder Gate; *see p46*) and the **Suijo water bus dock**. It's not hard to spot the vehicle – it's dressed as a panda, complete with ears on the roof and the front moulded in the shape of the bear's face.

Senso-ji, Asakusa Kannon is Tokyo's oldest temple, with origins so remarkably precise story has it, dating to 18 March 628. That was when two brothers fishing on the Sumida river caught a five-centimetre (two-inch) golden statue in their net. Clearly lacking wisdom, they threw the statue back in the river twice, only for it to reappear both times. At this point they twigged that something out of the ordinary was happening, and took the statue to the village chief. He enshrined it in his house, and in 645 a hall was built for this image of Kannon, the Buddhist goddess of mercy, on the spot where today's temple stands. The complex also houses a Shinto shrine, **Asakusa Jinja**, which was established in 1649 to honour the two fishermen and the village headman.

In later years, Asakusa flourished because of its proximity to Yoshiwara, the biggest area of licensed prostitution in Edo (as Tokyo was known from 1600 to 1868). Seeking a little refreshment before the evening's main activities, Yoshiwara's clientele could find that and plenty of other diversions in Asakusa – from acrobats and magicians to comedians and performing monkeys. In particular, the area flourished as the centre of *kabuki* theatre, a vastly popular form of entertainment whose leading actors were idolised like rock stars.

SIGHTS

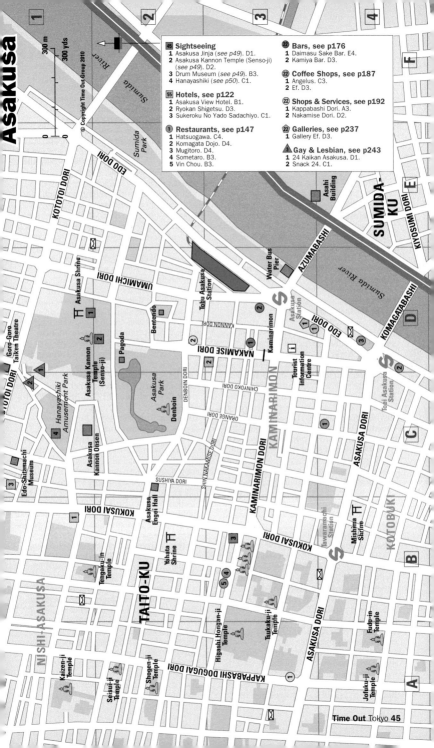

Asakusa

© Copyright Time Out Group 2010

Sumida River

0 300 m
0 300 yds

45 Sightseeing
1 Asakusa Jinja (*see p49*). D1.
2 Asakusa Kannon Temple (Senso-ji) (*see p49*). D2.
3 Drum Museum (*see p49*). B3.
4 Hanayashiki (*see p50*). C1.

55 Hotels, see p122
1 Asakusa View Hotel. B1.
2 Ryokan Shigetsu. D3.
3 Sukeroku No Yado Sadachiyo. C1.

1 Restaurants, see p147
1 Hatsuogawa. C4.
2 Komagata Dojo. D4.
3 Mugitoro. D4.
4 Sometaro. B3.
5 Vin Chou. B3.

22 Bars, see p176
1 Daimasu Sake Bar. E4.
2 Kamiya Bar. D3.

22 Coffee Shops, see p187
1 Angelus. C3.
2 Ef. D3.

22 Shops & Services, see p192
1 Kappabashi Dori. A3.
2 Nakamise Dori. D2.

22 Galleries, see p237
1 Gallery Ef. D3.

⚠ Gay & Lesbian, see p243
1 24 Kaikan Asakusa. D1.
2 Snack 24. C1.

Time Out Tokyo **45**

SIGHTS

Nowadays, Asakusa is home to numerous festivals, both old and new. Tokyo's oldest and biggest festival, in May, is the **Sanja Festival** (*see p222*), a frenzied procession of more than a hundred *mikoshi* (portable shrines). The most modern is the **Asakusa Samba Carnival** (*see p223*) in late August, when hundreds of Brazilian and Japanese dancers parade through the streets. The **Sumida River Fireworks** (*see p223*), Japan's biggest annual summertime fireworks display, is held at the end of July and is broadcast on national TV.

The Asakusa subway line station sits adjacent to the Sumida river at the end of Asakusa Dori; a few hundred metres north, next to Azumabashi (Azuma Bridge), is the Ginza line station, at the end of Kaminarimon Dori. Across the road, next to the Tobu Isesaki line station, stands Tokyo's oldest Western-style hostelry, **Kamiya Bar** (*see above* **Inside Track**), built in 1880.

The alcoholic vein continues when you look over Azumabashi to the Bubble-era **Asahi Building**, home of one of Japan's four main brewing companies, and the **Flamme d'Or** bar. Designed by Philippe Starck, this odd building is topped by a large golden sculpture whose shape causes many locals to refer to it as the *unchi-biru* ('turd building'). In the face of such architectural extravagance, the local constabulary clearly didn't want to be left out, so the police box near the bridge sports a pagoda-style roof. North of the pier is **Sumida Koen**, a riverside park that is popular during cherry-blossom season.

The approach to Asakusa Kannon temple begins about 100 metres (300 feet) up Kaminarimon Dori from the bridge. It's impossible to miss the main gate to the temple, the **Kaminarimon** (Thunder Gate), with its gigantic red paper lantern. Even in Edo days, this lantern was one of the city's most distinctive sights. Between 1856 and 1858, the great *ukiyo-e* woodblock artist Hiroshige published a set of prints called *One Hundred Views of Edo*. Among those evocative depictions of the old city, the Kaminarimon lantern is about the only one that could be identified by a modern-day Tokyoite. Black-garbed rickshaw drivers cruise the

entrance looking for tourists to ferry around. Across the road is the **Asakusa Culture & Sightseeing Centre** (3842 5566, open 9.30am-8pm daily), which has maps and information, and runs free one-hour tours on Sundays (at 11am and 2pm).

From the gate stretches the lively thoroughfare of **Nakamise Dori** (*see p200*). For centuries, this street was lined with stalls catering to the crowds on their way to and from the temple. Today, there are about 150 stalls along its 300-metre (984-foot) length, selling such traditional goods as combs, fans, dolls, kimono, paper crafts, clothing, toys and snacks, many of which would be instantly recognisable to any resident of old Edo. Absent from the scene are the former archery galleries. These were presided over by attractive young women, whose make-up and manner made it clear that when they escorted a male customer into their back room it wasn't with a view to stringing up his bow.

The temple is the main attraction in Asakusa, but there are plenty of other sights of interest. Heading north through the temple precincts will lead you to Kototoi Dori; turn left and you'll walk past the **Goro-Goro Taiken Theatre**, famous for displays of highly stylised swordsmanship. Turning left again at a small shopping street called Hisagao Dori brings you to the entrance of Japan's oldest amusement park, **Hanayashiki**. Nearby is the small **Edo-Shitamachi Traditional Crafts Museum** (2-22-13 Asakusa, 3842 1990, open 10am-8pm daily, admission free), which displays traditional crafts made by local artists.

Just to the west beyond Hanayashiki is the small district of **Rokku**, centred on Rokku Eigagai. This was Edo and Tokyo's prime entertainment area, though, today, sadly, it's a pale imitation of its former self. Japanese folk music drifts from the open doorways of **Asakusa Engei Hall**, the home of *rakugo* – traditional comic storytelling. Garish posters of 1960s yakuza gangster films are pasted outside the Shin-Gekijo, Meiga-za and Toho cinemas. Further south, on Kokusai Dori opposite the police box, is the delightful **Drum Museum**, located on the second floor of a shop selling musical instruments and Buddhist shrines.

Aside from the temple grounds and brash culture of Rokku, Asakusa's busy shopping streets are great places for an idle wander to see a slice of traditional life. You might chance upon a kimono shop owner kneeling at his counter in front of variegated bolts of cloth; or a half-dozen *sembei* (rice cracker) makers chatting as they toast crackers on a charcoal grill; or a tea merchant, with jade-green wares displayed in woven baskets and the delicious smell of roasting fresh tea wafting from his shop.

Asakusa Kannon Temple (Senso-ji) & Asakusa Jinja. *See p49.*

Suijo water-bus.

Shopping of a more specialised kind can be found by walking west (away from the river) to **Kappabashi Dori** (*see p199*), Tokyo's main wholesale district for the restaurant industry. This is far more interesting than it sounds: it's where caterers come to buy all those (surprisingly expensive) plastic models of foodstuffs that you see in restaurant windows. All manner of kitchen hardware is on sale, from small fish knives to cauldron-sized pots. It's a good place to pick up some lacquerware or ceramic souvenirs. Shops line either side of Kappabashi Dori; look for the 12-metre (39-foot) high chef's head atop the Niimi Building.

Further south and back towards the river are other wholesale districts, specialising in dolls, stationery and fashion accessories – the nearest stations are Kuramae and Asakusabashi. Near the latter is the **Japanese Stationery Museum**, where you can explore the history of writing and calculating implements.

ON THE RIVER

Asakusa can also be the starting point for a cruise on the **Sumida river**. One option is to take the , which leaves every 20-45 minutes from the pier next to Azumabashi, heading south under 13 bridges en route to the beautiful Hama-Rikyu Detached Garden (*see p60*). There's a network of five water-bus lines; for more details, *see p310*.

Or you could take a *yakata-bune* boat tour. These are leisurely cruises around Tokyo Bay on floating restaurants – and nicest at night. Several companies operate tours; try **Amisei** (3844 1869). Tickets are ¥8,000-¥10,000, but

include as much food (tempura, sushi, yakitori) and drink (beer, saké, juice) as you can consume. Reservations are advisable.

RYOGOKU

Just across the Sumida river is Ryogoku, where sumo tournaments have been held for 300 years. You'll spot a few small statues of wrestlers outside the Ryogoku JR station and maybe a couple of souvenir stalls, but it's generally a nondescript area. It's home to the **Ryogoku Kokugikan** (*see p280*), the stadium where three of sumo's Grand Tournaments are held, in January, May and September, and various stables (*heya*), where the wrestlers live and train. Restaurants specialising in *chanko-nabe*, the stews the wrestlers eat, also cluster here; a good one to visit is **Yoshiba** (*see p147*).

If you're in town when no tournaments are in progress, it's possible to visit a stable to see the wrestlers in their daily morning practice sessions. There are over 40 stables in Tokyo, most situated close to the Kokugikan. Most allow visitors, on condition that they remain quiet – call ahead (in Japanese) to ask for permission. The stables let you in for free, but take along a small gift – such as a bottle of saké – for the stable master to show your appreciation. Photos are usually permitted, but don't point your feet towards the ring. Be warned: the day starts early. Junior wrestlers are up and about at 4am, and practice sessions start at around 5am. The higher-ranked wrestlers appear at around 8am.

Recommended stables are **Azumazeki** (4-6-4 Higashi Komagata, Sumida-ku, 3625 0033),

Dewanoumi (2-3-15 Ryogoku, Sumida-ku, 3633 4920), **Musashigawa** (4-27-1 Higashi-Nippori, Arakawa-ku, 3801 6343) and **Oshiogawa** (2-17-7 Kiba, Koto-ku, 3643 8156). There's also an up-to-date list of addresses at www.accesscom.com/~abe/03haruheya.html.

If you couldn't care less about sumo, the excellent **Edo-Tokyo Museum** is located next door to the Kokugikan. There's also the **Tokyo Metropolitan Memorial & Tokyo Reconstruction Museum** and **Popeye** (*see p186*), the city's best beer bar.

FURTHER AFIELD

Asakusa thrived in the Edo era because of its proximity to **Yoshiwara**, but little survives of the red-light district today. What was once a huge, walled pleasure area is now the home of massage parlours, 'soaplands' and love hotels. What does remain, though, is the sad structure of the **Jokan-ji** temple, close to Minowa station (from Asakusa station, take the Ginza line to Ueno station, then the Hibiya line two stops to Minowa). The image of Yoshiwara may have a rakish, exotic appeal, but Jokan-ji presents the other side of the coin: this is where more than 11,000 prostitutes, mostly in their early 20s, were buried in a common grave.

From Minowa it is possible to experience another aspect of old Tokyo in the form of the **Arakawa Streetcar Line** (*see p70*). Old-fashioned green and cream trams trundle westwards along a 12-kilometre (eight-mile) route from Minowabashi station to Waseda, not far from Ikebukuro.

★ FREE Asakusa Kannon Temple (Senso-ji) & Asakusa Jinja

2-3-1 Asakusa, Taito-ku (3842 0181 temple, 3844 1575 shrine). Asakusa station (Asakusa, Ginza lines), exits 1, 3, 6, A4. **Open** *Temple* Oct-Mar 6.30am-5pm daily; Apr-Sept 6am-5pm daily. *Grounds* 24hrs daily. **Admission** free. **Map** p45.

The lively focus of traditional life in Tokyo, Asakusa Kannon is the city's most vivid reminder of the Edo era. Although the current buildings are constructed in a distinctly un-Edo-like ferro-concrete, they do offer an indication of the older city that lurks beneath the modern jacket of Tokyo.

Most people enter from the south, through the main gate, Kaminarimon, past the stalls of Nakamise Dori and then through the two-storey Hozomon gate into the temple grounds proper. To the left stands a five-storey, 55m (180ft) pagoda, the second-highest in Japan; ahead are the magnificent sweeping roofs of the Main Hall, with the gold-plated Gokuden shrine inside. Behind and to the right is Asakusa Jinja, the starting point of the Sanja Matsuri.

A huge bronze incense burner stands in front of the Main Hall. The smoke is believed to have curative powers, and visitors usually stop to 'bathe' in it, often directing the smoke towards a troubled part of the body. You can make a wish, pick your fortune or buy good-luck charms from stalls. Other buildings and gardens occupy the extensive grounds. *Photo p47*.

Drum Museum
Taiko-kan
Miyamoto Unosuke Shoten, Nishi-Asakusa Bldg 4F, 2-1-1 Nishi-Asakusa, Taito-ku (3842 5622,

SIGHTS

Hanayashiki. See p50.

www.tctv.ne.jp/members/taikokan). Tawaramachi station (Ginza line). **Open** 10am-5pm Wed-Sun. **Admission** ¥300; ¥150 reductions; free under-6s. **No credit cards. Map** p45.

With a clay drum from Mexico, an *udekki* from Sri Lanka and hundreds of other drums from around the world, this interactive museum is a fine place to visit. Find your own rhythm by banging on many of them (a blue dot means it's allowed, a red one means it's not).

★ Edo-Tokyo Museum

1-4-1 Yokoami, Sumida-ku (3626 9974, www.edo-tokyo-museum.or.jp). Ryogoku station (Oedo line), exits A3, A4; (Sobu line), west exit. **Open** 9.30am-5.30pm Tue-Fri, Sun; 9.30am-7pm Sat. **Admission** ¥600; free-¥480 reductions; additional fee for special exhibitions. **No credit cards.**

This large museum's outlandish architectural style may not appeal to everyone, but the building houses the city's best collection of displays dealing with the history of Tokyo. Highlights include large-scale reconstructions of Nihonbashi bridge and a *kabuki* theatre, as well as detailed models of quarters of the city in different eras. Exhibits outline lifestyles and show how disasters, natural and man-made, altered the city's landscape. The English labelling is good.

Hanayashiki

2-28-1 Asakusa, Taito-ku (3842 8780, www. hanayashiki.net). Asakusa station (Asakusa, Ginza lines), exit 3. **Open** 10am-6pm daily. **Admission** ¥900; free-¥400 reductions. **No credit cards. Map** p45.

Hanayashiki has been in business since 1885 and still draws crowds. There are around 20 rides, more appealing for nostalgia than thrills – including

---

Old Soaks

Relax in a traditional hot-spring bath.

The global spa boom hasn't neglected Japan. Slick modern complexes are popping up across the capital – try the **Spa at Mandarin Oriental Tokyo** (*see p127*), which offers high-rise views of the city as the staff pamper you. But a more authentically Japanese experience awaits you at one of the traditional *onsen* or *sento*. Onsen are Japan's hot springs, taking advantage of the nation's volcanic geology for piping-hot, mineral-rich water that is renowned for its healing effects. *Sento* (literally, 'penny baths') are the artificial equivalent – using heated tap water – and there are around 1,000 of them in Tokyo (look for short curtains with a sign that resembles flames emerging from a frying pan). Both baths are throwbacks to an era when the local public tub was the only place to wash, and while some places look as though they haven't had a facelift since that time, there are some great spots in the city to soak your stresses away.

The baths are communal, and segregated by sex, so you'll likely be bathing with a handful of naked locals. Most *sento* also have a cashier who sits in a stall with a perfect view of both changing rooms, but dutifully avoids gazing into either.

If you're heading for **Hakone** (*see pp292-295*), you'll find myriad *onsen*, many of them boasting spectacular views. High-end traditional inns often have private hot springs (*kashikiri onsen*), which can make the communal bathing experience more fun.

BATHING ETIQUETTE

Having paid and entered the relevant changing room – signs are written only in *kanji*, but often colour-coded red and blue – strip off completely and put your clothes in a locker. Proceed into the bathing area and start showering. This being communal bathing, it's considered essential to be spotlessly clean before you enter the bath, so be visibly diligent in scrubbing yourself. Then climb into the tub, relax, and always keep your head above water.

Be warned that the water temperature can, for the uninitiated, be extremely hot. Sluice yourself first to get acclimatised, then ease yourself into the bath. Lie back and enjoy.

ONSEN

Asakusa Kannon Onsen

2-7-26 Asakusa, Taito-ku (3844 4141). Asakusa station (Asakusa, Ginza lines), Kannosamma exit. **Open** 6.30am-6pm Mon, Tue, Thur-Sun. **Admission** ¥700. **No credit cards.**

This classic bathhouse's waters are reportedly good for rheumatism and nervous disorders.

Seta Onsen

4-15-30 Seta, Setagaya-ku (3707 8228, www.setaonsen.co.jp). Futako Tamagawa station (Tokyu Denentoshi, Tokyu Oimachi,

Japan's oldest steel-track rollercoaster. Most have been upgraded over the years, but their scope is limited due to the park's small size. *Photo p49.*

FREE Japan Stationery Museum
1-1-15 Yanagibashi, Taito-ku (3861 4905). Asakusabashi station (Asakusa, Sobu lines), east exit. **Open** 1-4pm Mon-Fri. **Admission** free.
Exhibits range from flints and a tablet from Mesopotamia through Egyptian papyrus to abacuses and typewriters with interchangeable *kanji* keys. One highlight is a 14kg (31lb) brush made from the hair of over 50 horses. Descriptions are all in Japanese.

FREE Tokyo Metropolitan Memorial & Tokyo Reconstruction Museum
2-3-25 Yokoami, Sumida-ku (3623 1200). Ryogoku station (Oedo line), exits A3, A4;
(Sobu line), west exit. **Open** *Memorial Museum* 8.30am-4.30pm Tue-Sun. *Reconstruction Museum* 9am-4.30pm daily. **Admission** free.
Following the Great Kanto Earthquake of 1923, some 40,000 people who had fled their homes perished on this site when sparks set clothing and bedding alight. The fire raged for nearly a day and a half, destroying three-quarters of the city and killing 140,000 people. Seven years later, a three-storey pagoda-topped memorial building was erected; after World War II, the memorial's name was changed to include the 100,000 people who died in Tokyo's air raids.

The Reconstruction Museum in a nearby building in the park contains wartime mementos. Both buildings are pretty run-down and receive little attention. Most of what they do receive is concentrated on the controversial Yasukuni Shrine (*see p80*), which honours the war dead. Memorial services are held on 10 March and 1 September at 10am.

Tokyu Shin-Tamagawa lines) then 10mins walk or shuttle bus. **Open** 10am-11pm daily. **Admission** ¥2,300; ¥1,260 after 9pm. **No credit cards**.
A large-scale, family-friendly *onsen* in a lovely garden setting. There are communal outdoor pools (these are the only baths in town that demand swimwear) and, best of all, an outdoor bar. The view isn't great, but when you're sipping cocktails in the open-air hot spring, you won't care.

SENTO
The price of all *sento* baths is set at a standard ¥450, though it usually costs extra to use the sauna.

Aqua
4-9-22 Higashi-Nakano, Nakano-ku (5330 1126). Higashi-Nakano station (Chuo, Oedo lines), east exit. **Open** 3pm-midnight Tue-Sun. **No credit cards**.
A modern *sento* with a variety of baths, including a *rotenburo* and sauna. Usefully, it stocks cold beers. The sauna costs an extra ¥500.

Daikoku-yu
32-6 Senju Kotobuki-cho, Adachi-ku (3881 3001). Kita-Senju station (Chiyoda, Hibiya lines), west exit then 15mins walk. **Open** 3pm-midnight Tue-Sun. **No credit cards**.
This majestic, temple-like building is probably the most attractive *sento* in Tokyo. Cleaner than most of its peers

and boasting its own *rotenburo* (outdoor *sento*), it also has cold beer in stock.

Komparu-yu
8-7-5 Ginza, Chuo-ku (3571 5469). Ginza station (Ginza, Hibiya lines), exit A2. **Open** 2-11pm Mon-Fri; 2-10pm Sat. **No credit cards**.
A few doors from Kyubei – one of Tokyo's most famous (and famously expensive) sushi restaurants – in ritzy Ginza, this tiny old bathhouse dates back to Edo days. There are two baths: *atatakai* (hot) and *nurui* (lukewarm) – lukewarm is hot enough for most.

Shimizu-yu
3-12-3 Minami-Aoyama, Minato-ku (3401 4404). Omotesando station (Chiyoda, Ginza, Hanzomon lines), exit A4. **Open** noon-midnight Tue-Fri; noon-11pm Sat, Sun. **No credit cards**.
A soak in the heart of Omotesando. Stash your shopping and unwind with a bath.

Tamano-yu
1-13-7 Asagaya-Kita, Suginami-ku (3338 7860). Asagaya station (Chuo line), north exit. **Open** 3.30pm-1am Tue-Sun. **No credit cards**.
A recently renovated, traditional *sento* with a number of novelty tubs, including one that ignores all sane advice and pumps electricity into the bath water for a tingling sensation.

SIGHTS

Ebisu & Daikanyama

Cool cafés and funky fashion await in this upmarket patch of Tokyo.

Within a stone's throw of Shibuya, dining destination **Ebisu** comes alive at night, when hordes of young Tokyoites flock to its myriad bars and restaurants. Meanwhile, the self-contained plaza of Ebisu Garden Place is liveliest on weekends, when shoppers and daytrippers crowd its stores, galleries and museums.

The weekend is also **Daikanyama**'s appointed hour, as young – mainly female – shoppers descend upon its scores of boutiques for essential wardrobe updates. This prim neighbourhood is, refreshingly, one of the few districts in Japan that has managed to resist the rise of the big chain burger bars and their Japanese equivalents.

Just to the south of Ebisu is **Meguro** station – the starting point for some unusual and entertaining diversions.

Map p53	**Restaurants** p148
Hotels p123	**Bars** p177

SIGHTS

EBISU

Getting there: Ebisu station is on the Yamanote line and the Hibiya subway line.

The area of Ebisu (sometimes also spelled Yebisu) is renowned for its wealth of restaurants and bars, and as one of Tokyo's top spots for rowdy *go-kon* (group blind dates). Ebisu began life as the home of brewer Sapporo, who built a brewery here in 1887. There are still strong ties to the liquid gold – Ebisu's biggest attraction is **Ebisu Garden Place**, a mall development backed by Sapporo that serves as the location for the company's headquarters, a Sapporo Beer Hall and the **Beer Museum Yebisu**. A five-minute

'Skywalk' via a moving sidewalk from Ebisu station, the mall is a well-heeled mini city, housing dozens of shops, including a small branch of Mitsukoshi department store. It's also home to a host of restaurants, foremost among which is chef extraordinaire Joël Robuchon's palatial **Taillevent Robuchon** (5424 1338, www.taillevent.com/japon), housed in a bright-yellow, mock-French château complete with wine shop and pâtisserie. Also figured into the development are the **Westin Tokyo** hotel (*see p125*), office towers, apartment buildings and the **Tokyo Metropolitan Museum of Photography**.

Venture out of the station through either the east or west exits, and you are plunged into a buzzing mélange of restaurants, cafés such as the **Time Out Café** (*see p187*), pubs including **What the Dickens** (*see p177*), a smattering of bars and nightclubs, and, underlining the area's suitability as a dating spot, even a couple of love hotels.

FREE Beer Museum Yebisu

B1F 4-20-1 Ebisu Garden Place, Shibuya-ku (www.sapporobeer.jp/brewery/y_museum). Ebisu station (Yamanote line), east exit; (Hibiya line), exit 1. **Open** 11am-6.30pm Tue-Sun. **Admission** free. *Beer* ¥200. **No credit cards.**

> **INSIDE TRACK**
> **BREWING UP A NAME**
>
> Some beers take their name from the area in which they were brewed, but for Ebisu it was the reverse. Ebisu is a corruption of Yebisu, the beer brewed by Sapporo. The eponymous train station was built in 1901 as a freight station for the precious liquid cargo.

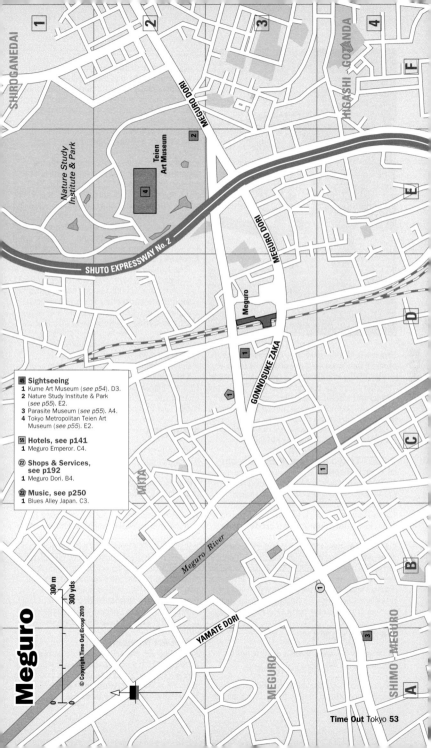

Meguro

SHIROGANEDAI

MEGURO DORI

SHUTO EXPRESSWAY No. 2

Nature Study Institute & Park

Teien Art Museum

Meguro

GONNOSUKE ZAKA

MITA

Meguro River

YAMATE DORI

MEGURO

SHIMO-MEGURO

HIGASHI-GOZANDA

45 Sightseeing
1 Kume Art Museum (*see p54*). D3.
2 Nature Study Institute & Park
   (*see p55*). E2.
3 Parasite Museum (*see p55*). A4.
4 Tokyo Metropolitan Teien Art
   Museum (*see p55*). E2.

55 Hotels, see p141
1 Meguro Emperor. C4.

22 Shops & Services,
   see p192
1 Meguro Dori. B4.

22 Music, see p250
1 Blues Alley Japan. C3.

300 m
300 yds

© Copyright Time Out Group 2010

Daikanyama.

There are no big overseas brands here – Daikanyama kids prefer cutesy home-grown designer labels to logo-laden merchandise. The area offers many opportunities for observing the often risible outfits of Japan's most deeply afflicted fashion victims from the comfort of numerous open-air cafés.

If you're not shopping for young fashion, Daikanyama will have limited appeal, but there are several good places for picking up souvenirs. Anyone who appreciates the Japanese aesthetic will find something of interest at **Okura** (20-11 Sarugakucho, 3461 8511, open 11am/11.30am-8.30pm daily), where indigo-dyed T-shirts with traditional patterns are lined up alongside carefully crafted accessories in traditional materials such as bamboo, hemp and silk. Also here is a branch of Tokyo's number-one hat emporium, **CA4LA** (*see p208*), at 17-5 Daikanyamacho.

The **Eataly** complex (20-23 Daikanyama-cho, Shibuya-ku, 5784 2736, www.eataly.co.jp) is a good place to take a break, with a café and posh grocery store selling Italian ingredients, and plenty of al fresco seating. For something more substantial, try **Sobateria** (2F, 16-2 Daikanyama-cho, Shibuya-ku, 6416 9028, www.tokyosoba.com), which gives the humble buckwheat noodle a trendy Daikanyama treatment.

One station down the tracks from Daikanyama is Naka-Meguro (*see p114*), a picturesque neighbourhood perennially at the centre of a 'hip, has-been or back again?' debate.

Sapporo built this museum – commemorating the brewery that stood on the space it now occupies – along with the slightly starchy mall in which it sits. Past the historical photographs, beer labels, old posters and video displays, there's a virtual reality tour of the brewing process and, at last, a lounge where you can sample the product.

▶ *Beer fans will have even more fun sampling the vast selection at Popeye (see p186).*

★ FREE Tokyo Metropolitan Museum of Photography

Ebisu Garden Place, 1-13-3 Mita, Meguro-ku (3280 0099, www.syabi.com). Ebisu station (Yamanote line), east exit; (Hibiya line), exit 1. **Open** 10am-6pm Tue, Wed, Sat, Sun; 10am-8pm Thur, Fri. **Admission** free. **No credit cards.** Occupying a four-floor building in one corner of Ebisu Garden Place, this is Tokyo's premier photography showcase. It has a large permanent collection and brings in leading lights of the photography world for regular star-studded shows. The small Images & Technology Gallery in the basement presents a multimedia history of optics, featuring tricks such as morphing, and the occasional media art exhibition.

DAIKANYAMA

Getting there: Daikanyama station is on the Tokyu Toyoko line.

Almost every square metre of Daikanyama is devoted to clothing, mostly for girls in their 20s.

MEGURO

Getting there: Meguro station is on the Yamanote line.

The area around Meguro station isn't rich in tourist attractions, but there are a couple of interesting museums in the area: the **Kume Art Museum**, next to the station's west exit, and the **Tokyo Metropolitan Teien Art Museum**, a short walk from the east exit. The latter is a 1930s French art deco house, once a prince's residence and now a beautiful blend of architectural showpiece, art museum and landscaped garden. Adjacent to the museum you'll find the botanical wonders of the **Nature Study Institute & Park**.

Further away to the east of the station is the world's only **Parasite Museum**.

Kume Art Museum

Kume Bldg 8F, 2-25-5 Kami-Osaki, Shinagawa-ku (3491 1510, www.kume-museum.com). Meguro station (Yamanote line), west exit. **Open** 10am-5pm Tue-Sun. **Admission** ¥500; ¥200-¥300 reductions. **No credit cards. Map** p53.

SIGHTS

Nature Study Institute & Park.

Keiichiro Kume was one of the first Japanese artists to embrace the Impressionist style. This museum has changing displays of his paintings.

Nature Study Institute & Park

5-21-5 Shirokanedai, Minato-ku (3441 7176, www.ins.kahaku.go.jp). Meguro station (Yamanote line), east exit or Shiroganedai station (Mita, Nanboku lines), exit 1. **Open** *May-Aug* 9am-5pm Tue-Sun. *Sept-Apr* 9am-4pm Tue-Sun. **Admission** ¥300; free reductions. **No credit cards. Map** p53.

A primeval forest in central Tokyo? Yes, it's a remnant of the ancient Musashino plain. Established as a scientific study area in 1949, the park contains myriad plants, birds and insects. Admission is limited to a few hundred people at a time, so that visitors can enjoy the turtle-filled ponds and forested hills in peace. The one-room museum at the entrance is hardly a destination in itself, but it has a couple of interesting points, such as a map showing how the greenery in Tokyo has decreased since 1677, largely as a result of dwindling temple grounds.

FREE Parasite Museum

4-1-1 Shimo-Meguro, Meguro-ku (3716 1264). Meguro station (Yamanote line), west exit. **Open** 10am-5pm Tue-Sun. **Admission** free. **Map** p53.

This unusual venture was opened in 1953 by Satoru Kamegai, a doctor whose practice was overwhelmed by patients afflicted by parasites (caused by the poor sanitary conditions that were widespread in post-war Japan). The museum displays some 300 samples of 45,000 parasites he collected, 20 of which were discovered by his foundation. The second floor has a display of an 8.8m (29ft) tapeworm taken from the body of a 40-year-old man, with a ribbon next to it showing you just how long 8.8m really is.

► *The shop sells parasites preserved in plastic keyrings: ideal gifts for your nearest and dearest.*

★ Tokyo Metropolitan Teien Art Museum

5-21-9 Shirokanedai, Minato-ku (3443 0201, www.teien-art-museum.ne.jp). Meguro station (Yamanote line), east exit or Shiroganedai station (Mita, Nanboku lines), exit 1. **Open** 10am-5.30pm daily. Closed 2nd & 4th Wed of mth. **Admission** *Exhibitions* varies. *Garden* ¥200; free-¥160 reductions. **No credit cards. Map** p53.

This 1933 art deco mansion, fronted by both a Western-style rose garden and a Japanese strolling garden, was once the home of Prince Yasuhiko Asaka – the uncle of Emperor Hirohito – and his wife, Princess Nobuko – the eighth daughter of Emperor Meiji. The prince returned from a three-year stint in 1920s Paris enamoured of art deco and decided to build a modern residence. Henri Rapin designed most of the interior, while René Lalique added his touch to the crystal chandeliers and the doors. The edifice was completed by architects of the Imperial Household Department, foremost among them Yokichi Gondo. Regularly changing temporary shows are spread through the museum and double as house tours.

SIGHTS

Ginza

Bring your credit cards – this could get expensive.

Ginza is, was and always will be the epitome of Tokyo extravagance. It's here that ladies saunter the wide streets, dressed head to toe in luxury brands, shopping for more of the same. This is where you'll find politicians and businessmen on bottomless expense accounts quaffing overpriced drinks in the company of kimono-clad bar staff.

Crammed into Ginza's eight main blocks (*chome*) are over 10,000 shops, many of them selling goods at Bubble-era prices. Here are small, old-school specialist stores selling the best of their chosen craft, from kimonos to confectionery, as well as the dazzling flagships of the international super-brands. And though a coffee or a cocktail doesn't come cheap here, Ginza is home to some of the most extraordinary eating and drinking in this gastronomic city.

Map p59	**Restaurants** p150
Hotels p125	**Bars** p177

EXPLORING GINZA

Getting there: The Ginza area is well served by trains. There's Yurakucho station (JR Yamanote and Yurakucho subway lines), Hibiya station (Chiyoda, Hibiya and Mita subway lines), and Ginza station (Ginza, Hibiya and Marunouchi subway lines).

The area's reputation for exclusivity stretches back to the 19th-century Meiji period, when Ginza became the first part of Tokyo to be rebuilt in red brick rather than wood. Red brick was thought to offer greater protection from natural disasters, a theory disproved in 1923 when the area was razed by the Great Kanto Earthquake. Unfortunately, not one single red brick from Ginza's first golden era survives today.

INSIDE TRACK
GINZA'S GALLERIES

It's easy to get caught up in the commerce and fine dining of Ginza, but don't miss the area's gallery scene, one of the capital's best. For reviews of the top venues, *see p238*.

What does survive, though, is the Tokyo pastime of 'Ginbura', or Ginza strolling. The area has unusually wide pavements – and from noon at weekends, cars are banned from the main street, **Chuo Dori** – creating what is known as *hokousha tengoku* ('pedestrian heaven'). Buskers and café seating in the middle of the road lend the area a relaxed feel.

Foreign retail chains tend to choose to have their first Japanese outlets in prestigious Ginza before opening up elsewhere. The first to arrive were the luxury giants – Gucci, Prada, Hermès, Louis Vuitton – all of whom commissioned celebrity architects to give their stores fancy façades. They've been joined in recent years by the likes of H&M, Abercrombie & Fitch and Uniqlo, which all have flagship stores on the strip; and even these lower-end retailers have made respectable efforts to blend into their architecturally eye-popping surroundings.

There's also a mix of affordability and luxury at **RagTag** (*see p208*), a six-storey second-hand clothing shop that deals only in the biggest brands. Ginza's fickle fashion crowd keeps the store stocked with barely worn garments from recent catwalk collections.

For dining, too, you'll find bargains in Ginza if you look hard enough (though if it's budget dining you're looking for, head instead to the

SIGHTS

neighbouring district of Shinbashi; *see p58*). As elsewhere in Tokyo, most restaurants offer set-lunch deals, the difference here being that you have a chance to eat food for around ¥2,000 that might cost ten times as much in the evening. Most restaurants are off the main drag, many of them in basements, so take a walk around the backstreets and check out the prices, which are usually posted on boards outside (if they're not, it's because the prices would make you weep).

Yurakucho station is a good starting point to explore Ginza; the **Tokyo TIC** (*see p318*) tourist office is almost next door. Take the exit for Ginza and walk down the narrow arcade, then straight through the the Mullion complex with its cinemas. You'll emerge at a multi-directional zebra crossing known as Sukiyabashi (Sukiya Bridge). Confusingly, there is no bridge. There used to be one from the present-day Sukiyabashi Hankyu department store toward Hibiya, across the old outer moat of Edo Castle (now the Imperial Palace), but both bridge and waterway were casualties of 1960s road construction. Today, a small monument marks the spot where the bridge once stood.

Standing with Sukiyabashi Hankyu department store on your right, you will see a Sony sign on the other side of the crossing. The electronic giant's eight-storey showcase, the **Sony Building** (*see p203*), will appeal to both technology and gaming fans. All the latest Sony models are on display, with staff eager to talk you through them. The sixth floor is a free PlayStation arcade where you can try the latest games; it's packed with kids at weekends, but more tolerable midweek. The basement holds two floors of Sony Plaza, a chain that stocks import snacks, cosmetics and other colourful goodies. The narrow tower next door, made of semi-translucent gold glass bricks that seem to glow from within at night, is the **Hermès** flagship, designed by Renzo Piano.

Walk down Sotobori Dori (Outer Moat Avenue, once part of Edo Castle's waterway defences), towards Ginza Ha-chome and Shinbashi. Ginza streets are named and laid out in a grid, so it's difficult to get lost. Stop off at some of the small art galleries, most of which are free to enter. When you reach the boundary of Ginza at Gomon Dori, turn left toward Ginza Dori and the narrower streets of Sony Dori, Namiki Dori, Nishi Gobangai Dori and Suzuran Dori. Whichever route you take back to **Harumi Dori** (the other major thoroughfare), the atmospheric streets between Ginza Dori and Sotobori Dori are the best pottering area in Ginza. Zigzag toward the area's main crossroads: the intersection of Ginza Dori and Harumi Dori – known as Yon-chome crossing.

Each corner of the crossing has its landmark, the most famous being **Wako**, a watch and jewellery department store famous for its window displays and clocktower. In Ozu's classic film *Tokyo Story* (1953), two women are driven past Wako, the store representing the high-class, modern face of Tokyo.

Facing Wako, on the other side of Ginza Dori, is upscale department store **Mitsukoshi** (*see p195*; the bronze lion at its entrance is a popular meeting point). The **Nissan Gallery** occupies another corner, with the latest models exhibited on the ground floor, and on the fourth corner you will find the cylindrical **San-ai Building**, with **Le Café Doutor Ginza** offering cheap coffee and great views. Next door is the famous paper specialist **Kyukyodo** (*see p212*).

From the Yon-chome crossing, with your back to Wako, heading left along Ginza Dori will take you past more high-class stores – spectacular at night when the neon signs are switched on – and, eventually, into Kyobashi, where you'll find the **Metropolitan Police Department Museum** and the **National Film Centre**.

If you take Harumi Dori instead, you'll eventually reach **Tsukiji Fish Market**, one of the world's largest wholesale markets and an unmissable sight (*see p61* **Something Fishy**).

On the northern side of the Yamanote line tracks, opposite the **Imperial Hotel** (*see p126*), is the **Takarazuka** (*see p273*), a theatre that's home to an all-female musical revue.

Sony Building.

Takarazuka is imbued with less tradition and history than *kabuki*, but it's an equally unique experience. Next door is a large park, **Hibiya Koen**. Once the parade ground for the Japanese army, it was turned into the country's first Western-style park in 1903, complete with rose gardens, a bandstand and open-air theatre. It's a great spot for an impromptu picnic or romantic late-night stroll. At the northern end of the park is a moat, which surrounds the expansive grounds of the **Imperial Palace** (*see p74*).

FREE Metropolitan Police Department Museum

Matsushita Denko Tokyo Honsha Bldg B2-2F, 3-5-1 Kyobashi, Chuo-ku (3581 4321, www. keishicho.metro.tokyo.jp). Kyobashi station (Ginza line), exit 2. **Open** 10am-6pm Tue-Sun. **Admission** free. **Map** p59.

With a reputation lying somewhere between inept and corrupt, Japan's police force needs a little more than this drab collection of artefacts to turn things around. The absence of anything relating to modern crime-fighting might alarm more than reassure visitors, and the most exciting-looking exhibit is an arcade-style gaming machine that, disappointingly, turns out to be a safe-driving simulator. Still, if you've been dragging your kids around designer boutiques all day, you might redeem yourself here: diminutive visitors can dress as mini officers, sit on a Kawasaki police motorcycle with flashing lights, peer into a helicopter and meet force mascot Pipo-kun.

National Film Centre

3-7-6 Kyobashi, Chuo-ku (3561 0823, www. momat.go.jp/english). Kyobashi station (Ginza line), exit 1. **Open** 11am-6.30pm Tue-Fri. *Library* 10am-6.30pm Tue-Sun. **Admission** ¥500; ¥100-¥300 concessions; free under-6s; additional charge for special exhibitions. **No credit cards. Map** p59.

Japanese and foreign films – 19,000 of them – star at the country's only national facility devoted to the preservation and study of cinema. Fans throng to its two cinemas for series focusing on, for example, DW Griffith or Korean films from the 1960s. Visitors can also check out the library of film books on the fourth floor or exhibitions of photos, graphic design and film-related items (often drawn from its own collection) in the gallery on the seventh floor.

SHINBASHI & SHIODOME

Getting there: Shinbashi is on the Yamanote, Asakusa and Ginza lines, while Shiodome is on the Oedo subway and Yurikamome monorail.

At the southern limits of Ginza is Shinbashi, the yang to Ginza's yin. It's a rough and tumble district with plenty of cheap eats and old-time Tokyo atmosphere. Wander the side streets and you'll see salarymen in crumpled suits

INSIDE TRACK
HIGH-RISE HONEY

Though you wouldn't know it to walk past the **Kami Palupu Kaikan** (Paper & Pulp Building), its rooftop is home to the Ginza Honeybee Project and its 300,000 winged workers. The bees collect nectar from nearby gardens, including those of the **Imperial Palace** (*see p74*) and return to their rooftop hives to make honey that ends up in candles, cakes and cocktails in Ginza's shops and bars. The pâtisserie **Henri Charpentier** (3562 2721, www.henri-charpentier.com) has a Ginza honey Madeline, while **Bar 5517** (3289 5676) has Ginza honey cocktails.

45 Sightseeing
1 Metropolitan Police Department Museum (*see above*). E1.
2 National Film Centre (*see above*). F1.

55 Hotels, see p125
1 Ginza Mercure. E2.
2 Hotel Com's Ginza. C4.
3 Hotel Seiyo Ginza. E2.
4 Imperial Hotel. B2.

① Restaurants, see p150
1 Azumitei. D2.
2 Bangkok Kitchen. C3.
3 Bird Land. D2.
4 Dhaba India (*see p161*). E1.
5 Kondo. D3.
6 Les Saisons. B2.
7 Little Okinawa. C4.
8 Ohmatsuya. C3.
9 Oshima. D3.
10 Robata. C2.

11 Shin-Hinomoto. C2.
12 Shunju Tsugihagi. B2.
13 Sushi no Midori. C3.
14 Ten-Ichi. C3.
15 Tokachiya. C3.

22 Bars, see p177
1 Bar High Five. C3.
2 Lion Beer Hall. D4.
3 Peter. C2.
4 Rockfish. C3.

22 Coffee Shops, see p188
1 Benisica. C2.
2 Café Fontana. D3.
3 Café Paulista. C4.
4 Cha Ginza (*see p191*). D3.
5 Ki No Hana. E4.

22 Shops & Services, see p192
1 Akebono. D3.
2 Familiar. D3.
3 Ginza Kanematsu. C3.
4 Ginza Natsuno. C3.

5 Hakuhinkan. C4.
6 Ito-ya. E2.
7 Kimuraya. D3.
8 Kyukyodo. D3.
9 Matsuya. E3.
10 Matsuzakaya. D3.
11 Mikimoto. D3.
12 Mitsukoshi. D3.
13 Mujirushi Ryohin. D1.
14 Nail Bee. D2.
15 Niwaka. E2.
16 Sayegusa. D4.
17 Sony Building. D3.
18 Tanagokoro. E2.
19 Tasaki Shinju. D3.
20 Uniqlo. D3.
21 Wako. D3.

22 Children, see p227
1 Royal Baby Salon. E1.

22 Film, see p232
1 Ciné Pathos. E3.
2 Ciné Switch Ginza. D3.
3 Ginza Théâtre Cinema. E2.

22 Galleries, see p238
1 Arataniurano. F3.
2 Forum Art Shop. D1.
3 Galleria Grafica Tokyo. D4.
4 Gallery Koyanagi. E2.
5 Ginza Graphic Gallery. C4.
6 INAX Gallery. F1.
7 Maison Hermès. D3.
8 Megumi Ogita. F3.
9 Nishimura Gallery. D2.
10 Shiseido Gallery. C4.
11 Tokyo Gallery. C4.

22 Music, see p250
1 Hibiya Yagai Ongakudo. A3.
2 Someday. A4.
3 Tokyo International Forum. D1.

22 Performing Arts, see p269
1 Shinbashi Embujo. E4.
2 Tokyo Takarazuka Gekijo. B2.

munching yakitori or tonkatsu and guzzling cheap beers. After the shiny and sometimes overwhelming consumer excess of its neighbour, Shinbashi feels refreshingly real.

However, this wouldn't be Tokyo without something modern thrusting skywards, and the area has not escaped the attentions of the developers. A collection of skyscrapers known as **Shiodome** opened in 2003 on the site of a former Japan Railways goods yard. With spacious plazas, mid-range dining and a couple of top-end hotels, it sits in gleaming contrast to the rest of the neighbourhood. The commercial and cultural impact of Shiodome was muted, however, by the almost simultaneous opening

Hama-Rikyu Detached Garden.

of the larger, ritzier Roppongi Hills (*see p198*). Having failed to attract as many upmarket restaurants or designer boutiques, Shiodome doesn't draw the crowds that its cross-town competitor does.

One of the skyscrapers is home to Dentsu, Japan's largest advertising agency; in the basement lies the **ADMT Advertising Museum Tokyo**, a great, interactive look at over 300 years of ads in Japan. The museum is at the rear of **Caretta Shiodome** (*see p197*), a shopping and dining arcade that also houses **Shochu Authority** (Caretta Shiodome B2F, 1-8-2 Higashi-Shinbashi, 5537 2105, open 11am-10pm daily), a spacious shop with over 3,200 varieties of Japan's domestic distillate (*see p181* **Local Potions**) and knowledgeable staff on hand.

Sitting quietly between the skyscrapers of Shiodome is a fascinating glimpse of the area's past. The **Old Shinbashi Station** is a reconstruction of one of Tokyo's first railway stations, the foundations of which are now visible through the glass floor.

After shopping and eating your way around all this gleaming modernity, take a five-minute walk to **Hama-Rikyu Detached Garden**, a one-time duck-hunting ground and the most picturesque spot in the Ginza area.

★ FREE ADMT Advertising Museum Tokyo

Caretta Shiodome B1F-B2F, 1-8-2 Higashi-Shinbashi, Minato-ku (6218 2500, www.admt.jp). Shinbashi station (Yamanote line), Shiodome exit; (Asakusa, Ginza lines), exit 6 or Shiodome station (Oedo, Yurikamome lines), exit 6. **Open** 11am-6.30pm Tue-Fri; 11am-4.30pm Sat, Sun. **Admission** free.

This fab museum is devoted to Japanese advertising, from fascinating 17th-century woodblock prints to modern product-placement techniques. Although English explanations are limited, the images largely speak for themselves. Inspired technology allows touch-screen browsing of historic ads, and on-demand viewing of award-winning commercials from the past three decades. The museum also contains a library of over 100,000 digitised images.

★ Hama-Rikyu Detached Garden
Hama-Rikyu Onshi Teien

1-1 Hama-Rikyu Teien, Chuo-ku (3541 0200). Shiodome station (Oedo, Yurikamome lines), exit 10 or Suijo water bus. **Open** 9am-5pm daily. **Admission** ¥300; ¥150 concessions. **No credit cards**.

This tranquil garden, once a hunting ground for the Tokugawa shogunate, now cowers in the shadow of the new Shiodome development. The garden's main appeal lies in the abundance of water in and around it and the fact that it feels deceptively spacious,

SIGHTS

Something Fishy

The sights and smells of Tsukiji fish market.

Take advantage of your jet lag and pay an early morning visit to one of Tokyo's most memorable sights, the wholesale fish market at Tsukiji. Colourful, cacophonous and chaotic – it's a fascinating spectacle. Some 50,000 workers and 14,000 retailers come daily to do business here. Over 1,600 stalls sell 450 varieties of seafood – fresh, frozen, smoked, dried, pickled – and much of it is totally unfamiliar. If it lives in water, you'll find it here.

There's been a fish market in Tokyo since 1590, but Tsukiji's current location is much younger, established in 1935. It comprises an inner and an outer market.

The inner section, strictly wholesale, is where the auction (and the action) happens. The tuna auction starts at around 5am and is finished by 6.30am. Auctions of vegetables and fruit follow, and the bulk of the market's business is done by midday. It's worth noting that flash photography is not permitted during auctions.

The market workers have a prickly attitude to tourists, so be careful to give way to their vehicles and stay inconspicuous during the auction. The market announces periodic bans on tourists viewing the auction, and since May 2010 has limited the number of visitors to 140 per day. The market office now issues tickets to visitors on a first-come, first-served basis, though the policy changes frequently and at short notice, so ask the TIC for the latest info. Even if the auction is out of bounds, it's still worth a visit to the outer market, which is packed with market stalls as well as sushi bars for the freshest breakfast you'll ever eat.

Tsukiji is open six days a week (closed Sundays, national holidays, two Wednesdays per month, New Year, and Obon in August). Tsukijishijo station (exit A2) on the Oedo subway line is on the doorstep; to find the auction area, walk straight through the market from the main gate to the end. You can pick up a useful map from the tourist offices (*see p318*) or visit the website www.tsukiji-market.or.jp/tukiji_e.htm.

For several years there have been murmurings of the market moving to newer, larger premises nearby, though as of 2010, no firm decision has been made.

thanks to beautiful landscaping. Situated on an island, it is surrounded by an ancient walled moat with only one entrance, over the Nanmon Bridge; it's also possible to reach Hama-Rikyu by boat from Asakusa. The focal points are the huge pond, which contains two islands (one with a teahouse) connected to the shore by charming wooden bridges, and a photogenic 300-year-old pine tree.
► *For more about the garden's teahouse, see p191 Teashops.*

FREE **Old Shinbashi Station**
1-5-3 Higashi-Shinbashi, Minato-ku (3572 1872). Shinbashi station (Yamanote line), Shiodome exit; (Asakusa, Ginza lines), exits 3, 4 or

Shiodome station (Oedo, Yurikamome lines), exits 3, 4. **Open** 11am-6pm Tue-Sun. **Admission** free.
This is a reconstruction of the Shinbashi passenger terminus, part of the first railway in Japan, which opened in 1872. The current structure (opened in 2003) stands on the foundations of the original. These were uncovered during excavations, and can be viewed through a glass floor in the basement. Those of ironic bent may notice that Londoners still use stations every day that would be considered archaeological treasures in Tokyo, but quibbles aside, this is a great project, with a permanent railway history exhibition hall and English labelling. There's also a pleasant café.

Harajuku & Aoyama

Trendsetting teens, big-brand boutiques and a spectacular Shinto shrine.

The tree-lined boulevard of Omotesando runs through two of Tokyo's biggest fashion districts. The **Aoyama** end, around Omotesando subway station, is where you'll find the fanciest stores stocking international mega-brands, some eye-catching architecture and the **Omotesando Hills** retail complex.

Going the other way, the street stretches downhill to Meiji-Jingumae subway station and Harajuku JR station. **Harajuku** is arguably the heart of the city's vibrant youth fashion scene, and it's the best place to shop for the latest

Map p65   Bars p179
Restaurants p154

urban brands. Explore the side streets off lower Omotesando here for funkier independent boutiques and upcoming labels. Just beyond is the green expanse of **Yoyogi Park** and the **Meiji Jingu** complex, Tokyo's largest Shinto shrine.

SIGHTS

AOYAMA

Getting there: Omotesando station is on the Chiyoda, Ginza and Hanzomon subway lines.

After Ginza (*see p56*), this is where all the big-name global brands want to put their flag-ship Tokyo stores. **Christian Dior**, **Ralph Lauren**, **Louis Vuitton** and **Tod's** are all represented, but **Prada**, with its bubble-glass high-rise, is still the highlight of the area. And things got better – or worse, depending on your point of view – with the opening of the Ando Tadao-designed **Omotesando Hills** (*see p197*) in 2005. The brainchild of the corporation behind multi-use mini-city

Roppongi Hills (*see p198*), the far smaller Omotesando version is almost entirely devoted to retail, with flashy fashion brands such as YSL and Dolce & Gabbana hogging the bulk of the floorspace. Unless you're heading to one of the posh eateries inside, this monument to Mammon is best experienced from the other side of the street, preferably after dark when the glass panels of its façade emit their chameleon-like ambient glow.

Head downhill and, on the opposite side of the road, is the traditional façade of **Oriental Bazaar** (*see p214*). A godsend for souvenir hunters, the store's three floors are stuffed with all manner of Japanese goods. Best of all, everything is quite cheap, probably less than half the price you'd pay at an average department store. Nearby is toy megastore **Kiddyland** (*see p202*). The centre of cute, cuddly, crazy and comical Japan, it offers myriad toys, games and dolls; be prepared for sensory overload.

Head uphill from Omotesando Hills and you'll find **Anniversaire** (3-5-30 Kita-Aoyama, Minato-ku), with three floors of upscale shopping, a fancy French restaurant and a Parisian-style café. The café's outdoor seats are prime people-watching territory, but do watch out: you'll pay through the nose for a cup of coffee.

Further along, Omotesando intersects with Aoyama Dori, where there is a great deal to explore. Head south (towards Shibuya), and you'll soon pass, on the left, the white exterior of **Spiral** (*see p239*), one of Tokyo's key art and design spaces. Just beyond is a turning into another key shopping street, Kotto Dori, which runs down to join Roppongi Dori. It has upmarket fashion houses next to effete French restaurants, plus some posh clubs and bars. A stroll along here at night should reveal a mix of well-to-do partiers, hard-core ravers and average folk out for a good time. For a healthy dose of whimsy, pop into the **Okamoto Taro Memorial Museum**, about halfway down Kotto Dori and one block to the left. Not far away is Aoyama's prime art oasis, the **Nezu Museum**, which is set in tranquil woods that come complete with ponds, stone trails and teahouses.

Further along Aoyama Dori is the massive **United Nations University Centre** and, next door, the **National Children's Castle** (*see p229*), a great resource for local parents. Among other attractions here are a video library, fine-arts studio, computer playroom and a very popular rooftop playport.

Heading in the opposite direction along Aoyama Dori (towards Akasaka) leads to the giant necropolis of **Aoyama Cemetery**, to the south of Gaienmae subway station. Occupying some of the most expensive land in Tokyo, it was once part of the local *daimyo*'s estate and became a cemetery in 1872 after a brief stint as a silk farm. It contains more than 100,000 graves and is an excellent place to go for cherry-blossom viewing in April. On the

**INSID[...]
FORBID[...]**

Tempted by the [...] of Omotesando H[...] there if you like, but [...] for one of the city's od[...] boutiques, **Bedrock** (*see* [...])

other side of the main road is **Meiji [...] Outer Garden** and various sports fac[...] that were built for the 1964 Olympics, inc[...] the **National Stadium** (*see p277*) and **Jing[...] Baseball Stadium** (*see p277*). Also in the vicinity is the **Watari-Um Museum of Contemporary Art**.

★ Nezu Museum

6-5-1 Minami-Aoyama, Minato-ku (3400 2536, www.nezu-muse.or.jp). Omotesando station (Chiyoda, Ginza, Hanzomon lines), exit A5. **Open** 10am-5pm Tue-Sun. **Admission** ¥1,000; ¥700 reductions. **No credit cards.**
In late 2009, the Nezu unveiled a makeover by architect Kengo Kuma, with a sleek, minimalist design that references traditional Japanese motifs such as bamboo, *washi* paper and temple eaves. The building still houses the impressive collection of oriental art amassed by rail magnate Kaichiro Nezu, including seven national treasures. And it's still set in 20,000sq m (five acres) of lush Japanese garden, with pagodas, teahouses and stone Boddhisatvas furnishing a very photogenic scene. The grounds probably take more curation than the museum, and are worth the entry price alone.

Harajuku.

...ari-Um Museum
...ontemporary Art

...*Jingumae, Shibuya-ku (3402 3001,*
...*watarium.co.jp). Gaienmae station (Ginza*
...*exit 3.* **Open** 11am-7pm Tue, Thur-Sun;
...-9pm Wed. **Admission** ¥1,000; ¥800
...tions. **No credit cards**. **Map** p65.
...) Botta designed this small art museum for the
...ri family in 1990. It holds four exhibitions a
...some of which originate at the museum, while
...s are brought in from abroad. There's a good
...okshop and a pleasant café in the basement.

...RAJUKU

...*g there: Harajuku station is on the*
...*inote line and nearby Meiji-Jingumae*
...*the Chiyoda and Fukutoshin lines.*

(Chiyoda, Ginza, Hanzomon lines), exit D1. **Open**
10am-6pm Mon, Wed-Sun. **Admission** ¥600;
¥300 reductions. **No credit cards**.
This two-storey museum just off Kotto Dori was
once the studio of artist Taro Okamoto, who died in
1996. The adjoining café looks into a lovely tropical
garden packed with his wacky sculptures.
▶ *You can also see a massive example of*
Okamoto's work in Shibuya Station, near
the Inokashira line entrance.

FREE United Nations University Centre
United Nations University Bldg, 5-53-70
Jingumae, Shibuya-ku (3499 2811, 5467 1359
library, www.unu.edu/ctr.html). Omotesando
station (Chiyoda, Ginza, Hanzomon lines), exit
B2. **Open** 10am-1pm, 2-5.30pm Mon-Fri.
Admission free. **Map** p93.
The UNU Centre houses a permanent UN staff, hosts
conferences on global problems and offers classes.
On the eighth floor is a good library on human-rights
issues and global concerns. The galleries on the first
and second floors are also worth checking out.

It's rammed, noisy, lurid and often obnoxious,
but **Takeshita Dori** (*see p200*) is Harajuku's
iconic thoroughfare. This narrow pedestrianised
lane of small clothes shops and crêpe stands is
teen heaven. It's a solid mass of humanity at
weekends, and a shuffle through is a must.
Takeshita Dori starts on the opposite side of
the road from quaintly old-fashioned Harajuku
station and stretches to Meiji Dori. The
surrounding side streets are crammed with
one-off clothing shops, quirky jewellery stores
and eateries, and are well worth a wander.

Key stores include **Laforet** (*see p204*), on
the corner of Meiji Dori and Omotesando. A
popular meeting spot, it offers five floors of
teeny-bopper shopping heaven, with an art
museum/event space as the cherry on top.
Behind Laforet lies another universe – the
'floating world' of *ukiyo-e* woodblock prints in
the small, dimly lit and tatami-floored **Ukiyo-e
Ota Memorial Museum of Art**. Leave your
shoes in a locker at the entrance, and don't miss
the basement gift shop. Fans of contemporary

48 Sightseeing
1 Meiji Shrine & Inner Garden (see p67). B1.
2 Ukiyo-e Ota Memorial Museum of Art (see p67). C2.
3 Watari-Um Museum of Contemporary Art (see above). F2.

① Restaurants, see p154
1 Agaru Sagaru Nishi Iru Higashi Iru. D2.
2 L'Artémis. D1.
3 Le Bretagne. E3.
4 Crayon House Hiroba. E4.
5 Fonda de la Madrugada. D1.
6 Fumin. E4.
7 Ghungroo. E4.
8 Hannibal Deux. C1.
9 Harem. F2.
10 Kurkku Kitchen. E1.

11 Maisen. E3.
12 Pure Café. E4.
13 Restaurant-I. D1.

㉒ Bars, see p179
1 Harajuku Taproom. C1.

㉒ Coffee Shops, see p188
1 Daibo. F4.
2 Volontaire. C3.

㉒ Shops & Services, see p192
1 A Bathing Ape. F4.
2 ADD. D2.
3 Ainz Tulpe. C2.
4 Atelier Shinji. E4.
5 Bedrock. D3.
6 Billionaire Boys Club/ Ice Cream Store. D2.
7 BørneLund. D1.
8 Boudoir. E1.

9 CA4LA. C3.
10 Comme des Garçons. F4.
11 Franc Franc. F3.
12 Fuji Torii. D3.
13 Gallery Samurai. F2.
14 Higashiya. F4.
15 Issey Miyake. F4.
16 Kampo Boutique Aoyama. F3.
17 Kinokuniya International. F3.
18 Laforet Harajuku. C3.
19 LIMI Feu Prankster. C3.
20 Loveless. F4.
21 Marvin's Vintage. C4.
22 Mister Hollywood. D3.
23 Neighborhood. D2.
24 Omotesando Hills. D3.
25 Oriental Bazaar. D3.
26 Oshmans. C2.
27 Override 9999. C4.
28 Pass the Baton. D3.
29 Peek-a-Boo Ext. E3.
30 Takeshita Dori. C2.
31 UnderCover. F4.

32 Uniqlo UT. C3.
33 Yohji Yamamoto. F4.

㉒ Galleries, see p239
1 Gallery 360°. E4.
2 Spiral. E4.

㉒ Music, see p250
1 Astro Hall. D2.
2 Cay. E4.
3 Crocodile. B4.
4 Eggman. A4.

㉒ Nightlife, see p263
1 Le Baron de Paris. F3.
2 Mix. E4.

㉒ Sport & Fitness, see p276
1 Gold's Gym Harajuku. C3.
2 National Yoyogi Stadium 1st Gymnasium. B3.

Harajuku & Aoyama

Gotta Have Faith

Shinto and Buddhism are both big in Japan.

Meiji Shrine.

SIGHTS

Japanese adherents of Shinto number around 106 million, while those regarding themselves as Buddhists amount to 95 million. This tally of over 200 million is not bad for a country with a population of less than 130 million. Clearly, when it comes to religion, the Japanese believe there's no harm in hedging one's bets. It's common for people to have their rites-of-passage ceremonies in a Shinto shrine, their marriage in a Christian chapel and their funeral in a Buddhist temple.

Though the majority of Japanese people happily embrace both native Shinto and imported Buddhism, these are about as different as two faiths could be. For example, Shinto is unconcerned with matters of afterlife, which is a major concern in Buddhism.

Shinto is an old faith: it imparts no ethical doctrine and possesses no scriptures. It is at heart a system of animistic belief in natural spirits (*kami*) – the religious system of an ancient nation of rice farmers that has survived into the modern age.

Some of the Shinto religion's most visible features are its numerous festivals, many of which double up as fertility rites,

architecture should visit the **GA Gallery**, located north of Harajuku station, between the railway tracks and Meiji Dori.

Harajuku is also justly famous for the largest Shinto shrine in the city. The entrance to the **Meiji Shrine** is through an 11-metre (36-foot) *torii* (gate), the largest in the country, built from 1,600-year-old Japanese cypress trees imported from Taiwan. A wide gravel path winds through the thickly wooded Inner Garden, with various smaller paths leading off into the dense overhanging foliage, before reaching the shrine's buildings. As with the Imperial Palace and its grounds, this huge patch of green is instantly recognisable from observation decks across the city. The serene atmosphere, punctuated by birdsong, is a world away from the mayhem of Harajuku's shops.

Each Sunday, a collection of garishly dressed 'cosplay' (costume play) aficionados display themselves on the bridge beside Harajuku station, in front of the entrance to the Meiji Shrine's Inner Garden. Don't be shy about taking their photos – that's the highest form of flattery for cosplay queens. The costumes range from cool to inventive to bizarre, often

employing some combination of cartoon, fairytale and horror.

Adjoining the Inner Garden are the lush expanses of **Yoyogi Park**, a favourite with couples and families, who spend warm afternoons lounging on the grass. Formerly a residential area for US military, then the site of the Olympic Village in 1964, it became a park in 1967. It's known for its autumn foliage, especially the golden gingko trees. At the southern end of the park, across Inokashira Dori, lie the headquarters of state broadcaster NHK and architect Kenzo Tange's **Yoyogi National Stadium** (*see p279*), also built for the Olympics and still one of Tokyo's most famous modern landmarks.

GA Gallery

3-12-14 Sendagaya, Shibuya-ku (3403 1581, www.ga-ada.co.jp). Yoyogi station (Yamanote line), east exit; (Oedo line), exit A1. **Open** 10am-6.30pm Tue-Fri; noon-6.30pm Sat, Sun. **Admission** ¥500; free reductions. **No credit cards.**
Global Architecture's annual 'GA Houses' and 'GA Japan' exhibitions make this one of Tokyo's best

supplicating the deities to bestow a bountiful rice crop on the community.

Purity has long been a major feature of Shinto, and this is evident at the place of worship (conventionally termed 'shrine' in English, to distinguish it from Buddhist temples). After passing through the shrine's distinctive torii (gate), worshippers often ritually wash their hands and mouth with water from a stone basin before offering their prayers at the main hall.

Talismans play an important role, too, so stalls at the shrine sell amulets for luck in health, love, exams and even driving. You'll also see collections of small wooden plaques (ema) on which people write wishes, white fortune-telling slips of paper (omikuji) tied around trees in the grounds, and sometimes colourful strings of 1,000 origami cranes (senbazuru).

By the time Buddhism arrived in Japan from Korea in the sixth century AD, it was already 1,000 years old, and in its long journey across Asia from India had picked up rituals, symbols and tenets that would have seemed utterly alien to its original founders. Mahayana Buddhism, as practised in Japan, introduced the notion of bodhisattvas, who put off their own salvation in order to bring enlightenment to others. Kannon is a popular bodhisattva, as is Jizo, who is often seen by roadsides and in temples as a small stone figure wearing a red bib.

Temples are often ornate and brightly coloured, while shrines tend to be more muted. At both, people make offerings, often with a ¥5 coin, which is considered lucky. Temples also sell good-luck charms, and commonly feature incense burners; you'll see people directing the smoke, which is deemed to have beneficial powers, over themselves.

You can't enter the main buildings at temples or shrines, but otherwise there are no off-limit areas, and locals won't be offended by sightseers. Photography is widely permitted, though it may be forbidden indoors at some temples – look for signs. You may be required to take off your shoes before entering some buildings.

Must-see religious sites in Tokyo are the **Meiji Shrine** (*see below*) and the **Asakusa Kannon (Senso-ji) Temple** (*see p49*); if you're really keen, head to the temple towns of **Kamakura** (*see pp295-299*) or **Nikko** (*see pp300-303*).

SIGHTS

places for modern and contemporary Japanese and international architecture. The building also houses an excellent architecture bookshop.

★ FREE Meiji Shrine & Inner Garden

1-1 Yoyogi-Kamizonocho, Shibuya-ku (3379 5511, www.meijijingu.or.jp). Harajuku station (Yamanote line), Omotesando exit or Meiji-Jingumae station (Chiyoda, Fukutoshin lines), exit 2. **Open** *Shrine & Inner Garden* spring, autumn 5.10am-5.50pm daily; summer 5am-6.30pm daily; winter 6am-4.10pm daily. *Meiji Shrine Garden* Mar-Oct 9am-5pm daily; Nov-Feb 9am-4pm daily. **Admission** *Shrine & Inner Garden* free. *Meiji Shrine Garden* ¥500. *Treasure house* ¥200. **No credit cards. Map** p65.
Opened in 1920, the shrine is dedicated to Emperor Meiji – whose reign (1868-1912) coincided with Japan's modernisation – and his consort, Empress Shoken. Exceedingly popular, especially at New Year, when it draws crowds of a million-plus, the shrine hosts numerous annual festivals, including two sumo dedicatory ceremonies (in early January and at the end of September). Shinto weddings take place here regularly. The current main building dates from 1958, a reconstruction after the original

was destroyed during World War II. It is an impressive example of the austere style and restrained colours typical of Shinto architecture.

Just off the main path to the shrine, through the wooded Inner Garden, are two entrances to another garden, the Meiji Jingu Gyoen. It's neither large nor especially beautiful, but it is quiet – except in June, when the iris field attracts many admirers. Vegetation is dense, limiting access to the few trails, which lead to a pond and teahouse.

★ Ukiyo-e Ota Memorial Museum of Art
Ota Kinen Bijutsukan

1-10-10 Jingumae, Shibuya-ku (3403 0880, www.ukiyoe-ota-muse.jp). Harajuku station (Yamanote line), Omotesando exit or Meiji-Jingumae station (Chiyoda, Fukutoshin lines), exit 5. **Open** 10.30am-5.30pm Tue-Sun. Closed 27th-end of mth. **Admission** ¥700; ¥500 reductions. **No credit cards. Map** p65.
The late Seizo Ota, chairman of Toho Mutual Life Insurance, began collecting *ukiyo-e* prints after he saw that Japan was losing its traditional art to Western museums and collectors. Temporary exhibitions drawn from his 12,000-strong collection often include works by masters such as Hiroshige and Hokusai.

Ikebukuro

Despite its frumpy image, there's lots going on.

Ikebukuro ranks third behind Shinjuku and Shibuya as one of the main commercial sub-centres of Tokyo, but it's way down the list as a tourist destination. It has a resolutely uncool reputation and very little visual charm, though this actually works in its favour, making the area unpretentious and more laid-back than the other big hubs. But laid-back doesn't mean quiet: it's crammed with shops, bars, restaurants, karaoke rooms, cinemas, love hotels and other 'entertainment' establishments.

Map p69   **Restaurants** p158
Hotels p127   **Bars** p180

NAVIGATING IKEBUKURO

Getting there: Ikebukuro station is on the Yamanote line and the Fukutoshin, Marunouchi and Yurakucho subway lines, as well as the JR Saikyo, Seibu Ikebukuro and Tobu Tojo train lines. The Toden Arakawa tram line does not serve the station directly, but makes stops in eastern Ikebukuro, including Higashi-Ikebukuro Yonchome, outside Higashi-Ikebukuro station on the Yurakucho line.

The nerve centre of Ikebukuro is one of Tokyo's largest train stations, served by two subway lines, two private railways and numerous JR lines. While this makes it an easy place to reach, it can be a difficult place to get around, as the station is devoid of significant landmarks. Among more than 40 exits, the most popular meeting spot is the Ike Fukuro ('Lake Owl') statue at the bottom of the stairs inside exit 22.

Once you escape the station, though, navigation gets easier. Look north to spot the

---

INSIDE TRACK THE BIG HOUSE

The **Sunshine City** skyscraper (*see p72*) occupies the former site of Sugamo Prison, where General Hideki Tojo, Japan's wartime prime minister, was hanged in 1948. A small monument on the northern corner of the block marks where the gallows stood.

30-storey phallic cement chimney of the local garbage incineration plant, and use this as your guide to the **Ikebukuro Sports Centre** (*see p284*), in the building immediately next door to the plant. The centre's tenth-floor gym and 11th-floor swimming pool will give you a bird's-eye impression of how Ikebukuro is laid out while you work out.

Since most of the above-ground railway lines run north–south, Ikebukuro itself divides into east and west. Each side is dominated by a huge department store half next to, and half on top of, the train station. This is the result of a feud between wealthy arch-rival half-brothers Yasujiro Tsutsumi and Kaichiro Nezu, who developed the two private rail lines – the Seibu Ikebukuro and Tobu Tojo lines, respectively – that serve the area. Each encouraged local growth by building a department store. Both stores grew to be among the largest in the world.

Confusingly, the department store **Seibu** (*see p195* – whose name originates from 'west area railway line' – is located on the east side of the station, and **Tobu** (*see p195*) – the 'east area railway line' – has the west side covered.

WEST SIDE

Before World War II, the area to the west of Ikebukuro station was known in some circles as 'the Montparnasse of Tokyo'. Its cheap homes were occupied by artists and writers, including Edogawa Rampo (1894-1965), the revered detective novelist whose name is a Japanised pronunciation of Edgar Allan Poe.

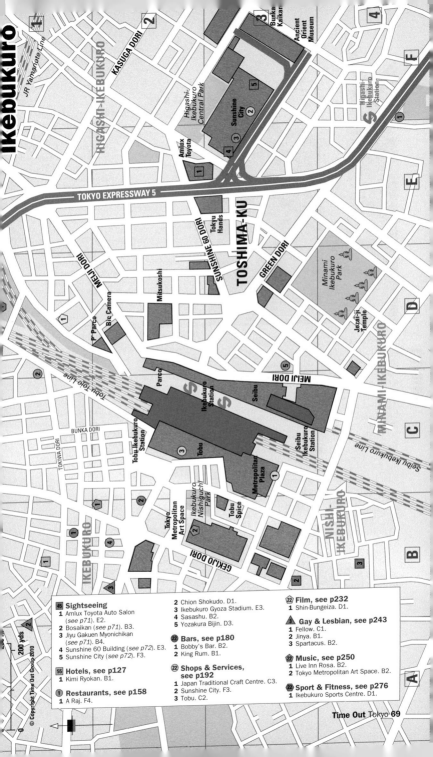

Ikebukuro

Higashi-Ikebukuro

Toshima-Ku

Minami-Ikebukuro

Nishi-Ikebukuro

JR Yamanote Line

KASUGA DORI

Ancient Orient Museum

Bunka Kaikan

Higashi-Ikebukuro Central Park

Sunshine City

Amlux Toyota

Higashi-Ikebukuro Station

TOKYO EXPRESSWAY 5

MEIJI DORI

SUNSHINE 60 DORI

Tokyu Hands

GREEN DORI

Minami Ikebukuro Park

Jozaiji Temple

Mitsukoshi

Bic Camera

P'Parco

Tobu Tojo Line

BUNKA DORI

TOKIWA DORI

Parco

Ikebukuro Station

Tobu Ikebukuro Station

Tobu

Seibu

Seibu Ikebukuro Station

MEIJI DORI

Seibu Ikebukuro Line

Metropolitan Plaza

Ikebukuro Nishiguchi Park

Tobu Spice

Tokyo Metropolitan Art Space

IKEBUKURO

GEKIJO DORI

200 yds

© Copyright Time Out Group 2010

Sightseeing
1 Amlux Toyota Auto Salon (see p71). E2.
2 Bosaikan (see p71). B3.
3 Jiyu Gakuen Myonichikan (see p71). B4.
4 Sunshine 60 Building (see p72). E3.
5 Sunshine City (see p72). F3.

Hotels, see p127
1 Kimi Ryokan. B1.

Restaurants, see p158
1 A Raj. F4.
2 Chion Shokudo. D1.
3 Ikebukuro Gyoza Stadium. E3.
4 Sasashu. B2.
5 Yozakura Bijin. D3.

Bars, see p180
1 Bobby's Bar. B2.
2 King Rum. B1.

Shops & Services, see p192
1 Japan Traditional Craft Centre. C3.
2 Sunshine City. F3.
3 Tobu. C2.

Film, see p232
1 Shin-Bungeiza. D1.

Gay & Lesbian, see p243
1 Fellow. C1.
2 Jinya. B1.
3 Spartacus. B2.

Music, see p250
1 Live Inn Rosa. B2.
2 Tokyo Metropolitan Art Space. B2.

Sport & Fitness, see p276
1 Ikebukuro Sports Centre. D1.

East Side.

is the **Bosaikan**, an earthquake simulation centre designed to teach citizens how to survive the impending Big One.

EAST SIDE

There are two main exits on this side of the station – the east exit and the Seibu exit. Turn left out of either, and you will come to **Parco**, which is part of the Seibu complex. **P' Parco**, slightly further along, is one source of the wild fashions worn in the trendier parts of Tokyo. One block further up the main street, Meiji Dori, is the Ikebukuro branch of **Bic Camera**, an electronics megastore so big it occupies more than one building.

If you think this area is mobbed, just try making your way to the main centre of Ikebukuro – **Sunshine 60 Dori**, the wide tree-lined street that heads due east. The thoroughfare is packed with tiny shops, many selling discount clothing, as well as restaurants and cinemas. The **Sanrio** shop is worth a giggle – two whole floors offering Hello Kitty goods, cooed over by grown women.

Sunshine 60 Dori is so called because it ultimately leads to the **Sunshine 60 Building**, part of the **Sunshine City** complex. In the building's massive mall are all kinds of fashion shops and restaurants, and within the complex, an observatory, an aquarium, a planetarium, a theme park and the Ancient Orient Museum (among other attractions). To check out other aspects of modern-day Japan, visit the **Amlux Toyota** automobile showroom, as well as the **Animate** manga emporium just next door.

A few blocks further to the east a more old-fashioned experience awaits, in the form of the **Arakawa Streetcar Line** – one of Tokyo's last two surviving tram lines. Small, one-car trams – *chin-chin densha* ('ding-ding trains') – trundle through picturesque residential areas, sometimes slipping behind rows of houses or joining cars and buses on the streets. Hop aboard for an unhurried look at non-tourist Tokyo – it's possible to stand behind the driver and look over his shoulder for the best view. There's a standard fare of ¥160, and stops along the 12-kilometre (eight-mile) route include **Asukayama Park** and its three small museums, **Zoshigaya Cemetery** and the nearby **Zoshigaya Missionary Museum**, and Waseda University. The tram connects with the JR lines at Oji and Otsuka stations, while Sunshine City is only a few blocks' walk from Mukohara station.

FURTHER AFIELD

Thanks to its profusion of railway lines, Ikebukuro is a good staging point for excursions to other areas. Two of Tokyo's

SIGHTS

Even today, much of western Ikebukuro consists of quiet residential neighbourhoods, though few pre-war buildings remain. One survivor is **Jiyu Gakuen Myonichikan**, a school building designed by Frank Lloyd Wright in 1921. It and the nearby **Mejiro Teien** garden provide an oasis of tranquillity that makes a welcome contrast to the bustle of Ikebukuro station. Contributing to that bustle are thousands of students from **Rikkyo University**, also located to the west of the station. The campus is unremarkable most of the year, but around Christmas its red-brick buildings are decked out with festive lights.

The other major department store on this side is **Marui**, directly down the street perpendicular to the station's main west exit. Metropolitan Plaza, home to the **Japan Traditional Craft Centre** (*see p212*) – a good place for learning more about Japanese arts and crafts – is right next to Tobu.

Directly opposite the Metropolitan exit is **Tobu Spice**, a building full of restaurants. In the basement of the building behind that is the **Dubliners** (*see p185*) – a branch of one of the city's ever-expanding number of Irish pubs. The Dubliners' entrance faces a broad stone plaza that is the only significant car-free open space in the area. You may find buskers or old men hunched over *shogi* and *go*-boards. On the west side of the plaza stands the airy, glass-enclosed **Tokyo Metropolitan Art Space** (*see p253*), used for classical concerts, plays and ballets. A block south of the plaza main amusement parks are accessible from here: **Toshimaen** (*see p72*) and **Tokyo Dome City** (*see p228*). A more peaceful option lies next door to Tokyo Dome: **Koishikawa Korakuen**, the oldest garden in the city, laid out in the 17th century.

FREE Amlux Toyota Auto Salon

3-3-5 Higashi-Ikebukuro, Toshima-ku (5391 5900, www.amlux.jp/english/floorguide). Ikebukuro station (Yamanote line), east exit; (Marunouchi, Yurakucho lines), exit 35. **Open** *B1F & 1F* 11am-9pm Tue-Sun. *2F-4F* 11am-7pm Tue-Sun. **Admission** free. **Map** p69.

Toyota claimed this was the world's biggest car showroom until it opened an even bigger one in Odaiba. But Amlux still echoes with the sound of slamming doors as scores of petrolheads hop in and out of the 70 or so vehicles on display – essentially Toyota's entire consumer line. More amazing is that you can test drive any vehicle as long as you have a valid driving licence (Japanese or international). Rates start at ¥250 for 30 minutes.

▶ *For Toyota's larger showroom in Odaiba, see p84 Mega Web.*

Asukayama Park

1-1-3 Oji, Kita-ku (3916 1133). Asukayama station (Toden Arakawa line) or Oji station (Keihin Tohoku line), south exit; (Namboku line), exit 1. **Open** *Museums* 10am-5pm Tue-Sun. **Admission** *Individual museum* ¥300; ¥100 reductions. *All museums* ¥720; ¥240 reductions. **No credit cards**.

This wooded hilltop park was formerly the estate of Shibusawa Eiichi (1840-1931), president of Japan's first modern bank. Former US President Ulysses Grant was treated to a ju-jitsu demonstration here in 1879 while staying as Shibusawa's guest. The towering mansion is long gone, but a few outbuildings still remain. The park's main

attractions are the 'Asukayama Three Museums', which stand in a row at the park's eastern edge.

The Paper Museum (www.papermuseum.jp) displays items related to paper art, papermaking technology and the history of paper, and sometimes holds participatory workshops. The Kita City Asukayama Museum (3916 1133) focuses on local archaeological finds, including a dugout canoe from the Jomon period, Japan's Stone Age. English signage is minimal, but the displays are largely self-explanatory. The Shibusawa Memorial Museum (3910 0005, www.shibusawa.or.jp) praises the achievements of Shibusawa Eiichi. Most of the exhibits are old documents, some in English – including a signed letter from Thomas Edison.

★ FREE Bosaikan

2-37-8 Nishi-Ikebukuro, Toshima-ku (3590 6565, www.tfd.metro.tokyo.jp/ts/ik/ikeb.htm). Ikebukuro station (Marunouchi, Yurakucho lines), exit 3. **Open** 9am-5pm Mon, Wed-Fri. Closed 3rd Wed of mth. **Admission** free.

This earthquake-prone city is long overdue for a devastating tremor, so the Tokyo Fire Department has created this 'life safety learning centre' in its HQ to simulate a real emergency. There's first-aid training and survival tips, but the real fun is the shaking room, the smoke maze and the only chance you'll ever have to play with fire extinguishers without getting reprimanded. The whole thing takes around two hours, and while you can just drop in and take part, it's advisable to reserve a place.

Jiyu Gakuen Myonichikan

2-31-3 Nishi-Ikebukuro, Toshima-ku (3971 7535, www.jiyu.jp/index-e.html). Ikebukuro station (Yamanote line), Metropolitan exit; (Marunouchi, Yurakucho lines), exit 3. **Open** 10am-4pm Tue-Sun. **Admission** ¥600. **No credit cards**. **Map** p69.

SIGHTS

Jiyu Gakuen Myonichikan.

Architect Frank Lloyd Wright's Imperial Hotel in Tokyo was famously demolished in 1968, but few people realise that a smaller Wright building – a private school – still stands in Ikebukuro. Now used as an alumni meeting hall rather than for classes, it is open for tours (but it's wise to call ahead first, especially at weekends, when it's regularly booked for weddings). Viewed from the outside, the unusual geometry of the window frames is the clearest indication of Wright's signature.

★ Koishikawa Korakuen

1-6-6 Koraku, Bunkyo-ku (3811 3015). Iidabashi station (Namboku, Oedo lines), exit C3 or Korakuen station (Marunouchi line), exit 2. **Open** 9am-5pm daily. **Admission** ¥300. **No credit cards.**

Koishikawa Korakuen was first laid out in 1629. It's now only a quarter of its original size, but it's still beautiful, with a range of walks, bridges, hills and vistas (often the miniatures of more famous originals) that encourage quiet contemplation. The entrance, tucked away down a side street, can be a little difficult to find.

FREE Mejiro Teien

3-20-18 Mejiro, Toshima-ku (5996 4810). Ikebukuro station (Yamanote line), south exit; Marunouchi, Yurakucho lines), exit 39 or Mejiro station (Yamanote line). **Open** *Jan-June, Sept-Dec* 9am-5pm daily. *July, Aug* 9am-7pm daily. Closed 2nd & 4th Mon of mth. **Admission** free.

This small garden a short walk from Wright's school building creates the illusion of greater space by way of a deep artificial valley with a pond at the bottom. The gazebo over the pond and a grassy area behind some trees are good spots for a picnic lunch.

Sunshine 60 Building

3-1-1 Higashi-Ikebukuro, Toshima-ku (3989 3331, www.sunshinecity.co.jp). Ikebukuro station (Yamanote line), east exit; (Marunouchi, Yurakucho lines), exit 35 or Higashi-Ikebukuro station (Yurakucho line), exit 2. **Open** *Observatory* 10am-9pm daily. *Namjatown* 10am-10pm daily. **Admission** *Observatory* ¥620; ¥310 reductions. *Namjatown* ¥300; ¥200 reductions; 1-day passport ¥3,900; ¥3,300 reductions. **No credit cards. Map** p69.

One of the fastest lifts in the world will whisk you to the observatory on the top floor of this 60-storey skyscraper in around 35 seconds. The building's lower floors house the World Import Mart shopping mall and Namjatown, an unbelievably tacky indoor amusement park.

▶ *Sunshine 60 is also home to the Ikebukuro Gyoza Stadium (see p158).*

Sunshine City

3-1-3 Higashi-Ikebukuro, Toshima-ku (3989 3466, www.sunshinecity.co.jp). Ikebukuro station (Yamanote line), east exit; (Marunouchi, Yurakucho lines), exit 35 or Higashi-Ikebukuro station (Yurakucho line), exit 2. **Open** *Aquarium* 10am-6pm daily. *Planetarium* 11am-8pm daily. *Ancient Orient Museum* 10am-5pm (last entry 4pm) daily. **Admission** *Aquarium* ¥1,800. *Planetarium* ¥800. *Museum* ¥500. **No credit cards. Map** p69.

As well as the Sunshine 60 Building (*see above*), the Sunshine City complex contains the world's first aquarium in a high-rise building, with more than 20,000 fish and shows by performing seals. There's also a planetarium. The Ancient Orient Museum in the Bunka Kaikan building focuses on western Asia, especially Iran and Pakistan – check out the Parthian-era bull-shaped ceremonial drinking vessel, with nipple-spouts on its chest.

Toshimaen

3-25-1 Koyama, Nerima-ku (3990 8800, www.toshimaen.co.jp). Toshimaen station (Oedo line), exit A2. **Open** *Mid July-Aug* 10am-8pm daily. *Sept-mid July* 10am-5pm Fri-Sun. *Toshimaen Garden Spa* 10am-11pm daily. **Admission** *Entry only* ¥1,000. *Entry & ride pass* ¥3,800. *Toshimaen Garden Spa* ¥2,000; ¥1,200 after 9pm. **Credit** AmEx, DC, JCB, MC, V.

Every summer this old, uninspiring amusement park becomes much more fun with the opening of Hydropolis, a waterpark that includes a surf pool and a very elaborate set of waterslides. Next door you'll find a year-round mineral-water spa.

FREE Zoshigaya Cemetery

4-25-1 Minami-Ikebukuro, Toshima-ku (3971 6868). Zoshigaya station (Toden Arakawa line). **Open** 24hrs daily. **Admission** free.

This tree-shaded cemetery is the final resting place of such notables as John Manjiro (1827-98), the legendary Edo-era link between East and West, in plot 1-2-10-1, and writer Lafcadio Hearn (1850-1904), who is buried in plot 1-1-8-35 under his Japanese name, Koizumi Yakumo. In plot 1-14-1-3 lies Natsume Soseki (1867-1916), one of Japan's best-loved novelists. Disgraced general Tojo Hideki is buried in plot 1-1-12-6.

FREE Zoshigaya Missionary Museum

1-25-5 Zoshigaya, Toshima-ku (3985 4081, http://humsum.cool.ne.jp/cho-41.html). Higashi-Ikebukuro station (Yurakucho line), exit 5 or Zoshigaya station (Toden Arakawa line). **Open** 9am-4.30pm Tue-Sun. Closed 3rd Sun of mth. **Admission** free.

Few homes of early foreign Tokyo residents have escaped the ravages of time. This one, built in 1907, belonged to American missionary JM McCaleb. When it was threatened with demolition a few years ago, residents campaigned to save it. The white clapboard building is strangely displaced, time-warped from old America to the hubbub of modern Tokyo.

SIGHTS

How to Play Pachinko

A guide to the Japanese gambling machines.

Pachinko parlours are Japan's version of the bookies. Nobody boasts about spending the day there, but plenty of people do. In fact, you'll usually see a line of people waiting for a parlour to open, based on the belief that some machines are luckier than others (and are usually placed nearer the door).

A *pachinko* machine resembles a cross between a pinball and a slot machine, and uses zillions of mini steel balls. Gaudily decorated, ear-splittingly noisy parlours are scattered all over Tokyo, from the bustling shopping areas to the hushed suburbs.

If you enter a *pachinko* parlour and take in the cacophony of bleeps and whirrs, it will be hard to believe that the game is, technically, illegal. But it is. So there are a few hoops to jump through to circumvent the law. First, you need to buy a prepaid card from a machine near the entrance (so you'll be gambling points rather than money). Slip your card into the slot, push the ball-eject button, turn the handle to flick the balls, and you're rolling.

Now comes the tricky part. The balls have to land in the centre hole to start the numbers on the screen revolving. This is done by inching the handle back and forth to find the optimum setting. Once you're satisfied the balls are going in (aim for at least ten hits every ¥500), wedge a coin

into the handle to hold it in place and wait to win. In the meantime, you're free to read a book, call a friend or write a short story. Any sudden ejaculation of steel balls means you're a winner: cash them in or continue playing.

In the unlikely event that your machine pays out, you'll have to carry your little balls to a desk where you can exchange them for a variety of prizes. The least enticing ones may look like taped-up lumps of rock, others may resemble gold bars. Opt for these 'special prizes' anyway, and take them to a small window somewhere off-premises (look on the counter for a map), where someone will repurchase them for yen.

Winning at *pachinko* is largely a matter of luck, but there are some pointers. First, don't just plonk yourself at any old machine. Instead, reconnoitre, suss out the parlour; see who's winning, which machines haven't paid out. Once you've picked, throw a pack of cigarettes into the trough to mark your spot – smoking is compulsory.

Most serious players believe the machines are rigged, sometimes in the player's favour. You'll notice that the people seated by the entrance are on incredible winning streaks. The battle for a door seat explains why you'll see long lines of people waiting up to two hours each morning for the parlours to open.

Marunouchi

Even the financial sector is a shopaholic's paradise.

Tokyo's fastest-changing area is the focus of massive spending by Mitsubishi, which owns most of the land. For decades, the conglomerate was happy to leave the area as a characterless business district, enlivened only by its proximity to the Imperial Palace and Gardens.

All that changed with the new millennium. The dowdy Naka Dori reinvented itself as a luxury retail boulevard, and a series of high-rise commercial complexes sprang up, all of them financed by Mitsubishi.

In 2010, the group created Brick Square, a low-rise, eye-pleasing plaza with red-brick architecture. It's a transformation as unlikely as Roppongi's, but Marunouchi has finally become a credible tourist destination rather than merely the route to the palace.

Map p77	**Restaurants** p158
Hotels p127	**Bars** p180

SIGHTS

NAVIGATING MARUNOUCHI

Getting there: Tokyo station is the terminus of the JR Chuo line and is on the JR Yamanote and Keihin Tohoku lines, as well as the Marunouchi subway line. It is also the main terminus for shinkansen bullet trains. Other subways stations dot the area. It's walking distance from Ginza.

Tokyo station has plenty to keep shoppers amused, including the **Daimaru** department store (*see p192*) beside the Yaesu exit, and the new Ecute shopping centre, stocking food and interiors items. The area's top tourist attraction, the **Imperial Palace**, is accessed via the station's central exit. The moat, stone walls and outer gardens still divide the palace from the city. The building is out of bounds, except on 2 January and 23 December (the emperor's birthday), when the non-imperial masses are allowed into part of the grounds to wave flags and listen to a brief speech. Otherwise, the closest you can get is to take photos of the scenic Nijubashi (Double Bridge), with part of the palace buildings in the background. You can also stroll around the landscaped **Imperial Palace East Gardens**, which house a few historical remains and a Japanese-style garden.

At the north end of the gardens, across the main road, is another park, **Kitanomaru**

Koen. This slightly unkempt section of the imperial grounds is home to the **Nippon Budokan** (*see p257 and p279*), the **Japan Science Foundation Science Museum** and the **National Museum of Modern Art**. The park's cherry trees make a popular, postcard-perfect sight at blossom time in April.

Other cultural outposts include the **Idemitsu Museum of Arts**, opposite the southern corner of the Imperial Palace site; the **Bridgestone Museum of Art**, east of Tokyo station; and the **Communications Museum**, just to the north of the station.

For fans of modern architecture, one of the area's most striking constructions is the **Tokyo International Forum** (*see p253*), which stands close to Yurakucho station. It is divided into two buildings, the most eye-catching being the ship-shaped Glass Hall Building, designed by Rafael Vinoly, which has a glass roof and 60-metre (197-foot) glass wall. The adjacent building is far less impressive but hides an interior bustling with people attending conventions and other social events. The three main halls are increasingly used for concerts, film premières and festivals.

To the east – go under the train tracks – is Pacific Century Place, opened in 2001, which contains Tokyo's second **Four Seasons** hotel (*see p127*) and plenty of restaurants and coffee bars. From here it's easy walking distance to

Kyobashi and Nihonbashi, areas that give
a taste of the way Tokyo was before the swanky
consumer complexes popped up. For sightseers,
there's the **Tokyo Stock Exchange**, **Kite
Museum**, Meiji Memorial Museum, **Bank
of Japan** and adjacent **Currency Museum**.

MARUNOUCHI'S HISTORY

Nothing of what is currently Marunouchi lives
up to its name, which means 'within the moat
or castle walls'. But the world that was once
within the walls was the most influential in
Japan. Tokyo has been home to the Japanese
royal family since 1868, and the Imperial Palace
occupies a chunk of prime real estate in the
centre of the city, on part of the former site
of Edo Castle, seat of the Tokugawa shogun.

Edo came to life in 1457 as warrior poet
Dokan Ota settled where the palace now stands.
When shogun Ieyasu Tokugawa decided to rule
from here too, he chose Ota's castle as his base,
and Marunouchi became the centre of the city.
Tokugawa then decreed that all *daimyo* (feudal
lords) must live in Edo for half the year, turning
Marunouchi into a political centre. Even
today, the district remains a political, imperial,
economic and geographical centre of Tokyo.

Marunouchi went through a second heyday
in the Meiji era (1868-1912), when it became
the economic centre of the country and famous
for its buildings. This showcase of foreign
architecture was then dubbed 'London Town'.
It was not only the pride of the city, but also
a sign that Japan had opened up to the world.
The main remaining example of buildings from
this era is **Tokyo station**, built to resemble
Amsterdam's Centraal station.

The third era began in the 21st century,
with an urban transformation designed to lure
consumer yen. The 36-storey **Marunouchi
Building** (*see p197*) the first structure ever
to overlook the grounds of the Imperial Palace,
showed that commerce trumps tradition in
modern Japan. It was soon followed by the Sir
Michael Hopkins-designed **Shin Marunouchi
Building** (*see p198*), the shopping, dining
and office centre **Oazo** (*see p197*), and the
eye-pleasing oasis of Brick Square. Meanwhile,
the area's main transport hub, Tokyo station,
is getting an overhaul to return it to its pre-
war look, adapt the old building to modern
earthquake-proofing standards, and create
a more tourist-friendly walkway to the palace.

FURTHER AFIELD

Within easy reach of Marunouchi are a couple
of worthwhile sights. **Akihabara** is devoted

SIGHTS

Nihonbashi.

to electronic goods (*see p202*) and geek culture (*see pp39-42* **Otaku**). **Ochanomizu**, an area famous for sports shops and universities, also boasts **Nikolai Cathedral** (4-1 Kanda-Surugadai, Chiyoda-ku, 3291 1885, open to visitors 1-3.30pm Tue-Fri, Japanese service 10am Sun). This cruciform Russian Orthodox church, complete with an onion dome, was designed by British architect Josiah Conder and completed in 1891. The original, larger dome was destroyed in the 1923 Great Kanto Earthquake. The cathedral occupies the site of a former Edo-era watchtower and offers visitors a commanding view of the area.

FREE Bank of Japan
2-1-1 Nihonbashi-Hongokucho, Chuo-ku (3279 1111, www.boj.or.jp). Mitsukoshimae station (Ginza, Hanzomon lines), exits A8, B1. **Tours** (1hr; book 1wk ahead) 9.45am, 11am, 1.30pm, 3pm Mon-Fri. **Admission** free. **Map** p77.
The Bank of Japan has two buildings, descriptively named Old and New. The New Building is where all the banking activities occur, and the Old Building… well, it just looks nice. The first Western-style construction by Japanese builders, the Old Building is said to be modelled on London's Bank of England.

Bridgestone Museum of Art
1-10-1 Kyobashi, Chuo-ku (5777 8600, www.bridgestone-museum.gr.jp). Tokyo station (Yamanote, Chuo, Marunouchi, Sobu lines), Yaesu (central) exit. **Open** 10am-8pm Tue-Sat; 10am-6pm Sun. **Admission** ¥800; ¥500-¥600 reductions; free under-12s. **Credit** AmEx, JCB, MC, V. **Map** p77.
Ishibashi Shojiro, founder of the giant Bridgestone Corporation, wheeled his private collection into this museum back in 1952. Impressionism, European

modernism and Japanese Western-style paintings form the core holdings, but exhibitions cover genres ranging from Ancient Greek to 20th-century abstraction. For a taste of what's inside, stroll past the artworks displayed in the street-level front windows.
▶ *There's a tearoom on the first floor.*

Communications Museum
2-3-1 Otemachi, Chiyoda-ku (3244 6811). Otemachi station (Chiyoda, Hanzomon, Marunouchi, Mita, Tozai lines), exit A5. **Open** 9am-4.30pm Tue-Sun. **Admission** ¥110; ¥50 reductions. **Credit** (shop, over ¥3,000 only) AmEx, JCB, MC, V. **Map** p77.
This massive museum relays the stories and technological histories of national public broadcasting company NHK, telecoms giant NTT and the now-defunct Post & Telecommunications Ministry. Philatelists can peruse 280,000 old and new stamps from everywhere from Afghanistan to Zimbabwe (including an 1840 English penny black). Kids can race post-office motorbikes in a video game, compare international postboxes and ogle a room-sized mail sorter. On the telecommunications floor, ample interactive displays teach how the telephone works. A full range of historic public payphones – from pink to yellow to green – is sealed behind glass. The gift shop sells vintage postcards and collectable stamps.

FREE Currency Museum
1-3-1 Nihonbashi-Hongokucho, Chuo-ku (3277 3037, www.imes.boj.or.jp/english). Mitsukoshimae station (Ginza, Hanzomon lines), exits A5, B1. **Open** 9.30am-4.30pm Tue-Sun. **Tours** (1hr) 1.30pm Tue, Thur. **Admission** free. **Map** p77.
Run by the Bank of Japan, this museum traces the history of money in the country, from the use of Chinese coins in the late Heian period (12th century) to the creation of the yen and the central bank in

▣ Sightseeing	Memorial Museum	7 Isegen. E1.	10 Takashimaya. E4.
1 Bank of Japan	(*see p80*). A1.	8 Izumo Soba Honke. C1.	11 Yamamoto Yama. E3.
(*see above*). E3.		9 Kanda Yabu Soba. E1.	
2 Bridgestone Museum	▣ Hotels, see p127	10 Shisen Hanten. A4.	㉒ Film, see p232
of Art (*see above*). E4.	1 Four Seasons Hotel Tokyo	11 Takara. D4.	1 Institut Franco-Japonais. A1.
3 Communications Museum	at Marunouchi. D4.	12 Tapas Molecular Bar. E2.	2 Iwanami Hall. C1.
(*see above*). D2.	2 Hilltop Hotel. D1.		3 National Film Centre. E4.
4 Currency Museum	3 Hotel Kazusaya. E2.	㉒ Bars, see p180	
(*see above*). E3.	4 Hotel Moneterey Hanzomon	1 Mandarin Bar. C1.	㉒ Galleries, see p239
5 Idemitsu Museum of Arts	(*see p139*). A2.		1 Base Gallery. F3.
(*see p78*). D4.	5 Hotel Nihonbashi Saibo. F3.	㉒ Coffee Shops,	2 Galerie Sho
6 Imperial Palace East	6 Kayabacho Pearl Hotel. F4.	see p189	Contemporary Art. E4.
Gardens (*see p78*). C3.	7 Mandarin Oriental Tokyo. E2.	1 Marunouchi Café. D4.	3 Zeit-Foto Salon. E4.
7 Japan Science Foundation	8 Marunouchi Hotel. D3.	2 Mironga. C1.	
Science Museum	9 Ryokan Ryumeikan		㉒ Music, see p250
(*see p78*). B2.	Honten. D1.	㉒ Shops & Services,	1 Casals Hall. D1.
8 Kite Museum (*see p78*). F3.	10 Sakura Hotel. C1.	see p192	2 Cotton Club. D4.
9 Mitsubishi Ichigokan	11 Shangri-La. E3.	1 American Pharmacy. D3.	3 Nippon Budokan. B1.
Museum (*see p78*). D4.		2 Daimaru. E3.	4 Tokyo TUC. F1.
10 Mitsui Memorial Museum	❶ Restaurants,	3 Ebisu-Do Gallery. C1.	
(*see p80*). E2.	see p158	4 Hara Shobo. C1.	㉒ Performing Arts,
11 National Museum of Modern	1 A16. D4.	5 Marunouchi Building. D4.	see p269
Art (*see p80*). C2.	2 Aroyna Tabeta. D4.	6 Maruzen. D3.	1 National Theatre. A3.
12 Tokyo Stock Exchange	3 Bar de España Muy. D3.	7 Oazo. D3.	
(*see p80*). F3.	4 Botan. E1.	8 Pokemon Centre. E4.	㉒ Sport & Fitness,
13 Yasukuni Shrine	5 Brasserie aux Amis. D4.	9 Shin Marunouchi	see p276
& Yushukan War-Dead	6 Ieyasu Hon-jin. C1.	Building. D3.	1 Chiyoda Kuritsu Sogo
			Taiikukan Pool. E2.

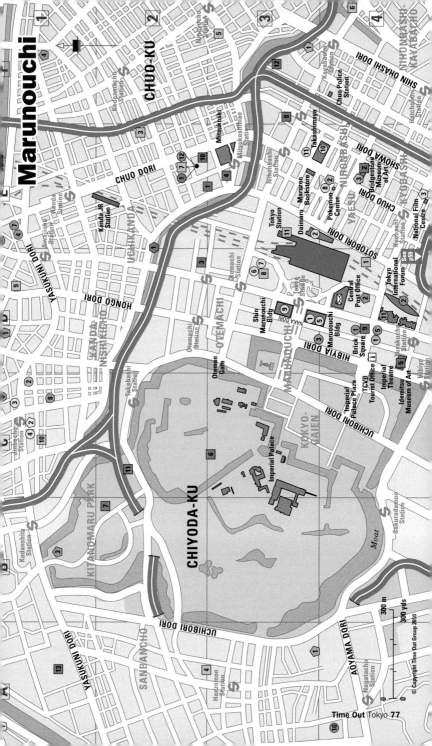

Marunouchi

CHUO-KU

CHIYODA-KU

NIHOMBASHI-KAYABACHO

NIHOMBASHI

KYOBASHI

YAESU

MARUNOUCHI

KOKYO-GAIEN

KITANOMARU PARK

SANBANCHO

YASUKUNI DORI

HONGO DORI

CHUO DORI

UCHIKANDA

KANDA-NISHIKICHO

SHIN-NIHOMBASHI DORI

SHOWA DORI

SOTOBORI DORI

NAKA DORI

HIBIYA DORI

UCHIBORI DORI

AOYAMA DORI

UCHIBORI DORI

Kodenmacho Station

Awajicho Station

Kanda Station

Kanda JR Station

Ogawamachi Station

Mitsukoshimae Station

Mitsukoshi

Ningyocho Station

Kayabacho Station

Chuo Police Station

Hatchobori Station

Nihombashi Station

Takashimaya

Maruzen Bookstore

Pokémon Center

Bridgestone Museum of Art

Kyobashi Station

National Film Centre

See p.59

Tokyo Station

Daimaru

Tokyo Station

Central Post Office

Tokyo International Forum

Yurakucho Station

Otemachi Station

Otemachi Station

Shin Marunouchi Bldg

Marunouchi Bldg

Brick Square

Imperial Theatre

Imperial Palace Plaza

Idemitsu Museum of Art

TCVB Tourist Office

Imperial Palace

Otemon Gate

Takebashi Station

Kudanshita Station

Jimbocho Station

Hanzomon Station

Nagatacho Station

Sakuradamon Station

Moat

300 m

300 yds

© Copyright Time Out Group 2010

Imperial Palace.

the second half of the 19th century. See beautiful, Edo-era, calligraphy-inscribed gold oblongs, occupation-era notes from Indonesia and the Philippines, Siberian leather money and Thai leech coins. Or get the feel for some serious dosh by lifting ¥100 million, safely stored inside a perspex box.

Idemitsu Museum of Arts

Tei Geki Bldg 9F, 3-1-1 Marunouchi, Chiyoda-ku (3213 9404, www.idemitsu.co.jp/museum). Hibiya station (Chiyoda, Hibiya, Mita lines), exit B3. **Open** 10am-5pm Tue-Thur, Sat, Sun; 10am-7pm Fri. **Admission** ¥800; free-¥700 reductions. **Credit** (shop only) MC, V. **Map** p77.

Idemitsu Sazo, founder of Idemitsu Kosan Co, collected traditional Chinese and Japanese art for more than 70 years. This museum (opened in 1966) features displays drawn from a permanent collection of ceramics, calligraphy and painting (for example, Rimpa-style irises painted by Hoitsu Sakai on a six-fold screen). There's a good view of the Imperial Palace.

FREE Imperial Palace East Gardens
Kokyo Higashi Gyoen

Chiyoda, Chiyoda-ku (www.kunaicho.go.jp/eindex. html). Otemachi station (Chiyoda, Hanzomon, Marunouchi, Mita, Tozai lines), exits C10, C13B. **Open** *Mar-mid Apr, Sept, Oct* 9am-4.30pm Tue-Sat. *Mid Apr-Aug* 9am-5pm Tue-Sat. *Nov-Feb* 9am-4pm Tue-Sat. **Admission** free (token collected at gate to be submitted on leaving). **Map** p77.

This is the main park of the Imperial Palace, accessible through three old gates: Otemon (five minutes from Tokyo station), Hirakawamon (close to Takebashi bridge) and Kita-Hanebashimon (near Kitanomaru Park).There are few historical features in the manicured park, except for two old watch-houses, the remains of the old dungeon at the northern end (near Kita-Hanebashimon) and, at the exit into the next area, a wall of hand-carved stones dropping a great height into the water. There's also the small Museum of Imperial Collections.

Japan Science Foundation Science Museum
Kagaku Gijutsukan

2-1 Kitanomaru Koen, Chiyoda-ku (3212 8544, www.jsf.or.jp). Kudanshita station (Hanzomon, Shinjuku, Tozai lines), exit 2 or Takebashi station (Tozai line), exit 1A. **Open** 9.30am-4.50pm daily. **Admission** ¥600; ¥250-¥400 reductions. **No credit cards. Map** p77.

This museum takes to extremes the maxim 'learning by doing'. The unique five-spoke building, in a corner of Kitanomaru Park, consists of five floors of interactive exhibits. Its drab, dated entrance belies the fun displays inside. Children can learn the rudiments of scientific principles while standing inside a huge soap bubble, lifting a small car using pulleys and generating electricity by shouting. There's not a lot of English used, but much of it doesn't need translation.

Kite Museum

Taimeiken 5F, 1-12-10 Nihonbashi, Chuo-ku (3271 2465, www.tako.gr.jp). Nihonbashi station (Asakusa, Ginza, Tozai lines), exit A4, C5. **Open** 11am-8.30pm Mon-Fri; 11am-8pm Sat, Sun. **Admission** ¥200; ¥100 reductions. **No credit cards. Map** p77.

This cornucopia of kites includes Indonesian dried leaves, giant woodblock-print samurai and a huge styrofoam iron. The former owner of the first-floor restaurant (one of Tokyo's earliest forays into Western-style dining) spent a lifetime collecting the 3,000 kites now layering the walls, packing display cases and crowding the ceiling. Don't expect detailed explanations of the exhibits; this is more of a private hobby on public display – as often happens in Tokyo. The museum is not clearly marked – look for the long white sign on the building.

★ Mitsubishi Ichigokan Museum

2-6-2 Marunouchi, Chiyoda-ku (5777 8600, www.mimt.jp/english). Tokyo station (JR, Keiyo, Marunouchi lines), Marunouchi South exit; Nijubashimae station (Chiyoda line), exit 1.

Walk Old Tokyo

A half-day promenade through the city's imperial heart.

Leaving Kudanshita station from exit one, walk up the hill (a prime cherry-blossom area) until you reach the bridge over the moat that is below on your left. From here, either continue up the slope and cross the road for the **Yasukuni Shrine** (*see p80*) and the Yushukan, its controversial museum, or turn left over the bridge, head past the guard and through the impressive Edo-era gates into **Kitanomaru Park**.

The park, once a part of the Imperial Palace, is home to two museums and the **Nippon Budokan** (*see p257 and p279*) – built for the 1964 Olympics and now a multi-use venue that regularly hosts big-name foreign music stars. Kitanomaru Park also contains plenty of picnic spots, and is a popular place for joggers trying to avoid exhaust fumes.

Following the road past the Budokan, you eventually come to the Soviet-style **Japan Science Foundation Science Museum** (*see p78*), just north of which is a bronze statue of post-war prime minister Shigeru Yoshida. The museum itself has an underwhelming concrete exterior, while the lobby could be that of an East German hotel circa 1970. Inside, however, there are plenty of interactive treats and displays, perfect for killing an hour or two.

Carrying on down the road takes you over an expressway and to the perimeter of the Imperial Palace. On your left is the **National Museum of Modern Art** (*see p80*). On your right, you should be able to spot the red-brick **Crafts Gallery**, which has revolving exhibits of Japanese and foreign handicrafts.

To continue into the **Imperial Palace East Gardens** (*see p78*), use the footbridge to cross the road and walk straight up through the Kita-Hanebashimon gate. Past the policeman, just inside the gate, is a booth, at which you will be given a returnable coupon.

The gardens are spacious and well designed for meandering. In addition to a large number of stone bases that used to support *donjons* (towers), the gardens also house the **Museum of Imperial Collections**, a small concert hall and hundreds of trees that are at their most picturesque in autumn.

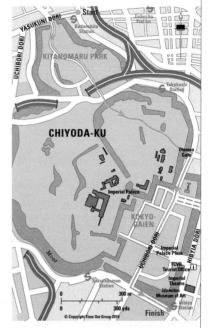

Leaving the gardens via the Otemon gate brings you right back to the present, with the skyscrapers of the Otemachi and Marunouchi business districts looming large. Turn right and walk along the front of the palace until you hit its Outer Gardens. Here, the combination of trimmed pine trees and a vast, empty plaza looks a cross between London's Horseguard's Parade and a giant bonsai collection.

Continuing south along Uchibori Dori across the plaza, the Imperial Palace moat finally turns right, at which point you can cross into **Hibiya Park**. Entering the park through the north entrance, you should see an outdoor café on your left, which, among other things, serves decent fish and chips at prices comparable to Tokyo's British pubs.

But from here it's only a short walk through the garden's main east exit towards Yurakucho and Ginza, where you'll find countless other drinking, eating and entertainment options.

SIGHTS

Open 10am-6pm Tue, Sat, Sun; 10am-8pm Wed-Fri. **Admission** ¥1,500; ¥500-¥1,000 reductions. **No credit cards**. **Map** p77.
The red-brick home of Marunouchi's latest museum is a faithful recreation of an 1890 building by British architect Josiah Conder and inspired the name of the adjoining plaza, Brick Square. It opened in spring 2010 with a heavyweight Manet exhibition, and plans to focus on major 19th-century art. The museum's collection includes over 200 works by Toulouse-Lautrec.
▶ *For more Josiah Conder architecture, visit the Kyu Iwasaki-tei House & Gardens (see p109).*

Mitsui Memorial Museum
Mitsui Main Bldg 7F, Nihonbashi Muromachi 2-1-1, Chuo-ku (5777 8600, www.mitsui-museum.jp). Mistukoshimae station (Ginza, Hanzomon lines), exit A7. **Open** 10am-5pm Tue-Sun. **Admission** ¥1,200; ¥700 reductions. **No credit cards**. **Map** p77.
The Mitsui family turned a 17th-century miso store into one of Japan's biggest conglomerates and a pioneer of modern commerce. The group now has tentacles in banking, construction, real estate, shipping, mining and engineering among many other industries. It also has a museum to show off its impressive collection of around 4,000 Japanese treasures and works of art. The most famous item in the collection is a shinoyaki tea bowl, one of only two tea bowls in the country to be designated a National Treasure.

★ National Museum of Modern Art
3-1 Kitanomaru Koen, Chiyoda-ku (5777 8600, www.momat.go.jp/english). Takebashi station (Tozai line), exits 1A, 1B. **Open** *Art Museum* 10am-5pm Tue-Thur, Sat, Sun; 10am-8pm Fri. *Crafts Gallery* 10am-5pm Tue-Sun. **Admission** ¥420; ¥70-¥130 reductions; free seniors, under-16s; additional charge for special exhibitions. Free to all 1st Sun of mth. **Credit** (shop only) AmEx, JCB, MC,V. **Map** p77.
This is an alternative-history MoMA, one consisting mostly of Japanese art from the turn of the 20th

century onwards. Noteworthy features of the permanent collection are portraits by early Japanese modernist Kishida Ryusei and grim wartime paintings by Tsuguharu Fujita. The 1969 building, designed by Yoshiro Taniguchi was renovated to the tune of ¥7.8 billion in 2001. Its location next to the moat and walls of the Imperial Palace makes it a prime stop for viewing springtime cherry blossoms and autumn foliage. Nearby is the Crafts Gallery, an impressive 1910 European-style brick building, once the base for the legions of guards who patrolled the Imperial Palace.

FREE Tokyo Stock Exchange
Tokyo Shoken Torihiki Sho
2-1 Nihonbashi-Kabutocho, Chuo-ku (3665 1881, www.tse.or.jp). Kayabacho station (Hibiya, Tozai lines), exit 11. **Open** 9am-4.30pm Mon-Fri. *Tours* (English) 1.30pm daily. **Admission** free. **Map** p77.
Sadly, you won't be able to witness much wailing and gnashing of teeth here, since the TSE, home to global giants such as Toyota and Sony, abolished its trading floor in 1999. The stock market of the world's second-largest economy is now run almost entirely by sophisticated computers, which means the building is eerily quiet, the former trading floor taken over by a huge glass cylinder with the names and real-time stock prices of listed companies revolving at the top. If you want to catch what little action is left, visit on a weekday during trading hours (9-11am, 12.30-3pm). The 40-minute guided tour includes a video explaining the history and function of the TSE.

★ Yasukuni Shrine & Yushukan War-Dead Memorial Museum
3-1-1 Kudankita, Chiyoda-ku (3261 8326, www.yasukuni.or.jp). Kudanshita station (Hanzomon, Shinjuku, Tozai lines), exits 1, 3 or Ichigaya station (Chuo, Nanboku, Shinjuku, Sobu, Yurakucho lines), exits A3, A4. **Open** *Grounds* 6am-6pm daily. *Museum* 9am-5pm daily. **Admission** *Shrine* free. *Museum* ¥800; ¥300-¥500 reductions. **No credit cards**. **Map** p77.
Yasukuni is one of Tokyo's grandest shrines, conceived by Emperor Meiji to commemorate those who died defending him against the shogun. It is also the nation's most controversial landmark. It houses the souls of almost 2.5 million war dead, but 14 in particular have brought the shrine notoriety. World War II leaders such as Iwane Matsui, the general who ordered the destruction of Nanking, are enshrined here, with the reasoning that their Class A war criminal status is a Western construct and irrelevant to the Shinto religion. The neighbouring Yushukan war museum stokes the flames with an intriguing take on historic events, arguing, for example, that the Russo-Japanese War (1904-05) inspired Mahatma Gandhi, and suggesting that the Pearl Harbor attack saved the US economy. Former PM Junichiro Koizumi made annual visits to the shrine, delighting nationalists but provoking anger from Japan's neighbours and wartime victims. His successors have chosen not to.

Odaiba

Oh, they do like to play beside the bayside.

You'll either love or hate Odaiba. Its wide avenues give a spacious feel, and what with entertainment galore, the water of Tokyo Bay and an awesome view of the rest of the city, it's a much-loved dating spot for young Tokyoites. But this pristine playground also feels artificial – primarily because it is.

The area started out as a Bubble-era project to develop Tokyo Bay on reclaimed land, with the name being taken from the cannons placed offshore by the Tokugawa shogunate in the late Edo period to protect Japan from invasion. Over the past decade, it's turned into something of a community apart from the rest of Tokyo, at its busiest on summer weekends. But just ten years since much of the area came into being, the leases are up and the wrecker's ball is hovering.

Map p83   **Hotels** p131

ODAIBA ORIENTATION

Getting there: Odaiba is on the Yurikamome monorail line (a one-day travel pass costs ¥800) and the Rinkai line. You can also get there by water bus (see p310).

First, a word of caution. Though the listings and map are correct at time of writing, 2010 was set to be the year that much of Odaiba was razed. The ten-year lease ran out on the Palette Town area – which includes the Stream of Starlight Ferris wheel, the music venue **Zepp Tokyo** (*see p258*), **Mega Web** (*see p84*), **Venus Fort** (*see p198*) and **Oedo Onsen Monogatari** (*see p84*)

INSIDE TRACK
BAYSIDE BOOZE

Odaiba is home to the headquarters of drink giant Suntory – you'll find a classy bar in the building's basement. **Malt Bar Whisky Voice** (B1, 2-3-3 Daiba, Minato-ku, 3529 6381, http://r.gnavi. co.jp/g851525) offers all the usual drink staples, plus some rare (and mightily expensive) Suntory whiskies.

– and the city sold the land to Toyota and Mori Buildings (the people behind Roppongi Hills, Omotesando Hills and dozens of other constructions). The new owners declared their intention to demolish the lot to make room for a high-rise office, retail and leisure complex. The global financial crisis iced those plans temporarily, but the terms of the sale stipulated that the new complex must be open by 2015. If you're coming to Odaiba to see any of the sights between Tokyo Teleport station and Aomi station, check they still exist before you set out.

The most scenic way to reach Odaiba is via the elevated, driverless Yurikamome monorail from Shinbashi or Shiodome stations and watching the view unfold. The gateway to Odaiba is **Rainbow Bridge**, named after the illuminations that light it up after dark. It's become one of the most impressive additions to Tokyo's skyline, along with the ever-changing psychedelic patterns of the enormous Ferris wheel that hopefully still rotates in the distance behind it. If you want to take things slower, you can walk across the bridge in about 30 minutes.

As you come over the bridge, the first sight you'll see is the extravagant 25-storey structure of the **Fuji TV** headquarters, designed by acclaimed Japanese architect Kenzo Tange and crowned by a 1,200-tonne glittering metal

SIGHTS

Rainbow Bridge. *See p81.*

sphere. Inside the sphere is an observation deck that, on clear days, gives breathtaking views.

Get off at Odaiba Kaihin-Koen station if you want to visit the Fuji TV building, or to explore the nearby shopping and entertainment centre of **Decks** (www.odaiba-decks.com). Inside this nautical-themed centre you'll find the Island and Seaside Malls, the Joypolis Game Centre and several restaurants. The Decks Tokyo Brewery, on the fifth floor, is notable for the Daiba brand micro-beer brewed on site.

Follow the signs to 'Daiba-Itchome Shotengai', on the fourth floor, and you'll find one of Odaiba's most intriguing attractions: a loving re-creation of 1960s Japan. Wander down dark and twisty corridors, and visit shops covered in old movie posters and selling food and toys from the post-war days. On the floor above is Little Hong Kong, a cluster of Chinese restaurants surrounded by mock-ups of 1940s railway stations.

Next to Decks is another mall, **Aqua City** (www.aquacity.co.jp). Here you'll find yet more shops, cafés and restaurants and the 13-screen Mediage cinema. In front of Aqua City, next to the water, is – oddly enough – a small-scale replica of the **Statue of Liberty**, built in France and erected in 2000. From here you can walk (or jump back on the monorail to Aomi station) to **Palette Town** – if it's still there.

There are also several museums in Odaiba – including the **Museum of Maritime**

Science, **National Museum of Emerging Science & Innovation** and **Tokyo Metropolitan Waterworks Science Museum** – all of which have their charms.

Beyond the science museum stands the imposing blue-glass arch of the **Telecom Center**, a major telecommunications hub with an observation deck (2-38 Aomi, Koto-ku, 11.30am-9.30pm daily, admission ¥600). And next to this lies the **Oedo Onsen Monogatari**, a hot-spring theme park with customers in *yukata* (dressing gowns) strolling around.

Odaiba is also home to **Tokyo Big Sight**, Japan's largest exhibition and convention centre. There's a scattering of parks; the most pleasant is **Odaiba Seaside Park** in front of Decks and Aqua City, which includes a man-made sand beach. This is also where the Suijo Bus boats stop (*see p310*).

Fuji TV Building

2-4-8 Daiba, Minato-ku (5500 8888, www.fujitv. co.jp). Daiba station (Yurikamome line). **Open** 10am-8pm Tue-Sun. **Admission** *Studios & observation deck* ¥500. **Credit** (gift shop only) MC, V. **Map** p83.

The headquarters of the Fuji TV corporation, one of Japan's nationwide commercial channels, has exhibitions (mostly in Japanese with occasional English subtitles) on popular programmes and guided tours around studios in use. Entrance is free, but you have to pay to get into the studios and observation deck.

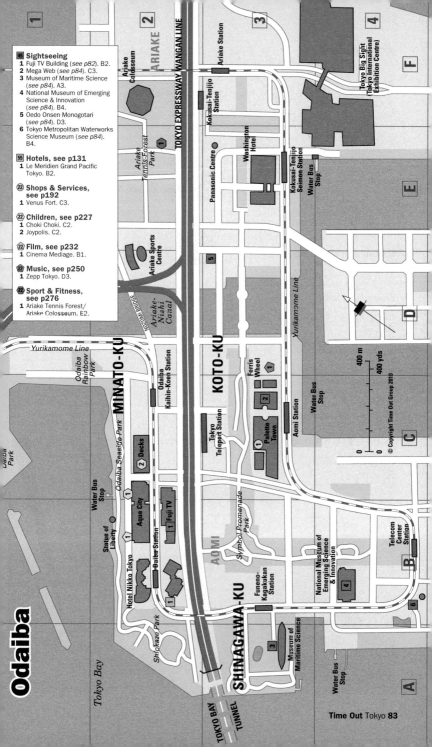

Odaiba

Sightseeing
1 Fuji TV Building (*see p82*). B2.
2 Mega Web (*see p84*). C3.
3 Museum of Maritime Science (*see p84*). A3.
4 National Museum of Emerging Science & Innovation (*see p84*). B4.
5 Oedo Onsen Monogotari (*see p84*). D3.
6 Tokyo Metropolitan Waterworks Science Museum (*see p84*). B4.

Hotels, see p131
1 Le Meridien Grand Pacific Tokyo. B2.

Shops & Services, see p192
1 Venus Fort. C3.

Children, see p227
1 Choki Choki. C2.
2 Joypolis. C2.

Film, see p232
1 Cinema Mediage. B1.

Music, see p250
1 Zepp Tokyo. D3.

Sport & Fitness, see p276
1 Ariake Tennis Forest/ Ariake Colosseum. E2.

ARIAKE

Ariake Coliseum

Ariake Station

Tokyo Big Sight (Tokyo International Exhibition Centre)

TOKYO EXPRESSWAY WANGAN LINE

Kokusai-Tenjijo Station

Ariake Tennis-Forest Park

Panasonic Centre

Washington Hotel

Kokusai-Tenjijo Seimon Station

Water Bus Stop

Ariake Sports Centre

Ariake-Nishi Canal

Yurikamome Line

NOZOMI BRIDGE

MINATO-KU

KOTO-KU

Ferris Wheel

Water Bus Stop

Yurikamome Line

Odaiba Rainbow Park

Odaiba Kaihin-Koen Station

Palette Town

Aomi Station

© Copyright Time Out Group 2010

Daiba Park

Odaiba Seaside Park

Tokyo Teleport Station

2 Decks

Water Bus Stop

Aqua City

Fuji TV

Daiba Station

Symbol Promenade Park

AOMI

Telecom Center Station

Statue of Liberty

Hotel Nikko Tokyo

SHINAGAWA-KU

Funeno-Kagakukan Station

National Museum of Emerging Science & Innovation

Shiokaze Park

Museum of Maritime Science

Water Bus Stop

Tokyo Bay

TOKYO BAY TUNNEL

400 m

400 yds

Time Out Tokyo **83**

FREE Mega Web

*1-3-2 Aomi, Koto-ku (3599 0808, 0800 0800
489 test-drive reservations, www.megaweb.gr.jp).
Aomi station (Yurikamome line) or Tokyo
Teleport station (Rinkai line).* **Open** *Toyota City
Showcase & History Garage 11am-9pm daily.*
Admission free. **Map** p83.

Part of the huge Palette Town development that
opened in 1999, Mega Web certainly lives up to its
name. Its giant Ferris wheel – at 115m (383ft) one of
the tallest in the world – is visible for miles, and lit
with amazing kaleidoscopic patterns at night.
Beneath it is the world's largest car showroom, the
Toyota City Showcase. Here you can sit in the
newest models, take a test drive (¥300) on the two-
lap track (Japanese or international driver's licence
required) or see the company's latest prototypes.
Expect a queue for tickets, especially at weekends.

Museum of Maritime Science
Funeno Kagakukan

*3-1 Higashi-Yashio (Odaiba), Shinagawa-ku
(5500 1111, www.funenokagakukan.or.jp).
Funeno-Kagakukan station (Yurikamome line).*
Open *10am-5pm Tue-Sun.* **Admission** ¥700;
¥400 reductions. **Credit** (restaurant only) V.
Map p83.

Attractions include displays on marine exploration
and replicas of ancient Japanese ships.

★ National Museum of
Emerging Science & Innovation
Nihon Kagaku Miraikan

*2-3-6 Aomi, Koto-ku (3570 9151, www.miraikan.
jst.go.jp). Funeno-Kagakukan station or Telecom
Center station (both Yurikamome line).* **Open**
10am-5pm Mon, Wed-Sun. **Admission** ¥600;
¥200 reductions; free under-6s. **No credit
cards. Map** p83.

Upon entering, the visitor beholds a globe 6.5m (22ft)
in diameter above the lobby, with 851,000 LEDs on
its surface showing real-time global climatic
changes. The museum holds interactive displays on
robots, genetic discoveries and space travel and, perhaps most bizarre of all, a model using springs and
ball bearings to explain the operating principle of
the internet. There are ample explanations in
English, and a good gift shop.

★ Oedo Onsen Monogatari

*2-6-3 Aomi, Koto-ku (5500 1127, www.ooedo
onsen.jp). Telecom Center station (Yurikamome
line).* **Open** *11am-9am daily (last entry 2am).*
Admission *11am-6pm* ¥2,900; *after 6pm*
¥2,000; *extra charge after 2am* ¥1,700. **Map** p83.

This hot-spring theme park does a pretty good job
of recreating an Edo-period bathhouse, with numerous bathing areas, indoor and out, plus hot-sand
baths and saunas. The admission fee includes
yukata and towels. People with tattoos are banned.

Tokyo Metropolitan Waterworks
Science Museum

*3-1-8 Ariake, Koto-ku (3528 2366, www.water
works.metro.tokyo.jp/pp/kagakukan/kagaku.html).
Kokusai Tenjijo-Seimon station (Yurikamome
line).* **Open** *9.30am-5pm Tue-Sun.* **Admission**
free. **Map** p83.

This museum underwent a facelift in 2010, and was
about to reopen as this guide went to press. If it's
anything like the previous incarnation, expect displays and interactive games relating to water.

Tokyo Big Sight. *See p82.*

Roppongi

Where crass, commerce and culture collide.

Roppongi today betrays little of its roots. Until the 17th century, the area was no more than a thoroughfare for Shibuya's residents, but things changed in 1626, when shogun Hidetaka chose Roppongi for his wife's burial ground. The four Buddhist priests who oversaw her funeral were each handed generous rewards by the grateful leader. All four spent their riches building new temples in the area, giving Roppongi its first image – as a centre of spirituality.

Map p87	**Restaurants** p161
Hotels p131	**Bars** p181

Today, the name Roppongi carries a very different resonance. There's nothing much spiritual about the massage parlours, clubs and bars that fill Old Roppongi. But that's not all there is: the Roppongi Hills and Tokyo Midtown developments are many ways the antithesis of Old Roppongi; here it's all about luxury and style.

NAVIGATING ROPPONGI

Getting there: Roppongi station is on the Hibiya and Oedo subway lines. A concourse from exit 1C of the Hibiya line takes you direct to the heart of Roppongi Hills, in front of the Mori Tower. Azabu-Juban is on the Oedo and Nanboku lines, and Hiroo on the Hibiya line.

Take exit 3 from Roppongi station and you'll find yourself at Roppongi Crossing, where the streets **Roppongi Dori** and **Gaien-Higashi Dori** cross. Heading left from the exit, along Roppongi Dori, will take you to Roppongi Hills and, eventually, Nishi-Azabu (*see p88*). Heading up Gaien-Higashi Dori, between the Panasonic LCD screen and the UFJ bank, will take you to Tokyo Midtown on the right, and a few blocks of largely insalubrious entertainment on the left. Further ahead is **Nogi Jinja** (*see p89*) a reminder of the role that ritual suicide once played in Japan. In the other direction, with the Tokyo Tower ahead of you, you're heading right into Old Roppongi, the party zone, where the street is lined with massage parlours, cheap restaurants, rowdy clubs and bars that play music loud enough to make your brain and ears bleed. You'll probably also meet several touts, though

they aren't nearly as numerous or aggressive as they once were, thanks to a 2009 ordinance that threatens heavy fines for soliciting any kind of business on the street.

ROPPONGI HISTORY

In the mid 18th century, Roppongi, then a site of temples and spirituality, had an official population of 454. It wasn't until the late 19th century that the modern area began to take shape. The government moved a division of the Imperial Guard to the area, heralding the start of a long military association. Following World War II, the US occupiers also picked Roppongi as a base, and it developed to serve the various visceral needs of military men. For over half a century, Roppongi has been the place to go for sleazy revelry, deafening music and drink-till-you-hurl tomfoolery.

As a result, Tokyo's leading property magnate Minoru Mori raised a few eyebrows when, in 1995, he announced plans to build a huge, multibillion-yen, upmarket urban development right next to the bedlam. **Roppongi Hills** opened to great fanfare in April 2003, and its popularity has yet to wane. Official figures claim 100,000 visitors each weekday, rising to 300,000 each weekend. When **Tokyo Midtown** opened in 2007, even closer

Roppongi-Itchome Station.

to the party streets, with a lookalike blueprint of retail, art, dining, hotel and high-end residences, Roppongi's new split personality was confirmed. It's still the place to indulge your vices, but you can now also enjoy high art, fine dining and posh boutiques.

ROPPONGI HILLS

The complex is designed as a 'city within a city', housing more than 200 cafés, restaurants and shops, hundreds of Conran-designed serviced apartments, a major art museum, the nine-screen **Toho Cinemas** (*see p236*), the Ashahi TV studio, a park and the sumptuous **Grand Hyatt Tokyo** (*see p131*). With an emphasis on the luxururious side of life, Roppongi Hills has only one thing in common with the Old Roppongi – the distinctly foreign feel; anyone looking for traditional Japan won't find it here.

Reaching Roppongi Hills is easy – the Hibiya and Oedo subway lines are on its doorstep – but navigating the complex is close to impossible,

even with the official map. The layout swirls with corridors, escalators and floor plans so complex that you could almost believe the architects (who also designed Las Vegas's Bellagio casino-hotel) were instructed to disorientate visitors. In the middle is Mori's eponymous 54-storey tower – the top supposedly modelled on a samurai helmet – home to the world-class **Mori Art Museum** and an observation deck, **Tokyo City View** (both on the 52nd floor; *see p88*), and a wallet-busting private members' club. Louise Bourgeois's huge spider sculpture, *Maman*, crouches in front of the tower. For more details of what the complex contains, visit www.roppongihills.com.

TOKYO MIDTOWN

Like Roppongi Hills, Midtown is loosely based on the vertical cities proposed by Le Corbusier and others in the inter-war years. At its centre is a 248-metre (813-foot) monolith named, rather perfunctorily, **Midtown Tower**. Unlike

46 Sightseeing
1 21_21 Design Sight (*see p88*). C1.
2 Mori Art Museum & Tokyo City View (*see p88*). B3.
3 National Art Center Tokyo (*see p88*). B2.
4 Nogi Jinja (*see p89*). B1.
5 Okura Shukokan Museum of Fine Art (*see p90*). F1.
6 Suntory Museum of Art (*see p90*). B2.
7 Tokyo Tower (*see p90*). F4.

55 Hotels, see p131
1 ANA Intercontinental Tokyo. E1.
2 Grand Hyatt Tokyo. B4.
3 Hotel Arca Torre Roppongi. C3.
4 Hotel Ibis. C2.
5 Hotel Okura Tokyo. F2.
6 Ritz-Carlton Tokyo. C2.

Restaurants, see p161
1 L'Atelier de Joël Robuchon. B4.
2 Bangkok. C3.
3 Brasserie Paul Bocuse Le Musée. B2.
4 China Café Eight. B4.
5 Coriander. A3.
6 Fukuzushi. C3.
7 Gonpachi. A4.
8 Harmonie. A4.
9 Inakaya. C2.
10 Maimon. A4.
11 Nihonryori Ryugin. B3.
12 Nodaiwa. F4.
13 Oak Door. B4.
14 Pierre Gagnaire Tokyo. E1.
15 Pintokona. B3.
16 Roti. C3.

Bars, see p181
1 A971. C2.
2 Agave. B3.
3 Bauhaus. C3.
4 Cask. C2.

5 Cavern Club. C3.
6 L Garden. D3.
7 Mado Lounge. B4.
8 Super-deluxe. B3.
9 These. A3.
10 Tokyo Sports Café. B2.

Shops & Services, see p192
1 Jennifer Hair & Beauty. B4.
2 Koyasu Drug Store. F1.
3 Restir. D2.
4 Roppongi Hills. B4.
5 Roppongi Pharmacy. C3.
6 Serendipity. B2.
7 Tokyo Midtown. C2.

Children, see p227
1 Kids Square. B3.

Film, see p232
1 Cinem@rt. C3.
2 Haiyu-Za. C2.
3 Toho Cinema Roppongi Hills. B4.

Galleries, see p240
1 Gallery Ma. B1.

Music, see p250
1 Alfie. C3.
2 Billboard Live. B1.
3 STB139. C3.
4 Suntory Hall. E2.

Nightlife, see p264
1 328 (San Ni Pa). A4.
2 Alife. A3.
3 Bar Matrix. C3.
4 Bullet's. A3.
5 Eleven. A3.
6 Feria. B2.
7 Muse. A4.

Performing Arts, see p269
1 Tokyo Comedy Store. B1.
2 Tokyo International Players. E4.

Roppongi

Aoyama Cemetery

MINAMI-AOYAMA

Aoyama Park

Hinokicho Park

National Arts Center

Tokyo Midtown

GAIEN-HIGASHI DORI

ROPPONGI DORI

AKASAKA

ARK HILLS

Ark Mori Building

EXPRESSWAY NO 3 SHIBU

MINATO-KU

Kamiyacho Station

SAKURADA DORI

Shiba Park

Tokyo Tower

Hotel Okura Tokyo

Roppongi-Itchome Station

Roppongi Cemetery

Roppongi Station

GAIEN-HIGASHI DORI

HIGASHI-AZABU

IMAHI-ZAKI

ROPPONGI

Asahi TV

Roppongi Hills

to Azabu-Juban Station

NISHI-AZABU

Nogizaka Station

© Copyright Time Out Group 2010

0   300 yds

Roppongi Hills, it is easy to navigate and a model of how to use Japanese design elements in a modern commercial centre. The designers, Skidmore, Owings and Merrill, claim the layout is based on a traditional Japanese rock garden. Whether or not you can see that, the bamboo, washi paper and light wood interior, and the flowering cherry trees in the garden, all nod emphatically to a Japanese sensibility.

The complex features offices, apartments, shops and restaurants, as well as the Ritz-Carlton Tokyo hotel, the Suntory Museum of Art and 21_21 Design Sight, a design gallery housed in a futuristic building inspired by the fabrics of fashion maestro Issey Miyake. What really distinguishes Midtown from its rivals, though, is the four hectares of greenery in which all these amenities are housed. Roppongi Hills has grass, but not on the scale of the beautifully landscaped Hinokicho Park, which covers 40 per cent of the grounds. In the summer, grab a takeaway from the food stores in the basement and have a picnic.

This is Tokyo's most upmarket mega-mall experience, with jewellery from Harry Winstone and fashion from the Restir boutique (*see p205*). The restaurants and cafés are some of Tokyo's best, and the basement food court is packed with gourmet brand names.

Exit 8 from Roppongi station will deliver you right into the Midtown complex.

NISHI-AZABU, AZABU-JUBAN & HIROO

Before Roppongi Hills came along, **Nishi-Azabu** was the chalk to Roppongi's cheese. Loaded with stylish bars, restaurants and clubs, it pulls a sophisticated crowd. Like Roppongi, Nishi-Azabu lights up at sundown; unlike Roppongi, there's always an atmosphere of calm about the place. It's the perfect location for dates or entertaining clients. Nishi-Azabu has no station, so access is via Roppongi station. Take exit 1 and walk down Roppongi Dori towards Shibuya. When you reach a crossroads with Hobson's ice-cream shop opposite you, that's the heart of Nishi-Azabu.

Further east is **Azabu-Juban**, another district rich in restaurants, though with a more traditional feel. This Azabu has a station on the Nanboku and Oedo subway lines, and each August hosts one of the capital's most congested festivals, the Azabu-Juban Noryo Festival (*see p223*), featuring *taiko* drumming and traditional dancing. It's also home to import food store **Nissin** (*see p211*). Also in the area, although not within walking distance, is **Hiroo**, an expat haven thanks to the numerous embassies nearby. Its shops, cafés and restaurants betray strong Western influences, and most employ English-speaking staff.

★ 21_21 Design Sight

9-7-6 Akasaka, Minato-ku (3475 2121, www.2121designsight.jp). Roppongi station (Hibiya, Oedo lines), exit 8. **Open** 11am-8pm Mon, Wed-Sun. **Admission** ¥1,000; free-¥800 reductions. **Credit** AmEx, DC, JCB, MC, V.
Design heavyweights Issey Miyake and Naoto Fukasawa are behind Japan's first modern design museum. Appropriately enough for a city where nothing seems fixed, it has no permanent collection; instead, it hosts thematic exhibitions of work from established names and promising designers. The building is a Tadao Ando creation inspired by Miyake's clothing. From the outside it looks like a mere sliver of a building, but it descends underground, always twisting and folding.

★ Mori Art Museum & Tokyo City View

Mori Tower 52F-53F, 6-10-1 Roppongi, Minato-ku (6406 6100, www.mori.art.museum/ html/eng/index.html). Roppongi station (Hibiya, Oedo lines), exit 1. **Open** 10am-10pm Mon, Wed, Thur; 10am-5pm Tue; 10am-midnight Fri-Sun. **Admission** ¥1,500. **Credit** AmEx, DC, JCB, MC, V. **Map** p87.
The exhibitions are world-class, focused mainly on contemporary culture, but the secrets of the Mori Art Museum's success are location (part of the popular Roppongi Hills complex), location (on the 52nd and 53rd floors of the Mori Tower, offering spectacular views) and location (within a two-floor 'experience' that includes a bar, café, shop and panoramic observation deck). One ticket allows access to all areas, and the late opening hours maximise accessibility. Exhibitions are deliberately varied, with past shows including Bill Viola's video art and an exhibition about humour in contemporary art. The vista from Tokyo City View isn't quite 360°, and it's expensive compared to the free Tokyo Metropolitan Government building observatory (*see p104*), but the views are arguably better, especially at night with the city lit up; you can see it while sipping a drink from Mado Lounge (*see p183*).

★ National Art Center Tokyo

7-22-2 Roppongi, Minato-ku (6812 9900, www.nact.jp). Nogizaka station (Chiyoda line), exit 6. **Open** 10am-6pm Mon, Wed, Thur, Sat, Sun; 10am-8pm Fri. **Admission** varies. **Credit** AmEx, DC, JCB, MC, V.
Tokyo's largest art museum opened in 2007 with a whopping 14,000sq m (150,000sq ft) of exhibition space. It has no permanent collection, but stages temporary exhibitions that are usually impressive, if not always as innovative as you'll find at the nearby Mori Art Museum. The architecture, by the late Kisho Kurokawa, is one of Tokyo's most photogenic modern creations, with an undulating glass façade hiding a lobby that could have been plucked from the *Star Wars* set.

SIGHTS

New Otani Museum

*Hotel New Otani, Garden Court 6F, 4-1 Kioicho,
Chiyoda-ku (3221 4111, www.newotani.co.jp/
group/museum/index.html). Akasaka-Mitsuke
station (Ginza, Marunouchi lines), exit D or
Nagatacho station (Hanzomon, Nanboku,
Yurakucho lines), exit 7.* **Open** 10am-6pm
Tue-Sun. **Admission** ¥500; ¥200 reductions;
free hotel guests. **No credit cards**.

The museum inside the New Otani houses a collection of Japanese and Japanese-inspired woodblock
prints, plus a selection of traditional Japanese and
modern European paintings (including works by
Vlaminck and School of Paris artists). The place is
small, consisting of two rooms near the hotel reception, but often has shows not seen elsewhere.

NHK Broadcast Museum

*2-1-1 Atago, Minato-ku (5400 6900, www.nhk.
or.jp/museum/index.html). Kamiyacho station
(Hibiya line), exit 3 or Onarimon station (Mita
line), exit 2.* **Open** 9.30am-4.30pm Tue-Sun.
Admission free.

This museum is run by the national public broadcasting company. The nation's first radio station
began broadcasting in July 1925 from this location,
although NHK itself has since moved to bigger digs
in Shibuya. There are two floors of early electronic
equipment, and vintage TV shows and news broadcasts play throughout the museum and can also be
viewed in the video library.

Nogi Jinja

*8-11-27 Akasaka, Minato-ku (3478 3001/
house enquiries 3583 4151, www.nogijinja.
or.jp). Nogizaka station (Chiyoda line), exit 1
or Roppongi station (Hibiya, Oedo lines),
exit 7.* **Open** *Walkway* 8.30am-5pm daily.
House 9.30am-5pm 12, 13 Sept. **Admission**
free. **Map** p87.

When Emperor Meiji died, on 13 September 1912,
General Nogi Maresuke and his wife proved their
absolute loyalty to their divine ruler by joining him
in death; he killed himself by *seppuku* (ritual disembowelment), she by slitting her throat with a knife.
The house in which they died is situated adjacent to

Mori Art Museum & Tokyo City View.

SIGHTS

Local View Joi Ito

A technophile hungers for old school.

I love the little eateries inside the Toyokawa Inari shrine in Akasaka. They serve *oden* and soba, are very quaint and kitsch and are a pretty mellow way to feel very rural in the middle of Akasaka.

There's a trio of stores just inside the main entrance (watch out for pigeon droppings). The middle one is my favourite. Order *oden* and *kitsune soba* (buckwheat noodles with deep-fried tofu). They also sell all kinds of weird little trinkets, and you can grab some traditional Japanese junk food on the way out.

Toyokawa Inari Shrine
1-4-7 Moto-Akasaka, Minato-ku (3408 3414). Akasaka-Mitsuke station (Ginza, Marunouchi lines), exit D. **Open** dawn-dusk daily. *Shop & cafés* 11am-5pm daily.

● *Cousin of Cornelius (see p218) and godson of Timothy Leary, Ito is a board member of the Mozilla Foundation, Creative Commons and the Open Source Initiative, and runs a popular blog at http://joi.ito.com.*

the Nogi Shrine, which is dedicated to his memory. The house itself is open on only two days a year, namely the eve and anniversary of their deaths, but an elevated walkway allows you to peek in through the windows, one of which provides a glimpse of Nogi's bloodstained shirt.

Okura Shukokan Museum of Fine Art
Hotel Okura, 2-10-4 Toranomon, Minato-ku (3583 0781, www.okura.com/tokyo/info/shukokan.html). Roppongi-Itchome station (Nanboku line), exits 2, 3. **Open** 10am-4.30pm Tue-Sun. **Admission** ¥800; ¥400-¥500 reductions; free hotel guests. **No credit cards.** **Map** p87.
This two-storey Chinese-style building sits in front of the retro-modern Hotel Okura Tokyo (*see p132*). Inside there's a small mix of Asian antiquities: paintings, calligraphy, Buddhist sculpture, textiles, ceramics, swords, archaeological artefacts, lacquerware and metalwork. The exhibitions change five or six times a year.

Suntory Museum of Art
Tokyo Midtown Gardenside, 9-7-4 Akasaka, Minato-ku (3479 8600, www.suntory.com/
culture-sports/sma). Roppongi station (Hibiya, Oedo lines), exit 8. **Open** 10am-8pm Wed-Sat; 10am-6pm Mon, Sun. **Admission** varies.
Drink giant Suntory has one of the most distinguished private collections of Japanese art and antiquities, and since it moved to the Tokyo Midtown complex it now also has a polished, elegant home. It's not huge, but it's large enough for all but the most serious connoisseur.

Tokyo Tower
4-2-8 Shiba-Koen, Minato-ku (3433 5111/2, www.tokyotower.co.jp). Kamiyacho station (Hibiya line), exit 1 or Onarimon station (Mita line), exit A1 or Akabanebashi station (Oedo line), Akabanebashi exit. **Open** *Tower* 9am-10pm daily. *Other attractions* 10am-9pm daily. **Admission** *Main Observatory* ¥820; ¥310-¥460 reductions. *Special Observatory* ¥600; ¥350-¥400 reductions. *Waxwork Museum* ¥870; ¥460 reductions. *Trick Art Gallery* ¥400; ¥300 reductions. *Mysterious Walking Zone* ¥410; ¥300 reductions. *Combined ticket* ¥1,900; ¥950-¥1,100 reductions. **No credit cards. Map** p87.
The resemblance to the Eiffel Tower is deliberate, as is the superior height – 13m (43ft) taller than the Parisian structure. Back in 1958, when it was built, it must have been impressive. Nowadays, the Mori Tower and Shinjuku's Tocho both offer more impressive views, as will the Tokyo Sky Tree from 2012. The tower still functions as a radio and TV mast, but its days as the observation deck of choice are long gone. The attractions inside, including a wax museum and trick art gallery, only serve to highlight how dated the tower has become. But it remains Tokyo's most recognisable structure and, ironically, its most striking attraction when viewed at night from any of the other observation decks.

Zojo-ji Temple
4-7-35 Shiba Koen, Minato-ku (3432 1431, www.zojoji.or.jp/en/). Shiba-Koen station (Mita line), exit A4 or Daimon station (Asakusa, Oedo lines), exit A6. **Open** *Temple* 6am-5.30pm daily. *Grounds* 24hrs daily. **Admission** free.
The main temple of the Buddhist Jodo sect in the Kanto area, Zojo-ji was built in 1393 and moved to its present location in 1598. In the 17th century, 48 temples stood on this site. The main hall has been destroyed three times by fire in the last century, the current building being a 1970s reconstruction. The most historic element is the Sangedatsumon main gate: dating back to 1605, it's the oldest wooden structure in Tokyo. Each of its three sections represents three of the stages that are necessary to attain nirvana. A mausoleum in the grounds contains the tombs of six Tokugawa shoguns. There's also a cemetery, with row upon row of small statues of the bodhisattva Jizo, guardian of (among other things) stillborn, aborted or miscarried babies.

Shibuya

Teenage kicks right through the day and night.

Shibuya is the bright, brash centre of Tokyo's teen culture. The city's youths have made Shibuya their playground, and the area's innumerable shops, cafés, clubs, bars and restaurants largely cater to their tastes. This is a fast, fun and affordable part of town.

The entire nation's youth culture stems from Shibuya and, whether they know it or not, these kids also supply the rest of the world with fashion cues. The English footballers' WAG look? Very late '90s Shibuya. Car-crash mismatching of colours and styles? It happened here first.

| **Map** p93 | **Restaurants** p165 |
| **Hotels** p133 | **Bars** p183 |

During the day, the area is all about shopping, with music and fashion dominating its stores. But when darkness falls and the neon flicks on, myriad clubs, bars, cinemas, performance venues and less salubrious establishments keep the area throbbing till dawn.

NAVIGATING SHIBUYA

Getting there: Shibuya is on the JR Yamanote and Saikyo train lines and the Fukutoshin, Ginza and Hanzomon subway lines, as well as the Keio Inokashira, Tokyu Toyoko and Denentoshi suburban rail lines.

Traditionally, Shibuya's action has been limited to the wedge of land west of the Yamanote line train tracks, but thanks to the economic and cultural triumph of Tokyo's youth, and ongoing improvements in transport links, the fun is expanding in all directions. The JR station's Hachiko exit is still the gateway to most of the area's attractions, but it's now worth wandering elsewhere for some great gems of nightlife or independent stores.

In the paved square outside the exit is a small bronze statue of the eponymous **Hachiko**, a dog of legendary loyalty who walked to Shibuya to meet his owner at the end of each day, then travelled in vain to the station for a further seven years after the old man's death. He too passed on in 1935, earning obituaries in national newspapers and the honour of his statue becoming Shibuya's most popular – and thus overcrowded – meeting spot.

Next to the square is the world's busiest pedestrian crossing, also named Hachiko, across which a scuttling horde pours every three minutes. To a backdrop of blaring video screens and neon-clad buildings, this is the Tokyo of popular imagination, the first choice of foreign TV crews looking for an instant symbol of the manic city. You can watch it all from the second floor of Starbucks.

Beside Starbucks, on the far side of Hachiko crossing, is the entry to **Center Gai** (*photo p94*),

INSIDE TRACK SHIBUYA STATION – ALL CHANGE!

In a collaboration between the rail companies and various levels of government, much of Shibuya's century-old station building will be razed and the rail lines altered. The Tokyu department store will be demolished and Hachiko Square expanded by 50 per cent. The new station's 33-storey complex will house shops, offices, an exhibition hall and a 2,000 capacity theatre when completed in 2012.

SIGHTS

SIGHTS

a pedestrian street lined with cheap chain restaurants, mobile-phone vendors and trainer shops. It's also a catwalk for Tokyo's teen trendsetters, who mill around in the latest garish fashions. The likely source of their threads is **109** (*see p204; photo p97*). This ten-storey cylindrical collection of boutiques, a block to the left of Center Gai, is not so much a store as a way of life for the area's flamboyantly attired teenage girls. The store's most accessorised ambassadors are known as

---

INSIDE TRACK
JUST PROTEST IT

In 2006, when a music venue was renamed CC Lemon Hall after a popular drink, it raised barely an eyebrow. So Shibuya council likely expected an easy ride when they sold Nike the rights to rename and redesign Miyashita Park, a little-loved patch of dirt on Meiji Dori, near Shibuya station. As part of its ten-year, ¥170 million lease, Nike plans to build a climbing wall, skate ramps and futsal courts under the name **Miyashita Nike Park**. But locals opposed to the idea of a foreign corporation stamping their brand on a public space, and advocates of the homeless people currently living in the park, are against the idea as well. The protestors succeeded in delaying the start of construction in April 2010, but Nike still aims to open its new facilities by year's end.

---

gyaru – an approximation of the English 'gal'. The staff (usually drawn from the store's customers) – are powerful players on the teen fashion scene, often doubling as stylists for magazines and going on to launch their own boutiques or labels. It's a retailing phenomenon lubricated by just-in-time production, cheap Chinese manufacturing and the hard-earned yen of their elders and betters. Whether or not such clothing is to your taste, a visit to see the young shoppers in action is an essential experience.

The street that forks to the right of 109 leads to **Bunkamura**, a massive arts centre owned by the same corporation (Tokyu) as the fashion superstore, but catering to a very different crowd. It's an oasis of calm that contains, among other things, **Le Cinema** (*see p233*), the performance spaces **Theatre Cocoon** (*see p275*) and **Orchard Hall** (*see p251*) and a good museum.

Just before reaching Bunkamura you'll notice the six-storey emporium **Don Quixote**. In a two-fingered salute to the traditional retail format, the layout is deliberately bewildering, with sex toys sitting beside shoes, and 'mini-skirt police' costumes mixed in with travel bags. Food, jewellery, electronics, furniture and toys are just some of the products piled high and sold cheap here. The shop assistants double as buyers and have remarkably free rein to order anything they think might sell, so the selections are eclectic and fast-changing.

A right turn at Bunkamura should lead you back to the bustle. The Shibuya BEAM building on the right-hand side is home to a large basement branch of manga/*anime* specialist **Mandarake** (*see p212*). Teens

---

45 Sightseeing
1 Bunkamura The Museum (*see p94*). A2.
2 Parco Museum of Art & Beyond (*see p96*). C2.
3 TEPCO Electric Energy Museum (*see p97*). C1.
4 Tobacco & Salt Museum (*see p97*). C1.
5 United Nations University Centre (*see p64*). F1.

55 Hotels, see p133
1 Central Land Shibuya (*see p140*). B4.
2 Cerulean Tower Tokyu Hotel. C4.
3 Excel Hotel Tokyu. C3.
4 Granbell Hotel. D5.
5 Hotel Unizo. B1.
6 P&A Plaza. B4.
7 Villa Giulia. B3.

1 Restaurants, see p165
1 Beacon. B2.
2 Don Ciccio. F3.
3 Gaya. F2.
4 Kanetanaka-so. C4.
5 Legato. B4.
6 Negiya Heikichi. B2.

7 Respekt Café. E2.
8 Sushi Ouchi. F2.
9 Underground Mr Zoogunzoo. F2.
10 Uogashi Nippon-Ichi. C2.

20 Bars, see p183
1 Bello Visto. C4.
2 Chandelier Bar/Red Bar. E2.
3 Pink Cow. F1.
4 Quons (*see p179*). E2.
5 Shirokuma. B2.

22 Coffee Shops, see p189
1 Lion. B3.
2 Satei Hato. D2.

22 Shops & Services, see p192
1 109. C3.
2 ABC Mart. D1.
3 Dance Music Record. B2.
4 Hatch. C3.
5 Mark City. B3.
6 Opening Ceremony. C2.
7 Parco. C2.
8 RagTag. C1.
9 RanKing RanQueen. D3.
10 Recofan. B2.
11 Seibu. C2.
12 Technique. B2.

13 Tokyu Hands. B1.
14 Zoff. C3.

22 Children, see p227
1 Kids World. A3.
2 National Children's Castle. F2.
3 Tokyo Metropolitan Children's Hall. D2.

22 Film, see p232
1 Le Cinema. A2.
2 Cinema Rise. B2.
3 Ciné Quinto. C2.
4 Ciné Saison Shibuya. B3.
5 Euro Space. C4.
6 Theatre Image Forum. F2.
7 Theatre N Shibuya. C4.

22 Galleries, see p241
1 Gallerie Le Déco. E4.
2 Tokyo Wonder Site. C1.

▲ Gay & Lesbian, see p243
1 Chestnut & Squirrel. E4.

22 Music, see p250
1 Club Quattro. B2.
2 DeSeO. D4.
3 JZ Brat. C4.
4 La.mama Shibuya. B4.

5 Orchard Hall. B2.
6 Shibuya O-East. A3.
7 Shibuya O-West. A3.

22 Nightlife, see p265
1 Club Asia. A3.
2 Club Atom. A3.
3 Club Bar Family. E2.
4 Club Camelot. C1.
5 Club Hachi. F3.
6 La Fabrique. C2.
7 Harlem. A3.
8 Loop. F2.
9 Microcosmos. B2.
10 Module. B2.
11 Organ Bar. B1.
12 Rockwest. B1.
13 Room. D4.
14 Ruby Room. B2.
15 Womb. A3.

22 Performing Arts, see p269
1 Aoyama Round Theatre. F1.
2 Cerulean Tower Noh Theatre. C4.
3 Theatre Cocoon. A2.

22 Sport & Fitness, see p276
1 Esforta. C4.

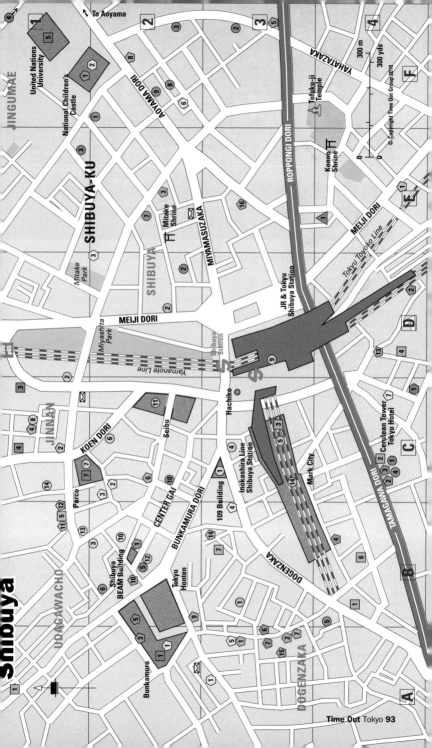

Shibuya

Center Gai. *See p91.*

can browse old comics, adults can indulge their nostalgia with some vintage Nintendo games, while high-rolling geeks can snap up original *anime* cells from Hayao Miyazaki's Studio Ghibli. The staff have been known to perform song and dance routines in full *anime* costume to celebrate big purchases.

Continue to the next T-junction, head left and you'll find yet another Tokyu-run institution – **Tokyu Hands** (*see p217*). Often misleadingly termed a stationery or hardware store, it hawks everything from stereos to Halloween masks, and is the best place to find the latest, only-in-Japan novelties. Vinyl enthusiasts should explore the surrounding streets, where dozens of vinyl-only music stores, some little larger than a cupboard, offer 'Shibuya taste' discs: mainly hip hop, house, techno and reggae.

Between Tokyu Hands and the next main street, Koen Dori, is another teen haven, **Parco** (*see p205*). The hip division of Seibu department store, Parco takes up three separate buildings (Part 1, Part 2 and Part 3). At the top of Part 3 is the **Parco Museum of Art & Beyond**, which hosts an eclectic mix of trendsetting shows.

The rest of Shibuya is a winding maze of streets. It can be a disorienting experience – but that's half the fun – though with each of the main roads leading downhill to the station, it's hard to become seriously lost.

If you tire of consumerism, check out Shibuya's quirky museums, including the **Tobacco & Salt Museum** and the **TEPCO Electric Energy Museum** (both north of Parco). Further west in the Shoto area, quiet contemplation is the order of the day at two small art museums: the **Toguri Museum** and the **Shoto Museum**. Nearby is the unusual **Gallery Tom** (2-11-1 Shoto, 3467 8102, open 10.30am-5.30pm Tue-Sun, admission ¥600), which has been catering for the visually

impaired for two decades. It's the only gallery in town where visitors are encouraged to get touchy-feely with the sculptures and 3-D art.

Further out, a couple of stops from Shibuya on the Keio Inokashira line, is the low-key **Japan Folk Crafts Museum**.

When the shops close, head back towards Bunkamura and turn left. This takes you uphill to the hub of Shibuya's nightlife, home to several of Tokyo's best-known clubs (**Womb, Vuenos, Club Asia, Ruby Room, Neo**; for reviews of nightclubs, *see pp262-268*), as well as a great many of its love hotels. At these, from around ¥3,000, you can 'rest' with a friend for a couple of hours. Alternatively, you might prefer to fork out ¥30,000 for a night at the luxury love hotel **P&A Plaza**, where room 901 has a private swimming pool and room 902 comes complete with its own cave (*see p141* **Love Hotels**).

After a long period of looking like its main function is as an after-hours youth club, Shibuya has started to push its image upmarket. The **Mark City** shopping centre (*see p197*) and upmarket **Excel** (*see p134*) and **Cerulean Tower** (*see p133*) hotels were the beginning of a massive revamp that will see Shibuya station become another multi-purpose mega venue (*see p92* **Inside Track**).

Some lament the loss of the area's downbeat charm. But the same protests have been heard since the original Tokyu department store rose up beside the station in 1934 (some of the original shops displaced by Tokyu still operate underneath Hachiko), and Shibuya has never been a place to stand still.

★ Bunkamura The Museum

Bunkamura B1, 2-24-1 Dogenzaka, Shibuya-ku (3477 9111, www.bunkamura.co.jp). Shibuya station (Yamanote, Ginza lines), Hachiko exit; (Hanzomon line), exit 3A. **Open** 10am-7pm

Walk People-watching

Witness the fashion parade of Tokyo's youthful tribes.

Save this three-hour walk for a sunny Sunday when the city's youths come out in force – and in costume. Dive in at the deep end by taking the Hachiko exit from Shibuya station. With luck, you'll find local kids squatting on the street hawking all manner of wares and services, from artistic calligraphy to 'listening to your story for five minutes'.

Facing you on the far side of the world's busiest pedestrian crossing is the **Q-Front** building, with its four-storey projection of pop videos and high-tempo ads. Directly to the left is **Centre Gai**, the pedestrianised hub for tarted-up teens, including the 'Centre Guys' and perhaps their super-tanned, brightly dressed female counterparts.

Once you're past the congested street entrance, the human traffic eases, and you can stroll along perusing the latest fashions. Turn right at the far end of the street, continue to the end of the street and turn left. Ahead of you is the city's vinyl district. The spacious **DMR** store on the left draws the DJs, while the tiny cubby-holes in the Noa building above offer rarer, pricier treats for collectors.

Turn right at the **Tokyu Hands** shop and walk to the main intersection with Koen Dori ('Park Street'). Straight ahead is the **Tokyo Wonder Site** (*see p241*) for a cultural diversion. Take a left; as you walk up the hill, a detour a block to the right leads to numerous outlets for urban and vintage fashion, including **RagTag** (*see p208*). Cross the street at the top of Koen Dori and you'll find yourself on a pedestrianised avenue. At weekends, it's lined with performers and their audiences. Most of the acts are unsigned bands looking to pick up new fans. You might also spot some stand-up comedians, puppeteers or, more disturbingly, wannabe 'idols' offering their cuteness to admiring huddles of middle-aged men.

At the end of the avenue lies a plaza. There are frequent festivals held here, often with regional themes. The best of the lot is the massive **Thai Festival**, which takes place each May (*see p222*).

From the plaza, take the footbridge into **Yoyogi Park**. This spacious, verdant spot is a great place to relax after the bustle of Shibuya, but if you still want some action

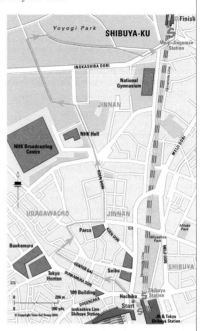

amid the azaleas, there's more fun to be had by veering right, to the park entrance. Each Sunday afternoon, a dozen or so rockabillies in greaser gear and pompadours descend on the area, crank out stripped-down 1950s rock 'n' roll from their sound systems, and spend the afternoon twisting and spinning for the crowd of onlookers.

The fun continues just around the corner towards Harajuku station, where the 'cosplay' (costume play) kids hold court. The bridge just south of the station is the main venue for masquerading the elaborate, often handmade costumes. The 'gothloli' look (a mash-up of 'Gothic' and 'Lolita') is a favourite. Most cosplayers are delighted to pose for photos.

If your people-watching urge is sated, escape via Harajuku station. If not, the backstreets of Harajuku offer a take on urban fashion that's a shade less brassy than that of Shibuya.

(For more on Tokyo's most colourful and unique characters, *see pp39-42* **Otaku**.)

SIGHTS

Mon-Thur, Sun; 10am-9pm Fri, Sat. **Admission** usually ¥1,000. **Credit** (shop only) AmEx, JCB, MC, V. **Map** p93.

One of the best museums in Tokyo is, perhaps appropriately, run by a department-store chain (it's owned and operated by the Tokyu corporation, which also runs 109, Tokyu Hands and part of Mark City). Bunkamura hosts international art blockbusters featuring subjects and artists ranging from Tintin to Picasso. Elsewhere in this major shopping and cultural centre are boutiques, an art-house cinema, two theatre/music spaces, an art bookshop and various restaurants.

Japan Folk Crafts Museum
Mingei-kan

4-3-33 Komaba, Meguro-ku (3467 4527, www.mingeikan.or.jp). Komaba-Todaimae station (Keio Inokashira line), west exit. **Open** 10am-5pm Tue-Sun. **Admission** ¥1,000; ¥200-¥500 reductions. **Credit** MC, V.

Kyoto University professor Yanagi Soetsu created this museum in 1936 to spotlight *mingei*, literally 'arts of the people'. The criteria for inclusion in the collection were that objects should be made anonymously, by hand, and in large quantities. Yanagi collected ceramics, metalwork, woodwork, textiles, paintings and other everyday items from Japan, China, Korea and Taiwan at a time when their beauty wasn't always recognised. Handwritten labels (in Japanese) and simple wooden display cases complement the rustic feel.

★ Parco Museum of Art & Beyond

Parco Part 3 7F, 15-1 Udagawacho, Shibuya-ku (3464 5111, www.parco-art.com). Shibuya station (Yamanote, Ginza lines), Hachiko exit; (Hanzomon line), exits 3A, 6, 7. **Open** (during exhibitions only) 10am-8.30pm. **Admission** ¥500; ¥400 reductions. **Credit** AmEx, DC, JCB, MC, V. **Map** p93.

This top-floor gallery's programming policy perfectly fits the Shibuya demographic, with regularly changing exhibitions on pop-culture themes, plus work by only the trendiest photographers and designers from Japan and overseas. Past shows have featured photos by the dog-loving William Wegman, and that enduring pop icon, Che Guevara.

Animania

Everywhere you look, businesses seem to require a cutesy mascot.

Although they might look like the bastard offspring of children's TV and a porn channel, the mission of the **Noppon brothers** is far more mundane. The pink creatures are the official mascots of the Tokyo Tower. If you're wondering why the city's most instantly recognisable structure might need mascots, let alone ones resembling cuddly phalluses, it's all thanks to Tokyo's mania for cartoon characters.

The inexplicably grizzly face of national broadcaster NHK is the toothy cuboid known as **Domo-kun**, who, we're told, shares a cave with an elderly rabbit and can't eat apples because of a quirk in his DNA. And NHK isn't the only company getting in on the mascot act. Daikin, one of the nation's leading manufacturers of air conditioners, uses a cheerful water droplet called **Pichon-kun**.

The cartoon face of the NTT Docomo mobile-phone company, meanwhile, is a beady-eyed fungus called **Docomodake**. Even the police are in on the character craze with a little Smurf-like creature called **Pipo-kun** (after the onomatopoeia for a police siren), who reminds citizens how to behave themselves.

And, not to be outdone, the fire department has **Kyuta-kun**, who looks like a wide-eyed young firefighter with an oversized helmet and horns.

The most successful characters, such as Japan Railway's **Suica Penguin** (the cutesy public face of its magnetised travel card), develop fan bases who buy branded merchandise and sport the symbol.

At the other end of the spectrum are the *yuru chara* (loose characters), whose tenuous existence bring more ridicule than affection. These Z-list beasts are often the creations of local towns or minor-league bureaucratic enterprises. Contenders for the *yuru chara* crown include **Earth-kun,** the smiling face of the Tokyo Bureau of Sewage, and the truly bizarre mascot of neighbouring Chiba prefecture's Environmental Regeneration Foundation: a yellow dog named **Chiba-Ken,** whose prefecture-shaped head looks like the result of a horrible environmental tragedy.

So when the marketing minds behind the Tokyo Tower suggested that the 332-metre (1,090-foot) structure needed a pointy-headed pink icon, they were only following the lead of hundreds of other companies and government ventures in giving Tokyoites what they crave: a cute, comforting face to deal with. Nothing this cute could ever let you down.

Shoto Museum of Art

2-14-14 Shoto, Shibuya-ku (3465 9421). Shinsen station (Keio Inokashira line), north exit. **Open** 9am-5pm Tue-Sun. **Admission** ¥300; ¥100 reductions; free children Sat. **No credit cards**.
The Shoto's rough stone exterior gives way to curved walls encircling a central fountain. It's no Guggenheim, but this odd bit of ageing architecture (owned by Shibuya ward) sometimes hosts inspired shows. It's also inexpensive and quiet.

TEPCO Electric Energy Museum

Denryoku-kan

1-12-10 Jinnan, Shibuya-ku (3477 1191, www.denryokukan.com). Shibuya station (Yamanote, Ginza lines), Hachiko exit; (Hanzomon line), exits 6, 7. **Open** 10am-6pm Mon, Tue, Thur-Sun. **Admission** free. **Map** p93.
'Let's make friends with electricity' is the slogan of this energy giant's six-storey homage to the joy of electrons and protons. Adults might tire quickly of the corporate message, but it's a great place to keep the kids busy. Teaching your offspring to play with electricity might not seem the sagest of lessons, but the innovative games and multimedia activities will keep them genuinely entertained.

109. *See p92.*

Tobacco & Salt Museum

1-16-8 Jinnan, Shibuya-ku (3476 2041, www.jti.co.jp/Culture/museum). Shibuya station (Yamanote, Ginza lines), Hachiko exit; (Hanzomon line), exits 6, 7. **Open** 10am-6pm Tue-Sun. **Admission** ¥100; ¥50 reductions. **No credit cards**. **Map** p93.
The rationale for this pairing of themes is that both were once nationalised commodities. Tobacco gets most exposure, with two of the four floors devoted to the history, manufacture and culture of the killer leaf. Besides the gallery of packet designs, collection of pipes and videos of cigarette production, one of the most fascinating aspects of the museum is the number of families that bring their kids to learn about the marvel of smoking. On the third floor, a 1.2-tonne block of Polish salt and a model *Cutty Sark* crafted from crystals are among the sodium-based exhibits. The top floor is often the best, with changing exhibitions that have, in the past, ranged from tequila production to 19th-century prostitutes' wigs. The gift shop sells a range of cigarettes.

Toguri Museum of Art

1-11-3 Shoto, Shibuya-ku (3465 0070, www.toguri-museum.or.jp). Shibuya station (Yamanote, Ginza lines), Hachiko exit; (Hanzomon line), exit 3A or Shinsen station (Keio Inokashira line). **Open** 9.30am-5.30pm Tue-Sun. **Admission** ¥1,000; ¥200-¥500 reductions. **Credit** AmEx, DC, JCB, MC, V.
The art of porcelain is the focus of this quiet museum. Its 11,000 antique Chinese and Japanese pieces rotate through four shows a year. All displays are accompanied by captions in English.

Shinjuku

The neon-lit Tokyo you've seen in the movies.

Tokyo's largest sub-centre is by far its most cosmopolitan area, with fancy department stores, sleazy strip clubs, smoky jazz bars, government offices and gay porn shops all just a few blocks from each other.

The area is divided into two contrasting east and west sections by the JR Yamanote and Chuo train lines. The clean-cut west is home to the city government, corporate skyscrapers and the luxurious **Park Hyatt Tokyo** (*see p135*), while the cacophonous east offers everything from big-brand shopping to neon-lit sex parlours.

Map p101	**Restaurants** p167
Hotels p135	**Bars** p184

Shinjuku is also a major transport hub. In fact, its station is the busiest in the world. Those photos you've seen of commuters being pushed on to crowded trains by uniformed guards in rush hour? Shinjuku station, every morning of the week. And with over 50 exits, miles of tunnels and several different levels, it's also the station you're most likely to get lost in.

NAVIGATING SHINJUKU

Getting there: Shinjuku is served by something approaching a dozen railway lines, including the JR Yamanote, Chuo, Saikyo and Sobu lines, and the Keio line, the Odakyu line and the Seibu Shinjuku line. What's more, it's also on the Marunouchi, Oedo and Shinjuku subway lines. Tochomae (on the Oedo line) is the closest station to the TMG headquarters, while Shinjuku-Sanchome (Fukutoshin, Marunouchi and Shinjuku lines) is convenient for Kabuki-cho and Ni-chome.

INSIDE TRACK
SPORTING SHINJUKU

Not everything in Kabuki-cho is sleazy. The area also has two baseball batting centres, several ten-pin bowling centres, pool halls, snooker tables and some of Tokyo's largest game arcades. Most of the sporting attractions surround the main square, though the batting centres are further north.

EAST AND SOUTH SHINJUKU

Head out of the east exit from the Yamanote line station, and you'll see the main street of **Shinjuku Dori** (*photo p103*). Facing you will be the large video screen of **Studio Alta** – a multi-storey shopping centre specialising in young girls' fashion, but more popular as Shinjuku's meeting spot. The east side is where the action is. It's home to most of the shopping, as well as Japan's largest red-light area, Kabuki-cho, the gay district of Ni-chome (two-chome) and the vibrant bars of San-chome (three-chome).

Kabuki-cho lies north of Yasukuni Dori and contains hundreds of restaurants, bars, sex clubs, *pachinko* parlours and love hotels – if you're male, you won't get five yards before a tout tries to lure you into their strip-club or brothel. It's almost certainly the safest red-light district in the world, but it's still smart to keep your wits about you. Adjoining it is **Golden Gai**, a collection of minuscule, timeworn watering holes. Not all welcome foreigners; *see p185* **Golden Gai** for those that do.

Occupying a substantial plot between Golden Gai and Meiji Dori is the large **Hanazono Shrine**. Erected in the 16th century, the shrine has been rebuilt many times but still retains the

Manga Mania

The Japanese are drawn to comic books.

The Japanese love their comics. Known as manga (a term coined by Hokusai in 1814 and meaning 'crazy drawings'), they account for almost 40 per cent of everything published in Japan. You can find manga magazines as thick as phone directories, and epic stories that take numerous volumes to complete. The 400-page *Shonen Jump* magazine, costing a mere ¥250, shifts three million copies a week. Manga cover every subject under the sun, from child-rearing to porn.

While manga have clearly been influenced by Western comics and animation, they also draw on Japan's long tradition of visual entertainments, such as *ukiyo-e* ('floating world' prints) and erotic *shunga* prints.

The man principally responsible for starting this all-consuming love affair is Tezuka Osamu (1928-89), creator of *Tetsuwan Atomu* (aka Astro Boy) and founder of the post-war manga and *anime* (animated cartoons) industries. Since World War II, manga have evolved into Japan's unique popular literary form with their own iconic vocabulary; manga magazines are the sources of many of the country's most successful films and TV series, both animated and live-action. Much of this success stems from the dizzying diversity of their stories, styles and subjects, and their appeal to both sexes and every age group and taste.

Traditionally, the biggest sellers have been the *shonen* titles for boys and the more adult *seinen* ranges for men, but there are some 40 *shojo* magazines for girls and, more recently, over 50 *redikomi* aimed at women. Written and drawn mainly by women, these cover everything from 'office lady' lifestyles, pregancy advice and sex therapy to raunchy erotica and the gloriously titled 'Truly Horrifying Mother-in-Law and Daughter-in-Law Comics', which tackle the trials of newlywed wives.

That's not counting niche titles covering such subjects as golf, *pachinko*, military history or the unique genre of *shonen ai* – stories about gay boys that are hugely popular with teenage girls. And don't forget *dojinshi* (self-published fanzines); Tokyo's twice-yearly Comiket fairs for *dojinshi* attract nearly half a million visitors.

Most manga are printed in black or one-colour ink on white or tinted newsprint, with perhaps a small full-colour section. They are read from what Westerners consider the 'back', and from right to left across the page. Most casual readers discard the magazines or leave them for others on trains or in cafés. What the Japanese prefer to buy and put on their shelves are the compact, usually paperback books that compile several episodes of a story in one volume.

Manga are widely available in most of Tokyo's bookshops, and department stores often dedicate large areas, sometimes entire floors, to them. Devoted readers may prefer specialist or second-hand outlets such as **Tora no Ana** (*see p201*) and **Mandarake** (*see p212*), while whole boutiques are dedicated to specific creators like Tezuka or characters like Doraemon. Myriad spin-off products range from figurines to clothes emblazoned with manga heroes and heroines.

There are also numerous 24-hour manga cafés in Tokyo, where you can read from a vast quantity of manga books, both old and new, for a modest charge.

You will struggle to find English-language editions in Japan, but they are increasingly available in the West – manga has been the fastest-growing book category in the US for a number of years.

● *Paul Gravett wrote* Manga: Sixty Years of Japanese Comics *(Laurence King, 2004).*

SIGHTS

Tokyo Metropolitan Government Building No.1. See p104.

It may surprise some that for all Shinjuku's consumerist dazzle, the area is also steeped in counter-culture. **Ni-chome** is the most active and open gay and lesbian district in the country, with queer literature, ads and goods openly displayed (something unusual for Japan) on airy side streets (*see p243*). The little alleyways between Kabuki-cho and Golden Gai are home to avant-garde performance houses, as well as tiny bars frequented by young intellectuals. Indeed, Shinjuku was the explosive epicentre of Japan's active and demonstrative youth movement in the 1960s (something that can be viewed in director Nagisa Oshima's 1968 classic *Diary of a Shinjuku Thief*). This feeling has never left some of the smaller byways of the east side.

Further east and south of Shinjuku Dori is the vast green lung of **Shinjuku Gyoen**, one of Tokyo's largest parks. It's a spectacular sight at *hanami* (cherry-blossom viewing), when its 1,500 trees paint the whole place pink. And to the north of Kabuki-cho, centred on Shin-Okubo station, is Tokyo's 'Koreatown', catering to the city's enduring interest in Korean culture – especially the edible kind.

WEST SHINJUKU

The west side offers a clutch of skyscrapers, a plethora of banking, insurance and other company headquarters, and some smart hotels. Among the corporate high-rises are the **Sompo Japan Museum**, worth a look for some of its famous (and famously expensive) paintings, and the **Toto** showroom, where you can view the latest in Japan's celebrated toilet technology.

The area's tallest building is the Tokyo government's headquarters, known as Tocho and designed by Kenzo Tange. Completed in 1991, the twin-towered centrepiece of

SIGHTS

gripping presence of a historical monument that is very active. With striking orange pillars, railings and *torii* (gates), it holds numerous lively festivals, notably a three-day event at the end of May and a pre-New Year's fest in November.

Shinjuku is also a major shopping district. It has more department stores than any other district, with every major company represented. The grandaddy of them all, and the expat's favourite for its larger-than-usual clothes, is **Isetan** (*see p193*). It's also a good place to pick up electronic goods if you don't fancy the trek to Akihabara. Shinjuku was already shifting close to ¥200 billion in electronics per year when the ten-storey **LABI** (*see p203*) opened in 2010 and prompted speculation of an impending price war.

45 Sightseeing
1 Bunka Gakuen Costume Museum (*see p103*). A2.
2 Shinjuku Gyoen (*see p104*). F4.
3 Sompo Japan Museum (*see p104*). B1.
4 Tokyo Metropolitan Government Building No.1 (*see p104*). A3.
5 Toto Super Space (*see p104*). B2.

55 Hotels, see p135
1 Hilton Tokyo. A1.
2 Keio Plaza Hotel. B2.
3 Park Hyatt Tokyo. A4.
4 Shinjuku Kuyakusyo-Mae Capsule Hotel (*see p140*). E1.
5 Shinjuku Washington Hotel. A4.
6 Star Hotel Tokyo. C1.

① Restaurants, see p167
1 China Grill – Xenlon. C4.
2 New York Grill. A4.
3 Tsunahachi. D2.

㉒ Bars, see p184
1 African Bar Esogie. E2.
2 Albatross. C1.
3 Albatross G. E1.
4 Dubliners. D2.
5 La Jetée. E1.
6 Shot Bar Shadow. E1.
7 Zoetrope. C1.

㉒ Coffee Shops, see p190
1 Bon. C1.
2 Tajimaya. C1.

㉒ Shops & Services, see p192
1 Disk Union. E2.
2 Don Quixote. D1.
3 Dub Store. C1.
4 Isetan. E2.

5 Keio. C2.
6 Kinokuniya Bookstore. D2.
7 LABI. C1.
8 Lumine Est. D2.
9 No.1 Travel. D1.
10 Odakyu. C2.
11 Yamaya. A4.

㉒ Film, see p232
1 Shinjuku Wald 9. E2.

◢ Gay & Lesbian, see p243
1 24 Kaikan Shinjuku. F2.
2 Advocates Bar. F2.
3 Advocates Café. F2.
4 Arty Farty. F2.
5 Business Hotel S. F2.
6 Dragon. F2.
7 Fuji. F2.
8 GB. F2.
9 Go Round. F2.
10 Hijouguchi. F2.
11 Hug. F2.
12 King of College. F2.

13 Kinsmen. F2.
14 Kinswomyn. F2.
15 Kusuo. F2.
16 Monsoon. F2.
17 Motel #203. F3.
18 Papi Chulos. F2.
19 Tac's Knot. E2.

㉒ Music, see p250
1 Antiknock. E3.
2 Shinjuku Loft Plus One. D1.
3 Shinjuku Pit Inn. F2.

㉒ Nightlife, see p268
1 Garam. D1.
2 Open. F3.
3 Rags Room Acid. F3.

㉒ Performing Arts, see p269
1 Suehiro-tei. E2.

㉒ Sport & Fitness, see p276
1 Tipness. C1.

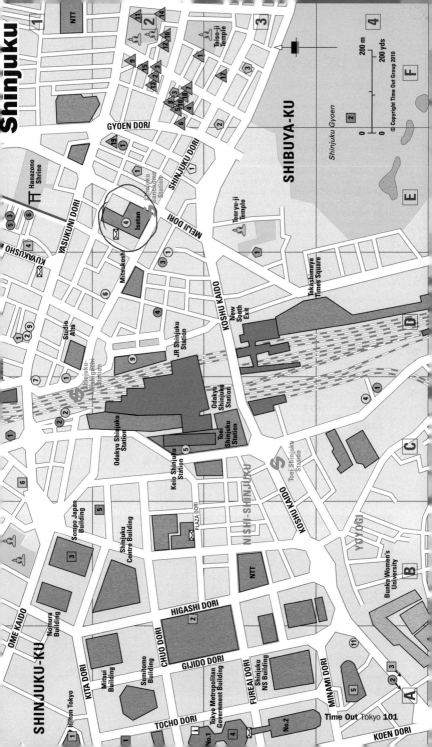

Shinjuku

NTT

2

Taiso-ji Temple

3

4

F

© Copyright Time Out Group 2010

200 m
200 yds

SHIBUYA-KU

Shinjuku Gyoen

E

GYOEN DORI

SHINJUKU DORI

Hanazono Shrine

YASUKUNI DORI

KUYAKUSHO

Shinjuku Sanchome Station

Isetan

MEIJI DORI

Mitsukoshi

Tenryu-ji Temple

KOSHU KAIDO

New South Exit

Studio Alta

Takashimaya Times Square

D

Shinjuku Nishiguchi Station

JR Shinjuku Station

Odakyu Shinjuku Station

Shinjuku Station

Odakyu Shinjuku Building

Toei Shinjuku Station

Keio Shinjuku Station

Toei Shinjuku Station

PLAZA DORI

NISHI-SHINJUKU

KOSHU KAIDO

YOYOGI

C

Sompo Japan Building

Shinjuku Centre Building

NTT

Bunka Women's University

B

SHINJUKU-KU

OME KAIDO

Nomura Building

HIGASHI DORI

Hilton Tokyo

KITA DORI

Mitsui Building

Sumitomo Building

CHUO DORI

GIJIDO DORI

Tokyo Metropolitan Government Building

FUREAI DORI

Shinjuku NS Building

MINAMI DORI

No.1

TOCHO DORI

No.2

KOEN DORI

A

Hey, Big Spender?

Platinum-card options – and the thrifty alternatives.

When Suntory launched its Yamazaki 50 Years Old whisky, the entire run sold out in hours despite being priced at ¥1million per bottle. This is a city of luxury tastes, but it also has plenty of options for the frugal visitor. While **Bespoke Tokyo** (www.bespoketokyo.jp) offers top-end tours for ¥200,000 a day, the **Tokyo Metropolitan Government** offers volunteer-guided tours (up to ¥3,540 per person, depending on numbers) of the major tourist areas (www.tourism.metro.tokyo.jp). Here are some other ways to splash out or save:

EAT

The ¥10,000 ramen You need to book at least three days in advance for a bowl of 'Imperial ramen', the only dish on the menu at Fujimaki Gekijo (3-36-28 Kami-Meguro, Meguro-ku, 3792 7743, www.fujimaki gekijou.jp). With shanks of beef and pork, crabs, clams, shrimp, ham and chicken in a spicy, Chinese soup, it's the world's priciest ramen.

The ¥290 ramen The Kourakuen ramen chain has branches throughout the city, all of which offer bowls of *chukka soba* ramen, with slices of pork, bamboo, spring onions and nori in a soy-based broth for just ¥290.

DRINK

The ¥1.8 million cocktail It's a glass of Grey Goose vodka with a twist of lime and a one-carat Bulgari diamond at the bottom. What girl doesn't dream of gems that reek of vodka? For one of the the Ritz-Carlton's (*see p132*) more sensible extravagances, try the Cigar Martini, a blend of Louis XIII cognac and 40 Years Old Taylor's port for just ¥38,000.

The ¥50 beer At Botan (1-24-7 Higashi-Gotanda, Shinagawa-ku 5739 0333), a grubby *izakaya* in the Gotanda district, beers cost just ¥50 a glass, meaning it's cheaper to drink here than at home. You're obliged to buy food too, but that won't test your budget either.

STAY

The ¥2,000,000 hotel room It's the Ritz-Carlton (*see p132*) again. The city's highest hotel also boasts its loftiest prices. A 24-hour stay in the 300-square-metre (3,229-square-foot) Ritz Carlton Suite on the 53rd floor will set you back ¥1,388 a minute.

The ¥1,500 bed for the night Bangkok this isn't, but that doesn't mean you can't find cheap digs. A bunk in a 12-person shared dorm at the Khaosan Tokyo Asakusa Annex (www.khaosan-tokyo.com, 3842 8286) near the Sumida river is cheap enough to make the stingiest backpacker smile.

LOOK

The ¥90,000 city view Charter a helicopter from Excel Air (www.excel-air.com) and fly up to five people over Tokyo by day or night. As the chopper tilts from side to side, you can look straight down on the chaos below. The tours leave from Urayasu Heliport near Maihama station on the JR Keiyo line.

The free city view The observatories on the 45th floors of the Tokyo Metropolitan Government Building No.1 (*see p104*) offer near-panoramic views of the city and don't cost a yen.

Ritz-Carlton Tokyo.

SIGHTS

Shinjuku Dori. *See p98.*

this impressive complex is the **Tokyo Metropolitan Government Building No.1**: a must-visit, both architecturally and for the great – and free – views from its two observation decks. Directly behind the TMG site is **Shinjuku Chuo Park**, better known for its homeless community than its scenery.

In stark contrast to the gleaming high-rises is **Omoide Yokocho**, just outside the station's north-west exit. This narrow alleyway lined with ramshackle eateries, each with seating for no more than a handful of customers, is the last remnant of a vanished world. It dates from the post-war years, when Shinjuku was the site of a thriving black market; whatever you needed, you could find here. Omoide Yokocho occupies prime real estate and may not defy the developers for much longer.

South of the main road of Koshu Kaido is women's fashion college Bunka Gakuen, which founded the small **Bunka Gakuen Costume Museum** on its 60th anniversary in 1979. Further west lies the **Tokyo Opera City** complex, containing halls for classical music (*see p251*), one of the city's best-funded private contemporary art galleries (*see p241*) and the **NTT Inter Communication Centre**, a museum of media arts. Adjacent is the **New National Theatre, Tokyo** (*see p250*).

ELSEWHERE

Shinjuku is also a good jumping-off point for other neighbourhoods. To the south, **Yoyogi** is a large area that abuts Yoyogi Park and the **Meiji Shrine** complex (*see p67*) and contains the **Sword Museum**.

Heading east, back towards Chiyoda-ku, is **Yotsuya**, home to one of Tokyo's more surprising buildings. The **Akasaka Detached Palace** (aka Geihinkan, 2-1-1 Moto-Akasaka, Minato-ku) is a hybrid of Versailles and Buckingham Palace. Its construction, in the early 20th century, was intended to prove that Japan could do anything the West could. Emperor Hirohito lived here when he was crown prince, but sadly it's only open to the public for ten days and 20,000 visitors each summer, with places allocated by lottery (apply, in Japanese only, via www8.cao.go.jp/geihinkan). Nearby is the Tokyo Fire Department-owned **Fire Museum**, which offers an insight into the key role fire has played in the development of the city.

Bunka Gakuen Costume Museum

3-22-7 Yoyogi, Shibuya-ku (3299 2387, www. bunka.ac.jp/museum/hakubutsu.htm). Shinjuku station (Yamanote, Chuo, Sobu lines), south exit; (Oedo, Shinjuku lines), exit 6. **Open** 10am-4.30pm Mon-Sat. **Admission** ¥500; ¥200-¥300 reductions. **No credit cards. Map** p101.
The small collection includes examples of historical Japanese clothing, such as an Edo-era fire-fighting coat and a brightly coloured, 12-layer *karaginumo* outfit. Kamakura-period scrolls illustrate the types of dress worn by different classes of people. The displays change four or five times a year.

FREE Fire Museum

3-10 Yotsuya, Shinjuku-ku (3353 9119, www. tfd.metro.tokyo.jp/ts/museum.htm). Yotsuya-Sanchome station (Marunouchi line), exit 2. **Open** 9.30am-5pm Tue-Sun. **Admission** free.

This museum traces the cultural history of fire-fighting, with exhibits ranging from decorative uniforms to vintage ladder trucks to the elaborate pom-poms used to identify neighbourhood brigades. Between 1603 and 1868, 97 major conflagrations swept through Tokyo. Scale models, sound and lights recreate an Edo-period blaze in miniature. Video monitors show footage of the fires that destroyed the city after the 1923 Great Kanto Earthquake and World War II fire bombing. Elsewhere, cartoon stories (in Japanese) teach children what to do in case fire breaks out at home. Kids also love climbing onto the rooftop helicopter.

FREE NTT Inter Communication Centre

Tokyo Opera City Tower 4F, 3-20-2 Nishi-Shinjuku, Shinjuku-ku (0120 144 199, www.ntticc.or.jp). Hatsudai station (Keio New line), east exit. **Open** 11am-6pm Tue-Sun. Closed 2nd Sun Feb, 1st Sun Aug. **Admission** free; additional charge for special exhibitions. **Credit** (shop) AmEx, DC, JCB, MC, V.

Opened by telecoms giant NTT in 1996, this museum is at the leading edge of media design and arts. The permanent collection includes a timeline of art videos and interactive installations.

Shinjuku Gyoen

11 Naito-cho, Shinjuku-ku (3350 0151, www.shinjukugyoen.go.jp). Shinjuku-Gyoenmae station (Marunouchi line), exit 1. **Open** *Park* 9am-4.30pm Tue-Sun; daily during cherry blossom (early Apr) and chrysanthemum (early Nov) seasons. *Greenhouse* 11am-3pm Tue-Sun. **Admission** ¥200; ¥50 reductions. **No credit cards. Map** p101.

Shinjuku Gyoen opened as an imperial garden in 1906, during Japan's push for Westernisation, and was the first place in the country where many non-indigenous species were planted. The fascination with the West is evident in the garden's layout: there are both English- and French-style sections, as well as a traditional Japanese garden.

▶ *The park is one of the most popular places for cherry-blossom viewing, see p220.*

Sompo Japan Museum

Sompo Japan Bldg 42F, 1-26-1 Nishi-Shinjuku, Shinjuku-ku (3349 3081, www.sompo-japan.co.jp/museum). Shinjuku station (Yamanote, Chuo, Sobu lines), west exit; (Marunouchi line), exits A16, A17; (Shinjuku line), exit 3 or Shinjuku-Nishiguchi station (Oedo line), exit D1. **Open** 10am-6pm Tue-Sun. **Admission** ¥500; ¥300 reductions; free under-15s; additional charge for special exhibitions. **No credit cards. Map** p101.

The views from this 42nd-floor museum are spectacular. Perhaps to compete, the owner, insurance company Yasuda (as the firm was previously called), purchased Van Gogh's 1889 *Sunflowers* in 1987 for the then record-breaking price of over ¥5 billion

(£24 million). There is now some concern that it may not be authentic, but no one is certain. This symbol of Japan's Bubble years hangs alongside Cézanne's *Pommes et Serviette* (bought in 1990). The museum's core work is by Japanese artists, specifically Seiji Togo (1897-1978), who donated 200 of his own pieces and 250 items from his art collection.

Sword Museum

4-25-10 Yoyogi, Shibuya-ku (3379 1386). Sangubashi station (Odakyu line). **Open** 10am-4.30pm Tue-Sun. **Admission** ¥525; free reductions. **No credit cards.**

The confiscation of swords as offensive weapons during the American occupation after World War II threatened the traditional Japanese craft of sword-making. To safeguard it, the Society for the Preservation of Japanese Art Swords was established in 1948. Twenty years later, it opened this museum to display its collection of centuries-old swords and fittings. Even non-enthusiasts may find themselves mesmerised.

FREE Tokyo Metropolitan Government Building No.1

2-8-1 Nishi-Shinjuku, Shinjuku-ku (5321 1111, 5320 7890 Observatory, www.yokoso.metro.tokyo.jp). Tochomae station (Oedo line), exit 4. **Open** *North Observatory* 9.30am-11pm Tue-Sun. *South Observatory* 9.30am-5pm Mon, Wed-Sun. **Admission** free. **Map** p101.

Two of the best views over Tokyo have the added bonus of being free. Each of the TMG twin towers (243m/797ft tall) has an observation deck on the 45th floor, affording a 360° panorama interrupted only by the other tower – on a clear day you can see Mount Fuji. Admire the cityscape while sipping a coffee from the cafeteria in the centre of the vast floor. The south observatory is the best choice by day; after dark, the view from the north deck is preferable. The easiest way to get to the TMG complex from Shinjuku station is by underground tunnel; it's well signposted. Other buildings in west Shinjuku with free viewing areas include the Shinjuku Centre Building (53F) and the Nomura Building (49F).

▶ *For other city views, try the Mori Tower's City View (see p88), the Tokyo Tower (see p90) or, from 2011, the Tokyo Sky Tree (see p38).*

FREE Toto Tokyo Center Showroom

L-Tower Bldg 26F-27F, 1-6-1 Nishi-Shinjuku (3345 1010). Shinjuku station (Yamanote, Chuo, Sobu lines), west exit; (Marunouchi line), exits A16, A17; (Shinjuku line), exit 3 or Shinjuku-Nishiguchi station (Oedo line), exit D1. **Open** 10am-5pm daily. Closed 1st & 3rd Wed of mth. **Admission** free. **Map** p101.

There aren't many corporate showrooms that suit sightseeing, but this one, from toilet maker Toto, is worth a look. The company shows off its latest innovations in waste disposal and nether-region hygiene.

Ueno

It's not the Tokyo of your fantasy, but Ueno has plenty of charm.

With a bustling street market, the city's largest park, historic shrines and some major art museums, how does Ueno not feature on every tourist itinerary? Probably because it's distinctly 'old Tokyo', slow to change and doesn't fit the template of Tokyo as neon-wrapped, breakneck-pace supercity. Which, of course, is why you should visit. It's a glimpse of the city's past, earthier than the skyscraper sectors, resistant to fleeting trends and oozing old-fashioned atmosphere. But it's also walking distance from high-tech Akihabara.

| **Map** p107 | **Restaurants** p169 |
| **Hotels** p137 | |

Map p107 Restaurants p169 Hotels p137

NAVIGATING UENO

Getting there: Ueno is on the Yamanote line, and Ginza and Hibiya subway lines; if you're heading for the park, arriving via the Yamanote line is the best option. At the northern end of the park is Uguisudani station, which is also on the Yamanote line; and at the southern end, Keisei-Ueno station, on the Kesei line. Yushima and Nezu stations, on the Chiyoda line, are not far away.

Long before feng shui gained a foothold in the West, China's ancient rules of geomancy were being strictly applied in feudal Japan. And it is thanks to feng shui that Ueno, one of Tokyo's main sub-centres, came into being. Around the start of the 17th century, shogun Ieyasu Tokugawa began assiduously building a new administrative capital out of the fishing village

in a swamp that came to be known as Tokyo. His successor, Hidetada, was advised that he ought to build a great temple north-east of Edo Castle to guard against the evil spirits that were apt to enter from that inauspicious direction. So, in 1625, he duly installed a massive complex of 36 temples in Ueno.

Only a hint of his complex remains today, but the land that the temples occupied is home to the feature for which Ueno is now best known – its park. **Ueno Koen** (Ueno Park) was Tokyo's first public park when it opened in 1873, but just five years earlier it had been the site of the bloody Battle of Ueno between supporters of the new Meiji government and warriors still loyal to the Tokugawa shogun. The government won, but in the process **Kanei-ji**, the centre of the temple complex where six of Japan's 15 shoguns are buried, was destroyed. Today, the site holds a temple and three cemeteries.

The park contains a slew of attractions – from museums to shrines and temples to a zoo. It lacks lawns and picnic areas, but is famed for its collection of cherry trees. Enormous throngs of Tokyoites gather here every spring in blossom season, though these raucous affairs tend to focus more on portable karaoke machines than flowers. The groundsheets that the partygoers sometimes leave behind get reused for shelters by the homeless people who live in the park.

If you arrive at the JR station, head to the main (above-ground) hall, one of the few station

INSIDE TRACK
BIRTHPLACE OF JUDO

Martial arts fans should take the Ginza line one stop north of Ueno to Inaricho station. Take a left out of exit 3, and you will find the blink-and-you'll-miss-it temple of **Eishoji** (the second building on the left). It was here, in 1882, that Jigoro Kano first began teaching a technique he named 'judo'.

buildings in Tokyo to have largely survived Japan's decades of redevelopment. The high ceilings and grandiose architectural style recall a time when this was one of the city's main transport hubs, ferrying people in from the north before the *shinkansen* dragged most passengers away to the main terminus at Tokyo station. That was when the east side of Tokyo was king, and Asakusa and Ueno were the city's playgrounds, before the action started to drift westwards, to Shibuya and Shinjuku. The first subway line in the whole of Asia opened in 1927 to link Asakusa to Ueno, and is now part of the Ginza line.

There's more to Ueno than its park, though. Near the station is the area's other great attraction: a lively, exciting street market that offers a real flavour of the Tokyo of yesteryear. To the north of Ueno, across Kototoi Dori, is Yanaka (*see p111*), another of Tokyo's *shitamachi* ('low city') districts; it's a short walk from the northern end of Ueno Park into Yanaka Cemetery and its environs.

INSIDE UENO PARK

Take the park exit from the station, cross the road and pick up an English map from the information booth. Ueno Koen is home to some of Japan's greatest cultural assets and Tokyo's best collection of museums, so you'll need one. The first you'll come to is the Le Corbusier-designed **National Museum of Western Art**. Next door is the **National Science Museum** (*see p230*) and, north of that, the **Tokyo National Museum**, the grandest museum in the park. The **University Art Museum** and **Ueno Royal Museum** are both within easy striking distance, as is the **Tokyo**

Metropolitan Art Museum, though the last is going to be closed until 2012.

The park also contains **Ueno Zoo** (*see p229*), the most famous in the country, with a diverse selection of critters, from Asian lions to wolf-like *dholes* and bison, alongside more familiar animals. The zoo occupies the western section of the park. Near to its main entrance, just around from the kiddies' amusement park, is the approach to **Toshogu Shrine**, the finest of the park's historical monuments.

The most attractive part of Ueno Park is the southern area around **Shinobazu Pond** (Shinobazunoike). Given its present inland position, it may be difficult to imagine that this large pond was once part of an inlet of Tokyo Bay. Causeways divide the pond, which is now freshwater, into three: one section is part of Ueno Zoo and has a large colony of cormorants, one is a boating pond, and the third is home to a great diversity of waterfowl and comes alive with pink lotus flowers in summer. At the centre of the three causeways is an island on which sits **Bentendo**, a strong contender for the title of most charming temple in Tokyo. It is dedicated to Benten (also called Benzaiten), the goddess of music and feminine beauty, and the only female among the Seven Deities of Good Fortune (these auspicious figures are especially evident at New Year). You can nourish more earthy parts at the food stalls that line the approach to the temple.

From Bentendo, cross over Dobutsuen Dori (the main path that bisects the park) to reach the red **Kiyomizu Kannondo** temple. It is dedicated to Kannon and modelled on the famous Kiyomizu-dera temple in Kyoto. This was completed in 1631, and is one of the few

Ameyoko Market. *See p108.*

45 Sightseeing
1 Daimyo Clock Museum (*see p113*). A3.
2 Kyu Iwasaki-teiHouse & Gardens (*see p109*). B5.
3 National Museum of Western Art (*see p109*). C4.
4 Shitamachi Museum (*see p109*). C5.
5 Tokyo National Museum (*see p110*). C3.
6 Toshogu Shrine (*see p110*). B4.
7 Ueno Royal Museum (*see p110*). C4.
8 University Art Museum (*see p110*). B3.
9 Yokoyama Taikan Memorial Hall (*see p110*). B5.

55 Hotels, see p137
1 Hotel Edoya. B6.
2 Ryokan Katsutaro. B3.
3 Ryokan Sawanoya. A3.
4 Ueno First City Hotel. B6.
5 Ueno Tsukuba Hotel. D5.

1 Restaurants, see p169
1 Hantei. A4.
2 Ikenohata Yabu Soba. B5.
3 Nezu Club. A3.
4 Sasanoyuki. D2.

2 Shops & Services, see p192
1 Ameyoko Market. C5.

22 Children, see p227
1 National Science Museum. C4.
2 Ueno Zoo. B4.

22 Galleries, see p241
1 Gallery Jin. A3.
2 SCAI The Bathhouse. B3.

3 Gay & Lesbian, see p243
1 24 Kaikan Ueno. D4.

22 Music, see p250
1 Tokyo Bunka Kaikan. C4.

Ueno & Yanaka

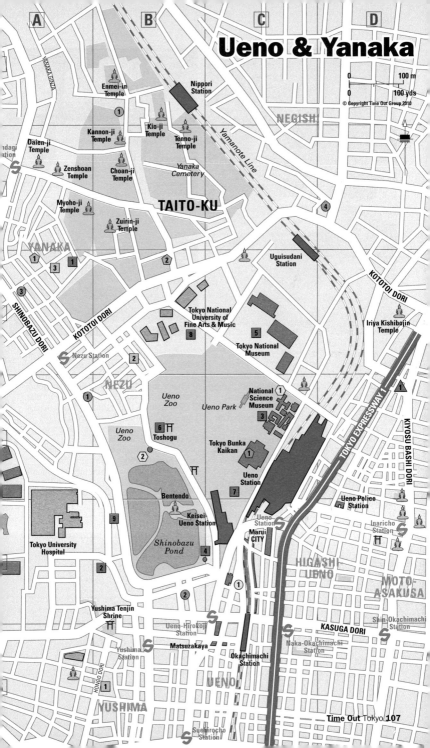

A **B** **C** **D**

0   100 m
0   100 yds
© Copyright Time Out Group 2010

NEGISHI

Enmei-in Temple

Nippori Station

Yamanote Line

Kannon-ji Temple

Kio-ji Temple

Tenno-ji Temple

Daien-ji Temple

Zenshoan Temple

Choan-ji Temple

Yanaka Cemetery

TAITO-KU

Myoho-ji Temple

Zuirin-ji Temple

YANAKA

SHINOBAZU DORI

KOTOTOI DORI

Uguisudani Station

KOTOTOI DORI

Iriya Kishibojin Temple

Tokyo National University of Fine Arts & Music

Tokyo National Museum

Nezu Station

NEZU

Ueno Zoo

Ueno Park

National Science Museum

TOKYO EXPRESSWAY 1

KIYOSU BASHI DORI

Ueno Zoo

Toshogu

Tokyo Bunka Kaikan

Ueno Station

Ueno Police Station

Inaricho Station

Bentendo

Keisei-Ueno Station

Ueno Station

Shinobazu Pond

Tokyo University Hospital

Marui CITY

HIGASHI UENO

MOTO-ASAKUSA

Yushima Tenjin Shrine

Ueno-Hirokoji Station

Matsuzakaya

Okachimachi Station

KASUGA DORI

Naka-Okachimachi Station

Shin-Okachimachi Station

Yushima Station

HONGO DORI

UENO

YUSHIMA

Suehirocho Station

Shitamachi Museum.

temple buildings to have survived the destruction of the Battle of Ueno.

Nearby, in the south-east corner of this side of the park, stands the statue of **Takamori Saigo**, a fascinating figure and the person on whom Katsumoto, the warrior played by Ken Watanabe in *The Last Samurai*, is based. Saigo played an instrumental role in the Meiji restoration of 1868, which ended the reign of the shoguns and brought into power a new imperial government. Later, Saigo became disenchanted with the government he had done so much to create, and got mixed up with an ill-fated rebellion, which ended with Saigo and his supporters committing *hara-kiri*. It is this rebellion that formed the basis for the Tom Cruise film. Of course, Hollywood presents Katsumoto as a virile warrior, whereas by the time of his rebellion, Saigo was so obese he had to be carried around in a chair. His statue in Ueno Park (unveiled in 1898) depicts him in a deliberately unmilitary mode, in a kimono taking his dog for a walk.

Further south, at the corner of the pond next to the main road, stands the **Shitamachi Museum**. *Shitamachi* refers to the low-lying areas of Tokyo inhabited by the hoi polloi, and this small gem of a place recreates the city as it was in the 19th and early 20th centuries.

OUTSIDE THE PARK

History of a very different kind is to be found in the area around **Ameyoko** (*see p199*), which begins close by Ueno station on the other side of

the main road from the park. The name nicely hints at the place's history: the 'Ame' in Ameyoko originally referred to 'sweets', and the name meant 'confectioner's alley'. But during the occupation following World War II this became a major area for black-market goods, many of which came from the US military. Thus the 'Ame-rican' aspect to the name took on significance.

Ameyoko is home to Tokyo's liveliest market (*photo p106*), with more than 500 stalls somehow shoehorned into a 400-metre (quarter-mile) stretch that leads south to Okachimachi station. The weekend crowds can be so thick that progress is at a snail's pace (if you go, watch out for your valuables: this is inevitably a popular spot for pickpockets). As well as myriad fishmongers, and fruit and vegetable stalls, there are scores of small shops selling cheap jeans, T-shirts and goods 'inspired' by international designers. It is also a reliable source of hard-to-find foods and spices. Families from south and south-east Asia stock up on chillies, basmati rice and coriander, while homesick Americans seek solace in Milky Way bars or Hershey's chocolate imported from their homeland.

At a fork in the road that lies roughly 100 metres (300 feet) into the market is a somewhat dubious-looking building that contains an amazing basement food hall selling whole frogs, durian fruit and other difficult-to-get delicacies from around the world.

Meanwhile, under the railway tracks, cheap watches and electronic goods are the order of the day, along with lots of bootleg CDs.

A couple of additional attractions are located across the western side of the park. Beyond the pond's boating area, on the other side of the main road, is **Yokoyama Taikan Memorial Hall**, which is dedicated to the life and work of one of Japan's greatest painters of the modern era. Following the road above the hall in a southerly direction will bring you to **Kyu Iwasaki-tei House & Gardens**, which was built by influential British architect Josiah Conder, one of many Westerners to bring Western learning to Japan in the 19th century.

Kyu Iwasaki-tei House & Gardens

1-3-45 Ikenohata, Taito-ku (3823 8033, www. tokyo-park.or.jp/english/park/detail_06.html). Yushima station (Chiyoda line), exit 1. **Open** 9am-4.30pm daily. **Admission** ¥400; ¥200 reductions. **No credit cards. Map** p107.
Built in 1896 for Hisaya Iwasaki, who was the son of the founder of the Mitsubishi industrial conglomerate, this compound reveals the fin-de-siècle sheen beneath Ueno's grimy surface. Josiah Conder designed the recently renovated main residence – a two-storey wooden structure with Jacobean and Pennsylvanian country- house elements (and the first Western-style toilet in Japan) – and the adjacent billiards room in the form of a log cabin. In the large tatami rooms, visitors can sip green tea and admire *fusuma* (sliding doors) painted with seasonal motifs by Gaho Hashimoto.

National Museum of Western Art
Kokuritsu Seiyo Bijutsukan
7-7 Ueno Koen, Taito-ku (3828 5131, www. nmwa.go.jp). Ueno station (Yamanote line), park exit; (Ginza, Hibiya lines), Shinobazu exit. **Open** 9.30am-5pm (until 5.30pm mid Mar-early Dec) Tue-Thur, Sat, Sun; 9.30am-8pm Fri. **Admission** ¥420; free-¥210 reductions; additional charge for special exhibitions. Free 2nd & 4th Sat of mth. **No credit cards. Map** p107.
The core collection housed in this 1959 Le Corbusier-designed building, Japan's only national museum devoted to Western art, was assembled by Kawasaki shipping magnate Kojiro Matsukata in the early 1900s. Considering that the collection was begun so recently, it is surprisingly good, ranging from 15th-century icons to Monet to Pollock.

Shitamachi Museum
Shitamachi Fuzoku Shiryokan
2-1 Ueno Koen, Taito-ku (3823 7451, www. taitocity.net/taito/shitamachi). Ueno station (Yamanote, Ginza, Hibiya lines), Shinobazu exit. **Open** 9.30am-4.30pm Tue-Sun. **Admission** ¥300; ¥100 reductions. **No credit cards. Map** p107.

INSIDE TRACK
PRESERVING LE CORBUSIER

The Japanese government was taken by surprise when the French announced plans to recommend a building by Le Corbusier for UNESCO World Heritage status. Why? Because the building was in Tokyo. The boxy **National Museum of Western Art** (*see left*) was one of 22 buildings nominated as part of 'Le Corbusier's architectural and urban work.' After much talk of how 'unusual' a third-party nomination would be, the government got behind the bid, fast-tracking its classification as an Important Cultural Property and giving it a major facelift. Alas, UNESCO denied the application – at least for the time being.

Toshogu Shrine. *See p110.*

INSIDE TRACK STOCK TRADER

If you want to try your hand at Japanese cooking, you'll need some *katsuobushi*, the bonito stock that forms the base of so much of the country's cuisine. One of the best places to buy it is **Iseoto**, in Ameyoko (6-4-10 Ueno, Taito-ku, 0120 10 8888, www.iseoto. com). Its *hongare katsuo honbushi* is made from only local, line-caught, early-season bonito from Japanese waters.

This museum presents the living environment of ordinary Tokyoites between the pivotal Meiji restoration of 1868 and the Great Earthquake of 1923. Take off your shoes and step into re-creations of a merchant's shop, a coppersmith's workshop and a sweet shop. Everything has a hands-on intimacy: open up a drawer and you'll find a sewing kit or a children's colouring book. Upstairs are traditional toys that even today's children still delight in.
▶ *This is a small counterpart to the large-scale Edo-Tokyo Museum (see p50) in Ryogoku.*

★ Tokyo National Museum
Tokyo Kokuritsu Hakubutsukan
13-9 Ueno Koen, Taito-ku (3822 1111, www.tnm.go.jp). Ueno station (Yamanote line), park exit; (Ginza, Hibya lines), Shinobazu exit. **Open** 9.30am-5pm Tue-Sun. **Admission** ¥600; free-¥400 reductions; additional charge for special exhibitions. **Credit** (gift shop only) DC, JCB, MC, V. **Map** p107.
If you have just one day to devote to museum-going in Tokyo and are interested in Japanese art and artefacts, this is the place to visit. Japan's oldest and largest museum houses nearly 90,000 items. Past the ornate gateway, there's a wide courtyard and fountain surrounded by three main buildings. Directly in front is the Honkan, or main gallery, dating from 1937, which displays the permanent collection of Japanese arts and antiquities. The 25 rooms regularly rotate their exhibitions of paintings, ceramics, swords, kimonos, sculptures and the like. The Toyokan building, to the right, features three floors of artworks from other parts of Asia. The Hyokeikan, the 1909 European-style building to the left, is only open for special events. Behind the Hyokeikan is the Gallery of Horyu-ji Treasures, which houses some of Japanese Buddhism's most important and ancient artefacts, from the seventh-century Horyu-ji temple in Nara. The Heiseikan, behind the Honkan, holds month-long temporary blockbuster exhibitions of Japanese and Asian art. There are also plenty of places to eat around the complex, and a good gift shop.
▶ *The museum stays open until 8pm Fridays and 6pm weekends during some special exhibitions.*

★ FREE Toshogu Shrine
9-88 Ueno Koen, Taito-ku (3822 3455, www. uenotoshogu.com). Ueno station (Yamanote line), park exit; (Ginza, Hibya lines), Shinobazu exit. **Open** 9am-sunset daily. **Admission** *Grounds* free. *Garden* ¥600. **No credit cards. Map** p107.
Toshogu is dedicated to the first Tokugawa shogun, Ieyasu, and is similar to the shrine in Nikko (also called Toshogu; *see p300*) where he is buried. Ueno Toshogu was built in 1627, then remodelled in 1651. It has withstood earthquakes, fires and the Battle of Ueno, and is one of Tokyo's oldest buildings. The huge lantern on the left before the first gate is one of the largest in Japan. Karamon, the front gate of the temple, is famous for its dragon carvings. Note: the main building is closed until 2013. *Photo p109.*

FREE Ueno Royal Museum
Ueno no Mori Bijutsukan
1-2 Ueno Koen, Taito-ku (3833 4195, www.ueno-mori.org). Ueno station (Yamanote line), park exit; (Ginza, Hibya lines), Shinobazu exit. **Open** 10am-5pm daily (until 6pm during special exhibitions). **Admission** varies; usually free. **No credit cards. Map** p107.
This medium-sized *Kunsthalle* in the woods of Ueno Park holds the annual VOCA exhibition of emerging Japanese artists, as well as touring shows from the likes of New York's MoMA and Barcelona's Picasso Museum. It has no permanent collection, and its temporary exhibitions are sporadic.

University Art Museum
12-8 Ueno Koen (5685 7755, www.geidai.ac.jp/ museum). Ueno station (Yamanote line), park exit; (Ginza, Hibya lines), Shinobazu exit. **Open** 10am-5pm Tue-Sun. **Admission** ¥300; ¥100 reductions; additional charge for special exhibitions. **No credit cards. Map** p107.
The museum connected to Japan's most prestigious national art and music school has an impressive collection of over 40,000 objects, ranging from Japanese traditional art to Western paintings and photos. The large new building, opened in 1999, holds both permanent collections and some temporary exhibitions.

Yokoyama Taikan Memorial Hall
1-4-24 Ikenohata, Taito-ku (3821 1017, www.tctv.ne.jp/members/taikan). Yushima station (Chiyoda line), exit 1. **Open** 10am-4pm Thur-Sun. **Admission** ¥500; ¥200 reductions. **No credit cards. Map** p107.
Regarded as one of Japan's great modern painters, Yokoyama Taikan was born at the beginning of the Meiji restoration and lived through 89 years of change. In his house overlooking Shinobazu Pond, Yokoyama practised *nihonga* (traditional Japanese painting), taking images from nature as his inspiration. If his paintings don't impress, his gardens will. The house closes in bad weather and occasionally during the summer.

Yanaka

Tokyo's slow lane.

When the frantic pace of Tokyo starts
to wear you down, head to **Yanaka**,
a picturesque spot where life seems to
potter along just as it did a century ago.
Low-key, low-rise Yanaka, together with
the neighbouring districts of **Nezu** and
Sendagi, forms a rough-shaped lozenge
north-west of Ueno Park. But it's a world
away from the grand museums and
huge, brash street market of Ueno.

The area is home to Tokyo's highest
concentration of temples, which were
moved here following the 1657 Long
Sleeves Fire. Yanaka has led something

| Map p107 | Restaurants p169 |
| Hotels p137 | |

of a charmed life ever since. First as a playground for the wealthy, and then
almost a living museum of old Tokyo, escaping destruction in both the Kanto
Earthquake of 1923 and the air raids in World War II.

A WALKING TOUR OF YANAKA

*Getting there: Nippori station is on the
Yamanote line. Other stations in the area
include Sendagi and Nezu, both on the Chiyoda
line, and Nishi-Nippori, on both lines.*

The best way to see Yanaka is on foot. If
you're prepared to risk getting lost, there's
a lot to be discovered in its steep, winding
backstreets. But you might want to avoid
Yanaka on Mondays and Wednesdays, when
this sleepy corner gets even sleepier as many
of its cafés and museums close.

To start, take the Yamanote line to Nippori
station. Leave by the west exit, which will
bring you to a narrow footpath at the foot of
a flight of steps. In front of you at the top of
the steps is the main street through Yanaka
Cemetery, but before heading there take a look
at **Tenno-ji** temple at the start of the road.
The temple was founded over 700 years ago
and once covered a far larger area. Its star
attraction is the bronze Buddha, cast in 1690,
that overlooks the temple gate. The temple
gained notoriety in the early 19th century,
when it was one of the few places where people
could buy lottery tickets. Naturally, it became
a very popular spot – until the government
spoiled all the fun and closed the business

down. Tenno-ji is also dedicated to Bishamonten,
one of the Seven Deities of Good Fortune.

Leave the temple grounds and head down the
central avenue of **Yanaka Cemetery** (opened
1874), one of Tokyo's largest graveyards and,
along with Aoyama Cemetery, one of its most
picturesque. These days the avenue is usually
quiet, but over 150 years ago it was a den of
iniquity, lined with tea shops that doubled as
brothels and illegal gambling dens. However,
the cemetery does become rather popular
during cherry-blossom time. The Japanese are
oddly fond of holding blossom-viewing parties
in the grounds of the city's cemeteries, and
Yanaka is noted for its blooming cherry trees.

The cemetery contains the remains of many
prominent figures, including Soseki Natsume
(1867-1916), usually regarded as the Japanese
as their finest modern writer. Yanaka Cemetery
is also the resting place of the last Tokugawa
shogun, Yoshinobu (1837-1913), who
surrendered power to the emperor in 1868.

Continue down the path until the *koban*
(police box). To the left and slightly behind
the *koban* is a small fenced-off area. The rubble
inside is all that's left of Yanaka's five-storey
pagoda, once the tallest building in Edo.
Constructed in 1644, it burned down in 1772
and was rebuilt. It burned down for the last
time in 1957, part of a macabre lovers' suicide

Nezu.

pact. Turn right at the police box; the path you are on ends in a T-junction just past some modern houses. Facing you at the end of the street is **Choan-ji** temple, dedicated to Jurojin, a god of long life.

Turn right at the junction and on your left, down a side street, you will catch a glimpse of a traditional Japanese slate wall, part of the complex surrounding **Kannon-ji** temple, where two of the famous 47 *ronin* (*see p24* **Suicidal Samurai**) studied. Inside the grounds on the right is a small pagoda dedicated to their memory.

Turn left out of the temple and continue along the main road. Shortly afterwards, you'll reach **Sandara** (7-18-6 Yanaka, 5814 8618, open 10.30am-6pm Tue-Sun), a charming little shop that sells traditional Japanese pottery. On the other side of the road, a little further on, is **Ryusen-ji**, a minor but picturesque temple with bending trees and sloping roofs. An alternative refuelling stop is **Jinenjyo** (5-9-25 Yanaka, 3824 3162, open 11.30am-9.30pm Tue, Fri, Sat; 11.30am-5.30pm Wed, Thur, Sun), a quaint little coffee shop further up the road on your left. Its speciality is *'yakuzen'* curry', which contains traditional Chinese medicines thought to be good for the circulation.

Further down, on the right, is the **Asakura Choso Museum** (closed until 2015 for renovations); it's situated in the black concrete building that was once the house and studio of sculptor Fumio Asakura. From the museum, turn right and continue along the street, passing on your right an alleyway lined with small drinking dens, or *nomiya*. This is **Hatsunei Komichi**, one of the last wooden-roofed arcades in Tokyo.

At the end of the street, turn left (to return to Nippori station, turn right) and follow the road to the right, down a flight of steps. On the way,

you'll pass eccentric Persian/Turkish restaurant **Zakuro** (3-13-2 Nishi-Nippori, 5685 5313, http://zakuro.oops.jp, open 11am-11pm Mon, Tue, Thur-Sun). Turn right at the bottom of the steps, and 50 metres (150 feet) down the road stands **Midori-ya** (3-13-3 Nishi-Nippori, 3828 7522, open 10am-5pm or 6pm Tue-Sun), which is a traditional maker of hand-woven basketware. Prices range from ¥500 for trinkets to over ¥30,000 for handbags. Return to the foot of the steps and turn right, into the incongruously named **Yanaka Ginza**, the area's main (pedestrianised) shopping street. A surprising number of traditional businesses still survive; notable among these is **Goto no Ame** (3-15-1 Nishi-Nippori, 3821 0880, open 10.30am-7pm daily), which sells traditional sweets, many made on the premises. Other shops offer such wares as *geta* (Japanese wooden shoes), green tea, rice crackers, pottery or tofu.

Turn left at the bottom of Yanaka Ginza, and walk straight on, past the **Ryokan Katsutaro** (*see p137*), until you reach the traffic lights at the end of the street. Turn left at the lights and walk up the hill to **Daien-ji** temple, established in 1591. This is a highly unusual building in that it consists of two symmetrical halves. The left half was intended to serve as a Shinto shrine, the right as a Buddhist temple, but such plans were rejected by the shogunate, which enforced the separation of Buddhism and Shinto. The temple is famous for its colourful chrysanthemum festival in mid October.

Leave the temple, turn left, cross the road at the pedestrian crossing and turn right by the large white school building with a pagoda. Continue straight down this road, bearing left when it forks, to reach the **Daimyo Clock Museum**, which showcases the Japanese-style clocks made for Edo-era *daimyo* feudal lords.

Return to the main street from the museum, turn left and then next left, down a slope with a wonderful Japanese inn, **Ryokan Sawanoya** (*see p137*), close by a crossroads. Take the road to the right at this junction and follow the small street for about 500 metres (a third of a mile). This brings you out to Sansaki-zaka, and just to the left is **Isetatsu** (2-18-9 Yanaka, 3823 1453, open 10am-6pm daily). This shop sells fine decorated papers, whose patterns are made from intricately carved wooden blocks.

Following Sansaki-zaka down brings you to Sendagi station (on the Chiyoda line). The walk can be ended here, or you can go on to **Nezu Shrine**, which is about 400 metres (a quarter of a mile) away: turn left on to the main road, Shinobazu Dori, and then right at the first main junction. Dating from 1706, the shrine is a colourful spot with a giant painted gate and landscaped gardens stretching up a hillside. For most of the year it's an attractive peaceful spot, but in April, when the hillside azalea bushes bloom, the whole place swarms with camera-toting visitors. An interesting time to visit throughout the year is 6.30am, when scores of locals gather to go through their daily communal exercises, all directed by a voice on a crackly radio.

Three art museums are located nearby. Return to Shinobazu Dori, turn right and then continue as far as the big junction with Kototoi Dori. Turn right and walk for 300 metres until you reach a largish junction; take the road to the left, and you will soon see the **Tachihara Michizo Memorial Museum**, followed by the **Takeshisa Yumeji Museum of Art** and **Yayoi Museum of Art**.

Daimyo Clock Museum

2-1-27 Yanaka, Taito-ku (3821 6913). Nezu station (Chiyoda line), exit 1. **Open** 10am-4pm Tue-Sun. Closed July-Sept. **Admission** ¥300; ¥100-¥200 reductions. **No credit cards**. **Map** p107.
Daimyo feudal lords were the only people who could afford the clocks displayed here. Before Japan adopted the solar calendar in 1870, there was a set number of hours between sunrise and sunset, with the result that the length of an hour was longer in summer than in winter. Times were named after the animals of the Chinese zodiac. This one-room museum displays dozens of other timepieces, from alarm clocks to watches worn with a kimono.

Tachihara Michizo Memorial Museum

2-4-5 Yayoi, Bunkyo-ku (5684 8780, www.tachihara.jp). Nezu station (Chiyoda line), exit 1. **Open** 10am-5pm Thur-Sun. **Admission** ¥400; ¥200-¥300 reductions. **No credit cards**.
One of three small museums facing a historic gate of Tokyo University. This one is dedicated to Michizo Tachihara, an artist noted for his pastels. Unfortunately, the museum does not supply English translations, though it is still worth a look.

Takeshisa Yumeji Museum of Art & Yayoi Museum of Art

2-4-3 Yayoi, Bunkyo-ku (5689 0462 Takeshisa Yumeji Museum, 3812 0012 Yayoi Museum, www.yayoi-yumeji-museum.jp). Nezu station (Chiyoda line), exit 1. **Open** 10am-5pm Tue-Sun. **Admission** ¥900; ¥400-¥800 reductions. **No credit cards**.
This building houses two museums, both of them dedicated to the history of Japanese manga (comics) and illustrations.

Asakura Choso Museum.

Further Afield

Step outside the main loop for some of Tokyo's funkiest neighbourhoods.

Just off the tourist radar sit several lively, characterful neighbourhoods that are worth checking out. **Naka-Meguro** – arguably Tokyo's coolest area right now – is the spiritual home of its design-conscious twentysomethings. **Shimo-Kitazawa** is young, vibrant and one of the cheapest places for a decent night out, while **Futako Tamagawa** has a couple of tucked-away finds.

The first handful of stations along the **Chuo line**, one of the city's longest and most crowded commuter lines, also offer pockets of interest. Beyond that, we've included a selection of attractions dotted about other parts of the metropolitan area.

SIGHTS

FUTAKO TAMAGAWA

Getting there: Futako Tamagawa station is on the Denentoshi line (from Shibuya station).

This upmarket suburb got a major facelift in 2010, with a high-rise commercial complex transforming the skyline of what is otherwise a photogenic riverside location. There's plenty of high-end shopping here, but nothing you can't find elsewhere in Tokyo. Still, the area is worth a visit for two reasons: **Seta Onsen** (*see p50* **Old Soaks**), Tokyo's only natural hot spring with communal bathing – and also the only one with a bar attached – and the unforgettable **Gyokushin Mitsuin** temple, hidden in a back street a few blocks from the *onsen*. There's also plenty of dining; in the summer months, eating pizza by the river at **Peace Café** (Hyogojima Koen, 3-2-1 Tamagawa, 3709 0220, www.peacetokyo.com, open 11.30am-9.30pm daily, closed Dec-Mar) is one of the area's highlights. For something lighter, **Chichi Café** (Hyogojima Koen, 1-2-8 Tamagawa, 6411 7958, www.chichicafe.com, open 11am-10pm, closed 2nd Mon of mth) is stylish, friendly and one of the few places in Tokyo you can try *kopi luwak*, the Indonesian coffee that has been semi-digested by a civet.

★ **FREE** **Gyokushin Mitsuin**
4-13-3 Seta, Setagaya-ku (3700 2561). Futako-Tamagawa station (Denentoshi line). **Open** 9am-5pm daily. **Admission** Temple free. Tunnel ¥100.

Popularly known as Tamagawa Daishi, this looks like just another tiny local temple from the outside. But step inside (after removing your shoes) and look to your left. The steps lead to a 100m (330ft) underground tunnel, much of it winding in pitch darkness. Feel your way along the stone corridor until you emerge into a room of 300 candle-lit boddhisattvas. It's a sight to rival anything at the major tourist attractions, but don't bother asking anyone outside the area about it – this is one of Tokyo's best-kept secrets.

NAKA-MEGURO

Getting there: Naka-Meguro station is the first stop on the Hibiya subway line and two stops from Shibuya on the Tokyu Toyoko line.

Naka-Meguro has been blessed and cursed by years of being called Tokyo's hippest neighbourhood. It certainly attracts a trendy crowd of young artists, designers and musicians, and, crucially for a land in which shopkeeping is considered an art form, upcoming retailers. But the days are long gone when you could stumble across a hidden gem in this area: everyone has already found it, swamped it and tweeted it to death. On weekends, you'll be competing for space at the best cafés, restaurants and bars, but the attractions are dispersed enough that the area never feels crowded.

The Meguro river, which defines this district, is lined with small cafés, boutiques and interior outfitters. These establishments are almost all owned and run by entrepreneurs rather than big corporations – rare for Japan – and the cool spaces they have created are what fuels the hype surrounding this trendy tract.

Art aficionados have the **Museum of Contemporary Sculpture**. Fans of café culture, meanwhile, should visit **Chano-ma** (Kangyo Bldg 6F, 1-22-4 Kami-Meguro, 3792 9898, open noon-2am Mon-Thur, Sun, noon-4am Fri, Sat). Located just across from the train station, this urban haven has clever lighting, Eames chairs and elevated mattress-seating for socks-off sprawling.

For hearty dining, several rowdy *izakaya* are situated by the river, close to the station; **Aguri** (*see p171*) is worth a visit. But to sample the local speciality *nabe* (hotpot), follow the train tracks away from the river to the famed *motsu nabe* (offal hotpot) restaurant **Torigoya** (3-5-22 Kami-Meguro, 3710 6762, open 5pm-2am Mon-Sat, noon-midnight Sun), run by a camp amateur *enka* singer. The area is also home to the city's two most acclaimed pizzerias: **Seirinkan** (*see p173*) and **Pizzeria e Trattoria da Isa** (1-28-9 Aobadai, 5768 3739, www.da-isa.jp, open 11.30am-10.30pm Tue-Sat, closed afternoons).

Mizuma Art Gallery (*see p242*) has a well-connected curator who brings in a steady stream of Tokyo's hottest upcoming artists. Visit **Cow Books** (1-14-11 Aobadai, 5459 1747, www.cowbooks.jp, open 1-9pm Tue-Sun) – facing the river – for out-of-print books and vintage magazines, and **Buro-stil** (1-6-19

Higashiyama, 3794 9955, open 11am-8pm daily, closed 2nd & 3rd Tue of mth) for wacky retro furniture.

There's plenty of fashion here too. In addition to a dozen or so second-hand stores and a handful of posh boutiques pushing upmarket European prêt-à-porter, there are some excellent home-grown labels that are worth a browse. Check out the eye-opening oufits on offer at the flagship store of geeky teen favourite **Frapbois** (1-20-4 Aobadai, 6415 4688, www.frapbois.jp, open 11am-8pm daily) and, behind it, **Venom** (MS Bldg B1F, 1-19-7 Aobadai, 5728 4765, www.metalburger.com, open noon-8pm daily) is the home of the Metal Burger brand, a punkish monochrome streetwear label. The out-there vintage selection at hole in the wall **Waingman Wassa** (1-23-5, Aobadai, 5773 5586, www.waingman.com, open 1-9pm daily) perfectly encapsulates the area's irreverent style.

FREE Museum of Contemporary Sculpture

4-12-18 Naka-Meguro, Meguro-ku (3792 5858, www.museum-of-sculpture.org). Naka-Meguro station (Hibiya, Tokyu Toyoko lines), central exit. **Open** 10am-5pm Tue-Sun. Closed 20 Dec-14 Jan. **Admission** free.

The Watanabe Collection includes more than 200 pieces by 56 contemporary Japanese artists. Three outdoor areas filled with large, mostly conceptual works complement two storeys of figurative studies. The marble tombstones in the adjacent graveyard provide an interesting counterpoint.

SIGHTS

Edo-Tokyo Open-Air Architecture Museum. *See p117.*

Mandarake.

SHIMO-KITAZAWA

*Getting there: Shimo-Kitazawa station is on
the Keio Inokashira line (from Shibuya station)
and the Odakyu line (from Shinjuku station).*

Shimo-Kitazawa, a short train ride from both
Shibuya and Shinjuku, is a favourite among
young Tokyoites looking for something a little
less trashy than Shibuya. It's loaded with cool
shops, cafés and bars, though things are about
to change dramatically due to a controversial
plan to divide the area in two with a large
highway. Despite fierce local opposition,
demolition and construction began in 2010;
it's slated to end in 2014, when the area will
have several high-rise commercial centres in
addition to the new highway. Whether or
not Shimo-Kitazawa will retain its quirky,
independent personality remains to be seen.

The creative impetus behind the area's
growth came from the *sho-gekijou* (small
theatre) movement of the 1960s, which was
born of frustration with the way theatres
were dominated by either Western realism
or tradition-bound *kabuki* and *Noh*. Its theatres
gave younger actors and directors the freedom
to express themselves, and a large number of
them came to be concentrated here. Legendary
theatre directors such as Ninagawa Yukio and
Mori Hajime have staged productions on the
area's illustrious boards.

As well as theatre, the neighbourhood
has become famous for its 'live houses' –
the dark, dynamic, box-like venues where
Tokyo's aspiring bands hone their skills.
At weekends, the better-known venues,

including **Shelter Shimo-Kitazawa**
(*see p261*), **Club Que** (*see p259*) and
Club 251 (*see p259*), are rammed.

Shimo-Kitazawa station has two exits
– north and south – both of which lead to areas
of interest. From the north exit, turn right and
after about 200 metres (650 feet), you'll come
to the first set of crossroads. The street that
stretches away to both sides takes you past
boutiques selling new and second-hand
clothes ranging from cute to bizarre, with
everything in-between.

Keep walking, and you'll get to another
crossroads. Turning right leads back to the
train tracks, and straight-ahead down a small
alleyway will take you past **FxG** (*see p215*) –
the shop that spearheaded the current wave of
cheap, stylish opticians – to Ichibangai Dori.

Over on the other side of the station, you'll
find plenty of life after dark, as this is where
local residents and visitors come to eat, drink
and mosh themselves into a happy, eardrum-
ringing haze. Directly opposite the station's
south exit is the area's main street, Minami
Shotengai, which is packed full of fast-food
shops, *pachinko* parlours and cheap boutiques.
Halfway down the street the area's distinctive
character starts to reveal itself, with its
second-hand book, game and CD shops.
A road branching off to the right, with
Mr Donuts on the corner, points the way to a
quiet, leafy street with one of the best *izakaya*
in the area – the stately **Shirube** (3413 3785,
open 5.30pm-midnight Sun-Thur; 5.30pm-2am
Fri, Sat). Right opposite Shirube is English pub
Heaven's Door (*see p186*), a haven for those
looking for a decent pint and British football.

SIGHTS

Going back to the main street and walking to the bottom, you'll find streets leading off in five directions. These streets contain numerous little bars and restaurants, many serving ethnic food and drink.

Back at the south exit, turn left and head down the street that has a Starbucks on the corner. Halfway down is the basement venue Club Que, while at the end is Chazawa Dori, with Shelter off to the left and Club 251 about ten minutes' walk to the right. The streets between the Minami Shotengai and Chazawa Dori are worth a wander, as they host several 'natural-food' *izakaya* and the most famous *sho-gekijou* in the area, the **Honda Theatre** (2-10-15 Kitazawa, Setagaya-ku, 3468 0030, www.honda-geki.com).

THE CHUO LINE

The JR Chuo line heads west in the evening from its first station, Tokyo, stopping at the key business hubs of Ochanomizu, Yotsuya and Shinjuku before trekking out to the 'bedtowns' and suburbs of western Tokyo and the cities beyond. Its cargo is a mass of sleeping, occasionally drunk, always exhausted commuters heading home. In the morning, it all happens in reverse: the Chuo line picks up the same crew of wage slaves and spits them out again into the bowl of central Tokyo for another day at Japan Inc.

The Chuo line is one of the most crowded in all of Japan, with commuters jammed in so tightly it's – almost – worth joining in for the experience. Wise travellers, however, avoid it between 7.30am and 9.30am (into the city) and 6pm and 9pm (out of the city). The last train of the night from Shinjuku station, at around 12.30am, is a great way to come face to face – literally – with the locals, and redefine your concept of personal space.

The first two stations out of Shinjuku – Okubo and Higashi-Nakano – contain little of note. The most interesting locales are between Nakano and Kichijoji stations. These stations are served by two types of train: the yellow-coloured local (Sobu line) and the orange-coloured express (Chuo line). The Sobu line starts in Chiba prefecture and stops at all stations (including Shinjuku), but goes no further west than Mitaka. From Shinjuku, the Chuo line plonks down first at Nakano before going station by station out to various termination points, the furthest located deep in the suburbs of west Tokyo.

Trains run between roughly 6am and midnight, and their frequency makes it easy to hop from one destination to another; stations are only a few minutes apart. If you're exploring at the weekend, take the Sobu line – because Chuo trains stop only at Ogikubo, rather than at every station between Nakano and Mitaka.

Further along the line are more delights, such as the historic buildings held at the open-air branch of the **Edo-Tokyo Open-Air Architecture Museum** in Musashi-Koganei.

Nakano

Although best known these days for its cheap shopping, Nakano was once home to 80,000 dogs. The fifth shogun, Tokugawa Tsunaiyasho, was particularly fond of mutts, and in 1695 built an *inuyashiki* (dog castle) across the whole of Nakano to keep his tens of thousands of canine mates in comfort. Dogs can still be seen today, wandering the streets, unaware of their providence.

A must-see for fans of manga, *anime* and 'cosplay' (costume play) is the sprawling empire of **Mandarake** (*see p212*). What was once one shop selling recycled manga comics has slowly spread its Akira-like tentacles across **Nakano Broadway** (*see p200*), the town's main shopping mall next to the station's north exit. Now, 14 shops on three floors of the four-storey centre sell comics, figurines, vintage toys, animation cells, CDs, video games, posters, cosplay costumes – in fact, anything related to Japan's *otaku* phenomenon (*see pp39-42*). Begin on the third floor at comic HQ, and lose an afternoon wandering around. Key rings and tiny figurines start at ¥100, and make cheap and unique souvenirs. Japanese schoolgirl dresses can be had for a bigger outlay. Broadway is also home to a host of discount shoe and fashion shops, with prices far below those charged a five-minute train ride away in Shinjuku.

The warren of streets around the Broadway complex has scores of restaurants, bars and *izakaya*, many offering food at bargain prices.

Slightly out of Nakano centre is the quirky **Tetsugakudo Park**.

🆓 Tetsugakudo Park

1-34-28 Matsuoka, Nakano-ku (3954 4881, www.tetsugakudo.jp). Arai Yakushi-mae station (Seibu Shinjuku line), north exit then 12mins walk or Nakano station (Chuo line), north exit then bus to Tetsugakudo. **Open** *Apr-Sept* 8am-6pm daily. *Oct-Mar* 9am-5pm daily. **Admission** free.

A hillside park founded by philosopher Enryo Inoue, who wanted to enshrine philosophical theory in physical form. The park contains 77 spots that symbolise different doctrines. On the top of the hill are six Meiji-era buildings that are open to the public during *hanami* (cherry-blossom viewing) and in October on public holidays and at weekends.

SIGHTS

Koenji

Koenji is home to a youthful live music scene and plenty of students. A cluster of bars around both sides of the station exit provide a window into a selection of musical styles – mainly punk/grunge, but also jazz, country and western, and soul. The best of these, **Inaoiza** (2F Sunny Mansion, 2-38-16 Koenjikita, 3336 4480, www.freepe.com/i.cgi?inaoi, open 8pm-2am daily), is a decades-old bar that serves up many a random meal. Local talent plays most evenings from 8pm, and entry is ¥1,500, or free if no one is jamming.

Also worth a visit is **Las Meninas** (see p186), run by affable Geordie Johnny Miller, whose Spanish fare and English banter are so popular it's almost always packed. Prices are half what you would pay in central Tokyo. Ask for a map at the police box just outside the north exit – staff are used to directing foreigners.

Koenji also has a reputation as Tokyo's centre for all things associated with the southern Japanese island of Okinawa. Tuck into some Okinawan food at the Tokyo-famous **Dachibin** (3-2-13 Koenji-Kita, 3337 1352, open 5pm-5am daily). Most of the cooking is *chanpuri* (mixed fried things) and many dishes feature the bitter flavours of the Okinawan vegetable *goya* – *chanpuri goya* is a good start. If you tire of the pedestrian flavours of Orion, the island's own beer, then ask for *awamori* – Okinawan saké. It comes in two strengths: five-year-old 35 per cent and the older 45 per cent. Drink with respect.

Asagaya

This area's well-founded reputation for jazz grows every year as its Jazz Street festival, held in October, continues to develop both in size and composition. A number of bars showcase local jazz players throughout the year.

Scribblers of all types laid the foundations for Asagaya's self-important world view. The Asagaya-kai was a group of prominent Japanese authors who spent much of their time in the area from 1910 to the early 1950s. The group's leader, Masuji Ibuse, gained international fame with his novel *Black Rain*, the story of a Hiroshima woman's struggle with radiation poisoning. From the 1970s, the area enjoyed an art renaissance when it became a draw for Japan's best manga artists. These days, though, its wealthy residents spend rather than create, and a little ambulatory effort will unearth good restaurants and cramped but homey bars.

It's worth seeing the aged trees lining Nakasugi Dori, the main street under the railway tracks, which are at their most gloriously green from May to June. Film buffs note: the square on the south side of the station was a backdrop in the original version of horror movie *The Ring*.

Ogikubo

Key word: ramen. One of Tokyo's best-known ramen shops is in Ogikubo, and people travel from all over Japan to eat there. **Harukiya** (1-4-6 Kami-Ogi, 3391 4868, open 11am-9pm daily) seats only 16 people, and there's usually a small queue. Ask for *chuka soba* or, for extra slices of pork, *chashumen*. Harukiya was established in 1952, on the heels of a black market that sprang up after World War II. There's also a good daily fish, meat and veg market in the area, sprawling over the basement of the Ogikubo Town 7 shopping centre.

Although not a particularly pretty place, Ogikubo retains a bustling, working-class feel and, more than at most stations on the Chuo line, a sense of history.

Nishi-Ogikubo

In the 1960s, peaceful 'Nishi Ogi' rose to heights of civil disobedience as a gathering point for organic, veggie-loving hippies. Two cults have also risen from these nondescript surroundings – the most notorious was Aum Shinrikyo, the religious sect responsible for the 1995 subway sarin gas attacks that killed 12 people.

Now, fortunately, the area is best known for its antiques and bric-a-brac shops – around 75 of them, in fact. Take the north exit from the station and head for the *koban* (police box). Stride up to the policeman and say '*antiku mapu onegai shimasu*'. He'll pull a map from his desk, and you'll be on your way to a pleasant day strolling the backstreets. You'll find Western and Japanese antiquities on sale, but don't expect bargains. The north-west section of the walk has the best furniture, lighting and antiques shops, and there are also a few eccentric second-hand bookshops that may reward your browsing.

Kichijoji

On the edge of Tokyo's 23 wards, Kichijoji often tops lists of the most livable districts in Tokyo. It has everything – shopping galore, hundreds of quality independent cafés, bars and restaurants, the spacious **Inokashira Park**, plenty of music venues and and an energy that beats most of the Chuo line's other destinations.

Jazz venues and ethnic restaurants are something of a speciality, while digging deep among the streets outside the station's north exit will turn up numerous bars and eateries. This plethora of choice makes Kichijoji an excellent night-time excursion.

SIGHTS

Inokashira Park.

SIGHTS

A good choice for dinner is **Toaun** (B1, 2-16-17 Kichijoji-honcho, 0422 29 7660, www.frontier-one.co.jp/touan, open 11.30am-12.30am daily, closed afternoons), which specialises in tofu and free-range chicken, but has a menu that encompasses everything from sashimi to soba to gyoza. The setting is pure Old Japan, with a dark wood interior, private tatami rooms and a Japanese garden.

For something a little more unusual, try **Café Russia** (B1, 1-4-10 Kichijoji-honcho, 0422 23 3200, http://caferussia.web.fc2.com, open 11.30am-10pm daily), next to the station. The authentic Georgian and Russian food is uniformly good, and the warm service compensates for the horrifying all-pink interior.

Vegetarians should head for **Deva Deva Café** (2-14-7 Kochijoji-honcho, 0422 21 6220, www.devadevacafe.com, open 11am-8pm daily), for a vast menu of veggie burgers.

Inside the park itself, **Pepecafe Forest** (4-1-5 Inokashira-Koen, 0422 42 7081, open noon-10pm Mon, Wed-Sun) lies across from the central bridge over the lake. The café's plastic walls roll up in summer, making it the ideal place for evening beers.

In between the park and Mitaka (further up the Chuo line) lies the **Ghibli Museum**, a showcase for the Oscar-winning animation studio of the same name.

Ghibli Museum

1-1-83 Shimo-Renjaku, Mitaka-shi (0570 05 5777, www.ghibli-museum.jp). Kichijoji station (Chuo line), north exit then 15mins walk or *Mitaka station (Chuo line), south exit then community bus.* **Open** 10am-6pm Mon, Wed-Sun. **Admission** ¥1,000; ¥400-¥700 reductions. **Credit cards** (gift shop only) AmEx, DC, JCB, MC, V.

Hayao Miyazaki's studio has produced some of Japan's most popular and complex animation classics, from *My Neighbour Totoro* to *Princess Mononoke* and *Spirited Away*. You need a bit of dedication to visit Miyazaki's museum. Not only is it a trek from central Tokyo, but you need to purchase tickets in advance (which can be done from overseas, check the website, or at Lawsons convenience stores in Japan), then show up on the prescribed day with your ticket and some ID. You will be escorted into another world: you can view original prints, play in rooms with painted ceilings and walls, and watch short animations in the cinema. The gift shop sells original animation cells.

FREE Inokashira Park

1-18-31 Gotenyama, Musashino-shi (0422 47 6900). Kichijoji station (Chuo line), park exit then 10mins walk. **Open** 24hrs daily.

Located just 15 minutes from the centre of Tokyo, Inokashira park has more than enough to occupy you for an afternoon, including a zoo (not the greatest in the world; *see p128*), a pond with amusingly shaped rental boats, and enough playground facilities to keep the little ones happy for hours. At weekends, the park comes alive with street traders, musicians and artists. In late March and early April, it fills with people enjoying *hanami* (cherry-blossom viewing), and it's well worth making the trip to join them.

OTHER SIGHTS

Beyond the neighbourhoods covered in this guide, there are a number of individual attractions that are worth making a special trip.

★ Edo-Tokyo Open-Air Architectural Museum
Edo-Tokyo Tatemono-en

3-7-1 Sakuracho, Koganei Ishi (042 388 3300, www.tatemonoen.jp). Musashi Koganei station (Chuo line), north exit then any bus from bus stops 2 or 3 to Koganei Koen Nishi-Guchi. **Open** *Apr-Sept* 9.30am-5.30pm Tue-Sun. *Oct-Mar* 9.30am-4.30pm Tue-Sun. **Admission** ¥400; free-¥200 reductions. **No credit cards.**

Tokyo's architectural heritage is well preserved in a hoard of buildings at this branch of the Edo-Tokyo Museum (*see p50*). As well as swanky private residences and quaint old town shops, there's a host of one-offs, such as an ornate bathhouse and a mausoleum built for a shogun's wife. Even the visitors' centre once served as a ceremonial pavilion in front of the Imperial Palace. Be prepared for lots of slipping in and out of shoes if you want to visit the interiors.

▶ *You can grab a Zen – and vegetarian – lunch at nearby Sanko-in (see p171).*

FREE Kasai Seaside Park

6-2 Rinkai-cho, Edogawa-ku (3686 6911, www.senyo.co.jp/kasai). Kasai-Rinkai Koen station (Keiyo line) or by Suijo water bus. **Open** *Park* 24hrs daily. *Birdwatching centre & visitors' centre* 9.30am-4.30pm daily. *Beach* 9am-5pm daily. *Big wheel* 10am-7.40pm Mon-Fri; 10am-8.40pm Sat, Sun. *Tokyo Sea Life Park* 9.30am-5pm Tue-Sun. **Admission** free. *Big wheel* ¥700. *Tokyo Sea Life Park* ¥700. **No credit cards.**

Located by the water at the eastern edge of the city, close to the Tokyo Disney Resort (*see below*), this is one of Tokyo's biggest parks and was built to re-create a natural seashore environment. Inside are the Tokyo Sea Life Park, two small beaches, a Japanese garden and a lotus pond. The birdwatching area includes two ponds and tidal flats.

Museum of Contemporary Art, Tokyo (MoT)

4-1-1 Miyoshi, Koto-ku (5245 4111, www.mot-art-museum.jp). Kiba station (Tozai line), exit 3 then 15mins walk. **Open** 10am-6pm Tue-Sun. **Admission** ¥500; ¥200-¥400 reductions; free under-12s; additional charge for special exhibitions. **Credit** (shop only) JCB, MC, V.

This huge, city-owned showpiece opened in 1995 on reclaimed swampland in a distant part of Tokyo. Its collection of 3,500 international and Japanese artworks has its moments, but the temporary exhibitions are the main reason to visit. Visitors can access the database, extensive video library, and magazine and catalogue collection (all available in English).

★ Rikugien

6-16-3 Hon-komagome, Bunkyo-ku (3941 2222, www.tokyo-park.or.jp/english/park/detail_08.html). Komagome station (Nanboku, Yamanote lines). **Open** 9am-5pm daily. **Admission** ¥300. **No credit cards.**

It feels more like Kyoto than Tokyo inside this stunning landscape garden. Rikugien was built in 1702 at a shogun's behest, and recreates several of the country's most celebrated beauty spots. It's rare in Tokyo to find such natural beauty without enormous skyscrapers distractingly piercing the background.

▶ *For other great gardens, visit Hama Rikyu (see p60) and Sankeien (see p289).*

FREE Sengaku-ji Temple

2-11-1 Takanawa, Minato-ku (3441 5560, www.sengakuji.or.jp). Sengaku-ji station (Asakusa line), exit A2. **Open** *Temple* 7am-5pm (Apr-Sept until 6pm) daily. *Museum* 9am-4pm daily. **Admission** free.

The most interesting thing about the Sengaku-ji Temple is its connection to one of Japan's most famous stories – that of the 47 samurai attached to Lord Ako (*see p24* **Suicidal Samurai**). After he drew his sword on a rival, Yoshinaka Kira, in Edo Castle, Lord Ako was ordered to commit *seppuku* (death by ritual disembowelment). He was buried here. His 47 loyal followers then became *ronin*, or samurai without a master, bent on avenging his death. They killed Kira and were then themselves permitted to die in the same manner as their master, and to be buried close to him at Sengaku-ji. Their tombs are at the top of a flight of steps. Follow the smoke trails from the incense left by well-wishers.

▶ *On 14 December, the anniversary of the samurai's revenge attack, Sengaku-ji holds a festival to celebrate: the 47 Ronin Memorial Service (see p225).*

Tokyo Disney Resort

1-1 Maihama, Urayasu-shi, Chiba (045 683 3333, www.tokyodisneyresort.co.jp/index_e.html). Maihama station (Keiyo, Musashino lines), south exit. **Open** varies. **Admission** (per park) *1-day passport* ¥5,800; ¥3,900-¥5,100 reductions. Off-peak, 2-day passports also available. **Credit** AmEx, DC, JCB, MC, V.

Sitting on a huge tract of land in Tokyo Bay, the Tokyo Disney Resort comprises two adjacent but separate theme parks: Disneyland and DisneySea. The latter, opened in 2001, gave the whole enterprise a massive shot in the arm, since the rest of the park was starting to show its age. Disneyland's seven main zones contain 43 attractions, while DisneySea has 23 water-based attractions. Disney has a special place in the hearts of many Japanese people, so the queues can be horrendous. Go early, and preferably on a weekday.

Consume

Hotel Villa Fontaine Shiodome. *See p126.*

Hotels	122
Tokyo's Best Hotel Bars	131
Tatami Treats	134
Love Hotels	141

Restaurants	143
A Guide to	
Japanese Cuisine	144
Queue Tips	150
Super Bowls	157
Shojin Ryori	172
Menu Reader	174

Bars	176
Local Potions	181
Japanese Whisky	182
Golden Gai	185

| Coffee Shops | 187 |

Shops & Services	192
Duty-free Goods	193
Treats Abound	
Underground	194
Automatic for the People	201
The Rag Trade	206
Present Perfect	213
Local View Cornelius	218

Hotels

High-rises with high prices – but there are still affordable options.

If the last decade was all about the luxury behemoths arriving in force, this one looks set to be about a boom in elegant, affordable accommodation.

Until recently, you got what you paid for in Tokyo, meaning that budget accommodation was only for the desperate, and mid-range hotels were likely to be drab affairs. Now, hotels such as the **Granbell Hotel** (*see p134*), the **Hotel Unizo** (*see p134*), **Citadines Tokyo Shinjuku** (*see p136*) and the **Villa Fontaine** chain (*see p125*) all offer stylish decor and great service for under ¥25,000 per night.

STAYING IN TOKYO

If you're looking for luxury, Tokyo has more than ever. Gone are the days when the **Park Hyatt Tokyo** (*see p135*) could scoop up all the 'haves'. In the last decade, the city has welcomed a Ritz-Carlton, a Grand Hyatt, a Conrad, a Peninsula, a Four Seasons and a Shangri-La. And as this guide goes to print, the Tokyu hotel chain is preparing to reopen its Tokyo flagship hotel in a shell by star architect Kengo Kuma. If the economy can rebound and bring tourism with it, expect plenty of competition by the purveyors of luxe to out-sparkle each other.

Tokyo's budget options are still limited. The **capsule hotels** (*see p140*) are the last resort of the drunk, desperate and male (most are men-only). They offer cheap accommodation in a tube that's barely big enough to swing a room key. It's something to try for the experience, but do not plan on an extended stay. For couples, love hotels (*see p141* **Love Hotels**) are a more comfortable and kitsch option, though you'll be kicked out with all your luggage each morning. **Minshuku** (*see p140*) are Japan's version of the B&B and usually a friendly, no-frills, futon-on-the-floor option. For a more sumptuous Japanese experience, you'll need a *ryokan* – the Japanese-style inns that can be pricey but usually include an extravagant dinner.

WHERE TO STAY

Tokyo is a massive, sprawling metropolis, so where you stay will have a big impact on your enjoyment of the city. If you plan to indulge in the city's nightlife, Shibuya or Roppongi will suit you. Prefer culture? Try Asakusa or Ueno. For easy access to anywhere in the city, Shinjuku is hard to beat.

PRICES

The prices given in this chapter refer to the rack rates for standard double rooms. The rates should give an indication of what you can expect to pay, but note that rates can vary wildly according to the season. At peak season, rooms can be as much as double the off-peak rate.

SALES TAX

All room rates are subject to Japan's usual five per cent sales tax, but if your bill climbs to the equivalent of over ¥15,000 per night (including service charges), you will be liable to pay an additional three per cent tax. Then there's a flat-rate surcharge of ¥100 per night for rooms costing ¥10,000-¥14,999, rising to ¥200 for rooms costing ¥15,000 or over. This money goes to help the metropolitan government promote Tokyo as a tourist destination.

No tipping is expected in any Tokyo hotel, although most high-end places include a standard service charge of 10 to 15 per cent in their room rates. Ask when booking.

ASAKUSA
Expensive

Asakusa View Hotel
3-17-1 Nishi-Asakusa, Taito-ku (3847 1111, www.viewhotels.co.jp/asakusa). Tawaramachi station (Ginza line), exit 3. **Rooms** 338. **Rates** ¥27,300-¥29,400 double. **Credit** AmEx, DC, JCB, MC, V. **Map** p45.

With its uniformed staff and marble lobby somewhat incongruous in this downtown, working-class neighbourhood, the Asakusa View offers a fairly high standard of accommodation, though the style is from a bygone era. If you want to make the hotel live up to its name, go for a room as high up as you can: the view from the top over Asakusa and the Sumida river is worth catching.

Bars (3). Concierge. Disabled-adapted rooms. Japanese & Western rooms. No-smoking rooms. Parking (¥1,000/night). Pool (indoor). Restaurants (3). Room service (7am-11pm). ▶ Non-visitors can also pop in for a drink in the Belvedere lounge on the 28th floor.

Moderate

Ryokan Shigetsu

1-31-11 Asakusa, Taito-ku (3843 2345, www. shigetsu.com). Asakusa station (Asakusa line), exit A4; (Ginza line), exits 1, 6. **Rooms** 23. **Rates** ¥17,000-¥26,000 double. **Credit** AmEx, MC, V. **Map** p45.

Barely 30 seconds from Asakusa's market and temple complex, yet surprisingly peaceful, the Shigetsu offers a choice of comfortable rooms in Japanese and Western styles in an elegant downtown setting. All rooms have their own bathrooms, although there is also a Japanese-style communal bath on the top floor. Recent years have seen a shift back to Japanese-style rooms, with 15 of the 23 now featuring traditional tatami and futon furnishings.

Internet (shared terminal). Japanese & Western rooms. No-smoking rooms. Restaurant.

Sukeroku No Yado Sadachiyo

2-20-1 Asakusa, Taito-ku (3842 6431, www.sadachiyo.co.jp). Asakusa station (Asakusa line), exit A4; (Ginza line), exits 1, 6 or Tawaramachi station (Ginza line), exit 3. **Rooms** 20. **Rates** ¥19,000-¥28,000 double. **Credit** MC, V. **Map** p45.

This smart, modern *ryokan* is wonderfully situated just five minutes' walk from Asakusa's temple. From the outside, the building resembles a cross between a European chalet and a Japanese castle, but inside it's pure Japanese, with receptionists shuffling around the reception area dressed in kimonos. Staff are obliging, but speak only minimal English. All of the rooms are Japanese-style and come in a variety of sizes, the smallest being just five mats. The communal Japanese baths should help make a stay here a memorable and incredibly relaxing experience.

Internet (shared terminal). Japanese rooms only. Room service (7.30am-10pm).

Budget

Sakura Ryokan

2-6-2 Iriya, Taito-ku (3876 8118, www.sakuraryokan.com). Iriya station (Hibiya line), exit 1. **Rooms** 18. **Rates** ¥9,000-¥11,000 double. **Credit** AmEx, DC, JCB, MC, V.

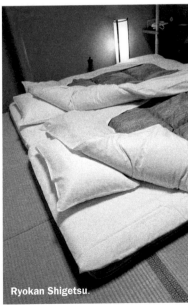

Ryokan Shigetsu.

CONSUME

Ten minutes' walk north from Asakusa's temple complex, in the traditional downtown area of Iriya, the Sakura is a friendly, traditional, family-run *ryokan*. Of the Japanese-style rooms, only two have their own bathrooms, while seven of the Western-style rooms each have a bath. The Sakura also has a communal bath on each floor.
Internet (shared terminal). Japanese & Western rooms. Parking (¥1,000/night).

EBISU
Deluxe

Westin Tokyo
1-4-1 Mita, Meguro-ku (5423 7000, www. westin-tokyo.co.jp). Ebisu station (Yamanote, Hibiya lines), east exit. **Rooms** 445. **Rates** ¥65,100-¥76,650 double. **Credit** AmEx, DC, JCB, MC, V.
The Westin, at the far end of Ebisu's giant Garden Place development, opened in 1994. Its spacious lobby attempts to re-create the feeling of a European palace, while all guest rooms are palatial in size and feature soft lighting and antique-style furniture. A good view is pretty much guaranteed. The setting is quiet, but it's within strolling distance from the bars and restaurants of Ebisu.
Bars (3). Business centre. Concierge. Disabled-adapted rooms. Internet (high-speed). No-smoking rooms. Parking (¥1,000/night). Restaurants (6). Room service (24hr).

Moderate

Hotel Excellent
1-9-5 Ebisu-Nishi, Shibuya-ku (5458 0087, www.soeikikaku.co.jp). Ebisu station (Yamanote line), west exit; (Hibiya line), exit 3. **Rooms** 127. **Rates** ¥11,550 double. **Credit** DC, MC, V.
A thoroughly basic but phenomenally popular business hotel offering no-frills accommodation in small, functional and bland rooms. The main reason for its success is its location, one stop away from Shibuya on the Yamanote line and in the heart of the lively Ebisu area.
Bar. Internet (high-speed). No-smoking rooms. Restaurants (2).

GINZA & AROUND
Deluxe

Conrad Tokyo
Tokyo Shiodome Bldg, 1-9-1 Higashi-Shinbashi, Minato-ku (6388 8000, www.conradtokyo.co.jp). (Ginza line), exit 2; Shinbashi station (Yamanote, Asakusa lines), exit 1; Shiodome station (Oedo, Yurikamome lines), exit 9. **Rooms** 290. **Rates** ¥37,000-¥67,000 double. **Credit** AmEx, DC, JCB, MC, V.

Hotel Villa Fontaine Shiodome.
See p126.

The Conrad opened in 2005, occupying the top ten floors of the 37-storey Tokyo Shiodome Building. Its rooms feature modern Japanese design brightened by floor-to-ceiling windows, and have plasma-screen TVs and wireless internet. The Conrad is also home to Gordon Ramsay's first restaurant in Japan.
Bar. Business centre. Concierge. Gym. Internet (high-speed, wireless). No-smoking rooms. Parking. Pool (indoor). Restaurants (3). Room service (24hr). Spa.
▶ *For our restaurant review of Gordon Ramsay at Conrad Tokyo, see p154.*

★ Hotel Seiyo Ginza
1-11-2 Ginza, Chuo-ku (3535 1111, www.seiyo-ginza.com). Ginza-Itchome station (Yurakucho line), exits 7, 10. **Rooms** 77. **Rates** ¥40,000-¥60,000 double. **Credit** AmEx, DC, MC, V.
Map p59.
The Rosewood-owned Seiyo is smaller than most of its upscale peers, meaning impeccable, personal service. The rooms are furnished not in the clean lines and nature tones that seem de rigueur at this price range, but in a more flowery classic European style that will look homey to some and horrifying to others. The location, on Ginza's main drag, is a huge amenity, and the bar, open only to hotel guests and members, is one of the best hotel bars in Tokyo, if sometimes choked with cigar smoke.
Bars (2). Business centre. Concierge. Gym. Internet (high-speed). No-smoking floors. Parking (free). Restaurants (3). Room service (24hr).

Kimi Ryokan.

CONSUME

Imperial Hotel
1-1-1 Uchisaiwaicho, Chiyoda-ku (3504 1111, *www.imperialhotel.co.jp). Hibiya station (Chiyoda, Hibiya, Mita lines), exits A5, A13 or Yurakucho station (Yamanote, Yurakucho lines), Hibiya exit.* **Rooms** 1,052. **Rates** ¥40,000-¥90,000 double. **Credit** AmEx, DC, JCB, MC, V. **Map** p59.
There has been an Imperial Hotel on this site overlooking Hibiya Park since 1890. This 1970 tower block-style building replaced the glorious 1923 Frank Lloyd Wright creation that famously survived the Great Kanto Earthquake on its opening day. It's had a recent overhaul, but still isn't quite in the same luxury league as the famous foreign chains.
Bars (3). Business centre. Concierge. Disabled-adapted room. Gym. Internet (high-speed). No-smoking rooms. Parking (free). Pool (indoor). Restaurants (14). Room service (24hr).

Expensive

Ginza Mercure
2-9-4 Ginza, Chuo-ku (4335 1111, www.mercure. com). Ginza-Itchome station (Yurakucho line), exit 11. **Rooms** 209. **Rates** ¥32,340 double. **Credit** AmEx, DC, JCB, MC, V. **Map** p59.
This French-owned hotel opened in 2004 in a great central location, just behind Matsuya department store. Niftily converted from an existing office building, it has the feel of a European boutique hotel, featuring smart cherry-wood furniture, stylish wallpaper and black and white photos of old Paris. All the rooms

vary in size (numbers 16 and 18 are the biggest), and there are 18 special 'ladies' rooms' on the eight, ninth and tenth floors. The breakfast room doubles as a French bistro, and staff speak English. A good choice for both business and independent travellers.
Bar. Business centre. Concierge. Disabled-adapted room. Internet (high-speed). No-smoking rooms. Parking (¥2,000/night). Restaurant.
Other locations Mercure Hotel Narita, 818-1 Hanazaki-cho, Narita, Chiba-ken (0476 23 7000).

Hotel Com's Ginza
8-6-15 Ginza, Chuo-ku (3572 4131, www.hotel coms.jp/ginza). Shinbashi station (Yamanote, Asakusa, Ginza lines), Ginza exit. **Rooms** 267. **Rates** ¥25,000-¥28,800 double. **Credit** AmEx, DC, JCB, MC, V. **Map** p59.
Hotel Com's is an unassuming, practical choice on the edge of Ginza. Rooms are quite small and spartan, but reasonable value, and the buffet breakfast is impressive for this price category. The hotel's proximity to Ginza's nightlife quarter means it's often filled with Japanese businessmen and kimono-clad hostesses on their way to or from work.
Bar. Internet (high-speed). No-smoking floor. Parking (¥1,500/night). Restaurants (5).

★ Park Hotel Tokyo
Shiodome Media Tower, 1-7-1 Higashi Shinbashi, Minato-ku (6252 1111, www.park hoteltokyo.com). Shiodome station (Oedo, Yurikamome lines). **Rooms** 273. **Rates** ¥26,250-¥23,700 double. **Credit** AmEx, DC, JCB, MC, V.
It's got the service and style of a deluxe hotel, but the rooms are a touch smaller and so is the price. The location, attached to Shiodome station and a short walk from Ginza, is convenient enough and the views will knock you out.
Bar. Business centre. Concierge. Disabled-adapted room. Internet (high-speed). No-smoking rooms. Parking (¥2,000/night). Restaurants (3).

Moderate

★ Hotel Villa Fontaine Shiodome
1-9-2 Higashi-Shinbashi, Minato-ku (3569 2220, www.villa-fontaine.co.jp). Shiodome station (Oedo line), exit 10; (Yurikamome line), Shiodome Sumitomo Bldg exit. **Rooms** 497. **Rates** ¥14,000-¥18,000 double. **Credit** AmEx, DC, JCB, MC, V.
The Villa Fontaine chain has mushroomed across the city in the last few years. Prices are surprisingly low, and many of its hotels offer unique options such as women-only floors. This branch, opened in 2004, sits in the gleaming Shiodome complex. Interiors are bold and modern, and the well-designed rooms make the most of their small size. Free broadband internet access is a bonus. Shame about the disappointing buffet breakfast. This is the smartest of the hotel's ever-increasing number of locations in the metropolis. *Photo p125.*

Business centre. Disabled-adapted room. Internet (high-speed). No-smoking rooms. Parking (¥2,100/night). **Other locations** throughout the city (5339 1200 central reservations).

IKEBUKURO
Budget

Kimi Ryokan
2-36-8 Ikebukuro, Toshima-ku (3971 3766, www.kimi-ryokan.jp). Ikebukuro station (Yamanote, Marunouchi, Yurakucho lines), exits west, C6. **Rooms** 38. **Rates** ¥6,500-¥7,500 double. **No credit cards. Map** p69.
A *ryokan* that caters almost exclusively to foreign visitors, the Kimi offers simple, small, Japanese-style rooms. Bathing and toilet facilities are communal but are very clean; there's even a Japanese bath for use at set times. Downstairs in the communal lounge, you'll likely find backpackers and travellers exchanging gossip. Booking is advised. *Japanese rooms only.*
▶ *Kimi Ryokan also runs an information and accommodation service for foreigners apartment-hunting in Tokyo (3986 1604), and a telephone answering service for businesspeople (3986 1895).*

Mandarin Oriental Tokyo.

MARUNOUCHI & AROUND
Deluxe

Four Seasons Hotel Tokyo at Marunouchi
Pacific Century Place, 1-11-1 Marunouchi, Chiyoda-ku (5222 7222, www.fourseasons. com/marunouchi). Tokyo station (Yamanote, Marunouchi lines), Marunouchi south exit. **Rooms** 57. **Rates** ¥39,000-¥60,000 double. **Credit** AmEx, DC, JCB, MC, V. **Map** p77.
The Four Seasons, in the heart of the city's business district, is decorated in cool, modern timber and is beautifully lit. The rooms are among the biggest of any Tokyo hotel, and some have great views. Service is multilingual and impeccable, as you're entitled to expect for the price. Each room comes with high-speed internet access, a 42in plasma-screen TV with surround sound and a DVD player. *Bar. Business centre. Concierge. Gym. Internet (high-speed). No-smoking rooms. Parking (¥5,000/night). Restaurant. Room service (24hr). Spa.*

Mandarin Oriental Tokyo
2-1-1 Nihonbashi-Muromachi, Chuo-ku (3270 8800, www.mandarinoriental.com/tokyo). Mitsukoshimae station (Ginza line), exit A7. **Rooms** 157. **Rates** ¥45,000-¥55,000 double. **Credit** AmEx, DC, JCB, MC, V.
The Mandarin is the antidote to that feeling that luxury hotels are the same the world over. Many of the materials are sourced from artisans local not just to Tokyo but the to Nihonbashi district in which the hotel sits. The lobby and rooms all hint at traditional Japanese motifs, from the *torii* shrine gates and *washi* paper lanterns to the woven fabrics that hang in place of paintings. The view from the rooms trumps most of its top-end rivals, with a mosaic of lights from the business district in the foreground, and Mt Fuji straight ahead. Facilities include a trio of restaurants with a Michelin star apiece. *Bar. Business centre. Concierge. Disabled-adapted room. Gym. Internet (high-speed). Non-smoking floors. Parking (¥5,000/night). Restaurants (4). Spa.*

Shangri-La
Marunouchi Trust Tower, 1-8-3 Marunouchi, Chiyoda-ku (6739 7888). Tokyo station (Yamanote, Marunouchi lines), Yaesu North exit. **Rooms** 200. **Rates** ¥38,000-¥48,000 double. **Credit** AmEx, DC, JCB, MC, V. **Map** p77.
Tokyo's newest luxury hotel adjoins Tokyo station – a convenient, if somewhat uninspiring, location. It's another high-rise hotel, offering impressive views of the city or Tokyo Bay. It also provides the flawless service you would expect, with a decor that strikes the right balance between sparkle and comfort, and a sensual palette of maroon and wood in the rooms. *Bar. Business centre. Concierge. Disabled-adapted room. Gym. Internet (high-speed). No-smoking rooms. Parking (¥3,000/night). Restaurant. Room service (24hr). Spa.*

CONSUME

World Class

Perfect places to stay, eat and explore.

Expensive

Hilltop Hotel

1-1 Kanda-Surugadai, Chiyoda-ku (3293 2311, www.yamanoue-hotel.co.jp). Ochanomizu station (Chuo, Marunouchi lines), Ochanomizubashi exit. **Rooms** 74. **Rates** ¥18,900-¥25,200 double. **Credit** AmEx, DC, JCB, MC, V. **Map** p77.

Not many hotels in Tokyo can be said to exude genuine charm, so the Hilltop deserves some credit for retaining its old-fashioned traditions, with antique writing desks and small private gardens for the more expensive suites. That said, its seventh storey, called the Art Septo Floor, offers funky furniture and decor, plus large-screen TVs and enhanced stereos. Known throughout Tokyo as a literary hangout, the Hilltop tries to boost the concentration of those with writer's block by pumping ionised air into every room.

Bars (3). Internet (high-speed). Japanese & Western rooms. Parking (¥1,000/night). Restaurants (5). Room service (7am-2am).

Marunouchi Hotel

1-6-3 Marunouchi, Chiyoda-ku (3217 1111, www.marunouchi-hotel.co.jp). Tokyo station (Yamanote line), Marunouchi north exit; (Marunouchi line), exit 12. **Rooms** 205. **Rates** ¥26,765-¥44,400 double. **Credit** AmEx, DC, JCB, MC, V. **Map** p77.

There's been a Marunouchi Hotel since 1924; its latest incarnation opened in the Oazo (*see p197*) complex in 2004. The lobby is on the seventh floor, from where a spectacular atrium soars through the centre of the hotel. Rooms (which vary considerably in size) are on the ninth to 17th floors – hence some fantastic views over the train tracks of neighbouring Tokyo station – and major in sumptuous materials in a palette of browns and golds. Altogether a classy joint. *Photo p130.*

Bar. Disabled-adapted rooms. Internet (high-speed). No-smoking rooms. Parking (¥1,500/night). Restaurants (6). Room service (7am-10pm).

Moderate

Hotel Kazusaya

4-7-15 Nihonbashi-Honcho, Chuo-ku (3241 1045, www.h-kazusaya.co.jp). Kanda station (Yamanote, Ginza lines), east exit; Mitsukoshimae station (Ginza, Hanzomon lines), exit A10 or Shin-Nihonbashi station (Sobu Kaisoku line), exit 8. **Rooms** 71. **Rates** ¥10,500-¥12,600 double. **Credit** AmEx, DC, JCB, MC, V. **Map** p77.

You'd be hard pushed to know it from the modern exterior of the current building, but there has been a Hotel Kazusaya in Nihonbashi since 1891, located in what is now one of the last *shitamachi* areas in the heart of Tokyo's business district. Inside, you'll find good-sized, functionally furnished rooms, including one Japanese-style tatami room (¥22,050-¥25,200 for

three to four guests). Service is obliging, although only minimal English is spoken by most staff.
Internet (high-speed). Japanese & Western rooms. No-smoking rooms. Parking (¥2,100/ night). Restaurant.

Kayabacho Pearl Hotel

1-2-5 Shinkawa, Chuo-ku (3553 8080, www. pearlhotel.co.jp/kayabacho). Kayabacho station (Hibiya, Tozai lines), exit 4B. **Rooms** 268. **Rates** ¥10,500-¥12,600 double. **Credit** AmEx, DC, JCB, MC, V. **Map** p77.

A business hotel in the heart of the business district, the Pearl has good-sized, well-furnished rooms and reasonable service. Staff speak some English. An unexpected plus is the canalside location.
Business centre. No-smoking rooms. Parking (¥1,500/night). Restaurant.

Ryokan Ryumeikan Honten

3-4 Kanda-Surugadai, Chiyoda-ku (3251 1135, www.ryumeikan.co.jp/honten.html). Ochanomizu

Hilltop Hotel.

Marunouchi Hotel. *See p129.*

station (Chuo, Marunouchi lines), Hijiribashi exit. **Rooms** 12. **Rates** ¥17,000-¥18,000 double. **Credit** AmEx, DC, JCB, MC, V. **Map** p77.

Just south of Ochanomizu's Russian Nikolai Cathedral, this *ryokan* is modern and clean, with helpful staff and good-sized Japanese rooms. In an architectural sense, though, it's a nightmare, occupying part of a modern office block that blends completely into the surrounding skyscrapers. The interior is a testament to how ingeniously the Japanese can disguise the shortcomings of a building to produce a pleasant atmosphere, but you still might find yourself wishing you'd stayed somewhere a little more traditional. The branch in Nihonbashi is slightly cheaper and more imposing.

Internet (high-speed). Japanese rooms only. Parking (free). Restaurant. Room service (7.30am-10pm).

Other locations Hotel Yaesu Ryumeikan, 1-3-22 Yaesu, Chuo-ku (3271 0971).

Budget

Hotel Nihonbashi Saibo

3-3-16 Nihonbashi-Ningyocho, Chuo-ku (3668 2323, www.hotel-saibo.co.jp). Ningyocho station (Asakusa, Hibiya lines), exit A4. **Rooms** 126. **Rates** ¥10,920 double. **Credit** AmEx, DC, JCB, V. **Map** p77.

The good news for anyone looking to stay in this quiet area not far from Tokyo station is that while the Saibo has remodelled its interior and guest

rooms – rooms are still small and services sparse, however – the bargain rates have been retained. A good bet for solo travellers looking for functional and relatively modern accommodation.

Internet (high-speed, shared terminal). Restaurants (2).

Sakura Hotel

2-21-4 Kanda-Jinbocho, Chiyoda-ku (3261 3939, www.sakura-hotel.co.jp). Jinbocho station (Hanzomon, Mita, Shinjuku lines), exits A1, A6. **Rooms** 43. **Rates** ¥8,200 double. **Credit** AmEx, DC, JCB, MC, V. **Map** p77.

Of all the budget hotels and *ryokan* in Tokyo, this is the most central, located in the Jinbocho district just a mile or so north of the Imperial Palace. Small groups can use the dorm rooms, which sleep six. Rooms are tiny but clean, and all are no-smoking. Staff are on duty 24 hours a day and speak good English. Book well in advance.

Internet (shared terminal). No smoking. Restaurant.

YMCA Asia Youth Centre

2-5-5 Sarugakucho, Chiyoda-ku (3233 0611, www.ymcajapan.org/ayc). Suidobashi station (Chuo line), east exit; (Mita line), exit A1. **Rooms** 55. **Rates** ¥9,240-¥11,550 double. **Credit** JCB, MC, V.

Part of the Korean YMCA in Japan, this centre offers many of the same facilities and services you'd expect at a regular hotel, a fact reflected in its relatively

high prices. In terms of location, it shares many advantages with the nearby Hilltop Hotel (*see p129*). The smallish singles, twins and triples are Western in style, with their own bathrooms.
Internet (shared terminals). Restaurant.

ODAIBA
Deluxe

Le Meridien Grand Pacific Tokyo
2-6-1 Daiba, Minato-ku (5500 6711, www.grand pacific.jp/eng). Daiba station (Yurikamome line). **Rooms** 884. **Rates** ¥39,000-¥57,000 double. **Credit** AmEx, DC, JCB, MC, V. **Map** p83.
Location is both the strength and weakness of this decade-old luxury hotel. Odaiba makes a lousy base for touring Tokyo, but the island offers spectacular views of Rainbow Bridge and the Tokyo skyline. Perhaps to compensate for the lack of local character, the hotel supplies some of its own with a photography gallery and a 30th-floor bar with great views. It is also one of the few Tokyo hotels to boast of having an outdoor pool.
Bars (3). Business centre. Concierge. Disabled-adapted rooms. Gym. No-smoking rooms. Parking (¥1,000/night). Pools (indoor, outdoor). Restaurants (7). Room service (6am-1am). Spa.

ROPPONGI & AKASAKA
Deluxe

Grand Hyatt Tokyo
6-10-3 Roppongi, Minato-ku (4333 1234, www.tokyo.grand.hyatt.com). Roppongi station (Hibiya line), exit 1C; (Oedo line), exit 3. **Rooms** 390. **Rates** ¥32,000-¥44,000 double. **Credit** AmEx, DC, MC, V. **Map** p87.

Though it shares a celebrity buzz with its sister hotel the Park Hyatt, the effortlessly sleek Grand is pleasingly low-key. Its location in the upmarket Roppongi Hills complex might not suit those who like their Tokyo served straight up, but by the same token it provides a restful retreat. And having high-end shops and restaurants, a 53-floor panorama and world-class art on your doorstep can be considered quite an amenity. As is the Nagomi spa (though there's a charge for guests), which, in addition to the usual list of artful treatments, has a lap pool, steam and sauna, and a luminous white jacuzzi. Its palette is taupe and cream, marble and wood – as it is in the relatively modest number of guest rooms. Though not flashy, these are extremely comfortable and well thought out, with dimmable lights, Bose stereos and free high-speed internet, and a tub you could park your car in.
Bars (3). Business centre. Concierge. Gym. Internet (high-speed). No-smoking rooms. Parking (¥3,000/night). Pool (indoor). Restaurants (7). Room service (24hr). Spa.

Hotel New Otani Tokyo
4-1 Kioi-cho, Chiyoda-ku (3265 1111, www.newotani.co.jp/en/tokyo). Akasaka-Mitsuke station (Ginza, Marunouchi lines), exit D or Nagatacho station (Hanzomon, Nanboku, Yurakucho lines), exit 7. **Rooms** 1,600. **Rates** ¥34,000-¥40,000 double. **Credit** AmEx, DC, JCB, MC, V.
The New Otani sprawls like a mini metropolis over a vast area that's just ten minutes' walk west of the Imperial Palace. From the outside, the building bears the unattractive hallmarks of its 1969 construction (capacity was increased in the late '70s by the addition of a 40-storey tower block). Inside, however, the dim lighting and spacious foyers produce the feeling of a luxury cruise ship. To the rear

---

Tokyo's Best Hotel Bars
Nothing lost in translation here...

Bar à Vins Tateru Yoshino
Park Hotel Tokyo. *See p126*.
Not only is this an outpost of the Scotch Malt Whisky Society, with an extraordinary menu of malts, but head bartender Takayuki Suzuki runs an on-site school teaching the cocktail craft to other bartenders.

G1
Hotel Seiyo Ginza. *See p125*.
The moodiest hotel bar in Tokyo is also the most exclusive. This small, barely lit room with a black and gold colour scheme is open only to hotel guests or members, who must be over 35 and pay ¥30,000 a year.

New York Bar
Park Hyatt Tokyo. *See p135*.
Familiar to viewers of *Lost in Translation*, this is the only hotel bar in Tokyo that can truly be called an institution. The view, demure lighting, drinks, superb service and background jazz add up to pure romance.

Polestar
Keio Plaza Hotel. *See p136*.
The Keio Plaza bartenders utterly dominate the annual Japan Hotel Bartending Association, winning about 50 per cent of the national competitions. You won't find better cocktails in another Tokyo bar.

of the hotel is a beautifully laid-out and lovingly tended Japanese garden. Within the garden stand several of the hotel's numerous restaurants, which include the only branch of the legendary Parisian eaterie La Tour d'Argent.

Bars (6). Business centre. Concierge. Disabled-adapted rooms. Gym. Internet (high-speed). Japanese & Western rooms. No-smoking rooms. Parking (free). Pools (indoor, outdoor). Restaurants (26). Room service (6am-1am). Spa.

Hotel Okura Tokyo

2-10-4 Toranomon, Minato-ku (3582 0111, www.okura.com/tokyo). Roppongi-Itchome station (Nanboku line), exit 3 or Tameike-Sanno station (Ginza, Nanboku lines), exit 13. **Rooms** 858. **Rates** ¥42,000-¥126,000 double. **Credit** AmEx, DC, JCB, MC, V. **Map** p87.

The Okura, next door to the US Embassy, doesn't appear to have changed much in the last half century. The huge wooden lobby's gold and beige decor evokes a bygone era, while the guest rooms offer an antiquated fusion of European and Japanese styles. But the Okura is taking steps to modernise itself, such as two 'Relaxation Floors' that feature jet baths, saunas and massage services in plush new rooms.

Bars (3). Business centre. Concierge. Disabled-adapted rooms. Gym. Internet (high-speed). No-smoking rooms. Parking (free). Pools (indoor, outdoor). Restaurants (9). Room service (24hr). Spa.

★ Ritz-Carlton Tokyo

Tokyo Midtown, 9-7-1 Akasaka, Minato-ku (3423 8000, www.ritzcarlton.com). Roppongi station (Hibiya, Oedo lines), exit 8. **Rooms** 248. **Rates** ¥45,000-¥70,000 double. **Credit** AmEx, DC, JCB, MC, V. **Map** p87.

Ten years ago, nobody would have believed that a Ritz-Carlton could exist in the party heartland of Roppongi – but what a difference a decade makes. This carnival of opulence is a perfect fit for the luxurious Tokyo Midtown complex. The hotel has a towering lobby, Bulgari amenities, bathrooms big enough to live in, and, with rooms all on the 47th floor or higher, unforgettable city views guaranteed. If you pick the Ritz, be sure to book a club room. It's only a small hike in the rate and you get access to the plush Club Lounge where you can take breakfast in style and enjoy free bubbly in the evening. Anything less just wouldn't be the Ritz.

Bar. Business centre. Concierge. Disabled-adapted rooms. Gym. Internet (high-speed). No-smoking floors. Parking (¥5,000). Pool (indoor). Restaurants (2). Room service (24hr). Spa.

Expensive

★ ANA InterContinental Tokyo

1-12-33 Akasaka, Minato-ku (3505 1111, www.anaintercontinental-tokyo.jp). Tameike-Sanno station (Ginza, Nanboku lines), exit 13. **Rooms** 901. **Rates** ¥26,000-¥36,000 double. **Credit** AmEx, DC, JCB, MC, V. **Map** p87.

In 2007, owners All Nippon Airways joined forces with the InterContinental chain and rebranded this 29-storey hotel. Its airy lobby has been redone in gleaming marble and cherry wood, with the modern space broken up by cascading waterfalls and artworks. Spacious, well-equipped rooms have all been renovated, and by snaring Pierre Gagnaire to open a restaurant the hotel has signalled its intention to compete with the luxury leaders. The hotel provides stunning views on a clear day – you can see Mt Fuji from the open-air rooftop pool.

Bars (3). Business centre. Concierge. Disabled-adapted room. Gym. Internet (high-speed). No-smoking rooms. Parking (¥1,000/night). Pool (outdoor). Restaurants (6). Room service (6am-2am). Spa.

Hotel Avanshell

2-14-4 Akasaka, Minato-ku (3568 3456, www.avanshell.com). Akasaka station (Chiyoda line), exit 2 or Tameike-Sanno station (Ginza, Nanboku lines), exit 10. **Rooms** 71. **Rates** ¥26,000 double. **Credit** AmEx, DC, JCB, MC, V.

The Avanshell is the latest incarnation of a one-time serviced apartment building on a side street in Akasaka, a fact that's reflected in the mini kitchens and other apartment-style touches. Long-term stays are encouraged, with a range of electronics and other items available to rent. Rooms are designed around five themes, with names such as Zen, Primo and Ultimo, and are pleasingly spacious, with large living and work areas in addition to separate bedrooms.

Internet (high-speed). Japanese & Western rooms. No-smoking floors. Parking (¥1,575/night). Restaurant. Room service (5.30-10pm).

Tokyo Prince Hotel Park Tower

4-8-1 Shibakoen, Minato-ku (5400 1111, www.princehotels.co.jp/parktower-e). Akabanebashi station (Oedo line), Akabanebashi exit. **Rooms** 673. **Rates** ¥20,000-¥25,000 double. **Credit** AmEx, DC, JCB, MC, V.

Occupying the corner of Shiba Park next to the Tokyo Tower, this 33-storey luxury hotel opened in spring 2005, offering everything from a jazz bar to a natural hot-spring spa. All rooms have internet service, jet baths and balconies with views across the park and as far as Mt Fuji, plus all the amenities you'd expect for the price. The Royal Suite even comes with a full-time butler.

Bars (3). Business centre. Concierge. Disabled-adapted rooms. Gym. Internet (high-speed). Japanese & Western rooms. No-smoking rooms. Parking (¥1,500). Pool (indoor). Restaurants (7). Room service (24hr). Spa.

CONSUME

Ritz-Carlton Tokyo.

Moderate

Hotel Arca Torre Roppongi

6-1-23 Roppongi, Minato-ku (3404 5111, www. arktower.co.jp/arcatorre). Roppongi station (Hibiya, Oedo lines), exit 3. **Rooms** 77. **Rates** ¥14,700-¥17,850. **Credit** AmEx, DC, MC, V. **Map** p87.

Arca Torre is a smart, bright, high(ish)-rise business hotel sandwiched between the adults' playground of Roppongi and the Roppongi Hills complex. Rooms are small and functional. The vibe is vaguely Italian, with lots of marble flourishes and a first-floor café. For nightlife lovers, the hotel's location is hard to beat, but light sleepers will bemoan the noisy streets. *Disabled-adapted room. No-smoking rooms. Restaurants (2).*

Hotel Ibis

7-14-4 Roppongi, Minato-ku (3403 4411, www. ibis-hotel.com). Roppongi station (Hibiya, Oedo lines), exit 4A. **Rooms** 182. **Rates** ¥17,000-¥21,000 double. **Credit** AmEx, DC, JCB, MC. **Map** p87.

Hard to believe, but less than a decade ago, this was the closest hotel to the centre of Roppongi. Now, with all the competition, Hotel Ibis is looking a little worn, and customers may well be enticed elsewhere. That said, it's always clean, functional and good value. And perhaps no other can claim to embody Roppongi more effectively, with a gentlemen's club off the front desk, a karaoke lounge downstairs, plus Italian and Vietnamese restaurants thrown into the mix. *Bar. Disabled-adapted rooms. Internet (shared terminal). No-smoking rooms. Parking (¥2,100/night). Restaurants (3).*

Budget

Asia Center of Japan

8-10-32 Akasaka, Minato-ku (3402 6111, www. asiacenter.or.jp). Nogizaka station (Chiyoda line), exit 3. **Rooms** 173. **Rates** ¥8,820-¥11,130 double. **Credit** AmEx, JCB, MC, V.

Founded by the Ministry of Foreign Affairs in the 1950s as a cheap place for visiting students to stay, this has long since outgrown its origins and offers comfortable, no-frills accommodation to all visitors on a budget. A new building was added in 2003, presenting a greater variety of Western-style rooms, with clean if unexciting furnishings. The in-house dining hall offers a gathering place and a decent breakfast buffet for a reasonable ¥945. A good choice for those who don't want to sacrifice location in favour of price, the Asia Center of Japan is conveniently situated for the Aoyama area. *Disabled-adapted rooms. Internet (high-speed). No-smoking floor. Parking (¥1,500/night). Restaurant.*

SHIBUYA

Deluxe

Cerulean Tower Tokyu Hotel

26-1 Sakuragaokacho, Shibuya-ku (3476 3000, www.ceruleantower-hotel.com). Shibuya station (Yamanote, Ginza lines), south exit; (Fukutoshin, Hanzomon lines), exit 8. **Rooms** 411. **Rates** ¥41,000-¥81,500 double. **Credit** AmEx, MC, V. **Map** p93.

CONSUME

Tatami Treats

Bed down in a traditional Japanese inn.

If you can bear to forgo a small number of home comforts, then staying in a *ryokan* (traditional Japanese inn) is a great choice, particularly since they tend to be cheaper than Western-style hotels. *Ryokan* also make excellent lodgings for groups: you can have as many futons as you can fit on the tatami (straw mat) floor, for an extra charge that is significantly less than the price of another room.

There are a few matters of *ryokan* etiquette. First, remove your shoes when entering. Staff will show you to your room, and introduce you to the waiting flask of hot water and green tea. Decor will include a *shoji* (sliding paper screen) and a *tokonoma* (alcove), which is for decoration, not for storing luggage. Inside the cupboard you will find a *yukata* (dressing gown) and *tanzen*

(bed jacket), which can be worn inside the inn and double as pyjamas. When putting on a *yukata*, put the left side over the right.

By day the futons are folded away in a cupboard. Staff will make up the futons at around 8pm. They'll be back the following morning at about 8am with breakfast. More expensive *ryokan* usually have private bathrooms, but at the cheaper end of the scale you'll be expected to bathe Japanese-style in a communal bath. (For tips on bathing etiquette, *see p50* **Old Soaks**.)

Most *ryokan* are family-run businesses, so many impose a curfew of 11pm. If you're going to be out later, be sure to tell your hosts. If a curfew doesn't suit you, check with the individual *ryokan* in advance. We've listed some of the best choices in this chapter.

It may be outshone in the luxury market by the myriad new entrants, but the Cerulean is Shibuya's lone top-end establishment and, with rooms on the 19th to 37th floors of the area's tallest building, it offers grandstand views. In addition to the usual restaurants and bars, it has a *Noh* theatre (*see p271*) and a jazz club, JZ Brat (*see p255*). Room furnishings are a step down from the likes of the Grand Hyatt, but so is the price. Except, that is, for the 35th to 37th Executive Floors, which offer free access to the gym, newspapers, web TV and refreshments in the salon. *Bars (2). Business centre. Concierge. Disabled-adapted rooms. Gym. Internet (high-speed). Japanese & Western rooms. No-smoking rooms. Parking (¥2,000). Pool (indoor). Restaurants (6). Room service (24hr). Spa.*

Expensive

Excel Hotel Tokyu

Shibuya Mark City, 1-12-2 Dogenzaka, Shibuya-ku (5457 0109, www.tokyuhotelsjapan.com). Shibuya station (Yamanote, Ginza, Hanzomon lines). **Rooms** 408. **Rates** ¥24,255-¥28,875 double. **Credit** AmEx, DC, JCB, MC, V. **Map** p93.
Situated in the Mark City complex attached to Shibuya station, the Excel is very popular with domestic visitors wanting to spend their stay in the capital in the heart of Shibuya. Pleasant and clean, with spacious rooms and nice views, it's one of few good-quality hotels in this part of town. There are six special floors: two for women only, with added security; three for business travellers; and a 'Healing Floor', with aromatherapy, soothing music and relaxation programmes.

Bar. Concierge. Disabled-adapted rooms. Internet. No-smoking floors. Parking (¥2,000/ night). Restaurants (2). Room service (7-10am; 9pm-midnight). Spa.

Moderate

★ Granbell Hotel

15-17 Sakuragaoka-cho, Shibuya-ku (5457 2681, www.granbellhotel.jp). Shibuya station (Yamanote, Ginza lines), south exit; (Fukutoshin, Hanzomon lines), exit 8. **Rooms** 55. **Rates** ¥21,000-¥26,000 double. **Credit** AmEx, JCB, MC, V. **Map** p93.
With an enviable location, quality service and fun interiors that mix minimalist chic with a splash of pop art, the Granbell has a lot to offer. The single rooms may be on the small side, but the doubles are comfortable and are excellent value.
Bar. Internet (high-speed). No-smoking rooms. Restaurant. Room service (24hr).

★ Hotel Unizo

4-3 Udagawa-cho, Shibuya-ku (5457 7557, www.hotelunizo.com). Shibuya station (Yamanote, Ginza lines), Hachiko exit; (Fukutoshin, Hanzomon lines), exit 3a. **Rooms** 186. **Rates** ¥14,000-¥23,000 double. **Credit** AmEx, DC, JCB, MC, V. **Map** p93.
If you like waking up in the middle of the action, you won't find many hotels better placed than this one. It's in the heart of Shibuya's shopping and nightlife districts, and just a couple of blocks from Yoyogi Park. It's also elegantly furnished with modern Japanese taste, and though the singles and doubles are small, the twins start to look great value. There's

a ladies-only floor to make single women feel safer. The downside: it's a ten-minute trek from the station. *Internet. No-smoking rooms. Restaurant.*
▶ *For visits to Yoyogi Park, see p66.*

SHINJUKU
Deluxe

Hilton Tokyo
6-6-2 Nishi-Shinjuku, Shinjuku-ku (3344 5111, www.hilton.com). Nishi-Shinjuku station (Marunouchi line), exit C8 or Tochomae station (Oedo line), exit C8. Free bus from Keio department store (bus stop 21), Shinjuku station, west exit. **Rooms** 806. **Rates** ¥30,000-¥41,000 double. **Credit** AmEx, DC, JCB, MC, V. **Map** p101.
A luxury hotel in west Shinjuku, the Hilton opened in 1984 after vacating its previous premises in Akasaka. Rooms are of a good size, although the views from some – blocked by other towers in the area – can be disappointing. As you'd expect, the standard of service is high. For business travellers, the hotel offers five executive floors, with separate check-in, a fax machine in each room and their own guest relations officers on hand to help out and advise. The Hilton is also one of few Tokyo hotels to have its own tennis courts.
Bar. Business centre. Concierge. Disabled-adapted rooms. Gym. Internet (high-speed). Japanese & Western rooms. No-smoking rooms. Parking (¥1,500/night). Pool (indoor). Restaurants (6). Room service (24hr).
Other locations Hilton Tokyo Bay, 1-8 Maihama, Urayasu-shi, Chiba-ken (047 355 5000).

★ Park Hyatt Tokyo
3-7-1-2 Nishi-Shinjuku, Shinjuku-ku (5322 1234, http://tokyo.park.hyatt.com). Shinjuku station (Yamanote, Marunouchi lines), west exit; (Shinjuku line), exit 6 or Tochomae station (Oedo line), exit A4. Free shuttle bus from in front of Shinjuku L Tower, Shinjuku station, west exit. **Rooms** 178. **Rates** ¥53,000-¥65,000 double. **Credit** AmEx, DC, JCB, MC, V. **Map** p101.
The original top-end Tokyo hotel is still, for many, the best. Though the decor hasn't changed in a decade and a half, it still looks fresh and elegant. The rooms are huge, the furnishings first-class and the city views impressive (the hotel is located atop a skyscraper) – running on a treadmill in the fitness centre at night looking over the city is unforgettable. But it's the service that makes the Park Hyatt stand out: with 15 years of practice, it has mastered the art of hospitality. The downside: it's a shuttle-bus ride or ten-minute walk to the nearest station. But when that station is the world's busiest, it's hard to call it too inconvenient.
Bars (2). Business centre. Concierge. Disabled-adapted rooms. Gym. Internet (high-speed). No-smoking rooms. Parking (free). Pool (indoor). Restaurants (3). Room service (24hr). Spa.

Do not disturb.

Granbell Hotel.

CONSUME

Keio Plaza Hotel.

Expensive

Keio Plaza Hotel

2-2-1 Nishi-Shinjuku, Shinjuku-ku (3344 0111, www.keioplaza.com). Shinjuku station (Yamanote line), west exit; (Marunouchi line), exit A17; (Shinjuku line), exit B1 or Tochomae station (Oedo line), exits A1, B1. **Rooms** 1,450. **Rates** ¥24,000-¥34,000 double. **Credit** AmEx, DC, JCB, MC, V. **Map** p101.

The lavish decor that once made this Tokyo's most prestigious hotel now looks seriously dated compared to its new luxury rivals. The location, however, is still pretty tough to beat: a stone's throw from the world's busiest train station, with upper floors offering superb views of the metropolis. It's gradually renovating its rooms, meaning there's a choice of modern, elegant furnishings or gruesome '80s designs. Be sure to specify a renovated room. The Polestar bar is famous nationwide for its top-class bartending.

Bars (4). Business centre. Disabled-adapted rooms. Gym. Internet (high-speed). No-smoking rooms. Parking (¥1,000/night). Pool (outdoor). Restaurants (13). Room service (24hr).

Moderate

★ Citadines Tokyo Shinjuku

1-28-13 Shinjuku, Shinjuku-ku (5379 7208, www.citadines.com). Shinjuku San-chome station (Fukutoshin line), exit C7 or Shinjuku Gyoen-mae station (Marunouchi line), exit 2. **Rooms** 160. **Rates** ¥21,000-¥23,100 double. **Credit** AmEx, DC, JCB, MC, V.

Had Ikea designed this hotel, it would probably look much the same as this. Simple, bright and practical furnishings give the rooms an airy feel. Fully equipped kitchens let you self-cater, which can

make trips to the Tsukiji market or the department store food floors a lot more fun. For travellers on a budget, this hotel offers exceptional value.

Gym. Internet (high-speed). Restaurant.

Shinjuku Washington Hotel

3-2-9 Nishi-Shinjuku, Shinjuku-ku (3343 3111, www.wh-rsv.com/english/shinjuku). Shinjuku station (Yamanote, Marunouchi lines), south exit; (Oedo, Shinjuku lines), exits 6, 7. **Rooms** 1,296. **Rates** ¥15,000-¥19,200 double. **Credit** AmEx, DC, JCB, MC, V. **Map** p101.

A step down in price and luxury from other west Shinjuku hotels, the Washington nonetheless offers a high standard of accommodation and service. Its main target market is business travellers, so rooms tend to be small and blandly furnished. Also, there is now a women-only floor, and a business floor with upgraded amenities. The newer annex (containing 337 rooms) offers roughly the same level of service, with more modern decor.

Bar. Disabled-adapted rooms. Internet (high-speed). No-smoking rooms. Parking (¥100-¥250/ 30mins). Restaurants (2). Room service (main building 6-11pm; annex 6-10pm).

▶ For the new sister property, the Akihabara Washington Hotel, see p139.

Star Hotel Tokyo

7-10-5 Nishi-Shinjuku, Shinjuku-ku (3361 1111, www.starhotel.co.jp/city/tokyo.html). Shinjuku station (Yamanote line), west exit; (Marunouchi, Shinjuku lines), exit D4 or Shinjuku-Nishiguchi station (Oedo line), exit D4. **Rooms** 214. **Rates** ¥14,700-¥17,850 double. **Credit** AmEx, JCB, MC, V. **Map** p101.

In terms of position, the Star offers everything its more expensive west Shinjuku rivals do. Tucked

among all-night restaurants on a noisy main road, it's a great location from which to base your Tokyo explorations, with the red-light district of Kabuki-cho on one side and access to the rest of the city via Shinjuku station on the other. Rooms are tiny and frill-free, but the Star has made some cosmetic upgrades and remains one of the best options on its side of Shinjuku.
Bar. Internet (high-speed). No-smoking rooms. Parking (¥1,500/night). Restaurants (3). Room service (5-10pm).

UENO & AROUND
Moderate

★ Homeikan Honkan/Daimachibekkan
5-10-5 Hongo, Bunkyo-ku (3811 1181 Honkan, 3811 1186 Daimachibekkan, www.homeikan. com). Hongo-Sanchome station (Marunouchi line), Hongo-Nichome exit; (Oedo line), exit 2 or Kasuga station (Mita line), exits A5, A6. **Rooms** *Honkan 24; Daimachibekkan 30.* **Rates** ¥11,500 double. **Credit** AmEx, DC, JCB, MC, V.
This wonderful old *ryokan* in the sleepy streets of Hongo looks just like a Japanese inn ought to: wooden, glass-fronted and with an ornamental garden at the front. And its owners plan to keep it that way following the *ryokan*'s designation as an important cultural property by the Ministry of Education. Be sure to have a word with Homeikan's cordial, English-speaking manager Kunio Koike when making a reservation – he can help you choose a room and, if need be, direct you away from the rowdy Japanese students who often lodge here. The inn is divided into two buildings, which face each other, with another branch a five-minute walk away. The only drawback is its location, around 20 minutes' walk from the nearest real action around Ueno or Ochanomizu stations. Long-stay rates are available.
Internet (shared terminal). Parking (free). Room service (7am-10pm).
Other locations Morikawabekkan, 6-23-5 Hongo, Bunkyo-ku (3811 8171).

Ueno First City Hotel
1-14-8 Ueno, Taito-ku (3831 8215, www.uenocity-hotel.com). Yushima station (Chiyoda line), exit 6. **Rooms** 77. **Rates** ¥11,500-¥13,600 double. **Credit** AmEx, DC, JCB, MC, V. **Map** p107.
A cut above the normal business hotel, this place offers comfortable Western- and Japanese-style accommodation in a modern, red-brick block not far from Ueno Park and its myriad attractions.
Bar. Internet. Japanese & Western rooms. No-smoking rooms. Restaurant.

Budget

Hotel Edoya
3-20-3 Yushima, Bunkyo-ku (3833 8751, www. hoteledoya.com). Yushima station (Chiyoda line),

exit 5. **Rooms** 49. **Rates** ¥8,540-¥12,930 double. **Credit** AmEx, DC, JCB, MC, V. **Map** p107.
This mainly Japanese-style *ryokan*, not far from Ueno Park, offers a good standard of accommodation at reasonable prices. There's a small Japanese tearoom and garden on the first floor, and the roof has an open-air hot bath for both men and women.
Japanese & Western rooms. Parking (free). Restaurant.

Ryokan Katsutaro
4-16-8 Ikenohata, Taito-ku (3821 9808, www. katsutaro.com). Nezu station (Chiyoda line), exit 2. **Rooms** 7. **Rates** (for 2 people) ¥8,400-¥9,600. **Credit** AmEx, MC, V. **Map** p107.
In a backstreet on the northern side of Ueno Park, Katsutaro is a small, friendly *ryokan* with good-sized rooms and the atmosphere of a real family home (which it is). Rooms come with or without bath and can be occupied by up to four people, at an extra charge of roughly ¥4,000 per person. The owner speaks a little English, but have a phrasebook handy if you want the conversation to progress. Just a short walk away is the Annex (¥10,500-¥12,600 double), which is more modern and has more facilities.
Internet (high-speed, shared terminal). Japanese rooms only. Parking (free).
Other locations Annex, 3-8-4 Yanaka, Taito-ku (3828 2500).

Ueno Tsukuba Hotel
2-7-8 Moto-Asakusa, Taito-ku (3834 2556, www.hotelink.co.jp/tsukuba). Inaricho station (Ginza line), exit 2. **Rooms** 111. **Rates** ¥6,600 double. **No credit cards**. **Map** p107.
A basic business hotel in Ueno, the Tsukuba is clean and offers good value. Rooms are tiny, so opt for a Japanese-style room, where the futon is cleared away in the morning. Western-style rooms have baths, but if you stay in a Japanese room you'll be expected to bathe Japanese-style in the communal bath on the ground floor. The hotel is two minutes' walk from Inaricho station on the Ginza line.
Internet (high-speed, wireless). Japanese & Western rooms. Parking (¥2,000/night).
Other locations Iriya Station Hotel, 1-25-1 Iriya, Taito-ku (3872 7111).

YANAKA
Budget

Ryokan Sawanoya
2-3-11 Yanaka, Taito-ku (3822 2251, www. tctv.ne.jp/members/sawanoya). Nezu station (Chiyoda line), exit 1. **Rooms** 12. **Rates** ¥9,240-¥9,870 double. **Credit** AmEx, MC, V. **Map** p107.
One of the few *ryokan* to cater almost exclusively for foreign visitors, Sawanoya has a small library of English-language guidebooks and provides its own map of the old-style Yanaka area. Rooms are small

CONSUME

but comfortable, and there are signs in English reminding you how to behave and how to use the bath. More expensive rooms have their own bath; cheaper ones have access to the communal bath and shower. There's also a small coffee lounge. The couple who own the place will do everything possible to make your stay enjoyable.

Internet (high-speed, shared terminal). Japanese rooms only. No smoking.

ELSEWHERE IN CENTRAL TOKYO

Deluxe

Four Seasons Hotel Tokyo at Chinzan-so

2-10-8 Sekiguchi, Bunkyo-ku (3943 2222, www.fourseasons.com/tokyo). Mejiro station (Yamanote line), then 61 bus or Edogawabashi station (Yurakucho line), exit 1A. **Rooms** 283. **Rates** ¥43,000-¥69,000 double. **Credit** AmEx, DC, JCB, V.

Inconveniently located in the wilds of northern Tokyo, this is a breathtakingly opulent and beautiful hotel that's popular with locals on weekend escapes and celebrities seeking privacy away from the bright lights of the city. Take a stroll around the Japanese garden – with its own firefly population, as well as ancient statues from Nara and Kamakura – then enjoy the wide open spaces of the lobby area. Everything is immaculate, from the service to the decor of the rooms, a mixture of old Japanese and European styles.

Bars (2). Business centre. Concierge. Disabled-adapted rooms. Gym. Internet (high-speed). No-smoking rooms. Parking (free). Pool (indoor). Restaurants (4). Room service (24hr). Spa.

InterContinental Tokyo Bay

1-16-2 Kaigan, Minato-ku (5404 2222, www.interconti-tokyo.com). Hamamatsucho station (Yamanote line), south exit or Takeshiba station (Tokyo monorail). **Rooms** 336. **Rates** ¥36,000-¥43,000 double. **Credit** AmEx, DC, JCB, MC, V.

The InterContinental opened in the mid 1990s in the hitherto little-explored area that fronts Tokyo's Sumida river. Amid the grim industrial surroundings, the luxurious hotel and the adjoining New Pier Takeshiba shopping and dining complex stand out like a diamond in a cowpat. If its location is the hotel's main shortcoming, then its prime selling point must certainly be the view over the river and across the spectacular Rainbow Bridge to the island of Odaiba (*see pp81-84*). All of the rooms – and their bathrooms – have a river prospect.

Bars (2). Business centre. Concierge. Internet (high-speed). No-smoking rooms. Parking (¥1,500/night). Restaurants (5). Room service (24hr). Spa.

Strings Hotel Tokyo

Shinagawa East One Tower 26F-32F, 2-16-1 Konan, Minato-ku (5783 1111, www.intercontinental-strings.jp). Shinagawa station (Yamanote line), Konan exit. **Rooms** 206. **Rates** ¥27,000-¥72,000 double. **Credit** AmEx, DC, JCB, MC, V.

When it opened in 2003, ANA's Strings Hotel brought a bit of class to the revitalised Shinagawa district. Its rooms occupy the top floors of a gleaming new skyscraper and are decked out in soothing earth tones. The 59 higher-end Club Rooms offer sparkling views over Tokyo Bay, as well as extra amenities, including one complimentary meal per day. The hotel's convenient location just off the JR Tokaido *shinkansen* tracks also makes it a great base for travelling between cities. Shame the service isn't always as polished as the rooms.

Bar. Business centre. Concierge. Disabled-adapted rooms. Gym. Internet. No-smoking rooms. Parking (¥2,500/night). Restaurants (2). Room service (24hr).

Expensive

Le Meridien Hotel Pacific Tokyo

3-13-3 Takanawa, Minato-ku (3445 6711, www.pacific-tokyo.com). Shinagawa station (Yamanote line), Takanawa exit. **Rooms** 800. **Rates** ¥24,000-¥27,000 double. **Credit** AmEx, DC, JCB, MC, V.

This 1971 monolith benefits from a pleasant garden that gives it a sense of space that many Tokyo hotels lack. The hotel might look its age from the outside, and the decor is a mix of bland and garish, but there's no faulting the facilities. Rooms are of a good size and kept bang up to date thanks to what appears to be a constant process of renovation and redecoration. The Shinagawa area hasn't got much to recommend it, though it's a short hop into the centre via the Yamanote line, and the bullet train line makes it a popular choice for business travellers. This is one of the hotels frequently used by travel companies for package tours and stopovers.

Bars (3). Business centre. Concierge. Disabled-adapted rooms. Internet (high-speed). No-smoking rooms. Parking (free). Pool (outdoor). Restaurants (6). Room service (6am-midnight). Spa.

Takanawa Prince Hotel, New Takanawa Prince Hotel & Sakura Tower
3-13-1 Takanawa, Minato-ku (3447 1111, www.princehotels.com/en/takanawa). Shinagawa station (Yamanote line), Takanawa exit then free shuttle bus. **Rooms** *Takanawa Prince 414. New Takanawa Prince 946. Sakura Tower 309.* **Rates** ¥24,000 double. **Credit** AmEx, DC, JCB, MC, V.
The Takanawa Prince, the New Takanawa Prince and the Sakura Tower – all part of the same chain – operate as separate hotels but are linked by glorious landscaped grounds. Guests can use the facilities of all three. The oldest, the Takanawa Prince, recently remodelled its rooms with new wallpaper, carpeting and furniture, as well as air-con units and LCD TVs. It has also added a number of rooms especially for women. The New Takanawa Prince is gaudy from the outside but impressive within, while the Sakura Tower, a pink monster of a building, offers the most up-to-date facilities and the priciest accommodation. The services listed are for all three hotels combined.
Bars (5). Business centre. Concierge. Disabled-adapted rooms. Gym. Internet (high-speed). Japanese & Western rooms. No-smoking rooms. Parking (free). Pools (2, outdoor). Restaurants (7). Room service (24hr). Spa.

P&A Plaza. *See p141.*

Moderate

Akihabara Washington Hotel
1-8-3 Sakumacho, Kanda, Chiyoda-ku (3255 3311, www.wh-rsv.com/english/akihabara). Akihabara station (Sobu line), Showa Dori exit; (Hibiya line), exit 3. **Rooms** 369. **Rates** ¥17,000-¥19,000 double. **Credit** AmEx, DC, MC, JCB, V.
The Washington hotel chain closed its dowdy Akihabara dive in 2009 and reopened in spring 2010 in brand new digs to attract the geek-culture tourists. Rooms are simple but infinitely more stylish and comfortable than the previous incarnation. There is also a women-only floor.
Bar. Business centre. Internet (high-speed). Restaurant.

Hotel Bellegrande
2-19-1 Ryogoku, Sumida-ku (3631 8111, www.hotel-bellegrande.co.jp). Ryogoku station (Oedo line), west exit. **Rooms** 150.
Rates ¥12,600-¥16,800 double.
Credit AmEx, DC, JCB, V.
A modern, business-style hotel barely a wrestler's stride from the sumo stadium in Ryogoku – a quiet, traditional area that comes alive during the city's three annual sumo tournaments. The unglamorous location is reflected in the prices of the rooms, which are small but comfortable. There are ten designated rooms for women with a few added amenities.
Bar. No-smoking rooms. Parking (¥1,500/night). Restaurants (5).
▶ *For more about sumo wrestling and where you can watch a match, see p280.*

Hotel Monterey Hanzomon
23-1 Ichibancho, Chiyoda-ku (3556 7111, www.hotelmonterey.co.jp/hanzomon). Hanzomon station (Hanzomon line), exit 5. **Rooms** 340.
Rates ¥9,200-¥22,000 double. **Credit** AmEx, DC, JCB, MC, V.
Opened in mid 2006 a stone's throw from the British Embassy and Imperial Gardens, the latest Monterey is a stylish place with rooms elegantly decorated in what they describe as 'Edo taste'. In practice, this means colourful rooms of pinks and yellows, with touches of classic Japanese design. This isn't designer living to the degree offered at Claska, Grand Hyatt Tokyo or the Mandarin Oriental, but it's a comfortable, peaceful option.
Internet (high-speed). No-smoking rooms. Parking (¥1,500). Restaurant.
Other locations Hotel Monterey Ginza, 2-10-2 Ginza, Chuo-ku (3544 7111); Hotel Monterey Lasouer Ginza, 1-10-18 Ginza, Chuo-ku (3562 7111).

Budget

Tokyo International Youth Hostel
Central Plaza 18F, 1-1 Kagurashiki, Shinjuku-ku (3235 1107, www.tokyo-ih.jp). Iidabashi station

CONSUME

(Sobu line), west exit; (Nanboku, Oedo,
Tozai, Yurakucho lines), exit 2B. **Rooms** 33.
Rates ¥3,860 per person; ¥2,000 children.
No credit cards.
Shared rooms (men and women sleep separately
here) are the order of the day at this hostel, which
occupies the 18th and 19th floors of a skyscraper
above Iidabashi station. All rooms are perfectly
spotless, and the entire place is no-smoking. Guests
are not allowed into the building between 10am and
3pm. The excellent website is regularly updated
with room availability information; weekends tend
to be booked up ages in advance. And remember
to watch out for that 11pm curfew.
*Disabled-adapted rooms. Japanese & Western
rooms. No smoking.*

FURTHER AFIELD
Expensive

Claska
*1-3-18 Chuo-cho, Meguro-ku (3719 8121,
www.claska.com). Gakugei-Daigaku station
(Tokyu Toyoko line) then 10mins walk.*
Rooms 9. **Rates** ¥22,145-¥98,000 double.
Credit AmEx, DC, JCB, MC, V.
Nine rooms occupying two floors: hotels don't get
much more exclusive than the Claska. Add the
funky designer vibe, and you have Tokyo's only true
boutique hotel. Having opened in 2003 in a refurbished business hotel, the Claska prides itself on
offering a new style of living. Each room is set up
and styled differently, with the most expensive
boasting a 41sq m (441sq ft) terrace. The 'East meets
West' Tatami room is particularly fun. The rest of
the building is taken up by a hip bar/restaurant,
gallery, dog-grooming salon, bookshop and open-
plan workspace. Claska is also one of the city's least
convenient hotels, located a ten-minute walk from
a minor train station.
*Bar. Internet (high-speed). Parking (free).
Restaurant. Room service.*

Budget

Hotel New Koyo
*2-26-13 Nihonzutumi, Taito-ku (3873 0343,
www.newkoyo.jp). Minowa station (Hibiya line),
exit 3.* **Rooms** 75. **Rates** ¥4,800 double.
Credit AmEx, MC, V.
Clean and friendly, with facilities that put more
expensive accommodation to shame (kitchens on
each floor, laundry machines, a Japanese-style
bath), the New Koyo may offer the cheapest
overnight stay in Tokyo. Rooms are tiny, however,
and the place is slightly out of the way, although
central Tokyo is easily accessible from the nearby
Hibiya line station.
*Internet (shared terminal). Japanese
& Western rooms.*

▶ *The owners also run a more traditional
and upmarket Japanese-style inn, the Andon
(www.andon.co.jp), in the same area.*

Juyoh Hotel
*2-15-3 Kiyokawa, Taito-ku (3875 5362,
www.juyoh.co.jp). Minami-Senju station
(Hibiya line), south exit.* **Rooms** 76.
Rates ¥6,400 double. **No credit cards.**
Another cheap option in Taito-ku, the Juyoh caters
almost exclusively for foreign visitors. The rooms
really are minuscule, and since only three of them
are doubles, early booking (via the website) is
essential. The second floor is reserved for female
guests only. Bath and shower facilities are shared.
The hotel has no curfew, setting it apart from quite
a few of its competitors.
*Internet (wireless, shared terminals).
No-smoking rooms.*

OTHER OPTIONS
Minshuku (B&Bs)

Expect to pay around ¥5,000 per night.
You should book at least two days in advance.

Japan Minshuku Centre
*103 Toka Bldg, 3-11-8 Hirai, Edogawa-ku (3683
3396, www.minshuku.jp). Hirai station (JR Sobu
line), south exit.* **Open** 11am-9pm Mon-Sat.

Minshuku Association of Japan
*KS Axe Bldg 3F, 27-6 Haraikatamachi,
Shinjuku-ku (5225 9577, www.minshuku.or.jp).
Ushigome Kagurazaka station (Oedo line),
exit A1.* **Open** noon-5pm Mon-Fri.

Capsule hotels

Central Land Shibuya
*1-19-14 Dogenzaka, Shibuya-ku (3464 1777,
3464 7771, www.shibuyadogenzaka.com
/capsule). Shibuya station (Yamanote,
Ginza, Hanzomon lines), Hachiko exit.*
Capsules 140. **Rates** ¥3,700-¥4,000.
No credit cards. Map p93.

Shinjuku Kuyakusyo-Mae Capsule Hotel
*1-2-5 Kabuki-cho, Shinjuku-ku (3232 1110,
www.toyo-bldg.ne.jp/hotel). Shinjuku station
(Yamanote line), east exit; (Marunouchi line),
exit B7; (Oedo, Shinjuku lines), exit 1.*
Capsules 460. **Rates** from ¥4,200.
No credit cards. Map p101.

Love hotels

In addition to those listed here, there are
also predominantly gay love hotels (*see p249*).

Bron Mode

2-29-7 Kabuki-cho, Shinjuku-ku (3208 6211,
www.hotel-guide.jp/shop/bronmode). Shinjuku
station (Yamanote, Chuo, Sobu lines), east exit;
(Marunouchi line), exit B7; (Shinjuku line),
exit 1 or Shinjuku-Nishiguchi station (Oedo line),
exit D3. **Rates** ¥6,000-¥10,290 rest; ¥11,000-
¥20,790 stay. **Credit** AmEx, DC, JCB, MC, V.
Flashy and futuristic-looking, the Bron Mode fan-
cies itself as a little bit upmarket. Rooms have
karaoke, jet bath/jacuzzi and sauna, and gay and
lesbian couples are welcome.

Hotel Listo

2-36-1 Kabuki-cho, Shinjuku-ku (5155 9255).
Shinjuku station (Yamanote, Chuo, Sobu lines),
east exit; (Marunouchi line), exit B7; (Shinjuku
line), exit 1 or Shinjuku-Nishiguchi station (Oedo
line), exit D3. **Rates** ¥5,200-¥14,700 rest; ¥9,500-
¥28,000 stay. **Credit** AmEx, JCB, MC, V.
A love hotel in Kabuki-cho, this establishment is
surrounded by fir trees, meaning that a certain
level of clandestine discretion is assured.

Meguro Emperor

2-1-6 Shimo-Meguro, Meguro-ku (3494 1211,
www.meguroemperor.com). Meguro station
(Yamanote, Mita, Nanboku lines), west exit.
Rates ¥5,800-¥12,800 rest; ¥9,800-¥19,800
stay. **Credit** AmEx, MC, V. **Map** p53.
A famous Tokyo love hotel, standing on its own
like a fairytale palace. Check in and pay via a
machine in the foyer. Rooms are huge and well furnished. Karaoke, jet bath/sauna and free drinks are
standard, as are microwave ovens. Don't ask.

P&A Plaza

1-17-9 Dogenzaka, Shibuya-ku (3780 5211,
www.paplaza.com). Shibuya station (Yamanote,
Ginza lines), south exit; (Hanzomon line), exit 5.
Rates ¥5,600-¥16,000 rest; ¥9,800-¥29,600 stay.
Credit AmEx, DC, JCB, MC, V. **Map** p93.
One of the most famous love hotels in the capital,
located in Dogenzaka near Shibuya station. The
P&A's top-priced suite contains a swimming pool.
A jet bath or jacuzzi comes as standard in all rooms.
Photo p139.

Love Hotels

Where to spend a few stolen moments.

Japan's chronic lack of any real privacy –
and the thinness of its rice-paper walls –
has helped create a thriving tradition of 'love
hotels'. These short-stay establishments
(usually rented in two-hour blocks) are
ubiquitous, with entire sections of the
capital's neighbourhoods devoted to them.
And while slightly risqué, the use of such
places has much in common with sex in
general in Japan – not talked about openly,
but widely indulged. Love hotels offer such
a quintessentially Japanese experience
that any couple travelling to Tokyo should
try one out, if only for the afternoon.
(For a few suggestions, *see above*.)

The system for using a love hotel varies
from place to place, but the basics are
simple enough. Open around the clock,
they offer rates for different blocks of
time. Overnight rates are relatively cheap
compared to other hotels (so they can
be used as emergency accommodation),
but most will not admit overnight guests
until after 11pm at the earliest, so as
to maximise profit from the day trade.

On entering a hotel, you are typically
faced with pictures of each room with their
prices listed beneath – the cheaper is for
a short 'rest', the higher for an overnight
stay. Only the illuminated rooms are
unoccupied. Push the button on the room

of your choice, then go to the front desk
to collect the key. In cheaper love hotels,
all rooms may be the same, and you simply
go to the service window (you are usually
unable to see the clerk and vice versa)
and pay for the required time. Some hotels
are fully automatic, with machines printing
out room numbers so that guests can avoid
the potential embarrassment of interacting
with another human. Go to your room, lock
the door, and the rest is up to you.

As with any hotel, the more you pay,
the more you're likely to get. Prices for
a two-hour visit range from around ¥3,500
for a room with a bed, TV, bathroom and
nothing more, to ¥15,000-plus for a room
with its own swimming pool, swings and
bondage paraphernalia. All love hotels
have immaculate bathrooms, some with
jacuzzi or sauna, since the Japanese like
to wash before jumping in the sack. When
you leave, pay the person at the desk;
in automatic hotels, simply feed your
money into the talking machine by the door.

The highest concentrations of love hotels
in Tokyo are to be found in the Kabuki-cho
district in Shinjuku, Dogenzaka in Shibuya
and by the railway tracks near Ikebukuro
station, although there are clusters in many
other areas too. You'll even find a sprinkling
in swankier neighbourhoods, such as Ebisu.

CONSUME

Villa Giulia

2-27-8 Dogenzaka, Shibuya-ku (3770 7781).
Shibuya station (Yamanote, Ginza lines),
Hachiko exit; (Hanzomon line), exit 1. **Rates**
¥3,900-¥10,900 rest; ¥7,900-¥19,900 stay.
Credit AmEx, JCB, MC, V. **Map** p93.
From the outside, Villa Giulia looks rather like an
Italian restaurant. Inside, it's clean and fully auto-
matic. Push a button, take a slip for your room, then
follow the spoken (Japanese) instructions to pay.

LONG-TERM ACCOMMODATION

Finding long-term accommodation in Tokyo
can be a nightmare for foreigners. Many
Japanese landlords refuse to deal with the non-
Japanese, so specialist companies have stepped
into the breach to let to foreigners, sometimes
by the week. If you do find something suitable,
it probably won't be cheap. You will be required
to pay a damage deposit (*shikikin*), usually
equivalent to between one and three months'
rent, a brokerage fee (*chukairyo*) to the agent,
usually another month's rent, and finally key
money (*reikin*), usually one or two months' rent
– a non-refundable way of saying thank you
to the landlord for having you. You then have
to find a month's rent in advance.

Deterred by the cost of finding a place of
their own, many foreigners fall back on so-called
gaijin houses – apartment buildings full of
foreigners sharing bathrooms, cooking facilities
and, in some cases, rooms. All the operations
listed below are used to dealing with foreigners
and offer a full range of accommodation.

Asahi Homes

3-2-13 Nishi-Azabu, Minato-ku (3583 7544,
www.asahihomes.co.jp). Roppongi station (Hibiya,
Oedo lines), exit 1b. **Credit** AmEx, DC, MC, V.
Upmarket agency offering fully serviced apartments
in well-chosen locations, with a minimum stay of one
week. Weekly rent starts from ¥80,850 for a studio,
rising to ¥345,450 for a three-bedroom apartment,
including internet access and weekly maid service.

Bamboo House

Office Bamboo Nippori 1F, 2-5-4 Nishi-Nippori,
Ararkawa-ku (3805 3278, www.bamboo-
house.com). Mikawashima station (Joban line).
Rates from ¥3,500 daily; from ¥58,000 monthly.
Credit AmEx, MC, V.
A chain of serviced apartments and guesthouses
scattered across the less fashionable parts of Tokyo
and Chiba. The rooms are 9-12sq m (32-43sq ft), and
have shared facilities.

Cozy House

3-15-11 Ichikawa, Ichikawa City, Chiba-ken
(047 379 1539, www.cozyhouse.net). Konodai
station (Keisei line) then 10mins walk. **Rooms** 7.

Rates from ¥1,200 daily; from ¥57,000 monthly.
Credit (deposit only) MC, V.
Cozy House has two locations: a cheaper one in
more central Kita-ku, and this main branch, slightly
out of the way in Chiba. Its aim is to bring foreigners in Japan together, to which end the incredibly
friendly owner lays on demonstrations of Japanese
crafts and traditions. Cozy House is just a 15-minute
train ride from Tokyo station.
Other locations 15-1 Sakae-cho, Kita-ku
(090 8176 0764).

Hoyo Tokyo

4-19-7 Kita-Shinjuku, Shinjuku (3362 0658,
www.hoyotokyo.jp). Okubo station (Chuo, Sobu
lines), north exit. **Open** 9.30am-6.30pm Mon-Fri.
No credit cards.
An agency with around a thousand units, Hoyo
offers studio apartments from ¥42,000 per week
(plus a deposit of ¥50,000) or ¥135,000 per month.
Family apartments cost from ¥300,000 a month
(¥100,000 deposit).

Oak House

4-8-3 Ikebukuro, Toshima-ku (3981 0091, www.
oakhouse.jp). Ikebukuro station (Yamanote line),
west exit. **No credit cards**.
This guesthouse agency offers private rooms starting from ¥39,000 per month, as well as dorm-style
accommodation, shared rooms and private apartments around the city.

Sakura House

K1 Bldg 2F, 7-2-6 Nishi-Shinjuku, Shinjuku-ku
(5330 5250, www.sakura-house.com). Shinjuku
station (Yamanote line), west exit; (Marunouchi
line), exit D5; (Oedo, Shinjuku lines), exit 3.
Open 8.50am-8pm Mon-Sat. **Credit** DC, MC, V.
Owned by the people who operate the Sakura Hotel
(*see p130*), which is in itself a mark of quality, this
agency offers guesthouses and apartments in 83
locations around the city.

Tokyo Apartment

4-16-2 Kita-Shinjuku, Shinjuku-ku (3367 7117,
www.tokyoapt.com). Okubo station (Sobu line).
Open 9am-6pm Mon-Fri. **Credit** DC, MC, V.
An agency that deals exclusively with foreigners,
and offers everything from one-night backpacker
deals to fully fledged, long-term apartment contracts. Apartments start at ¥100,000 per month.

Weekly Center

5950 1111 central reservations, www.weekly
center.co.jp. **Rates** ¥25,000-¥60,000/wk.
No credit cards.
This budget chain has a dozen locations dotted
around Tokyo, offering weekly stays for around the
same price as top hotels charge for one night.
Monthly rates are also available. The cheapest central branch is in Ochanomizu.

CONSUME

Restaurants

In Tokyo, the food's so fresh it wriggles.

Welcome to the dining capital of the world. With thousands of restaurants and bars, Tokyo offers an astonishing panoply of choice – from the cypress-walled enclave of a sushi master to the smoke-in-the-eye sizzle of a yakitori joint.

Michelin keeps heaping praise on the high-end dining experiences (topping 200 stars at the last count), but they won't tell you that the budget dining can be just as special. Even if you have the stomach for a ¥40,000 meal, be sure also to try the ¥800-a-pop ramen, rice bowl or yakitori that stir just as much passion in local gourmets.

EATING OUT IN TOKYO

The genre-encompassing Japanese restaurants found in the West are rare here and never the best options. Most restaurants pick one type of food in which to specialise. Chefs study for decades to become masters of sushi, sashimi, tempura or sukiyaki, and don't stray from their chosen field. If you've come to sample the very best of a given cuisine, look for a specialist restaurant and, where available, the *omakase* course, leaving the chef to choose the dishes.

There's plenty of international dining, too, some of it every bit as good as you'd find in New York or London. You'll find world-class French, Italian and Chinese food here, though you may have to lower your expectations for other nations' fare. The foreign superstar chefs (Ramsay, Gagnaire, Ducasse, Robuchon) have all turned up, in name if not in person, for a slice of the profits, but the real buzz surrounds the Japanese chefs, especially Yoshihiro Narisawa of **Les Créations des Narisawa** (*see p155*), Chikara Yamada of **Yamada Chikara** (*see p163*) and Seiji Yamamoto of **Ryugin** (*see p162*), who inject cutting-edge science and a modern Japanese sensibility into their menus.

Adventurous eaters will find plenty to please, from the rarefied multi-course banquets known as *kaiseki*, to the anything-goes *chanko-nabe* stews that give sumo wrestlers their physiques. There are also ingredients to raise the eyebrow or turn the stomach of all but the most intrepid eater, including horse sashimi, live fish and offal galore.

At the other end of the spectrum, a recent proliferation of macrobiotic and vegetarian restaurants is good news for herbivores, though neither term is well understood outside of their still-narrow scenes.

And at least once, be sure to try an *izakaya* (literally, 'saké places'), a catch-all term covering the gamut from raucous, crowded taverns to elegant drinking and dining establishments. What they all have in common is their suitability as places to unwind at the end of the day. As in tapas bars, you need only order a couple of dishes at a time with your beer, saké or *shochu*. Food quality varies greatly, but the smaller, independent *izakaya* are usually the best bets.

If you haven't decided what to eat, and haven't made reservations, it's not a bad idea to head to one of the retail and dining super-complexes, such as **Tokyo Midtown** (*see p198*), **Roppongi Hills** (*see p198*), **Omotesando Hills** (*see p197*) or the **Marunouchi Building** (*see p197*), where you'll find restaurant floors offering everything from burger bars to fine dining.

ETIQUETTE

You don't have to worry too much about dining etiquette, but there are a few no-nos. Don't stick your chopsticks vertically into your rice or use them to pass food directly to another person's chopsticks (both are funerary customs). Don't spear food with your chopsticks or wave them around in the air. Remove your shoes in a Japanese-style restaurant. Tipping is not expected anywhere. Learning a few Japanese

CONSUME

A Guide to Japanese Cuisine

Get to know your oden from your udon.

The staple food in Japan is rice. Indeed, the word for meal (*gohan*) literally means 'cooked rice'. In farming communities rice is still eaten three times a day (sometimes noodles are substituted), along with a simple side dish, a bowl of miso soup and some pickles. This is a Japanese meal at its most basic.

Until 150 years ago, meat-eating (especially from four-legged animals) was shunned, and Japanese cooking is still weighted towards seafood and products made from protein-rich soya beans, such as tofu, *yuba* (soya milk skin), *natto* (fermented beans), soy sauce and miso.

There is a strong emphasis on fresh ingredients, so the varieties of seafood, vegetables and mushrooms vary throughout the year, reflecting the season. In addition, each region of the country, from Hokkaido down to Okinawa, has its own specialities; all are available in Tokyo. Food quality and hygiene standards are always excellent.

Below is a guide to Japan's amazingly diverse cuisine. For a glossary of food terms, *see pp174-175* **Menu Reader**.

KAISEKI RYORI

Japan's haute cuisine developed from the highly formalised light meals that were served with the tea ceremony. Kaieski consists of a sequence of small dishes, apparently simple but always immaculately prepared and presented to reflect the seasons. Courses follow each other at a slow pace: a one-hour meal would be quick.

The order of the meal is: starter (often highly elaborate); sashimi; clear soup; then a series of dishes prepared in different styles (grilled; steamed; served with a thick dressing; deep-fried; served with a 'salad' with a vinegar dressing); and finally rice and miso soup, with a light dessert to clear the palate at the end. *Kaiseki* can be very pricey, though some restaurants serve simplified versions for around ¥5,000.

KUSHI-AGE

Pieces of meat, seafood or vegetables are skewered and deep-fried till golden brown in a coating of fine breadcrumbs. Usually eaten with a sweetened soy-based sauce, salt or even a dab of curry powder, washed down with beer, and rounded off with rice and miso soup.

NABEMONO & ONE-POT COOKING

One-pot stews cooked at the table in casseroles (*nabe*) of iron or heavy earthenware are delicious and warming in winter. Everyone is served (or helps themselves) from the one pot: you just pluck out what you want using long chopsticks, and dip into the sauce provided. Favourite *nabe* styles include chicken *mizutaki*; duck meat; *yose* (mixed seafood and vegetables); and *chanko*, the sumo wrestlers' stew into which anything goes.

NOODLES: SOBA, UDON & RAMEN

There are two main indigenous varieties of noodle: soba (thin, grey, made from buckwheat mixed with wheat flour) and udon (chunkier wheat noodles, usually white). These are eaten chilled, served on a bamboo tray with a soy-based dipping sauce; or hot, usually in a soy-flavoured broth. Accompaniments include tempura, grated *daikon* (radish) or sweetened tofu. Chinese-style ramen noodles are even more popular. These crinkly, yellowish noodles are served in a rich, meat-based soup flavoured with miso, soy sauce or salt, and topped with vegetables or *cha-shu* (sliced, barbecued pork).

ODEN

Fish cakes, tofu, vegetables, whole eggs and *konnyaku* (devil's tongue) are simmered long and slowly in a *shoyu*-flavoured broth and eaten with a dash of hot mustard. This simple wintertime dish goes wonderfully with saké, and is often served at outdoor *yatai* (street stalls). Cheap versions can smell chokingly pungent, but the subtle flavour of *oden* in fine restaurants can be a revelation.

SASHIMI

Raw fish, delicately sliced and artfully arranged, is an essential course in most Japanese meals. It is usually served with a dip of soy sauce, plus a dab of pungent green wasabi (or sometimes grated ginger). Best appreciated with some good saké.

SHOJIN RYORI

Japan's long tradition of vegetarian cooking lives on in *shojin ryori* – Buddhist temple cuisine that generally follows the same lines as mainstream *kaiseki*, except that

CONSUME

no fish is used in the cooking stocks (shiitake mushrooms and *konbu* seaweed are used instead); garlic and onion are also banned. Tofu and *yuba* (soya milk skin) feature prominently in *shojin* meals and also in *fucha ryori*, a variant with more Chinese influence. See p172 **Shojin Ryori**.

SUKIYAKI & SHABU-SHABU
These meat dishes, both cooked at the table, have evolved over the last century to become key parts of Japanese cuisine. Sukiyaki combines tender cuts of meat (usually beef, but sometimes pork, horse or chicken) with vegetables, tofu and other ingredients, such as *shirataki* (jelly-like *konnyaku* noodles), which are lightly cooked in a sweetened soy-sauce broth. As they cook, you fish them out and dip them into beaten raw egg.

Shabu-shabu is paper-thin slices of beef quickly dipped into a boiling cooking stock, usually in a special copper pot. The name derives from the sound made as the meat is swished to and fro in the broth.

SUSHI
The classic style of arranging raw fish or other delicacies on patties of vinegared rice dates back to the 18th century, when sushi became a popular street food in Edo. Top sushi shops can be daunting, as they don't post their prices, and customers are expected to know their *uni* (sea urchin) from their *ikura* (salmon roe). The easiest (and cheapest) way to learn your way around the etiquette and vocabulary is to explore the many *kaiten* (conveyor belt) sushi shops, where prices are fixed and you can take what you want without having to order. Another style of sushi popular in Osaka and western Japan is *chirashi-zushi* – large bowls of sushi rice with morsels of fish, egg and vegetables scattered on top.

TEMPURA
The Portuguese are credited with introducing the idea of deep-frying seafood and vegetables in a light, crisp batter – and also with the name itself. But in Japan the technique has been elevated to a fine art. Premium tempura, cooked one morsel at a time in top-quality sesame oil, should never taste too oily.

TEPPANYAKI, OKONOMIYAKI & MONJA
Beef is never cheap in Japan, but Japanese beef (especially Kobe *wagyu* beef) is a luxury item. The marbled fat lends itself perfectly to being cooked on a flat *teppan* grill – Japan's contribution to the art of the steak. Seafood and vegetables are also cooked the same way in front of you.

Okonomiyaki ('grilled whatever you like') is a cross between a pancake and an omelette, stuffed with meat, beansprouts, chopped cabbage and other goodies. Many *okonomiyaki* restaurants also do *yaki-soba* (fried Chinese-style noodles). Originally from western Japan (Hiroshima and Osaka both lay claim to it), *okonomiyaki* is cheap, robust and satisfying. The Tokyo version is known as *monja*.

TOFU CUISINE
Tofu and other soya-bean derivatives are celebrated for their protein content and versatility, and feature strongly in Japanese cooking. The silky *kinu* tofu is considered the most refined version, which you can expect to be served in a top *kaiseki* meal. The firmer *momen*, or cotton, tofu is the versatile version. *Izakaya* will often serve *atsuage*, a deep-fried cotton tofu topped with bonito flakes.

TONKATSU
The *katsu* in *tonkatsu* means 'cutlet', a very popular dish first introduced during the Meiji period, when meat-eating began to catch on. The *katsu* is now almost always pork, usually lean cuts of sirloin, dredged in flour, dipped in egg, rolled in breadcrumbs and deep-fried.

UNAGI
Another of Japan's great delicacies. Fillets of freshwater eel are basted and very slowly grilled (often over charcoal). The delectably rich, fatty white meat is considered a restorative and is said to improve stamina, eyesight and even virility.

YAKITORI
Yakitori ('grilled bird') is the Japanese version of the kebab: skewered morsels of chicken cooked over a grill, seasoned either with salt or a slightly sweet soy-based glaze. Most yakitori shops also do wonderful things with vegetables.

CONSUME

phrases will add to your dining experience, especially *sumimasen* (excuse me); *o kaikei onegaishimasu* (the bill please); and *gochisou sama deshita* (thank you for the meal).

For more useful translations, *see p174* **Menu Reader** and *see p321* **Vocabulary**.

TIMES & PRICES

Lunch is usually served between 11.30am and 2.30pm, but most workers dine from noon to 1pm, so it gets crowded then. Dinner is typically from about 6pm to 11pm, with last orders at 10pm or 10.30pm – though you can get fed much later in Roppongi and Shibuya.

Prices listed below are for an average dinner with one drink; budget venues are marked ¥. We've noted if you can get a menu in English; some (usually cheaper) restaurants also display realistic plastic models of dishes in their windows, so you can point at what you want. Though the information listed here was correct at the time of writing, Tokyo's restaurant scene is fast-changing, so call ahead to confirm before making a long trek.

ASAKUSA

Japanese

¥ Hatsuogawa

2-8-4 Kaminarimon, Taito-ku (3844 2723). Asakusa station (Asakusa, Ginza lines), exits 1, 2, 3, A3, A4. **Open** noon-2pm, 5-8pm Mon-Sat; 5-8pm Sun. **Average** ¥3,000. **No credit cards. Map** p45. Unagi
Stones, plants, bamboo latticework and a white *noren* (shop curtain) mark the entrance to this venerable eel shop. The *unaju* box set is delicious; or try *kabayaki* – skewered eel with the rice served separately.

¥ Komagata Dojo

1-7-12 Komagata, Taito-ku (3842 4001, www.dozeu.com). Asakusa station (Asakusa, Ginza lines), exit A1. **Open** 11am-9pm daily. **Average** ¥2,500. **Credit** AmEx, DC, JCB, MC, V. **English menu. Map** p45. **Traditional Japanese**
You dine here much as you would have done a century ago – sitting on thin cushions at low tables that are little more than polished planks on the rush matting floor. The menu revolves around *dojo* – small, plump, eel-like fish served (in ascending order of delectability) as *nabe* hotpots; *yanagawa* (in a runny omelette); or *kabayaki* (grilled, like eel). Not a gourmet delicacy, perhaps, but Komagata Dojo is an absolute Asakusa institution.

¥ Mugitoro

2-2-4 Kaminarimon, Taito-ku (3842 1066, www.mugitoro.co.jp). Asakusa station (Asakusa, Ginza lines), exits A1, A3, A4. **Open** 11.30am-

10.30pm daily (last orders 9pm). **Average** ¥3,000. **Credit** AmEx, DC, JCB, MC, V. **Map** p45. **Traditional Japanese**
The speciality at this Japanese restaurant is rice cooked with barley and served with a bowl of grated yam (so gooey it must be healthy). There are lots of other options too, ranging from simple lunches to full evening meals.

Otafuku

1-6-2 Senzoku, Taito-ku (3871 2521, www.otafuku.ne.jp). Iriya station (Hibiya line), exits 1, 3. **Open** *Feb-Sept* 5-11pm Tue-Sat; 5-10pm Sun. *Oct-Jan* 5-11pm Mon-Sat; 4-10pm Sun. **Average** ¥3,500. **Credit** AmEx, DC, JCB, MC, V. **English menu. Oden**
This place has been serving *oden* since the Meiji era. The chef takes great pride in his special Kansai-style version (with a much lighter broth than the Tokyo version). Otafuku also specialises in saké, which complements the delicate flavour of the vegetables and fish cakes that make up *oden*.

¥ Sometaro

2-2-2 Nishi-Asakusa, Taito-ku (3844 9502). Tawaramachi station (Ginza line), exit 3. **Open** noon-10pm daily. **Average** ¥2,500. **No credit cards. English menu. Map** p45. **Okonomiyaki**
Comfort food in a funky wooden shack, within easy walking distance of Asakusa's tourist sights. It can get incredibly sweaty in summer, but when you're sitting round the *okonomiyaki* pan, the intimate atmosphere is wonderfully authentic.

Yoshiba

2-14-5 Yokoami, Sumida-ku (3623 4480). Ryogoku station (Oedo line), exit A1; (Sobu line), east exit. **Open** 11.30am-1.30pm, 5-10pm Mon-Sat; also 5-10pm Sun during sumo tournaments. **Average** ¥4,000. **No credit cards. Hotpot**
Chanko-nabe is the legendary food of sumo wrestlers, said to help them put on those extra tonnes – but only if eaten in huge amounts late at night. For the rest of us, it's just a warming, mixed casserole. Nowhere makes a more atmospheric sampling spot than Yoshiba, a former sumo stable where you sit around the hard-packed mud of the ring where wrestlers used to practise.

Non-Japanese

Vin Chou

2-2-13 Nishi-Asakusa, Taito-ku (3845 4430, www.vinchou.jp). Tawaramachi station (Ginza line), exit 3. **Open** 5-10.30pm Mon, Tue, Thur-Sun. **Average** ¥4,500. **Credit** MC, V. **Map** p45. **Grill**
Call it French yakitori. This rustic eaterie is an offshoot of the nearby French bistro La Chèvre, which explains the charcoal-grilled Bresse chicken, quail

and a fine range of wines and cheese. Casual and simple, Vin Chou serves some of the best food that you'll find in the neighbourhood.

EBISU & DAIKANYAMA
Japanese

Chibo
Yebisu Garden Place Tower 38F, 4-20-3 Ebisu, Shibuya-ku (5424 1011, www.chibo.com). Ebisu station (Yamanote line), east exit; (Hibiya line), exit 1. **Open** 11.30am-3pm, 5-10pm Mon-Fri; 11.30am-10pm Sat, Sun. **Average** ¥4,000. **Credit** AmEx, DC, JCB, MC, V. **English menu.** Okonomiyaki

This branch of one of Osaka's top *okonomiyaki* restaurants replicates the original Kansai-style recipes. In addition to the usual meats and seafood, stuffings include asparagus, *mochi* (rice cakes), cheese and, of course, mayonnaise. Friendly staff, reasonable prices, a large menu and a gorgeous view make this a popular place.
Other locations 108-7 Ginza, Chuo-ku (5537 5900); BIC Camera 6F, 1-11-1 Yurakucho, Chiyoda-ku (5288 8570).

¥ Ippudo
1-3-13 Hiroo, Shibuya-ku (5420 2225, www.ippudo.com). Ebisu station (Yamanote line), west exit; (Hibiya line), exit 1. **Open** 11am-4am daily. **Average** ¥2,000. **No credit cards.** Ramen

Once you get past all the ordering choices – red or white pork broth; noodles soft-cooked, medium or al dente; with or without *chashu* pork – you can settle in and appreciate all the little touches that make Ippudo different from other ramen shops. The layout is simple and open, with lots of plain wood; you can add your own condiments (spicy beansprouts, sesame seeds and garlic that you grind yourself); and there are unlimited pots of *rooibos* (red bush) tea to quench your thirst.
Other locations throughout the city.

Jinroku
6-23-2 Shirokane, Minato-ku (3441 1436, www.jinroku.jp). Hiroo station (Hibiya line), exits 1, 2. **Open** 6pm-3am (last orders 1.30am) Tue-Sat; 6-11pm Sun. **Average** ¥3,500. **Credit** AmEx, MC, V. **English menu.** Okonomiyaki
Jinroku has raised *okonomiyaki* to a new and superior level, and as an indication of that change, put it on show in gleaming upmarket surroundings. Besides the standard pancakes, the chefs at this restaurant also fry up great *gyoza* dumplings, teppanyaki seafood, tofu steaks and *yaki-soba* (fried noodles). In particular, be sure to try the *negi-yaki*, which uses chopped green leeks in place of the usual Chinese cabbage. Help it all down with cheap Chilean cabernet.

¥ Kookaï
3-49-1 Ebisu, Shibuya-ku (3440 1272, www.kookai-web.com). Hiroo station (Hibiya line), exits 1, 2. **Open** 11am-11pm daily. **Average** ¥2,000. **No credit cards. English menu.** Ramen
There's plenty of good ramen in Ebisu, but this branch of the reliable Kookaï chain is hip, clean and foreigner-friendly – although bear in mind that it is a fairly long walk from any station. As a change from the usual soup-style noodles, try the *tsukemen*, served on a tray with various garnishes and a hot dipping broth on the side.

★ Tachimichiya
B1, 30-8 Sarugakucho, Shibuya-ku (5459 3431). Daikanyama station (Toyoko line). **Open** 6pm-4am Mon-Fri; 6pm-midnight Sat, Sun. **Average** ¥4,000. **No credit cards.** Izakaya
This could almost be a template for the perfect rustic *izakaya* – rough-hewn wooden tables; tatami-floored attic; saké galore; a smoky, bouncy atmosphere; and first-rate Japanese pub grub – except the walls are covered in posters for the Ramones and the Sex Pistols, and the music is usually Japanese rock or punk. If that sounds intolerable, it's not. Tachimichiya is a great *izakaya* that happens to rock.
▶ *For more on Tokyo's vibrant music scene, see p250.*

Non-Japanese

Bistrot des Arts
4-9-5 Ebisu, Shibuya-ku (3447 0408). Ebisu station (Yamanote line), east exit; (Hibiya line), exit 1. **Open** 11.30am-3am Mon-Sat; 11.30am-11pm Sun. **Average** ¥4,000. **Credit** AmEx, DC, JCB, MC, V. French
Forsaking the usual clichés of checked tablecloths and the like, Bistrot des Arts espouses a chic, modern look complemented with rotating exhibitions of contemporary art. The cuisine is well above the bistro norm, and the late-night hours make it a great stop-off for a glass of wine and a light meal – try their *confit de canard*, or a comforting bowl of classic French onion soup.

Cardenas Charcoal Grill
1-12-14 Ebisu-Nishi, Shibuya-ku (5428 0779, www.cardenas.co.jp/charcoal). Ebisu station (Yamanote line), west exit; (Hibiya line), exit 4. **Open** 6-10.30pm Mon-Sat; 6-10pm Sun. **Average** ¥5,000. **Credit** AmEx, JCB, MC, V. **English menu.** Fusion
This is the most stylish and satisfying of the three Californian-style restaurants that share the Cardenas name and its distinctive take on Pacific Rim fusion food. The centrepiece is the grill, which serves up chicken, steak, fish and seafood, backed up by a strong selection of US West Coast wines.

CONSUME

Gonpachi. *See p161.*

Other locations Cardenas Ginza Kanematsu Bldg 7F, 6-9-9 Ginza, Chuo-ku (5537 5011); Cardenas Chinois 5-22-3 Hiroo, Shibuya-ku (5447 1287).

¥ La Casita
Selsa Daikanyama 2F, 13-4 Daikanyama, Shibuya-ku (3496 1850, www.lacasita.co.jp). Daikanyama station (Toyoko line). **Open** 5-10pm Mon; noon-10pm Tue-Sun. **Average** ¥3,000. **No credit cards**. **English menu**. Mexican
Like most of Tokyo's south-of-the-border restaurants, La Casita isn't authentically Mexican. But the heady aroma of corn tortillas grabs you upon entering this airy 'little house' and won't let go until you've sampled the near-perfect *camarones al mojo de ajo* (grilled shrimp with garlic, Acapulco-style) or the *enchiladas rojas* bathed in spicy tomato sauce.

Khumbila
1-9-11 Ebisu-Minami, Shibuya-ku (3719 6115, www.khumbila.com). Ebisu station (Yamanote line), west exit; (Hibiya line), exit 4. **Open** 11.30am-2.30pm, 5-10.30pm Mon-Fri; 11.30am-3pm, 5-11.30pm Sat, Sun. **Average** ¥3,500. **Credit** DC, MC, V. **English menu**. Nepalese
There are other Nepalese places around town, but none in the same league as Khumbila, housed in a quirky building by oddball local architect Hideo Horikawa. Whether you order the Indian-accented curries or the Tibetan-style *momo* dumplings, it's all carefully adapted to suit Japanese tastes. Non-smokers enjoy a floor to themselves, but the best seats in the house are at the top, sitting on the floor under the dome-like roof.

Lohotoi
3-48-1 Ebisu, Shibuya-ku (3449 8899, www.long-fu-fong.com). Hiroo station (Hibiya line), exits 1, 2. **Open** 11.30am-3pm, 6-11pm Mon, Tue, Thur-Sun. **Average** ¥5,000. **Credit** AmEx, DC, JCB, MC, V. Chinese
Neither too funky nor too pristine, Lohotoi occupies a welcome middle ground, producing flavourful, satisfying Hong Kong cuisine. The dim sum – all prepared in-house by the HK-born chefs – are excellent, as are the seafood dishes and sweet-sour spare ribs.

Ninniku-ya
1-26-12 Ebisu, Shibuya-ku (3446 5887). Ebisu station (Yamanote line), west exit; (Hibiya line), exit 1. **Open** 6-10.30pm Tue-Fri; 6-11pm Sat, Sun. **Average** ¥5,000. **Credit** AmEx, JCB, MC, V. **English menu**. International
Ninniku is the Japanese word for garlic, and everything on the menu here is laced with it. The odours of towering garlic bread, viciously flavourful curries and mouth-watering pasta and rice dishes, with Chinese, Thai, Indian and other ethnic twists, waft out on to the street.

INSIDE TRACK
EAT YOUR GREENS

Vegetarian visitors to Tokyo should check the website www.vege-navi.jp, where you'll learn that the metropolis is far more herbivore-friendly than you might ever have imagined.

CONSUME

Queue Tips

Food that's worth the wait.

It's not just the arm-and-a-leg, mortgage your kids dining scene that makes Tokyo great. The fanaticism for detail and dedication to fresh, seasonal ingredients trickle all the way down to the places most Tokyoites actually visit: the ramen shops, the gyoza joints, the udon restaurants and the confectioners. And these everyday eateries (and shops) have their own version of the fancy restaurant's waiting lists: queues. If a meal is good, Tokyoites will line up in sun or rain to get to it. Along with **Tetsu** (*see p157* **Super Bowls**), these are some of the current favourites.

Meat Shop Sato
1-1-8 Kichijoji-honcho, Musashino-shi (042 222 3130). Kichijoji station (Chuo, Sobu, Tozai, Inokashira lines), north exit. **Average wait** 30mins.
This butcher shop's speciality is just a ball of beef, onions and lard, and it creates lines of up to 200 people. To be fair, it's juicy Matsuzaka beef and it's cooked so

precisely that you need to wait a few minutes after purchasing the cutlet to let the heat reach the middle. So popular are Sato's cutlets that customers are limited to 20 pieces each on a weekday, and ten each on a weekend or holiday. They often sell out by mid afternoon.

Ozasa
1-1-8 Kichijoji-honcho, Musashino (042 222 7230, www.ozasa.co.jp). Kichijoji station (Chuo, Sobu, Tozai, Inokashira lines), north exit. Closed Tue. **Average wait** 3-4hrs.
They call the confectionery at this shop *maboroshi youkan*, which roughly translates as 'bloody hard to get hold of bean-paste jelly'. Ozasa makes just 150 little blocks per day, and if you'd like to try one, start queuing from around 5am on a clement day, or around 7am if it's pouring with rain. At 8.30am, staff distribute tickets for the ¥580-a-piece jellies, up to five per person, and ask you to return between 10am and 6pm to pick up your purchase.

Tableaux
11-6 Sarugakucho, Shibuya-ku (5489 2201, www.tableaux.jp). Daikanyama station (Tokyu Toyoko line). **Open** 5.30pm-1am daily (last orders 11pm). **Average** ¥8,000. **Credit** AmEx, MC, V. **English menu.** Fusion
There is more than a touch of kitsch to the decor, but the eclectic Pac-Rim fusion food is serious. Tableaux is a favourite port of call with the Daikanyama set, who drop by for a Havana in the cigar bar.

Tio Danjo
1-12-5 Ebisu, Shibuya-ku (5420 0747). Ebisu station (Yamanote line), east exit; (Hibiya line), exit 1. **Open** 2pm-midnight Mon-Sat **Average** ¥6,000. **No credit cards.** Tapas
Owner-chef 'Uncle' Keita Danjo is a dyed-in-the-wool Iberophile, and has assembled a great range of tapas recipes and wines from all over Spain. The second-floor restaurant is not particularly atmospheric, but his ground-floor tapas bar remains lively till late.

GINZA & AROUND
Japanese

Azumitei
Ginza Inz 1 Bldg 2F, 3-1-saki Ginza-Nishi, Chuo-ku (5524 7890, www.azumi-food.com/ginza). Yurakucho station (Yamanote, Yurakucho lines),

Sukiyabashi exit. **Open** 5-11pm daily. **Average** ¥6,000. **Credit** AmEx, DC, JCB, MC, V. **Map** p59. Sukiyaki
This sleek, modern restaurant specialises in premium sukiyaki and *shabu-shabu*, prepared with finely marbled beef from Japanese *wagyu* steer. The full-course dinners (¥6,300 and up) make a great introduction to contemporary Japanese cuisine, but you can also order more simply from the à la carte menu. Try to nab one of the semi-private booths in the centre of the restaurant.

★ Bird Land
Tsukamoto Sozan Bldg B1F, 4-2-15 Ginza, Chuo-ku (5250 1081). Ginza station (Ginza, Hibiya, Marunouchi lines), exit C6. **Open** 5-10pm Tue-Fri; 5-9.30pm Sat. **Average** ¥6,000. **Credit** AmEx, DC, JCB, MC, V. **English menu.** **Map** p59. Yakitori
Bird Land was one of the first places to offer upmarket yakitori, served with imported beers and fine wines. Grill master Wada Toshihiro uses top quality, free-range bantam chickens that are so tasty you can enjoy their meat raw as sashimi. Start off with the chicken-liver pâté and don't miss the superb *sansai-yaki* (breast meat grilled with Japanese pepper). It's a small place – just a few tables and a U-shaped counter – and so popular that reservations are hard to get. But seats usually start freeing up by around 8pm, so it's always worth trying your luck.

Sushi no Midori
See p153 **Average wait** 30mins.
There are six main branches of Midori
sushi, and they all come with queues,
though the Ginza branch usually has the
longest lines. Courses start from as little
as ¥840 for the ten-piece *umenigiri* plate,
which is about as cheap as it gets for sushi
in Ginza. But the biggest draws are the
anago ipponzuke, a ball of rice with a whole
eel draped over it (¥630), and the *daimyo
midorimaki*, an oversized maki roll stuffed
with cucumber, egg and mashed whitefish
(¥1,890). In the winter, the store hands out
hot pads to customers in the queue.

Tamahide
See p171. **Average wait** 45mins.
This is the birthplace of *oyakodon*, the
chicken-and-egg rice bowl. Tamahide
was founded in 1760 as a chicken
hotpot specialist, but the wife of the fifth-
generation chef created a dish that became
a Japanese classic and came to define the
restaurant. If you're seated for dinner at
Tamahide, you'll need to wait until the end
of the meal for the famous dish. At lunch,
though, you can dive straight into the
oyakodon as long as you don't mind the
wait. If you don't start queuing by noon,
you won't be getting in.

Yanagiya
See p173. **Average wait** 45mins.
Back in 1916, Yanagiya began making
taiyaki (fish-shaped, griddle-baked bean
paste in batter), and with over 90 years
of practice, they've become pretty good
at it. The batter is made fresh daily and is
used sparingly, which gives the snack an
unusually thin and crispy shell (so eat fast,
before it goes soft). Inside, there's *koshian*
(skinless azuki bean paste), sweet but not
cloying. Yanagiya is one of the 'big three'
taiyaki outlets in Tokyo (along with Wakaba
in Yotsuya and Naniwaya Souhonten in
Azabu Juban) and uses moulds that pre-
date World War II.

¥ Kagaya

*B1F, 2-15-12 Shinbashi, Minato-ku (3591 2347,
www1.ocn.ne.jp/~kagayayy). Shinbashi station
(Yamanote, Asakusa lines), Karasumori exit;
(Ginza line), exit 8; (Yurikamome line), exit 6.*
Open 6pm-midnight Mon-Sat; by appt only Sun.
Average ¥4,000. **No credit cards**. Casual
Japanese
If you're looking for the goofy side of Tokyo, make
this your first stop. It's run by 'Mark', the Japanese
equivalent of Robin Williams, whose crackpot
behaviour has made Kagaya famous. The drinks
menu features beverages and country names.
Choose one of each and Mark will disappear into his
cupboard to re-emerge in a costume that reflects
your choice. The food menu might be performed as
a mime, drinks come in glasses that move, shake or
gurgle, and you can, if you wish, dress as a frog or
giant teddy bear. In a setting such as this, the food
is really almost incidental, but you'll get decent
home-style Japanese grub. It's a small place, so reservations are recommended.

Kondo

*Sakaguchi Bldg 9F, 5-5-13 Ginza, Chuo-ku
(5568 0923). Ginza station (Ginza, Hibiya,
Marunouchi lines), exits A3, A4.* **Open** noon-
8.30pm Mon-Sat. **Average** ¥9,000. **Credit**
AmEx, DC, JCB, MC, V. **English menu**.
Map p59. Tempura

Sit at the counter and marvel as chef Fumio Kondo
and his assistants deliver a succession of exquisite
morsels of golden, batter-fried seafood and vegetables. A kimono-clad waitress is always on hand,
hovering attentively and constantly replacing the
paper mats that absorb excess oil. Kondo is a tempura artist of the old school, but his restaurant is less
formal (and more affordable) than other traditional
tempura shops. The view over the Ginza rooftops is
a further bonus.

Little Okinawa

*8-7-10 Ginza, Chuo-ku (3572 2930, www.little-
okinawa.co.jp). Shinbashi station (Yamanote
line), Ginza exit; (Asakusa line), exit A3; (Ginza
line), exit 3.* **Open** noon-1.30pm, 5pm-3am Mon-
Fri; noon-1.30pm, 4pm-midnight Sat, Sun.
Average ¥3,500. **Credit** AmEx, DC, JCB, MC, V.
English menu. **Map** p59. Okinawan
This cheerful, busy hole-in-the-wall serves the foods
of Japan's southernmost islands. The Chinese influence is strong, especially in the emphasis on noodles
and pork. Among the more accessible dishes are
deep-fried chips of *goya* (bitter gourd), *jimami-dofu*
(a creamy peanut mousse) and *rafuti* (delectable,
slow-simmered pork belly). Once you've had a few
shots of *awamori*, the local rice-based, rocket-fuel
hooch, you'll be ready for more exotic offerings such
as *mimiga* (gelatinous pig's ear) or *umi-budo*
(crunchy seaweed).

CONSUME

Ohmatsuya

*Ail d'Or Bldg 2F, 6-5-8 Ginza, Chuo-ku
(3571 7053). Ginza station (Ginza, Hibiya,
Marunouchi lines), exit B9.* **Open** *5-10pm
Mon-Sat.* **Average** ¥9,000. **Credit** AmEx,
DC, JCB, MC, V. **English menu. Map** p59.
Traditional Japanese
Ohmatsuya serves the foods of rural Yamagata prefecture, but it does so in swish Ginza style. The decor
is faux rustic, with wooden beams and farmhouse
furniture. Every table has a charcoal fireplace on
which fish, vegetables, mushrooms and delicious
wagyu beef are grilled as you watch. The rest of the
menu features plenty of wild mountain herbs and
fresh seafood from the Japan Sea coast, not to mention some of the best saké in the country.

Oshima

*Ginza Core Bldg 9F, 5-8-20 Ginza, Chuo-ku
(3574 8080). Ginza station (Ginza, Hibiya,
Marunouchi lines), exits A3, A4.* **Open** *11am-
10pm daily.* **Average** ¥6,000. **Credit** AmEx,
DC, JCB, MC, V. **Map** p59. **Traditional
Japanese**
Oshima serves traditional Japanese food from the
Kaga (Kanazawa) area, all of it expertly prepared
and beautifully presented. There's a wide range of
set meals, including tempura, *shabu-shabu* and *nabe*
(hotpot) courses.
Other locations Odakyu Halc Annex 8F, 1-5-1
Nishi-Shinjuku, Shinjuku-ku (3348 8080); Hotel
Pacific Tokyo 3F, 3-13-3 Takanawa, Minato-ku
(3441 8080).

Robata

*1-3-8 Yurakucho, Chiyoda-ku (3591 1905).
Hibiya station (Chiyoda, Hibiya, Mita lines),
exit A4.* **Open** *5-11pm daily.* **Average** ¥10,000.
No credit cards. Map p59. **Japanese grill**
This venerable *izakaya* provides one of the most
charming dining experiences in central Tokyo.
Perch yourself on one of the wooden seats and pick
from the freshly prepared dishes arrayed in huge
bowls on the giant counter. The food is a curious mix
of Japanese and Western – salads, pork in cream
sauce, tofu dishes and tomato-based veggie stews –
which goes just as well with wine as with saké.

Shin-Hinomoto

*2-4-4 Yurakucho, Chiyoda-ku (3214 8021).
Yurakucho station (Yamanote, Yurakucho lines),
Hibiya exit.* **Open** *5pm-midnight daily.* **Average**
¥4,000. **No credit cards. English menu.
Map** p59. **Izakaya**
Tucked under the Yamanote line tracks and shud-
dering every time a train passes overhead, Shin-
Hinomoto delivers the classic *izakaya* experience.
That means it's cramped, boisterous and smoky,
and serves a good range of cheap, honest grub with
plenty of saké and *shochu* to wash it down. What
makes it unique is that the master of the house is an
English expat.

Shunju Tsugihagi

*Nihon Seimei Bldg B1F, 1-1-1 Yurakucho,
Chiyoda-ku (3595 0511, www.shunju.com/ja/
restaurants/tsugihagi). Hibiya station (Chiyoda,*

CONSUME

Hibiya, Mita lines), exit A13. **Open** 11.30am-2.30pm, 5-11pm Mon-Sat; noon-2.30pm, 5-9.30pm Sun **Average** ¥7,000. **Credit** AmEx, DC, JCB, MC, V. **English menu**. **Map** p59. Izakaya
From the ever-reliable Shunju group, a modern *izakaya* offering everything from home-made tofu and country-style vegetable dishes to premium seafood and grilled meats. Be warned: it's pricier than other branches of Shunju, reflecting the upscale ambience and neighbourhood.

Sushi Bun
Chuo Shijo Bldg No.8, 5-2-1 Tsukiji, Chuo-ku (3541 3860, www.tsukijinet.com/tsukiji/kanren/susibun/eng.html). Tsukiji station (Hibiya line), exit A1. **Open** 6.30am-2.30pm Mon-Sat. **Average** ¥3,500. **No credit cards. English menu.** Sushi
If the fish market finally moves out of Tsukiji, Sushi Bun and the other barrow boys' sushi shops will be lost – so go now before it's too late. Like the others, Bun is cramped (the counter seats just 12) and invariably full from first light until closing time. For fish this fresh, the set meal (¥3,500) is brilliant value.
▶ *For more on the Tsukiji fish market, see p61 Something Fishy.*

Sushi no Midori
Corridor Gai, 7-108 Ginza, Chuo-ku (5568 1212, www.sushinomidori.co.jp). Ginza station (Ginza, Hibiya, Marunouchi lines), exit C2. **Open** 11am-2pm, 4.30-10pm Mon-Fri; 11am-10pm Sat; 11am-9pm Sun. **Average** ¥3,000. **Credit** AmEx, DC, JCB, MC, V. **Sushi**

Nihonryori Ryugin. *See p162.*

For review, *see p150* **Queue Tips**.
▶ *When you've eaten your sushi, head across the street to Rockfish (see p179) or Bar High Five (see p177) for a drink.*

★ Ten-Ichi
6-6-5 Ginza, Chuo-ku (3571 1949, www.tenichi.co.jp). Ginza station (Ginza, Hibiya, Marunouchi lines), exits C3, B6. **Open** 11.30am-9.30pm daily. **Average** ¥10,000. **Credit** AmEx, DC, JCB, MC, V. **English menu**. **Map** p59.
Tempura
Top-quality tempura, served direct from the wok to your plate, is one of the finest delicacies in Japan's cuisine. It really must be tried and you won't find it prepared better than at Ten-Ichi, Tokyo's best-known tempura house. The atmosphere is tranquil and pampering, the tempura light and aromatic. A full-course meal also includes sashimi, salad, rice and dessert. This Ginza flagship is the most refined member of the restaurant chain (it regularly hosts visiting dignitaries and film stars), but other branches all guarantee similar quality.
Other locations throughout the city.

★ Tokachiya
Corridor Gai, 6-2 Ginza, Chuo-ku (3573 7373, www.tokachiya.com/tokachiya.shtml). Ginza station (Ginza, Hibiya, Marunouchi lines), exit C2. **Open** 5.30-11pm Mon; 11.30am-2pm, 5.30-11pm Tue-Sat. **Average** ¥4,500. **Credit** AmEx, DC, JCB, MC, V. **English menu**. Izakaya
Tokachiya is billed as a showcase for the food of Hokkaido, Japan's second-largest island. But since the island is known for produce as diverse as dairy, root vegetables, soybeans, seafood, wheat, beef, wine and beer, the geographical designation gives the chefs plenty to play with. The menu is simple but inventive (pressed-pork 'sushi', head of cabbage in anchovy sauce), the setting chic and cosy. And where else can you order 'potato of the day'? Reservations essential.

Non-Japanese

Bangkok Kitchen
Corridor Gai, 8-2 Saki Ginza, Chuo-ku (5537 3886). Ginza station (Ginza, Hibiya, Marunouchi lines), exit C1 or Shinbashi station (Yamanote line), Ginza exit; (Asakusa line), exit A3; (Ginza line), exit 3. **Open** 11am-2.30pm, 5.30-11.15pm Mon-Fri; 11.30am-3pm, 5.30-11.30pm Sat, Sun. **Average** ¥3,500. **Credit** AmEx, DC, JCB, MC, V. **Map** p59. Thai
Contemporary Bangkok touches down in the heart of Ginza and makes itself at home. Besides the Thai noodles promised by the sign outside, you will find plenty of fiery curries, pungent soups and spicy Isaan specialities, prepared with finesse. The kitchen crew and most of the waiters are Thai, so the ambience is as authentic as the flavours.

CONSUME

Gordon Ramsay at Conrad Tokyo
The Conrad Tokyo, Tokyo Shiodome Bldg 28F,
1-9-1 Higashi-Shinbashi, Minato-ku (6388 8000,
www.gordonramsay.jp). Shinbashi station
(Yamanote, Asakusa lines), exit 1; (Ginza line),
exit 2 or Shiodome station (Oedo line) exit 9.
Open 11.30am-2pm, 5.30-9pm Tue-Sat. **Average**
¥18,000. **Credit** AmEx, DC, JCB, MC, V. **French**
Ramsay's Japanese outlet has a Michelin star, and
there's nothing to fault about this high-rise hotel
eaterie. The signature dishes are all present and correct: *mosaïque* of foie gras, lobster ravioli, cannon of
lamb, expertly recreated by chef-in-residence Shinya
Maeda. But it feels reliable rather than dazzling, and
there are better ways to spend your yen.

Les Saisons
Imperial Hotel 2F, 1-1-1 Uchisaiwaicho,
Chiyoda-ku (3539 8087). Hibiya station (Chiyoda,
Hibiya, Mita lines), exits A5, A13 or Yurakucho
station (Yamanote, Yurakucho lines), Hibiya exit.
Open 7-10am, 11.30am-2.30pm, 5.30-10pm daily.
Average ¥20,000. **Credit** AmEx, DC, JCB,
MC, V. **Map** p59. **French**
Always one of Tokyo's top French restaurants, Les
Saisons – the Imperial Hotel's flagship restaurant –
has been soaring under the direction of the brilliant
Thierry Voisin (formerly of Les Creyères in Reims).
The dining room is ample and luxurious, the service
supremely professional, the wine cellar extensive,
and Voisin's haute cuisine outstanding (especially
his autumn *gibiers*). It all adds up to classic heavy-
weight dining.

HARAJUKU & AOYAMA
Japanese

¥ Crayon House Hiroba
3-8-15 Kita-Aoyama, Minato-ku (3406 6409,
www.crayonhouse.co.jp). Omotesando station
(Chiyoda line), exit A1; (Ginza, Hanzomon lines),
exit B2. **Open** 11am-11pm daily. **Average**
¥2,500. **Credit** AmEx, DC, JCB, MC, V.
Map p65. **Modern Japanese**
Sitting next to a natural food shop, Crayon House is
not exclusively vegetarian, but serves up a good

INSIDE TRACK DINING SOLO

Eating out alone is easier in Tokyo than
in most cities, thanks to the popularity
of counters. You'll blend in seamlessly
in most sushi bars and ramen shops,
but also at **Inakaya** (*see p162*), **L'Atelier
de Joël Robuchon** (*see p163*) and the
Tapas Molecular Bar (*see p161*), which
was designed as a sushi bar but switched
direction shortly before opening.

---

selection of wholesome, well-prepared dishes, many
with organic ingredients. It consists of two mini
restaurants: Hiroba, offering Japanese food, and
Home, offering Western dishes.

¥ Kyushu Jangara Ramen
Shanzeru Harajuku Ni-go-kan 1F-2F,
1-13-21 Jingumae, Shibuya-ku (3404 5572,
www.kyushujangara.co.jp). Harajuku station
(Yamanote line), Omotesando exit or Meiji-
Jingumae station (Chiyoda line), exit 3. **Open**
10.45am-2am Mon- Thur; 10.45am-3am Fri;
10am-3am Sat; 10am-2am Sun. **Average**
¥1,500. **No credit cards. Ramen**
Kyushu ramen from Fukuoka City is the speciality
here, and how you have it is entirely up to you. At
this bright and breezy noodle house, customers can
specify particular broths (lighter or heavier), types
of noodles (thin, thick or in between), quantities and
toppings. There are often queues snaking down the
stairs, but don't worry – with 73 seats, an opening
will soon appear.
Other locations 2-11-8 Uchi Kanda, Chiyoda-ku
(3512 4059); 1-7-7 Nihonbashi, Chuo-ku (3281 0701).

¥ Maisen
4-8-5 Jingumae, Shibuya-ku (3470 0071,
http://members.aol.com/maisenpr). Omotesando
station (Chiyoda, Ginza, Hanzomon lines), exit
A2. **Open** 11am-10pm daily. **Average** ¥3,000.
Credit DC, JCB, MC, V. **English menu.**
Map p65. **Tonkatsu**
The main branch of this *tonkatsu* chain is built
around a converted bathhouse. If you're able to get
a seat in the huge and airy dining room in the back,
you'll notice several telltale signs of the building's
origins: very high ceilings and a small garden pond.
You can't go wrong with any of the set meals that
are on offer here; standard *rosu katsu* or lean *hire
katsu* are both good choices, and each comes with
rice, soup and pickled radish.
Other locations 1-9-1 Marunouchi, Chiyoda-ku
(6638 6871).

¥ Natural Harmony Angolo
3-38-12 Jingumae, Shibuya-ku (3405 8393).
Gaienmae station (Ginza line), exits 2, 3. **Open**
11.30am-2.30pm, 6-9pm Tue-Sun. **Average**
¥1,200-¥1,500. **No credit cards. English
menu. Map** p65. **Modern Japanese**
Still Tokyo's best natural-food restaurant, this no-
smoking venue has a simple, wood-clad interior and
an additive-free menu. The food, mostly in a Japanese
vein, is tasty, and although some fish is served, the
ethos is strongly vegetarian. The baked aubergine is
fantastic; the wholewheat pizzas less so.

Restaurant-I
1-4-20 Jingumae, Shibuya-ku (5772 2091,
www.restaurant-i.jp). Harajuku station (JR line),
Takeshita exit or Meiji-Jingumae station (Chiyoda

CONSUME

line), exit 5. **Open** 11.30am-3pm, 6-10pm daily. **Average** ¥9,000. **Credit** AmEx, DC, JCB, MC, V. **Modern Japanese**
Keisuke Matsushima is best known for his eponymous 'eco-gastro' restaurant in Nice, France, but he has returned to his roots with this restaurant, situated in the tranquil shadow of the Togo shrine, a short hop from where his career began. Matsushima uses French, Italian and Chinese techniques to put an international flavour on traditional Japanese dishes such as *bonbon d'iwanori* (sweet dumplings wrapped in iwanori seaweed) or *thon marine zuke*, an Edo-style *maguro* marinade. Ingredients are mainly local and organic.

Tama
CI Plaza 2F, 2-3-1 Kita-Aoyama, Minato-ku (5772 3933, www.bigriver.co.jp). Gaienmae station (Ginza line), exit 4. **Open** 11.30am-2pm, 5.30-11pm Mon-Fri; noon-3pm, 6-11pm Sat; noon-3pm, 5-11pm Sun. **Average** ¥3,500. **Credit** AmEx, DC, JCB, MC, V. **English menu.** Izakaya
Tama serves inventive *izakaya* food rejigged for the new century and backed up with an exemplary selection of saké and *shochu*. Unlike so many similar saké-centric spots, Tama is hip enough to appeal to design-conscious Aoyama types while also remaining refreshingly affordable.

Non-Japanese

Adding:blue
6-3-16 Minami-Aoyama, Minato-ku (5485 2266, www.addingblue.com). Omotesando station (Chiyoda, Ginza, Hanzomon lines), exit B1. **Open** 5.30-11pm Mon-Fri; 3-10pm Sat. **Average** ¥5,000. **Credit** AmEx, DC, JCB, MC, V. **English menu.** Mediterranean
One part casual café-wine bar, two parts sleek, contemporary restaurant, adding:blue is run by, and located a stone's throw from, the Blue Note jazz club, hence the name and hip typography. Chef Takahisa Nagasawa's modern Mediterranean cuisine really excels. The place also has a refreshing lack of attitude and a relaxed open terrace that makes the experience even more pleasant.
▶ *For the Blue Note Tokyo jazz club, see p255.*

L'Artémis
2-31-7 Jingumae, Shibuya-ku (5786 0220, www.artemisjp.com). Harajuku station (Yamanote line), Omotesando exit or Meiji-Jingumae station (Chiyoda line), exit 5. **Open** noon-2pm, 6-9.30pm Mon, Tue, Thur-Sun. **Average** ¥5,000. **Credit** AmEx, DC, JCB, MC, V. **Map** p65. **French**
L'Artémis showcases the excellent skills of Yusuke Nakada, one Tokyo's most able young chefs (and a protégé of Regis Marcon). His ¥3,990 Menu Pétillant includes his signature smoked-salmon salad (with

poached egg and caviar) and superb scrambled egg with *uni* (urchin). The tables are a bit cramped, but at these prices, who cares?

Benoit
La Porte Aoyama 10F, 5-51-8 Jingumae, Shibuya-ku (6419 4181, www.benoit-tokyo.com). Omotesando station (Chiyoda, Ginza, Hanzomon lines), exit B2. **Open** 11.30am-2.30pm, 5.30-9.30pm daily. **Average** ¥9,000. **Credit** AmEx, DC, JCB, MC, V. **English menu.** Bistro
Alain Ducasse presents a fine example of his inventive Mediterranean bistro cuisine. Benoit is relaxed and informal, but everything runs like clockwork. Drop in during the afternoon for a salad or a bowl of the delectable *soupe de poisson*. It's also worth keeping an eye out for the special monthly Wine Days, when all bottles are discounted.

Le Bretagne
3-5-4 Jingumae, Shibuya-ku (3478 7855, www.le-bretagne.com). Omotesando station (Chiyoda, Ginza, Hanzomon lines), exit A2. **Open** 11am-11pm Mon-Sat; 11am-10pm Sun. **Average** ¥4,000. **Credit** AmEx, DC, JCB, MC, V. **English menu. Map** p65. Crêperie
Owner Bertrand Larcher is a native Breton, so it's no surprise that his buckwheat *galettes* are authentically tasty. The sweet crêpes are excellent too. So close to swanky Omotesando, Le Bretagne's homely wood-clad interior makes a welcome break from fashion-store façades.

★ Les Créations de Narisawa
2-6-15 Minami-Aoyama, Minato-ku (5785 0799, www.narisawa-yoshihiro.com). Aoyama-Itchome station (Ginza, Hanzomon, Oedo lines), exit 5. **Open** noon-1pm, 6.30-9pm Mon-Sat. **Average** ¥25,000. **Credit** AmEx, DC, JCB, MC, V. **French**
Yoshihiro Narasawa learned his craft in the kitchens of Paul Bocuse, Joël Robuchon and Frédy Girardet, but his cuisine is entirely his own, as the restaurant's name reminds us. Dishes often resemble miniature landscapes, sometimes accompanied by whimsies such as a waft of smoke trapped under a glass dome, but always emphasising seasonality in ingredients and plating. The Pellegrino awards named this Asia's best restaurant in 2009 and 2010, and Michelin elevated it to two-star status in 2010.

Fonda de la Madrugada
Villa Bianca B1, 2-33-12 Jingumae, Shibuya-ku (5410 6288, www.fonda-m.com). Harajuku station (Yamanote line), Omotesando exit or Meiji-Jingumae station (Chiyoda line), exit 5. **Open** 5.30pm-2am Mon-Thur, Sun; 5.30pm-5am Fri, Sat. **Average** ¥4,500. **Credit** AmEx, DC, JCB, MC, V. **English menu. Map** p65. Mexican
When a restaurant has in-house mariachi players, you'd be forgiven for deciding to steer well clear. But

though the vibe might be a little Disneyesque, the food is decent and as authentic as you can expect to find in Tokyo. It might not be Guadalajara, but it could almost be Cancùn.

Fumin

Aoyama Ohara Bldg B1F, 5-7-17 Minami-Aoyama, Minato-ku (3498 4466). Omotesando station (Chiyoda, Ginza, Hanzomon lines), exit B1. **Open** 11.30am-2.30pm, 6-9.30pm Mon-Fri; 11.45am-2.30pm, 5.30-9pm Sat. Closed 1st Mon of mth. **Average** ¥4,000. **No credit cards**. **Map** p65. Chinese

This much-loved Chinese restaurant serves full-flavoured home-style cooking, and in generous servings too. The *negi* (spring onion) wonton, *kaisen gyoza* (seafood dumplings) and the house special Fumin noodles are so popular that you'll almost certainly have to wait in line.

Ghungroo

Seinan Bldg 2F, 5-6-19 Minami-Aoyama, Minato-ku (3406 0464, www.ghungroo-jp.com). Omotesando station (Chiyoda, Ginza, Hanzomon lines), exit B1. **Open** 11.30am-10.30pm Mon-Fri; noon-10.30pm Sat; noon-9.30pm Sun. **Average** ¥3,500. **Credit** AmEx, DC, JCB, MC, V. **English menu**. **Map** p65. Indian

The closest you can get in Tokyo to an upscale British-style Indian curry house, Ghungroo is divided into two rooms, the inner chamber being the more inviting. The menu contains few surprises, but the chicken dishes and okra curry are especially good. As with most Indian cooking in Japan, the rice is Japanese-style short grain – best to stick with the naan, fresh from the tandoor.

Hannibal Deux

Harajuku Miwa Bldg B1F, 3-53-3 Sendagaya, Shibuya-ku (3479 3710, www.hannibal.cc). Harajuku station (Yamanote line), Omotesando exit or Meiji-Jingumae station (Chiyoda line), exit 5. **Open** 5.30-11pm daily. **Average** ¥4,500. **Credit** AmEx, DC, JCB, MC, V. **Map** p65. Tunisian

Chef Mondher Gheribi's Tunisian home cooking adds another dimension to this colourfully cosmopolitan area. He draws on influences from around the Mediterranean, but his best dishes are the ones that hail from his homeland – *mechoui* salad, excellent roast chicken stuffed with banana and herbs, and home-made *khobz* bread served with red-hot harissa sauce.

Harem

CI Plaza B1, 2-3-1 Kita-Aoyama, Minato-ku (5786 2929, www.harem.co.jp). Gaienmae station (Ginza line), exit 4. **Open** 11.30am-2.30pm, 5.30-11pm Mon-Sat. **Average** ¥5,000. **Credit** AmEx, DC, JCB, MC, V. **English menu**. **Map** p65. Turkish

The atmosphere here is more refined than at most of Tokyo's mom-and-pop Turkish eateries, and so is the cuisine. Among the standouts: the excellent meze, *imam bayildi* (aubergine) and *hunkar gebendi* ('His Majesty's favourite') lamb. Food fit for a sultan.

Kaikatei

7-8-1 Minami-Aoyama, Minato-ku (3499 5872). Omotesando station (Chiyoda, Ginza, Hanzomon lines), exit B1. **Open** 11am-2pm, 6-10pm Mon-Sat. **Average** ¥3,500. **No credit cards**. Chinese

Visiting Kaikatei is like stepping back in time to 1930s Shanghai: old beer posters, wooden clocks, dated LPs and odd murals of barbarian foreigners lend an air of wartime mystery. The shrimp in crab sauce is delicately flavoured, and a good match for mildly spicy Peking-style chicken with cashew nuts and rich black-bean sauce.

Kurkku Kitchen

2-18-21 Jingumae, Shibuya-ku (5414 0944, www.kurkku.jp/english/kitchen.html). Harajuku station (Yamanote line), Omotesando exit or Meiji-Jingumae station (Chiyoda line), exit 5. **Open** 11.30am-2pm, 6-10pm Tue-Sun. **Average** ¥4,500. **Credit** AmEx, DC, JCB, MC, V. **English menu**. **Map** p65. International

The centrepiece of an ambitious project marrying quality food, contemporary architecture and green thinking, Kurkku Kitchen bases its French-Japanese hybrid cuisine on organic produce and meat. Most of the food is cooked over a charcoal grill, and it's all delectable.

Lauburu

6-8-18 Minami-Aoyama, Minato-ku (3498 1314). Omotesando station (Chiyoda, Ginza, Hanzomon lines), exit B3. **Open** 6-11pm Mon-Sat. **Average** ¥5,000. **Credit** AmEx, DC, JCB, MC, V. French

Chef Shinichiro Sakurai has mastered the sturdy, heart-warming cuisine of France's Basque country in all its glory. His intimate restaurant is simple and rustic, much like his cooking. Look no further to find the heartiest cassoulet in all of Asia, and back it up with the sturdy wines of Madiran and south-west France.

¥ Pure Café

5-5-21 Minami-Aoyama, Minato-ku (5466 2611, www.pure-cafe.com). Omotesando station (Chiyoda, Ginza, Hanzomon lines), exit B3. **Open** 8.30am-10.30pm daily. **Average** ¥2,000. **Credit** AmEx, DC, JCB, MC, V. **English menu**. **Map** p65. Vegetarian

Pure Café melds health-conscious, near-vegan principles with a bright, contemporary interior (it's part of the glass-fronted Aveda holistic spa complex). The menu offers a mix of East and West, along with organic wines and beer.

► *For a bigger menu by the same people, search out the secluded Café Eight (see p173).*

Super Bowls

A fanatic's guide to the city's best ramen.

Fifty years ago, Momofuku Ando created instant ramen and forever changed the world. College students across the globe had an effort-free staple food, and their wallets were thankful. Unfortunately, this all but ruined the image of ramen outside Japan. A wonderful meal was reduced to a three-minute last resort.

But Tokyo is the place to restore your faith in ramen. Think handmade noodles, soup that takes days to make, and lots and lots of pork.

Not every joint is a gem: ramen in Tokyo runs the gamut from delicious to almost inedible, but here are five favourites.

A good place to start is **Manpuku** (2-13-13 Ginza, Chuo-ku, 3541 7210). Dating back to the early 1920s, this Ginza joint is one of the oldest and most traditional ramen shops in town. The base is a simple, hearty soy broth, accentuated by shiitake, konbu seaweed and the secret ingredients that they've been using for the last 90 years. It's reminiscent of 'Oriental flavour' instant noodles, but a whole lot better.

Across town, in Shinjuku's Golden Gai drinking district, is another shop offering soy-based ramen. But **Nagi** (2F, 1-1-10 Kabukicho, Shinjuku-ku, 3205 1925) takes a fresher approach. The soup packs a strong fishy taste, thanks to copious amounts of *niboshi* (dried sardines). The noodles are cut wide; some are more lasagne than linguine.

Around the year 2000, *tsukemen* made a huge impact on the Tokyo ramen scene.

These thick, wheaty noodles are served dry, with a separate pork and fish soup for dipping. Depending on how many oily fish bits the chef uses, the dip ranges in consistency from light broth to motor oil. One of the best *tsukemen* shops, evident by the 45- to 90-minute wait, is **Tetsu** (4-1-14 Sendagi, Bunkyo-ku, 3827 6272). Go for the *atsumori* option. You'll be given the standard bowl of cold noodles, plus a bowl of hot ones, plus the soup, plus a red-hot stone to reheat the broth, plus extra soup. It's a complicated process, made simple by a tableside manga-style instruction card.

Tokyo is no stranger to fusion cuisine, the ramen world included. **Basanova** (1-4-18 Hanegi, Setagaya-ku) executes the concept flawlessly with its green-curry ramen. It's not just noodles with a spicy sauce: Basanova blends a traditional pork soup with Thai herbs and spices. The result is like nothing you've tasted before, and goes great with a cold beer.

Picking a miso ramen shop can be daunting, with so much choice and such variable quality. But **Kururi** (3-2 Ichigaya Tamachi, Shinjuku-ku; 3269 0801) consistently makes the top three in rankings by TV shows, magazines and websites. The chef fries up nine kinds of miso before adding the rich soup to create a ramen that's a little sweet and a lot salty. It's then reduced a little, giving Kururi one of the biggest impacts in town.

● *Brian MacDuckston blogs about ramen at www.ramenadventures.com.*

CONSUME

IKEBUKURO
Japanese

¥ Ikebukuro Gyoza Stadium
*2-3F Namjatown, World Importmart,
3 Higashi-Ikebukuro, Toshima-ku (5950 0765,
www.teamnamja.com/ftp/ikebukuro_gyoza).
Ikebukuro station (Yamanote, Marunouchi,
Yurakucho lines), east exit.* **Open** 10am-10pm
daily. **Average** ¥2,000. **No credit cards.**
Map p69. Gyoza
One of Tokyo's most bizarre experiences. Inside a
Japanese ghost theme park lies this arcade of booths
serving *gyoza* – Japan's take on Chinese-style
dumplings (mostly pan-fried). Upstairs you'll find
Dessert Republic and Ice Cream City, both of them
serving frozen desserts from all over Japan in weird
and wonderful local flavours (grilled chicken-wing
ice-cream, anyone?)

Yozakura Bijin
*1-21-2 Minami-Ikebukuro, Toshima-ku (5952
5860, www.diamond-dining.com/yozakura).
Ikebukuro station (JR, Marunouchi, Seibu, Tobu,
Yurakucho lines), east exit.* **Open** 5pm-4am Mon-
Sat; 5-11pm Sun. **Average** ¥5,000. **Credit**
AmEx, DC, JCB, MC, V. Izakaya
The decor makes a bigger impression than the food
here. It's a make-believe 19th-century Tokyo, with
a checklist of traditional motifs – cherry blossom,
folding fans, washi paper, kimono fabric – and a
passion-red colour scheme. Kitsch it may be, but it's
also gorgeous and cosy. The menu offers the gamut
of *izakaya* fare, from tempura to sashimi to *shabu-
shabu*, always good enough, never dazzling.

Non-Japanese

¥ A Raj
*2-42-7 Minami-Ikebukuro, Toshima-ku (3981
9688). Higashi-Ikebukuro station (Yurakucho
line), exit 3.* **Open** 11.30am-2pm, 6-10.30pm Mon,
Wed-Sun. **Average** ¥2,500. **Credit** AmEx, DC,
JCB, MC, V. **English menu. Map** p69. Indian
With its colourful wall hangings of Ganesha,
Hanuman and Shiva, this modest Indian diner is a
welcome find in a barren location (it's situated
underneath an expressway overpass). Besides the
fine range of well-priced curries, chef A Raj also
delivers good *dosas, idli, uppama* and other South
Indian exotica. Not worth crossing town for, but nice
if you're nearby.

¥ Chion Shokudo
*1-24-1 Ikebukuro, Toshima-ku (5951 8288).
Ikebukuro station (Yamanote, Marunouchi,
Yurakucho lines), east exit.* **Open** 11am-2pm,
6pm-2.30am Mon-Fri; 6pm-2.30am Sat, Sun.
Average ¥3,000. **No credit cards. Map** p69.
Chinese

Specialising in the fiery cuisine of Sichuan, this basement eaterie is run by and for the local Chinese community. Watch Chinese satellite TV as you tuck into
spicy *tantan-men* noodles. Prices are as low as you'd
expect, with Tsingtao beer just ¥380 per bottle.

Shilingol
*4-11-9 Sengoku, Bunkyo-ku (5978 3837).
Sugamo station (Yamanote line), south exit;
(Mita line), exit A2 or Sengoku station (Mita
line), exit A4.* **Open** 6-10.30pm daily. **Average**
¥3,500. **No credit cards. English menu.**
Mongolian
As much a Mongolian cultural centre as a restaurant, this converted coffee shop serves little that isn't
made with mutton. You can have it stuffed in
dumplings, skewered on kebabs, stewed with spuds,
swished in *shabu-shabu* style or simply boiled on the
bone. To help it down, there's Genghis Khan vodka
and live performances of folk music on the two-
stringed 'horse-head' cello. Totally transporting.

MARUNOUCHI & AROUND
Japanese

Botan
*1-15 Kanda-Sudacho, Chiyoda-ku (3251 0577).
Kanda station (Yamanote line), east exit; (Ginza
line), exits 5, 6 or Awajicho station (Marunouchi
line), exit A3 or Ogawamachi station (Shinjuku
line), exit A3.* **Open** 11.30am-8pm Mon-Sat.
Average ¥7,000. **Credit** AmEx, DC, JCB, MC, V.
Map p77. Sukiyaki
Botan's charm lies in its timeworn wooden interior
as much as its food. There's only one thing on the
menu: chicken sukiyaki. You will be well taken care
of by matrons in kimonos, who bring glowing charcoal to the grill atop your low table, set a small iron
dish on top, then begin cooking: chicken, onion, tofu
and vegetables, all in the rich, sweet house sauce.

Ieyasu Hon-jin
*1-30 Kanda-Jinbocho, Chiyoda-ku (3291 6228).
Jinbocho station (Hanzomon, Mita, Shinjuku
lines), exit A7.* **Open** 5-10pm Mon-Fri. **Average**
¥5,000. **No credit cards. Map** p77. Yakitori
Amiable host Taisho bangs the drum behind the bar
to greet each new customer to this cosy, top-class
yakitori bar named after the first of the Tokugawa
shoguns. There are only a dozen seats, so everyone
crowds around the counter, where a wide choice of
food lies in glass cases, already on sticks, ready to
be popped on the coals and grilled. The food is excellent, as is the saké. Avoid the 6-8pm after-work rush
and don't go in a group of more than three.

Isegen
*1-11-1 Kanda-Sudacho, Chiyoda-ku (3251 1229).
Kanda station (Yamanote line), east exit; (Ginza
line), exits 5, 6 or Awajicho station (Marunouchi*

line), exit A3 or Ogawamachi station (Shinjuku line), exit A3. **Open** 11.30am-2pm, 5-10pm Mon-Fri (also Sat from Oct to Apr). **Average** ¥5,000. **No credit cards. Map** p77. **Hotpot**
Isegen's legendary *anko nabe* (monkfish casserole) is basic but warming – in fact, exactly like the sprawling wooden premises. The *anko* season runs from September to April, which is thus the best time of year for a hearty hotpot. The rest of the year the menu revolves around *ayu* (a trout-like sweetfish) and other freshwater fish.

¥ Izumo Soba Honke
1-31 Kanda-Jinbocho, Chiyoda-ku (3291 3005, www.izumosoba.jp). Jinbocho station (Hanzomon, Mita, Shinjuku lines), exit A7. **Open** 11.30am-8.30pm Mon-Fri; 11.30am-6.30pm Sat. **Average** ¥3,000. **Credit** AmEx, DC, JCB, MC, V. **Map** p77. **Soba**
The hand-chopped soba noodles here are some of the best that can be found in town: wholesome and robust, prepared in the country style popular in Shimane (western Japan). The classic way to eat them is cold, served in stacks of five small trays with a variety of condiments. A good range of hot soba in broth is also available.

Kandagawa Honten
2-5-11 Soto-Kanda, Chiyoda-ku (3251 5031, www.unagidaisuki.com/mkandagawa.html). Ochanomizu station (Chuo, Marunouchi lines), Hijiribashi exit or Suehirocho station (Ginza line). **Open** 11.30am-1.30pm, 5-7.30pm Mon-Sat. Closed 2nd Sat of mth. **Average** ¥5,000. **Credit** DC, MC, V. **Unagi**
In this splendid old townhouse, kimono-clad waitresses serve succulent, tender eel grilled over charcoal and basted with thick, sweet soy sauce. It's all excellent, but you really shouldn't miss the *unaju*: eel served on a bed of white rice inside an ornate lacquered box. A classic dish of old Tokyo, and eaten in a setting to match. Kandagawa is just steps from the electronic frazzle of Akihabara, but a world away in atmosphere. Advance reservations are essential here.

¥ Kanda Yabu Soba
2-10 Kanda-Awajicho, Chiyoda-ku (3251 0287). Kanda station (Yamanote line), east exit; (Ginza line), exits 5, 6 or Ogawamachi station (Shinjuku line), exit A3 or Awajicho station (Marunouchi line), exit A3. **Open** 11.30am-7.30pm daily. **Average** ¥2,500. **No credit cards. English menu. Map** p77. **Soba**
Like a living museum dedicated to the traditional art of the buckwheat noodle, Kanda Yabu Soba is housed in a low Japanese house with a small garden, decorated inside with *shoji* screens, tatami and woodblock prints. Besides its excellent soba, Yabu serves tasty side dishes if you fancy joining the locals in some beer or saké.

Takara
Tokyo International Forum B1 Concourse, 3-5-1 Marunouchi, Chiyoda-ku (5223 9888, www.t-i-forum.co.jp). Tokyo station (Marunouchi lines), Tokyo Forum exit. **Open** 11.30am-2.30pm, 5-11pm Mon-Fri; 11.30am-3pm, 5-10pm Sat, Sun. **Average** ¥4,500. **Credit** AmEx, DC, JCB, MC, V. **English menu. Map** p77. **Izakaya**
Takara offers welcome sanctuary in the echoing concrete of the International Forum's basement. The food is standard modern *izakaya* fare, although bolstered with a few Spanish-style tapas, but the main draw here is the brilliant selection of saké from throughout Japan, plus fine microbrewed ales and a better than expected wine list. The place also serves good set lunches.

Non-Japanese

A16
Park Bldg, Marunouchi Brick Square, 2-6-1 Marunouchi, Chiyoda-ku (3212 5215, http://c113skl3.securesites.net/a16). Tokyo station (Yamanote, Chuo lines), Shin Marubiru exit; (Marunouchi line), exit 5. **Open** 11am-11pm Mon-Sat; 11am-10pm Sun. **Average** ¥4,000. **Credit** AmEx, DC, JCB, MC, V. **English menu. Map** p77. **Italian**
It doesn't feel as if you're in Japan when you're sitting on the patio, eating Italian and staring at a Henry Moore on a lawn, but the new Brick Square enclave is a Zen-like sanctum and this restaurant is yet another sign of Tokyo's growing appetite for top-quality pizza.

¥ Aroyna Tabeta
3-7-11 Marunouchi, Chiyoda-ku (5219 6099, www.tabeta.com/yurakucho). Tokyo station (Yamanote, Marunouchi lines), Tokyo Forum exit. **Open** 11am-10.30pm Mon-Sat; 11am-10pm Sun. **Average** ¥1,500. **No credit cards. English menu. Map** p77. **Thai**
Nowhere in Tokyo makes Thai street food that's as authentic and cheap as at this funky little diner that's located under the train tracks near the International Forum. The simple set meals (including curries, fried noodles and the house speciality, of braised pork) are just ¥630 each: a veritable bargain, especially for somewhere in this upwardly mobile stretch of the city.

Bar de España Muy
Tokyo Bldg Tokia 2F, 2-3-3 Marunouchi, Chiyoda-ku (5224 6161, www.spain-bar.jp/muy). Tokyo station (Yamanote, Marunouchi lines), Marunouchi South exit. **Open** 11.30am-2.30pm, 5.30-11pm Mon-Wed; 11.30am-2.30pm, 5.30pm-midnight Thur; 11.30am-4pm, 5.30-11pm Fri; 11.30am-4pm, 5.30-10pm Sun. **Average** ¥4,000. **Credit** AmEx, DC, JCB, MC, V. **Map** p77. **Tapas**

CONSUME

CONSUME

Ukai Tofuya. *See p162.*

Chic and contemporary Barcelona-style tapas served in a setting of steel, glass and polished wood. The bar runs half the length of the building, giving brilliant views over the passing trains as you sip cava and nibble *albondigas*, fresh-made mini-tortillas or ink-black paella. There's even a small outside terrace looking up at the dramatic International Forum. ▶ *For more on the local surroundings, see p253 Tokyo International Forum.*

Brasserie aux Amis
Shin-Tokyo Bldg 1F, 3-3-1 Marunouchi, Chiyoda-ku (6212 1566, www.auxamis.com/brasserie). Tokyo station (Yamanote, Marunouchi lines), Marunouchi exit or Yurakucho station (Yamanote, Yurakucho lines), International Forum exit. **Open** 11am-10.30pm Mon-Sat; 11.30am-9.30pm Sun. **Average** ¥4,500. **Credit** AmEx, DC, JCB, MC, V. **Map** p77. French
A slice of Paris in Marunouchi, right down to the red banquettes, brass fittings and menu chalked on the large wall mirrors. There's a small bar by the door, for a quick espresso or a glass of *vin ordinaire*, as well as a top-notch wine list to go with the authentically hearty brasserie food.

★ Dhaba India
2-7-9 Yaesu, Chuo-ku (3272 7160, www.dhabaindia.com). Kyobashi station (Ginza line), exit 5. **Open** 11.15am-3pm, 5-11pm Mon-Fri; noon-3pm, 5-10pm Sat, Sun. **Average** ¥4,000. **Credit** AmEx, DC, JCB, MC, V. **English menu**. **Map** p59. Indian
One of the few places serving South Indian specialties. Delicious masala dosas, curries and thali meals, served with real basmati rice (evenings only), prepared by ever-friendly staff. The interior is also a breath of fresh air, without the elephant carvings and Bollywood videos that seem de rigueur elsewhere.

Shisen Hanten
Zenkoku Ryokan Kaikan 5F-6F, 2-5-5 Hirakawa-cho, Chiyoda-ku (3263 9371, www.sisen.jp). Nagatacho station (Hanzomon, Nanboku, Yurakucho lines), exit 5. **Open** 11.30am-2pm, 5-9pm daily. **Average** ¥5,000. **Credit** AmEx, DC, JCB, MC, V. **English menu**. **Map** p77. Chinese
Good Szechuan cuisine, albeit with the spices toned down for Japanese palates, from chef Kenichi Shin, best known for his appearances in the Iron Chef TV cooking shows. His classic dish is *mabo-dofu* (spicy minced meat with tofu), but in summer, queues form for his *hiyashi chuka*, chilled Chinese-style noodles and chopped vegetables that are topped with sesame or vinegar sauce. **Other locations** throughout the city.

Tapas Molecular Bar
Mandarin Oriental Hotel 38F, 2-1-1 Nihonbashi-Muromachi, Chuo-ku (3270 8800, www.mandarinoriental.com/Tokyo/dining).

Mitsukoshimae station (Ginza, Hanzomon lines), exit A8. **Open** (by reservation only) 6pm, 8.30pm. **Average** ¥12,000. **Credit** AmEx, DC, JCB, MC, V. **English menu**. **Map** p77. Fusion
Tokyo's first outpost of molecular gastronomy, high up in the Mandarin Oriental tower. It's no rival to Spain's El Bulli or the UK's Fat Duck in either scale or creativity, but it's still remarkable culinary theatre, watching as your food – 25 courses or more – emerges from syringes or super-chilled distilling retorts. The chef has been producing more seasonal fare since winning a Michelin star in 2009. You'll need to book well ahead: this bar has only eight seats and two sittings per night.

ROPPONGI & AZABU
Japanese

Banrekiryukodo
2-33-5 Higashi-Azabu, Minato-ku (3505 5686, www.banreki.com). Azabu-Juban station (Nanboku, Oedo lines), exit 3. **Open** 11.30am-1.30pm, 6-9pm Mon-Sat. **Average** ¥9,000. **Credit** AmEx, DC, JCB, MC, V. **English menu**. Modern Japanese
Banreki (as it's known to its many admirers) offers an excellent, contemporary take on Japanese cuisine. Its interior melds traditional craftsmanship with cutting-edge design, and its *kaiseki*-style meals are multi-course gourmet taste adventures that go just as well with wine as premium saké. The ground-floor dining area consists of a single huge wooden counter. If you want more privacy, try to book the beautiful tea-ceremony-style tatami room downstairs. Reservations are essential.

Fukuzushi
5-7-8 Roppongi, Minato-ku (3402 4116, www.roppongifukuzushi.com). Roppongi station (Hibiya, Oedo lines), exit 3. **Open** 11.30am-2pm, 5.30-11pm Mon-Sat; 5.30-10pm Sun. **Average** ¥7,000. **Credit** AmEx, DC, JCB, MC, V. **English menu**. **Map** p87. Sushi
Tokyo may have more exclusive (and even pricier) sushi shops than Fukuzushi, but few are as welcoming or accessible. Superlative seafood in an elegant yet casual setting that feels miles away from the gritty hubbub of Roppongi.

★ Gonpachi
1-13-11 Nishi-Azabu, Minato-ku (5771 0170, www.global-dining.com). Roppongi station (Hibiya, Oedo lines), exit 1. **Open** 11.30am-5am daily. **Average** ¥5,500. **Credit** AmEx, DC, JCB, MC, V. **English menu**. **Map** p87. Izakaya/sushi.
Dominating the Nishi-Azabu crossing like a feudal Japanese castle, Gonpachi was supposedly an inspiration for the film *Kill Bill*. Sit at rustic wooden tables or in private booths and sup on simple country-style

CONSUME

cooking, such as yakitori, grilled pork or soba noodles. The waiters dress in folksy *happi* coats, and traditional festival music plays over the speakers. The separate third-floor sushi restaurant is more sophisticated, in both atmosphere and food, and has an open-air terrace. *Photo p149.*

Other locations Mediage 4F, 1-7-1 Daiba, Minato-ku (3599 4807); E Spacetower 14F, 3-6 Maruyamacho, Shibuya-ku (5784 2011); 1-23 Ginza, Chuo-ku (5524 3641).

★ Inakaya

4-10-11 Roppongi, Minato-ku (5775 1012, www.roppongiinakaya.jp/en/map_west.html). Akasaka station (Chiyoda line), exit 6 or Roppongi station (Hibiya line), exit 6; (Oedo line), exit 7. **Open** 5-11pm daily. **Average** ¥8,000. **Credit** AmEx, DC, JCB, MC, V. **Map** p87. **Japanese grill**

Most of the ingredients are laid out in front of you here. Point to whatever you fancy – seafood, meat, tofu or vegetables – and one of the two chefs will cook your choice over charcoal in front of you, passing it to you across the counter on long wooden paddles. It's theatrical, fun and remarkably tasty, but the bill escalates fast, especially if you order sole or sirloin, so don't get carried away by the tempo of the place.

Other locations 5-3-4 Roppongi, Minato-ku (3408 5040); 8-7-4 Ginza, Chuo-ku (3569 1708).

★ Itosho

3-4-7 Azabu-Juban, Minato-ku (3454 6538). Azabu-Juban station (Nanboku, Oedo lines), exit 1. **Open** noon-1pm, 5.30-7.30pm Mon-Sat. **Average** ¥8,000. **No credit cards**. **Shojin ryori**

For review, *see p172* **Shojin Ryori**.

Maimon

6-1-3 Roppongi, Minato-ku (3408 2600, www.maimon.jp). Roppongi station (Hibiya, Oedo lines), exit 3. **Open** 11.30am-2.30pm, 6pm-midnight daily. **Average** ¥8,000. **Credit** AmEx, DC, JCB, MC, V. **English menu**. **Map** p87. **Oyster bar**

This über-stylish oyster bar (run by the same company behind New York's Megu) offers an astounding 40 varieties of the mollusc, served either raw in the shell or cooked in numerous ways. Alternatives include yakitori and other charcoal-grilled delicacies (beef tongue, pork, shellfish and more), with a great range of saké and *shochu*.

Other locations 1-1-10 Ebisu-Minami, Shibuya-ku (3715 0303); 8-3-saki Ginza, Chuo-ku (3569 7733).

★ Nihonryori Ryugin

7-17-24 Roppongi, Minato-ku (www.nihonryori-ryugin.com). Roppongi station (Hibiya, Oedo lines), exits 2, 7. **Open** 6pm-1am (last orders 10.30pm). **Average** ¥25,000. **Credit** AmEx, DC, JCB, MC, V. **English menu**. **Map** p87. **Modern Japanese**

Ryugin built its considerable reputation with molecular gastronomy, but it took a more traditional turn in 2010 with less of the eye-catching chemistry and more back-to-basics Japanese fare. It's done nothing to dampen the buzz, and there's now an à la carte menu (from 9pm) for those that don't have the stomach or wallet for the full 12-course extravaganza. The service is exceptional. *Photo p152.*

Nodaiwa

1-5-4 Higashi-Azabu, Minato-ku (3583 7852, www.geocities.co.jp/Milkyway/8859/nodaiwa). Akabanebashi station (Oedo line), Akabanebashi exit or Kamiyacho station (Hibiya line), exit 1. **Open** 11am-1.30pm, 5-8pm Mon-Sat. **Average** ¥4,000. **Credit** MC, V. **English menu**. **Map** p87. **Unagi**

Housed in a converted *kura* storehouse transported from the mountains, Nodaiwa is the most refined *unagi* shop in the city. It only uses eels that have been caught in the wild, and the difference is noticeable in the texture, especially if you try the *shirayaki* (grilled without any added sauce and eaten with a dip of soy sauce and wasabi).

Pintokona

Hollywood Plaza B2F, 6-4-1 Roppongi, Minato-ku (5771 1133). Roppongi station (Hibiya, Oedo lines), exit 1. **Open** 11am-11pm daily. **Average** ¥4,500. **Credit** AmEx, DC, JCB, MC, V. **Map** p87. **Sushi**

A conveyor-belt sushi bar with a difference. Here, you can either help yourself to whatever's going past, or peruse the menu, sing out your order and wait for it to be prepared and delivered straight to you. Quality and freshness are definitely superior, but so too are the prices.

T

Atago Shrine, 1-5-3 Atago, Minato-ku (5777 5557, www.tasaki-shinya.com). Kamiyacho station (Hibiya Line), exit 3 or Toranomon station (Ginza Line), exit A1. **Open** 11.30am-2pm, 5-10pm Tue-Sun. **Average** ¥5,000. **Credit** AmEx, DC, JCB, MC, V. **Modern Japanese**

Just about everything you eat and drink at T (pronounced 'Tay') is grown, netted or brewed inside Greater Tokyo, mostly in the rural area to the west of the city or the Izu islands to the south. The menu offers simple but beautifully prepared dishes, with plenty of fresh seafood. The location makes it even more special – a low building on top of a wooded knoll in the middle of the city, in the precincts of a Shinto shrine.

★ Ukai Tofuya

4-4-13 Shiba Koen, Minato-ku (3436 1028, www.ukai.co.jp/shiba). Shiba-Koen station (Mita line), exit A4. **Open** 11am-8pm daily. **Average** ¥8,000. **Credit** AmEx, DC, JCB, MC, V. **Tofu**

Pierre Gagnaire Tokyo. *See p165.*

With its wooden architecture, miniature gardens and koi-filled ponds, Ukai Tofuya evokes the spirit of traditional Japan. The illusion is broken when you look up and see Tokyo Tower right over you. If you don't have time to get out to Ukai Toriyama, the parent restaurant in the Ukai group, this makes a very worthy second-best. *Photo p160.*
▶ *For the original, see p171 Ukai Toriyama.*

★ Yamada Chikara

1-15-2 Minami-Azabu, Minato-ku (5942 5817, www.yamadachikara.com). Azabu Juban station (Namboku, Oedo lines), exit 1. **Open** 6pm-midnight daily. **Average** ¥18,000. **Credit** AmEx, DC, JCB, MC, V. **Modern Japanese**
Japan loves its brands, and there's no dining brand bigger than Chef Yamada's former employer, El Bulli. After two years at the Catalan legend, he returned to Japan and, with his wife alongside, opened a restaurant that's beginning to carve a big mark on this city's dining scene. It's refined dining, with signatures including powdered foie gras over a beef consommé. Reservations essential.

Non-Japanese

★ L'Atelier de Joël Robuchon

Roppongi Hills Hillside 2F, 6-10-1 Roppongi, Minato-ku (5772 7500, www.robuchon.com). Roppongi station (Hibiya, Oedo lines), exit 1. **Open** 11.30am-2.30pm, 6-10pm daily. **Average** ¥8,000. **Credit** AmEx, DC, JCB, MC, V. **Map** p87. **French**
Robuchon now has his 'casual' (a relative term, here) counter-style Atelier restaurants on three continents,

and the Tokyo operation is a perfect match with upmarket Roppongi Hills. You sit at the plush counter looking in at the open kitchen, ordering one or two dishes at a time as if it were a sushi counter or a tapas bar (the Spanish influence is also strong in the cuisine). Set dinners start from ¥4,800. Reservations are accepted, but only for the first sitting at 6pm; after that, it's first come, first served.

¥ Bangkok

Woo Bldg 2F, 3-8-8 Roppongi, Minato-ku (3408 7353). Roppongi station (Hibiya, Oedo lines), exit 1. **Open** 11.30am-2pm, 5-10pm Mon-Sat; 11.30am-9pm Sun. Closed 3rd Sun of mth. **Average** ¥2,500. **No credit cards. English menu. Map** p87. **Thai**
This funky second-floor diner is worth tracking down, as it produces good Thai street food without fuss or delay. Among the highlights are *tom kha kai* soup in traditional clay pots, and the minced-meat *larb* 'salads', generously spiked with chillies, lemongrass, mint and onion.

Brasserie Paul Bocuse Le Musée

National Art Center 3F, 7-22-2 Roppongi, Minato-ku (5770 8161, www.nact.jp/english/ restaurant). Nogizaka station (Chiyoda line), exit 6. **Open** 11am-9pm Mon, Wed, Thur, Sat, Sun; 11am-10pm Fri. **Average** ¥7,500. **Credit** AmEx, DC, JCB, MC, V. **French**
Perched dramatically atop a grey concrete cone inside the National Art Center, this brasserie looks like a pastiche of a *Star Wars* set. Unfortunately, the drama doesn't transfer to the plates, with the food falling far short of the standards set by Bocuse in Lyon.

CONSUME

China Café Eight

3-2-13 Nishi Azabu, Minato-ku (5414 5708, www.cceight.com). Roppongi station (Hibiya, Oedo lines), exit 3. **Open** 24hrs daily. **Average** ¥3,500. **Credit** AmEx, DC, JCB, MC, V. **English menu**. **Map** p87. **Chinese**

The staff can be surly and the seating cramped, but you won't find cheaper Peking duck in town. The suggestive decor has novelty value, and the location – right across from the sumptuous Grand Hyatt – makes it feel even more surreal, especially in the wee hours, when it fills up with clubbers.

Cicada

5-2-40 Minami-Azabu, Minato-ku (5447 5522, www.cicada.co.jp). Hiroo station (Hibiya line), exit 3. **Open** 6-11pm Mon, Sun; noon-3pm, 6pm-3am Tue-Sat. **Average** ¥7,000. **Credit** AmEx, DC, JCB, MC, V. **English menu**. **Spanish**

Spain may provide the main inspiration, but the whole of the Mediterranean area is reflected in the excellent modern cooking of American chef David Chiddo. Hugely popular with the expat community (and quite deservedly so), Cicada always generates a great atmosphere. The large dining room is smoke-free, though the bar is anything but. Booking is highly recommended.

Coriander

B1F, 1-10-6 Nishi-Azabu, Minato-ku (3475 5720, www.simc-jp.com/coriander). Roppongi station (Hibiya, Oedo lines), exit 2. **Open** 11.30am-2pm Mon-Fri; 6-11pm Mon-Sat. **Average** ¥5,000. **Credit** AmEx, DC, JCB, MC, V. **English menu**. **Map** p87. **Thai**

A cosy basement restaurant that markets itself as 'new Thai', Coriander serves tasty dishes that are lighter on the chillies than their more authentic cousins and often contain unusual ingredients, as with the carrot *tom yam* soup. The decor is pleasant, heavy on the cushions, greenery and incense, and service is keen if not always efficient.

Garçon de la Vigne

5-17-11 Hiroo, Shibuya-ka (3445 6626, www.le-garcon.jp). Hiroo station (Hibiya line). **Open** noon-2pm, 6-10.30pm Mon-Sat. **Average** ¥6,000. **Credit** AmEx, DC, JCB, MC, V. **Bistro**

As the name suggests, this upmarket bistro focuses on the wine list as much as it does the food, but unusually (for Tokyo), it shuns Bordeaux in favour of Burgundy and the Loire Valley. Dinner menus start from just ¥1,600, and the food is good enough to warrant splurging on a decent bottle.

Harmonie

4-2-15 Nishi-Azabu, Minato-ku (5466 6655). Hiroo station (Hibiya line), exit 1 or Roppongi station (Hibiya, Oedo lines), exit 1. **Open** noon-3pm, 5pm-2am Mon-Sat. **Average** ¥6,000. **Credit** AmEx, DC, JCB, MC, V. **English menu**. **Map** p87. **Bistro**

With an astounding cellar of burgundies, this bistro excels at matching its casual menu with fine wine.

Beacon. *See p166.*

CONSUME

The winter menu features *gibiers* (boar, venison and wild fowl). The cosy, wood-clad second-floor dining room is entirely no-smoking, but if you're gasping you can head to his intimate stand-up bar downstairs for your Cohiba and armagnac.

¥ J's Kitchen
5-15-22 Minami-Azabu, Minato-ku (5475 2727, www.js-kitchen.com). Hiroo station (Hibiya line), exit 1. **Open** 11am-9pm Mon-Sat; 11am-5pm Sun. **Average** ¥3,000. **Credit** AmEx, DC, JCB, MC, V. **English menu.** Macrobiotic
Owner Ueki Kumiko set up this casual deli/restaurant to provide the kind of wholesome food she wanted to serve her young son Jerome (after whom the place is named). Organic, additive-free and entirely vegan, the macrobiotic fare here speaks with a pronounced southern California accent.

Oak Door
Grand Hyatt Hotel 6F, 6-10-3 Roppongi, Minato-ku (4333 8784, www.grandhyatttokyo.com/ cuisine/oakdoor.htm). Roppongi station (Hibiya, Oedo lines), exit 1. **Open** 11.30am-10.30pm daily. **Average** ¥8,000. **Credit** AmEx, DC, JCB, MC, V. **English menu. Map** p87. Steak
A huge selection of premium steaks (each *wagyu* steer individually identified), cooked to order in wood-burning ovens, and a gleaming cellar of New World wines: no wonder Oak Door is so popular with the expense-account expat community.

Pierre Gagnaire Tokyo
ANA Intercontinental Tokyo, 1-12-33 Akasaka, Minato-ku (03 3505 1111, www. anaintercontinental-tokyo.jp/pierre_gagnaire). Tameike Sanno station (Ginza, Nanboku lines), exit 13. **Open** 11.30am-2pm, 6-9pm Tue-Sun. **Average** ¥25,000. **Credit** AmEx, DC, JCB, MC, V. **English menu.** French
The godfather of modern French dining took a second stab at Tokyo's dining scene when he opened this 36th-floor restaurant in a luxury hotel. His first Tokyo outpost closed in 2009, but he bounced back eight months later with the same chef and same style, serving multiple dishes for every course and pairing flavors that only a Gagnaire eaterie could ever pull off. It's the same extraordinary dining experience, but now with a much better view. *Photo p163.*
▶ *To stay, see p132 ANA Intercontinental Tokyo.*

★ Roti
Piramide Bldg 1F, 6-6-9 Roppongi, Minato-ku (5785 3671, www.rotico.com). Roppongi station (Hibiya, Oedo lines), exit 1. **Open** 11.30am-5pm, 6-10pm Mon-Fri; 11.30am-5pm, 6-11pm Sat; 11am-5pm, 6-10pm Sun. **Average** ¥4,500. **Credit** AmEx, DC, JCB, MC, V. **English menu. Map** p87. American
The speciality at this casual, self-styled 'modern American brasserie' is the rotisserie chicken. There's

a good selection of New World wines and American microbrews to provide appropriate lubrication. **Other locations** Galeria Garden Terrace, Tokyo Midtown, 9-7-2 Akasaka, Minato-ku (5413 3655).

SHIBUYA & AROUND
Japanese

Kaikaya
23-7 Maruyama-cho, Shibuya-ku (3770 0878, www.kaikaya.com). Shinsen station (Inokashira line). **Open** (weekends by reservation only) 11.30am-2pm, 5-11.30pm Mon-Thur; 11.30am-2pm, 5pm-4am Fri; 5pm-4am Sat; 5-11.30pm Sun. **Average** ¥5,000. **Credit** AmEx, DC, JCB, MC, V. **English menu.** Modern Japanese
There's always a friendly welcome at this laid-back Japanese-style diner on the fringes of Shibuya. Owner-chef Tange Teruyuki combines his love of the ocean (that's his surfboard on the wall) and cooking to offer an excellent seafood menu, plentiful saké and reasonable prices.

Kanetanaka-so
Cerulean Tower Tokyu Hotel 2F, 26-1 Sakuragaoka-cho, Shibuya-ku (3476 3420, www.kanetanaka.co.jp/so). Shibuya station (Yamanote, Ginza lines), west exit; (Fukutoshin, Hanzomon lines), exit 8. **Open** 7-10.30am, 11.30am-3pm, 5.30-11pm daily. **Average** ¥11,000. **Credit** AmEx, DC, JCB, MC, V. **Map** p93. Kaiseki
Kanetanaka is one of Tokyo's most exclusive *ryotei* (traditional restaurants), but this sleek, chic offshoot is thoroughly modern and totally accessible. Instead of tatami mats and *washi* paper screens, it's furnished with tables and chairs, and blinds of silvery metal. The multi-course *kaiseki* meals give Japan's traditional haute cuisine an inventive contemporary slant.
▶ *The Cerulean Tower Hotel also contains a Noh theatre – see p271 Cerulean Tower Noh Theatre – and a jazz club, JZ Brat (see p255).*

Negiya Heikichi
36-18 Udagawa, Shibuya-ku (3780 1505, www.kiwa-group.co.jp/restaurant/a100118.html). Shibuya station (Yamanote, Ginza lines), Hachiko exit; (Fukutoshin, Hanzomon lines), exits 6, 7. **Open** 11.30am-2.30pm, 5-11pm Mon-Sat; 11.30am-2.30pm, 5-10pm Sun. **Average** ¥5,000. **Credit** AmEx, DC, JCB, MC, V. **English menu. Map** p93. Izakaya
A welcome retreat from Shibuya's brash Center-gai, Heikichi has a rustic, retro feel. The menu is typical of a modern *izakaya*, with one major difference – just about everything features *negi* (Japanese leeks). Unless you're a big fan of the vegetable, then the ¥4,000 set dinner may be overkill. But don't miss the *negi-no-kuroyaki* (charcoal-charred leek).

CONSUME

★ Soranoniwa

4-17 Sakuragaoka-cho, Shibuya-ku (5728 5191). *Shibuya station (Yamanote, Ginza lines), east exit; (Fukutoshin, Hanzomon lines), exit 8.* **Open** 5-11pm Mon-Sat; 5-10.30pm Sun. **Average** ¥6,000. **No credit cards. English menu.** Tofu

Presenting one of Japan's most traditional foods with a modern twist, Soranoniwa specialises in tofu and other soy foods. The highlight of the menu is the tofu cooked in a wooden box at your table. Tofu never tastes better than when it's freshly set, and this smart restaurant is definitely the best place at which to try it.

★ Sushi Ouchi

2-8-4 Shibuya, Shibuya-ku (3407 3543). *Shibuya station (Yamanote, Ginza lines), east exit; (Hanzomon line), exit 11.* **Open** 11.40am-1.40pm, 5.30-11.30pm daily. **Average** ¥7,000. **No credit cards. Map** p93. Sushi

Owner-chef Hisashi Ouchi ensures all his seafood is wild, adds no sugar or MSG to his rice, uses only free-range eggs and shuns all artificial additives. This is no gimmick. Ouchi's sushi is wonderful, and so are the premises, a homely room with wooden beams and antique furniture.

¥ Uogashi Nippon-ichi

25-6 Udagawacho, Shibuya-ku (5728 5451, www.uogashi.jp). Shibuya station (Yamanote, Ginza lines), Hachiko exit; (Fukutoshin, Hanzomon lines), exits 6, 7. **Open** 11.30am-11pm daily. **Average** ¥1,500. **No credit cards. Map** p93. Sushi

The sushi here is surprisingly good considering the rock-bottom prices. There are branches of this chain in many parts of Tokyo, but this one is a welcome oasis of quality among the fast-food joints of Shibuya's Center-gai.

Non-Japanese

Beacon

1-2-5 Shibuya, Shibuya-ku (6418 0077, www. tyharborbrewing.co.jp/index_e.html). Omotesando station (Chiyoda, Ginza, Hanzomon lines), exit B2. **Open** 11.30am-2pm, 6-10pm Mon-Fri; 11.30am-3pm, 6-10pm Sat; 11.30am-3pm, 6-9pm Sun. **Average** ¥9,000. **Credit** AmEx, DC, JCB, MC, V. **English menu. Map** p93. Grill

The latest venture by David Chiddo – the man behind Cicada (*see p164*) and TY Harbor Brewery (*see p173*) – is described as an 'urban chop-house'. That means prime steaks from grain-fed Aussie Angus cattle, free-range chicken, Loch Fyne salmon and more, all grilled expertly over charcoal. The look at Beacon is sleek and understated, the cellar is stocked with New World wines and the adjoining bar pours killer cocktails. Just the place for celebrating or entertaining. *Photo p164.*

Buchi

9-7 Shinsen-cho, Shibuya-ku (5728 2085). *Shinsen station (Inokashira line).* **Open** 11.30am-2pm, 5pm-3am daily. **Average** ¥3,500. **Credit** AmEx, DC, JCB, MC, V. **Tapas**

An artsy, well-dressed crowd props up the counters and spills out on to the street at this chic standing-only bar. They come to drink – wine as much as saké – but also because the food menu is so vast. Raw oysters, sashimi, terrines, pappardelle, steaks and more. The location could be more convenient, though.

Don Ciccio

2-3-6 Shibuya, Shibuya-ku (3498 1828). Shibuya station (Yamanote, Ginza lines), east exit; (Fukutoshin, Hanzomon lines), exit 11. **Open** 6pm-midnight Mon-Sat. **Average** ¥7,500. **Credit** AmEx, DC, JCB, MC, V. **Map** p93. Italian

Friendly and casual, this new mid-market trattoria specialises in the *cucina* and *vini* of Sicily. The pastas and hearty main dishes (both seafood and meat) are excellent, though desserts are not so special. There may be cheaper Italian places in town, but few can match the quality of the ingredients or the enthusiasm of the staff here.

★ Gaya

2-2-5 Shibuya, Shibuya-ku (3498 8810, www.gaya.co.jp). Shibuya station (Yamanote, Ginza lines), east exit; (Fukutoshin, Hanzomon lines), exit 12. **Open** 5.30pm-11:30pm daily. **Average** ¥4,500. **Credit** AmEx, DC, JCB, MC, V. **Map** p93. Macrobiotic

Gaya calls itself a macrobiotic *izakaya*, but it will elevate your impression of both terms. It's neither pious nor discernibly health-oriented, with lots of fried food and plenty of alcohol. And the swank black and wood interior is classier than the average *izakaya*. Most of the menu is macrobiotic, vegetarian and organic, though you probably won't notice. The original branch, in Yoyogi Uehara, serves similar fare but is rowdier and smokier. *Photo p168.* **Other locations** 3-11-6 Nishihara, Shibuya-ku (3481 5255).

Legato

E Space Tower 15F, 3-6 Maruyama-cho, Shibuya-ku (5784 2121, www.legato-tokyo.jp). Shibuya station (Yamanote, Ginza lines), Hachiko exit; (Fukutoshin, Hanzomon lines), exit 1. **Open** 11.30am-2pm, 5.30-10.30pm Mon-Fri; 5.30pm-midnight Sat, Sun. **Average** ¥7,000. **Credit** AmEx, DC, JCB, MC, V. **English menu. Map** p93. Fusion

Trust the Global Dining Group – also behind Tableaux (*see p150*) – to do things in style. Legato occupies the top floor of a tower at the top of Dogenzaka hill, and its food is as theatrical as the lavish decor. The menu mixes Asian and Western influences, in accordance with Tokyo's current

CONSUME

vogue, and features Vietnamese spring rolls and Chinese noodles alongside lamb chops and pizza. There's also a bar/lounge open until 4am on weekdays and 6am on weekends.

¥ Respekt Café

2F, 1-11-1 Shibuya, Shibuya-ku (6418 8144, www.cafecompany.co.jp). Shibuya station (Yamanote, Ginza lines), east exit; (Fukutoshin, Hanzomon lines), exit 11. **Open** 11.30am-2am Mon-Thur; 11.30am-5am Fri, Sat; 11.30am-midnight Sun. **Average** ¥2,000. **Credit** AmEx, DC, JCB, MC, V. **English menu**. **Map** p93. *Café*

Respekt is an enormous café that somehow manages to feel intimate. It sells cheap-as-chips food that's a huge leap above most café fare (the rice bowls are great). With designer seating, jazzy house music, free Wi-Fi and friendly staff, it's no surprise that Respekt is thriving.

▶ *The Cafe Company runs a string of big-scale cafés in Tokyo – Respekt Café is the best of them.*

Underground Mr Zoogunzoo

Aoyama City Bldg B1, 2-9-11 Shibuya, Shibuya-ku (3400 1496, www.unitedf.com/zoogunzoo). Shibuya station (Yamanote, Ginza lines), east exit; (Fukutoshin, Hanzomon lines), exit 11. **Open** 6pm-2am (restaurant 6pm-11pm) Mon-Sat. **Average** ¥5,000. **Credit** AmEx, DC, JCB, MC, V. **English menu**. **Map** p93. *Italian/Australian*

This cosy basement wine bar has decor every bit as eccentric as its name. The cuisine is modern (meaning here a Japanese take on Italian), and portions are modest, but there's a great cellar, focusing exclusively on Antipodean wines, with half a dozen always available by the glass. The lights stay dimmed, the welcome is friendly, and hectic Tokyo always feels a long way away.

SHINJUKU & AROUND
Japanese

Tsunahachi

3-31-8 Shinjuku, Shinjuku-ku (3352 1012, www.tunahachi.co.jp). Shinjuku station (Yamanote line), east exit; (Marunouchi line), exit A6; (Oedo, Shinjuku lines), exit 1 or Shinjuku-Sanchome station (Marunouchi, Shinjuku lines), exits A1-A5. **Open** 11am-10.30pm daily. **Average** ¥5,000. **Credit** AmEx, DC, JCB, MC, V. **English menu**. **Map** p101. **Tempura**

Who says tempura has to be expensive? Surviving amid the gleaming modern buildings of Shinjuku, Tsunahachi's battered wooden premises are a throwback to the early post-war era – as are the prices. The whole place is filled with the whiff of cooking oil, but the food is perfectly good enough for everyday fare.

Other locations throughout the city.

Yukun-tei

3-13 Samoncho, Shinjuku-ku (3356 3351, www.akasakayukun.com). Yotsuya-Sanchome station (Marunouchi line), exit A4. **Open** 11.30am-1.30pm, 5-10.30pm Mon-Sat (Sat by reservation only). **Average** ¥7,500. **Credit** AmEx, DC, JCB, MC, V. *Izakaya*

This friendly *izakaya* serves Kyushu and southern Japanese cuisine (which revolves around seafood, pork and *shochu* spirits). The lunch sets are truly fantastic: *onigiri teishoku* features two enormous *onigiri* (rice balls), while *inaka udon teishoku* is a very generous bowl of udon noodles with rice and tasty side dishes. In the evening, the place does good sashimi, and grilled and simmered dishes, and offers a good range of saké. Don't miss out on the succulent *kakuni* pork.

Other locations Seio Bldg B1F, 2-2-18 Ginza Chuo-ku (3561 6672); Tokyo Tatemono Dai 5 Yaesu Bldg B1F, 1-4-14 Yaesu, Chuo-ku (3271 8231); Akasaka Tokyu Plaza 3F, 2-14-3 Nagatacho, Chiyoda-ku (3592 0393).

Non-Japanese

¥ Angkor Wat

1-38-13 Yoyogi, Shibuya-ku (3370 3019). Yoyogi station (Yamanote line), west exit; (Oedo line), exit A1. **Open** 11am-2pm, 5-10pm daily. **Average** ¥2,500. **No credit cards**. *Cambodian*

What this bustling little restaurant lacks in ambience it makes up for in tasty Cambodian-Chinese cooking. It can feel a bit like a diner (indeed, the food is served with amazing speed), and there are queues outside at lunch. Start with the spring rolls and chicken salad, then ask the cheerful Cambodian waitresses (most of them relatives of the proprietor) to help you navigate the menu further.

China Grill – Xenlon

Odakyu Hotel Century Southern Tower 19F, 2-2-1 Yoyogi, Shibuya-ku (3374 2080, www.xenlon.com). Shinjuku station (Yamanote line), south exit; (Marunouchi, Oedo lines), exit A1;

INSIDE TRACK
FEARLESS EATING

If you want to stretch your palate, head to **Albatross** (*see p184*). This bar is surrounded by atmospheric, timeworn and less than pristine eateries, including **Asadachi** (literally, 'morning glory'), where you'll find sashimi of pig's testicles and barbecued salamander among a long list of unusual eats. It's located at 1-2-14 Shinjuku, Shinjuku-ku (3342 1083, www.shinjuku-omoide.com/asadachi).

CONSUME

(Shinjuku line), exit 6. **Open** 11.30am-11pm daily. **Average** ¥8,000. **Credit** AmEx, DC, JCB, MC, V. **English menu**. **Map** p101. **Chinese**
Impeccable service and impressive views of the neon skyline make this stylish Chinese restaurant well worth the splurge. The Cantonese menu, which nods toward Western rather than Japanese influences, includes excellent dim sum at lunchtime.
Other locations throughout the city.

¥ Hyakunincho Yataimura
2-20-25 Hyakunincho, Shinjuku-ku (5386 3320, www.yataimura.jp). Shin-Okubo station (Yamanote line). **Open** 11.30am-2.30pm, 5pm-2am Mon-Thur, Sun; 11.30am-4am Fri, Sat. **Average** ¥2,500. **Credit** AmEx, DC, JCB, MC, V. **English menu** (some stands). **Asian**
The cheerfully chaotic *Yataimura* ('food-stall village') provides a one-stop culinary tour of Asian street food. A score of small stands set around a large central eating area supply a choice of cuisines (Malaysian, Chinese, Thai, Vietnamese and Indian). The proprietors vie aggressively for your custom, so the best option is to quickly order beer and snacks while you consider the rest of your meal. Fun, funky and, best of all, cheap.

¥ Matsuya
1-1-17 Okubo, Shinjuku-ku (3200 5733). Shin-Okubo station (Yamanote line). **Open** 11am-2am daily. **Average** ¥3,000. **No credit cards**.
Korean

The name may sound Japanese, but the food is 100% Korean home-style cooking. Kick off your shoes, sit on the floor and tuck into Matsuya's rugged *kamjatang* hotpot, a delectable chilli-rich stew of potatoes and massive pork backbones. Subtle fare this is not, but it's great for keeping out the winter chill. Wash it all down with the milky (but undeniably potent) *makkoli* rice wine.

★ New York Grill
Park Hyatt Tokyo 52F, 3-7-1-2 Nishi-Shinjuku, Shinjuku-ku (5323 3458, www.parkhyatttokyo. com). Shinjuku station (Yamanote line), west exit; (Marunouchi line), exit A13; (Oedo, Shinjuku lines), exit 6. **Open** 11.30am-2.30pm, 5.30-10.30pm daily. **Average** ¥14,000. **Credit** AmEx, DC, JCB, MC, V. **English menu**. **Map** p101. **Grill**
The New York Grill offers sky-high power dining (and brilliant views) at the apex of the Park Hyatt hotel. The food – great seafood and meat dishes prepared in modern New World style – is consistently excellent, service is polished, and the well thought-out selection of North American wines unrivalled in Japan. Sunday brunch is an expat institution, as are evening cocktails in the adjoining New York Bar.

Thien Phuoc
Kotoku Bldg 2F, 3-11 Yotsuya, Shinjuku-ku (3358 6617). Yotsuya-Sanchome station (Marunouchi line), exit 2. **Open** 11am-3pm, 5-11pm Mon-Fri; noon-11pm Sat, Sun. **Average** ¥4,000. **No credit cards**. **Vietnamese**

Gaya. *See p166.*

Despite the humble location, tucked well back from the street, Thien Phuoc is worth searching out for its excellent Saigon street-stall food. Try the crisp *banh xeo* pancakes, spicy Hue-style beef *pho* noodles and memorable *cha gio* (spring rolls). Reasonable prices also make this a popular, but low-key, joint.

UENO
Japanese

Goemon
1-1-26 Hon-Komagome, Bunkyo-ku (3812 0900, www.tcn-catv.ne.jp/~goemon). Hakusan station (Mita line), exit A2 or Hon-Komagome station (Nanboku line), exit 2. **Open** *noon-2pm, 5-10pm Tue-Fri; noon-8pm Sat, Sun.* **Average** ¥6,000. **No credit cards.** Tofu
Hidden away in Hakusan, this Kyoto-style tofu restaurant is one of Tokyo's best-kept secrets. The entrance is lined with bamboo and the garden has a waterfall, carp ponds and a couple of rustic bowers where you can sit in clement weather. The winter speciality is *yudofu* (piping hot tofu in broth); in summer, try the *hiya yakko* (chilled tofu). This is not the place for a rushed meal; last orders are taken two hours before closing time.

Hantei
2-12-15 Nezu, Bunkyo-ku (3828 1440, www.hantei.co.jp). Nezu station (Chiyoda line), exit 2. **Open** *noon-2.30pm, 5-10pm Tue-Sat;*

4-9.30pm Sun. **Average** ¥4,500. **No credit cards.** **English menu.** **Map** p107.
Kushi-age
Kushi-age (skewers of meat, fish or vegetables) is not gourmet fare, but Hantei almost makes it refined. This is partly due to the care that goes into the preparation, but mostly because of the beautiful old wooden building. Staff bring course after course, stopping after every six to ask if you want more.

¥ Ikenohata Yabu Soba
3-44-7 Yushima, Bunkyo-ku (3831 8977, www.yabu-soba.com). Yushima station (Chiyoda line), exit 2. **Open** *11.30am-2pm, 4.30-8pm Mon, Tue, Thur-Sun.* **Average** ¥3,000. **No credit cards.** **English menu.** **Map** p107. Soba
Kanda Yabu Soba has spawned numerous shops run by former apprentices. This one does predictably good noodles at reasonable prices in a simple Japanese setting. There's also a range of snacks, and, in winter, suitably warming *nabe* hotpots.

YANAKA
Japanese

Nezu Club
2-30-2 Nezu, Bunkyo-ku (3828 4004, www.nezuclub.com). Nezu station (Chiyoda line), exit 1. **Open** *6-10pm Wed-Sat.* **Average** ¥6,500. **Credit** AmEx, DC, JCB, MC, V. **Map** p107.
Modern Japanese

Chef Etsuko Yamada's stylish Japanese cuisine is not as formal as *kaiseki*, but it is far more sophisticated than regular home cooking. She has a very creative modern touch that reflects the restaurant's innovative setting: a converted 30-year-old, metal-frame workshop tucked away down a narrow alley in this very traditional neighbourhood. The restaurant also doubles as a cooking school.

Sasanoyuki

2-15-10 Negishi, Taito-ku (3873 1145).
Uguisudani station (Yamanote line), north exit.
Open 11am-9.30pm Tue-Sun. **Average** ¥5,000.
Credit AmEx, DC, JCB, MC, V. **English menu**.
Map p107. **Tofu**
Tokyo's most famous tofu restaurant was founded way back in the Edo period by a tofu-maker lured from Kyoto by the Kanei-ji temple's imperial abbot. Despite its illustrious past, Sasanoyuki is as down to earth as the Nippori neighbourhood it sits in, with very reasonable prices.

ELSEWHERE IN CENTRAL TOKYO

Japanese

Buri

3-13-12 Akasaka, Minato-ku (3560 6322).
Akasaka station (Chiyoda line), exit 1. **Open**
11.30am-2pm, 5pm-midnight Mon-Sat. **Average**
¥4,000. **Credit** AmEx, DC, JCB, MC, V. **English**
menu. Izakaya
You won't find a friendlier place in Akasaka than this upscale *izakaya*, a grander relative of the Ebisu bar also called Buri (*see p177*). Sit at the counter and watch the chefs at work. Or just relax and enjoy the excellent seafood and other traditional dishes. There's a great selection of saké too, with tasting sets so you can compare different styles.

Daigo

Forest Tower 2F, 2-3-1 Atago, Minato-ku (3431 0811, www.atago-daigo.com). Kamiyacho station (Hibiya line), exit 3 or Onarimon station (Mita line), exit A5. **Open** 11.30am-3pm, 5-9pm daily.
Average ¥18,000. **Credit** AmEx, DC, JCB, MC, V. **English menu**. Shojin ryori
For review, *see p172* **Shojin Ryori**.

Jidaiya

Naritaya Bldg 1F, 3-14-3 Akasaka, Minato-ku (3588 0489). Akasaka station (Chiyoda line), exit 1. **Open** 11.30am-2.30pm, 5pm-4am Mon-Fri; 5-11pm Sat, Sun. **Average** ¥5,000. **Credit** AmEx, DC, JCB, MC, V. **Traditional Japanese**
Jidaiya recreates a rustic Japanese farmhouse, complete with tatami mats, dried ears of corn, fish-shaped hanging fireplace fixtures and heaps of old-looking wooden furniture. The atmosphere is a little contrived but fun nonetheless, and large shared

---

INSIDE TRACK MONJAYAKI TOWN

Step out of Tsukishima station (Oedo, Yurakucho lines) and you'll smell the local speciality. Almost every eatery in the area serves *monjayaki*, a sloppy, pungent dish that looks something like a half-digested *okonomiyaki*. Cooked on a hotplate at your table, it's a fun, sociable and cheap eat. It's also not to everyone's taste, but you'll be able to tell by the smell before you even enter a *monjayaki* joint.

---

tables contribute to the conviviality. The food is all Japanese, with an emphasis on seafood, meat and vegetables cooked at the table.

Ninja

Akasaka Tokyu Plaza 1F, 2-14-3 Nagatacho, Chiyoda-ku (5157 3936, www.ninja.tv). Akasaka-Mitsuke station (Ginza, Marunouchi lines), Sotobori Dori exit. **Open** 5.30pm-4am Mon-Sat; 5-11pm Sun. **Average** ¥5,000. **Credit** AmEx, DC, JCB, MC, V. **English menu**. Izakaya
Waiters dressed as ninjas usher you through a series of winding wooden corridors designed to evoke the interior of an ancient Japanese castle. Others sneak up with menus and food, and there's also an itinerant magician. It's good, harmless fun and very popular. Food is Japanese with plenty of Western tweaks.

Sakura Sakura

5-15-10 Shirokanedai, Minato-ku (3440 7316, www.sakura2.co.jp). Shirokanedai station (Nanbokui line). **Open** 11.30am-3pm, 5.30-11pm Tue-Sun. **Average** ¥7,000. **Credit** AmEx, DC, JCB, MC, V. **Traditional Japanese**
The multi-course meals (from ¥5,520) of Kyoto-style *obanzai* cuisine are light and flavourful, emphasising tofu, *yuba* and seasonal vegetables. It's a beautiful setting too: a small three-storey wooden house decorated with vermilion walls, black woodwork and kimono fabric over the windows.

Seigetsu

Kamiya Bldg 2F, 6-77 Kagurazaka, Shinjuku-ku (3269 4320, www.teshigoto.net). Kagurazaka station (Tozai line), Kagurazaka exit or Ushigome-Kagurazaka station (Oedo line), exit A3. **Open** 5-11.30pm Mon-Fri; 5-11pm Sat, Sun. **Average** ¥4,000. **Credit** AmEx, DC, JCB, MC, V. **English menu**. Izakaya
The open kitchen in this bustling, wood-clad *izakaya* produces a good range of seafood and side dishes – the charcoal-grilled fish and chicken are notable. Not only is there a fine selection of saké and *shochu*, but the place can also provide a list in English. There's even a (cramped) no-smoking section.

CONSUME

Torijaya
*4-2 Kagurazaka, Shinjuku-ku (3260 6661, www.
torijaya.com). Iidabashi station (Chuo, Sobu lines),
west exit; (Nanboku, Yurakucho lines), exit B3
or Kagurazaka station (Tozai line), Kagurazaka
exit or Ushigome-Kagurazaka station (Oedo line),
exit A3.* **Open** 11.30am-2pm, 5-9.30pm Mon-Sat;
11.30am-3pm, 4-9pm Sun. **Average** ¥6,000.
Credit AmEx, JCB, MC, V. **Yakitori/udon**
Kyoto-style cuisine is the focus of this traditional
restaurant. It's referred to as *udon kaiseki*, but things
never get too formal. The centrepiece of any meal
here is *udon-suki* – a hearty hotpot of chicken, vegetables and thick-cut wheat noodles.

Non-Japanese

Manuel Churrascaria
*2-3-22 Takanawa, Minato-ku (3443 5002,
www.pjgroup.jp/manuel). Takanawadai station
(Asakusa line), exit A1.* **Open** noon-2.30pm,
6-11pm Tue-Sun. **Average** ¥5,000. **Credit**
AmEx, DC, JCB, MC, V. **Portuguese**
The third and smallest of the three Manuel restaurants is a cosy, bistro-scale North Portuguese-style
grillhouse. The spicy African chicken is highly recommended, as are the spare ribs and sardines. There
are wines from Douro and Dao to wash it all down
with, and vintage port if you feel like lingering.

Stefano
*Terui Bldg 1F, 6-47 Kagurazaka, Shinjuku-ku
(5228 7515, www.stefano-jp.com). Kagurazaka
station (Tozai line), exit 1 or Ushigome-
Kagurazaka station (Oedo line), exit A3.* **Open**
11.30am-2pm, 6-11pm Tue-Sat; noon-3pm, 5.30-
9pm Sun. **Average** ¥6,000. **Credit** AmEx, DC,
JCB, MC, V. **English menu**. Italian
Chef Stefano Fastro hails from the Veneto, and his
culinary repertoire ranges from Venetian seafood to
the meaty, almost Austrian fare of the mountains.
It's a modest place and rather off the beaten track,
but many rate Stefano among their favourite Italian
restaurants in Tokyo. The gnocchi alone make it
worth seeking out.

Tribes
*10-7 Wakamiyacho, Shinjuku-ku (3235 9966,
www.tribes.jp). Kagurazaka station (Tozai line),
Kagurazaka exit or Ushigome-Kagurazaka
station (Oedo line), exit A3.* **Open** 6pm-midnight
Mon-Sat. **Average** ¥5,000. **Credit** AmEx, DC,
JCB, MC, V. **English menu**. African
African inspiration meets French cuisine meets
Tokyo style in the alleys of Kagurazaka. The result
is an original and chic little bar-restaurant with a
menu (and wine list) that ranges from Morocco down
to South Africa. Among the standouts: *pepe*, a
Nigerian stew seasoned with plenty of pepper, and
ostrich meat (the birds are raised in Japan) served
as kebabs or in rich sausages.

FURTHER AFIELD
Japanese

Aguri
*1-6-7 Kami-Meguro, Meguro-ku (3792 3792,
www.agurimeguri.com/nakameguro). Naka-
Meguro station (Hibiya, Toyoko lines).* **Open**
5.30pm-midnight daily. **Average** ¥4,000.
Credit AmEx, DC, JCB, MC, V. **Izakaya**
Friendly, casual and inexpensive, this large *izakaya*
close to the river has just enough style to raise it
above the average. Platters of prepared foods line
the counter in tapas style, while short-order cooks
stand ready to rustle up grilled fish and teppanyaki
meat or vegetables.
Other locations Dogenzaka Center Bldg 6F,
2-29-8 Dogenzaka, Shibuya-ku (3780 3788).

Bon
*1-2-11 Ryusen, Taito-ku (3872 0375,
www.fuchabon.co.jp). Iriya station (Hibiya line),
exit 3.* **Open** noon-3pm, 5.30-9pm Mon-Fri; noon-
9pm Sat; noon-8pm Sun. **Average** ¥7,000.
Credit MC, V. **English menu**. Shojin ryori
For review, *see p172* **Shojin Ryori**.

★ Higashiyama
*1-21-25 Higashiyama, Meguro-ku (5720 1350).
Naka-Meguro station (Hibiya, Toyoko lines).*
Open 6pm-1am Mon-Sat. **Average** ¥6,000.
Credit AmEx, DC, JCB, MC, V. **Izakaya**
Inventive traditional cuisine from a team of gifted
chefs, matched by a beautifully sleek, modern inte-
rior (the creation of Shinichiro Ogata): this is
Japanese contemporary designer dining at its best.
The staff is friendly and, since others appreciate the
quality too, reservations are essential.

Sanko-in
*3-1-36 Honmachi, Koganei-shi (042 381 1116).
Musashi-Koganei station (Chuo, Sobu lines),
north exit, then bus to Sankoinmae.* **Open** *Lunch*
noon Tue-Fri. Closed every 3rd Wed, 4th Fri, and
all of Aug.* **Average** ¥4,000. **No credit cards**.
Shojin ryori
For review, *see p172* **Shojin Ryori**.

Tamahide
*1-17-10 Nihonbashi Ningyocho, Chuo-ku (3668
7651, www.tamahide.co.jp). Ningyocho station
(Hibiya, Toei Asakusa lines), exit A2.* **Open**
11.30am-2pm, 5-10pm Mon-Fri; 11.30am-2pm,
4-9pm Sat. **Average** ¥9,000. **Credit** AmEx,
DC, JCB, MC, V. **Hotpot**
For review, *see p150* **Queue Tips**.

Ukai Toriyama
*Minami-Asakawa 3426, Hachioji-shi (0426 61
0739, www.ukai.co.jp/toriyama). Takaosan-Guchi
station (Keio line) then free shuttle bus.* **Open**

Shojin Ryori

Relax, you can find vegetarian – and Zen – dining in Tokyo.

You'd never believe it from a glance at today's menus, but Japan was once a vegetarian country. In the seventh and eighth centuries AD, shortly after Buddhism arrived in Japan, no fewer than four emperors issued decrees banning the consumption of flesh.

Needless to say, things are different today, and the veggie visitor is likely to encounter bemusement at best when describing their diet. But there is one legacy of the nation's more ardently Zen past that the modern herbivore can enjoy: *shojin ryori*. Devised almost 800 years ago by a monk named Dogen, this ceremonial Zen dining is based on a multitude of precepts that govern colour, taste, texture and nutrition, as well as more ethical concerns. Meat and fish are, of course, strictly forbidden, but so are onions and garlic, which are considered an assault on the senses and a threat to the Zen disciple's command of his or her desires.

As in *kaiseki* dining, the food is served in a procession of around a dozen small dishes, each an elegantly presented bite-size course. Expect the whole meal to take a couple of hours.

Since wasting food is a serious transgression in Zen thinking, most *shojin ryori* restaurants demand that bookings are made at least two days ahead to avoid over purchasing. And leaving food on your plate is unthinkable.

FOUR TO TRY

Bon (*see p171*) serves *fucha ryori*, a strand of *shojin* that gives a more obvious tip of the hat to its Chinese origins. The feel is almost rustic in its simplicity, and the meals are beautifully presented. The interior of this restaurant is stunning, with a cobbled stone corridor linking immaculate tatami rooms.

The priciest *shojin* spot in Tokyo, **Daigo** (*see p170*) is also the least authentic. The chefs use fish stock and onions, but if you can tolerate a little non-conformism, you'll enjoy dishes as complex and subtle as the finest *kaiseki* cuisine. Each meal comprises a dozen or more exquisite dishes, like edible brush paintings to be savoured with your eyes as much as your mouth. A meal here will linger in your memory for months – as will the bill.

Bon.

Itosho (*see p162*) is a central Tokyo spot that has been run for over three decades by a genial chef who happily describes each of the dishes being presented. The menu is a mix of orthodox and inventive, with the rice-grain tempura a particular highlight.

It's quite a trek (about an hour from Shinjuku station) to **Sanko-in** (*see p171*), but you can combine it with a visit to the nearby Edo-Tokyo Museum (*see p50*). Plus, you'll be rewarded with the most authentic and most affordable *shojin ryori*. The setting is a Buddhist nunnery, and the chef is an abbess who adheres tightly to *shojin* rules. The cuisine is simpler and more restrained than some *shojin* restaurants, but no less tasty.

CONSUME

11am-9.30pm Mon-Sat; 11am-9pm Sun. **Average** ¥6,000. **Credit** AmEx, DC, JCB, MC, V. **English menu**. Grill/sashimi

Here you sit in quaint teahouse-style cottages in a manicured, pond-filled garden, grilling your own *jidori* chicken over charcoal, or dining on other seasonal Japanese delicacies. Anyone visiting Mt Takao should make a special detour for a meal here. In fact, it's worth making a special trip, despite the long journey (50 minutes from Shinjuku by train, then ten minutes by bus). Reservations are highly recommended. Note that last orders is 90 minutes before the closing time.

Yanagiya

2-11-3 Nihonbashi Ningyocho, Chuo-ku (3666 9901). Ningyocho station (Hibiya, Toei Asakusa lines), exit A1. **Open** 12.30-6pm Mon-Sat. **Average** ¥500. **No credit cards**. Confectionery

For review, *see p150* **Queue Tips**.

Non-Japanese

¥ Café Eight

3-17-7 Aobadai, Meguro-ku (5458 5262, http:// cafe8.exblog.jp/i10). Ikejiri-Ohashi (Denentoshi line). **Open** 11am-10pm Tue-Sun. **Average** ¥3,000. **Credit** AmEx, DC, JCB, MC, V. **English menu**. Vegetarian

The healthy, vegetarian fusion food here is good enough to draw herbivores and healthy eaters out to this less-than-convenient location.

▶ *Pure Café (see p156), from the same people, has a more limited menu but a better location.*

★ ¥ Junkadelic

4-10-4 Kami-Meguro, Meguro-ku (5725 5020, http://junkadelic.jp). Naka-Meguro station (Hibiya, Toyoko lines). **Open** 6pm-2am daily. **Average** ¥3,000. **Credit** AmEx, DC, JCB, MC, V. **English menu**. Mexican

Day of the Dead figurines, primitive murals and battered, junk-shop furniture set the scene at Junkadelic. The frozen margaritas are large and lurid, while the kitchen turns out a strange Japanese take on Tex-Mex cantina food that's never less than tasty. It's a ten-minute trek from Naka-Meguro station, but it's worth it.

Other locations 2-21-2 Akasaka, Minato-ku (3224 0750).

¥ Makani & Lanai

2-16-11 Aobadai, Meguro-ku (5428 4222, www.zetton.co.jp/aloha/ml). **Open** 11.30am-3am Mon-Sat; 11.30am-midnight Sun. **Average** ¥3,000. **Credit** AmEx, DC, JCB, MC, V. **English menu**. Hawaiian

The food here – which, with names such as *pupu* and *ahi poke*, won't mean much unless just you flew in from Hawaii – is distinctly lightweight. But it's the

river location, right on cherry-lined Megurogawa, that establishes M&L's credentials. An ideal spot for chilling with a Kona beer or three.

Osteria La Luna Rossa

2-5-23 Naka-Meguro, Meguro-ku (3793 4310). Naka-Meguro station (Hibiya, Toyoko lines). **Open** 11.30am-2pm, 6-10pm Mon, Wed-Sun. **Average** ¥6,000. **Credit** AmEx, DC, JCB, MC, V. Spanish

The gentrification of the Meguro River banks continues apace with La Luna Rossa. Sleek tranquil decor, a massive subterranean wine cellar and outstanding *cucina* from the gifted young chef, Masaru Kawahara. Taste his delicate *fritti* or *pastella di scampi* and swoon.

★ ¥ Seirinkan

2-6-4 Kami-Meguro, Meguro-ku (3714 5160, www.seirinkan.jp). Naka-Meguro station (Hibiya, Toyoko lines). **Open** 11.30am-2pm, 6-9.30pm Mon-Fri; noon-3pm, 5-9.30pm Sat; noon-3pm, 5-9pm Sun. **Average** ¥3,000. **Credit** DC, JCB, MC, V. Pizzeria

Japan might be more famous for its bastardisation of the pizza format (cod roe and mayo, anyone?) but it's also home to a pizza joint that Naples would be proud of. Pizzaiolo Susumu Kakinuma only makes two kinds of pizza – margherita and marinara – but he makes them so perfectly that Seirinkan is the king of Tokyo's pizza scene.

▶ *Seirinkan has a mock speakeasy bar in the basement, though it's well hidden and is only open sporadically.*

TY Harbor Brewery

2-1-3 Higashi-Shinagawa, Shinagawa-ku (5479 4555, www.tyharborbrewing.co.jp). Tennozu Isle station (Tokyo monorail), central exit. **Open** 11.30am-2pm, 5.30-10pm Mon-Fri; 11.30am-3pm, 5.30-9pm Sat, Sun. **Average** ¥4,000. **Credit** AmEx, DC, JCB, V. **English menu**. American

Tokyo's best brewpub produces Californian-style ales and porters, and the attached restaurant serves up straightforward, if uninspired, diner fare. The canalside location is one of the few places in Tokyo where you can sit outside on the waterfront.

INSIDE TRACK
GO THE WHOLE HOG

Most dubious item on a Tokyo menu? The *tonkatsu* parfait, a waffle cone filled with ice-cream, fresh fruit and two sticks of deep-fried pork. You'll find it at **Tokyo Meatria**, a flesh-obsessed food court on the outskirts of Tokyo at 5F Minami-Osawa station (042 653-3729, www.keio-ekichika.com/tokyomeatrea).

Menu Reader

ESSENTIAL VOCABULARY

A table for..., please ...*onegai shimasu*

one/two/three/four
hitori/futari/san-nin/yo-nin

Is this seat free? ***kono seki aite masu ka***

Could we sit...? ...*ni suware masu ka*

over there ***asoko***

outside ***soto***

in a non-smoking area ***kin-en-seki***

by the window ***madogiwa***

Excuse me
sumimasen/onegai shimasu

May I see the menu, please
menyuu o onegai shimasu

Do you have a set menu?
setto menyuu/teishoku wa arimasu ka

I'd like... ...*o kudasai*

I'll have... ...*ni shimasu*

a bottle/glass...
...*o ippon/ippai kudasai*

I can't eat food containing...
...*ga haitte iru mono wa taberare masen*

Do you have vegetarian meals?
bejitarian no shokuji wa arimasu ka

Do you have a children's menu?
kodomo-yoo no menyuu wa arimasu ka

The bill, please
o-kanjyoo onegai shimasu

That was delicious, thank you
gochisou sama deshita

We'd like to pay separately
betsubetsu ni onegai shimasu

It's all together, please
issho ni onegai shimasu

Is service included?
saabisu-ryoo komi desu ka

Can I pay with a credit card?
kurejitto caado o tsukae masu ka

Could I have a receipt, please?
reshiito onegai shimasu

MAIN TYPES OF RESTAURANT

寿司屋　***sushi-ya***
sushi restaurants

イクラ　*ikura*　salmon roe

タコ　*tako*　octopus

マグロ　*maguro*　tuna

こはだ　*kohada*　punctatus

トロ　*toro*　belly of tuna

ホタテ　*hotate*　scallop

ウニ　*uni*　sea urchin roe

エビ　*ebi*　prawn

ヒラメ　*hirame*　flounder

アナゴ　*anago*　conger eel

イカ　*ika*　squid

玉子焼き　*tamago-yaki*　sweet egg omelette

かっぱ巻き　*kappa maki*　rolled cucumber

鉄火巻き　*tekka maki*　rolled tuna

お新香巻き　*oshinko maki*　rolled pickles

蕎麦屋（そば屋）　***soba-ya***
Japanese noodle restaurants

天ぷらそば うどん　*tempura soba, udon*
noodles in hot broth with prawn tempura

ざるそば うどん　*zaru soba, udon*
noodles served on a bamboo rack in a lacquer box

きつねそば うどん　*kitsune soba, udon*
noodles in hot broth topped with spring onion and
fried tofu

たぬきそば うどん　*tanuki soba, udon*
noodles in hot broth with fried tempura batter

月見そば うどん　*tsukimi soba, udon*
raw egg broken over noodles in hot broth

あんかけうどん　*ankake udon*
wheat noodles in a thick fish bouillon/soy sauce
soup with fishcake slices and vegetables

CONSUME

鍋焼きうどん   *nabeyaki udon*
noodles boiled in an earthenware pot with other ingredients and stock. Mainly eaten in winter.

居酒屋   ***izakaya***
Japanese-style bars

日本酒   *nihon-shu*   sake

冷酒   *rei-shu*   cold sake

焼酎   *shoochuu*   barley or potato spirit

チュウハイ   *chuuhai*
shoochuu with juice or tea

生ビール   *nama-biiru*   draught beer

黒ビール   *kuro-biiru*   dark beer

梅酒   *ume-shu*   plum wine

ひれ酒   *hirezake*
hot sake flavoured with blowfish fins

焼き魚   *yaki zakana*   grilled fish

煮魚   *ni zakana*
fish cooked in various sauces

刺し身   *sashimi*
raw fish in bite-sized pieces, served with soy sauce and wasabi

揚げ出し豆腐   *agedashi doofu*
deep fried plain tofu served with savoury sauce

枝豆   *edamame*
boiled green soybeans in the pod

おにぎり   *onigiri*
rice parcel with savoury filling

焼きおにぎり   *yaki onigiri*
grilled rice balls

フグ刺し   *fugusashi*
thinly sliced sashimi, usually spectacularly arranged and served with ponzu sauce

フグちり   *fuguchiri*
chunks of fugu in a vegetable stew

雑炊   *zosui*
rice porridge cooked in fuguchiri broth

焼き鳥屋   ***yakitori-ya***
yakitori restaurants

焼き鳥   *yakitori*
barbecued chicken pieces seasoned with sweet soy sauce

つくね   *tsukune*   minced chicken balls

タン   *tan*   tongue

ハツ   *hatsu*   heart

シロ   *shiro*   tripe

レバー   *reba*   liver

ガツ   *gatsu*   intestines

鳥皮   *tori-kawa*   skin

ネギ間   *negima*   chicken with leek

おでん屋   ***oden-ya***
oden restaurants or street stalls

さつま揚げ   *satsuma-age*   fish cake

昆布   *konbu*   kelp rolls

大根   *daikon*   radish

厚揚げ   *atsu-age*   fried tofu

OTHER TYPES OF RESTAURANT

料亭   *ryotei*
high-class, traditional restaurants

ラーメン屋   *ramen-ya*
ramen noodle shop

天ぷら屋   *tempura-ya*   tempura restaurants

すき焼き屋   *sukiyaki-ya*
sukiyaki restaurants

トンカツ屋   *tonkatsu-ya*
tonkatsu restaurants

お好み焼き屋   *okonomi yaki-ya*
okonomiyaki restaurants

CONSUME

Bars

Sky-high spirits, streetside saké and gallons and gallons of beer.

Whatever your drink, you're in for a treat in Tokyo. It's not just the quality and ranges on offer, it's also the extraordinary number of opportunities you'll have to indulge your taste buds. You won't look out of place sinking a drink in a cinema, bowling alley, temple grounds or hot spring.

Tokyoites pursue their alcoholic passions with such vigour that it's easy to find fellow drinkers in the wee hours of a weekday, and just as easy to find some top-quality booze to toast them with. If you're looking for the finest malts, rums, tequilas or wines, you'll find them in this metropolis.

WHERE TO DRINK

Ginza is the pinnacle of Japanese cocktail culture, but don't come looking for mixology: the master bartenders here are traditionalists who are more concerned with serving the classics perfectly than mixing something unheard of. **Shibuya** is young, fun and affordable, while neighbouring **Aoyama** is more upmarket. **Ebisu** offer unpretentious fun, as do some of the further afield locations such as Shimo-Kitazawa, Koenji and Kichijoji. **Shinjuku**, as usual, has the lot, from cocktail bars to **Golden Gai** (*see p185*).

Defining a 'bar' is not easy. Drinking and eating are such inseparable activities for Tokyoites that some of the best boozing spots are technically restaurants – including **TY Harbor Brewery** (*see p173*) – and many of the places listed below have impressive food menus. Most bars serve a mandatory snack called *otoshi*. This could be a handful of peanuts, a bowl of potato salad or something far less identifiable. Expect to pay ¥300-¥1,500 depending on the area and the style of the bar. The same dish is served to every customer – a service that is considered more sophisticated than demanding an entrance fee. This system can make bar-hopping an expensive pursuit unless you look for the 'no charge' signs (in English) posted outside most free bars.

ASAKUSA

Daimasu Sake Bar

1-2-8 Asakusa, Taito-ku (5806 3811, www.e-daimasu.com/bar). Asakusa station (Asakusa line), exit A4; (Ginza line), exit 1. **Open** noon-11.30pm daily. **Credit** AmEx, MC, V. **Map** p45.
As the name says, Daimasu serves saké. The atmosphere is surprisingly modern for an Akasaka bar, but the range of 100 rice brews fits right into this most traditional area. Tasting sets offer an easy intro to the drink.

★ Kamiya Bar

1-1-1 Asakusa, Taito-ku (3841 5400, www.kamiya-bar.com). Asakusa station (Asakusa line), exit A5; (Ginza line), exit 3. **Open** 11.30am-9.30pm Mon, Wed-Sun. **No credit cards. Map** p45.
Established in the late 1800s, Kamiya is something of a legend. It's the oldest Western-style bar in Tokyo and one of the friendliest to boot. The crowds certainly don't come here for the decor (think Formica tables and too-bright lighting), but the atmosphere – loud, smoky and occasionally raucous – is typical of this working-class neighbourhood. Try the house Denki Bran (Electric Brandy) – a sweet blend of wine, gin and brandy that's a lot nicer than it sounds.

INSIDE TRACK
HOPPY DAYS ARE HERE AGAIN

Showa chic – a throwback to the period of impoverishment that followed the war (*see p26*) – has revived the fortunes of Hoppy, a non-alcoholic beer-flavoured drink created in Tokyo in 1948. When mixed with discount shochu, it makes for one of the cheapest socially acceptable ways to drown worldly worries. You'll find the drink at grittier bars and *izakayas*.

CONSUME

EBISU & DAIKANYAMA

★ Buri
*1-14-1 Ebisu-Nishi, Shibuya-ku (3496 7744,
www.buri-group.com). Ebisu station (Yamanote,
Hibiya lines), west exit.* **Open** 5pm-3am daily.
Credit AmEx, JCB, MC, V.
Most saké menus are written in Japanese script, so
ordering a drink can be an arbitrary affair if you're
not fluent. Buri solves the problem by lining its walls
with single-serving 'one-cup' saké. Pluck a cup from
the wall, or order from the English menu, where
drinks are listed according to the location of the
brewery. This standing-only bar is always fun, often
full, and serves great yakitori and grilled veggies.

Dagashi
*1-13-7 Ebisu-Nishi, Shibuya-ku (5458 5150). Ebisu
station (Yamanote, Hibiya lines), west exit.* **Open**
6pm-4.30am daily. **Credit** AmEx, DC, MC, V.
A beautiful *izakaya* serving standard drinks alongside steaming dishes of Asian favourites. The twist
is the all-you-can-eat candy (*dagashi*), which is offered
free to every customer. Sweet-toothed boozers can
plunge their hand into the numerous buckets of trad
Japanese candies and crispy snacks. For an extra
¥500 you can take a bag home. The name outside is
only in Japanese, so look for the blazing orange signs.

Kissa Ginza
*1-3-9 Ebisu-Minami, Shibuya-ku (3710 7320).
Ebisu station (Yamanote, Hibiya lines), west
exit.* **Open** 10am-midnight Mon-Sat. **Credit**
AmEx, DC, JCB, MC, V.
Here's a recipe for postmodern kitsch, Tokyo-style.
Take a 40-year-old coffee shop, install a glitter ball,
two turntables and… absolutely nothing else.
Result: the blue-rinse set still come for coffee in the
daytime, but the evening brings lounge-loving
urban hipsters who love the laid-back grooves.

What the Dickens
*Roob 6 Bldg 4F, 1-13-3 Ebisu-Nishi, Shibuya-ku
(3780 2099, www.towncryer.jp/WTD.html).
Ebisu station (Yamanote, Hibiya lines), west exit.*
Open 5pm-1am Tue-Sat; 3pm-midnight Sun.
No credit cards.
The walls of this this popular British-style pub are
decorated with Dickens manuscripts (which have
been liberally recaptioned in the gents' toilets).
Unfortunately, the food is of genuine (old-school)
British pub standard. Local bands play nightly.

GINZA

★ Bar High Five
*No.26 Polestar Building 4F, 7-2-14 Ginza,
Chuo-ku (3571 5815). Ginza station
(Ginza, Hibiya, Marunouchi lines), exit C2.*
Open 6pm-2am Mon-Sat. **Credit** DC, JCB,
MC, V. **Map** p59.

INSIDE TRACK PECHA KUCHA

Six minutes 40 seconds – that's all the
time each presenter gets to talk about
their passions at Tokyo's premier creative
showcase, **Pecha Kucha**. The brainchild
of a pair of expat architects, Pecha Kucha
(a Japanese onomatopoeia for 'chit chat'),
invites 14 people to present 20 slides
for 20 seconds each on any topic they like.
The event has spawned replicas in over 50
cities worldwide, and attracted presenters
as varied as Rem Koolhaas and Joanna
Lumley, but it began, and still takes place,
in Roppongi's **Super-deluxe** (*see p183*).

Kamiya Bar.

CONSUME

Hidetsugu Ueno is one of the world's most in-demand bartenders, representing Japan on the judging panels of most big cocktail contests. When he's in town, he plies his trade at this cosy cocktail bar. Best known for his White Lady and his ice carving, Ueno is also the only top-tier Ginza bartender we know of who speaks fluent English.

Hibiki
Caretta Shiodome 46F, 1-8-1 Higashi-Shinbashi, Minato-ku (6215 8051). Shiodome station (Oedo line), exit A1; (Yurikamome line), Dentsu exit. **Open** 5-11.30pm daily. **Credit** AmEx, DC, JCB, MC, V.
A pleasantly upmarket *izakaya* with great Japanese food and even better views from atop a tower in the Shiodome complex. The food is Japanese grill fare, at around ¥800 a dish. The view over the river toward Odaiba is spectacular, taking in the Rainbow Bridge and beyond. Reserve ahead for window tables.

Lion Beer Hall
7-9-20 Ginza, Chuo-ku (3571 2590, www.ginza lion.jp). Ginza station (Ginza, Hibiya, Marunouchi lines), exit A4. **Open** 11.30am-11pm Mon-Sat; 11.30am-10.30pm Sun. **Credit** AmEx, MC, V. **Map** p59.
This 1930s beer hall, part of the Sapporo Lion chain, is a tourist attraction in itself. The tiled and wood-panelled interior looks as if it's been transplanted from Bavaria, and a menu laden with sausages adds to the effect. Friday night sessions have been known to descend into mass karaoke demonstrations.
▶ *There's also a cheap and cheerful restaurant upstairs serving Japanese and Western dishes.*

Peter
1-8-1 Yurakucho, Chiyoda-ku (6270 2763, www.peninsula.com). Hibiya station (Chiyoda, Hibiya, Mita lines), exit A6. **Open** noon-midnight Sun-Thur, noon-1am Fri, Sat. **Credit** AmEx, DC, JCB, MC, V. **Map** p59.
The Peninsula hotel could have played it safe with a by-the-numbers cocktail bar, but instead they made Peter, a spectacle of a venue. The entrance is bathed in a rainbow of lights, the long bar furnished with pod seats and chrome trees, and the 24th-floor city view is breathtaking at night. The Tokyo Joe cocktail is equally dramatic.

★ Rockfish
2F Polestar Bldg, 7-2-14 Ginza, Chuo-ku (5537 6900). Ginza station (Ginza, Hibiya, Marunouchi lines), exit C2. **Open** 3-11pm Mon-Fri; 3-9pm Sat, Sun. **No credit cards. Map** p59.
So famous is Rockfish for its highball (whisky and soda) cocktails that it's rare to see anyone drinking anything else. Kazunari Maguchi is such a perfectionist about his highballs that when Suntory stopped selling his favourite base whisky, he scoured the country for remaining stock before persuading the distiller to keep supplying him with it. With no cover, free bar snacks, a friendly vibe and not-very-Ginza prices, Rockfish fills up fast, so get there early.

HARAJUKU & AOYAMA

★ Harajuku Taproom
2F, 1-20-13 Jingumae, Shibuya-ku (6438 0450, www.bairdbeer.com/en/taproom/ harajuku-taproom). Harajuku station (JR line), Takeshita exit; Meiji-Jingumae station (Chiyoda, Fukutoshin lines), exits 3, 5. **Open** 5pm-midnight Mon-Fri; noon-midnight Sat, Sun. **Credit** AmEx, DC, JCB, MC, V. **Map** p65.
American expat Bryan Baird runs an acclaimed microbrewery in the hot-spring resort of Numazu, in Shizuoka prefecture. In late 2009, he opened this *izakaya*-esque Tokyo taproom, serving more than a dozen of his brews, along with *kushi-yaki* skewers of grilled chicken and veg. *Photo p180.*
Other locations Nakameguro GT Plaza C-Block 2F, 2-1-3 Kami-Meguro, Meguro-ku (5768 3025).

Office
Yamazaki Bldg 5F, 2-7-18 Kita-Aoyama, Minato-ku (5786 1052). Gaienmae station (Ginza line), exit 2. **Open** 7pm-3am Mon-Sat. **No credit cards.**
You'll find that theme bars of all description abound in Tokyo, but none has quite the same bizarrely unattractive concept as Office. With a photocopier by the window, power points for workaholics and bookshelves against the wall, the management seems not to have noticed that its bar offers the best view in the area. DJs play mellow tunes most nights, and the crowd are young, urban trendies.
▶ *Office is above Sign (see p180), both run by the same design company.*

Quons
2F 5-51-6 Jingumae, Shibuya-ku (5468 0633, www.quons.jp). Omotesando station (Chiyoda, Ginza, Hanzomon lines), exit B2. **Open** 6pm-3am daily. **Credit** AmEx, DC, JCB, MC, V. **Map** p93.

INSIDE TRACK
HIGH ON HIGHBALLS

At the start of 2008, whisky sales were in their 26th straight year of decline in Japan. But by 2010 they were rising again. The difference: an astoundingly successful marketing campaign by drink giant Suntory that sold the nation on whisky and sodas, or highballs as they are better known here. The city's most famous highball bar is **Rockfish** (*see left*) in Ginza, but you'll find the drink prominently placed on virtually every menu in the city.

Harajuku Taproom. *See p179.*

The interior here is by-the-numbers trendy bar, with designer sofas, hip music and artsy projections on the wall. But it's the roof that offers the best reason to spend an evening at Quons, if the weather allows. The cosy wooden top deck falls a bit short of the Balinese effect it seems to be aiming for, but it's still a great place to sip cocktails with a breeze on your cheeks.

Sign

2-7-18 Kita-Aoyama, Minato-ku (5474 5040, www.transit-web.com). Gaienmae station (Ginza line), exit 3. **Open** 11am-3am Mon-Fri; 11am-midnight Sat, Sun. **No credit cards**.

An unashamedly artistic and artsy bar cum restaurant cum gallery a stone's throw from the station, Sign manages to be all things to all punters. While nearby office workers treat it as their local, creative types flock to the basement gallery, and clubbers come to listen to the occasional shows by local DJs.

Two Rooms

5F AO Bldg, 3-11-7 Kita-Aoyama, Minato-ku (3498 0002, www.tworooms.jp). Omotesando station (Chiyoda, Ginza, Hanzomon lines), exit B2. **Open** 11.30am-2am Mon-Sat; 11.30am-10pm Sun. **Credit** Amex, DC, JCB, MC, V.

One of the 'two rooms' in question is an upmarket grill restaurant, but it's the other one that draws

the most visitors. The bar is formulaic: designer furniture + oversized art + multi-martini menu + glass-walled wine cellar = magnet for dressed-up, well-financed drinkers. But it's a formula that works, and the bar also has a terrace with a great view over the local rooftops.

IKEBUKURO

Bobby's Bar

Milano Bldg 3F, 1-18-10 Nishi-Ikebukuro, Toshima-ku (3980 8875, http://plaza.rakuten. co.jp/bobbysbar). Ikebukuro station (Yamanote, west exit. **Open** 6pm-2am/3am Mon, Tue, Thur-Sat; 6pm-midnight Sun. **No credit cards**. **Map** p69.

A small, foreigner-friendly place on the west side of Ikebukuro station, Bobby's Bar offers a fine selection of imported beers with live music most nights. It shares a building with the New Delhi Indian restaurant, which offers good food at reasonable prices, and is a conveniently placed bolt-hole after a few lagers.

King Rum

2-9-1 Ikebukuro, Toshima-ku (3980 2903, www.kingrum.jp). Ikebukuro station (Yamanote, Fukutoshin, Marunouchi, Yurakucho lines), west exit. **Open** 7pm-6am daily. **Credit** AmEx, JCB, MC, V. **Map** p69.

With over a hundred types of rum, from distilleries as far apart as Japan and Jamaica, King Rum is a great place to find out why it was Jamaica, not Japan, that became famous for its rum.

MARUNOUCHI

Mandarin Bar

37F Mandarin Oriental Tokyo, 2-1-1 Nihonbashi-Muromachi, Chuo-ku (3270 8800, www. mandarinoriental.com). Mitsukoshimae station (Ginza line), exit A7. **Open** 11.30am-midnight daily. **Credit** AmEx, DC, JCB, MC, V. **Map** p77.

INSIDE TRACK SNACK ATTACK

Take care if you see the word 'snack' outside a small Japanese bar. These are tamer versions of hostess bars, where the staff will drink away merrily on your bar tab. Prices are rarely displayed, so if you are not the guest of a regular customer you can expect to pay an arbitrary and sky-high sum at the end of the night.

Superb cocktails, impeccable design, faultless service: what else are you looking for? Local design hotshot Kosaka Ryu was asked to create 'something sexy, but like nothing you've seen before'. His spacious layout incorporating a Zen pool and an array of designer furnishings succeeds on both counts. The view of Nihonbashi's business district is impressive, but you might not even notice.

▶ *For a room within easy stumbling distance, see p127 Mandarin Oriental Tokyo.*

ROPPONGI

A971
Tokyo Midtown East, 9-7-2 Akasaka, Minato-ku (5413 3210, www.a971.com). Roppongi station (Hibiya, Oedo lines), exit 8. **Open** 10am-2am Mon-Thur; 10am-4am Fri, Sat; 10am-midnight Sun. **Credit** AmEx, DC. **Map** p87.
It's a love-it-or-loathe-it bar. To fans, it's an uptempo, flirtatious and airy DJ bar that spills out onto the Midtown terrace in the summer time. To the haters, it's a noisy meat market with brusque bartenders. Either way, it's easy to meet people here, which makes it a good place to start a night in Roppongi.

Agave
Clover Bldg B1F, 7-15-10 Roppongi (3497 0229, www.agave.jp). Roppongi station (Hibiya, Oedo lines), exit 4B. **Open** 6.30pm-1.30am Mon-Thur; 6.30pm-3.30am Fri, Sat. **Credit** AmEx, DC. **Map** p87.
From the orange stone walls to the snifters and sangritas, Agave is a perfect replica of an upmarket Mexican cantina in all ways but two: few cantinas stock 400 varieties of tequila and mezcal, and no joint in Mexico would charge so much for them. With single measures costing from ¥800 to an impressive ¥9,400, this is the only place in Roppongi where customers don't hurl their cactus juice straight down their throats.

Bauhaus
Reine Roppongi Bldg 2F, 5-3-4 Roppongi (3403 0092, www.e-bauhaus.jp). Roppongi station (Hibiya, Oedo lines), exit 3. **Open** 7pm-1am Mon-Sat. **Credit** AmEx, DC, JCB, MC, V. **Map** p87.
One of those 'only in Japan' experiences, this is a music venue that has featured the same band for over 20 years. Nowhere else in the world can you listen to flawless covers of the Rolling Stones, Pink Floyd or Madonna performed by men and women who can't speak three words of English, and then have them serve you food and drink between sets. It's on the pricey side, though, with a ¥2,835 music charge. There are sets every hour.

Cask
3-9-11 Roppongi, Minato-ku (3402 7373, www.cask.jp). Roppongi station (Hibiya, Oedo lines), exit 5. **Open** 6pm-late daily. **Credit** MC, V. **Map** p87.

Local Potions

Get into the spirits of Japan.

Japan is home to three key indigenous alcoholic drinks: *nihonshu*, *shochu* and *awamori*. The famous 'saké' is a synonym of *nihonshu*, but can also be a catch-all for booze in general, so *nihonshu* is the unambiguous way to order.

NIHONSHU (SAKE)
Nihonshu is brewed from rice, and fermented with an enzyme that converts the starches to sugar – a step that parallels malting barley in beer-making. This allows saké to rise to as high as 20 per cent alcohol – though it's almost always watered down again to around 16 per cent. *Nihonshu* can be served hot or cold, but in general it's the cheap stuff that's heated and the premium stuff that's best enjoyed chilled. For the best, unadulterated stuff, ask for *junmai*.

SHOCHU
Shochu (and *awamori*) are distinct in that both are distilled rather than brewed. Thus they're significantly more potent, at anything from 20 to 50 per cent alcohol. *Shochu* can be made from one of several raw materials, including barley, rice or the popular purple Satsuma sweet potato. If it's distilled only once, it's termed *honkaku shochu* ('the real thing') and bears the distinct fragrance of the source produce. But it can also be distilled multiple times into a clear liquor that's great for mixing with fruit juices. Japan's convenience store shelves are loaded with canned versions of just such a potion – called *chu-hai*. Premium *shochu* can be enjoyed in a number of ways: on the rocks, mixed with a little hot water, or with a pickled plum thrown in the glass.

AWAMORI
Awamori is also distilled but is made only with imported Thai long-grain rice, and it hails from the southern islands of Okinawa. It has a significantly more earthy flavour than *shochu*, thanks to the special mould that's used in the distilling process. *Awamori* can be drunk on the rocks, mixed with hot or cold water, or even straight (in small doses), but Okinawans drink it with ice and water. Look for the *kuusu*, a premium version aged for at least three years.

CONSUME

For whisky fans, this establishment is as good as it gets. Cask stocks over a thousand bottles of Scotch, and you'll struggle to spot any standard labels. The setting is a smart, cave-like basement, which somehow softens the blow of the bill. Drams here cost anything from ¥1,000 to ¥90,000, but the bartenders will warn you when you try to order anything too pricey.

▶ *If you'd rather try Japanese whisky, nip into specialist outfit Zoetrope (see p186).*

Cavern Club
Saito Bldg 1F, 5-3-2 Roppongi (3405 5207, www.cavernclub.jp). Roppongi station (Hibiya, Oedo lines), exit 3. **Open** 6pm-2.30am Mon-Sat; 6pm-midnight Sun. **Credit** AmEx, DC, JCB, MC, V. **Map** p87.
Tokyo's famous Beatles imitators play here most nights – look for the Silver Beats on the schedule. Some say they sound better live than the originals. In low light, if you're very drunk and wearing dark

Japanese Whisky

Giving the Glens a run for their money.

In Ian Fleming's *You Only Live Twice*, the Australian spy Dikko Henderson gets a vile hangover drinking Japanese whisky. James Bond, more of a martini man, is amazed that Dikko would even consider drinking that gutrot, saying 'I can't believe Japanese whisky makes a good foundation for anything.' That neatly sums up the attitude of most foreigners to Japanese whisky for most of its more than 80-year history.

In 2001, that all started to change when a 10-year-old Yoichi made by Nikka Whisky won the 'Best of the Best' title at *Whisky Magazine*'s annual awards. Since then, Japan has regularly scooped the top prizes at whisky competitions and has transformed its reputation. The Japanese spirit is spelled the Scottish way – 'whisky' not 'whiskey' – and belongs to the Scottish tradition, tracing its history to an epic journey by Masataka Taketsuru to learn Scotland's distilling secrets in 1919. There are currently seven active single-malt whisky distilleries:

YAMAZAKI
Yamazaki is Japan's oldest distillery, built in 1923, at a site famous for its pure water at the confluence of the Katsura, Kizu and Uji rivers, near Kyoto. Its malts often have a delicate fruitiness, with sweet spice, incense, and coconut aromas.

HAKUSHU
Perched in the Southern Japanese Alps, Hakushu is, at over 670 metres (2,200 feet) above sea level, one of the highest whisky distilleries in the world. Opened by Suntory in 1973, it makes clean, playful single malts with sweet fruity flavours often balanced by well controlled peppery or aniseed tastes.

YOICHI
Yoichi is Japan's second-oldest distillery. It was built by the founder of Japanese

whisky, Taketsuru, when he split from Suntory in 1934 to found Nikka whisky. High up on the north coast of Hokkaido, it spends much of the year deep in snow. Its whiskies are relatively 'masculine', with rich stewed fruit, nutty and coffee notes often balancing the assertiveness.

MIYAGIKYO
Nikka Whisky opened its second distillery at Miyagikyo, Miyagi Prefecture in 1969. Taketsuru thought the location, sandwiched between the Hirosegawa and Nikkawagawa rivers and surrounded by mountains, was ideal for whisky-making. Its products are typically softer and milder than Yoichi's.

FUJI GOTEMBA
With an iconic location at the foot of Mt Fuji, this Kirin-owned distillery takes its water from rain and melted snow running off the great volcano. Its malts are relatively light and elegantly balanced.

CHICHIBU
Chichibu in Saitama Prefecture was only established in 2008, and the majority of its spirit is still ageing. However, Ichiro Akuto, the man behind this tiny independent craft distillery, sells some superb whisky from his family's now-closed Hanyu distillery under the Ichiro's Malt brand.

WHITE OAK
White Oak is a small independent distillery by the sea in Hyogo prefecture, western Japan, owned by Eigashima Shuzo, a saké and shochu maker. Their single malts have a very mild, rounded flavour.

● *Chris Bunting writes* Nonjatta.com, *a blog about Japanese whisky, and is the author of* Drinking Japan *(2011, Tuttle), a guide to Japan's alcohol culture.*

CONSUME

enough glasses, you might even convince yourself you're back in '60s Liverpool. Music fee is ¥2,100 for men, ¥1,680 for women.

★ L Garden
3-15-15 Roppongi, Minato-Ku (3568 3313, www.l-garden-roppongi.com). Roppongi station (Hibiya, Oedo lines), exit 5. **Open** 6pm-2am Mon-Sat. **Credit** AmEx, DC, JCB, MC, V. **Map** p87.
It's one of those wonderful Tokyo juxtapositions: one block from Roppongi's rowdiest street is the 90-year-old former home of a wealthy restaurateur, which was closed up after his death, until reopening as a restaurant and bar in 2008. Sadly, the new owners decided to serve mediocre Italian food, so skip the restaurant but come for the bar, which occupies the entire top floor and still feels like someone's home. If the main bar is closed, try the one next door in what used to be the driver's house.

Mado Lounge
Mori Tower 52F, 6-10-1 Roppongi, Minato-ku (6406 6652, www.ma-do.jp). Roppongi station (Hibiya line), exit 1C; (Oedo line), exit 3. **Open** 11am-5pm, 6pm-midnight daily. **Credit** AmEx, DC, JCB, MC, V. **Map** p87.
Part of Roppongi Hills' Tokyo City View observation deck, Mado Lounge opened in 2006, supplementing the great view with booze and quality local DJs.
▶ *The elevator to the 52nd floor costs ¥1,500 but also allows you entrance to the Mori Art Museum (see p88).*

Super-deluxe
B1F, 3-1-25 Nishi-Azabu, Minato-ku (5412 0515, www.super-deluxe.com). Roppongi station (Hibiya, Oedo lines), exit 1B. **Open** varies. **Credit** V. **Map** p87.
Picked up by *Time* magazine as Asia's best spot for 'avant-garde idling', Super-deluxe is the brainchild of a pair of architects who envisaged the spot as 'a bar,

a gallery, a kitchen, a jazz club, a cinema, a library, a school…' and so on. Closer in atmosphere to an artists' salon than a bar, Super-deluxe offers something different every night, from slide shows to club nights. Also the home of the microbrew Tokyo Ale.

These
2F, 2-13-19 Nishi-Azabu, Minato-ku (5466 7331, www.these-jp.com). Roppongi station (Hibiya, Oedo lines), exit 1. **Open** 7pm-4am Mon-Sat; 7pm-2am Sun. **Credit** MC, V. **Map** p87.
As much library as bar – and pronounced 'tay-zay' – this strange establishment exudes the feel of a British gentlemen's club, but with superior service. The bar has shelves and shelves of magazines and books – both foreign and Japanese – for browsing, as well as a large central room where you are free to chat while indulging in one of the long list of whiskies. Harry Potter fans should keep an eye out for the secret room.

Tokyo Sports Café
Fusion Bldg 2F, 7-13-8 Roppongi, Minato-ku (5411 8939, www.tokyo-sportscafe.com). Roppongi station (Hibiya, Oedo lines), exits 2, 4. **Open** 6pm-5am Mon-Sat (closing time varies depending on matches). **Credit** DC, JCB, MC, V. **Map** p87.
One of the longest-established and largest sports bars in Tokyo, this place screens all major sporting events from around the world, with space to show two things at once. It offers an extensive range of beers – both domestic and imported – and cocktails. Happy hour lasts from 6pm to 8pm daily.

SHIBUYA

Bello Visto
Cerulean Tower Tokyu Hotel 40F, 26-1 Sakuragaoka-cho, Shibuya-ku (3476 3000, www.ceruleantower-hotel.com). Shibuya station

Super-deluxe.

(Yamanote, Ginza, Hanzomon lines), south exit. **Open** 4pm-midnight Mon-Fri; 3pm-midnight Sat, Sun. **Credit** AmEx, DC, JCB, MC, V. **Map** p93.

There are more luxurious hotel bars in town, but the enormous glass windows of the 40th-floor Bello Visto make this a spot worth checking out. The menu focuses on wine, with a frankly terrifying list of expensive tipples from all over the world. Prices start at ¥1,270 a glass, and a 10% service charge will be added to your bill. To ensure a seat by the window, booking is advisable.

▶ *If you want to be able to take the lift to your room, see p133 Cerulean Tower Tokyu Hotel.*

Chandelier Bar/Red Bar

1-12-24 Shibuya, Shibuya-ku. Shibuya station (Yamanote, Ginza, Hanzomon lines), east exit. **Open** 8pm-5am Mon-Thur, Sun; 8pm-11am Fri, Sat. **Map** p93.

Once the pick of Tokyo's late-night/early morning bars, this spot has lost some of its popularity due to the snooty staff and the fickle whims of Tokyo's trendies. But thanks to the generous opening times, it's still the number-one place in Shibuya to hit when everywhere else shuts. The dual-named bar is, appropriately, red and stuffed with chandeliers.

Pink Cow

Villa Moderna B1F, 1-3-18 Shibuya, Shibuya-ku (3406 5597, www.thepinkcow.com). Shibuya station (Yamanote, Ginza lines), Hachiko exit; (Fukutoshin, Ginza lines), exit 13. **Open** 5pm-late Tue-Thur, Sun; 5pm-3am Fri, Sat. **Credit** (min ¥5,000) AmEx, DC, JCB, MC, V. **Map** p93.

With an interior that's either garish or funky, depending on your taste, the Pink Cow is not the low-key venue its backstreet location would suggest. It's popular with artistic expats, and the regular events are as quirky and diverse as a knitting salon and a short-film festival. The food is good; the Friday and Saturday buffet is a reasonable ¥2,500.

★ Shirokuma

3F Kusuhara Bldg, 33-13 Udagawacho, Shibuya-ku (3464 4690, www.shirokuma.bz). Shibuya station (Yamanote, Ginza lines), Hachiko exit; (Fukutoshin, Ginza lines), exit 6. **Open** 6-11pm Mon-Thur, Sun; 6pm-1am Fri, Sat. **No credit cards. Map** p93.

The girls who run Shirokuma seem to have rummaged in their closets for all their long-lost junk, and then glued it to the walls of this endearing bar. The menu is even quirkier, with most cocktails built from Dita, Amaretto or similar girly liqueurs, and beers flavoured with anything from fresh ginger to pickled plums. It's wacky, but in a good way.

SHINJUKU

African Bar Esogie

3F Muraki Bldg, 3-11-2 Shinjuku, Shinjuku-ku (3353 3334, www4.point.ne.jp/~esogie). Shinjuku San-chome station (Marunouchi, Shinjuku lines), exit C3. **Open** 6pm-midnight Mon, Tue, Thur; 6pm-4am Fri, Sat; 6-11pm Sun. **No credit cards. Map** p101.

Shinjuku's San-chome district is crammed with tiny bars, most of them musically themed, and Esogie is arguably the pick of the bunch. Nigerian owner Lucky might just be the friendliest bartender in town, and the Afrobeat and highlife tunes make it easy to forget you're in a narrow black bar with minimal furnishings. Lucky gives *djembe* performances most nights, and invites customers to try their hand. The imported African beers aren't cheap, but – unusually for this area – there's no seating charge, and the authentic African dishes are reasonable.

★ Albatross

1-2-11 Nishi-Shinjuku, Shinjuku-ku (3342 5758, www.alba-s.com). Shinjuku station (JR, Shinjuku lines), west exit; (Marunouchi, Oedo lines), exit B16. **Open** 5pm-2am daily. **No credit cards. Map** p101.

Albatross.

Golden Gai

Shinjuku's concentrated drinking district.

Over 200 minuscule drinking dens are crammed into four ramshackle streets in east Shinjuku between Kuyakusho Dori and Hanazono shrine. Each place seats from half a dozen to two dozen guests, and each has a unique vibe, from post-war grittiness to high-end cocktails to hard rock. The area once catered to the underbelly of Tokyo (some of the bars are former brothels). It has also been long renowned as an unwelcoming place, but as leases change hands, newer, friendlier owners

have moved in. Most Golden Gai bars charge a seating fee of around ¥1,000, but this can rise to a staggering ¥4,000 at those wishing to discourage strangers. Here are three places to get you started:

Sister bar of the ever-popular Albatross, **Albatross G** (*see below*) is spacious by Golden Gai standards, with three stories, including a cute upper-tier lounge that we suspect was originally designed as a storage space. The ¥300 seating charge is about the cheapest in Golden Gai.

By contrast, **La Jetée** (*see below*) is a tiny Golden Gai institution. It's owned by a film fanatic (the place gets its name from the Chris Marker classic) who speaks fluent French but little English. Popular with French expatriates and creative types, it's also a favourite haunt of many visiting filmmakers, from Wim Wenders to Quentin Tarantino.

Also tiny is **Shot Bar Shadow** (*see below*). The master of this bar speaks Arabic, German, Russian and French, thanks to his time in the Foreign Legion. For you to be a member, and get in after midnight, he must be able to remember your name. It's a friendly place where six is a crowd.

Hidden among the tiny, rickety eateries of Omoide Yokocho, beside Shinjuku station, Albatross is a tiny three-storey salon that seats, in total, around 30 people. Customers seated on the middle floor place orders and receive drinks through a hole in the floor; an operation that becomes increasingly perilous as the night progresses and senses diminish. Up top, in lenient weather, the roof accommodates half a dozen more drinkers. The crowd is a genuinely eclectic mix of suits, artists, expats and students. Get there early.

The oldest and scruffiest of the Irish pub chain owned by Japanese brewer – and Guinness importer – Sapporo. Draught Guinness and cider (little known in Japan) accompany standard domestic beers, while the menu offers semi-authentic fish and chips. **Other locations** 2-29-8 Dogenzaka, Shibuya-ku (5459 1736); Sun Grow Bldg B1F, 1-10-8 Nishi-Ikebukuro, Toshima-ku (5951 3614); Sanno Park Tower B1F, 2-11-1, Nagatacho, Chiyoda-ku (3539 3615); 1-1-18 Toranomon, Minato-ku (5501 1536).

Albatross G
2F 5th Avenue, 1-1 Kabukicho, Shinjuku-ku (3202 3699, www.alba-s.com). Shinjuku station (Yamanote, Chuo lines), east exit; (Marunouchi line), exits B6, B7; (Oedo, Shinjuku lines), exit 1. **Open** 8pm-5am Mon-Sat. **No credit cards. Map** p101.
For review, *see above* **Golden Gai**.

Dubliners
Shinjuku Lion Hall 2F, 3-28-9 Shinjuku, Shinjuku-ku (3352 6606, www.dubliners.jp). Shinjuku station (JR lines), east exit; (Marunouchi, Oedo, Shinjuku lines), exit A8. **Open** noon-1am Mon-Sat; noon-11pm Sun. **Credit** AmEx, MC, V. **Map** p101.

La Jetée
1-1-8 Kabuki-cho, Shinjuku-ku (3208 9645). Shinjuku station (Yamanote, Chuo lines), east exit; (Marunouchi line), exits B6, B7; (Oedo, Shinjuku lines), exit 1. **Open** 7pm-late Mon-Sat. **No credit cards. Map** p101.
For review, *see above* **Golden Gai**.

Shot Bar Shadow
1-1-8 Kabuki-cho, Shinjuku-ku (3209 9530). Shinjuku station (Yamanote, Chuo lines), east exit; (Marunouchi line), exits B6, B7; (Oedo, Shinjuku lines), exit 1. **Open** 5pm-midnight Mon-Fri; 6pm-midnight Sat. Members only after midnight. **No credit cards. Map** p101.
For review, *see above* **Golden Gai**.

CONSUME

INSIDE TRACK
THE NEAR BEERS

If your beer is surprisingly cheap, there's a good chance you're drinking *happoshu* or *dai-san* beer, two categories of quasi-beers produced by Japan's brewers to circumvent the beer tax. *Happoshu* is a low-malt beer that some drinkers prefer for its '*nodogoshi*' – that throat-tingling refreshment that light beers offer. *Dai-san* beers, also known as *happosei*, are even cheaper, brewed from beans or peas, and universally taste awful.

Zoetrope

7-10-14 Nishi-Shinjuku, Shinjuku-ku (3363 0162, http://homepage2.nifty.com/zoetrope). (JR, Shinjuku lines), west exit; (Marunouchi, Oedo lines), exit D4. **Open** 7pm-4am Mon-Sat. **Credit** AmEx, MC, V. **Map** p101.

More than 300 whiskies and not a Laphroaig or Macallan in sight: Zoetrope is devoted to Japanese whiskies, and owner Atsushi Horigami has an encyclopaedic knowledge of the stuff. He also serves Japanese vodka, brandy and rum, but it's the whisky that's worth coming for.

▶ *If it's Scotch you're after, try Cask; see p181.*

FURTHER AFIELD

Combine

103 Riverside Terrace, 1-10-23 Naka-Meguro, Meguro-ku (3760 3939). Naka Meguro station (Toyoko line). **Open** noon-4am Mon-Sat; noon-2am Sun. **Credit** AmEx, DC, JCB, MC, V.

Naka-Meguro has no shortage of fashionable hangouts, but this one is a great spot day or night. Art is the chosen theme, with a wall of hundreds of art books in English and Japanese. There are also turntables that get an occasional airing. But the best things about Combine are its airy interior, riverside location and lack of affectation.

Other locations 28-10 Sarugakucho, Shibuya-ku (3770 3309).

Heaven's Door

Takimoto Bldg 2F, 2-17-10 Kitazawa, Setagaya-ku (3411 6774, www.heavensdoortokyo.com). Shimo-Kitazawa station (Keio Inokashira, Odakyu lines), south exit. **Open** 6pm-2am Mon-Sat; 4pm-2am Sun. **No credit cards.**

An extremely comfortable bar near Shimo-Kitazawa station run by charismatic Brit expat Paul Davies. Comfy sofas, a Joe Orton-style approach to interior design, a crowd of friendly regulars and a complete absence of food mark this place out. Heaven's Door also hosts a monthly alternative politics salon with English-language films.

★ Las Meninas

Plaza Koenji 2F, 3-22-7 Koenji-Kita, Suginami-ku (3338 0266). Koenji station (Chuo line), north exit. **Open** 6pm-late Tue-Sun. **Credit** AmEx, DC, JCB, MC, V.

Johnny the giant Geordie is the unlikely manager of this elegant tapas bar. Among the myriad late-night haunts of Koenji, Las Meninas stands out for the banter of the big man, and his cooking. A one-time chef, Johnny serves such reliably high-class, home-cooked fare that most customers ignore the menu and simply ask for 'food'. In an area known for cheap, friendly bars, this place is notable on both counts. The drink menu emphasises Spanish wines, sherries and beer.

Mother

5-36-14 Daizawa, Setagaya-ku (3421 9519). Shimo-Kitazawa station (Keio Inokashira, Odakyu lines), south exit. **Open** 5pm-2am daily. **No credit cards.**

The extreme kitsch of this Shimo-Kitazawa bar, which resembles a mix of gingerbread house, tree-house and pub, betrays what is in fact a classy establishment. There's a wide selection of bottled beers, as well as a high-quality menu of freshly made Okinawan and Thai dishes. The playlist consists mostly of legends such as Sly and the Family Stone, the Rolling Stones, Bob Dylan and the like, but you can bring your own CDs and staff will play them.

★ Popeye

2-18-7 Ryogoku, Sumida-ku (3633 2120, www. 40beersontap.com). Ryogoku station (JR line), west exit; (Oedo line), exit A5. **Open** 5-11.30pm Mon-Sat. **Credit** AmEx, JCB, MC, V.

Quite simply one of the best beer bars in the world. It boasts an astonishing 70 drafts, most of which are Japanese microbrews. Owner Tatsu Aoki is Japan's authority on all things malt and hops, with an obsessive attention to details such as glass shape and serving temperature. The ten-glass tasting sets are a great way to get to know Japan's best breweries.

S University of Tokyo

2F Mukougaoka Faculty House, 1-1-1 Yayoi, Bunkyo-ku (3813 0991, www.ginza-s.com/ group/s-location.html). Todaimae station (Nanboku line), exit 1. **Open** 11am-10pm Mon-Sat. **Credit** AmEx, JCB, MC, V.

It's a student bar on the campus of Japan's most prestigious university, but it's not like any student bar you've ever seen. The walls are dressed in top-grade cypress, the bartenders in waistcoats, and the shelf is packed with single-cask Scotches. It's the sister of a posh Ginza whisky bar, and the service is just as exemplary. If you're a member of the Scotch Malt Whisky Society, you'll get malts half price. It's well hidden on the campus: look for a new, white-walled building, and take the first set of stairs.

Other locations B2 Kaitou Bldg, 7-5-4 Ginza, Chuo-ku (3573 5074).

CONSUME

Coffee Shops

These cups don't come with a plastic lid.

For a nation of renowned tea-drinkers (*see p191* **Teashops**), the Japanese love their coffee. The city's first coffee shop opened in Ueno in 1888, when beans arrived from Brazil as free gifts (to get the nation hooked on the brew). And, as today's landscape shows, it worked like a charm.

The jazz and counter-culture booms of the '60s and '70s, when the country's youth looked West for inspiration, helped cement the role of the *kissaten* (coffee shop) as the place to hang out. The city's youth still look West for their coffee – but these days it's to the famous Seattle chain. The local equivalent, **Doutor**, is holding its own thanks to its lower prices and smoker-friendly outlets. The old-time *kissaten* are gradually disappearing, but it's still easy to find a coffee that tastes like coffee. It won't be the cheapest way to get your caffeine fix but you'll find that you get much more atmosphere.

ASAKUSA

Angelus

1-17-6 Asakusa, Taito-ku (3841 2208). Asakusa station (Asakusa, Ginza lines), exits 1, 3. **Open** 10am-9pm Tue-Sun. **No credit cards**. **Map** p45.
Perhaps, at some point in the distant past, this was the way local upmarket operations got to grips with handling new-fangled foreign delicacies. Out front is a smart counter selling a fancy selection of Western-style cakes; further inside, the coffee shop section is a more spartan affair of plain walls and dark wood trimmings.

Ef

2-19-18 Kaminarimon, Taito-ku (3841 0114, 3841 0442 gallery, www.gallery-ef.com). Asakusa station (Asakusa line), exit A5; (Ginza line), exit 2. **Open** *Café & gallery* 11am-7pm Mon, Wed-Sun. *Bar* 6pm-midnight Mon, Wed, Thur, Sat; 6pm-2am Fri; 6-10pm Sun. **No credit cards**. **Map** p45.
This retro-fitted hangout is a welcome attempt to inject a little Harajuku-style cool into musty Asakusa, but among its own more surprising attractions is a small art gallery converted from a 130-year-old warehouse. Duck through the low entrance at the back, and suddenly you're out of 1950s Americana and into tatami territory, with admittance to the main exhibits up a steep set of traditional wooden steps. A place to try when you're tired of the local temples.
► *For details about the gallery itself, see p237.*

EBISU

Time Out Café & Diner

3-16-6 Higashi, Shibuya-ku (5774 0440, www. timeoutcafe.jp). Ebisu station (JR line), west exit; (Hibiya line). **Open** 11.30am-11.30pm Mon-Fri; 1-11.30pm Sat; 1-10pm Sun. **No credit cards**.
Cheap café grub, free Wi-Fi, a library of Time Out books and a layout so spacious you won't believe you're in Tokyo... Sure, this may not be the most objective review, but the Time Out Café & Diner is worth a look if you're in the area.

GINZA

For teashops in the area, *see p191*.

Benisica

1-6-8 Yurakucho, Chiyoda-ku (3502 0848). Hibiya station (Chiyoda, Hibiya, Mita lines), exit A4. **Open** 9.30am-11.45pm Mon-Fri; 9am-11.45pm Sat, Sun. **No credit cards**. **Map** p59.
The traditional neighbourhood café is realised in ideal form just across the railway tracks from Ginza, with an extensive selection of meal-and-cake sets to boot. Benisica claims to be the original inventor of 'pizza toast' – a near cousin of Welsh rarebit – now featured on coffee-shop menus all over Japan.

Café Fontana

Abe Bldg B1, 5-5-9 Ginza, Chuo-ku (3572 7320). Ginza station (Ginza, Hibiya, Marunouchi lines), exits B3, B5. **Open** noon-11pm Mon-Fri; 2-11pm Sat; 2-7pm Sun. **No credit cards**. **Map** p59.
A typically genteel Ginza basement establishment, but one where the individually served apple pies come in distinctly non-dainty proportions. Each steaming specimen contains a whole fruit, thinly covered in pastry, then doused thoroughly with cream.

Café Paulista

Nagasaki Centre, 8-9-16 Ginza, Chuo-ku (3572 6160, www.paulista.co.jp). Ginza station (Ginza, Hibiya, Marunouchi lines), exits A3, A4, A5. **Open** 8.30am-10pm Mon-Sat; noon-7.30pm Sun. **No credit cards**. **Map** p59.
This Brazilian-themed Ginza establishment was founded back in 1914. The all-natural beans are imported directly from Brazil, keeping blend coffee prices down to ¥498, a bargain for the area. Low leather seats, plants and wall engravings catch the eye amid a general brown-and-green motif.

Ben's Café. *See p190.*

Ki No Hana

4-13-1 Ginza, Chuo-ku (3543 5280). Higashi-Ginza station (Asakusa, Hibiya lines), exit 5. **Open** 10.30am-8pm Mon-Fri, noon-6pm Sat. **No credit cards**. **Map** p59.
The pair of signed John Lennon cartoons on the walls is the legacy of a chance visit by the former Beatle one afternoon in 1978. With its peaceful atmosphere, tasteful floral decorations, herbal teas and lunchtime vegetarian curries, it isn't too difficult to understand Lennon's appreciation of the place. Apparently, the overawed son of the former owner also preserved the great man's full ashtray, including butts. Alas, he kept this as a personal memento, so it isn't on display.

INSIDE TRACK BEAN BAGS

Though vacuum-brewed siphon coffee is often associated with Japan, it wasn't invented here. Japan's true innovation was the 'nel drip' (from 'flannel drip'), a system that's even more unwieldy than the siphon. The brewer packs grounds into a cloth cone, then holds the cone over a pot as the water slowly filters through. It takes great skill to judge when and how to pour, but it offers greater control of the flavours than other drip methods. To try some, visit **Café de L'Ambre** (8-10-15 Ginza, Chuo-ku, 3571 1551, www.h6.dion.ne.jp/~lambre) or **Café Fouquet's** (Tamagawa Takashimaya S-C, 3-17-1 Tamagawa, Setagaya-ku, 3708 5038).

HARAJUKU & AOYAMA

★ A to Z Café

5F, 5-8-3 Minami-Aoyama, Minato-ku (5464 0281, www.jellyfish.bz). Omotesando station (Chiyoda, Ginza, Hanzomon lines), exit B1. **Open** noon-11.30pm daily. **No credit cards**.
Artist Yoshitomo Nara and design group Graf have teamed up together to produce what has been one of the capital's trendiest cafés since its opening in 2006. With an interior somewhere between tree-house and playpen, and local trendies occupying the mismatched wooden furniture, there are still no signs of this café's popularity waning. The menu is an east-west hotchpotch of dishes such as cod roe on toast, seafood croquettes and green tea sundaes, plus industrial strength coffee and teas from around the world. In the warmer months, the café extends to the rooftop.

Daibo

2F, 3-13-20 Minami-Aoyama, Minato-ku (3403 7155). Omotesando station (Chiyoda, Hanzomon, Ginza lines), exits A3, A4. **Open** 9am-10pm Mon-Sat; noon-8pm Sun. **No credit cards**. **Map** p65.

The biggest treat at this cosy, wood-bedecked outpost is the excellent milk coffee, which comes lovingly hand-dripped into large pottery bowls. Even the regular blend coffee reveals a true craftsman's pride and is available in four separate varieties. There's just one long wooden counter plus a couple of tables, but the restrained decoration and the low-volume jazz soundtrack combine to create a soothing and restful vibe.

Volontaire

2F, 6-29-6 Jingumae, Shibuya-ku (3400 8629). Meiji-Jingumae station (Chiyoda line), exit 4. **Open** 1-7pm Mon-Sat. *Bar* 7pm-midnight Mon-Sat. **No credit cards**. **Map** p65.

A hole-in-the-wall, old-style coffee and jazz joint handily near the Omotesando crossing. There's only a single counter for seating, but the area behind the bar bulges with old vinyl. Volontaire switches to bar mode in the evening, with a hefty cover charge.

MARUNOUCHI

Marunouchi Café

Shin Tokyo Bldg 1F, 3-3-1 Marunouchi, Chiyoda-ku (3212 5025, www.marunouchicafe.com). Yurakucho station (Yamanote line), Tokyo International Forum exit; (Yurakucho line), exit A1 or Nijubashimae station (Chiyoda line), exit B7. **Open** 8am-9pm Mon-Fri; 11am-8pm Sat, Sun. **No credit cards**. **Map** p77.

Despite the name, this place isn't quite a café in the usual sense: guests can bring their own food or drink to consume on the premises as they browse the extensive library, make use of the Wi-Fi or take in an exhibition. It's funded by Mitsubishi as a promotion for the area, but run by design firm Idée.

Mironga

1-3 Kanda-Jinbocho, Chiyoda-ku (3295 1716). Jinbocho station (Hanzomon, Mita, Shinjuku lines), exit A7. **Open** 10.30am-10.30pm Mon-Fri; 11.30am-7pm Sat, Sun. **No credit cards**. **Map** p77.

Probably the only place in Tokyo where non-stop (recorded) tango provides seductive old-style accompaniment to the liquid refreshments. Argentina's finest exponents of the dance feature in the impressive array of fading monochromes on the walls, and there's also a selection of printed works on related subjects lining the bookshelves. Of the two rooms, the larger and darker gets the nod for atmosphere. As well as a wide range of coffees, Mironga proffers a good selection of imported beers and reasonable food.

SHIBUYA

Lion

2-19-13 Dogenzaka, Shibuya-ku (3461 6858, http://lion.main.jp). Shibuya station (Yamanote, Ginza, Hanzomon lines), Hachiko exit. **Open** 11am-10.30pm daily. **No credit cards**. **Map** p93.

There's a church-like air of reverence at this sleepy shrine to classical music. A pamphlet listing stereophonic offerings is laid out before you, seating is in the form of pew-style rows facing an enormous

CONSUME

pair of speakers, and conversations are discouraged. If you must talk, then do so in whispers. The imposing grey building is an unexpected period piece amid the gaudy love hotels of Dogenzaka.

Satei Hato

1-15-19 Shibuya, Shibuya-ku (3400 9088). Shibuya station (Yamanote line), east exit; (Ginza line), Toyoko exit; (Hanzomon line), exit 9. **Open** 11am-11pm daily. **No credit cards**. **Map** p93.
Step through the marble-tiled entrance and into top-grade *kissaten* territory of a traditionalist bent. A huge collection of china cups stands behind the counter, while sweeping arrangements of seasonal blooms add colour to a dark wood interior that recalls an earlier age. The most expensive coffee on the menu is Blue Mountain at ¥1,000.

SHINJUKU

Bon

Toriichi Bldg B1, 3-23-1 Shinjuku, Shinjuku-ku (3341 0179). Shinjuku station (Yamanote, Chuo, Sobu lines), east exit; (Marunouchi line), exit A5; (Oedo, Shinjuku lines), exit 1. **Open** 1-11.30pm daily. **No credit cards**. **Map** p101.
The search for true coffee excellence is pursued with surprising vigour at this pricey but popular Shinjuku basement. The cheapest choice from the menu will set you back a cool ¥1,000, but at least the cups will be bone china – selected from an enormous collection. Special tasting events are held periodically for connoisseurs.

Tajimaya

1-2-6 Nishi-Shinjuku, Shinjuku-ku (3342 0881, www.shinjuku.or.jp/tajimaya). Shinjuku station (Yamanote, Chuo, Sobu lines), west exit; (Marunouchi line), exit A17; (Oedo, Shinjuku lines), exit 3. **Open** 10am-11pm daily. **No credit cards**. **Map** p101.

Caught between the post-war grunge of its immediate neighbours and the bustle of Shinjuku, Tajimaya responds with abundant bone china, coffees from all over the world, non-fetishist use of classical music, and milk in the best copperware. Scones on the menu provide further evidence of advanced sensibilities, but the deeply yellowed walls and battered wood could be smartened up for the sake of appearances.

UENO

Miro

2-4-6 Kanda-Surugadai, Chiyoda-ku (3291 3088). Ochanomizu station (Chuo, Sobu lines), Ochanomizu exit; (Marunouchi line), exit 2. **Open** 9am-7pm Mon-Fri; 11am-6pm Sat. **No credit cards**.
This spot is named after Catalan surrealist artist Joan Miró, several of whose works adorn the walls. Both ambience and decor appear untouched by the passing decades. The location is pretty well hidden, down a tiny alley opposite Ochanomizu station.

ELSEWHERE IN CENTRAL TOKYO

★ Ben's Café

1-29-21 Takadanobaba, Shinjuku-ku (3202 2445, www.benscafe.com/en). Takadanobaba station (Yamanote line), Waseda exit; (Tozai line), exit 3. **Open** 11.30am-11.30pm Mon-Thur, Sun; 11.30am-12.30am Fri, Sat. **No credit cards**.
Great food, great coffee, friendly staff and Wi-Fi make this New York-style café a local favourite. Ben's also hosts occasional art shows, weekend poetry readings and live music. The friendly staff speak English and the coffee is great. *Photos pp188-189.*

FURTHER AFIELD

★ Bear Pond Espresso

2-36-12 Kitazawa Setagaya-ku (5454 2486, www.bear-pond.com). Shimokitazawa station (Inokashira, Odakyu lines), north exit. **Open** 9am-6.30pm Wed-Mon. **No credit cards**.
The espresso at Bear Pond is often hailed as the city's best, though it might not be to everyone's taste. Katsu Tanaka pulls a single mouthful of extraordinarily intense, mouth-puckering coffee that unfurls a gorgeously long, chocolatey finish.

Café Bach

1-23-9 Nihonzutsumi, Taito-ku (3875 2669, www.bach-kaffee.co.jp). Minami-Senju station (Hibiya line), south exit. **Open** 8.30am-9pm Mon-Thur, Sat, Sun. **No credit cards**.
All the beans are roasted on the premises of this dedicated coffee specialist in suburban Minami-Senju in northern Tokyo. Café Bach supplied the coffee for the G8 summit that took place in Okinawa in 2000, a meeting commemorated on the Japanese ¥2,000 note.

CONSUME

Teashops

Tea-drinking in Japan is both a daily routine and a highly ritualised art. Exquisite tearooms at the **Imperial Hotel** (3504 1111, www.imperialhotel.co.jp/e) and the **Hotel New Otani** (3265 1111, www.newotani.co.jp/en), or the Meiji-era teahouse at picturesque event venue **Happo-en** (3443 3775, www.happo-en.com/english) stage full, elaborate tea ceremonies (reservations essential).

At the other end of the tea-drinking spectrum, the **Koots** chain (www.koots.jp) applies the Starbucks model to the classic drink, albeit with quirky modern takes such as green-tea mocha or frozen tea shakes.

For something in between, try one of these.

Cha Ginza (Uogashi-Meicha)

2F & 3F, 5-5-6 Ginza, Chuo-ku (3571 1211, www.uogashi-meicha.co.jp/shop_01.html). Ginza station (Ginza, Hibiya, Marunouchi lines), exit B5. **Open** 11am-7pm Tue-Sun. **No credit cards**. **Map** p59.

Buy a ¥500 ticket at the street-level tea shop and head upstairs to the wine-bar-esque second floor for *sencha* (green leaf tea) served with a sip of saké. Alternatively, have *matcha* (powered green tea) on the glass-ceilinged third floor where staff whisk a thick, frothy tea in a simplified ceremony that begins with a sip of water to cleanse the palate. As a considerate extra touch, all tea is served with a seasonal Japanese sweet.

★ Nakajima no Ochaya (Hamarikyu Onshi Teien)

1-1 Hamarikyu Teien, Chuo-ku (3541 0200, www.tokyo-park.or.jp/english/park/detail_04.html). Shinbashi station (Yamanote line), Karasumori exit; (Ginza line), exit 2; (Asakusa line), exit 5 or Shiodome station (Oedo line), exit 5. **Open** 9am-4.30pm daily. **No credit cards**.

Located on a tidal pond in Hama-Rikyu Garden, this teahouse with traditional tatami mats boasts the best view of our teashop picks. Remove your shoes, take a seat on the red felt and gaze out at the one-time falconry ground while you wait for your tray of *matcha* and a traditional sweet. Outdoor seating is available.
► *Note that you have to pay the park admission (¥300). For more information about visiting the Hama-Rikyu Detached Garden, see p60.*

Saryo Tsujiri

B2F Caretta Shiodome, 1-8-2 Higashi-Shinbashi, Minato-ku (5537 2217, www.giontsujiri.co.jp/saryo). Shinbashi station (Yamanote line), Karasumori exit; (Ginza line), exit 4; (Asakusa line), Shiodome exit or Shiodome station (Oedo line), exit 6; (Yurikamome line). **Open** 11am-10.30pm Mon-Fri; 11am-9.30pm Sat; 11am-9pm Sun. **Credit** AmEx, DC, JCB, MC, V.

And you thought green-tea ice cream was creative. At this Tokyo outlet of a legendary Kyoto café, expect long lines for green-tea desserts that include sorbet, mousse, jelly and cakes, all in vivid green tones. You can also try tea-flavoured noodle dishes and, if you still fancy it, tea.

Cha Ginza (Uogashi-Meicha).

CONSUME

Shops & Services

Where to spend, spend, spend in the capital of consumerism.

Japan's reputation for consumer culture is well deserved, and the crowded shops and streets of Ginza, Shibuya, Shinjuku, Omotesando, Ikebukuro and other retail centres are a great place to gain an insight into this island nation.

You'll find an extraordinary range of shops and products, from ritzy department stores and high-end international designer flagships to quirky boutiques and tiny outlets offering traditional crafts. You'll also find Tokyo more affordable than ever.

THE SHOPPING SCENE

Hard economic times have seen a proliferation of budget retailers, including pile 'em high, sell 'em cheap chain **Don Quixote** (*see p216*). Budget clothing brand **Uniqlo** (*see p208*) is as popular as ever, and second-hand shops (just look for the word 'recycle') such as **RagTag** (*see p208*) have become more visible in a nation that had never previously taken to the idea of used goods. Yet none of this has affected the popularity of the top brands, whose fortunes have soared in parallel with the bargain-shopping boom. Since the economy began rebounding, the biggest names in fashion have been gobbling up retail space across the city.

OPENING HOURS, SALES AND TAX

With more money floating around, opening times are inching longer and longer. The standard is still 10am or 11am until 8pm, but many places now stay open until 9pm or 10pm, especially in areas such as Shinjuku and Shibuya. Independent shops may close for one day, usually Monday or Wednesday. Sunday trading is the norm in Tokyo, as the day has no religious significance – in fact, it's one of the busiest shopping days. The only day that many shops take off is New Year's Day.

Most shops (except the traditional, craft-oriented ones) are open on national holidays – but if you're heading for a specific place, it's wise to call ahead before you go. Christmas is a normal working day with ordinary office hours. What's more, the Christmas decorations come down at the stroke of midnight on the 24th, to make space for the more traditional New Year celebrations. Sales are held seasonally, with the biggest at New Year and in early July.

Prices include a consumption tax of five per cent, which is levied on all goods and services. For information on tax refunds, *see right* **Duty-free Goods**.

General

DEPARTMENT STORES

All Japanese *depato* share certain basic features. Food halls (*depachika*) – hectic places featuring branches of internationally famous pâtisseries, confectioners and delis – are always in the basement. The first few floors sell women's clothing and accessories, with menswear beginning directly above. The top levels include restaurants (*depa-resu*) that stay open at night after the main store has closed, and many of the rooftops are used as beer gardens in the summer. Most *depato* have Japanese craft and souvenir sections, and some offer worldwide delivery services. Almost all stores offer a tax-exemption service for purchases (mainly clothing, kitchenware and electrical goods) that total over ¥10,000 – you'll need your passport. Floor guides in English are available at the information desk.

Daimaru

1-9-1 Marunouchi, Chiyoda-ku (3212 8011, www. daimaru.co.jp/english/tokyo.html). Tokyo station (Yamanote, Chuo lines), Yaesu central exit; (Marunouchi line), exits 1, 2. **Open** 10am-8pm daily. **Credit** AmEx, DC, JCB, MC, V. **Map** p77.

The first six floors of this store located inside Tokyo station are devoted to fashion and accessories; Japanese souvenirs are on the seventh and tenth, restaurants on the eighth, and the Daimaru Museum on the 12th. 'Gochiso Paradise', on floor B1 by the Yaesu central exit, contains Japanese confectionery shop Shirotae, and Kihachi, an extremely popular cake outlet. The currency-exchange and tax-exemption counters are on the seventh floor. A shipping service is also available.

★ Isetan

3-14-1 Shinjuku, Shinjuku-ku (3352 1111, www.isetan.co.jp/iclub). Shinjuku-Sanchome station (Marunouchi, Shinjuku lines), exits B3, B4, B5 or Shinjuku station (Yamanote, Chuo lines), east exit; (Oedo line), exit 1. **Open** 10am-8pm daily. **Credit** AmEx, DC, JCB, MC, V. **Map** p101.

Tokyo's trendiest and friendliest department store is located in Shinjuku, spread out over eight buildings very close to one another. The most noteworthy are the main building and men's building. The overseas shipping service is in the basement of the main building, and the tax-exemption counter is on the eighth floor of the annex. Isetan also runs the I-Club, a free service for foreign residents in Japan. The club's monthly newsletter contains news of sales, discounts and special promotions, plus details of the Clover clothing range, available in larger sizes than the standard Japanese ones. Ask for membership details at the foreign customer desk on the eighth floor of the men's building.

Other locations 1-11-5 Kichijoji Honcho, Musashino-shi (0422 211 111).

Keio

1-1-4 Nishi-Shinjuku, Shinjuku-ku (3342 2111, www.keionet.com). Shinjuku station (Yamanote line), west exit; (Marunouchi line), exits A12-A14; (Oedo, Shinjuku lines), exit 3. **Open** 10am-8pm daily. **Credit** AmEx, DC, JCB, MC, V. **Map** p101.

Keio has womenswear and accessories on the first four floors of the store; menswear on the fifth; kimonos, jewellery and furniture on the sixth; children's clothes and sporting goods on the seventh; and office supplies on the eighth. The store also offers a range of clothing in Westerner-friendly larger sizes called Lilac. The tax-exemption counter is located on the sixth floor.

Other locations Keio Seiseki-Sakuragaoka, 1-10-1 Sekido, Tama-shi (042 337 2111).

Lumine Est

3-38-1 Shinjuku, Shinjuku-ku (5269 1111, www. lumine.ne.jp/est). Shinjuku station (Yamanote, Chuo, Marunouchi lines), above the east exit; (Oedo, Shinjuku lines), exit 1. **Open** 11am-10pm Mon-Fri; 10.30am-10pm Sat, Sun. **Credit** AmEx, DC, JCB, MC, V. **Map** p101.

Wako. *See p195.*

Duty-free Goods

How to get the tax back.

Foreign visitors can reclaim the five per cent sales tax at shops that have duty-free counters. These include most department stores and many electrical goods shops in **Akihabara** (*see p202*). Exempted items include food, beverages, tobacco, pharmaceuticals, cosmetics, film and batteries.

To qualify, your total purchases must cost more than ¥10,000, and your passport must show that you have been in Japan for less than six months. Take the paid-for goods and receipts to the store's tax-refund counter, along with your passport; the refund will be paid on the spot. When you leave Japan, make sure you have your purchases with you (preferably in your carry-on bag, as Customs may ask to see them).

Situated above the east exit of Shinjuku station, Lumine Est is chiefly notable for the Shunkan gourmet restaurant area, created by celebrated designer Takashi Sugimoto, on the seventh and eighth floors. The lower floors are laid out in a series of corridors that are fun for people-watching.

▶ *For more restaurants in Shinjuku, see p167.*

Matsuya

3-6-1 Ginza, Chuo-ku (3567 1211, www.matsuya. com). Ginza station (Ginza, Hibiya, Marunouchi lines), exits A12, A13. **Open** 10am-8pm daily (but closing time varies by month). **Credit** AmEx, DC, JCB, MC, V. **Map** p59.

Matsuya is notable for having in-store boutiques from the famous triumvirate of Japanese fashion revolutionaries: Issey Miyake, Yohji Yamamoto and Comme des Garçons, all of which are situated on the third floor. Traditional Japanese souvenirs are on the seventh, and shopping services for foreigners – tax exemption and overseas delivery – are on the third. The bureau de change counter is on the first floor. **Other locations** 1-4-1 Hanakawato, Taito-ku (3842 1111).

Treats Abound Underground

In department stores, head downstairs for foodie delights.

The word *depachika* is a fusion of *depa*, meaning 'department store', and *chika*, the Japanese word for 'basement', and it's these nether regions of Tokyo's vast stores that cater to the nation's foodies. This is the place to come for glistening pieces of sushi, top-grade green tea, delicate Japanese *wagashi* confectionery and those famously overpriced melons.

Shops and stalls are grouped together by product, so wandering the *depachika* is a sensory treat as the yeasty bakery smell gives way to sweet pickle, fresh fish, a fruity tang or a subtle sugary whiff.

There's a dizzying array of seafood – raw, dried or cured – including slabs of the famous *otoro* (fatty tuna). In the meat section, look for the marbled cuts of beef from cows that have enjoyed a lifestyle of massages and, more bizarrely, beer.

And if you're souvenir shopping, check out the exquisite Japanese confectioneries. They look like mini works of art and are usually studded with seasonal motifs.

Some of Japan's most beloved brands, such as Toraya, renowned for its adzuki-bean *yokan* cakes, have been hawking their wares downstairs for generations. But they now compete with an increasing number of major international purveyors, including Fauchon, Harrods, Hediards and all the big-name chocolatiers.

The basement of **Tobu** (*see right*) in Ikebukuro offers the widest selection, with well over 200 stalls, but more renowned destinations include **Isetan** (*see p193*) in Shinjuku and **Mitsukoshi** (*see right*) in Ginza.

And when you've finished with the food, head upstairs, where most stores offer quality lacquerware, ceramics and tools.

The *depachika* in **Takashimaya**. *See right.*

Matsuzakaya

10-1 Ginza, Chuo-ku (3572 1111, www.
matsuzakaya.co.jp/ginza). Ginza station (Ginza,
Hibiya, Marunouchi lines), exits A1-A4. **Open**
10.30am-7.30pm daily. **Credit** AmEx, DC, JCB,
MC, V. **Map** p59.

The main Matsuzakaya store is actually in Ueno, but
the most convenient branch for shopaholics is this
one, located on Ginza's main drag near Mitsukoshi
and Matsuya. The tax-exemption and currency-
exchange counters are on the sixth floor, as are
kimonos. The annex contains a beauty salon, art
gallery and even a ladies' deportment school.
Other locations 3-29-5 Ueno, Taito-ku
(3832 1111).

Mitsukoshi

4-6-16 Ginza, Chuo-ku (3562 1111, www.
mitsukoshi.co.jp). Ginza station (Ginza, Hibiya,
Marunouchi lines), exits A7, A8, A11. **Open**
10am-8pm daily. **Credit** AmEx, DC, JCB,
MC, V. **Map** p59.

The oldest surviving department store chain in
Japan (founded 1673), Mitsukoshi has its gargantuan flagship store in Nihonbashi, but the Ginza
branch (opposite Wako) is more convenient and, with
the autumn 2010 unveiling of a new 13-storey wing,
the largest department store in the Ginza-Yurakucho
area. The bronze lion outside Mitsukoshi's main
entrance is a popular meeting place.
Other locations 1-4-1 Muromachi, Nihonbashi,
Chuo-ku (3241 3311); 3-29-1 Shinjuku, Shinjuku-ku
(3354 1111); 1-5-7 Higashi-Ikebukuro, Toshima-ku
(3987 1111); 4-20-7 Ebisu, Shibuya-ku (5423 1111);
1-19-1 Honcho, Kichijoji, Musashino-shi (0422
29 1111); 1-46-1 Ochiai, Tama City (0423 35 7711).

Odakyu

1-1-3 Nishi-Shinjuku, Shinjuku-ku (3342
1111, www.odakyu-dept.co.jp). Shinjuku station
(Yamanote, Chuo lines), west exit; (Marunouchi
line), exits A12-A14; (Oedo, Shinjuku lines),
exit 3. **Open** 10am-8pm daily. **Credit** AmEx,
DC, JCB, MC, V. **Map** p101.

Odakyu is split into two buildings connected by an
elevated walkway and underground passageways.
The main building has women's clothing on the first
six floors, kimonos on the fifth, and furniture on the
eighth, while the annex offers menswear, sportswear, four floors of the electronics retailer Bic
Camera, and a Troisgros delicatessen in the basement food hall. The top three floors of the main
building contain restaurants; the second holds the
tax-exemption counter.

Seibu

21-1 Udagawa-cho, Shibuya-ku (3462 0111, www.
seibu.co.jp). Shibuya station (Yamanote, Ginza
lines), Hachiko exit; (Hanzomon line), exits 6, 7.
Open 10am-8pm Mon-Wed, Sun; 10am-9pm Thur-
Sat. **Credit** AmEx, DC, JCB, MC, V. **Map** p93.

The Shibuya store is split into two buildings,
Annexes A and B, which face each other across the
street. Annex A sells mainly womenswear; Annex
B menswear, children's clothes and accessories.
The tax-exemption counter is on the seventh floor
of Annex A. Seibu also runs retailers Loft and
Movida, both of which are within easy walking dis-
tance of the store. Aimed at a young crowd, Loft
sells interior decorations and various knick-knacks,
while Movida houses fashion boutique Opening
Ceremony (*see p205*).
Other locations 1-28-1 Minami-Ikebukuro,
Toshima-ku (3981 0111); 2-5-1 Yurakucho,
Chiyoda-ku (3286 0111); Shinjuku Loft,
4F-6F Mitsukoshi Bldg, 3-29-1 Shinjuku,
Shinjuku-ku (5360 6210).

Takashimaya

2-4-1 Nihonbashi, Chuo-ku (3211 4111, www.
takashimaya.co.jp). Nihonbashi station (Asakusa
line), exit D3; (Ginza, Tozai lines), exits B1, B2.
Open 10am-8pm daily. **Credit** AmEx, DC, JCB,
MC, V. **Map** p77.

This Nihonbashi branch is a great place to pick up
some edible souvenirs – head to the basement floors.
There is also an overseas shipping service on the
first basement floor. The massive Shinjuku branch
– Takashimaya Times Square – contains a host of
boutiques and restaurants, a branch of hardware
shop Tokyu Hands, Kinokuniya International
Bookshop in the annex and the Times Square
Theatre on the 12th.
Other locations Takashimaya Times Square,
5-24-2 Sendagaya, Shibuya-ku (5361 1111);
3-17-1 Tamagawa, Setagaya-ku (3709 3111).

Tobu

1-1-25 Nishi-Ikebukuro, Toshima-ku (3981 2211,
www.tobu-dept.jp). Ikebukuro station (Yamanote
line), west exit; (Fukutoshin, Marunouchi,
Yurakucho lines), exits 4, 6. **Open** 10am-8pm
daily. **Credit** AmEx, DC, JCB, MC, V. **Map** p69.

The main building houses clothing for all occasions
on the lower floors (including kimonos on the ninth),
with an enormous selection of restaurants from the
11th to 17th floors. The central building sells clothing in larger sizes, plus a good range of interior
goods and office supplies. The plaza building contains the designer collection. The currency-exchange
and tax-exemption counters are on the basement
first floor of the central building.
▶ *In the basement is Tokyo's largest food hall;*
see left, Treats Abound Underground.

Wako

4-5-11 Ginza, Chuo-ku (3562 2111, www.wako.
co.jp). Ginza station (Ginza, Hibiya, Marunouchi
lines), exits A9, A10, B1. **Open** 10.30am-6pm Mon-
Sat. **Credit** AmEx, DC, JCB, MC, V. **Map** p59.

This prestigious department store is located on the
corner of Ginza Yon-chome, across from Mitsukoshi.

CONSUME

SEE MORE. BE MORE.

This is NEW YORK CITY™

Book Now. Get More.

★ travelocity®

Book your trip to NYC today with Travelocity on **nycgo.com**. Get the most out of your stay with special offers on hotels, dining, shopping, museums, arts, entertainment and more.

NYC
nycgo.com

The building's grand exterior – with its landmark clock tower – is matched only by the hushed ambience of the interior. As well as fine jewellery, porcelain and crystal, Wako sells designer apparel and accessories. *Photo p193.*
Other locations 5-6-6 Hiro, Shibuya-ku (3473 0200).

MALLS

The urban landscape of Tokyo has changed considerably in the past few years thanks to a series of gargantuan multi-use constructions that serve not just as shopping malls, but also incorporate high-class office space, hotels, restaurants and even art galleries. They are theme parks of conspicuous consumption, with breathtaking exteriors designed by internationally renowned architects.

The pioneer of this new movement is the Mori Corporation, which operates **Roppongi Hills** (incorporating the Grand Hyatt hotel, exclusive apartment buildings, restaurants and an art museum) and **Omotesando Hills**, a glorified mall designed by starchitect Tadao Ando. Both these developments, however, have been outshone by **Tokyo Midtown** – until recently the tallest building in Tokyo at 248 metres (813 feet) – which occupies the former site of the Defense Agency, just a stone's throw from Roppongi Hills. This shopping, entertainment, residential and business concept has co-opted architects Tadao Ando, Kengo Kuma and Jun Aoki.

Caretta Shiodome
1-8-2 Higashi-Shinbashi, Minato-ku (6218 2100, www.caretta.jp). Shiodome station (Oedo line), exits 5, 6. **Open** varies.
Just across from the Conrad Tokyo, this 47-storey skyscraper offers a relatively uninspiring mix of more than 60 shops, cafés and restaurants as well as housing the head office of advertising giant Dentsu, the ADMT Advertising Museum (*see p60*) and the Dentsu Shiki Theatre (*see p273*).

Mark City
1-12-1 Dogenzaka, Shibuya-ku (3780 6503, www.s-markcity.co.jp). Shibuya station (Yamanote, Ginza lines), Hachiko exit; (Hanzomon line), exits 5, 8. **Open** *Shops* 10am-9pm daily. *Restaurants* 11am-11pm daily. **Map** p93.
Shibuya's version of the multi-purpose mall is a relatively modest affair, housing a handful of boutiques and lifestyle stores in a building opposite Shibuya station. Casual restaurants and cafés are on the third and fourth floors.

Marunouchi Building
2-4-1 Marunouchi, Chiyoda-ku (5218 5100, www.marunouchi.com/marubiru/english). Tokyo station (Yamanote, Chuo lines), Shin Marubiru exit; (Marunouchi line), exit 5. **Open** *Shops* 11am-9pm Mon-Sat; 11am-8pm Sun. *Restaurants* 11am-11pm Mon-Sat; 11am-8pm Sun. **Map** p77.
While essentially an office tower, 'Marubiru', as it is affectionately known by patrons, devotes its first four floors and basement to a 'Shopping Zone', while the fifth, sixth, 35th and 36th floors belong to the 'Restaurant Zone'. The basement food hall has an emphasis on big-name gourmet products, and there are also branches of American Pharmacy and upmarket grocery store Meidi-ya. Just across the street is the New Marunouchi Building (opened in 2007), whose first nine floors are dedicated to retail.

Oazo
1-6-4 Marunouchi, Chiyoda-ku (5218 5100, www.oazo.jp). Tokyo station (Yamanote, Chuo lines), Marunouchi north exit; (Marunouchi line), exits 10, 12, 14. **Open** *Shops* 11am-9pm daily. *Restaurants* 11am-11pm daily. **Map** p77.
This gleaming glass complex of shops, restaurants and offices opposite Tokyo station is affiliated with the nearby Marunouchi Building. Pride of place goes to Maruzen's flagship bookstore (with a good English-language section; *see p200*). Also here is the Japan Aerospace Exploration Agency's showroom.

Omotesando Hills
4-12-10 Jingumae, Shibuya-ku (3497 0310, www.omotesandohills.com). Harajuku station (Yamanote line), Omotesando exit,

Omotesando Hills.

Tokyo Midtown.

or Omotesando station (Chiyoda, Ginza, Hanzomon lines), exit A2. **Open** *Shops* 11am-9pm Mon-Sat; 11am-8pm Sun. *Restaurants* 11am-9.30pm Mon-Sat; 11am-9pm Sun. **Map** p65.
The low-rise little sister of Roppongi Hills is a six-storey, 100-store concrete creation from Tadao Ando. Though not a must-visit destination, it has a few interesting shops and bars, most notably Bedrock (*see p204*) and Pass the Baton (*see p216*).

Roppongi Hills

6-10 Roppongi, Minato-ku (6406 6000, www. roppongihills.com). Roppongi station (Hibiya line), exit 1C; (Oedo line), exit 3. **Open** varies. **Map** p87.
Opened in 2003, this mammoth shopping and entertainment development received more than 49 million visitors in its first year alone. The brainchild of Tokyo property magnate Mori Minoru, Roppongi Hills is an entire mini city – with 200 shops and restaurants, the Grand Hyatt hotel, private apartment buildings, a multiplex, a TV studio and the colossal Mori Tower.
▶ *For the excellent Mori Art Museum and Tokyo City View observation deck, both atop the Mori Tower, see p88.*

Shin Marunouchi Building

1-5-1 Marunouchi, Chiyoda-ku (www. marunouchi.com/shinmaru/english). Tokyo station (Yamanote, Chuo lines), Shin Marubiru exit; (Marunouchi line), exit 5. **Open** *Shops* 11am-9pm Mon-Sat; 11am-8pm Sun. *Restaurants* 11am-11pm Mon-Sat; 11am-10pm Sun. **Map** p77.

A block away from the Marunouchi Building, and owned by the same people, the tower nicknamed 'Shinmaru Biru' was designed by the team behind London's Olympic velopark. It's better looking than its neighbour, and offers slightly more upmarket dining options, four floors of fashion, and a basement of luxury food items.

Sunshine City

3-1 Higashi-Ikebukuro, Toshima-ku (3989 3331, www.sunshinecity.co.jp). Ikebukuro station (Yamanote line), east exit; (Marunouchi, Yurakucho lines), exits 43, 44 or Higashi-Ikebukuro station (Yurakucho line), exit 2. **Open** *Shops* 10am-8pm daily. *Restaurants* 11am-10pm daily. **Map** p69.
The prototype for the huge malls that dominate Tokyo's retail scene, Sunshine City lacks much of the glossy glamour of its subsequent rivals. Most of its shops and restaurants are in the Alpa Shopping Centre. The complex also hosts the Ancient Orient Museum, an indoor theme park called Namja Town and the Gyoza Stadium (a collection of restaurants devoted to Japan's beloved dumplings).
▶ *For sightseeing details about Sunshine City and Ikebukuro's east side, see p70.*

★ Tokyo Midtown

9-7-1 Akasaka, Minato-ku (3475 3100, www. tokyo-midtown.com). Roppongi station (Hibiya, Oedo lines), exit 8. **Open** *Shops* 11am-9pm daily. *Restaurants* varies. **Map** p87.

The best-looking consumer complex in the entire city occupies almost 20 acres in the middle of Roppongi. Though its format is remarkably similar to the nearby Roppongi Hills (luxury hotel, big-name art museum, posh restaurants, designer boutiques, offices and residences), it eschews the navigation nightmares in favour of eye-pleasing architecture from SOM, Tadao Ando and Kengo Kuma. With lawns and spacious terraces, you could spend a day here.

▶ Highlights include 21_21 Design Sight (see p88), Suntory Museum of Art (see p90) and Restir (see p205).

Urban Dock LaLaport Toyosu

2-4-9 Toyosu, Koto-ku (6910 1234). Toyosu station (Yurakucho Line), exit 2. **Open** Shops 10am-9pm daily. Restaurants 11am-11pm daily.
Tokyo's largest shopping mall, covering almost 100,000sq m (1 million sq ft), LaLaport has little to excite in the shopping stakes, but it does have a few other attractions worth recommending. Top of the list is Kidzania (see p228), a career role-playing amusement park that offers children the chance to simulate a working day with pint-sized reproductions of grown-up jobs. It also has a Hello Kitty-themed amusement arcade and a cluster of shops for children, including Snoopy Town and Børnelund, as well as a cinema and a small gallery devoted to ukiyo-e. LaLaport's Tokyo Bay location offers impressive views of the city.

▶ To experience its full visual impact, the mall is best visited by the Suijo bus (see p48), the futuristic ferry designed by anime mastermind Leiji Matsumoto, on the Tokyo Water Cruise from Asakusa to Toyosu along the Sumida River.

Venus Fort

Palette Town, 1 Aomi, Koto-ku (3599 0700, www.venusfort.co.jp). Aomi station (Yurikamome line) or Tokyo Teleport station (Rinkai line). **Open** Shops 11am-9pm Mon-Fri, Sun; 11am-10pm Sat. Restaurants 11am-11pm daily. **Map** p83.
A women-oriented shopping centre in a faux-classic Graeco-Roman style was designed to evoke the feeling of strolling through Florence or Milan (it even has an artificial sky that changes colour with the time of day outside). In December 2009, the third floor became an outlet centre with 49 fashion and lifestyle stores, including Armani, Coach, Galliano and Wedgwood, offering bargain prices.

▶ The future of this shopping mall is uncertain, given the redevelopment in the area; see p81.

Yebisu Garden Place

4-20 Ebisu, Shibuya-ku & 13-1/4-1 Mita, Meguro-ku (5423 7111, www.gardenplace.co.jp/english). Ebisu station (Yamanote line), east exit; (Hibiya line), exit 1. **Open** Shops 11am-8pm Mon-Sat; 11am-7.30pm Sun. Restaurants varies.

Within the spacious precincts of Yebisu Garden Place you'll find the Atre shopping arcade, Westin Hotel, Tokyo Metropolitan Museum of Photography (see p54) and Beer Museum Yebisu (see p52). A large number of boutiques are located in the stylish, self-enclosed shopping centre, Glass Square, which also has an oyster bar.

SHOPPING STREETS

Shopping streets, or shotengai, exist in various forms around Tokyo. Often near railway stations, they are home to long-established shops and markets, and provide a less sanitised retail experience than the super-shiny malls.

★ Ameyoko Plaza
Food & Clothes Market

www.ameyoko.net. Ueno station (Yamanote, Ginza lines), Shinobazu exit; (Hibiya line), exits 6, 7 or Okachimachi station (Yamanote line), north exit. **Open** varies. **Map** p107.
This maze of streets next to the railway tracks between Ueno and Okachimachi stations comprises two markets: the covered Ueno Centre Mall and open-air Ameyoko itself. The mall sells an array of souvenirs and clothes, while the 500 stalls of jam-packed Ameyoko – one of Tokyo's greatest street markets – specialise in fresh food, especially fish.

▶ For more about the Ameyoko area, see p108.

Kappabashi Dori

Tawaramachi station (Ginza line), exit 1 or Asakusa station (Asakusa, Ginza lines), exits 1, 2, 3, A4. **Open** varies. **Map** p45.
If you're visiting Asakusa's Senso-ji temple (see p49) and Nakamise Dori (see below), take a short detour to this area devoted to wholesale kitchenware shops. You'll find low-cost crockery, rice cookers, knives, grills… indeed, everything you need to set up a restaurant, including the realistic-looking plastic models of dishes that are displayed in restaurant windows. The shops run along Shinbori Dori, from the corner of Asakusa Dori; look for the giant chef's head on the top of the Niimi store.

Meguro Dori

Toritsu Daigaku station (Tokyu Toyoko line). **Open** varies. **Map** p53.
From its intersection with Yamate Dori, running about two miles south-west, Meguro Dori is dotted with dozens of quirky, independently run shops specialising in home furnishings. It's been nicknamed 'Interior Dori', as the street offers every imaginable type of furnishing, from tatty antiques to fashionably minimalist Italian kitchens. Most of what's on offer is imported from Europe or the States, but there's still plenty of Made in Japan merchandise to be found. It's not the easiest area to access, but catch the Toyoko line to Toritsu Daigaku and walk towards Meguro.

CONSUME

Nakamise Dori
*www.asakusa-nakamise.jp. Asakusa station
(Asakusa, Ginza lines), exits 1, 3, A4.* **Open**
8am-8pm daily. **Map** p45.
This avenue of stalls and tiny shops leading up to
the entrance to Senso-ji temple in Asakusa sells all
manner of Japanese souvenirs, some of them dating back to the Edo era. It also sells the kind of food
that is associated with festivals, and traditional
snacks such as *kaminari-okoshii* (toasted rice crackers) and *ningyo-yaki* (red bean-filled buns moulded
into humorous shapes).
▶ *For more about the street, see p46.*

Nakano Broadway
*3387 1610, 3388 7004, www.nbw.jp.
Nakano station (Chuo, Tozai lines), north exit.*
Open varies.
Walk down the cathedral-like *shotengai* and you'll
reach the covered Broadway section. This contains
numerous outlets of Mandarake (*see p212*), specialising in new and second-hand manga; branches of
Fujiya Avic, the second-hand CD/DVD/*anime* store
offering rarities and bootlegs; and a large number of
shops selling collectable action figures.

Nishi-Ogikubo
*www.sugishoren.com/street/400.htm. Nishi-
Ogikubo station (Chuo, Sobu lines), north exit.*
Open varies.
The area around the four main roads that cross at
the Zenpukuji river is home to around 75 antiques,
second-hand and 'recycle' shops. These sell everything from Japanese ceramics to 1950s American
memorabilia. Take the station's north exit, stop at
the *koban* (police box) and ask an officer for a copy
of the *'antikku mappu'*.

Takeshita Dori
*www.harajuku.jp/takeshita. Harajuku station
(Yamanote line), Takeshita exit or Meiji-
Jingumae station (Chiyoda, Fukutoshin lines),
exit 2.* **Open** varies. **Map** p65.
Takeshita Dori is a clogged artery of teen culture.
Along this narrow sloping street (which runs from
Harajuku station to Meiji Dori) you'll find stalls selling photos of fresh-faced 'idols' to star-struck schoolgirls, boutiques offering hip-hop clothing, cosplay
outfits or retro-punk fashions, and eateries at
teenager-friendly prices. A must-see. Visit at the
weekend for the full-on experience.

Specialist
BOOKS & MAGAZINES
The shops listed below are the best sources
for books in English and other languages, on
any subject. If you're looking for curiosities or
bargains and have a day to spare, head for the

Kanda-Jinbocho area (Jinbocho station) and
the second-hand bookshops of Yasukuni Dori.
English-language newspapers are available
from kiosks around train stations, as well as
selected convenience stores. **Tower Records**
in Shibuya (1-22-14 Jinnan, Shibuya-ku, 3496
3661) has a great selection of English-language
books, newspapers and magazines.

General
Kinokuniya Bookstore
*3-17-7 Shinjuku, Shinjuku-ku (3354 0131, www.
kinokuniya.co.jp). Shinjuku station (Yamanote,
Chuo lines), east exit; (Marunouchi line), exits
B7, B8; (Oedo, Shinjuku lines), exit 1.* **Open**
10am-9pm daily. **Credit** AmEx, DC, JCB, MC, V.
Map p101.
The best-known branch of this chain is on Shinjuku
Dori, but the branch behind the nearby Takashimaya
(on the south side of Shinjuku station) is bigger.
Kinokuniya has perhaps the largest selection in
Tokyo of new books in English, with novels and aca-
demic titles on offer. It also carries videos and soft-
ware. Note that not all branches sell English books.
Other locations throughout the city.

Maruzen
*Oazo 1F-4F, 1-6-4 Marunouchi, Chiyoda-ku
(5288 8881, www.maruzen.co.jp). Tokyo station
(Yamanote, Chuo lines), Marunouchi north
exit; (Marunouchi line), exits 10, 12, 14.*
Open 9am-9pm daily. **Credit** AmEx, DC,
JCB, MC, V. **Map** p77.
This flagship store inside the Oazo shopping complex (*see p197*) holds 200,000 books in English and
other languages. There are bilingual book advisers
on hand and a touch-screen computer search facility
(available in English).
Other locations throughout the city.

Manga
Manga is available wherever they sell printed
matter, from bookstores to station kiosks, but
there are a couple of specialist shops that are
particularly worth a visit – as is **Mandarake**
(*see p212*) in Nakano Broadway and Shibuya.
For more about Japan's love-affair with comics,
see p99 **Manga Mania**.

Manga no Mori
*3-10-12 Takada, Toshima-ku (5292 7748,
www.manganomori.net). Takadanobaba station
(Yamanote, Tozai lines), Waseda exit.* **Open**
11am-9pm daily. **Credit** AmEx, DC, JCB, MC, V.
The main branch of this chain sells a good range of
classic Japanese manga, the latest imported titles
from Marvel and DC, and a handful of action figures. The Ikebukuro branch listed below specialises
in manga for women.

Automatic for the People

Tokyo's marvellous vending machines.

Locals take the vending machines (*jidohanbaiki*) for granted, but first-time visitors will be impressed by their ubiquity, and the fact that they always work, are never vandalised and sell an astounding range of products.

The vast majority of vending machines in Tokyo sell soft drinks (hot and cold) or cigarettes, with a smaller, dwindling number selling alcohol (usually beer or saké).

Most machines operate 24 hours, but those selling tobacco switch themselves off from 11pm until 7am (ostensibly to combat under-age smoking, although curiously porn machines operate opposite hours). The drinks machines usually stop dispensing hot coffee or tea in the summer. Tobacco and alcohol vending machines now demand an ID card before they will dispense their goods.

If you venture outside the main shopping areas, you may find machines that sell more esoteric products. Batteries, condoms, rice, tights, ice-cream, sex toys – all have vending machines devoted to them somewhere in Japan. The saucier machines selling 'used' schoolgirls' knickers are not an urban legend; they did exist, but succumbed to a crackdown on sleaze.

The *jidohanbaiki* arrived during the Tokyo Olympics in 1964; there are now over six million machines across Japan. All accept coins and ¥1,000 notes, and many now take payment via the Suica or Pasmo magnetic travel cards (*see p309* **Tickets & passes**).

Other locations 1-28-1 Higashi-Ikebukuro, Toshima-ku (5396 1245); 6-16-16 Ueno, Taito-ku (3833 3411).

Tora no Ana

B1F-4F, 4-3-1 Soto-Kanda, Chiyoda-ku (5294 0123, www.toranoana.co.jp). Akihabara station (Yamanote, Sobu lines), Electric Town exit; (Hibiya line), exit 3. **Open** 11am-9pm Mon-Thur; 10am-9pm Fri-Sun. **Credit** DC, JCB, MC, V.
Look out for the giant cartoon mascot painted on the top of this flagship store in Akihabara. Inside the six-floor building it's a hive of activity as Japan's *otaku* (nerds) flip through the latest releases. In addition to the nation's bestselling new comics, the shop offers a selection of *dojinshi*, fanzines created by devoted manga amateurs, showcasing everything from Disney-esque fantasies to hard-core porn. **Other locations** 1-18-1 Nishi-Shinjuku, Shinjuku-ku (5908 1681); 1-13-4 Higashi-Ikebukuro, Toshima-ku (5957 7138); Akihabara Part 2, Kimura Bldg 2F-4F, 1-9-8 Soto-Kanda, Chiyoda-ku (5256 2055); Akihabara Part 3, Kyoeki Soto Kanda Bldg 4F-6F, 4-4-2 Soto-Kanda, Chiyoda-ku (3526 7211).
▶ *To find out more about 'otaku', see pp39-42.*

Specialist

Nellie's English Books

Sunbridge Bldg 1F-2F, 1-26-6 Yanagibashi, Taito-ku (3865 6210, 0120 071 329, www.nellies.jp). Asakusabashi station (Asakusa line), exit A3; (Sobu line), east exit. **Open** 10am-12.30pm, 1.15-6pm Mon-Fri. **Credit** AmEx, DC, JCB, MC, V.

Nellie's stocks a wide selection of materials that are useful for English-language teachers working in Japan. The range includes books, readers, videos, songbooks and software.

Used & antiquarian

Good Day Books

3F, 1-11-2 Ebisu, Shibuya-ku (5421 0957, www.gooddaybooks.com). Ebisu station (Yamanote line), east exit; (Hibiya line), exit 1. **Open** 11am-8pm Mon, Wed-Sat; 11am-6pm Sun. **No credit cards**.
Tokyo's oldest and best-known used English bookshop stocks more than 35,000 second-hand books and 7,000 new ones. There's also an extensive selection of second-hand books on Japan and Japanese-language texts. You can sell/trade your second-hand books and DVDs here too.

★ Totodo

Dai 2 Villa Aoyama 101, 5-7 Uguisudani-cho, Shibuya-ku (3770 7387, www.totodo.jp). Shibuya station (Yamanote, Ginza lines), west exit; (Fukutoshin, Hanzomon lines), exit 8. **Open** noon-8pm Mon-Sat. **Credit** AmEx, DC, JCB, MC, V.
This is probably the only book store in the entire world where you can purchase psychedelic poster art from the 1960s and also browse through a tome on the typefaces used in Edo-period shop signage. Opened in spring 2009, this compact store sells second-hand books covering the fields of art, architecture, photography and design, with a sizeable selection of English-language books, as well as a number of French and German works.

CONSUME

CHILDREN

Fashion

Casualwear chains such as **Gap**, Japan's **Muji** (*see p216* **Mujirushi Ryohin**) and **Uniqlo** (*see p208*), have outlets throughout the city.

Familiar

New Melsa Bldg B1F, 5-7-10 Ginza, Chuo-ku (3574 7111, www.familiar.co.jp). Ginza station (Ginza, Hibiya, Marunouchi lines), exit A2. **Open** 11am-8pm Mon, Tue, Thur-Sun. **Credit** AmEx, DC, JCB, MC, V. **Map** p59.

This upscale children's goods shop in Ginza handles everything from clothes, shoes and umbrellas to desks, beds, strollers and skincare. Prices are hefty, but quality is high.

Limi Feu Prankster

6-6-1 Jingumae, Shibuya-ku (5464 2025, www.limifeu.com). Harajuku station (Yamanote line), Omotesando exit or Meiji-Jingumae (Chiyoda, Fukutoshin lines), exit 4. **Open** noon-9pm daily. **Credit** AmEx, DC, JCB, MC, V. **Map** p65.

Tokyo's antidote to the frilly togs so often foisted on toddlers comes courtesy of Limi Feu Prankster, a store showcasing the children's line of Limi Yamamoto, daughter of fashion paragon Yohji. The whippersnappers can be left in a padded play area while mum and dad rummage through the funky threads. Mother-of-two Limi has a keen sense of what trendy Tokyo moms want their kids to wear, and this store is proving to be a big hit.

► *Limi Feu also does grown-up fashion. Check the website for store locations.*

Sayegusa

7-8-8 Ginza, Chuo-ku (3573 2441, www.sayegusa.com). Ginza station (Ginza, Hibiya, Marunouchi lines), exit A2. **Open** 10.30am-7.30pm daily. **Credit** AmEx, DC, JCB, MC, V. **Map** p59.

For the ultimate Tokyo children's clothing shopping experience, pay a visit to Ginza's Sayegusa, purveyors of finery for small fry since 1869. Housed in a four-storey Meiji-era building, this venerable establishment offers top-of-the-range baby and children's clothing and accessories on the first and second floors, party dresses and suits in the first basement floor, and a made-to-order clothing service on the floor beneath. Expect impeccable service and gut-churning prices.

Toys

Kiddyland (www.kiddyland.co.jp) is a Tokyo institution, however it is closed for renovations until 2012; check the website for the latest news.

BørneLund

Hara Bldg 1F, 6-10-9 Jingumae, Shibuya-ku (5485 3430, www.bornelund.co.jp). Harajuku station (Yamanote line), Omotesando exit or Meiji-Jingumae station (Chiyoda, Fukutoshin lines), exit 4. **Open** 11am-7.30pm daily. **Credit** AmEx, DC, JCB, MC, V. **Map** p65.

No electric or 'character' toys are sold at this small shop near Omotesando, which specialises in imported wooden toys. You can touch and play with most of the items on display. Sofas, and nursing and nappy-changing facilities are also provided.

Hakuhinkan

8-8-11 Ginza, Chuo-ku (3571 8008, www.hakuhinkan.co.jp). Shinbashi station (Yamanote line), Ginza exit; (Asakusa line), exit A3; (Ginza line), exit 1. **Open** 11am-8pm daily. **Credit** AmEx, JCB, MC, V. **Map** p59.

This multi-storey emporium in Ginza, one of Tokyo's biggest toy shops, is a showcase for the wacky, the cuddly and the cute, all with a Japanese twist. The basement is the headquarters of the Licca-chan Club (the Japanese equivalent of Barbie). There is a tax-exemption counter on the fourth floor.

Pokemon Center

3-2-5 Nihonbashi, Chuo-ku (5200 0707, www.pokemoncenter-online.com). Nihonbashi station (Asakusa line), exit D3; (Ginza, Tozai lines), exits B1, B2 or Tokyo station (Yamanote, Chuo, Marunouchi lines), Yaesu (north) exit. **Open** 11am-8pm Mon-Fri; 10am-7pm Sat, Sun. **Credit** AmEx, DC, JCB, V. **Map** p77.

'Pocket Monster' may have lost ground to Yu-Gi-Oh! and a variety of other games, but Pikachu's furry yellow paw still has an iron grip on Japanese pop culture. Come and see the monster-masters in their central Tokyo stronghold.

► *For more shops selling manga, see p200.*

ELECTRONICS & PHOTOGRAPHY

Akihabara, which likes to call itself 'Electric Town', is still the best place to buy electrical goods, but you'll find most mainstream items at identical prices in the superstores of Shibuya and Shinjuku. Tax exemption is available on purchases of ¥10,000 and over; take your passport, which needs to show that you've been in Japan for less than six months. Photography enthusiasts should take a stroll around the backstreets east of Shinjuku station, where there's a host of second-hand camera shops.

General

Akky

1-12-1 Soto-Kanda, Chiyoda-ku (5207 5027). Akihabara station (Yamanote, Sobu lines),

Loveless. See p204.

Electric Town exit; (Hibiya line), exit 3. **Open**
9.30am-8pm daily. **Credit** AmEx, DC, JCB, MC, V.
A well-presented store that sells all kinds of electrical appliances. All products are export models, sold
with an international warranty and English instructions, at duty-free prices. Overseas delivery service is
available. The staff speak a variety of languages.

LABI

*3-23-7 Shinjuku, Shinjuku-ku (3359 5566, www.
yamadalabi.com). Shinjuku station (JR lines), east
exit; (Marunouchi, Oedo, Shinjuku lines), exit
B13.* **Open** 10am-10pm daily. **Credit** AmEx,
DC, JCB, MC, V. **Map** p101.
The most aggressively expanding electronics
retailer in Japan opened this Shinjuku megastore in
2010, and plans to open a similar outlet on the other
side of the station in 2011. With nine floors, including one devoted to women's products, this ought to
satisfy most of your electronic desires.
Other locations throughout the city, including
2-29-20 Dogenzaka, Shibuya-ku (5456 6300);
1-12-9 Shinbashi, Minato-ku (3580 7191);
1-15-8 Soto-Kanda, Chiyoda-ku (5207 8060).

Laox: Duty Free Akihabara

*1-15-3 Soto-Kanda, Chiyoda-ku (3255 5301,
www.laox.co.jp). Akihabara station (Yamanote,
Sobu lines), Electric Town exit; (Hibiya line),
exit 3.* **Open** 10am-9pm daily. **Credit** AmEx,
DC, JCB, MC, V.
One of Japan's biggest suppliers of duty-free overseas-
model electronics and appliances. There are English-
language catalogues and instruction manuals for
most products. This branch is near the station, with
a huge sign outside, so it's hard to miss.
Other locations throughout the city.

Sony Building

*5-3-1 Ginza, Chuo-ku (3573 2563, www.
sonybuilding. jp). Ginza station (Ginza,
Hibiya, Marunouchi lines), exit B9.* **Open**
11am-7pm daily. **Credit** AmEx, DC, JCB,
MC, V. **Map** p59.
This eight-floor building – a landmark in Ginza –
contains showrooms for Sony's world-famous
products, including the AIBO robot hound,
PlayStation 3, VAIO, Cyber-Shot, Handycam and
others. The building also contains a number of
cafés and restaurants, and even an English pub.
▶ *For more on the Sony Building and sightseeing
in the surrounding area, see p57.*

Specialist

Tokyo IT Services

*Shinwa Bldg 5F, 2-6-8 Hamamatsucho, Minato-ku
(5733 4279, www.tokyo-it.com). Hamamatsucho
station (Yamanote line), south exit.* **Open** 10am-
6.30pm Mon-Fri; 11am-4pm Sat. **Credit** AmEx,
DC, JCB, MC, V.
Tokyo IT Services offers English-language support
to computer users in Tokyo, plus wireless network
installation, laptop rental from ¥500 a day, and a
computer repair service. For Macs and PCs.

User's Side 2

*Kanda Ishikawa Bldg. 4F, 4-9-8 Soto-Kanda,
Chiyoda-Ku (5207 7076, www.users-side.co.jp/2).
Akihabara station (Yamanote, Sobu lines),
Electric Town exit; Suehirocho station (Ginza
line), exit 1.* **Open** 11am-7pm Mon-Sat. **Credit**
AmEx, DC, JCB, MC, V.
User's Side 2 sells export models of Japanese technol-
ogy with English software. It also has an affordable

CONSUME

INSIDE TRACK
BEAUTIFUL ON THE INSIDE

Some stores are more memorable
for their interiors than for their products.
If you fancy a break from just shopping,
check out the decor at fashion boutiques
Bedrock, **Loveless**, **Opening Ceremony**
and **Restir** (for all, *see right*).

---

repair and troubleshooting service, with English-
language technical support and bilingual shop staff.
Other locations 3-9-2 Sotokanda, Chiyoda-ku
(5295 1011).

FASHION

Large tracts of the metropolis are devoted
to fashion retail, and each area has its
own individual character. Upmarket luxury
brands dominate the Ginza area and much
of 'brand boulevard' Omotesando, which runs
into the youth culture-oriented Harajuku.
For the latest teen trends, head to Shibuya
or neighbouring Daikanyama.

All Japanese clothing sizes are measured
in centimetres. Western visitors often find
Japanese sizes too small, though **Isetan** (*see
p193*) in Shinjuku caters for larger frames.

Boutiques

109

*2-29-1 Dogenzaka, Shibuya-ku (3477 5111,
www.shibuya109.jp). Shibuya station (Yamanote,
Ginza lines), Hachiko exit; (Fukutoshin,
Hanzomon lines), exit 3A.* **Open** 10am-9pm
daily. **Credit** varies. **Map** p93.
This landmark Shibuya store is the domain of the
joshikousei – the fashion-obsessed teenage girls who
don't just follow trends but start them. Take a stroll
around to see them in action and indulge in some
amateur anthropology.
▶ *Nearby 109-2, located at 1-23-10 Dogenzaka
(3477 8111), sells more of the same to pre-teens.*

ADD

*201, 3-20-1 Jingumae, Shibuya (3405 5090,
www.banalchicbizarre.com). Harajuku station
(Yamanote line), Takeshita exit or Meiji-
Jingumae station (Chiyoda, Fukutoshin lines),
exit 5.* **Open** noon-8pm daily. **Credit** AmEx,
DC, JCB, MC, V. **Map** p65.
Produced by design duo Banal Chic Bizarre (*see p205*
The Rag Trade) – quite possibly the best new
brand name around – ADD showcases their quirky
blend of utilitarianism and art-school bohemian. The
young designers also produce a quarterly publication, *root*, with a mission to depict Harajuku street

fashion through the eyes of those actually making it.
When available, this diminutive backstreet Harajuku
shop is the place to get the publication.

Bedrock

*West Building B1F, Omotesando Hills,
4-12-10 Jingumae, Shibuya-ku (3423 6969,
www.maniac-co.jp). Harajuku station (Yamanote
line), Omotesando exit or Omotesando station
(Chiyoda, Ginza, Hanzomon lines), exit A2.*
Open 11am-9pm daily. **Credit** AmEx, DC,
JCB, MC, V. **Map** p65.
Not even the Omotesando Hills store directory
admits that this boutique exists. It's hidden underneath an unassuming juice bar (take the stairs
beside the cash register), and the contrast between
the warm, fruity façade and the forbidding black cellar couldn't be starker. Enter through the prison
doors and behold the Ducati draped with a belt of
bullets, the chairs built from tusks, the hothouse of
giant cacti, and the skulls and chandeliers galore.
The clothing – think *Pirates of the Caribbean* meets
Marilyn Manson – is beside the point.
▶ *For more about Omotesando Hills, see p197.*

Blackflag

*5-4-24 Minami-Aoyama, Minato-ku (5778 1999).
Omotesando station (Chiyoda, Ginza, Hanzomon
lines), exit A5.* **Open** 11am-8pm daily. **Credit**
AmEx, DC, JCB, MC, V.
This hard-to-spot store is a collaboration between
the designers of a pair of popular street brands –
Neighborhood and W)taps. The shop's dark interior has a rustic 1930s American Midwest look,
contrasting with the combat gear-inspired apparel
and accessories on display.

Laforet Harajuku

*1-11-6 Jingumae, Shibuya-ku (3475 0411, www.
laforet.ne.jp). Harajuku station (Yamanote line),
Takeshita exit or Meiji-Jingumae station (Chiyoda,
Fukutoshin lines), exit 5.* **Open** 11am-8pm daily.
Credit AmEx, DC, JCB, MC, V. **Map** p65.
One of teenage Tokyo's hallowed sites, Laforet is
located in the heart of Harajuku, on the corner of
Omotesando and Meji Dori; look for the flower
sculptures outside. This multi-level emporium contains numerous small boutiques selling clothes and
accessories aimed at young wearers of garish,
eccentric fashion. Exhibitions and multimedia
events are also held here.

★ Loveless

*3-17-11 Minami-Aoyama, Minato-ku (3401
2301). Omotesando station (Chiyoda, Ginza,
Hanzomon lines), exit A4.* **Open** noon-10pm
Mon-Sat; noon-8pm Sun. **Credit** AmEx, DC,
JCB, MC, V. **Map** p65.
Men get the better deal here, with two dungeon-
like basement floors and a coffee counter, while
women make do with a comparatively ordinary

Restir.

entrance-level boutique. For either sex, the fashion is red-hot, frequently outlandish and includes upcoming Japanese labels that you surely won't find anywhere else. *Photo p203.*

▶ *Loveless's sister store, Colour by Numbers (20-23 Daikanyamacho, Shibuya-ku, 3770 1991), is also worth a visit.*

Nincompoop Capacity

2F, 3-4-11 Koenji-kita, Suginami-ku (3337 9401, www.geocities.jp/nincompoopcapacity). Koenji station (JR Chuo, Sobu lines), north exit. **Open** 1-11pm. **No credit cards**.

It's an apt name. The duo that runs this store takes second hand clothes and gives them heavy makeovers – gluing, drawing, stitching and nailing things where nobody else would think to put them. You need to be an extrovert to wear most of this gear, but it's very Tokyo.

Opening Ceremony

Seibu Movida, 21-1 Udagawa-cho, Shibuya-ku (6415 6700, www2.seibu.jp/020/shibuya-oc). Shibuya station (Yamanote, Ginza lines), Hachiko exit; (Fukutoshin, Hanzomon lines), exits 6, 7. **Open** 10am-8pm Mon-Wed. Sun; 10am-9pm Thur-Sat. **Credit** AmEx, DC, JCB, MC, V. **Map** p93.

The first international branch of the New York store has hands-down the best interior of any shop in Tokyo. Opening Ceremony give plenty of giggles with its surreal displays and oddball mannequins, but also comes through with a cutting-edge collection of labels, including Katherine Fleming purses and an exclusive Chloë Sevigny line.

Parco

15-1 Udagawa-cho, Shibuya-ku (3464 5111, www.parco.co.jp). Shibuya station (Yamanote, Ginza lines), Hachiko exit; (Fukutoshin, Hanzomon lines), exits 6, 7. **Open** *Parts 1, 2, 3* 10am-9pm daily; *Quattro* 11am-9pm daily. **Credit** AmEx, DC, JCB, MC, V. **Map** p93.

This mid-range clothing store occupies multiple buildings in Shibuya. Part 1 houses a theatre and an art bookshop, Part 2 specialises in fashion, and Part 3 has an exhibition space that hosts frequent shows by artists and designers from Japan and abroad. Another branch is the home of the concert hall Club Quattro (*see p259*).

Other locations 1-28-2 Minami-Ikebukuro, Toshima-ku (5391 8000); 1-5-1 Kichijoji-Honcho, Musashino-shi (0422 218 111).

★ Restir

Galeria, Tokyo Midtown, 9-7-4 Akasaka, Minato-ku (5413 3708, www.restir.com). Roppongi station (Hibiya, Oedo lines), exit 8. **Open** 11am-9pm daily. **Credit** AmEx, DC, JCB, MC, V. **Map** p59.

Restir appears to be a small store offering a very select range of clothing and accessories, but if the staff like the look of you, they'll slide open the wall

CONSUME

The Rag Trade

Who to wear for a Tokyo look.

Its fashion week may pale next to Paris's, but Tokyo is still a global style destination. In Harajuku, Aoyama, Daikanyama and Ginza, Tokyoites follow the sartorial tides with a gimlet eye and create styles that couldn't exist anywhere else. Here are six Tokyo originals worth getting on your back.

FACTOTUM
Designer Koji Udo.
The look Cosy menswear for the post-apocalyptic nomad.
Why it matters Factotum manages to push the envelope for menswear without veering into way-out-there territory. Udo cuts modern shapes, gets experimental, but doesn't alienate the wearer.
Where to buy it Factotum Flagship Shop, 11-3 Uguisudanicho, Shibuya-ku (6692 7426, www.factotum.jp).

MATOHU
Designers Hiroyuki Horihata, Makiko Sekiguchi.

The look Traditional Japanese fashions zoom into the 23rd century and get a minimalist makeover.
Why it matters Matohu is one of the few labels out there explicitly focusing on traditional Japanese elements without being stereotypical. The result is a satisfying fusion of culture, history and futurism.
Where to buy it Noriem Designers, Shinjuku Takashimaya Times Square 8F, 5-24-2 Sendagaya, Shibuya-ku (5361 1111, www.noriem.com).

MERCI BEAUCOUP
Designer Eri Utsugi.
The look If clothes were made out of Lego… bright colours, simple patterns and big shapes keep things relaxed and optimistic.
Why it matters This label has a bit of everything. It's got trend cachet but isn't too pricey, is always popular and has a look that says 'fun' without being silly – though it can go there.

to reveal one of the most over-the-top shopping experiences in Tokyo. You'll strut a catwalk lined with an audience of mannequins, past a DJ, and upstairs to a store that looks more like a nightclub. The high-end brands include more than a few home-grown labels.

Designer

Many European luxury brands have built architecturally impressive flagship stores in central Tokyo. The Ginza district and the 'brand boulevard' of Omotesando are the best places to visit, though expect to pay far more than at equivalent stores outside Asia.

The following are Japanese designer stores.

A Bathing Ape

5-5-8 Minami-Aoyama, Minato-ku (5464 0335, www.bape.com). Omotesando station (Chiyoda, Ginza, Hanzomon lines), exit A5. **Open** 11am-7pm daily. **Credit** JCB, MC, V. **Map** p65.
Founded by stylist, DJ and entrepreneur Nigo in 1993, this brand was once known for its impossible to find stores, but now seems to have gone to the other extreme with multi-storey shops marked by giant neon ape logos. Still worth a look, though.
Other locations 4-21-5 Jingumae, Shibuya-ku (5474 0204); 13-17 Udagawa-cho, Shibuya-ku (6415 6041).

Billionaire Boys Club/Ice Cream Store

4-28-22 Jingumae, Shibuya-ku (5775 2633, www.bbcicecream.com). Meiji-Jingumae station (Chiyoda, Fukutoshin lines), exit 5. **Open** 11am-7pm daily. **Credit** JCB, MC, V. **Map** p65.
A collaboration between hip hop artist and producer Pharrell Williams and A Bathing Ape street-fashion mogul Nigo, clothing label Billionaire Boys Club and sneaker brand Ice Cream have side-by-side shops on Propeller Street, one of Harajuku's hippest strips. Head here for high-quality sneakers, T-shirts, sweatshirts, parkas, shirts, jackets and jeans, all of them in bold colours and designs.

Comme des Garçons

5-2-1 Minami-Aoyama, Minato-ku (3406 3951). Omotesando station (Chiyoda, Ginza, Hanzomon lines), exit A5. **Open** 11am-8pm daily. **Credit** AmEx, DC, JCB, MC, V. **Map** p65.
Comme des Garçons' Rei Kawakubo is one of the pioneers who put Japanese designers on the fashion map. The extraordinary exterior of this flagship store beckons the shopper into a maze of psychedelic prints, classically themed suits and smart formal wear. Tax-exemption service available.

Issey Miyake

3-18-11 Minami-Aoyama, Minato-ku (3423 1407 men, 3423 1408 women, www.isseymiyake.com). Omotesando station (Chiyoda, Ginza, Hanzomon

CONSUME

Where to buy it Merci Beaucoup, 3-10-11 Kita-Aoyama, Minato-ku (6805 1790, www.mercibeaucoup.jp).

BANAL CHIC BIZARRE

Designers Shun Nakagawa, Ayano Ichige.
The look Harajuku fever dream. Think edgy oversized T-shirts, jackets and dresses that mix punky plaid with alien cocoon shapes, and black, black, black.
Why it matters Banal Chic Bizarre is 'the pulse of Tokyo street fashion', at least according to the designers. Certainly, you won't see most of these styles outside Harajuku, which makes them perfect for showing off some Tokyo fashion cred.
Where to buy it ADD (*see p204*).

@IZREEL

Designer Kazuhiro Takakura.
The look The Topshop men's department goes cyberpunk. The dresses are floaty but grounded; the jackets and trousers are sharp and dark, cut with flashes of pink, purple and other highlights for a touch of the street.
Why it matters It can be painfully trendy, but @IZREEL has a volume control. If the knit *obi* or man-skirts aren't you, the more functional jackets or trousers might be.
Where to buy it Parco (*see p205*).

MINT DESIGNS

Designers Hokuto Katsui, Yao Nagi.
The look A fairytale tailor with the cerebral humour of a modern art curator.
Why it matters This duo is the darling of Japan Fashion Week; the clothes hit all the right buttons with texture, colour and theme, and display attention to detail right down to the socks and mittens.
Where to buy it Parco (*see p205*).

● *Jennifer Geacone-Cruz is the English-language editor for* Time Out Tokyo*'s website and writes about fashion for* Harper's Bazaar Japan.

lines), exit A4. **Open** 11am-8pm daily. **Credit** AmEx, DC, JCB, MC, V. **Map** p65.
Issey Miyake is one of the big three designers, along with Yohji Yamamoto and Rei Kawakubo, who transformed Japanese fashion back in the late '80s. In his Tokyo store, you'll find original creations and collaborations between designers and artists that can't be seen anywhere else. There's a tax-exemption service available.

Mister Hollywood

4-13-16 Jingumae, Shibuya-ku (5414 5071, www.n-hoolywood.com). Harajuku station (JR line), Omotesando exit or Omotesando station (Chiyoda, Ginza, Hanzomon lines), exit A2. **Open** noon-8pm daily. **Credit** AmEx, DC, JCB, MC, V. **Map** p65.
Daisuke Obana's N.Hoolywood (sic) is one of the hottest menswear lines in Japan. His diverse influences have included space travel and the Vietnam War, with the collections changing drastically each season. His Tokyo flagship is this well-concealed mint-green house in backstreet Harajuku.

Neighborhood

4-32-5 Jingumae, Shibuya-ku (3401 1201). Harajuku station (Yamanote line), Omotesando exit or Meiji-Jingumae station (Chiyoda, Fukutoshin lines), exit 4. **Open** noon-8pm daily. **Credit** AmEx, DC, JCB, MC, V. **Map** p65.

'Death from Above' declare the red neon signs outside this minimalist urban fashion shop. Inside are men's jackets, shirts, jeans and accessories with a biker or military influence.

Number (N)ine

2-16-6 Ebisu, Shibuya-ku (5793 3799, www.numberniners.com). Ebisu station (Yamanote line), east exit. **Open** noon-8pm Mon-Sat; 11am-7pm Sun. **Credit** AmEx, DC, JCB, MC, V.
This grunge rock-inspired menswear brand has proven a huge hit in Europe and the States, with its Paris catwalk collections receiving rave reviews. The Tokyo store is generally host to an array of shoe-gazing young men with Kurt Cobain fixations. Worth an angst-ridden browse.

Undercover

Unimat Bleu Cinq Point Bldg, 5-3-18 Minami-Aoyama, Minato-ku (3407 1232). Omotesando station (Chiyoda, Ginza, Hanzomon lines), exit A5. **Open** 11am-8pm daily. **Credit** AmEx, DC, JCB, MC, V. **Map** p65.
Undercover designer Jun Takahashi commands a fanatically loyal army of punk fashion rebels who adore his edgy clothes. Enter his unsettling world at this store, and experience the artistic side of his dark fashion empire at gallery-cum-store Zamiang in the basement. *Photo p209.*

Uniqlo

5-7-7 Ginza, Chuo-ku. (3569-6781, www.uniqlo. co.jp). Ginza station (Ginza, Hibiya, Marunouchi lines), exit A2. **Open** 11am-9pm daily. **Credit** AmEx, DC, JCB, MC, V. **Map** p59.

UK residents will already be familiar with the name Uniqlo. This is the chain store that revolutionised retail in Japan with basic clothing at reasonable prices. But Uniqlo is in the process of going upmarket, and to that end it opened a huge flagship store in Ginza. The façade is a matrix of 1,000 illuminated cells, which form Tetris-style patterns.

Other locations throughout the city.

▶ *The store was designed by Klein Dytham, the architect owners of Super-deluxe (see p183).*

★ Uniqlo UT

6-10-8 Jingumae, Shibuya-ku (5468 7313, www.ut.uniqlo.com/store). Harajuku station (Yamanote line), Omotesando exit or Meiji-Jingumae station (Chiyoda, Fukutoshin lines), exit 4. **Open** 11am-9pm daily. **Credit** AmEx, DC, JCB, MC, V. **Map** p65.

Uniqlo's T-shirt store is designed to resemble an arcade of vending machines, with the Ts 'dispensed' in plastic capsules (though you still have to fork over your cash to an old-school human being). The designs change fast, and the variety is impressive, with Nobuyoshi Araki, Kim Jones, Vincent Gallo and even Disney contributing.

▶ *For more on Tokyo's array of vending machines, see p201 Automatic for the People.*

Yohji Yamamoto

5-3-6 Minami-Aoyama, Minato-ku (3409 6006, www.yohjiyamamoto.co.jp). Omotesando station (Chiyoda, Ginza, Hanzomon lines), exit A5. **Open** 11am-8pm daily. **Credit** AmEx, DC, JCB, MC, V. **Map** p65.

Paragon of conceptual fashion Yohji Yamamoto remains hugely respected by style commentators. This store not only stocks the dark, billowing creations on which his reputation was founded, but also his sportswear collaboration with Adidas Y-3.

Used & vintage

For vintage that's been heavily reconstructed, *see p205* **Nincompoop Capacity**.

Marvin's Vintage

High Nest Harajuku B1, 6-12-15 Jingumae, Shibuya-ku (5466 2390, www.marvins-jp.com). Meiji-Jingumae station (Chiyoda, Fukutoshin lines), exit 7. **Open** noon-8pm daily. **Credit** AmEx, DC, JCB, MC, V. **Map** p65.

Denim fetishists, look no further. Marvin's sells jeans and jackets from as far back as the 19th century, at prices from ¥20,000 to over ¥1 million. The shop also stocks vintage Hawaiian shirts, leather jackets and seriously retro sweatshirts.

RagTag

1-17-7 Jinnan, Shibuya-ku (3476 6848, www.ragtag.jp). Shibuya station (Yamanote, Ginza lines), Hachiko exit; (Fukutoshin, Hanzomon line), exit 6. **Open** noon-9pm daily. **Credit** AmEx, DC, JCB, MC, V. **Map** p93.

This Shibuya recycle shop is where fashion-obsessed types who have run out of closet space go to sell on their unwanted threads. An excellent browsing ground for those in search of designer labels at heavily discounted prices.

Other locations 3-3-15 Ginza (3535 4100); 1-7-2 Jingumae (3478 0287); 3-32-8 Shinjuku (5366 6722); 2-34-12 Shimokitazawa (5790 5976).

FASHION ACCESSORIES

Hats

CA4LA

6-29-4 Jingumae, Shibuya-ku (3406 8271, www.ca4la.com). Harajuku station (Yamanote line), Omotesando exit or Meiji-Jingumae station (Chiyoda, Fukutoshin lines), exit 4. **Open** 11am-8pm daily. **Credit** AmEx, DC, JCB, MC, V. **Map** p65.

Tokyo youths looking to stand out from the crowd head straight for Japan's trendiest hat-maker CA4LA (pronounced 'ka-shi-la'). The Harajuku flagship offers a vast selection of funky headgear – from woolly bobble hats to pink panamas. Prices are very reasonable.

Other locations 4-7-5 Ueno, Taito-ku (5807 7237); 2F Cinderella City, Isetan Main Building, 3-14-1 Shinjuku, Shinjuku-ku (3351 8138); 1-18-2 Jinnan, Shibuya-ku (3770 5051); 17-5 Daikanyamacho, Shibuya-ku (5459 0085).

Override 9999

6-29-3 Jingumae, Shibuya-ku (5766 0575, www.ovr.jp). Harajuku station (Yamanote line), Omotesando exit or Meiji-Jingumae station (Chiyoda, Fukutoshin lines), exit 4. **Open** 11am-8pm daily. **Credit** AmEx, DC, JCB, MC, V. **Map** p65.

Eye-catching headgear, as worn by the young bucks prowling the streets of Harajuku.

Other locations 6-29-3 Jingumae, Shibuya-ku (5467 0047); 7-5 Daikanyama-cho, Shibuya-ku (5428 5085).

Jewellery

Atelier Shinji

5-6-24 Minami-Aoyama, Minato-ku (3400 5211, www.ateliershinji.com). Omotesando station (Chiyoda, Ginza, Hanzomon lines), exit A5. **Open** 11am-7pm Mon-Fri; 11am-5pm Sat, Sun. **Credit** AmEx, DC, JCB, MC, V. **Map** p65.

This small Aoyama shop, located behind the Spiral building (*see p239*), sells the original creations of noted jeweller Shinji Naoi.
Other locations (factory store) 2-2-2 Iriya, Taito-ku (3872 7201).

Mikimoto

2-4-12 Ginza, Chuo-ku (3562 3130, www. mikimoto.com). Ginza station (Ginza, Hibiya, Marunouchi lines), exit A9. **Open** 11am-7pm daily. **Credit** AmEx, DC, JCB, MC, V. **Map** p59.
This second flagship store for cultured pearl brand Mikimoto was designed by Toyo Ito. Its amazing pink façade is a favourite with tourists; the expensive creations inside, not so much.
Other locations 4-5-5 Ginza, Chuo-ku (3535 4611).

Niwaka

2-8-18 Ginza, Chuo-ku. (3564 0707, www. niwaka.com). Ginza station (Ginza, Hibiya, Marunouchi lines), exit A13. **Open** 11am -8pm daily. **Credit** AmEx, DC, JCB, MC, V. **Map** p59.
This store's elegant, nature-inspired designs are created by a team of artisans in workshops in Kyoto. Engagement rings are packaged in gorgeous *washi* paper and a wood case that puts other high-end jewellers to shame.
Other locations 3-13-8 Minami Aoyama, Minato-ku (3796 0803); West Walk 3F, Roppongi Hills, 6-10-1 Roppongi, Minato-ku.

Tasaki Shinju

5-7-5 Ginza, Chuo-ku (3289 1111, www.tasaki. co.jp). Ginza station (Ginza, Hibiya, Marunouchi lines), exit A2. **Open** 10.30am-7.30pm daily. **Credit** AmEx, DC, JCB, MC, V. **Map** p59.
The flagship Ginza shop is known (with good reason) as the Jewellery Tower. Each floor of this huge building is devoted to a particular jewellery theme; the museum on the fifth floor is also worth a look.
Other locations throughout the city.

Shoes

Designer trainers are also available from the **Ice Cream Store** (*see p206*).

ABC Mart

1-11-5 Jinnan, Shibuya-ku (3477 0602, www. abc-mart.com). Shibuya station (Yamanote, Ginza lines), Hachiko exit; (Fukutoshin, Hanzomon lines), exits 6, 7. **Open** 11am-9pm daily. **Credit** AmEx, DC, JCB, MC, V. **Map** p93.
An incredibly cheap and busy chain of shops selling brand-name footwear and sportswear at a discount.
Other locations throughout the city.

Ginza Kanematsu

6-9-9 Ginza, Chuo-ku (3573 0077, www.ginza-kanematsu.co.jp). Ginza station (Ginza, Hibiya, Marunouchi lines), exit A4. **Open** 11am-9pm Mon-Sat; 11am-8pm Sun. **Credit** AmEx, DC, JCB, MC, V. **Map** p59.

Undercover. *See p207.*

CONSUME

Toraya.

Stylish shoes for both men and women, available in sizes larger than the usual Japanese ones. **Other locations** throughout the city.

CONSUME

FOOD & DRINK

The basements of department store food halls (*see p194* **Treats Abound Underground**) are also worth a look.

Confectionery

Wagashi – traditional Japanese sweets – originated in Kyoto and are steeped in culture. The *wagashi* most palatable to the Westerner's sweet tooth are *yokan* (thick jellied candies made from gelatin, sugar and adzuki beans), *monaka* (adzuki-bean paste sandwiched between two crisp wafers), *zangetsu* (ginger-flavoured round pancakes folded in half) and *wasanbon* (a luxury powdery sugar pressed into tablets). Products vary according to the season and most are meant to be eaten quickly, so ask how long they'll keep.

For **Ozasa**'s desirable *maboroshi youkan* bean-paste jellies, *see p150* **Queue Tips**.

Akebono

5-7-19 Ginza, Chuo-ku (3571 3640, www.ginza-akebono.co.jp). Ginza station (Ginza, Hibiya, Marunouchi lines), exit A1. **Open** 10am-9pm Mon-Sat; 10am-8pm Sun. **Credit** AmEx, DC, JCB, MC, V. **Map** p59.
This small but lively shop's variety of traditional Japanese sweets is also available in the basement food halls of all Tokyo's major department stores (*see p194* **Treats Abound Underground**). **Other locations** throughout the city.

★ Higashiya

3-17-14 Minami-Aoyama, Minato-ku (5414 3881, www.higashiya.com). Omotesando station (Chiyoda, Ginza, Hanzomon lines), exit A4. **Open** 10am-8pm daily. **Credit** DC, JCB, MC, V. **Map** p65.
For Japanese confectionery, this is as good as it gets. Though the store is barely bigger than a closet, the creations it offers are superlative, and the packaging is gift perfect (which is why some top hotels in Tokyo use Higashiya products).

Kimuraya

4-5-7 Ginza, Chuo-ku (3561 0091, www. kimuraya-sohonten.co.jp). Ginza station (Ginza, Hibiya, Marunouchi lines), exits A9, B1. **Open** 10am-9.30pm daily. **No credit cards. Map** p59.
This venerable shop one door away from the Wako department store is historically and culturally significant for being the first in Tokyo to sell *anpan* – bread rolls filled with adzuki-bean paste. Break up a Ginza shopping or sightseeing trip with a visit to Kimuraya and try them for yourself.
Other locations throughout the city.
▶ *For more about Wako, see p195.*

Toraya

4-9-22 Akasaka, Minato-ku (3408 4121, www.toraya-group.co.jp). Akasaka-Mitsuke station (Ginza, Marunouchi lines), exit A. **Open** 8.30am-8pm Mon-Fri; 8.30am-6pm Sat, Sun. **Credit** AmEx, DC, JCB, MC, V.
This highly distinguished shop provides *wagashi* to the Imperial Family. It has 70 branches throughout Japan, and one in Paris.
Other locations throughout the city, and in many department store basements.

Imported food

If you're pining for some tastes from home, the shops below may have what you're looking for – but it'll cost about twice the price you're used to paying.

Kinokuniya International

3-11-7 Minami-Aoyama, Minato-ku (3409 1231, www.e-kinokuniya.com). Omotesando station (Chiyoda, Ginza, Hanzomon lines), exit A3. **Open** 9.30am-9pm daily. **Credit** AmEx, DC, JCB, MC, V. **Map** p65.
No relation to the Shinjuku bookstore of the same name, this is the best-known and most prestigious of Tokyo's foreign-food specialists. It also sells English-language newspapers, magazines and cards. **Other locations** throughout the city.

National Azabu

4-5-2 Minami-Azabu, Minato-ku (3442 3181). Hiroo station (Hibiya line), exit 1. **Open** 9.30am-8pm daily. **Credit** AmEx, DC, JCB, MC, V.
This Hiroo supermarket has a long history of serving the international community with imported groceries galore. It's known for its vast and impressive cheese selection. There's also a bookstore and stationery shop on the second floor.

★ Nissin

2-34-2 Higashi-Azabu, Minato-ku (3583 4586). Azabu-Juban station (Nanboku line), exit 3; (Oedo line), exit 6. **Open** 9am-9pm daily. **Credit** AmEx, DC, JCB, MC, V.
This huge outlet in Azabu-Juban specialises in imported meat – rabbit, kangaroo, pheasant and lots of sausages – but also sells a wide range of imported groceries. Nissin's third-floor wine department is very good.

Yamaya

3-2-7 Nishi-Shinjuku, Shinjuku-ku (3342 0601, www.yamaya.jp). Shinjuku station (Yamanote, Chuo lines), south exit; (Marunouchi line), exits A16, A17; (Oedo, Shinjuku lines), exit 6. **Open** 10am-10pm daily. **Credit** AmEx, DC, JCB, MC, V. **Map** p101.
A medium-sized foreign-food and booze specialist with one unique feature for Tokyo: it's cheap. It has a vast selection of imported wines priced from a budget-beating ¥280, along with inexpensive cheeses and snack foods. Delivery of large orders within the 23 wards of central Tokyo costs ¥500. **Other locations** throughout the city.

Japanese tea

Department store basements usually have a wide selection of green tea in attractive packaging. For places to drink a cup, *see p191* **Teashops**.

Yamamoto Yama

2-5-2 Nihonbashi, Chuo-ku (3281 0010, www.yamamotoyama.co.jp). Nihonbashi station (Asakusa line), exit D3; (Ginza, Tozai lines), exit B4. **Open** 10am-6pm daily. **Credit** AmEx, DC, JCB, MC, V. **Map** p77.
Sells a wide selection of Japanese and Chinese teas and implements for *sado*, the tea ceremony. **Other locations** throughout the city.

Saké

There are many different types of Japan's rice spirit, depending on location, brewing method, amount of rice polished away and quantity of distilled alcohol added (for a primer, *see p181* **Local Potions**). The broad categories are *amakuchi* (sweet saké) and *karakuchi* (dry saké). Premium brands, known as *jizake*, are more expensive and highly sought after by connoisseurs. Saké shops can be found in the basements of most department stores (*see p194* **Treats Abound Underground**).

Shinanoya

1-12-9 Kabuki-cho, Shinjuku-ku (3204 2365, www.shinanoya.co.jp). Shinjuku station (Yamanote, Chuo lines), east exit; (Marunouchi line), exit B12; (Oedo, Shinjuku lines), exit 1. **Open** 11am-4am Mon-Sat; 11am-9pm Sun. **Credit** MC, V.
Saké and whisky from all over Japan, plus hundreds of single malt Scotches at prices cheaper than in the UK. There's also a small selection of foreign foods and snacks, and several imported beers.

Suzuden

1-10 Yotsuya, Shinjuku-ku (3351 1777). Yotsuya station (Chuo, Sobu lines), Yotsuya exit; (Marunouchi line), exit 1; (Nanboku line), exit 2. **Open** 9am-9pm Mon-Fri; 9am-6pm Sat. **Credit** AmEx, DC, JCB, MC, V.
Offers a wide selection of rare saké brands, with an area set aside for tasting.

GIFTS & SOUVENIRS

Many department stores sell kimonos, ceramics, chopsticks and other traditional souvenirs, while some of the shopping streets (*see p199*) – notably **Nakamise Dori** and **Kappabashi**, both in Asakusa – are great for gifts. For kids' presents, *see p202* **Toys**.

Bingo-Ya

10-6 Wakamatsu-cho, Shinjuku-ku (3202 8778, www.quasar.nu/bingoya). Wakamatsu-Kawada station (Oedo line), Kawada exit. **Open** 10am-7pm Tue-Sun. **Credit** AmEx, DC, JCB, MC, V.
Six floors of handmade traditional crafts, including pottery, fabrics, bamboo, lacquerware, glassware, dolls and folk art.

CONSUME

Ebisu-Do Gallery

Inagaki Bldg 4F, 1-9 Kanda-Jinbocho, Chiyoda-ku (3219 7651, www.ebisu-do.com). Jinbocho station (Hanzomon, Mita, Shinjuku lines), exit A5. **Open** 11am-6.30pm Mon-Sat. **Credit** AmEx, DC, JCB, MC, V. **Map** p77.

Here you can buy original *ukiyo-e* prints (from around ¥20,000) and reproductions (from ¥3,000) by masters such as Hiroshige, Hokusai and Harunobu.

Fuji Torii

6-1-10 Jingumae, Shibuya-ku (3400 2777, www.fuji-torii.com). Harajuku station (Yamanote line), Omotesando exit or Meiji-Jingumae station (Chiyoda, Fukutoshin lines), exit 4 or Omotesando station (Chiyoda, Ginza, Hanzomon lines), exit A1. **Open** 11am-6pm Mon, Wed-Sun. Closed 3rd Mon of mth. **Credit** AmEx, DC, JCB, MC, V. **Map** p65.

Fuji Torii sells a wide variety of Japanese antiques (screens, ceramics, sculptures), as well as designing and selling its own original artwork and crafts.

Gallery Samurai

4F, 2-7-18 Kita-Aoyama, Minato-ku (5474 6336, www.nihonto.co.jp). Omotesando station (Chiyoda, Ginza, Hanzomon lines), exits A3, A4. **Open** 11am-7pm daily. **Credit** AmEx, DC, JCB, MC, V. **Map** p65.

A small shop in the heart of Aoyama, crowded with antique swords, guns, armour and helmets, not to mention screens, statues, woodblock prints and less classifiable curios. Staff speak fluent English.

★ Ginza Natsuno

6-7-4 Ginza, Chuo-ku (3569 0952, www.e-ohashi.com/natsuno). Ginza station (Ginza, Hibiya, Marunouchi lines), exit A5. **Open** 10am-8pm Mon-Sat; 10am-7pm Sun. **Credit** AmEx, DC, JCB, MC, V. **Map** p59.

Japanese chopsticks make affordable and easily portable souvenirs, so make a beeline for this shop and its amazing, eclectic collection. Ginza Natsuno's premises are small, but there's a good array of stock and plenty to choose from.

Other locations 4-2-17 Jingumae, Shibuya-ku (5785 4721).

Hara Shobo

2-3 Kanda-Jinbocho, Chiyoda-ku (5212 7801, www.harashobo.com). Jinbocho station (Hanzomon, Mita, Shinjuku lines), exit A6. **Open** 10am-6pm Tue-Sat. **Credit** AmEx, DC, JCB, MC, V. **Map** p77.

Hara Shobo sells all kinds of woodblock prints, both old and new. The company issues a catalogue, *Edo Geijitsu* ('Edo Art'), twice a year. English spoken.

Ito-ya

2-7-15 Ginza, Chuo-ku (3561 8311, www.ito-ya.co.jp). Ginza station (Ginza, Hibiya,

Marunouchi lines), exit A13. **Open** 10am-8pm Mon-Sat; 10.30am-7pm Sun. **Credit** AmEx, DC, JCB, MC, V. **Map** p59.

This huge, very busy store in Ginza specialises in Japanese paper. The main shop (Ito-ya 1 Bldg) sells conventional stationery and calligraphic tools, while the annex (Ito-ya 3 Bldg) – directly behind it and reached by walking through the main store – has origami, traditional handmade paper (*washi*), writing paper and ink.

Japan Traditional Craft Center

Metropolitan Plaza 1F-2F, 1-11-1 Nishi-Ikebukuro, Toshima-ku (5954 6066, www.kougei.or.jp/english/center.html). Ikebukuro station (Yamanote line), Metropolitan exit; (Fukutoshin, Marunouchi, Yurakucho lines), exit 3. **Open** 11am-7pm daily (until 5pm every 2nd Tue; closed some Weds). **Credit** AmEx, MC, V. **Map** p69.

This organisation was founded with the aim of promoting awareness of Japan's traditional crafts. Learn about, then shop for, a broad cross-section of crafts (lacquer, ceramics, paper, kimonos, knives, textiles, stonework, household Buddhist altars and so on) at this showroom-cum-museum. There are permanent and temporary exhibitions, a reference library and even classes. The gift shop sells the work of craftspeople (who sometimes give demonstrations) from across the country.

Kimono Arts Sunaga

2-1-8 Azabu-Juban, Minato-ku (3457 0323). Azabu-Juban station (Oedo, Nanboku lines), exit 4. **Open** 11am-8pm Wed-Mon. **Credit** AmEx, DC, JCB, MC, V.

A friendly store offering tailor-made kimonos, as well as ready-to-wear versions, and a range of crafts and ornaments made from recycled kimono material.

Kyukyodo

5-7-4 Ginza (3571 4429, www.kyukyodo.co.jp). Ginza station (Ginza, Hibiya, Marunouchi lines), exit A2. **Open** 10am-7.30pm Mon-Sat; 11am-7pm Sun. **Credit** AmEx, DC, JCB, MC, V. **Map** p59.

Another Japanese paper specialist, Kyukyodo opened its first shop in Kyoto in 1663 and supplied incense to the Imperial Palace during the Edo period. Still run by the Kumagai family that founded it, the shop moved to Tokyo in 1880. This branch in Ginza, with its distinctive arched brick entrance, still sells incense, alongside a selection of seasonal gift cards and lots of small, moderately priced items (boxes, notebooks, picture frames) made from colourful *washi*.

Other locations 2-24-1 Shibuya, Shibuya-ku (3477 3111); 1-1-25 Nishi-Ikebukuro, Toshima-ku (3981 2211).

Mandarake

5-52-15 Nakano, Nakano-ku (3228 0007, www.mandarake.co.jp). Nakano station (Chuo, Tozai

CONSUME

Present Perfect

Tokyo offers big-game souvenir hunting.

There's a vast range of gifts and souvenirs, both ancient and modern, classy and kitsch, available in Tokyo: here are a few ideas. For one-stop shopping, **department stores** (*see p192*) are a good bet. If you're short of time and/or money, **Oriental Bazaar** (*see p214*) on Omotesando stocks all the classic Japanese goodies. But Tokyo is a shopper's paradise, so a little digging will turn up something special.

CLOTHING

The obvious garment is a **kimono**, new or second-hand, which can range in price from ¥4,000 to ¥1,000,000. A cheaper and easier-to-wear option is the **yukata**, a cotton gown that is used by both sexes. Designs are highly detailed and use seasonal motifs such as cherry blossom, plum blossom, maple and pine. For men, the **happi** coat is a short tunic used in festivals, and for both sexes there are **tabi** (split-toed socks) and **tenugui** (a towel worn around the head at festivals, often decorated with some form of heraldic symbol). Accessories include the **netsuke**, a small carved pouch that is hung from the kimono belt.

KITCHENWARE

Ceramic and pottery **tableware** comes in all shapes and sizes, and at all price ranges; or there's (often expensive) **lacquerware** (*urushi-nuri*) and, of course, **chopsticks** – all vary according to their region of origin. **Kappabashi Dori** (*see p199*) is the street to head for.

CULTURAL AND TRADITIONAL

Myriad antiques shops specialise in everything from **samurai swords** and **helmets** to **screens** – but you'll need a fat wallet, and they're difficult to transport. *Ukiyo-e* woodblock **prints** by Hiroshige, Hokusai or lesser-known artists are always popular; you can pay as little as ¥1,500 for a modern reproduction or tens of thousands for an original work. Head for a stationery/paper specialist for seasonal **greeting cards** and **calligraphy sets**, or for lanterns, fans, boxes and other ornamental goods made with colourful, handmade **washi** paper.

Fuuring (wind chimes) are a reminder of the cooling, melodic sound heard in the heat of the Japanese summer,

while **hagoita** (battledores), painted with decorative scenes from *kabuki* plays, are sold in November as household decorations for the New Year. Then there are the numerous implements used in the **tea ceremony**, and the *karuta* **card games** Hyakunin Isshu and Hanafuda. Stalls near shrines and temples sell all sorts of small, cheap **good-luck charms**. Look for the omnipresent *maneki neko* (lucky cat); a raised left paw is for business success; a raised right paw is for money – or hedge your bets and get one with both paws raised.

FOOD AND DRINK

There's a bewildering variety of comestibles to choose from, but **saké** and **green tea** are always reliable choices; head to the basement of a department store for the widest selection. Boxed **wagashi** (traditional Japanese sweets) are a thing of beauty, but they often have short shelf lives.

THE QUIRKY STUFF

Japan is undisputedly a world leader in bizarre inventions and offbeat novelties. The best place to shop is **RanKing RanQueen** (*see p214*), which stocks, and ranks, the hottest-selling goods. And, this being Tokyo, the hottest-selling goods are usually highly entertaining. At time of writing, these include beauty products such as a pocket tongue cleaner, a bottom cushion for the bath, and a 'lifting turban' headpiece that claims to smooth wrinkles. More practical (and inexpensive) gifts are the **hokaron** heat pads sold in pharmacies and most convenience stores.

CONSUME

Oriental Bazaar. こけし スプーン ¥245

lines), north exit. **Open** noon-8pm daily.
Credit AmEx, DC, JCB, MC, V.
Mandarake (pronounced 'Mandala-K') is the place to go for action figures related to obscure Japanese *anime*, retro US toys from the 1960s and '70s, manga, *dojinshi* (fanzines), animation cells and any kind of kitsch weirdness you care to name. It has numerous outlets in the Broadway shopping centre. The Shibuya branch is almost as vast.
Other locations throughout the city.

Noritake Shop Akasaka

7-8-5 Akasaka, Minato-ku (3586 0059, www. noritake.co.jp/eng/tableware). Akasaka station (Chiyoda line), exit 7. **Open** 10am-6pm Mon-Fri.
Credit AmEx, DC, JCB, MC, V.
Noritake is the name of one of Japan's oldest and most distinctive forms of pottery and china, and this is its flagship store.

★ Oriental Bazaar

5-9-13 Jingumae, Shibuya-ku (3400 3933). Harajuku station (Yamanote line), Omotesando exit or Meiji-Jingumae station (Chiyoda, Fukutoshin lines), exit 4 or Omotesando station (Chiyoda, Ginza, Hanzomon lines), exit A1.
Open 10am-7pm Mon-Wed, Fri-Sun. **Credit** (min ¥2,000) AmEx, DC, JCB, MC, V. **Map** p65.
Probably the best-known gift shop in Tokyo, this is a useful one-stop outlet for almost everything: dolls, china, kimonos, *yukata*, woodblock prints, furniture, antiques and books on Japan. Ideal for stocking up on presents and souvenirs. Prices are generally moderate, and the staff speaks good English.
Other locations No.1 Terminal Building 4F, Narita Airport (0476 329 333).

RanKing RanQueen

West Bldg 2F, Tokyu Department Toyoko branch, 2-24-1 Shibuya, Shibuya-ku (3770 5480, www.ranking-ranqueen.net). Shibuya station (Yamanote, Ginza lines), Hachiko exit; (Hanzomon line), exits 3, 3A. **Open** 10am-11.30pm daily. **Credit** AmEx, DC, JCB, MC, V.
Map p93.
The Japanese are obsessed with making lists and charts of what's popular, which they call 'rankings' – hence the puns in this shop's name. At RanKing, RanQueen, a shop inside Shibuya JR station, you'll find the top ten products for cosmetics, dieting aids,

Mandarake. *See p212.*

CDs, magazines and so on. It's worth a visit to get an intriguing insight into the mind of the Japanese consumer. *Photo p217.*
Other locations Shinjuku station, east exit (5919 1263); Jiyugaoka station, central exit (3718 8890).

Sagemonoya

Palais Eternal Bldg 704, 4-28-20 Yotsuya, Shinjuku-ku (3352 6286, www.netsuke.com). Shinjuku-Gyoenmae station (Marunouchi line), Ookidomon exit or Yotsuya-Sanchome station (Marunouchi line), exits 1, 2. **Open** 1.30-6pm Wed-Sat or by appt. **Credit** AmEx, DC, JCB, MC, V.
Sagemonoya specialises in *netsuke* and *sagemono* – the tiny, ornate accessories designed to hang from the belt of a kimono to hold tobacco, medicines and other small objects. This shop holds hundreds of collectibles, and staff can answer enquiries in English.

Tanagokoro

1-8-15 Ginza, Chuo-ku (3538 6555, www. tanagokoro.com). Ginza-Itchome station (Yurakucho line), exits 7, 9. **Open** 11am-8pm Mon-Fri; 11am-7pm Sat, Sun. **Credit** AmEx, DC, JCB, MC, V. **Map** p59.
Binchotan, a highly refined form of Japanese charcoal, is used to purify, dehumidify and deodorise the air of a room it's placed in. This shop, whose name means 'palm of the hand', sells products made from *binchotan*. Shoppers can also indulge in the curative powers of *binchotan*'s fragrance in the basement healing room.

INSIDE TRACK
DESIGNER GIFTS

For quality souvenirs, try the basement of **Parco Part 1** (*see p205*) in Shibuya, where the trendy **Claska** hotel (*see p140*) runs a store of designer home furnishings and tableware from around Japan.

HEALTH & BEAUTY
Hairdressers & barbers

Peek-a-Boo Ext
4-3-15 Jingumae, Shibuya-ku (5411 0848,
www.peek-a-boo.co.jp). Omotesando station
(Chiyoda, Ginza, Hanzomon lines), exit A2.
Open 9am-11pm daily. **Credit** AmEx, DC,
JCB, MC, V. **Map** p65.
This stylish chain of unisex salons has been an indispensable feature of Tokyo's style centre Aoyama since 1978. All forms of hair treatment are available.
Other locations throughout the Harajuku and Aoyama areas.

Serendipity
Powerhouse Bldg B2F, 7-12-3 Roppongi, Minato-
ku (5414 1717). Nogizaka station (Chiyoda line),
exit 3 or Roppongi station (Oedo line), exit 7;
(Hibiya line), exit 4A. **Open** noon-4am Mon-Sat;
noon-8pm Sun. **Credit** AmEx, DC, JCB, MC, V.
Map p87.
As well as reasonable prices, this hair salon near Roppongi has a unique selling point: it's open until 4am, six days a week.

Who-Ga
Akasaka Kyo Bldg 1F, 2-16-13 Akasaka, Minato-
ku (5570 1773, www.who-ga-newyork.com).
Akasaka station (Chiyoda line), exits 5A, 5B.
Open 11am-9pm Mon, Wed-Fri; 10am-7pm Sat,
Sun. **Credit** AmEx, DC, JCB, MC, V.
The helpful, bilingual staff here all trained at Who-Ga's sister salon in New York. There's a popular membership system available for female customers; privileges include discounts for haircuts, perms and colouring services, along with further price reductions if reservations are made at least one week in advance.

Opticians

In recent years, Tokyo has seen an increase in shops/opticians that specialise in selling stylish eyewear at discount prices. Eye tests are often free.

FxG (Face By Glasses)
2-35-14 Kitazawa, Setagaya-ku (5790 8027,
www.fxg.co.jp). Shimo-Kitazawa station (Keio
Inokashira, Odakyu lines), north exit. **Open**
11am-8pm daily. **Credit** AmEx, DC, JCB, MC, V.

Hatch
2-5-8 Dogenzaka, Shibuya-ku (5784 3888,
www.e-hatch.jp). Shibuya station (Yamanote,
Ginza lines), Hachiko exit; (Hanzomon line), exits
2, 4. **Open** 11am-8pm daily. **Credit** AmEx, DC,
JCB, MC, V. **Map** p93.
Other locations throughout the city.

Zoff
Mark City 4F, 1-12-5 Dogenzaka, Shibuya-ku
(5428 3961, www.zoff.co.jp). Shibuya station
(Yamanote, Ginza lines), Hachiko exit;
(Hanzomon line), exits 5, 8. **Open** 10am-9pm
daily. **Credit** AmEx, DC, JCB, MC, V. **Map** p93.
Other locations throughout the city.

Pharmacies

Basic items, such as sanitary towels, condoms and sticking plasters can be purchased at any convenience store (usually open 24 hours daily). However, few of these are permitted to sell pharmaceutical products.

The following pharmacies all have English-speaking staff (except Roppongi Pharmacy, which does, however, have a late-night service, until 1am daily). Under Japanese law, Western medicines are not generally available, but pharmacy staff can help to find the best possible Japanese equivalent. For emergency medical information, *see p313*.

American Pharmacy
Marunouchi Bldg B1F, 2-4-1 Marunouchi,
Chiyoda-ku (5220 7716, www.tomods.jp). Tokyo
station (Yamanote, Chuo lines), Shin Marubiru,
south exits; (Marunouchi line), Marunouchi Bldg
exit. **Open** 10.30am-9pm Mon-Sat; 10am-8pm
Sun. **Credit** AmEx, DC, JCB, MC, V. **Map** p77.

Koyasu Drug Store Hotel Okura
Hotel Okura Main Bldg B1F, 2-10-4 Toranomon,
Minato-ku (3583 7958). Roppongi-Itchome
station (Nanboku line), exit 3. **Open** 8.30am-
9pm Mon-Sat; 10am-9pm Sun. **Credit** AmEx,
DC, MC, V. **Map** p87.

Roppongi Pharmacy
6-8-8 Roppongi, Minato-ku (3403 8879).
Roppongi station (Hibiya, Oedo lines), exit 3.
Open 10am-1am daily. Closed 2nd Sun of mth.
No credit cards. Map p87.

Shops

Japan's three biggest cosmetics companies –
Kanebo (www.kanebo.com), **Shiseido**
(www.shiseido.co.jp) and **Shu Uemura**
(www.shu-uemura.com) – have stand-alone shops as well as stands in department stores throughout Tokyo and Japan.

Ainz Tulpe
1-13-14 Jingumae, Shibuya-ku (5775 0561,
http://ainz-tulpe.ainj.co.jp). Harajuku station
(Yamanote line), Meiji-Jingumae exit or Meiji-
Jingumae station (Chiyoda, Fukutoshin lines),
exit 3. **Open** 10am-11pm daily. **Credit** AmEx,
DC, JCB, MC, V. **Map** p65.

CONSUME

Ainz Tulpe is a boon for late-night shoppers, and provides a bedazzling introduction to the fascinating world of Japanese cosmetics and medicine. The two floors are filled with every conceivable kind of beauty and health product.
Other locations Seibu 7F, 1-28-1 Minami-Ikebukuro, Toshima-ku (5949 2745).

Kampo Boutique Aoyama
3-3-13 Kita-Aoyama, Minato-ku (5775 6932, www.nihondo.co.jp). Omotesando station (Chiyoda, Ginza, Hanzomon lines), exit A4. **Open** 11am-8pm daily. **Credit** AmEx, DC, JCB, MC, V. **Map** p65.
This shop, the brainchild of the Nihondo corporation, employs the *kampo* (traditional Chinese medicine) method of product development. It sells a wide range of products, including natural cosmetics, health foods and herbal teas.
Other locations throughout the city.

Spas & salons

Boudoir
Mansion Kawai 101, 2-25-3 Jingumae, Shibuya-ku (3478 5898, www.boudoirtokyo.com). Harajuku station (Yamanote line), Takeshita exit or Meiji-Jingumae station (Chiyoda, Fukutoshin lines), exit 5. **Open** 11am-8.30pm Mon-Fri; 10am-8pm Sat; 10am-6pm Sun. **Credit** AmEx, DC, JCB, MC, V. **Map** p65.
Boudoir's mostly non-Japanese beauticians offer a full range of beauty treatments, including massages, facials, manicures, waxing and relaxation therapy.

Jennifer Hair & Beauty International
Roppongi Hills West Walk 6F, 6-10-1 Roppongi, Minato-ku (5770 3611). Roppongi station (Hibiya line), exit 1C; (Oedo line), exit 4. **Open** 10am-9pm daily. **Credit** AmEx, DC, JCB, MC, V. **Map** p87.
Extensive hair, make-up and nail services, plus massages and relaxing treatments. The salon uses Kérastase products from Paris.

Nail Bee
Nishi Ginza B2F, 4-1 Ginza, Chuo-ku (5250 0018, www.nailbee.com). Ginza station (Ginza, Hibiya, Marunouchi lines), exit C8. **Open** 11am-8.30pm Mon, Tue, Sat; 11am-9pm Wed-Fri; 11am-8pm Sun. **Credit** AmEx, DC, JCB, MC, V. **Map** p59.
Tokyo's leading nail salon has been serving the international community's beauty needs for more than a decade. In addition to manicures and nail art, Nail Bee offers facials, massages, waxing, pedicures and even eyelash perms.
Other locations Minochi Bldg 4F, 3-11-8 Roppongi, Minato-ku (3470 9665); Marui-City Shibuya Bldg 3F, 1-21-3 Jinnan, Shibuya-ku (5458 0026).

HOUSE & HOME

The best place for interior shopping of all styles is the thoroughly inconvenient **Meguro Dori** (*see p199*). For more central options, see below.

Don Quixote
1-16-5 Kabuki-cho, Shinjuku-ku (5291 9211, www.donki.com). Shinjuku station (Yamanote, Chuo lines), east exit; (Marunouchi line), exits B12, B13; (Oedo, Shinjuku lines), exit 1. **Open** 24hrs daily. **No credit cards**. **Map** p101.
Pile 'em high, sell 'em cheap taken to the extreme. The aisles and shelves are cluttered, disorganised and disorienting. But you'll find everything from lingerie to washing machines if you look hard enough.
Other locations throughout the city.

Franc Franc
3-11-13 Minami Aoyama (5413 2511, www.francfranc.com). Omotesando station (Chiyoda, Ginza, Hanzomon lines), exit A4. **Open** 11am-10pm daily. **Credit** AmEx, DC, JCB, MC, V. **Map** p65.
When interior goods chain Franc Franc opened a new flagship store in 2010, they invited *Monocle* magazine to host a store-within-a-store. Shoppers now have the choice of the chain's cheap and cheerful products or the pricier, often exclusive products chosen by *Monocle* honcho Tyler Brûlé.
Other locations throughout the city.

Mujirushi Ryohin
3-8-3 Marunouchi, Chiyoda-ku (5208 8241, www.muji.net). Yurakucho station (Yamanote line), Kyobashi exit; (Yurakucho line), exit A9. **Open** 10am-9pm daily. **Credit** AmEx, DC, JCB, MC, V. **Map** p59.
The shop better known as Muji – the original no-brand designer brand. This is the biggest Tokyo outlet of the all-purpose, one-stop store that went on to conquer London and Paris.
Other locations throughout the city.

★ Pass the Baton
Omotesando Hills B2, 4-12-10 Jingumae, Shibuya-ku (6447 0707, www.pass-the-baton.com). Harajuku station (JR line); Omotesando station (Chiyoda, Ginza, Hanzomon lines), exit A2. **Open** 11am-9pm Mon-Sat, 11am-8pm Sun. **Credit** DC, MC, V. **Map** p65.
An outlet store, second-hand shop, antique shop, flea market, pawn shop and charity store all rolled into one, plus a store-within-a-store by Bape founder Nigo. Pass the Baton is built around the premise of 'waste not, want not' and buys up quality seconds from local fashion chains, stamps new designs on them and sells them off cheap. It also stocks Japanese and European antiques, from cutlery to a vintage carousel horse. Customers can sell their own wares, after applying via the web site with images

and a product bio. And Nigo gets his own room, where he is currently offloading branded tableware from his Bape Café.

Other locations Marunouchi Brick Square, 2-6-1 Marunouchi, Chiyoda-ku (6269 9555).

★ Tokyu Hands

12-18 Udagawa-cho, Shibuya-ku (5489 5111, www.tokyu-hands.co.jp). Shibuya station (Yamanote, Ginza lines), Hachiko exit; (Hanzomon line), exits 6, 7. **Open** 10am-8.30pm daily. **Credit** AmEx, DC, JCB, MC, V. **Map** p93.

From stationery to toilet-seat covers, this is the largest household goods store in Tokyo, packed with knick-knacks for the home. Particularly interesting is the party supplies section, which gives a unique glimpse into the Japanese sense of humour. It can be difficult to find your way around the multitude of floors.

Other locations 1-28-10 Higashi-Ikebukuro, Toshima-ku (3980 6111).

MUSIC & ENTERTAINMENT

Whatever your musical preference, Tokyo has a shop, or shops, that will cater for it. And the city is definitely a vinyl-lover's heaven. There are specialist stores selling endless rarities, bootlegs and classic discs, and all genres are represented. Rock fans should head to the alleyways off Otakibashi Dori, a short walk from Shinjuku station's west exit. For hip hop, house or techno, try Shibuya; while, away from the centre, Shimo-Kitazawa is rich in quirky stores hawking more obscure offerings.

For new releases, domestic CDs are actually more expensive than foreign ones; thus it's possible to buy imported, big-name CDs for ¥1,500 to ¥2,500, while albums produced by Japanese artists usually sell for something in the region of ¥3,000.

★ Dance Music Record

36-2 Udagawa-cho, Shibuya-ku (3477 1556, www.dmr.co.jp/company/shop/shop.html). Shibuya station (Yamanote, Ginza lines), Hachiko exit; (Hanzomon line), exits 3, 6. **Open** 1-10pm daily. **Credit** AmEx, DC, JCB, MC, V. **Map** p93.

Dance Music Record is the name and dance-music records are the game. The first floor is a wide, open space with a comprehensive collection of the latest vinyl releases, both domestic and international. House and hip hop dominate the shelves, but it's also great for jazz and R&B.

Disk Union

3-31-4 Shinjuku, Shinjuku-ku (3352 2691, www.diskunion.co.jp). Shinjuku station (Yamanote, Chuo lines), east, central exits; (Marunouchi line), exit A6; (Oedo, Shinjuku lines), exit 1. **Open** 11am-9pm Mon-Sat; 11am-8pm Sun. **Credit** AmEx, DC, JCB, MC, V. **Map** p101.

Stocking thousands of items, Disk Union deals mainly in second-hand CDs and vinyl. The Shinjuku main store is a tall, narrow building where each floor is devoted to a different genre, including world music, soundtracks and electronica. Branches nearby specialise in dance music, jazz, funk, punk and that much-maligned genre, progressive rock.

Other locations throughout the city.

Dub Store

7-13-5 Nishi Shinjuku, Shinjuku-ku (5348 2180). Shinjuku station (Yamanote, Chuo lines), west exit; (Marunouchi line), exits A16, A17;

RanKing RanQueen. *See p214.*

CONSUME

(Shinjuku line), exit 3 or Shinjuku-Nishiguchi station (Oedo line), exit D1. **Open** noon-9pm daily. **Credit** AmEx, JCB, MC, V. **Map** p101.
This is Tokyo's best reggae store, with every conceivable genre of reggae and ska on original vinyl. The stock is expertly and meticulously categorised, and customers are welcome to listen to any of it.

Fujiyama
2-35-2 Shimouma, Setagaya-ku (3795 7595). Sangenjaya station (Tokyu Denentoshi line). **Open** Tue-Sun (hours as per owner's whim). *See below* **Local View**.

Recofan
Shibuya Beam 4F, 31-2 Udagawa-cho, Shibuya-ku (3463 0090, www.recofan.co.jp). Shibuya station (Yamanote, Ginza lines), Hachiko exit; (Hanzomon line), exit 3A. **Open** 11.30am-9pm daily. **Credit** AmEx, DC, JCB, MC, V. **Map** p93.
Recofan has a policy of selling new releases at bargain basement rates – in some cases, half the retail price. Each branch also has an extensive selection of second-hand CDs covering all genres. Regular shoppers receive a loyalty card that gives them even bigger discounts.
Other locations throughout the city.

Technique
33-14 Udagawacho, Shibuya-ku (3464 7690, www.technique.co.jp). Shibuya station (Yamanote, Ginza lines), Hachiko exit; (Hanzomon line), exits

---

Local View Cornelius

The music-maker's music shop.

In Setagaya ward, where I'm from, there's a record shop called **Fujiyama** (*see above*). The place is so strange; it's open all hours, even if you go there in the middle of the night. It's run by just one person, and all that's on offer is self-produced indie stuff. He's got so many cassette tapes, but all just indie bands.

It's a place that looks like it should've closed years ago, but it's been going since the '80s and is just a weird shop that has stuff you'd never find anywhere else. Whenever someone comes to visit me, I think about taking them there. It's so unique.

● *Tokyo native Keigo Oyamada found national fame as a member of Shibuya-kei pop duo Flipper's Guitar, before adopting the moniker Cornelius and becoming one of Japan's most eminent experimental musicians.*

3, 6. **Open** noon-8pm Mon-Sat; noon-9pm Sun. **Credit** AmEx, DC, JCB, MC, V. **Map** p93.
Technique is the purveyor of all strands of dance-music vinyl – from progressive house to nu-jazz. Several listening decks and knowledgeable staff make this the store of choice for many local DJs.

SPORTS & FITNESS

Tokyo's high-street shops and department stores are the places to head for most mainstream brands of sportswear and equipment. In addition, Yasukuni Dori, near Ochanomizu station on the Chuo line, is lined with outlets specialising in quality ski and snowboard gear.

Oshmans
1-14-29 Jingumae, Shibuya-ku (3478 4888, www.oshmans.co.jp). Harajuku station (Yamanote line), Omotesando exit or Meiji-Jingumae station (Chiyoda line), exit 2. **Open** 11am-9.30pm daily. **Credit** AmEx, DC, JCB, MC. V. **Map** p65.
Stockist of sports equipment galore, Oshmans also has kit by Patagonia, Gramicci, Merrell, Maxim and many other brands.
Other locations throughout the city.

TICKETS

Agencies throughout Tokyo sell tickets for rock gigs, classical concerts, theatre shows, films, sporting events – and plenty more. The main agency is **Ticket Pia** (0570 029 111, http://t.pia.co.jp), which has numerous outlets throughout the city, often in department stores, and publishes a weekly magazine listing thousands of events. Other agencies include **CN Playguide** (5802 9999, www.cnplayguide.com), **e-plus** (http://eplus.jp) and convenience-store chain **Lawson** (www2.lawsonticket.com), which have ticket vending machines in most stores. None of the websites is in English, but Pia operators can handle enquiries in English.

TRAVELLERS' NEEDS

No.1 Travel
Don Quixote Bldg 7F, 1-16-5 Kabuki-cho, Shinjuku-ku (3200 8871, www.no1-travel.com). Shinjuku station (Yamanote, Chuo lines), east exit; (Marunouchi line), exit B13 or Shinjuku-Nishiguchi station (Oedo line), exit D1. **Open** 10am-6.30pm Mon-Fri; 11am-4.30pm Sat. **Credit** AmEx, DC, JCB, MC. V. **Map** p101.
No.1 has been in business for more than 20 years and specialises in last-minute, discounted tickets. The helpful and knowledgeable staff speak a number of European and Asian languages.
Other locations throughout the city.

Arts & Entertainment

Gallery Ma. *See p240.*

Calendar	**220**
Superstitions	224
Children	**227**
Film	**232**
Galleries	**237**
Gay & Lesbian	**243**
Love Father, Love Son	244
24-hour Party People	249
Music	**250**
Big in Japan	252
Nightlife	**262**
Performing Arts	**269**
Kabuki Stars	271
Noh Future?	272
Sport & Fitness	**276**
The Sumo Workout	280

Calendar

Things to do in Tokyo the whole year through.

With four distinct seasons, two religions and three major breweries, Japan is awash with festivals throughout the year.

In the capital, barely a weekend goes by without some sort of cultural happening or celebration, ranging from appreciation of natural beauty during the cherry-blossom season to commemorating suicidal samurai. Below we list the highlights of the annual calendar, but there are plenty of other festivities in between; contact the tourist offices (*see p318*) for more information about what's happening when you're in town.

HOLIDAY TIMES

The two big holiday periods are **Golden Week** (29 April to 5 May) and **New Year** (28 December to 4 January). The former contains four public holidays (Showa Day, Greenery Day, Constitution Day and Children's Day); people flee the city en masse, then all head home again at the same time. Tokyo remains relatively quiet, with many smaller shops and restaurants shut for the duration. Avoid travelling at this time, as prices increase and accommodation vacancies throughout Japan decrease. There's a similar problem at New Year, when many attractions, museums, shops and businesses shut until 5 January.

For information on Tokyo's climate, and the dates of Japan's 14 public holidays, *see p318*.

SPRING

Fire-Walking Ceremony
Hi-watari

Kotsu Anzen Kitosho (0426 61 1115, www.takaotozan.co.jp). Takaosan-guchi station (Keio line). **Date** 2nd Sun in Mar.

At the foot of Mt Takao, *yamabushi* (hard-core mountain monks) from Yakuoin Temple walk barefoot across burning coals while chanting incantations. Brave members of the public are then invited to test their own toughness of soul and sole by following in their footsteps (literally).

White Day

Date 14 Mar.

Invented by confectionery firms to make up for the fact that on Valentine's Day in Japan only guys receive chocs, White Day is just for the ladies. And it also helps to sell more chocolate, of course.
▶ *For further details about Valentine's Day in Japan, see p226.*

St Patrick's Day Parade

www.inj.or.jp. **Date** 17 Mar or nearest Sun.
Enthusiastic local devotees of Gaelic culture can be found demonstrating their baton-twirling, drumming, pipe-playing and dancing skills at this popular parade along Omotesando. Unsurprisingly, the celebrations at Tokyo's many Irish pubs continue well into the wee hours.

★ Cherry-Blossom Viewing
Hanami

Ueno Park, Sumida Park, Yasukuni Shrine, Shinjuku Gyoen, Aoyama Cemetery & other locations (3201 3331 Tourist Information Centre). **Date** late Mar-early Apr.
The great outdoor event of the year sees popular viewing spots invaded by hordes of nature-loving locals. The ideal time to admire the blossoms is at full bloom, when petals start to fall off in the breeze like pink snow. It is also a big drinking occasion, and by late afternoon many partygoers are no longer in a fit state to appreciate anything. Cases of alcohol poisoning are not unknown, and ambulance crews remain on alert.

Tokyo Motorcycle Show

www.motorcycleshow.org.
Date late Mar-early Apr.
Plenty of stuff to set any biker's pulse racing, with the latest models from Japan and abroad, as well as some great classics. It's held at the Tokyo Big Sight exhibition centre (*see p311*).

Festival of the Steel Phallus
Kanamara Matsuri
Kanayama Shrine, Kawasaki. Kawasaki Daishi station (Keikyu Daishi line). **Date** 1st Sun in Apr.
Locals parade giant phalluses through the street, while stalls sell penis-shaped candy and carved vegetables, as part of a Shinto fertility festival. It's usually phenomenally overcrowded.

Art Fair Tokyo
Tokyo International Forum, Hall B2, 3-5-1 Marunouchi, Chiyoda-ku (5771 4520, www.artfairtokyo.com). **Date** early Apr.
The largest art fair in Japan was launched in 2005 and features works from over 100 galleries, covering the art spectrum from *ukiyo-e* to avant-garde.
▶ *For year-round art galleries, see pp237-242.*

Start of the baseball season
Date early Apr.
The long road to the October play-offs usually starts with a three-game Central League series featuring the Giants, the city's perennial favourite. There's extra spice if the opposition is the Swallows – the capital's other big team – or the Giants' oldest rivals, the Hanshin Tigers. The games are held at either Tokyo Dome or Jingu Baseball Stadium (*see p277*).

★ Horseback Archery
Yabusame
5246 1111. **Date** mid Apr.
Mounted riders in full medieval samurai gear fire their bows at three stationary targets while galloping at full speed. The event is held at Sumida Park in Asakusa. There's also a big *yabusame* festival at

---

INSIDE TRACK
PARTYING IN YOYOGI PARK

The **Thai Festival** (*see p222*) is Yoyogi Park's biggest annual event, but there are plenty of others, including the **One Love Jamaica Festival** (www.onelove-jamaica-fes.org), the **Laos Festival** (www.laos-festival.info), **Earth Day Tokyo** (www.earthday-tokyo.org) and the **Festival Brasil** (www.festivalbrasil.jp).

Tsurugaoka Hachiman-gu (*see p296*) in Kamakura in September, and the practice can be seen during the Meiji Jingu Grand Autumn Festival (*see p224*).

Meiji Jingu Spring Festival
Haru no Taisai
3379 5511. **Date** 29 Apr-early May.
Free daily performances of traditional entertainment at the large Meiji Shrine & Inner Garden (*see p67*) in Harajuku, including *gagaku* and *bugaku* imperial court music and dance, plus *Noh* and *kyogen* drama.

Design Festa
3479 1433, www.designfesta.com. **Date** May, Nov.
A twice-yearly showcase of hundreds of young artists, musicians and performers, turning the Tokyo Big Sight convention centre (*see p311*) into an enormous art fair.

Kanda Festival
Organised from Kanda Myojin Shrine (3254 0753, www.kandamyoujin.or.jp). **Date** mid May.

Cherry-Blossom Viewing.

ARTS & ENTERTAINMENT

Kanda Festival. *See p221.*

Held in odd-numbered years, this is one of Tokyo's 'Big Three' festivals. In Edo days, it was a local favourite thanks to the shrine's links with popular tenth-century rebel Taira no Masakado. Events include *shinkosai* rites with participants parading in Heian costume, plus a gala procession that crosses the Kanda area with *mikoshi* portable shrines.

★ Sanja Festival
Organised from Asakusa Shrine (see p49).
Date 3rd weekend in May.
Tokyo's largest annual festival, Sanja attracts huge crowds to Asakusa and honours the three seventh-century founders of Senso-ji temple. It climaxes after several days of events with three huge *mikoshi*

portable shrines that carry the spirits of the three men as they are paraded around the streets.

Thai Festival
3447 2247, www.thaifestival.net.
Date Sat, Sun in mid May.
An annual festival of Thai food, drink, arts and culture in the southern part of Yoyogi Park (*see p68*), near the NHK Hall. The stage has demonstrations of Muay Thai boxing, dancing and Thai bands.

SUMMER

Iris Viewing
Meiji Shrine Inner Garden, Horikiri Iris Garden, Mizumoto Park & other locations (3201 3331).
Date mid June.
The annual blooming of the beautiful purple and white flowers falls during the not-so-beautiful rainy season, but is no less popular for the bad timing.

Ground-Cherry Market
Hozuchi-ichi
Date 9-10 July.
On these two days in July, prayers at Asakusa Kannon Temple (aka Senso-ji) are said to carry the equivalent of 46,000 days' worth at other times. Big crowds are attracted by this spiritual bargain. A ground-cherry market also takes place.
► *For sightseeing at the temple, see p49.*

Tokyo International Lesbian & Gay Film Festival
www.tokyo-lgff.org. **Date** mid July.
Launched in 1992, the annual LGFF lasts around five days and offers a rare chance for locals to catch up on the best of gay cinema. The main venue is Spiral (*see p239*) in Harajuku.

INSIDE TRACK
A WOMAN'S PLACE

Japanese women won medals in every Olympic marathon from 1992 to 2004, but the men haven't taken a medal since Kenji Kimihara won silver in 1968. One theory for the gender gap is the vast popularity of the **New Year Hakone Ekiden**. This relay marathon sees 20 college teams run a two-day race (2-3 Jan) from Tokyo to Hakone and back – and only men are allowed to take part. The race draws enormous audiences, with up to a million people lining the route and many more watching it on TV. So prestigious is the Ekiden that Japan's top male runners train for years to master the gruelling route with its mountainous inclines. The women, meanwhile, are left to train for other marathons.

Sumida River Fireworks

5246 1111. **Date** last Sat in July.
First held in 1733, this is the oldest, biggest and most crowded of Tokyo's summer fireworks events. Up to a million people pack the riverbank area in Asakusa to see around 20,000 *hanabi* ('flower-fires') light up the night. The popular waterfront spots are not for the claustrophobic.

Obon

Date 13-15 Aug.
The souls of the departed are said to return to the living world during this Buddhist festival honouring ancestral spirits. Observances include welcoming fires, Bon dances, night-time floating of lanterns on open water and the placing of horses made from vegetables on the doorsteps of rural homes to carry and sustain the ancestors' souls. It's not a public holiday, but many firms give workers time off to visit their relatives, leaving the capital unusually quiet.

War-End Anniversary

Date 15 Aug.
The annual anniversary of Japan's surrender to the Allied forces is still a source of diplomatic friction with neighbouring countries, as many leading Japanese politicians mark the day by visiting Yasukuni Shrine (*see p80*), where the souls of Japan's war dead, including those executed as war criminals, are honoured.

★ Azabu-Juban Noryo Festival

3451 5812, www.azabujuban.or.jp.
Date 3rd weekend in Aug.
Azabu-Juban's shopping street becomes a slowly shuffling throng of people snaking past a multitude of food, games and antiques stalls as they make their way to or from a taiko drum performance with traditional Bon dancing.

Asakusa Samba Carnival

3842 5566. **Date** last Sat in Aug.
Thousands of brilliantly plumed dancers, some of whose costumes don't leave much to the imagination, shake their stuff in the streets of old Asakusa. It's a startling and colourful spectacle, with a competition for the parade's top troupe. The sidelines of the route can get very busy, so allow plenty of time to claim a place; only tall latecomers can expect to get a good view of the action.
▶ *For sightseeing in Asakusa, see pp44-51.*

★ Awa Odori

3312 2728, www.koenji-awaodori.com/ indexEn.html. **Date** last weekend in Aug.
Street carnival Japanese-style. This annual shindig in Koenji (*see p118*) features a form of traditional Tokushima folk dance known as the Fool's Dance. As the raucous refrain of its light-hearted song puts it: 'You're a fool whether you dance or not, so you may as well dance.' *Photo p225*.

AUTUMN

Tokyo Game Show

3591 1421, http://tgs.cesa.or.jp. **Date** mid Sept.
A compulsive attraction for gamers of every breed, the biggest computer and video-game show on the planet is held at the Makuhari Messe convention centre (*see p257*) and launches plenty of eagerly awaited new releases.

Moon Viewing

Tsukimi
Date late Sept.
Parties to view the harvest moon have been held in the city since the Edo era, but light pollution in the city has proved problematic in the search for clear night skies, with less urban venues favoured nowadays. Those not wishing to travel may find solace in the annual *Tsukimi* burger promotion, recognising a distinctly lunar quality to the fried egg that comes as a seasonal extra.

Toray Pan Pacific Open Tennis Tournament

www.toray-ppo.co.jp/en. **Date** late Sept-early Oct.
This women-only indoor tennis tournament, played at the Tokyo Metropolitan Gymnasium (*see p281*), is usually well attended by the biggest names in the women's game. Maria Sharapova beat Jelena Jankovic in the final of the 2009 event.

Art-Link Ueno-Yanaka

http://artlink.jp.org. **Date** late Sept-mid Oct.
An annual art fair that includes exhibitions and events in galleries, shops and temples around the old cultural centre of Ueno and the artists' district of Yanaka. Keep an eye out for flyers or announcements in the media for details.

Takigi Noh

Date Sept-Oct.
Atmospheric outdoor performances of medieval *Noh* drama are staged at a number of shrines, temples and parks, illuminated by bonfires and torches.

CEATEC Japan

6212 5233, www.ceatec.com. **Date** early Oct.
Techie heaven. CEATEC Japan is the best place to see the latest consumer gadgets and communication technologies before they hit the shops. The fair is held at the Makuhari Messe convention centre (*see p257*) and attracts crowds keen to stay up to date with the latest digitial developments.

Japan Open Tennis

3481 2511. **Date** early Oct.
Early October sees the international tennis circus hit town for Japan's premier competitive event, held at the Ariake Tennis Forest (*see p281*) on Odaiba. Local interest tends to focus more on the women's section of the tournament.

ARTS & ENTERTAINMENT

Superstitions

As luck would have it…

Tokyo's shrines do a roaring trade in protective amulets, fortune-telling papers, lucky wooden rakes and (often sizeable) cash donations to ward off bad luck – an indication of just how seriously many Japanese people take their superstitions. Some themes will be familiar – unlucky numbers, prophetic cups of tea and stepping on cracks – but they all get a local twist. Here are some of the most popular:

● The numbers four and nine are always unlucky, thanks to their phonetic similarity to the words for death and suffering, respectively. It's why few things come packaged in fours, and hospitals often omit those room numbers.

● Money is a common gift in Japan, especially at weddings. But the figure has to be an odd number, since anything divisible by two portends a future split in the relationship.

● Bodies are traditionally buried with the head pointing north, so it's considered unlucky to sleep this way. And while not quite a superstition, Japanese kids also learn that if they lie down directly after a meal they will become a cow.

● Stepping on the gaps between tatami mats is as unlucky in Japan as pavement cracks are in the West.

● To become wealthy you'll need either thick earlobes or to have a dream involving a snake.

● If a tea stem is floating upright in your tea, it means good luck.

● When you see a funeral car, quickly hide your thumbs. A dangling thumb will prevent you from being present at your parents' deaths. (This stems from the name for thumbs in Japanese: 'parent fingers'.)

● You'll also miss your parents' deaths if you cut your fingernails in the evening, although only if you are a Tokyoite. People in other regions incur alternative forms of bad luck by nocturnal trimming.

● And finally, a superstition that borders on plain common sense: don't eat eels and pickled plums at the same time or you'll get stomach cramps.

Tokyo Motor Show
www.tokyo-motorshow.com. **Date** late Oct-early Nov.
Held annually at the Makuhari Messe (*see p257*) – and one of the major events in the automobile world's calendar – the Tokyo Motor Show provides a showcase for swish new products from both domestic and foriegn manufacturers. Cars and motorbikes feature in odd-numbered years, while commercial vehicles feature in even ones.

Chrysanthemum Festival
3379 5511. **Date** late Oct-late Nov.
The start of autumn was traditionally marked by the Chrysanthemum Festival on the ninth day of the ninth month of the old lunar calendar. These delicate pale blooms are also represented on the crest of Japan's imperial family. You'll find many blooms on display at the Meiji Shrine & Inner Garden (*see p67*). If you're in town at this time of year, they are well worth checking out.

Tokyo International Film Festival
www.tiff-jp.net. **Date** late Oct-early Nov.
The largest film festival in the country screens more than 300 films and attracts a glittering influx of international movie talent. The main venues are Roppongi Hills and Le Cinema (*see p233*) in the Bunkamura complex.

★ Meiji Jingu Grand Autumn Festival
3379 5511. **Date** 3 Nov.
This is the biggest annual festival at the Meiji Shrine, with performances of traditional music, theatre and *yabusame* (horseback archery).
▶ *For details about visiting the Meiji Shrine & Inner Garden, see p67.*

Tori no Ichi Fair
Chokoku-ji/Otori Jinja, Asakusa (www.torinoichi.jp). **Date** Nov.
Kumade are expensive, gaudily decorated bamboo rakes, reputed to bring their owners prosperity and good fortune. Their power only lasts a year, and each November on the days of the rooster (*tori*) according to the Chinese calendar, people replace their old rakes with new ones. Asakusa's Chokoku temple and Otori Shrine occupy adjacent spots and host the largest Tori no Ichi Fair, with over 200 stalls.

Seven-Five-Three Festival
Shichi Go San
3201 3331. **Date** 15 Nov.
During the Heian period (710-1185), children had their heads shaved from birth until they were three, when they could grow their hair. From the age of five boys could wear *hakama* and *haori* (traditional dress for men), and from seven girls could wear kimonos. These were special birthdays. Nowadays, the third

and seventh birthday are celebrated only by girls, the fifth by boys. Kids of these ages go to their local shrine on 15 November in their finest outfits, with important shrines besieged by junior hordes.

Autumn Leaves
Koyo
Shinjuku Gyoen, Ueno Park, Meiji Shrine Inner Garden & other locations (3201 3331).
Date 2nd half of Nov.
The spectacular golds and rusts of maple and gingko trees transform many of Tokyo's parks and gardens.

Japan Cup
Tokyo Racecourse, 1-1 Hiyoshi-cho, Fuchu-shi (0423 63 3141). Seimonmae station (Keio line).
Date late Nov.
Top horses and jockeys from around the world race over 2.4km (1.5 miles) in Japan's most famous horse race, held about half an hour by train from Tokyo.

WINTER
FIFA Club World Cup
www.fifa.com. **Date** mid Dec.
What was once the Toyota Cup, a one-off match between the winners of Europe's Champion's League and South America's Copa Libertadores, has been replaced by a tournament involving the club champions from all six continents.

47 Ronin Memorial Service
Ako Gishi-sai
3441 5560. **Date** 14 Dec (also 1-7 Apr).
The famous revenge attack by the masterless samurai known as the 47 *ronin* (*see p24* **Suicidal Samurai**) took place in the early hours of 31 January 1703, or 15 December 1702 by the old Japanese calendar. Two days of events, including dances, a parade in period costume and a Buddhist memorial ceremony, take place at Sengaku-ji Temple (*see p120*), where the warriors are buried alongside their former master. There's also a parade in Ginza, with participants in samurai outfits.

Battledore Market
Hagoita Ichi
3842 0181. **Date** 17-19 Dec.
Hagoita are paddle-shaped bats used to hit the shuttlecock in *hanetsuki*, the traditional New Year game. Ornamental versions come festooned with colourful pictures, and many temples hold markets selling them in December. The one at Asakusa Kannon Temple (*see p49*) is Tokyo's largest.

Emperor's Birthday
Tenno Tanjobi
Date 23 Dec.
This is the only day, apart from 2 January, when the general public is allowed to enter the inner grounds of the Imperial Palace (*see p78*).

Christmas Eve & Christmas Day
Date 24, 25 Dec.
Christmas Eve is the most romantic day of the year in Japan. Couples celebrate with extravagant dates involving dinners at fancy restaurants followed by visits to love hotels. Few locals mark Christmas Day, despite the battery of fairy lights, decorated trees and piped carols deployed by department stores. Neither day is a public holiday.

Year End
Date 28-31 Dec.
The last official day of work is 28 December, but all through the month companies have *bonenkai*, work-organised drinking parties to celebrate the end of the year. After work on the 28th, people begin a frantic round of last-minute house-cleaning, decoration-hanging and food preparation ready for the New Year's Eve festivities. Many stay at home to catch NHK's eternally popular TV show *Red & White Singing Contest*, although huge crowds also go out to shrines and temples for midnight, when bells are rung 108 times to dispel the 108 earthly desires that plague us all according to Buddhist teachings.

New Year's Day
Ganjitsu
3201 3331. **Date** 1 Jan.
Japan's most important annual holiday sees large crowds of people fill temples and shrines for that all-important first visit of the year; some of the more famous spots are rammed from midnight

Awa Odori. *See p223.*

onwards. Otherwise, New Year's Day tends to be a quiet family affair, except for postmen staggering under enormous sacks of New Year cards (*nengajo*), which all Japanese people send to friends and colleagues. Only the first day of the year is an official holiday, but people stay away from work for longer, with most shops and businesses shut until 4 January.

Emperor's Cup Final

www.jfa.or.jp/eng. **Date** 1 Jan.

The showpiece event of Japan's domestic football season is the climax of the main cup competition, at the National Stadium (*see p277*). It's become more popular since Japan co-hosted the 2002 World Cup.

New Year Congratulatory Visit
Ippan Sanga

Date 2 Jan.

The public is allowed into the inner grounds of the Imperial Palace (*see p78*) on two days a year, and this is one of them (the emperor's birthday in December is the other; *see p225*). Seven times during the day, between 9.30am and 3pm, the public face of the state appears on the palace balcony with other members of the royal family to wave to the crowds from behind bulletproof glass.

Tokyo Metropolitan Fire Brigade Parade
Dezome-shiki

3201 3331. **Date** 6 Jan.

In celebration of the city's firefighters, a display is put on by the Preservation Association of the old Edo Fire Brigade, at Tokyo Big Sight (*see p311*). They dress in traditional *hikeshi* firefighters' garb and perform acrobatic stunts at the tops of long ladders.

★ New Year Grand Sumo Tournament
Ozumo Hatsu Basho

3623 5111, www.sumo.or.jp/eng. **Date** mid Jan.

The first of the year's three full 15-day sumo tournaments (*basho*) held in Tokyo. The tournaments take place at the Ryogoku Kokugikan (*see p280*) from the second to the fourth Sundays in January, May and September. The other three *basho* take place in Osaka, Nagoya and Kyushu in March, July and November respectively.

Coming of Age Day
Seijin no Hi

Meiji Shrine & other locations (3201 3331). **Date** 2nd Mon in Jan.

Those reaching the age of 20 in the 12 months up to April head to shrines in their best kimonos and suits for blessings and photos. Some areas organise a ceremony at local school halls; in recent years, these have been interrupted by drunken youngsters (20 is the legal drinking age). The traditional date of 15 January generally coincides with New Year's Day under the old lunar calendar, so the ceremonies are held at this time to maintain a tie with the old system.

Chinese New Year

Yokohama Chinatown (045 641 4759, www. chinatown.or.jp). Ishikawacho station (Keihin Tohoku, Negishi lines), Chinatown exit. **Date** late Jan/early Feb.

Cymbals crash as dragon dancers weave their way along the restaurant-lined streets of Yokohama Chinatown for the local community's annual festival. The restaurants get packed, so be prepared for a long wait to get a table.

Setsubun

3201 3331. **Date** 3 Feb.

Much hurling of soybeans to cries of *oni wa soto, fuki wa uchi* ('demons out, good luck in') as the last day of winter – according to the lunar calendar – is celebrated in homes, shrines and temples. The tradition is to eat one bean for every year of one's age. Sumo wrestlers and other celebrities are among those doing the casting out in ceremonies at well-known Tokyo shrines, including Senso-ji (*see p49*) and Zojo-ji Temple (*see p90*).

Valentine's Day

Date 14 Feb.

Valentine's was introduced to Japan by confectionery companies as a day when women give chocolates to men. There are heart-shaped treats for that special someone, plus *giri choko* (obligation chocs) for a wider circle of male associates.

▶ *Men reciprocate by giving women chocolates on White Day, a month later; see p220.*

Plum Blossoms

Yushima Tenjin Shrine, 3-30-1 Yushima, Bunkyo-ku (3836 0753). Yushima station (Chiyoda line), exit 3. **Date** mid Feb-mid Mar.

The delicate white blooms on the city's plum trees arrive a little earlier than the better-known cherry blossoms, and are usually celebrated in a more restrained fashion, possibly because the weather is still on the cold side. Yushima Tenjin Shrine, a prime viewing spot south of Ueno Park, holds a month-long festival featuring traditional arts such as *ikebana* and tea ceremonies.

Daruma Fair

Jindai-ji Temple, 5-15-1 Jindaiji Motomachi, Chofu-shi (0424 86 5511). Tsutsujigaoka station (Keio line), north exit then 15mins bus ride to terminus at Jindai-ji Temple. **Date** 3-4 Mar.

After meditating in a cave for nine years, Bodhidharma, a Zen monk from ancient India, is reputed to have lost the use of all four limbs. The cuddly red figure of the Daruma doll, which is modelled after him, also lacks eyes. The first eye gets painted in when a difficult task is undertaken for good luck, the second when the task is successfully completed. Jindai-ji's Daruma Fair is one of the biggest and most crowded.

Children

The big city for small fry.

There's no shortage of stimuli for children in Tokyo. From amusement parks to zoos, from playgrounds to toy emporiums, there are myriad outlets in the metropolis that are aimed specifically at youngsters.

Large stores provide small (unstaffed) play areas, allowing parents to shop without worrying that their brood might be getting bored. Government-run children's halls provide purpose-built, free entertainment, and Tokyo's restaurants increasingly welcome families.

ESSENTIAL INFORMATION

Public transport is free for kids under six and half-price for under-12s. Most stations and major commercial facilities in downtown areas are equipped with lifts and escalators – though you may need help to locate them, particularly in the large and crowded terminal stations.

Nappy-changing facilities are available in indoor public toilets, although not in parks or playgrounds. Most commercial outlets have nursing facilities. You should be aware that the Japanese do not breastfeed in public, so be prepared to brave curious stares if you do.

Avoid the weekday rush hours, when trains and stations can be horribly packed. Facilities for kids can get very crowded at weekends and during school holidays (21 Mar-7 Apr, 20 July-31 Aug and 23 Dec-7 Jan), especially on wet or cold days.

For useful information and child-oriented tips, visit www.tokyowithkids.com, an online forum for English-speaking families living in Japan. Click on 'Discussions' at the top of the home page to link to a decent list of topics that includes shopping, education and playgroups.

For reviews of children's clothing boutiques and toy shops in Tokyo, *see p202.*

AMUSEMENT PARKS

Visiting amusement parks can be a pricey business, so it's worth noting that tickets are often available cheaply at *kinken* shops – discount ticket stores – sometimes at a fraction of the regular prices. In addition to the places listed below, the small **Hanayashiki** park

(*see p50*) has lots of old-fashioned charm and a 1953 rollercoaster, while **Toshimaen** (*see p72*) offers hours of splashing fun at its water park in summer and a spa in winter.

For the **Tokyo Disney Resort**, located out in Tokyo Bay, *see p120.*

Joypolis

Decks Tokyo 3F-5F, 1-6-1 Daiba, Minato-ku (5500 1801, www.sega.co.jp/joypolis/tokyo_e.html). Odaiba Kaihin Koen station (Yurikamome line) or Tokyo Teleport station (Rinkai line). **Open** 10am-11pm daily. **Admission** *1-day passport* ¥3,300; ¥3,100 7-14s. *Entry only* ¥500; ¥300 7-14s; each ride then costs ¥300-¥600. **Credit** AmEx, DC, JCB, MC, V. **Map** p83.

INSIDE TRACK BABY CAFE

To be allowed into the **Tokyo Baby Café** (B1 4-5-12 Jingumae, Shibuya-ku, 5474 8281, www.tokyobabycafe.com, Omotesando station (Chiyoda, Ginza, Hanzomon lines), exit A2), you must either be pregnant or accompanied by someone aged no more than seven. For those that qualify, the café offers food for guests as young as five months, toys and children's books, private spaces for nursing and a pushchair-friendly layout. The interior plays with the young guests' sense of scale with giant sofas and tiny tables. The café, in the tony Omotesando district, charges by the half-hour (¥500) on top of your food and drink bill.

You can simulate snowboarding in the half-pipe canyon or ride a virtual hang-glider through tropical islands at this indoor park in Odaiba packed with Sega's virtual-reality games. Bilingual instructions are provided for each game. The non-virtual highlight is the Spin Bullet, a whirling rollercoaster.

Kidzania

Lalaport Toyosu, 2-4-9 Toyosu, Koto-ku (3536 2100, www.kidzania.jp). Toyosu station (Yurakucho, Yurikamome lines). **Open** 9am-3pm, 4-9pm daily. **Admission** ¥1,900; ¥3,200-¥4,400 3-15s; ¥1,600-¥2,200 kids with disabilities. **Credit** AmEx, DC, JCB, MC, V.

If your kids have been misbehaving, why not reprimand them with a day at Kidzania, where they can spend time in a miniaturised, fully branded Coca-Cola bottling plant, a burger store or a bank, or they can emulate more exciting careers such as firefighter or magician. And if child labour and brand indoctrination aren't dubious enough themes, your offspring can spend their mock earnings via a Kidzania credit card. Kidzania is a Japanese-language theme-park, and some 'careers' require Japanese fluency to participate, but staff can assist international visitors. Activities are designed for ages two to 12.

Tokyo Dome City

1-3-61 Koraku, Bunkyo-ku (5800 9999, www.tokyo-dome.co.jp). Suidobashi station (Chuo line), west exit; (Mita line), exits A3, A4 or Korakuen station (Marunouchi, Nanboku lines),

Tokyo Dome City.

exit 2 or Kasuga station (Mita, Oedo lines), exit A1. **Open** *Dome City* 10am-10pm daily. *LaQua Spa* 11am-9am daily. *Toys Kingdom* 10am-6pm Mon-Fri; 9.30am-7pm Sat, Sun. **Admission** *Dome City* multi-ride ticket ¥3,000; individual rides ¥400-¥1,000. *LaQua Spa* ¥2,565 Mon-Fri; ¥2,680 Sat, Sun; ¥4,455 midnight-6am. *Toys Kingdom* 1st 3hrs ¥700-¥1,000; every subsequent 30mins ¥300-¥400. **No credit cards.**

The amusement park formerly known as Korakuen reopened in 2003 as part of an amusement complex, with baseball stadium Tokyo Dome (*see p277*) at its centre. The ultra-modern section, called LaQua, comprises a shopping centre, restaurants, the world's first spokeless Ferris wheel and a hot mineral bath theme park where spring water is pumped up from an incredible 1,700m (5,670ft) below ground. Topping it all off is the Thunder Dolphin, a stunning urban rollercoaster that starts off higher than the Dome, leaps to the roof of the main LaQua building and plunges through the centre of the Ferris wheel. For small kids, there's Toys Kingdom, with room after room of toys and educational equipment, making the place a great rainy-day solution.

▶ *Food options include a baseball-themed café.*

AQUARIUMS & ZOOS

There's also an aquarium inside Sunshine City (*see p72*), in Ikebukuro.

Inokashira Nature & Culture Park

1-17-6 Gotenyama, Musashino-shi (042 246 1100, www.tokyo-zoo.net/english). Kichijoji station (Chuo line), park (south) exit. **Open** 9.30am-5pm Tue-Sun. **Admission** ¥400; ¥150 13-15s; free under-13s. **No credit cards.**

A five-minute walk from Kichijoji station, this zoo is set in splendid Inokashira Park (*see p119*), with a pond, woods, playground and outdoor pool all close by. The zoo comprises two sections: one near the pond, housing an aviary and freshwater aquarium; the other near the wood, containing a zoo with a petting area, greenhouse and small amusement park. The entrance fee gets you tickets for both sections, which can be used separately.

Shinagawa Aquarium

3-2-1 Katsushima, Shinagawa-ku (3762 3431, www.aquarium.gr.jp). Omori Kaigan station (Keihin Kyuko line), east exit or Sujo water bus from Hinode Pier. **Open** 10am-5pm Mon, Wed-Sun. **Admission** ¥1,300; ¥600 7-15s; ¥300 4-6s. **No credit cards.**

Tokyo's best aquarium is in a rather inconvenient location, on the western edge of Tokyo Bay. The best feature is the water tank tunnel, which lets you walk under swimming green turtles, stingrays and scores of other fish. From another tank, huge sand tiger sharks peer out with cold, steely eyes. The aquarium also offers Tokyo's only dolphin shows, which take place at the outdoor stadium four or five times a day. They always attract huge crowds, so check the show schedule on arrival.

Tama Zoo
7-1-1 Hodokubo, Hino-shi (042 591 1611, www.tokyo-zoo.net/english). Tama Dobutsu Koen station (Keio line). **Open** 9.30am-5pm Mon, Tue, Thur-Sun. **Admission** ¥600; ¥200 13-15s; free under-13s. **No credit cards**.
The animals at this zoo in Hino City (an hour by train from central Tokyo) are displayed in a more natural setting than at Ueno Zoo (*see below*). Built over several low hills, Tama Zoo is divided into three ecological areas: Asiatic, African and Australian. The main attractions include koalas, lions in a 'safari' setting and, above all, a huge insectarium with butterflies, beetles and other creepy-crawlies. Enjoy the sensation of butterflies coming to rest their weary wings on your hand.

Tokyo Sea Life Park
6-2-3 Rinkai-cho, Edogawa-ku (3869 5152, www.tokyo-zoo.net/english). Kasai Rinkai Koen station (Keiyo line) or Sujo water bus from Hinode Pier. **Open** 9.30am-5pm Mon, Tue, Thur-Sun. **Admission** ¥700; ¥250 13-15s; free under-13s. **Credit** (gift shop only) JCB, MC, V.
Newer than Shinagawa Aquarium and located on the other side of Tokyo Bay, this place was built on the 190 acres of reclaimed land that constitute Kasai Seaside Park. The main attraction is a large doughnut-shaped water tank, home to 200 tuna.
▶ *For the nearby Tokyo Disney Resort see p120.*

Ueno Zoo
9-83 Ueno Koen, Taito-ku (3828 5171, www. tokyo-zoo.net/english). Ueno station (Yamanote, Ginza, Hibiya lines), park exit. **Open** 9.30am-5pm Mon, Tue, Thur-Sun. **Admission** ¥600; ¥200 13-15s; free under-13s. **Map** p107.
Japan's oldest zoo, established in 1882, is also Tokyo's most popular, thanks mainly to its central location in Ueno Park and its range of beasts, which include a Sumatran tiger, elephants, lions, gorillas, sea lions and assorted bears. Don't be discouraged by the crowds, though; the western section across the bridge is less busy and offers opportunities to interact with animals in a petting zoo and to watch a huge alligator relaxing in the reptile house.

CHILDREN'S HALLS

Run by the local authorities, children's halls (*jidokan*) are free indoor play facilities for residents (not short-term visitors). Designed to supplement formal education, they provide weekly play classes for pre-schoolers, and daily after-school programmes for school-age children of working parents. There are more than 500 *jidokan* within Tokyo's 23 wards,

including one run by the Tokyo Metropolitan Government, and another built by the welfare ministry, the National Children's Castle (the only one that charges a fee). For information about other *jidokan*, contact the Tokyo Metropolitan Government Foreign Residents' Advisory Centre (*see p312*).

0123 Kichijoji
2-29-12 Kichijoji Higashi, Musashino-shi (0422 20 3210, www1.parkcity.ne.jp/m0123hap/ kichijyoji). Kichijoji station (Chuo line), north exit. **Open** 9am-4pm Tue-Sat. **Admission** free.
This *jidokan* caters specifically for under-threes. Converted from a former kindergarten, it's a spacious building with a garden and a sandbox. Children can paint, or play with clay and a variety of toys handmade by the staff.

National Children's Castle
Kodomo no Shiro
5-53-1 Jingumae, Shibuya-ku (3797 5666, www.kodomo-shiro.or.jp). Shibuya station (Yamanote, Ginza, Hanzomon lines), Miyamasuzaka (east) exit or Omotesando station (Chiyoda, Ginza, Hanzomon lines), exits B2, B4. **Open** 12.30-5.30pm Tue-Fri; 10am-5.30pm Sat, Sun. **Admission** ¥500; ¥400 3-17s. **No credit cards**. **Map** p93.
A fabulous play hall halfway between Shibuya and Omotesando. Facilities include climbing equipment and a playhouse on the third floor, and a music lobby on the fourth floor where children can indulge their love of noise. The playport on the fifth-floor roof garden is the biggest attraction, combining a jungle gym with large ball pools, but it closes on rainy days. *Photo p231.*

★ Tokyo Metropolitan Children's Hall
1-18-24 Shibuya, Shibuya-ku (3409 6361, www. fukushihoken.metro.tokyo.jp/jidou/English). Shibuya station (Yamanote, Ginza, Hanzomon lines), Miyamasuzaka (east) exit. **Open** *July, Aug* 10am-5pm daily. *Sept-June* 10am-4pm daily. Closed 2nd & 4th Mon of mth. **Admission** free. **Map** p93.
Handily located not far from Shibuya station, this six-storey hall is packed with recreational and educational facilities. The second floor is reserved for pre-schoolers, with large climbing frames and wooden toys. The third floor has a handicraft section, the 'human-body maze' and a ball pool. There's a library on the fifth floor, while on the roof kids can try rollerskating and unicycling. Each floor has plenty of lockers to stash belongings.

MUSEUMS

Other child-friendly museums include the **Japan Science Foundation Science Museum** (*see p78*) in Marunouchi and Shinjuku's **Fire Museum** (*see p103*).

ARTS & ENTERTAINMENT

★ National Science Museum

7-20 Ueno Koen, Taito-ku (3822 0111, www. kahaku.go.jp/english). Ueno station (Yamanote line), park exit; (Ginza, Hibya lines) Shinobazu exit. **Open** 9am-5pm Tue-Thur; 9am-8pm Fri; 9am-5pm Sat, Sun. **Admission** ¥600; ¥70 reductions; free under-18s. **No credit cards.** Map p107.

At this museum inside Ueno Park, the exhibits of fossils, specimens and asteroids are now supplemented with touch screens providing videos and multilingual explanations. After checking out dinosaur bones and a prehistoric house built with mammoth tusks, you may want to taste the speciality of the museum's Musée Basara restaurant: a 'dinosaur's egg' croquette.

Tama Rokuto Kagakukan

5-10-64 Shibakubo, Nishi-Tokyo-shi (042 469 6100, www.tamarokuto.or.jp). Hana-Koganei station (Seibu Shinjuku line), north exit then 20mins walk, or take bus bound for Tama Rokuto Kagakukan from Hana-Koganei station (Seibu Shinjuku line), south exit (Sat, Sun & holidays) or Kichijoji station (Chuo line), north exit (Sun & holidays). **Open** 9.30am-5pm Tue-Sun. **Admission** ¥500; ¥200 4-18s. *Planetarium shows* ¥1,000; ¥400 4-18s. **No credit cards.**

Visitors can climb inside the scale model of a space shuttle that stands upright in the middle of this science museum an hour from Shinjuku. You can practise moving cargo with a robot arm simulator, while a moonwalker simulator recreates the low-gravity environment of the moon's surface. Star shows are held at the planetarium, one of the world's largest. While astronomy is the major focus, there are also geology and biology sections. The major drawback is poor public transport access, with infrequent bus services from local train stations.

PARKS & PLAYGROUNDS

Apart from **Yoyogi Park** *(see p68)* and **Shinjuku Gyoen** *(see p104)*, parks in central Tokyo are few and far between. Furthermore, they are often not ideal for picnics or playing – Ueno Park is more concrete than grass, for example. To find the best green spaces, you're better off grabbing a map and a rail pass and heading to the suburbs.

★ Koganei Park

1-13-1 Sekino-machi, Koganei-shi (042 385 5611, www.tokyo-park.or.jp/english). Musashi Koganei station (Chuo line), north exit then any bus from bus stop 2 or 3; get off at Koganei Koen Nishi-Guchi. **Open** 24hrs daily. **Admission** free.

You can explore the central part of this spacious park in western Tokyo by bicycle; about 120 bikes are available for pre-schoolers and their parents (¥100-¥200/hr). If your child tires of pedalling, they can try sledging down an artificial, turf-covered slope that's built into one of the park's grassy knolls. The 17° slope is wide enough for at least a dozen sledges to race down at the same time. Kids love it. You can buy a sledge or borrow one by queuing at the bottom of the slope. The park also houses the open-air branch of the Edo-Tokyo Museum *(see p50)*.

Nogawa Park

6-4-1 Osawa, Mitaka-shi (042 231 6457, www. tokyo-park.or.jp/english/park/detail_03.html). Shin-Koganei station (Seibu Tamagawa line) then 15mins walk (follow railway tracks south until you reach Nogawa river). **Open** *Park* 24hrs daily. *Nature centre* 9.30am-4.30pm Tue-Sun. **Admission** free.

A natural spring on the northern side of the Nogawa river bisects this picturesque park. The area around the spring is a popular paddling spot in summer. Upstream is a small nature centre where you can listen to recorded sounds of birds in Tokyo and learn about various insects. Climbing frames and other wooden play equipment dot the extensive grassy areas. It's a half-hour train ride from Shinjuku, followed by an easy walk.

Showa Kinen Park

3173 Midori-machi, Tachikawa-shi (042 528 1751, www.showapark.jp). Nishi-Tachikawa station (Ohme line). **Open** from 9.30am daily; closing time varies from 4.30pm midwinter to 7pm midsummer. **Admission** *Park* ¥400; ¥80 6-15s. *Park & Rainbow Pool* ¥2,200; ¥1,200 6-15s; ¥300 4-5s. **No credit cards.**

A paradise for athletic children, this park 40 minutes from Shinjuku has a large play area called Children's Forest, with giant trampoline nets, bouncy domes and 'foggy woods' that – as the name implies – get covered by clouds of artificial fog. The Forest House in the centre sells snacks and drinks and provides a welcome resting space. If it's too hot to walk to the Children's Forest from the main gate, pop into the Rainbow Pool for a paddle. Three pools contain waterfalls and squirt fish; bigger children have the choice of a current pool, a wave pool and water slides. ▶ *The park also has some lengthy cycling tracks; bike rental for three hours costs ¥250 for under-15s, ¥410 for adults.*

Trim Sports Centre
Jingu Gaien 'Jido Yuen'

1-7-5 Kita-Aoyama, Minato-ku (3478 0550, www.meijijingugaien.jp/english). Shinanomachi station (Sobu line). **Open** *Mar-Oct* 10am-5pm daily. *Nov-Feb* 10am-4.30pm daily. **Admission** ¥300; ¥100 2-12s. **No credit cards.**

Despite its compact size and central location, this popular playground within the Outer Garden of the Meiji Jingu has more play equipment than any other park in Tokyo. Children can try swings, slides and climbs of various sizes and shapes, and picnic at beautiful log houses equipped with large

National Children's Castle. *See p229.*

tables and chairs. The park has three areas, each for a different age group, but children are allowed to wander anywhere under parental supervision.

RESOURCES
Babysitting & nurseries

Staff at reputable hotels may be able to arrange babysitting. Alternatively, the following outfits come highly recommended by Tokyo parents. Expect to pay between ¥1,500 and ¥2,800 per hour. Some agencies demand a minimum of two hours at a set rate; you then pay for each additional hour, with different rates for late-night and early-morning services.

Japan Baby Sitter Service
3423 1251, www.jbs-mom.co.jp. **No credit cards.**
One of the oldest services in Tokyo, specialising in grandmotherly types. Bookings must be made by 5pm on the preceding day.

Kids Square
West Walk 6F, Roppongi Hills, 6-10-1 Roppongi, Minato-ku (5772 1577, 0120 086 720 freephone, www.alpha-co.com/english). Roppongi station (Hibiya, Oedo lines), exit 1. **Open** 11am-7pm daily. **No credit cards. Map** p87.
Located conveniently in the middle of the Roppongi business district, this is a spacious, well-equipped nursery. You can check your child via mobile phone or computer by hooking up to video cameras installed in the nursery. Book by 4pm the day before.

Other locations Ark Hills Side 3F, 1-3-41 Roppongi, Minato-ku (3583 9320); Tokyo Dome Hotel 7F, 1-3-61 Koraku, Bunkyo-ku (5805 2272).

Kids World
Pigeon Shoto Takada Bldg 2F, 1-28-11 Shoto, Shibuya-ku (5428 3630, www.pigeonhearts.jp/ kidsworld). Shibuya station (Yamanote, Ginza, Hanzomon lines), Hachiko exit or Shinsen station (Keio Inokashira line). **Open** 9am-6pm Mon-Fri. **No credit cards. Map** p93.
This English-language school for children also provides nursery care at its many branches in the city, including this one in Shibuya. Pigeon Hearts, which runs the school, can also arrange a babysitting service for those able to communicate in Japanese; phone for more details (0120 764 154 freephone).
Other locations throughout the city; details on 0120 001 537.

Little Mate
045 712 3253, www.tokyolm.co.jp.
Open 10am-6pm daily. **No credit cards.**
You can drop off your kids for an hour or more at a day nursery at one of three hotels: Hotel Okura, Roppongi (3586 0360); Keio Plaza Intercontinental, Shinjuku (3345 1439); or the Sheraton Grande Tokyo Bay Hotel (047 355 5720), which is near Tokyo Disneyland. Reservations are required by 6pm the previous day (by 4pm at the Hotel Okura).

Poppins Service
3447 2100, www.poppins.co.jp/english.
Open 7am-9pm Mon-Sat. **No credit cards.**
Expect either a young lady trained in early childhood education or a retired veteran teacher when you request a sitter from Poppins. Non-members pay a flat rate of ¥2,300 per hour (¥3,200 5-10pm), and bookings must be made two days in advance. If Japanese is not your – or your children's – strong point, speakers of English can be provided.

Royal Baby Salon
Ginza Kosumion Bldg 7F, 1-5-14 Ginza, Chuo-ku (3538 3238, www.royalbaby.co.jp). Ginza-Itchome station (Yurakucho line), exit 6. **Open** 10am-6pm daily. **Credit** (incurs extra charge) AmEx, DC, JCB, MC, V. **Map** p59.
An upmarket nursery in Ginza that also offers a babysitting service. Bookings must be made by 5pm on the preceding day.

Equipment rental

Duskin Rent-All
0120 100 100, www.kasite.net.
If you don't have access to second-hand childcare equipment, try Duskin. It hires out all sorts of kit, from car seats to cots, at very reasonable rates, and will deliver to your home. There are also ten central outlets, but you'll need to speak Japanese.

Film

Catch a flick in the land of anime and Godzilla.

Hollywood remakes have planted Japanese cinema firmly in the global consciousness, and added murderous videotapes and vengeful houses to the register of cinematic icons. But Japan's film industry stretches way back to the 19th century and a documentary entitled *Geisha no Teodori* ('Geisha's hand dance').

Japan's golden age of cinema ran from the 1930s to '50s (with a wartime intermission), and was followed by a Japanese take on the French *nouvelle vague*. In the last two decades, there's been a renaissance of fresh new work and the notable influence of *anime*.

JAPAN'S CINEMATIC HISTORY

Mass viewing of film began in the early 20th century with imported silent movies. Since the audience could not understand the foreign language inter-titles, a narrator (or *benshi*) was employed to explain things. *Benshi* soon became valued artists who narrated both Japanese and foreign work.

A film of particular note from this early era is *A Page of Madness* (*Kurutta Ippeiji*, 1926) by Teinosuke Kinogasa, about a janitor in a mental asylum. The film's images and techniques remain gripping today, testament to both Kinogasa's vision, as well as to the sophistication of early Japanese film.

INSIDE TRACK LOVE SEATS

Forget about back-seat romance at the movies – some Tokyo cinemas offer seats for two. The **Toho Cinemas Roppongi Hills** (*see p236*) has a premium theatre where the more luxurious seating includes several 'pair seats' designed for two (¥3,000 per person). The **Shinjuku Piccadilly** cinema (3-15-15 Shinjuku, Shinjuku-ku, 5367 1144, www.shinjukupiccadilly.com) takes the idea even further with Platinum Rooms (¥5,500 per person) – semi-private booths on the balcony, furnished with two-seater leather sofas and leg rests.

The 1930s marked the dawn of the 'golden age' of Japanese cinema. Gifted directors such as Yasujiro Ozu, Kenji Mizoguchi, Mikio Naruse and the less-heralded Hiroshi Shimizu produced work that exhibited a remarkable mastery of the craft. Although Ozu is best known for his post-war films, such as the famous *Tokyo Story* (*Tokyo Monogatari*, 1953), his pre-war work is edgier, more varied and equally accomplished.

This period also saw the rise of the Japanese studio system. Much like their Hollywood counterparts, large studios such as Shochiku, Toho, Daiei and Nikkatsu started to put directors under contract and control the content of their work. Filmmaking was a thriving and extremely profitable business, and the studios ruled it with an iron fist.

The hiccup of World War II limited film production to mainly jingoistic dreck, but the industry recovered its poise afterwards. The consensus holds that the golden age continued into the mid to late 1950s with Ozu, Mizoguchi and Naruse still active. In addition, new stars such as Akira Kurosawa – a man who would define Japanese cinema for the next 40 years – were rising fast. This period saw the emergence of talented auteurs Kon Ichikawa, Yasuzo Masumura and Hiroshi Teshigahara.

In the late 1950s and early '60s, the studio system thrived as never before, but it was challenged by youthful and radical directors of the '*nuberu bagu*' (from the French term *nouvelle vague*, or new wave) movement, despite the fact that major studio Shochiku had launched this movement to attract younger fans. Nagisa Oshima, Shohei Imamura, Susumu Hani, Yoshige Yoshida and others made films exposing Japan's social problems, questioning the assumption of Western values and materialism, and addressing taboo subjects such as sexuality. In addition, they broke the studios' grip on directors, eventually venturing out on their own and also forming the artistically noteworthy independent production company Art Theatre Guild (ATG).

The tapering-off of the *nuberu bagu* in the mid '70s triggered a crisis in Japanese cinema. Attendances had been falling for years, and there were few new acclaimed directors appearing (although Kurosawa, Oshima and Imamura, among others, were still active). The situation continued in this vein for much of the 1980s. Although nearly half of Japanese box-office receipts still derived from locally made fare (a claim that few countries could make), the studios continued to churn out formulaic, melodramatic pieces and were suffering financially – in 1972 Daiei went bankrupt and Nikkatsu turned to making soft-core porn.

Japanese cinema underwent an energetic rebirth in the 1990s with the arrival of young and/or fresh directors such as 'Beat' Takeshi Kitano – the most internationally successful of contemporary Japanese filmmakers – Shunji Iwai, Kiyoshi Kurosawa, Shinya Tsukamoto, Makoto Shinozaki and Jun Ichikawa. In addition, Japanese *anime* (animation), led by the genius of Hayao Miyazaki, started to conquer foreign markets and take huge profits at home – Miyazaki's *Spirited Away* (2001) is the highest-grossing film of all time in Japan.

TICKETS & INFORMATION

Visiting a cinema in Tokyo is expensive, with most cinemas charging a standard ¥1,800 for on-the-day admission (¥1,000-¥1,500 reductions). If you want to save money, you can buy advance tickets at convenience stores and ticket agencies for around ¥300-¥500 less (or go on the first day of the month, when admission is usually ¥1,000). The problem with this system is that tickets are sold for the film, not the cinema – so in theory any number of people can arrive to catch the latest blockbuster. Seats are not allocated, so people regularly arrive an hour in advance and then charge in as soon as the doors open to grab the best places. The cluster of cinemas in Shinjuku, Ginza, Shibuya and other busy areas all operate this system. Seats can be reserved through agencies such as Pia (*see p218* **Tickets**), but this adds an extra ¥200-¥1,000 to the price. Some cinemas are cheaper; we've given ticket prices for those below. Hope also comes in the form of the new breed of multiplexes, which offer allocated seating at point of sale for no extra cost.

Most Hollywood or other foreign films are screened in their original version with Japanese subtitles. Cinemas occasionally screen a Japanese film with English subtitles (usually the last showing on a Sunday). If you visit in the autumn, you may catch one of the two international film festivals – the **Tokyo International Film Festival** (*see p224*) and **Tokyo Filmex** (www.filmex.net) – both of which show Japanese films with English subtitles. For film listings, check the *Japan Times*, *Metropolis* or www.timeout.jp.

INDEPENDENT & REPERTORY

Athénée Français Cultural Center
4F, 2-11 Kanda Surugadai, Chiyoda-ku (3291 4339, www.athenee.net/culturalcenter). Suidobashi station (Chuo, Sobu lines), east exit; (Mita line), exit A1. **Tickets** vary. **Seats** 80. Screens classics and discovers new filmmakers.

Le Cinema
Bunkamura 6F, 2-24-1 Dogenzaka, Shibuya-ku (3477 9264, www.bunkamura.co.jp). Shibuya station (Yamanote, Ginza lines), Hachiko exit; (Fukutoshin, Hanzomon lines), exit 3A. **Seats** 150 & 126. **Map** p93.

Cinema Rise. *See p234.*

Uplink Factory. *See p236.*

This two-screener in the giant Bunkamura arts complex in Shibuya offers mainly French fare. It's the principal venue for the Tokyo International Film Festival (*see p224*).

★ Cinema Rise
13-17 Udagawacho, Shibuya-ku (3464 0051, www.cinemarise.com). Shibuya station (Yamanote, Ginza lines), Hachiko exit; (Fukutoshin, Hanzomon lines), exit 6. **Seats** 220 & 303. **Map** p93.
A champion of independent cinema, Rise mixes well-known international fare such as *Precious* with offbeat Japanese films such as a biography of Yayoi Kusama. Foreign students (with suitable ID) pay only ¥1,000. *Photo p233*.

Cinema Square Tokyu
Tokyu Milano Bldg 3F, 1-29-1 Kabuki-cho, Shinjuku-ku (3202 1189, www.tokyucinemas. net). Shinjuku station (Yamanote, Chuo lines), east exit; (Marunouchi line), exit B12; (Oedo, Shinjuku lines), exit 1. **Seats** 224.
The pioneer of arthouse cinemas in Tokyo shows mainly recent independent films.

Cinem@rt
3-8-15 Roppongi, Minato-ku (5413 7711, www.cinemart.co.jp). Roppongi station (Hibiya, Oedo lines), exit 5. **Seats** 165, 87 & 52. **Map** p87.
The best place to catch independent Asian cinema. It also hosts occasional plays and concerts.
Other locations Shinjuku Bunka Bldg 6F, 7F, 3-13-3 Shinjuku, Shinjuku-ku (5369 2831).

Ciné Pathos
4-8-7 Ginza, Chuo-ku (3561 4660). Ginza station (Ginza, Hibiya, Marunouchi lines), exit A6. **Seats** 177, 130 & 72. **Map** p59.
A three-screener with new films and classic revivals.

Ciné Quinto
Parco Part 3 8F, 14-5 Udagawa-cho, Shibuya-ku (3477 5905, www.cinequinto.com). Shibuya station (Yamanote, Ginza lines), Hachiko exit; (Fukutoshin, Hanzomon lines), exit 6. **Seats** 227. **Map** p93.
Quinto often screens new British films, and offers bizarre film-based discounts. For example, when Hong Kong film *The Eye* was on, anyone carrying a photo of a ghost got a discount of ¥800. Different rules are stipulated for each film. Keep your ticket stub to enter for just ¥1,000 on your next visit.

Ciné Saison Shibuya
The Prime 6F, 2-29-5 Dogenzaka, Shibuya-ku (3770 1721, www.cinemabox.com/schedule/ shibuya). Shibuya station (Yamanote, Ginza lines), Hachiko exit; (Fukutoshin, Hanzomon lines), exit 3A. **Seats** 221. **Map** p93.
Revivals, mini festivals and independent productions are the lifeblood of this comfortable cinema.

Ciné Switch Ginza
Ginza-Hata Bldg B1F, 4-4-5 Ginza, Chuo-ku (3561 0707, www.cineswitch.com). Ginza station (Ginza, Hibiya, Marunouchi lines), exit B2. **Seats** 273 & 182. **Map** p59.
Recent European and American films.

Ebisu Garden Cinema
Ebisu Garden Place, 4-20-2 Ebisu, Shibuya-ku (5420 6161, www.kadokawa-gardencinema.jp/ yebisu). Ebisu station (Yamanote line), east exit; (Hibiya line), exit 1. **Seats** 232 & 116.
A mix of American indies and foreign films are shown here. Filmgoers are summoned in numbered batches, according to when they purchased their tickets, so there's never any stampede for seats.
▶ *For details about Ebisu Garden Place and the surrounding attractions, see p52.*

Eurospace

Q-AX Bldg, 1-5 Maruyama-cho, Shibuya-ku (3461 0211, www.eurospace.co.jp). Shibuya station (Yamanote,Ginza lines), Hachiko exit; (Fukutoshin, Hanzomon lines), exit 5. **Seats** 92 & 145. **Map** p93.
An arthouse specialist with a lifespan of over two decades, playing independent films from Europe and Asia, and in a new location since January 2006.

Ginza Théâtre Cinema

Ginza-Théâtre Bldg 5F, 1-11-2 Ginza, Chuo-ku (3535 6000, www.cinemabox.com/schedule/ginza). Kyobashi station (Ginza line), exit 2 or Ginza-Itchome station (Yurakucho line), exit 7. **Seats** 150. **Map** p59.
Late-night shows with interesting programmes.

Haiyu-za

4-9-2 Roppongi, Minato-ku (3470 2880, www.haiyuzagekijou.co.jp). Roppongi station (Oedo line), exit 6; (Hibiya line), exit 4A. **Tickets** vary. **Seats** 300. **Map** p87.
Roppongi's venerable old fleapit opens irregularly, but when it does, its speciality is weird and avant-garde films from all continents. A Tokyo treasure that is worth a visit, if you can catch it open.

Iidabashi Ginrei Hall

2-19 Kagurazaka, Shinjuku-ku (3269 3852, www.ginreihall.com). Iidabashi station (Chuo, Sobu lines), west exit; (Oedo, Nanboku, Tozai, Yurakucho lines), exits B4A, B4B. **Tickets** ¥1,500; ¥1,000-¥1,200 reductions. **Seats** 206.
Special double features offer interesting combinations of second-run films. Pay ¥10,500 to join the Cinema Club and you can go as often as you like for a whole year without paying another yen.

Institut Franco-Japonais

15 Ichigaya-Funagawaramachi, Shinjuku-ku (5206 2500, www.institut.jp). Iidabashi station (Chuo, Sobu lines), west exit; (Oedo Nanboku, Tozai, Yurakucho lines), exit B3. **Tickets** ¥1,000. **Seats** 115. **Map** p77.
A pearl in the Japanese cinema scene, this French cultural centre shows contemporary French films at the weekend, often with English subtitles.

Iwanami Hall

Iwanami Jinbocho Bldg 10F, 2-1 Kanda-Jinbocho, Chiyoda-ku (3262 5252, www.iwanami-hall.com). Jinbocho station (Hanzomon, Mita, Shinjuku lines), exit A6. **Seats** 220. **Map** p77.
This highbrow cinema has been screening international works of social realism since the 1970s. The focus is on female directors and political work.

Kichijoji Baus Theatre

1-11-23 Kichijoji-Honmachi, Musashino-shi (0422 22 3555, www.baustheater.com). Kichijoji station (Chuo line), north exit. **Seats** 220, 50 & 106.

They screen everything from Hollywood blockbusters to Japanese independent films here, but with an emphasis on mainstream stuff these days. There are discounts for men on Mondays, women on Wednesdays and couples on Fridays – plus anyone celebrating a birthday.

Kineca Omori

Seiyu Omori 5F, 6-27-25 Minami-Oi, Shinagawa-ku (3762 6000, www.cinemabox.com/schedule/omori). Omori station (Keihin-Tohoku line), east exit. **Seats** 134, 69 & 40.
Kineca Omori has three screens showing predominantly Asian films from all genres.

Laputa Asagaya

Laputa Bldg 2F, 2-12-21 Asagaya-Kita, Suginami-ku (3336 5440, www.laputa-jp.com). Asagaya station (Chuo, Sobu lines), north exit. **Tickets** ¥1,200; ¥1,000 reductions; ¥1,000 Wed. **Seats** 50.
A charming, tiny cinema that shows everything from Japanese indies to experimental fare – stuff that's usually not shown anywhere else in Tokyo.

★ National Film Centre

3-7-6 Kyobashi, Chuo-ku (5777 8600, www.momat.go.jp). Kyobashi station (Ginza line), exit 1 or Takaracho station (Asakusa line), exit A4. **Tickets** ¥500. **Seats** 310 & 151. **Map** p77.
Part of the National Museum of Modern Art, this venue has two cinemas, a gallery, a library and a café. It holds a collection of 19,000 films, and often revives Japanese classics.
► *For details of the rest of the National Museum of Modern Art complex, see p80.*

Sangenjaya Chuo Gekijo

2-14-5 Sangenjaya, Setagaya-ku (3421 4610, http://movie.walkerplus.com/th569/schedule.html). Sangenjaya station (Tokyu Denentoshi line),

► *For details of the rest of the National Museum of Modern Art complex, see p80.*

INSIDE TRACK
MAMA'S CLUB

Toho-run cinemas, including **Cinema Mediage** (see p236) and **Toho Cinemas Roppongi Hills** (see p236), run Mama's Club screenings, when parents are welcome to bring kids of any age. The film's volume is turned down and the cinema lights are brighter than usual to avoid scaring the youngsters, and there are no rules on sitting still or staying quiet. The films are all child-friendly, though not necessarily aimed at the youngsters. Screenings are intermittent. Check the cinema websites for schedules.

ARTS & ENTERTAINMENT

**INSIDE TRACK
PRIVATE SCREENINGS**

Want to watch a film in peace? Then hire one of the two **Tsutaya** screens in Shibuya (3464 6277, www.theater-tsutaya.jp). For ¥30,000-¥60,000 per hour, you can rent the entire 172- or 264-seat theatres and screen any DVD you wish. In addition, you can also bring your Wii or PlayStation for big-screen gaming.

Setagaya Dori exit. **Tickets** ¥1,300; ¥800-¥1,100 reductions. ¥1,100 Fri; ¥1,000 1st of mth. **Seats** 262.
Second-run cinema with interesting double features.

Shimo-Takaido Cinema
3-27-26 Matsubara, Setagaya-ku (3328 1008, www.shimotakaidocinema.com). Shimo-Takaido station (Keio line), east exit. **Tickets** ¥1,600; ¥1,000-¥1,300 reductions; ¥1,000 women Wed and for all 1st of mth. **Seats** 126.
A repertory cinema with a varied programming policy, from revivals to recent major films.

Shin-Bungeiza
Maruhan-Ikebukuro Bldg 3F, 1-43-5 Higashi-Ikebukuro, Toshima-ku (3971 9422, www.shin-bungeiza.com). Ikebukuro station (Yamanote, Yurakucho lines), east exit; (Marunouchi line), exit 30. **Tickets** ¥1,300; ¥900-¥1,200 reductions. **Seats** 266. **Map** p69.
A legendary repertory house in Ikebukuro showing a wide range of films, from Japanese classics to Hollywood no-brainers.

Theatre Image Forum
2-10-2 Shibuya, Shibuya-ku (5766 0114, www.imageforum.co.jp). Shibuya station (Yamanote,Ginza lines), east exit; (Fukutoshin, Hanzomon lines), exit 12. **Tickets** vary. **Seats** 64 & 108. **Map** p93.
Cutting-edge contemporary films, classics, avant-garde features and experimental work.

Theatre N Shibuya
Tobu Fuji Bldg 2F, 24-4 Sakuragaoka-cho, Shibuya-ku (5489 2592, www.theater-n.com). Shibuya station (Yamanote,Ginza lines), west exit; (Fukutoshin, Hanzomon lines), exit 5. **Tickets** ¥1,800; ¥1,000-¥1,500 reductions. **Seats** 75 & 102. **Map** p93.
The two screens at this Shibuya picture house show Japanese and international indie fare.

Tollywood
2F, 5-32-5 Daizawa, Setagaya-ku (3414 0433, http://homepage1.nifty.com/tollywood).

Shimo-Kitazawa station (Keio Inokashira, Odakyu lines), south exit. **Tickets** ¥600-¥1,500. **Seats** 46.
Arthouse cinema specialising in shorts, famous directors' early works and new independent films.

★ Uplink Factory
Totsune Bldg 1F, 37-18 Udagawacho, Shibuya-ku (5489 0750, www.uplink.co.jp). Shibuya station (Yamanote,Ginza lines), Hachiko exit; (Hanzomon line), exit 3A. **Tickets** vary. **Seats** 70.
A fascinating mix, from Roman Polanski's early works to Eurotrash, plus lots of experimental and short work thrown in. Uplink also holds film workshops and live performances. *Photo p234.*

MULTIPLEXES

Cinema Mediage
Mediage, Aqua City 1F/2F, 1-7-1 Daiba, Minato-ku (5531 7878, www.mediage.jp/e). Daiba station (Yurikamome line). **Seats** 13 screens seating 114-612. **Map** p83.
The home of the super-premium love seat, designed for canoodling couples (¥6,000), Warners-owned Mediage provides a superior film-going experience, with all seats reserved at no extra charge.

Shinagawa Prince Cinema
Shinagawa Prince Hotel, Executive Tower 3F, 4-10-30 Takanawa, Minato-ku (5421 1113, www.princehotels.co.jp/shinagawa/cinema). Shinagawa station (Yamanote line), Takanawa exit. **Seats** 10 screens seating 96-219.
All the latest hits appear at this ten-screen giant. Premium screens have wide, high-backed seats (¥2,500), and parents can leave kids in the hotel's day nursery (9am-6pm; call ahead to get a place).

★ Shinjuku Wald 9
Shinjuku Sanchome East Bldg 9F, 3-1-2 Shinjuku-ku (5369 4955, www.wald9.com). Shinjuku station (JR lines), east exit or Shinjuku San-chome station (Fukutoshin, Marunouchi lines), exit C1. **Seats** 9 screens seating 69-429. **Map** p101.
This cinema complex is the first of its kind in Japan, with all nine screens equipped with digital projectors. And the acoustics are just as cutting-edge. Selected weekday screenings from 3.30pm to 6pm are only ¥1,200.

Toho Cinemas Roppongi Hills
6-10-2 Roppongi, Minato-ku (5775 6090, www.tohotheater.jp). Roppongi station (Hibiya line), exit 1C; (Oedo line), exit 3. **Seats** 9 screens seating 81-652. **Map** p87.
Virgin's nine-screen multiplex in Roppongi Hills offers all-night screenings on Thursdays, Fridays, Saturdays and days preceding national holidays. Very comfortable seats (¥1,800-¥3,000).

Galleries

Art on the move.

A lot has happened in Tokyo's art world in the past couple of years. Popular galleries have closed, new spaces have sprouted up in their place. The Roppongi nightlife district continues to scrub up its image with gleaming, high-profile museums, and events such as its Roppongi Art Night.

Elsewhere, a large number of galleries have pulled up stakes, only to touch down again in interesting combinations across the city. The good news for art-lovers is that it's never been easier to see so much quality artwork in an afternoon.

THE SCENE

Many of the galleries listed below are around the same area, along the same train line or even in the same building. **Ginza** has the highest concentration of art spaces in the country, whether for painting, photography, *nihonga* (traditional Japanese painting) or ceramics. Not far away, nestled between a park and a factory in a residential neighbourhood, you'll find four of Japan's most influential galleries under the same roof in the **Kiyosumi Complex**. And in the suburb of **Bakurocho**, a large number of young and fresh gallerists have begun occupying crumbling buildings and revitalising a faded business district. And in **Shirokane**, an upmarket residential district, you'll now find a building with some of the capital's most cutting-edge galleries. In Roppongi, art-lovers should also check out the temporary, usually contemporary exhibitions at the **Mori Art Museum** (*see p88; photo p239*) and its newer rival (and the city's largest art museum), the **National Art Center Tokyo** (*see p88*).

INFORMATION

The best web resources are **TAB** (www. tokyoartbeat.com) and **Real Tokyo** (www. realtokyo.co.jp/english). You'll also find listings in *Metropolis*, and on Fridays in the weekly art sections of the English-language newspapers (*see p315*). The major commercial galleries have a free pamphlet entitled *New Favorite*, released every two months as a guide to the biggest contemporary art exhibitions. TAB now has its own pamphlet with even wider distribution (in galleries, cafes & restaurants).

Called *Tokyo Art Map*, these freebies provide information on 50 popular events and include small but detailed maps of each area.

Note that many of the galleries below are open only when they have an exhibition on.

ASAKUSA

Gallery Ef
2-19-18 Kaminarimon, Taito-ku (3841 0442, www.tctv.ne.jp/get2-ef). Asakusa station (Asakusa line), exit A5; (Ginza line), exit 2. **Open** noon-7pm Mon, Wed-Sun. **Map** p45.
The beamed ceilings and lacquered floors of this extremely rare example of a 19th-century earthen-walled warehouse are tough competition for the con-temporary art that is shown here. The shows are mainly by lesser-known but interesting Japanese artists, with some international names joining in.
▶ *The gallery has a nice café, Ef (see p187).*

EBISU

G/P Gallery
NADiff A/P/A/R/T bldg 2F, 1-18-4 Ebisu Shibuya-ku (5422-9331, www.gptokyo.jp). Ebisu station (Yamanote line), East exit; (Hibiya line). **Open** noon-8pm daily during exhibitions.
The G/P Gallery concentrates on photography and is worth a look after a visit to the nearby Tokyo Metropolitan Museum of Photography (*see p54*).

NADiff
NADiff A/P/A/R/T bldg 3F, 1-18-4 Ebisu Shibuya-ku (3446 4977, www.nadiff.com). Ebisu station (Yamanote line), East exit; (Hibiya line). **Open** noon-8pm daily.

One of the city's top art bookstores (the flagship shop in a chain) is now located in a side street near Ebisu station, in the same building as the G/P Gallery (*see p237*). NADiff also has a cafe and its own small gallery showing hot young Japanese artists, often in order to promote their latest book.

GINZA

Arataniurano

3A, 2-2-5 Shintomi, Chuo-ku (3555 0696, www.arataniurano.com). Shintomicho station (Yurakucho line). **Open** 11am-7pm Tue-Sat.
Gaining momentum over the last few years, Arataniurano has become a significant player in the young contemporary scene.

Galleria Grafica Tokyo

Ginza S2 Bldg 1 2F, 6-13-4 Ginza, Chuo-ku (5550 1335, www2.big.or.jp/~adel/grafica.html). Ginza station (Ginza, Hibiya, Marunouchi lines), exit A3. **Open** 11am-7pm Mon-Sat. **Map** p59.
Two distinct spaces are housed within Galleria Grafica Tokyo. The ground floor is a rental space for up-and-coming artists, while the second floor is home to works by the likes of Picasso, Miró, Giacometti, Matisse and Man Ray, and concentrates mainly on lithographs and prints.

★ Gallery Koyanagi

1-7-5 Ginza, Chuo-ku (3561 1896). Ginza station (Ginza, Hibiya, Marunouchi lines), exit A13 or Ginza-Itchome station (Yurakucho Line), exit 7. **Open** 11am-7pm Tue-Sat. **Map** p59.
This long-established gallery may have a reputation for photography, but that's by chance rather than design. It still represents photographer Hiroshi Sugimoto as well as animation queen Tabaimo, and works with notable foreign artists such as Thomas Ruff and Sophie Calle.

★ Ginza Graphic Gallery

DNP Ginza Bldg 1F, 7-7-2 Ginza, Chuo-ku (3571 5206, www.dnp.co.jp/gallery). Ginza station (Ginza, Hibiya, Marunouchi lines), exit A2. **Open** 11am- 7pm Mon-Fri; 11am-6pm Sat. **Map** p59.
One of Japan's largest printing companies presents contemporary design and graphics here. Japanese designers are prominent, but major international talents appear from time to time.

INAX Gallery

INAX Ginza Showroom 9F, 3-6-18 Kyobashi, Chuo-ku (5250 6530, www.inax.co.jp/Culture/gallery/1_tokyo. html). Ginza-Itchome station (Yurakucho line), exit 7 or Kyobashi station (Ginza line), exit 2. **Open** 10am-6pm Mon-Sat. Closed 1wk Aug. **Map** p59.
Major ceramics-maker INAX has an architecture bookshop on the ground floor here and two galleries upstairs. One gallery caters for emerging artists with a craft edge, while the other deals with exhibitions of traditional craft techniques from around the world.

★ Maison Hermès

Maison Hermès 8F Forum, 5-4-1 Ginza, Chuo-ku (3289 6811). Ginza station (Ginza, Hibiya, Marunouchi lines), exit B7. **Open** 11am-7pm Mon, Tue, Thur-Sun. **Map** p59.
The rounded glass-block walls of this beautiful, Renzo Piano-designed building both filter daylight and magnify neon at night. The gallery on the eighth floor holds shows of both international artists (such as Sarah Sze) and domestic darlings (such as Kohei Nawa).

Megumi Ogita

B1, 2-16-12 Ginza, Chuo-ku (3248 3405, www.megumiogita.com). Shintomicho station (Yurakucho line). **Open** noon-7pm Tue-Sat.
Tucked into a backstreet near Arataniurano (*see left*), Megumi Ogita is another good venue to catch up-and-coming Japanese contemporary work.

Nishimura Gallery

3rd Floor, Nihombashi Nikko Bldg, 2-10-8 Nihonbashi Chuo-ku (5203 2800, www.nishimura-gallery.com). Nihonbashi station (Ginza, Tozai lines), exit B1. **Open** 10.30am-6.30pm Tue-Sat. **Map** p59.
Tadanori Yokoo, Chieko Oshie and David Hockney all feature among the artists, both Japanese and international, appearing here.

★ Ota Fine Arts

Kintomi Soko bldg,4B, 2-18-19 Kachidoki, Chuo-ku (6273 8611, www.otafinearts.com). Kachidoki station (Oedo line), exit A2. **Open** 11am-7pm Tue-Sat.
Some of Japan's best-known contemporary artists – such as Yayoi Kusama, Tsuyoshi Ozawa and others who deal with the politics of identity – show at this well-established gallery. It's a 30-minute walk or five-minute cab from central Ginza.

★ Shiseido Gallery

Tokyo Ginza Shiseido Bldg B1, 8-8-3 Ginza, Chuo-ku (3572 3901, www.shiseido.co.jp/gallery/html). Shinbashi station (Yamanote line), Ginza exit; (Asakusa line), exit A3; (Ginza line), exit 1. **Open** 11am-7pm Tue-Sat; 11am-6pm Sun. **Map** p59.
Like Maison Hermès (*see above*), this place – run by cosmetics giant Shiseido – is more of a *kunsthalle* than a commercial gallery. It hosts important group and solo shows by contemporary Japanese and international artists such as Masato Nakamura and Roman Signer, as well as occasional retrospectives (Man Ray, for instance) and fashion-related shows. The gallery is located in the basement of the company's Ricardo Bofill-designed headquarters.

Mori Art Museum. *See p237.*

Tokyo Gallery
Shunya Bldg 7F, 8-10-5 Ginza, Chuo-ku (3571 1808, www.tokyo-gallery.com). Shinbashi station (Yamanote line), Ginza exit; (Asakusa line), exit A3; (Ginza line), exit 1. **Open** 11am-7pm Mon-Fri; 11am-5pm Sat. **Map** p59.
Tokyo Gallery shows modern and contemporary Japanese, Chinese and Korean artists.

HARAJUKU & AOYAMA
Canadian Embassy Gallery
B2, 7-3-38 Akasaka, Minato-ku (5412 6200, www.canadanet.or.jp). Aoyama-Itchome station (Hanzomon, Ginza, Oedo lines), exit 4. **Open** 9am-5.30pm Mon, Tue, Thur, Fri; 9am-8pm Sat.
Canada's best artists appear in the spacious, high-ceilinged granite basement of the distinctive, award-winning Canadian Embassy building, designed by Moriyama & Teshima Architects.

Gallery 360°
2F, 5-1-27 Minami-Aoyama, Minato-ku (3406 5823, www.360.co.jp). Omotesando station (Chiyoda, Ginza, Hanzomon lines), exit B4. **Open** noon-7pm Mon-Sat. **Map** p65.
This well-located space emphasises works on paper and multiples by the likes of Lawrence Wiener and Takashi Homma, as well as examining the work of Fluxus, Buckminster Fuller and others.

Spiral
Spiral Bldg 1F, 5-6-23 Minami-Aoyama, Minato-ku (3498 1171, www.spiral.co.jp). Omotesando station (Chiyoda, Ginza, Hanzomon lines), exit B1. **Open** 11am-8pm daily. Closed 10 May, 1wk Aug, 1wk Dec-Jan. **Map** p65.
A ramp spirals around the circular open space at one end of this Fumihiko Maki-designed building, hence the gallery's name. A wide range of fashion, art and design shows are hosted at Spiral, and the building's also home to a café, bar, interior goods store and record/CD shop.

IKEBUKURO
Misako & Rosen
3-27-6 Kita-Otsuka, Toshima-ku (6276 1452, www.misakoandrosen.com/en). Otsuka station (Yamanote line). **Open** noon-7pm Tue-Sat; noon-5pm Sun.
This tiny space tucked into a residential area shows a wide range of contemporary painting and photography from young Japanese and international artists.

MARUNOUCHI
Base Gallery
Koura Bldg 1 1F, 1-1-6 Nihonbashi-Kayabacho, Chuo-ku (5623 6655, www.basegallery.com). Kayabacho station (Hibiya, Tozai lines), exits 7, 8 or Nihonbashi station (Asakusa, Ginza, Tozai lines), exit D2. **Open** 11am-7pm Mon-Sat. **Map** p77.
This well-established space represents blue-chip contemporary Japanese artists, such as painter Shinro Ohtake, and younger names, which include photographer Tsukasa Yokozawa.

Forum Art Shop

*B Block 1F, Tokyo International Forum,
3-5-1 Marunouchi, Chiyoda-ku (3286 6716,
http://paper.cup.com/forum). Yurakucho station
(Yamanote line), Tokyo International Forum
exit; (Yurakucho line), exit A4B.* **Open** 10am-
8pm daily. **Map** p59.

Inside architect Rafael Vinoly's landmark convention
and performance centre (*see p74*), this space showcases contemporary Japanese objets, arts and crafts.
It also doubles as a shop, selling funky gifts.

Gallerie Sho Contemporary Art

*Sansho Bldg B1F, 3-2-9 Nihonbashi, Chuo-ku
(3275 1008, www.g-sho.com). Tokyo station
(JR, Marunouchi lines), Yaesu Central exit;
Nihonbashi station (Ginza line), exit B3.*
Open 11am-7pm Mon-Fri; 11am-5pm Sat.
The works of brand-name artists like Haring,
Basquiat and Warhol can be found in this gallery's
collection, which also shows a number of both young
and unestablished Japanese artists.

Zeit-Foto Salon

*Matsumoto Bldg 4F, 1-10-5 Kyobashi, Chuo-ku
(3535 7188, www.zeit-foto.com). Tokyo station
(Yamanote, Marunouchi lines), Yaesu exit or
Kyobashi station (Ginza line), exit B6.* **Open**
10.30am-6.30pm Tue-Fri; 10.30am-5.30pm Sat.
Closed 1wk Aug, 2wks Dec-Jan. **Map** p77.

This space behind the Bridgestone Museum of Art
(*see p76*) claims to be the first photography gallery in
Japan (it opened in 1978). It's certainly one of the
strongest, with over 3,000 works in its possession.
Expect inspired, reliable and wide-ranging exhibitions by Japanese and international photographers.

ROPPONGI

Gallery Ma

*Toto Nogizaka Bldg 3F, 1-24-3 Minami-Aoyama,
Minato-ku (3402 1010, www.toto.co.jp/gallerma).
Nogizaka station (Chiyoda line), exit 3.* **Open**
11am-6pm Tue-Thur, Sat; 11am-7pm Fri. Closed
3wks Dec-Jan. **Map** p87.

SCAI The Bathhouse.

Sponsored by bathroom appliance-maker Toto, Gallery Ma holds some of the city's best modern and contemporary architecture shows. Foreign architects featured recently include Angelo Mangiarotti (from Italy), Seung H-Sang (Korea) and Yung Ho Chang (China). There's a small bookshop on site too.

SHIBUYA

Gallerie Le Déco
Le Déco Bldg, 3-16-3 Shibuya, Shibuya-ku (5485 5188, http://home.att.ne.jp/gamma/ledeco). Shibuya station (Yamanoko line), east exit; (Ginza line), Toyoko exit; (Hanzomon line), exit 9. **Open** 11am-7pm Tue-Sun. Closed 2wks Dec-Jan. **Map** p93.
Regular exhibitions of work by young Japanese artists working in a range of media fill the six floors of this rental space. There's also a café and lounge area on the ground floor.

Tokyo Wonder Site
1-19-8 Jinnan, Shibuya-ku (3463 0603, www.tokyo-ws.org/english/shibuya). Shibuya station (Yamanote, Ginza lines), Hachiko exit; (Hanzomon line), exit 7. **Open** 11am-7pm Tue-Sun. **Map** p93.
The most significant and convenient of a trio of government-funded sites that aim to nurture young creatives with gallery space, regular seminars, a café and an art market.
Other locations Cosmos Aoyama South 3F 5-53-67 Jingumae, Shibuya-ku (5766 3732); 2-4-16 Hongo, Bunkyo-ku (5689 5331)

SHINJUKU

Public art is relatively scarce in Tokyo, but near the west exit of Shinjuku station is **Shinjuku I-Land**, a collection of outdoor pieces by such big names as Daniel Buren, Luciano Fabro and Roy Lichtenstein.

Kenji Taki Gallery
102, 3-18-2 Nishi-Shinjuku, Shinjuku-ku (3378 6051, www.kenjitaki.com). Hatsudai station (Keio New Line), east exit. **Open** noon-7pm Tue-Sat.
In the shadow of Tokyo Opera City, Kenji Taki exhibits contemporary artists from home (Eiji Watanabe) and abroad (Wolfgang Laib).
▶ *Wako Works of Art (see right) is located in the same building.*

★ Tokyo Opera City Art Gallery
3-20-2 Nishi-Shinjuku, Shinjuku-ku (5353 0756, www.operacity.jp). Hatsudai station (Keio New Line), east exit. **Open** 11am-7pm Tue-Thur; 11am-8pm Fri, Sat.
With money from Odakyu Railways, NTT and other giant corporations, Opera City is one of the city's largest and best-funded private contemporary art

---

spaces. As well as its own exhibitions of Japanese and international artists, it brings in touring shows from around the world and has in recent years enjoyed success with architecture exhibitions.

Wako Works of Art
101, 3-18-2 Nishi-Shinjuku, Shinjuku-ku (3373 2860). Hatsudai station (Keio New Line), east exit. **Open** 11am-7pm Tue-Sat.
Wako shows blue-chip and/or conceptual contemporary artists, both Japanese and foreign. Among the big names to appear are Gerhard Richter and Wolfgang Tillmans.

YANAKA

Gallery Jin
Yamaoka Bldg 1F, 2-5-22 Yanaka, Taito-ku (5814 8118, www.galleryjin.com). Nezu station (Chiyoda line), exit 1. **Open** noon-7pm Wed-Sun.
This small space in the residential Yanaka neighbourhood shows both two- and three-dimensional works by young Japanese artists.

★ SCAI The Bathhouse
Kashiwayu-Ato, 6-1-23 Yanaka, Taito-ku (3821 1144, www.scaithebathhouse.com). Nippori station (Yamanote line), south exit. **Open** noon-7pm Tue-Sat. Closed 2wks Aug, 2wks Dec-Jan. **Map** p107.
Formerly a bathhouse (the building is over 200 years old), this high-ceilinged space in a charming neighbourhood near Ueno Park features contemporary Japanese artists (Tatsuo Miyajima) and international practitioners (Lee Bul, Julian Opie).

FURTHER AFIELD

Aoyama Hideki
2-30-6 Kami-Meguro, Meguro-ku (3711 4099, www.aoyamahideki.com). Naka-Meguro station (Hibiya, Toyoko lines). **Open** 11am-7pm Mon-Sat.

ARTS & ENTERTAINMENT

INSIDE TRACK ART APPS

For iPhone users, the Tokyo Art app and Tokyo Art Beat app both use Tokyo Art Beat's database to list and locate galleries and museums by genre, medium or area. They use geolocation information and maps to walk you right to galleries' doors, which can be very, very useful with hard-to-find spaces.

The Aoyama Hideki gallery excels in conceptual art and three-dimensional work, which includes the occasional architecture exhibition.

Hiromi Yoshii Gallery

6F, 1-3-2 Kiyosumi, Koto-ku (5620 0555, www.hiromiyoshii.com). Kiyosumi-Shirakawa station (Hanzomon, Oedo lines), exit A3. **Open** 11am-7pm Tue-Sat.
Yoshii specialises in two areas: very young Japanese artists and new talent from art fairs abroad.

Mizuma Art Gallery

Kagura Bldg 2F, 3-13 Ichigaya-Tamachi, Shinjuku-ku (3268 2500, www.mizuma-art.co.jp). Iidabashi station (JR lines), west exit; Ichigaya station (Nanboku, Yurakucho lines), exit 5. **Open** 11am-7pm Tue-Sat. Closed 2wks Dec-Jan.
In its new space in Ichigaya, the Mizuma Art Gallery gallery presents some of Japan's hottest contemporary artists, among them Makoto Aida and Muneteru Ujino.

★ Nanzuka Underground

Shirokane Art Complex, 3-1-15 Shirokane, Minato-ku (3400 0075, www.nug.jp). Shirokane-Takanawa station (Mita, Nanboku lines), exit 4. **Open** 1-8pm Wed-Sun. **Map** p93.
Nanzuka presents new generation art with a hip, urban edge. Illustrations, futuristic fashion and vintage record sleeves have all adorned the walls of this gallery. When Diesel wanted a curator to add art to its Aoyama store, it tapped Nanzuka to deliver suitably quirky work.

★ Radi-um

2-5-17 Nihonbashi-Bakurocho, Chuo-ku (3662 2666, www.roentgenwerke.com). Bakurocho station (JR Sobu line), exit 5; Bakuro-Yokoyama station (Shinjuku line), exit A1. **Open** 11am-7pm Tue-Sat. **Map** p87.
This interesting space has gone through several moves, name and size changes. It was originally called Roentgenwerke and located in Roppongi, before influential gallerist Tsutomu Ikeuchi moved his space to Bakurocho in 2008. Most of the exhibitions here are conceptual work by Japanese artists.

ShugoArts

5F, 1-3-2 Kiyosumi, Koto-ku (5621 6434, www.shugoarts.com). Kiyosumi-Shirakawa station (Hanzomon, Oedo lines), exit A3. **Open** noon-7pm Tue-Sat.
One of three major galleries in Kiyosumi's must-see art complex is ShugoArts, showing an eclectic range of contemporary Japanese and international artists, such as Shimabuku and Candice Breitz.

Soh Gallery

2-14-35 Midori-cho, Koganei City (042 382 5338, www.soh-gallery.com). Higashi-Koganei station (Chuo line), north exit. **Open** 1-7pm Fri-Sun; by appt Wed, Thur. Closed 1wk Dec-Jan.
Soh Gallery has long-standing relationships with top Japanese artists such as Yasumasa Morimura, Kishio Suga and Mika Yoshizawa.

★ Taka Ishii Gallery

5F, 1-3-2 Kiyosumi, Koto-ku (5646 6050, www.takaishiigallery.com). Kiyosumi-Shirakawa station (Hanzomon, Oedo lines), exit A3. **Open** 11am-7pm Tue-Sat.
Taka Ishii Gallery shows photography by major international and Japanese artists (Nobuyuki Araki, Naoya Hatakeyama, Thomas Demand).

Taro Nasu Gallery

1-2-11 Higashi-Kanda, Chiyoda-ku (5856 5713, www.taronasugallery.com). Bakurocho station (JR Sobu line), exit 2. **Open** 11am-7pm Tue-Sat. **Map** p87.
Works by young and emerging Japanese and international artists – the likes of Taiji Matsue – are displayed here, under Taro Nasu's unusually thin fluorescent strip lighting.

★ Tomio Koyama Gallery

7F, 1-3-2 Kiyosumi, Koto-ku (6222 1006). Kiyosumi-Shirakawa station (Hanzomon, Oedo lines), exit A3. **Open** 11am-7pm Tue-Sat.
One of Japan's most powerful contemporary galleries, Tomio Koyama has the clout to pick and choose whom it represents. It has chosen major Japanese artists, including Takashi Murakami and Yoshitomo Nara, as well as international figures such as American Dennis Hollingsworth. This is the fourth of the main spaces in the Kiyosumi complex.

★ Yamamoto Gendai

Shirokane Art Complex 3F, 3-1-15 Shirokane, Minato-ku (6383 0626, www.yamamoto gendai.org). Shirokane-Takanawa station (Mita, Nanboku lines), exit 4. **Open** 11am-7pm Tue-Sat.
The best-known of the galleries in this gallery-packed building, Yamamoto Gendai features such up-and-coming Japanese talent as Motohiko Odani, as well as controversial artists including Hermann Nitsch. The gallery also stages the occasional live performance and symposium.

Gay & Lesbian

The closet's bigger than it looks.

Appearances can be deceiving when it comes to homosexuality in Japan. Despite the growing visibility of celebrities who are openly (or at least seemingly) gay, a flourishing gay culture has yet to emerge at street level. The high pressure of social conformity keeps most Japanese gays and lesbians in the closet.

The main gay district, **Shinjuku Ni-chome**, is home to around 200 gay bars, yet remains a virtual ghost town until evening falls. But when the lights come on, the fun begins. When the nation's gays and lesbians are away from the prying eyes of family and co-workers, life is a cabaret.

THE SCENE

The power of the closet means that gay political and social organisations in Japan are tiny and few, and related awareness is low. For instance, while Western gays and lesbians almost universally support gender and racial equality, it is not unusual for queer establishments in Japan to exclude people because of race, gender or age.

Most bars for gay men in Tokyo can't comfortably hold more than 20 people, which makes visiting one an intimate experience; it's akin to being in the owner's living room. The atmosphere and decor are very much a reflection of his personality, and every visitor will have to speak to him – or a member or his one- or two-person staff – personally. The same holds true at the far smaller number of bars that cater specifically to women.

QUEER INFORMATION

You can find more in *Otoko Machi Map* (*OMM*), an annual guide to gay bars and venues nationwide, with thousands of listings and numerous maps. Since the 1990s, *OMM* has evolved from a staple-bound booklet into a glossy paperback of more than 300 pages. In 2004, it received the sincerest form of flattery when an imitator called *Gay Navi* appeared. Both are available at any gay bookshop, as are *G-Men*, *Samson* and *Badi*, brick-sized magazines whose photographs, cartoons and classified ads will give you

some idea of the scene. These magazines are worth a look even if you don't read Japanese.

These resources are aimed at men, but queer women in Tokyo have a valuable resource of their own, in the form of the bilingual lesbian website **Out Japan** (www.outjapan.com); cultural topics get random but up-to-date coverage on the bizarrely named **Tokyo Wrestling** (www.tokyowrestling.com).

BARS & CLUBS

Advocates Bar
7th Tenka Bldg B1F, 2-18-1 Shinjuku, Shinjuku-ku (3358 8638). Shinjuku-Sanchome station (Fukutoshin, Marunouchi, Shinjuku lines), exits C7, C8. **Open** 8pm-4am daily. **No credit cards. Map** p101.

INSIDE TRACK
TRANSGENDER POLITICS

Tokyo has had a transsexual politician since 2003. Aya Kamikawa, a councillor for the Setagaya Ward, ran on a platform advocating rights for women, gays and those with gender identity disorder. Though she ran as a woman, she left blank the gender section of her electoral application form, and the ministry in charge of elections insists she must be legally considered male. She won re-election in 2007.

This small and smoky basement dance bar has a separate entrance around the corner from its sister, Advocates Café (*see below*). Weekend DJ nights are hit and miss; follow the crowds from Advocates Café. There is sometimes a cover charge.

★ Advocates Café
7th Tenka Bldg 1F, 2-18-1 Shinjuku, Shinjuku-ku (3358 3988). Shinjuku-Sanchome station (Fukutoshin, Marunouchi, Shinjuku lines), exits C7, C8. **Open** 6pm-4am Mon-Sat; 6pm-1am Sun. **Credit** AmEx, DC, JCB, MC, V. **Map** p101.
With its zebra-striped walls and mirrored disco balls, this is not your average pavement café. But then Tokyo doesn't really do average pavement cafés: such places are still very rare, and this is one of the few spots in the city where punters spill

out on to the street. Happy hour is 6-9pm Monday to Friday, and there's also a 'beer blast' on Sunday (6-9pm; all the beer you can drink for ¥1,000). Open to all sexes and sexualities. A good place to find out where the crowds are heading.

★ Arty Farty
Dai 33 Kyutei Bldg 2F, 2-11-6 Shinjuku, Shinjuku-ku (3356 5388, www.arty-farty.net). Shinjuku-Sanchome station (Fukutoshin, Marunouchi, Shinjuku lines), exits C7, C8. **Open** 6pm-5am Tue-Thur; 7pm-5am Fri; 5pm-5am Sat; 5pm-3am Sun. **Admission** ¥800 Mon-Thur; ¥900-¥1,000 Fri-Sun. **Credit** AmEx, DC, JCB, MC, V. **Map** p101.
This bar with a dancefloor offers DJs on weekends and mint-flavoured beer any time. Arty Farty is

Love Father, Love Son

If you can't marry your partner, why not adopt them?

Same-sex marriage may be a hot issue in the Western world, but it's not even a faint blip on Japan's political radar. However, gays and lesbians here do have a way to form legally recognised families, and it's been around for generations. *Yoshiengumi*, or adult adoption, is a legal device whereby two men become father and son, or two women become mother and daughter. The older partner officially becomes the parent and the younger one the child, no matter what the age difference.

The adoption of infants is rare in Japan, but families seeking heirs – to run the family business, for instance – have often adopted adults. The same legal device is used by same-sex couples as a non-marital route to forming a family. One famous example was lesbian novelist Nobuko Yoshiya (1896-1973), who made a daughter of her beloved live-in 'secretary' Chiyo Monma, only three years her junior.

Otsuka 'Tac' Takuya – owner of Tac's Knot (*see p247*) – has published an introductory guide to the subject. He tells of a gay couple who bought a house together but could register only one owner. When that partner died, his blood relatives claimed the property, and the survivor lost everything. According to Otsuka, same-sex couples who apply for adoption do it mainly to avoid such negative outcomes, but there are also positive aspects to the arrangement. Many Japanese companies offer employee benefits that extend to immediate family members. More importantly, an adoptive relationship

guarantees a partner's right to make hospital visits and have a voice in medical decision-making, which might otherwise be vetoed by blood kin.

One of the drawbacks of adoption as an alternative to marriage is the unequal status of the partners, with one partner becoming the 'parent'. In their memoir *Love Upon the Chopping Board*, bi-national lesbian couple Marou Izumo and Claire Maree write that they considered adoption, but found the idea of one addressing the other as 'Mom' to be just a little too weird.

Another drawback to adoption is that it involves a name change for one partner. This essentially means coming out to one's family and – more significantly in Japan's conformist society – also to one's employer.

Inheritance laws also complicate the issue, with the outcome depending on whether it's the 'parent' or the 'child' who dies first. And trying to circumvent the laws by filing complementary wills doesn't necessarily work in Japan since, according to Otsuka, local officials who review the wills must reject anything contrary to the public interest – but the definition of 'public interest' is left to their discretion. Some couples' wishes tally with the public interest, others are less fortunate. In contrast, adult adoptions must be accepted if the paperwork is in order.

Adoption seems to hold more appeal for older couples. Younger ones tend to put it off in the hope that real marriage will one day be available. But until then, at least gay and lesbian couples in Japan have a plan B.

very popular among foreigners, including members of Gay Friends Tokyo, an international English-speaking social group that often meets here on Wednesdays. Women are allowed 'with their gay friends' on Fridays and Sundays. *Photo p246.*
► *For more about Gay Friends Tokyo, visit http://groups.yahoo.com/group/gayfriendstokyo.*

★ Chestnut & Squirrel
Ooishi Bldg 3F (Minx), 3-7 Shibuya, Shibuya-ku (090 9834 4842, http://2d-k.oops.jp/cs/cs.html). Shibuya station (Yamanote line), east exit; (Ginza line), Toyoko exit; (Hanzomon line), exit 9. **Open** 7pm-midnight Wed. **No credit cards. Map** p93.
Although open only one night a week, this small lesbian bar serves good food and draws a lively international crowd, including the occasional man. Mistress Chu speaks English and was one of the organisers of Team Japan at the 2002 Gay Games in Sydney. The name is a mischievous bilingual pun, as 'chestnut and squirrel' in Japanese is 'kuri to risu' – a homophone for 'clitoris'.

★ Dragon
Accord Bldg B1F, 2-11-4 Shinjuku, Shinjuku-ku (3341 0606). Shinjuku-Sanchome station (Fukutoshin, Marunouchi, Shinjuku lines), exits C7, C8. **Open** 6pm-4am Mon-Thur, Sun; 6pm-4am Fri, Sat. **Admission** free.
No credit cards. Map p101.
Until around 9pm each night, only the address, the neon and the small-screen erotica give any clue to this being a gay bar. Then the muscular staff strip to their sauciest attire for the benefit of the boys. It's larger than most Ni-chome joints, with a dancefloor and a few outdoor seats. The early evening beer or cocktail 'blast' is an all-you-can-drink special for ¥1,000. Dragon welcomes women and men.

Fellow
2-63-5 Ikebukuro, Toshima-ku (3971 5756). Ikebukuro station (Yamanote line), north exit; (Marunouchi, Yurakucho lines), exits 20A, 20B. **Open** 7pm-2am Mon-Wed, Fri, Sat. **No credit cards. Map** p69.
Drawing mainly middle-aged athletes, this is a good place for a refreshing cool-down drink after a workout at the Toshima Ward Sports Center, just one block away across the tracks. Master Naka is a very good cook, and walking through his door means you have ordered a plate of food that is likely to include quiche. Clientele and staff are friendly, but you'll need to speak at least some Japanese to make yourself understood.

Fuji
B1F, 2-12-16 Shinjuku, Shinjuku-ku (3354 2707). Shinjuku-Sanchome station (Fukutoshin, Marunouchi, Shinjuku lines), exits C7, C8. **Open** 8.30pm-3am Mon-Thur, Sun; 8.30pm-5am Fri, Sat. **No credit cards. Map** p101.

Shinjuku Ni-chome.

This long-standing basement karaoke bar has begun to draw a younger, more international crowd than in the past. Grab yourself a microphone and show them what you're made of.

GB
Shinjuku Plaza Bldg B1F, 2-12-3 Shinjuku, Shinjuku-ku (3352 8972, www.techtrans-japan.com/GB). Shinjuku-Sanchome station (Fukutoshin, Marunouchi, Shinjuku lines), exits C7, C8. **Open** 8pm-2am Mon-Thur, Sun; 8pm-3am Fri, Sat. **No credit cards. Map** p101.
Shinjuku's GB has long been the most famous bar in Tokyo for East/West encounters of the gay kind, and is also handily attached to a 'business hotel'. A large venue by Tokyo standards, GB has a less relaxed atmosphere than many places but is always pretty busy. It admits men only, except for one day of the year – Halloween.

Go Round
2-16-12 Shinjuku, Shinjuku-ku (3350 1050, www.bar-goround.com), Shinjuku-Sanchome station (Fukutoshin, Marunouchi, Shinjuku lines), exits C7, C8. **Open** 7pm-3am Mon-Thur, Sun; 6pm-5am Fri, Sat, holidays. **Credit** AmEx, DC, JCB, MC, V. **Map** p101.
Go Round is smaller inside than its corner location and wide, windowless façade would otherwise suggest. Its two-tone decor includes a black chandelier, a white merry-go-round horse, black and white walls and floors, and Guinness on tap (which goes for ¥500 until 8pm daily).

Hijouguchi
2-12-16 Shinjuku, Shinjuku-ku (3341 5445, www.hijouguchi.com), Shinjuku-Sanchome station

ARTS & ENTERTAINMENT

**INSIDE TRACK
A BITE ON THE SIDE**

When you get peckish in Ni-chome, head to **Cocolo Café** (2-14-6 Shinjuku, Shinjuku-ku, 5366 9899, www.akiplan.com/cocolo-cafe). The district's most popular eaterie has a huge menu of international fare and is usually packed. It's also a good place to pick up flyers for upcoming queer events.

(Fukutoshin, Marunouchi, Shinjuku lines), exits C7, C8. **Open** varies. **No credit cards. Map** p101.
'Hijoguchi' means 'Emergency Exit', but the English signage at this side-street bar just says 'Exit'. (The signs are done in factory-issue style, making them easy to miss.) The bartenders' island inside the main entrance leaves barely enough room for customers to squeeze around the edges. Make your own 'emergency exit' through the unmarked door at the rear to find a second bar area. Here, the drinks counter hugs one wall, and a DJ booth clings to another, leaving a surprisingly spacious (by Ni-chome standards) dance-floor in the middle. Hijouguchi has little personality of its own, but hosts a chameleon-like array of events, sometimes including the women-only party 'Girlfriend'. The food menu includes *izakaya*-style snacks such as spring rolls and sautéed gizzards.

Hug

2-15-8 Shinjuku, Shinjuku-ku (5379 5085). Shinjuku-Sanchome station (Fukutoshin, Marunouchi, Shinjuku lines), exits C7, C8. **Open** 9pm-6am Mon-Sat. **No credit cards. Map** p101.
A women-only karaoke bar that tends to attract a clientele that is mostly aged 30 and above.

Arty Farty. *See p244.*

★ Kinsmen

2F, 2-18-5 Shinjuku, Shinjuku-ku (3354 4949). Shinjuku-Sanchome station (Fukutoshin, Marunouchi, Shinjuku lines), exits C7, C8. **Open** 8pm-3am Tue-Thur; 7pm-3am Fri, Sat; 7pm-1am Sun. **No credit cards. Map** p101.
A fixture on the anglophone gay scene for more than two decades, this spacious bar is run by a jovial pair of guys who go by the unlikely names of Nori and Ebi (Seaweed and Shrimp). Beyond its famous, giant *ikebana* flower arrangements, you'll find scented candles, tiny cacti, antique-looking Western furniture and a piano that sometimes actually gets played. Men, women and foreigners are made to feel equally welcome at this very laid-back place.

Kinswomyn

Daiichi Tenka Bldg 3F, 2-15-10 Shinjuku, Shinjuku-ku (3354 8720). Shinjuku-Sanchome station (Fukutoshin, Marunouchi, Shinjuku lines), exits C7, C8. **Open** 8pm-4am Mon, Wed-Sun. **No credit cards. Map** p101.
Kinswomyn (a sibling of the nearby Kinsmen bar; *see above*) is a popular women-only bar. Old-guard butch-femme types occasionally drop by, but for the most part it's home to a cosy, relaxed crowd.

Kusuo

Sunflower Bldg 3F, 2-17-1 Shinjuku, Shinjuku-ku (3354 5050, www5.ocn.ne.jp/~kusuo), Shinjuku-Sanchome station (Fukutoshin, Marunouchi, Shinjuku lines), exits C7, C8. **Open** 8pm-4am Mon-Fri, Sun; 8pm-5am Sat. **No credit cards. Map** p101.
A karaoke cathedral and one of the biggest gay bars in Tokyo, Kusuo not only has plenty of room to dance the night away but sometimes offers tango or square-dancing lessons in the afternoon too. What it lacks in refined decoration – the walls and ceiling are sloppily painted black – it more than makes up for in abundant breathing room and an exuberant, foreigner-friendly staff. Another plus is that women are officially welcome, though their first drink will cost ¥1,500, compared to ¥1,000 for men.

Monsoon

Shimazaki Bldg 6F, 2-14-9 Shinjuku, Shinjuku-ku (3354 0470). Shinjuku-Sanchome station (Fukutoshin, Marunouchi, Shinjuku lines), exits C7, C8. **Open** 3pm-6am daily.
Credit AmEx, MC, V. **Map** p101.
Small and inexpensive, this formerly men-only bar now opens its doors to everyone. The bar's unusually long opening hours make it one of the few spots in Ni-chome where you can get a drink before sunset. The artwork on the walls changes every few months.

★ Motel #203

203 Sunny Corpo Bldg, 2-7-2 Shinjuku, Shinjuku-ku (6383 4649, www.bar-motel.com). Shinjuku-Sanchome station (Fukutoshin,

Papi Chulos.

Marunouchi, Shinjuku lines), exits C7, C8.
Open 8pm-4am Mon, Wed-Sat; 8pm-2am Sun.
No credit cards. **Map** p101.
It's women-only here, except on Thursdays, and the proprietress is a legend of the local lesbian scene for hosting the ever-popular Goldfinger and Girlfriend lesbian events. The bar is a cosy, slightly kitsch spot with leather sofas and a disco ball. The first drink will cost you ¥1,000, the rest will be a little cheaper.

Papi Chulos
M&T Bldg 8F, 2-12-15 Shinjuku, Shinjuku-ku (3356 9833). Shinjuku-Sanchome station (Fukutoshin, Marunouchi, Shinjuku lines), exits C7, C8. **Open** 6pm-5am daily. **No credit cards**. **Map** p101.
Papi Chulos is a friendly place, welcoming all genders and nationalities. The agreeable, young, English-speaking master, Masa, enjoys experimenting with cocktail recipes. A small open-air balcony and a loft with fur-draped sofas make this an unusually comfortable bar, while the window-box installation art makes it a quirky one as well.

Snack 24
2-28-18 Asakusa, Taito-ku (3843 4424). Asakusa station (Asakusa line), exit A3; (Ginza line), exits 7, 8. **Open** 6pm-2am daily. **Admission** ¥2,800 (incl 3 drinks). **No credit cards**. **Map** p45.
This bar, associated with the nearby branch of 24 Kaikan (*see p249* **24-hour Party People**), consists of two sections, with street clothes worn in one area and traditional Japanese loincloths in the other. Regular customers bring their own loincloths, but these can also be rented for ¥500, and first-timers will be taught how to tie one on. Occasional patrols by a flashlight-wielding barman ensure minimal

hanky-panky in the main areas – but there is a back room. The crowd tends to be mostly middle-aged or older. Wednesday nights are particularly popular as they offer all-you-can-drink deals for ¥2,800.

Tac's Knot
3-11-12 Shinjuku, Shinjuku-ku (3341 9404), www.asahi-net.or.jp/~km5t-ootk/tacsknot.html). Shinjuku-Sanchome station (Fukutoshin, Marunouchi, Shinjuku lines), exits C7, C8. **Open** 8pm-2am daily. **Admission** ¥1,200 (incl 1 drink). **No credit cards**. **Map** p101.
Each month, the walls of this tiny cocktail bar display the work of a different local gay artist. Master Tac is a local gay community leader and an artist of some note himself – his bejewelled reliquaries for pubic hair caused a stir back in the 1990s. Tac speaks some English, but prefers to get warmed up first in Japanese. *Photo p248.*

Tactics
Princess Ichiban-kan Bldg 3F, 3-22-3 Shinbashi, Minato-ku (070 5086 8839, www2c.airnet.ne.jp/ tactics), Shinbashi station (Yamanote line), Karasumori exit. **Open** 6pm-midnight Mon-Thur, Sat; 6pm-5am Fri. **No credit cards**.
West and south of Shinbashi station are hundreds of bars where hard-working Japanese businessmen drown the stresses of their day. At least 50 of those bars, including Tactics, are gay. The clientele here consists mostly of salarymen in their 30s, direct from the office in their suits and ties, while the staff are predominately younger guys in T-shirts. Foreign visitors are made to feel welcome, and long-term expats are also sometimes part of the scene. Drinks here cost ¥1,500 for the first, and ¥800 thereafter. **Other locations** 1F, 2-7-3 Shinjuku, Shinjuku-ku (3354 5050).

Tac's Knot. *See p247.*

SEX CLUBS

Dozens of Tokyo *hattenba* (sex clubs) are listed in *OMM*. They're usually small apartments or offices turned into 'cruising boxes', with flimsy partition walls, dim lighting and dodgy music. Some have themes (naked, swimwear, jockstraps and so on) on different nights – but the real theme is always the same. Those listed below accept foreign customers.

Pay close attention to the addresses, as external signage is often minimal or non-existent. Condoms are generally provided at the door, but it's wise to bring your own. When you arrive, a voice behind the counter may ask if you speak Japanese. Just say '*hai*'.

24 Kaikan
24 Kaikan Asakusa *2-29-16 Asakusa, Taito-ku (5827 2424). Asakusa station (Asakusa line), exit A3; (Ginza line) exits 7, 8.* **Admission** ¥2,300 5am-9pm; ¥2,800 9pm-5am. **Map** p45.
24 Kaikan Shinjuku *2-13-1 Shinjuku, Shinjuku-ku (3354 2424). Shinjuku-Sanchome station (Fukutoshin, Marunouchi, Shinjuku lines), exits C7, C8.* **Admission** ¥2,600 up to 13hrs. **Map** p101.
24 Kaikan Ueno *1-8-7 Kita-Ueno, Taito-ku (3847 2424). Ueno station (Yamanote line), Iriya exit; (Ginza, Hibiya lines), exit 9.* **Admission** ¥2,400 5am-9pm; ¥2,800 9pm-5am. **All** *www.juno.dti.ne.jp/~kazuo24.* **Open** 24hrs daily. **No credit cards**.
For details about the three 24 Kaikan mega sex clubs, *see right* **24-hour Party People**.

Jinya
2-30-19 Ikebukuro, Toshima-ku (5951 0995). Ikebukuro station (Yamanote line), west exit; (Marunouchi, Yurakucho, lines), exit C1.

Open 24hrs daily. **Admission** ¥2,200. **No credit cards. Map** p69.
This gay bathhouse may be smaller than the three 24 Kaikan, but it certainly dwarfs ordinary *hattenba*. Facilities include a refreshment/television room, a communal bath, a sauna, private rooms with beds and locking doors, futon rooms with curtained doorways, and a large porn-viewing lounge with sofas and futons. You'll be issued with a towel and bathrobe upon entering the premises.

Spartacus
MK Bldg 4F, 2-14-3 Ikebukuro, Toshima-ku (5951 6556). Ikebukuro station (Yamanote line), west exit; (Marunouchi, Yurakucho, lines), exit C1. **Open** 24hrs daily. **Admission** ¥1,500; ¥1,000 5am-11am. **No credit cards**. **Map** p69.
The adverts for Spartacus say nobody 'over 40 or ill-mannered' will be admitted. As the club is on the fourth floor of a lift-less building, your physical state on arrival may reveal whether you're over the age limit. Then the cashier can reveal whether he is feeling ill-mannered. On weeknights, the maze-like interior can be as dark and silent as a tomb, but it gets much busier at weekends. Rikkyo University is nearby. Dress code: nude.

Treffpunkt
Fukutomi Bldg 4F, 2-13-14 Akasaka, Minato-ku (5563 0523). Akasaka station (Chiyoda line), exits 2, 5A, 5B. **Open** noon-11pm daily. **Admission** ¥1,000. **No credit cards**.
A small club near Tokyo's business areas, laid out in such a way that it takes a while to explore all the nooks and crannies (including one alcove with a sling). Even on a Sunday evening, when the surrounding area is dead, Treffpunkt is likely to be busy, with many foreigners in the mix. Underwear is forbidden at weekends. It is worth noting that unlike most sex clubs, which are open 24 hours a day, Treffpunkt closes at 11pm.

HOST CLUBS

'Host bar' is Japanese English for a place to hire rent boys. Japan's prostitution laws – at least as applied – pertain only to certain heterosexual acts, leaving gay bordellos free to operate openly. There are at least 14 such establishments in Ni-chome alone. At the one listed below, hosts will service foreigners. Step inside, have a drink at the bar, look over the assembled staff and take your pick.

King of College
2-14-5 Shinjuku, Shinjuku-ku (3352 3930, www.kocnet.jp). Shinjuku-Sanchome station (Fukutoshin, Marunouchi, Shinjuku lines), exits C7, C8. **Open** 6pm-4am daily. **Credit** AmEx, DC, JCB, MC, V. **Map** p101.

24-hour Party People

A trio of sex clubs where men can be men.

Tokyo's gay bars tend to be tiny and intimate, and its sex clubs tend to be tiny and cramped. One astonishing exception is the **24 (Niju-Yon) Kaikan** *(see left)*, a sexual 'theme park' so big it occupies three whole buildings in Asakusa, Ueno and Shinjuku. One foreign customer calls it 'Tokyo's best-kept secret'.

The procedure is the same at each establishment. Put your shoes in a small locker out front, then hand in the key and the entrance fee (¥2,300 to ¥2,800 depending on the time and location) in exchange for a towel, bathrobe and key to a bigger locker for the rest of your clothes. Once inside, the first item on your agenda is a Japanese-style communal bath.

At the five-storey building in Asakusa, this means sitting between paintings on opposite walls by Tagame Gengoroh, the famous Japanese erotic artist. Both show fierce, heavily muscled men in loincloths riding *mikoshi* portable shrines (a reference to the annual Sanja Festival in Asakusa). The hyper-masculine Tagame type is unlikely to be seen in person, though, as the Asakusa clientele tends towards grey-haired, older men and a few long-haired 'new halfs' (transsexuals). The bath area also includes two saunas (one dark) and a suffocatingly hot steam room, as well as several two-man shower stalls with latching doors.

Over at the ten-storey building in Ueno, the baths are bigger and so are the men, with lots of bodybuilders and robust blue-collar types. (In fact, most of the tenth floor is a large, well-equipped weights room.) The wall above the main tub is adorned with a Tagame mural of seven virile men in various states of traditional undress. It gives the place a slight Baths of Pompeii atmosphere in which you can imagine that burly fellow with the ripples lapping his nipples to be a horny centurion. The shower area has double-occupancy stalls.

The seven-storey Shinjuku operation – which opened in 2003 – has the largest bath area of all, including more double shower cubicles than the other two places combined, some communicating with neighbouring stalls via glory holes. There are two saunas, a steam room, a mist room and a sling room equipped with showerheads. No artwork, but there's plenty to look at in terms of your fellow customers. It's a younger crowd on the whole, with the greatest variety in terms of age, nationality and body type.

All three buildings have car parking at street level, sunbathing on the roof and a free condom at the front desk (plus condom-vending machines). They also offer bunkrooms and open, futon-floored rooms where you may sleep, cuddle or 'play', as well as hotel-style private rooms available for an extra charge. Asakusa has a public room set up like a peephole-riddled maze, and Shinjuku has a 'starlight room' where ultraviolet light turns bodies into stark black shapes against glowing white bedding. You'll also find snack bars, tanning beds and multiple TV lounges, and a large karaoke bar at Asakusa.

Friendly, English-speaking staff make this place ideal. You can rent hosts (starting at ¥13,000 for 60 minutes on top of the ¥1,500 one-drink cover charge) in a free private room at the club or to take to your own home or hotel. The bilingual website has staff photos on the Japanese side.

LOVE HOTELS

For more about these, *see p141* **Love Hotels**.

Business Hotel S

2-12-3 Shinjuku, Shinjuku-ku (5367 2949). Shinjuku-Sanchome station (Fukutoshin, Marunouchi, Shinjuku lines), exits C7, C8. **Open** 24hrs daily. **Admission** ¥4,200 2hrs; ¥8,800 overnight. **No credit cards. Map** p101.

The word 'business' fools no one. This is a gay love hotel, pure and simple, conveniently located above GB *(see p245)*. Rooms are small and spartan, but include a coin-operated minibar full of beer, and *yukata* bathrobes for modest post-coital lounging.

Hotel Nuts

1-16-5 Shinjuku, Shinjuku-ku (5379 1044). Shinjuku-Sanchome station (Fukutoshin, Marunouchi, Shinjuku lines), exit C8. **Open** 24hrs daily. **Admission** ¥5,800-¥7,400 2hrs. **Credit** AmEx, JCB, V.

The best known of Tokyo's smattering of gay love hotels, located just outside Shinjuku's main gay bar area. The basic rooms are pink, spotlessly clean and have decent bathrooms. The management has been known to refuse entry if neither customer is Japanese.

ARTS & ENTERTAINMENT

Music

The best of the West, and lashings of local talent.

Whatever your taste in music, you'll find a scene for it in Tokyo. From hip hop to opera, funk to punk, northern soul to death metal, there's a thriving live scene, specialist record shops and great domestic acts for genres as apparently un-Japanese as afrobeat or ska.

This city is heaven for jazz fans, with nanoscale venues and flash dinner clubs sandwiching one of the world's best scenes. When the economy is favourable, Western acts flock to perform here. All you have to do is pick your listening pleasure.

CLASSICAL & OPERA

Tokyo has an outstanding collection of classical music venues. Flush with Bubble-era cash, corporate titans and politicians hired brand-name architects and launched them on a building spree that has left 21st-century Tokyo with a number of gleaming entertainment venues, including the **Tokyo Opera City** and **New National Theatre, Tokyo** (NNTT) complex (Tange Kenzo, 1996) and the **Tokyo International Forum** (Rafael Vinoly, 1996).

Perhaps less thought was given to how to fill these new halls, but with dozens of amateur and professional orchestras, Tokyo claims to offer more classical music events than any other city in the world. Classical music has been popular in Japan since the country opened to the outside world in the 19th century, and it has produced its own legitimate stars – from conductor Ozawa Seiji and composer Takamitsu Toru to pianist Uchida Mitsuko and violinist Midori.

Tokyo has no fewer than five symphony orchestras; the most distinguished are the **NHK Symphony Orchestra** (founded in 1926, www.nhkso.or.jp) and the **Tokyo Symphony Orchestra** (founded in 1946, www.tokyo symphony.com). As is common elsewhere in Japan, most are led by star conductors from overseas, but native conductors such as Takaseki Ken are beginning to make their mark.

Opera is represented by the **Fujiwara Opera Company**, founded in 1934 and specialising in Western opera, and the **Nihon Opera Kyokai**, specialising in Japanese opera; both operate under the auspices of the Japan Opera Foundation (www.jof.or.jp). The New

National Theatre, Tokyo has its own chorus and presents operas in conjunction with the Tokyo Symphony Orchestra.

INFORMATION

Check out the free weekly magazine *Metropolis* (*see p314*) for the most up-to-date English-language listings. Most of the larger venues have detailed listings in English online.

Main venues

★ New National Theatre, Tokyo

1-1-1 Honmachi, Shibuya-ku (5352 9999, www.nntt.jac.go.jp). Hatsudai station (Keio New line), central exit. **Capacity** *Opera House* 1,814. *Playhouse* 1,038. *The Pit* 468. **Box office** 10am-7pm daily. **Credit** AmEx, JCB, MC, V.

The National Theatre (*see p271*) focuses on traditional dance and theatre, while the New National Theatre (NNTT) caters to the modern generation. It calls its spaces the Opera House, the Playhouse and the Pit. The last two cater for mostly modern dance and drama, while the Opera House was purpose-built for opera, but sometimes hosts classical ballet performances. The complex that houses the spaces is worth a visit in its own right. Opera tickets cost from ¥3,150 to ¥21,000.

▶ *For more culture in the area, visit the Kenji Taki Gallery (see p241).*

NHK Hall

2-2-1 Jinnan, Shibuya-ku (3465 1751, www.nhk-sc.or.jp/nhk_hall). Harajuku station (Yamanote line), Omotesando exit or Meiji-Jingumae station (Chiyoda line), exit 1. **Capacity** 3,677. **No credit cards**.

Located next to Yoyogi Park, the main auditorium of national broadcaster NHK is home to the NHK Orchestra, but also hosts a range of other productions from opera to ballet to pop concerts. The modern hall is serviceable but lacks the grandeur and audacity of Tokyo's newer performance spaces.

Orchard Hall
Bunkamura, 2-24-1 Dogenzaka, Shibuya-ku (3477 9999, www.bunkamura.co.jp). Shibuya station (Yamanote, Ginza, Hanzomon lines), Hachiko exit. **Capacity** *2,150.* **Box office** 10am-5.30pm daily. **Credit** AmEx, JCB, MC, V. **Map** p93.
This is the largest shoebox-shaped hall in Japan, designed to produce the best possible acoustics – though some complain it's rather echoey. Classical, opera and ballet are the norm, but works in other genres are also staged.

Sumida Triphony Hall
1-2-3 Kinshi, Sumida-ku (5608 1212, www. triphony.com). Kinshicho station (Hanzomon, Sobu lines), north exit. **Capacity** *Large Hall* 1,801. *Small Hall* 252. **Box office** 10am-7pm daily. **No credit cards.**
Situated just across the Sumida river, this venue has a beautiful, old-fashioned lobby and a warm atmosphere. It's the home of the New Japan Philharmonic Orchestra, and it also plays host to international artists and events.

★ Suntory Hall
1-13-1 Akasaka, Minato-ku (3505 1001, www. suntory.co.jp/suntoryhall/english). Roppongi-Itchome station (Nanboku line), exit 3. **Capacity** *Large Hall* 2,006. *Small Hall* 432. **Box office** 10am-7pm Mon-Sat; 10am-6pm Sun. **Credit** AmEx, JCB, MC, V. **Map** p87.
Run by local drinks company Suntory, this two-space venue is used mainly for orchestral concerts and recitals. The huge, Austrian-made pipe organ is the most striking visual feature of the Large Hall, giving it an almost church-like appearance. The acoustics are superb, with legendary conductor Herbert von Karajan describing the place as 'truly a jewel host of sound'. Soloists and chamber groups appear in the Small Hall.

Tokyo Bunka Kaikan
5-45 Ueno Koen, Taito-ku (3828 2111, www. t-bunka.jp). Ueno station (Yamanote, Ginza, Hibiya lines), park exit. **Capacity** *Large Hall* 2,303. *Small Hall* 649. **Box office** 10am-7pm Mon-Sat; 10am-6pm Sun. **Credit** JCB, MC, V. **Map** p107.
Located in historic Ueno Park, these halls were Tokyo's classical music hub in the post-war period. Now more than 40 years old, they were refurbished at the end of the 1990s to make up for ground lost to newer, flashier venues. The main hall is one of the city's largest, and it is high enough to have four balconies. On the fourth floor of the building is Tokyo's main music library (open to the public).

Tokyo Opera City
3-20-2 Nishi-Shinjuku, Shinjuku-ku (5353 0770, www.operacity.jp). Hatsudai station (Keio New line), east exit. **Capacity** *Main Hall* 1,632. *Recital Hall* 286. **Box office** 10am-6pm Tue-Sun. **Credit** AmEx, JCB, MC, V.
Part of the same huge complex as the NNTT (*see left*), Tokyo Opera City presents all sorts of classical music events – but not much opera. The lobby's fusion of architectural styles is a sign of what's to come in the Main Hall; the base of the hall is in the prevalent shoebox shape but rises into a soaring pyramid topped by a skylight. Built for the most advanced sound technology, the auditorium has a bright oak interior with a 3,826-pipe organ as its centrepiece. There's a space for solo performances too, which has also been designed to give the best acoustics.

Other venues

Casals Hall
1-6 Kanda-Surugadai, Chiyoda-ku (3294 1229, www.nu-casalshall.com). Ochanomizu station (Chuo, Marunouchi, Sobu lines), Ochanomizubashi exit. **Capacity** *511.* **No credit cards.** **Map** p77.
This beautiful hall in the heart of Tokyo's university and bookshop district was designed exclusively for chamber music and small ensembles, and is recognised for its high-quality acoustics.

Hakuju Hall
1-37-5 Tomigaya, Shibuya-ku (5478 8700, www.hakujuhall.jp). Yoyogi-Hachiman station (Odakyu line) or Yoyogi-Koen station (Chiyoda line). **Capacity** *300.* **Box office** 10am-6pm Tue-Sat. **Credit** JCB, MC, V.

INSIDE TRACK LIVE IN JAPAN

The list of musicians with 'Live in Japan' on their discographies is long and growing. Shirley Bassey and John Coletrane both played and recorded at the recently closed Kosei Nenkin Hall in Shinjuku. Sarah Vaughan recorded *Live in Japan* at **Nakano Sun Plaza Hall** (*see p258*) in 1973; Primal Scream's *Live in Japan* was recorded at **Zepp Tokyo** (*see p258*) three decades later. Rodrigo y Gabriela's *Live in Japan* captures the Mexican duo at **Shibuya O-East** (*see p258*), while the rest of the list ranges from legends (George Harrison, Wilson Pickett, the Carpenters and Louis Armstrong), to the not quite so legendary (It Bites). And that's not to mention all those 'Live in Tokyo' recordings…

Opened in 2003 by the health-products company Hakuju, this small hall aims to provide an unrivalled musical experience. The acoustics are first rate, and every seat can be reclined (a world first!). You'll find mainly recitals and chamber groups, as well as some world music.

▶ *The open-air terrace on the ninth floor, open only to concert-goers, offers wonderful views over Yoyogi Park and Shinjuku.*

Kan'i Hoken Hall

8-4-13 Nishi-Gotanda, Shinagawa-ku (3490 5111, www.u-port.kfj.go.jp). Gotanda station (Yamanote, Asakusa lines), west exit. **Capacity** 1,803.
A mainstay of the scene for more than two decades, this acoustically impressive venue presents mainly classical music and ballet, but musicals, and rock and jazz concerts, plus crooners both local and international, also make the bill.

Sogetsu Hall

7-2-21 Akasaka, Minato-ku (3408 1129, www.sogetsu.or.jp/hall). Aoyama-Itchome station (Ginza, Hanzomon lines), exit A4. **Capacity** 530.
This smallish venue, which belongs to the *sogetsu-ryu* school of *ikebana* (flower arranging), stages classical music events, as well as Japanese music recitals, poetry readings and even film previews. The funnel-shaped design can be frustrating for concert-goers who have sharp ears, but it provides a much more intimate experience than other halls.

Big in Japan

A quartet of bands to listen out for.

Tokyo draws international bands of all statures, but there's plenty of quality domestic talent vying for local ears. Here are four of the best live acts right now.

AFURILAMPO

The Sound A mixture of thrash, noise and nursery rhymes.
The Band Like temperamental toddlers, this guitar and drum duo alternately scream and coo into the microphones, shifting gears on a whim. Crashing cymbals and shimmering walls of feedback may stop abruptly for a lullaby on a toy piano, or vice versa. They've been lazily compared to Shonen Knife, the Osaka duo who play Ramones-era punk, but the girls of Afurilampo create noise of a very different kind. If Shonen Knife are the girls in class who colour inside the lines, then Afulilampo are the kids eating crayons to see what the colours taste like.
Why you should see them Most shows are partly or completely improvised. The excitement of spontaneity is palpable, and what may sound jerky or uneven on record feels like being fired out of a catapult when performed live.
Listen to *Ursula in Japan* has some of their most melodic output, including their garage rock-inflected theme song.

DE DE MOUSE

The Sound Android unicorns in love.
The Artist Daisuke Endo, the man known as De De Mouse, is quickly clambering atop Tokyo's über-cute indie electro scene. Using fairy-like vocals for melody, Endo slowly builds layers of house beats, live drum breaks, washes of synth and sparkling piano riffs. The result sounds great in the club, in the shower or in Apple stores, where he has performed more than once.
Why you should see him He is at the peak of his powers now, with a major label contract, celebrity fans and a full house wherever he plays. His hipster cred and popularity with Japan's fashion and design circles make the crowds as interesting to watch as the background visuals created for him by designers such as Midori Kawano.
Listen to The *Tide of Stars* LP has many of De De Mouse's most propulsive hits to get the girls squealing.

EKD

The Sound Surf rock goes south of the border. Think Manu Chao meets Dick Dale.
The Band The core members have been playing the sounds of Mexico and the Caribbean for years, but the fiery licks of the lead guitarist add a muscularity that propels the band beyond kitsch. The full sound is delivered with a seven-piece band, including an accordionist and three (!) drummers, but you might also find EKD playing as a trio in tiny bars around town.
Why you should see them EKD's genre-mashing approach to the Latin sound is finding a passionate and growing following here. Catch them now before they start playing the big clubs.
Listen to *Fantasma* encapsulates their sound better than most debut records. Enjoyable at any volume level.

ARTS & ENTERTAINMENT

Tokyo International Forum

3-5-1 Marunouchi, Chiyoda-ku (5221 9000, www.t-i-forum.co.jp/english). Yurakucho station (Yamanote, Yurakucho lines), Tokyo International Forum exit. **Capacity** *A Hall* 5,000. *C Hall* 1,500. **Map** p59.

This soaring, ship-like edifice of concrete and glass was opened in 1997 by the Tokyo Metropolitan Government, in the middle of the Marunouchi business district. Designed by award-winning architect Rafael Vinoly, it's a huge, multi-purpose complex used for everything from conventions and trade fairs to exhibitions and pop concerts. Classical concerts are usually held in halls A and C; the former is vast, with seating for 5,000, but still manages to offer superb acoustics and a warm atmosphere.

Tokyo Metropolitan Art Space

1-8-1 Nishi-Ikebukuro, Toshima-ku (5391 2111, www.geigeki.jp). Ikebukuro station (Yamanote line), west exit; (Marunouchi, Yurakucho lines), exit 2B. **Capacity** *Main Hall* 1,999. *Medium Hall* 841. *Small Halls* 300 each. **Box office** 10am-6pm daily. **Credit** JCB, MC, V. **Map** p69.

The first thing that strikes you about this building is the long escalator, travelling from the ground floor up to the fifth floor. Not to be outdone, the halls also have some unusual features – the Middle Hall's UFO-like shape is especially peculiar. Full-scale orchestras play in the Large Hall, while the Middle Hall is used for musicals, plays and ballets, as well as for classical music.

SHIBUSA SHIRAZU

The Sound A chaotic mix of free jazz, ska, klezmer, heavy metal and traditional *enka* that barely holds together during the band's extended freak-outs.

The Band Conductor Fuwa Daisuke and friends began as theatre musicians, but exited the orchestra pit with a vengeance, picking up a variety of other musicians who wanted to moonlight from their main bands. The line-up is rarely the same two shows in a row. The group has performed as small as a trio, but when billed as 'The Shibusa Shirazu Orchestra', expect over 40 people on stage, including performance artists, *butoh* dancers, kids and go-go girls.

Why you should see them There's no show like it anywhere. Shibusa Shirazu concerts employ absurdist humour, fantastic costumes, oddball stage sets and an amazing array of musical talent.

Listen to *Shibu Hata* has many of the fan favourites that are regularly played live, but the songs may sound different, as they evolve over time.

Shibusa Shirazu.

ARTS & ENTERTAINMENT

Liquid Room. *See p258.*

JAZZ

Jazz was once banned in Japan, as the nation's wartime leaders worried about the cultural influence of this American import. The ban had limited success at the time, and six decades later the genre is arguably more popular in Japan than in its homeland. There are over 30 large clubs and 20 smaller ones devoted to some form of the genre, and they're crowded every night of the week.

In a comprehensive and diverse scene, you'll find Latin, bop, free, big-band, swing, fusion, experimental, jazz-funk and blues events, plus various open-air gigs during the summer. Club jazz has been a success story in recent years, with home-grown acts such as Jazztronik, Kyoto Jazz Massive and Soil and 'Pimp' Sessions building large followings among young Tokyoites. And for something more eclectic, the Shibusa Shirazu Orchestra (literally: 'no sense of cool orchestra') is a loose-knit troupe of around 20 talented musicians whose shows veer across genres and incorporate *butoh* dance performance (*see p274*). They were the first unsigned band ever to play the main stage of the UK's Glastonbury festival.

Unlike rock or classical music venues, where the admission price reflects the performer's pulling power, jazz clubs tend to have fixed entry charges (included here, where available). Doors usually open at least 30 minutes before the music starts. Many clubs have two sessions per evening, so check beforehand whether the entry fee covers you for both. Some of the bigger clubs accept credit cards, but in general expect to pay cash. In addition to the clubs, there are hundreds of jazz bars dotted around the city, with Shinjuku and Kichijoji boasting more than 25 such places between them. Many have extensive vinyl collections and bartenders who are happy to take music requests.

Also look out for the weekend **Tokyo Jazz** festival (www.tokyo-jazz.com) in late August. Past headliners have included Herbie Hancock, Chick Corea and Dave Holland.

INFORMATION

Metropolis magazine (*see p314*) tends to list only the bigger clubs. For wider coverage, the Shinjuku branch of record shop **Disk Union** (*see p217*) has an excellent jazz section, with flyers and jazz magazines advertising upcoming events. The haphazardly published *JazzNin* magazine is half-English, half-Japanese and worth seeking out, while Japanese-only magazines *Swing Journal* and *Jazzlife* are great sources if you've mastered the language.

Venues

Aketa no Mise

Yoshino Bldg B101, 3-21-13 Nishi Ogi Kita, Suginami-ku (3395 9507, www.aketa.org). Nishi-Ogikubo station (Chuo, Marunouchi lines), north exit. **Shows** 7.30-11pm Mon-Fri; 7.30pm-1.30am Sat. **Admission** ¥2,500 (incl 1 drink).
The name means 'open shop', and this place has been welcoming jazz fans for three decades. Old photos and posters line the dark walls of the basement space, creating an intimate atmosphere for some proper jazz listening. There is no set style for the acts; expect anything from free improv to Latin to piano trios. Shimada-san is the relaxed proprietor. Drinks start at a decent ¥400.

Alfie

Hama Roppongi Bldg 5F, 6-2-35 Roppongi, Minato-ku (3479 2037, http://homepage1.nifty. com/live/alfie). Roppongi station (Hibiya, Oedo lines), exit 1. **Shows** 8pm, 9.45pm Mon-Sat; 7.30pm, 9.15pm Sun; jam sessions after midnight Mon-Sat. **Admission** ¥3,500. **Map** p87.

A jazz oasis in drunken Roppongi, Alfie has a sleek interior and an upscale audience paying upscale prices to hear international musicians as well as top-flight local bands.

Blue Note Tokyo

Raika Bldg, 6-3-16 Minami Aoyama, Minato-ku (5485 0088, www.bluenote.co.jp). Omotesando station (Chiyoda, Ginza, Hanzomon lines), exit B3. **Shows** from 7pm, 9.30pm Mon-Sat; from 6.30pm & 9pm Sun. **Admission** ¥6,000-¥10,000.

The largest jazz club in Tokyo – with prices to match – is part of the international Blue Note chain and well supported by the local music industry. Jazz, Latin, world and soul acts all appear. Expect short sets, expensive food and strangers sharing your dining table. It's hard to love the venue, but the quality of international talent keeps the crowds coming.

Blues Alley Japan

Hotel Wing International Meguro B1F, 1-3-14 Meguro, Meguro-ku (5496 4381, www.blues alley.co.jp). Meguro station (Yamanote, Mita, Namboku lines), west exit. **Shows** from 7.30pm daily. **Admission** ¥3,500. **Map** p53.

Blues Alley showcases everything from jazz, big band, Latin, Brazilian, fusion and soul to pop and, yes, blues. The service is impeccable, the sound system crisp and the food tasty, but the atmosphere can be a bit on the sterile side.

Body & Soul

Anisu Minami Aoyama B1, 6-13-9 Minami Aoyama, Minato-ku (5466 3348, www.bodyand soul.co.jp). Omotesando station (Chiyoda, Ginza, Hanzomon lines), exit B1. **Shows** from 8.30pm daily. **Admission** ¥3,500-¥6,000.

Jazz and jazz only at this terrific but pricey club, which has been in business since 1974. The best musicians in the city love to play to the savvy crowd here. Good food and wine too.

Buddy

Futaba Hall B2F, Asahigaoka 1-77-8, Nerima-ku, (3953 1152, www.buddy-tokyo.com). Ekoda station (Seibu Ikebukuro line), south exit. **Shows** 7.30pm-midnight daily. **Admission** ¥1,500-¥4,000.

This largish venue is a little out of the way but worth the trip. The main focus is jazz, but tango or prog-rock groups are almost as common.

Gate One

Maruishi Bldg B1F, 2-8-3 Takadanobaba, Shinjuku-ku (3200 1452, www.h3.dion.ne.jp/ ~gateone). Takadanobaba station (Yamanote, Tozai lines), Waseda exit. **Shows** from 7pm daily. **Admission** from ¥1,000.

Gate One is a small basement jazz bar owned by a husband-and-wife guitarist/vocalist duo. The decor is nothing to write home about, but the music is great (with an emphasis on vocalists), and there are frequent jam sessions.

Intro

NT Bldg B1F, 2-14-8 Takadanobaba, Shinjuku-ku (3200 4396, www.intro.co.jp). Takadanobaba station (Yamanote, Tozai lines), Waseda exit. **Shows** from 6.30pm daily. **Admission** from ¥1,000.

Small, dark and with a superb vinyl collection stacked above the bar, Intro is one of the best jazz bars in Tokyo. It doesn't have scheduled music performances every night, but the Saturday jam session (which goes on until 5am) is not to be missed, and is also great value at only ¥1,000.

J

Royal Mansion B1, 5-1-1 Shinjuku, Shinjuku-ku (3354 0335, www.jazzspot-j.com). Shinjuku station (Yamanote, Marunouchi, Oedo, Shinjuku lines), east exit or Shinjuku-Sanchome station (Marunouchi, Shinjuku lines), exit C7. **Shows** from 7.15pm daily. **Admission** ¥1,500-¥2,000.

A fifteen-minute walk from central Shinjuku, this basement club is a classic Tokyo jazz spot. The venue specialises in up-and-coming talent, with vocalists particularly well represented.

Jirokichi

Koenji Bldg B1, 2-3-4 Koenji-kita, Suginami-ku (3339 2727, www.jirokichi.net). Koenji station (Chuo line), north exit. **Shows** from 7.30pm daily. **Admission** ¥2,100-¥4,000.

Jirokichi presents everything from klezmer to didgeridoo, jive blues to jazz piano trios. The place is well run and good fun, with a young and hip atmosphere. There's barely any room to dance, but people go ahead and do it anyway.

★ JZ Brat

Cerulean Tower Tokyu Hotel 2F, 26-1 Sakuragaoka-cho, Shibuya-ku (5728 0168, www. jzbrat.com). Shibuya station (Yamanote, Ginza, Hanzomon lines), south exit. **Shows** from 7.30pm daily. **Admission** from ¥4,200. **Map** p93.

This smart club, housed inside the sprawling Cerulean Tower Tokyu hotel, is expensive but worth it. The booking policy is consistently good, with occasional overseas players performing. The space is large, so you can move and chat while the music plays. Plus point: the bar is open until 4am on Fridays and Saturdays.

▶ *For a room that's almost within earshot, see p133 Cerulean Tower Tokyu Hotel.*

ARTS & ENTERTAINMENT

Naru

*Jujiya Bldg B1, 2-1 Kanda Surugadai,
Chiyoda-ku (3291 2321, www.jazz-naru.com).
Ochanomizu station (Chuo, Marunouchi, Sobu
lines), Ochanomizubashi exit.* **Shows** from
7.30pm daily. **Admission** from ¥2,500.
At this medium-sized venue, young, hot players
predominate, but you'll also find straight-ahead,
satisfying old faves doing their stuff. There's a
good selection of food and wine too.

★ Shinjuku Pit Inn

*Accord Shinjuku B1F, 2-12-4 Shinjuku,
Shinjuku-ku (3354 2024, www.pit-inn.com).
Shinjuku-Sanchome station (Marunouchi,
Shinjuku lines), exit C5.* **Shows** from 2.30pm,
7.30pm daily. **Admission** ¥1,300-¥3,000.
Map p101.
All chairs here face the stage, in reverence to the
most respected jazz groups in town, who offer their
latest to the adoring crowd. It's not a place for lingering or lounging – the atmosphere is too hallowed for that – but the music is always first-class.
An irregular afternoon slot at 2.30pm offers the
stage to newly emerging bands.

Someday

*1-20-9 Nishi Shinbashi, Minato-ku (3506 1777,
www.someday.net). Shinbashi station (Yamanote,
Asakusa, Ginza lines), Karasumori exit.* **Shows**
from 7.45pm daily. **Admission** ¥2,500-¥3,700.
Map p59.
Someday specialises in big-band and Latin groups.
The atmosphere isn't particularly notable, though the
crowd is knowledgeable and enthusiastic. There's an
extensive (as well as expensive) selection of whisky
to choose from, along with the usual Japanese snacks
and small pizzas to satisfy any hunger pangs.

Sometime

*1-11-31 Kichijoji Honcho, Musashino-shi
(0422 21 6336, www.sometime.co.jp/sometime).
Kichijoji station (Chuo line), north exit.* **Shows**
from 7.30pm daily. **Admission** from ¥1,600.
A Tokyo institution in jazz-filled Kichijoji. The stage
at this place sits in the centre of the club, so that you
can see and hear performers up close. Make sure that

**INSIDE TRACK
ROCKING OUT, PART 1**

Of Japan's two massive music festivals,
the biggest and best is the **Fuji Rock
Festival** (www.fujirockfestival.com),
which is held on the last weekend
of July. Inspired by the UK's Glastonbury,
it attracts a diverse range of big names
to the scenic mountains of Niigata,
around 90 minutes' travel from Tokyo.

---

you don't arrive late and get stuck sitting below the
band; it's cramped, and the sound is not as good.
Almost every top-notch player comes through
Sometime at some time, and the management has
kept the admission price reasonable for years.
► *In the daytime (from 11am), this jazz venue
operates as a café.*

STB139

*6-7-11 Roppongi, Minato-ku (5474 1395,
http://stb139.co.jp). Roppongi station (Hibiya,
Oedo lines), exit 3.* **Shows** from 8pm Mon-Sat.
Admission from ¥5,000. **Map** p87.
A dinner venue with world-class jazz, STB139 feels
ever so slightly less commercial than rivals such as
Blue Note Tokyo (*see p255*) and the Cotton Club (*see
p260*). The layout is much friendlier and the atmos-
phere a little more relaxed. Musically it takes in soul,
Latin and R&B, as well as straight-up jazz.

Strings

*TN Clum Bldg B1F, 2-12-13 Kichijoji-Honcho,
Musashino-shi (0422 28 5035, www.jazz-
strings.com). Kichijoji station (Chuo line),
north exit.* **Shows** from 8pm daily.
Admission ¥2,000-¥3,000.
Strings is a small venue with an emphasis on vocalists, plus Latin/bossa nova and some soul acts. If
you get hungry, try the delicious, reasonably priced
Italian food that's served here.

Tokyo TUC

*Tokyo Uniform Center, Honsha Biru B1F,
2-16-5 Iwamotocho, Chiyoda-ku (3866 8393,
www.tokyouniform.com/tokyotuc). Akihabara
station (Yamanote, Hibiya lines), Showa Dori
exit or Kanda station (Yamanote, Ginza lines),
north exit.* **Shows** from 7.45pm Fri; from 7pm
Sat. **Admission** ¥3,500-¥12,000. **Map** p77.
An excellent club, although it doesn't have jazz
playing every night. When it does (and if you can
find a place to sit or stand), expect to hear the best
musicians from Japan and overseas.

ROCK & POP

The sickly sweet sound of J-pop is by far
the biggest music market in Tokyo, but there
are passionate, vibrant scenes for all the less
saccharine sounds too. Rock, reggae and hip
hop are the most conspicuous forms, but
you won't have to look far to find first-rate
electronica, soul, metal or pretty much any
genre you can think of. Venues run the whole
gamut, from tiny crammed spaces to enormous
stadiums, from relaxed wine-and-dine seating
to trashy underground pits, with just about
every size and ambience in between.
    The larger places host whoever wants
to book them, but the smaller venues –
known locally as 'live houses' – often focus

on a particular genre to build a following, making it possible to take a gamble on a gig by virtue of the venue alone.

Gigs often start at 7pm, even at weekends, and you can expect to be heading home as early as 9pm. At a few live houses, events kick off at 11pm or midnight. Smaller venues often host three to four bands a night. Expect to pay ¥2,000-¥4,000 for a local gig, somewhat more for established medium-sized bands, and as much as ¥14,000 for the international legends.

INFORMATION

The free weekly *Metropolis* (*see p314*) provides pretty complete listings of upcoming events. The city's two biggest promoters also have useful gig guides, in English, on their websites: **Creativeman** (www.creativeman.co.jp) and **Smash** (www.smash-jpn.com).

Stadiums & large venues

Other venues sometimes used for rock and pop concerts include the **NHK Hall** (*see p250*) and **Tokyo International Forum** (*see p253*).

Makuhari Messe

2-1 Nakase, Mihama-ku, Chiba-shi, Chiba-ken (043 296 0001, www.m-messe.co.jp/index_e. html). Kaihin Makuhari station (Keiyo line), south exit. **Capacity** approx 4,000.
The acoustics at this huge convention complex in Chiba City are generally bad, the place is impersonal and it's some distance from downtown. Still, it's the home of the Summer Sonic rockfest, and big bands such as the Prodigy have entertained full houses here.

National Yoyogi Stadium

2-1-1 Jinnan, Shibuya-ku (3468 1171, www. naash.go.jp). Harajuku station (Yamanote line), Omotesando exit or Meiji-Jingumae station (Chiyoda line), exit 1. **Capacity** *Gymnasium 1* 13,600. *Gymnasium 2* 3,200.
Built for the 1964 Olympics, this place is used rarely and mainly for big-selling J-pop stars, and exhibitions are held from time to time. More interestingly, the adjacent public space near NHK has a live stage with irregular free gigs.

Nippon Budokan

2-3 Kitanomaru-koen, Chiyoda-ku (3216 5100, www.nipponbudokan.or.jp). Kudanshita station (Hanzomon, Shinjuku, Tozai lines), exit 2. **Capacity** 14,950. **Map** p77.
The classic Tokyo live venue (think 'Dylan at the Budokan'). Unfortunately, this lasting reputation allows what is a horrible space to continue to host major rock shows. Built for martial-arts competitions at the 1964 Olympics, it's still used for sports events. The acoustics are poor, the vibe sombre, and the huge, ever-present Japanese flag hanging from

the centre of the hall does not inspire a rock 'n' roll atmosphere. And if you're up in the balcony, you might as well be outside.

Tokyo Dome

1-3-61 Koraku, Bunkyo-ku (5800 9999, www. tokyo-dome.co.jp/e). Kasuga station (Mita, Oedo line), exit A1 or Korakuen station (Marunouchi, Namboku lines), exit 2 or Suidobashi station (Chuo line), west exit; (Mita line), exits A3, A4, A5. **Capacity** 55,000-63,000.
Japan's first domed stadium opened in 1988, though it existed before that without the roof (it's the home of the Yomiuri Giants baseball team). With a capacity of between 55,000 and 63,000, it's the biggest music venue in the Tokyo area, and used for the biggest acts (the Rolling Stones, Michael Jackson, Madonna). Tickets for performances usually cost in excess of ¥10,000. The acoustics are atrocious.
► *For the neighbouring spa, amusement centre and other attractions, see p228 Tokyo Dome City.*

Yokohama Arena

3-10 Shin-Yokohama, Kohoku-ku, Kanagawa-ken (045 474 4000, www.yokohama-arena.co.jp/ english). Shin-Yokohama station (Yokohama, Shinkansen, Tokaido lines), north exit. **Capacity** 17,000.
An increasingly popular venue with good acoustics. Lady Gaga, the Rolling Stones and the two most famous Jacksons have all played here, as have most of Japan's musical superstars.

Medium venues

Studio Coast (www.studio-coast.com), which operates club nights as **Ageha** (*see p268*), also hosts the occasional rock act; Pavement and the Arctic Monkeys have both played there.

Club Citta Kawasaki

1-26 Ogawacho, Kawasaki-ku, Kawasaki-shi, Kanagawa-ken (044 246 8888, http://clubcitta. co.jp). Kawasaki station (Keihin Tohoku, Tokaido lines), east exit. **Capacity** 1,300.

INSIDE TRACK
ROCKING OUT, PART 2

More accessible than the Fuji Rock Festival, within easy reach of Tokyo, is **Summer Sonic** (www.summersonic.com), held each August at the Makuhari Messe convention centre (*see p257*). The line-up is more rock and pop-oriented, and the drab venue offers none of its competitor's atmosphere, but it still draws impressive names, including Jay-Z, Stevie Wonder and Beyoncé in recent years.

Halfway to Yokohama, Club Citta Kawasaki is a great hive of activity, with a large hall for gigs. The lighting gear and stageside speaker stacks are put to good use, mainly by loud and proud rock acts. Club Citta is an aggressive promoter too; some foreign bands only play this venue. Sometimes it turns into a cinema with all-night festivals.

Hibiya Yagai Ongakudo

1-3 Hibiya Koen, Chiyoda-ku (3591 6388). Kasumigaseki station (Chiyoda, Hibiya, Marunouchi lines), exits B2, C4. **Capacity** 3,100. **Map** p59.

In operation since 1923, this outdoor theatre in Hibiya Park puts enjoyment at the mercy of the weather. Umbrellas are not allowed, but if you turn up on a nice day, you'll be able to enjoy one of Tokyo's few open-air venues. Unfortunately, it is an ode to concrete, including the seats, even though it was rebuilt 20 years ago.

★ Liquid Room

3-16-6 Higashi, Shibuya-ku (5464 0800, www. liquidroom.net). Ebisu station (Yamanote, Hibiya lines), west exit. **Capacity** 1,100.

Liquid Room was born as a scruffy venue for gigs and club nights in Shinjuku's seedy Kabukicho district. It's since moved to the more upmarket Ebisu, but still offers the same mix of clubbing and straight-up live events. A long, rectangular room with a few seats in the back, it's a great place to catch a show. It also has the Time Out Café (*see p187*) as a chill-out space. *Photo p254.*

Nakano Sun Plaza Hall

4-1-1 Nakano, Nakano-ku (3388 1151, www.sunplaza.jp/hall). Nakano station (Chuo, Tozai lines), north exit. **Capacity** 2,200.

An unassuming venue located a few stops from Shinjuku, this hall has hosted top bands, including the Clash, PiL and the Pogues, as well as many blues, folk rock (Suzanne Vega) and world-music artists. The list of prohibitions recited before any concert is far more suited to a classical music hall, but the venue does still offer popular stuff. The acoustics are good.

Shibuya AX

2-1-1 Jinnan, Shibuya-ku (5738 2020, www. shibuya-ax.com). Harajuku station (Yamanote line), Omotesando exit or Meiji-Jingumae station (Chiyoda line), exit 1. **Capacity** 1,000.

Conveniently located on the edge of Shibuya, this venue regularly hosts hot indie acts, both foreign and local: Sigur Ros and Hard-Fi are two recent bookings. The acoustics and sight lines are good.

Shibuya CC Lemon Hall

1-1 Udagawacho, Shibuya-ku (3463 3022, www.shibuko.com/english). Shibuya station (Yamanote, Ginza, Hanzomon lines), Hachiko exit. **Capacity** 2,300.

Known as Shibuya Kokaido before an advertising agency rebranded it in celebration of a lemon-flavoured fizzy drink – most locals still use the old name. This is another 1964 Olympics structure, surviving decades of rock thanks to super acoustics.

Shibuya O-East

2-14-8 Dogenzaka, Shibuya-ku (5458 4681, www.shibuya-o.com). Shibuya station (Yamanote, Ginza, Hanzomon lines), Hachiko exit. **Capacity** 1,300. **Map** p93.

The O-East complex houses a number of clubs and bars. The biggest is simply called Shibuya O-East, and is where international rock bands and DJs play.

Stellar Ball

Epson Shinagawa Aqua Stadium (Shinagawa Prince Hotel), 4-10-30 Takanawa, Minato-ku (3440 1111, www.princehotels.co.jp/shinagawa/ aquastadium/livehall). Shinagawa station (Yamanote line), Takanawa exit. **Capacity** 1,884.

The Shinagawa Prince Hotel – part of the huge Prince chain – opened this concert hall in 2005. A long, thin stage allows a prime view from any part of the room, and high-quality lighting and acoustics add to the appeal. Yo La Tengo and the Yeah Yeah Yeahs both picked Stellar Ball for their recent Tokyo gigs.

Zepp Tokyo

Palette Town 1F, 1 Aomi, Koto-ku (3599 0710, www.zepp.co.jp/tokyo). Aomi station (Yurikamome line) or Tokyo Teleport station (Rinkai line). **Capacity** 2,700. **Map** p83.

Part of a chain with locations in four other cities in the country, this large and rather sterile venue in Odaiba has become a well-used spot for more popular foreign rock and electronic acts, including Bob Dylan and the Killers. It has an industrial atmosphere, and looks temporary, which is apt since it may meet the wrecking ball soon.

▶ *For more on the major developments slated for Odaiba, see p81.*

Small venues

Antiknock

Ray Flat Shinjuku B1F, 4-3-15 Shinjuku, Shinjuku-ku (3350 5670, www.antiknock.net). Shinjuku station (Yamanote, Marunouchi lines), new south exit; (Oedo, Shinjuku lines), exits 1, 2. **Capacity** 300. **Map** p101.

A small club near Takashimaya Times Square, where Tokyo's colourful punks gather. It aims to present 'original' music, but, more importantly, the music has to rock. Need to vent your frustration with the Shinjuku-station hordes? Pop down here.

Astro Hall

New Wave Harajuku Bldg B1F, 4-32-12 Jingumae, Shibuya-ku (3401 5352, www.astro-hall.com). Harajuku station (Yamanote line),

*Takeshita exit or Meiji-Jingumae station
(Chiyoda line), exit 5.* **Capacity** 400. **Map** p65.
When it opened in 2000, this was the venue of choice
for many local indie bands, and it's been holding
steady ever since. Some foreign acts trying to break
Japan also play here. Very intimate and generally
well laid out, it's a good place to catch a show.

★ Billboard Live

*Garden Terrace 4F, Tokyo Midtown, 9-7-4
Akasaka, Minato-ku (3405 1133, www.billboard-
live.com). Roppongi station (Hibiya, Oedo lines)
exit 8.* **Capacity** 300. **Map** p87.
Billboard's venue is modelled on the Blue Note and
Cotton Club's format of musicians serenading you
as you dine on marked-up mid-range fusion fare.
But it trumps the Blue Note with a far superior
atmosphere and a well-thought-out floorplan, and
it beats the Cotton Club by booking genres as broad
as the magazine's coverage, and acts that aren't
only big in Japan. Sergio Mendes and the Roots
have both played Billboard Live.

Cay

*Spiral Bldg B1F, 5-6-23 Minami-Aoyama,
Minato-ku (3498 5790, www.spiral.co.jp).
Omotesando station (Chiyoda, Ginza, Hanzomon
lines), exit B1.* **Capacity** 600. **Map** p65.
Multidisciplinary Cay is a restaurant that regularly
turns into a live (and sometimes all-night) venue.
Cay is located in the Spiral Building (*see p239*), a
centre for contemporary arts and design, and the

music is a perfect match for the setting, with new
electronica, world music-influenced and 'fusion' acts.

Club 251

*SY Bldg B1F, 5-29-15 Daizawa, Setagaya-ku
(5481 4141, www.club251.co.jp). Shimo-
Kitazawa station (Keio Inokashira, Odakyu
lines), south exit.* **Capacity** 350.
One of the main venues in Shimo-Kitazawa and a
reliable place to drop in. There are no restrictions on
musical styles, but gigs tend to be rock-oriented. It's
a black, bare place showing its age, but that's a sign
of popularity rather than neglect.

Club Quattro

*Parco 4F, 32-13 Udagawa-cho, Shibuya-ku
(3477 8750, www.club-quattro.com). Shibuya
station (Yamanote, Ginza, Hanzomon lines),
Hachiko exit.* **Capacity** 750. **Map** p93.
On the top floor of the Parco 4 fashion store, Club
Quattro is a superior venue with high-quality performers. It's not limited by genre, offering varied
overseas acts, plus top local bands, even ones that
would usually prefer to play at bigger halls. Despite
some view-restricting pillars on the main floor, this
is one of the most appealing music venues in town.

Club Que

*Big Ben Bldg B2F, 2-5-2 Kitazawa, Setagaya-ku
(3412 9979, www.ukproject.com/que). Shimo-
Kitazawa station (Keio Inokashira, Odakyu lines),
south exit.* **Capacity** 250.

ARTS & ENTERTAINMENT

Shinjuku Loft. *See p261.*

Unit.

This place has built a strong reputation over the past decade and, in spite of its smallish size, some not-so-small local indie bands sometimes appear. Irregular, early-afternoon gigs are held on weekends and holidays, and the place becomes a late-night DJ club at weekends.

Cotton Club
Tokyo Building Tokia 2F, 2-7-3 Marunouchi, Chiyoda-ku (3215 1555, www.cottonclubjapan. co.jp). Tokyo station (Yamanote, Chuo, Sobu lines), Marunouchi South exit; (Marunouchi line), exit 4. **Shows** *5.30pm, 8.30pm Mon-Sat; 4pm, 6.30pm Sun.* **Capacity** *180.* **Map** *p77.*
This sister venue of the Blue Note operates in much the same way: pay ¥8,000-¥10,000 to enter, order your pricey dinner, then sit back for just under an hour of Tito Jackson or Sheena Easton. The artists span the soul to jazz spectrum via funk, disco and R&B, though if you've heard of them, they're probably well past their glory years.
▶ *For information about jazz concerts at Blue Note Tokyo, see p255.*

Crocodile
New Sekiguchi Bldg B1F, 6-18-8 Jingumae, Shibuya-ku (3499 5205, www.crocodile-live.jp). Harajuku station (Yamanote line), Omotesando exit or Shibuya station (Yamanote, Ginza, Hanzomon lines), Miyamasusaka (east) exit or Meiji-Jingumae station (Chiyoda line), exit 4. **Capacity** *120-200.* **Map** *p65.*

Although Crocodile bills itself as a modern music restaurant, it's best to skip the food and stick to the sounds. The venue presents anything from salsa to country, rock and jazz, plus combos of any of these.

DeSeO
Dai 2 Okazaki Bldg 1F, 3-3 Sakuragaoka-cho, Shibuya-ku (5457 0303, www.deseo.co.jp). Shibuya station (Yamanote, Ginza, Hanzomon lines), south exit. **Capacity** *250.* **Map** *p93.*
This small live house along the JR tracks is another spot for bands warming up for bigger things. Some more established acts perform intermittently too.

Eggman
1-6-8 Jinnan, Shibuya-ku (3496 1561, www.eggman.jp). Shibuya station (Yamanote, Ginza, Hanzomon lines), Hachiko exit. **Capacity** *350.* **Map** *p65.*
Eggman is a Shibuya institution. Most nights you'll find local bands playing, particularly those with one eye on a record deal, so you should be able to catch some upcoming talent. A good venue for assorted rock-oriented music styles.

Heaven's Door
Keio Hallo Bldg B1F, 1-33-19 Sangenjaya, Setagaya-ku (3410 9581, www.geocities.jp/ xxxheavensdoorxxx). Sangenjaya station (Tokyu Denentoshi line), south exit. **Capacity** *300.*
Heaven's Door is another institution, in a rites of passage sense, for many loud Tokyo bands. Only a

few established acts play here, yet everybody knows about it. There's not much decoration, but the speakers are huge, and that's what matters.

La.mama Shibuya

Premier Dogenzaka B1F, 1-15-3 Dogenzaka, Shibuya-ku (3464 0801, www.lamama.net). Shibuya station (Yamanote, Ginza, Hanzomon lines), south exit. **Capacity** 120-250. **Map** p93.
La.mama has been presenting bands at the start of (one hopes) successful careers for more than 20 years. It tends to host more J-pop and commercial rock than other venues in the area.

Live Inn Rosa

Rosa Kaikan B2F, 1-37-12 Nishi-Ikebukuro, Toshima-ku (5956 3463, www.live-inn-rosa.com). Ikebukuro station (Yamanote line), west exit; (Marunouchi, Yurakucho lines), exit 12. **Capacity** 100-300. **Map** p69.
Proudly J-pop, this Ikebukuro venue also presents other types of music – including events combining bands and DJs, and artists on their first appearances.

Mandala 2

2-8-6 Kichijoji Minami-cho, Musashino-shi (0422 42 1579, www.mandala.gr.jp). Kichijoji station (Chuo line), south exit. **Capacity** 60.
More of a music venue than its sister in Minami-Aoyama, this branch of the mini Mandala empire specialises in experimental music. It's a hotbed of activity (one of the live CDs on John Zorn's Tzadik label was recorded here), where local stars sometimes show up unannounced for one-off gigs with friends.
Other locations Mandala Minami-Aoyama, MR Bldg B1F, 3-2-2 Minami-Aoyama, Minato-ku (5474 0411).

★ Shelter Shimo-Kitazawa

Senda Bldg B1F, 2-6-10 Kitazawa, Setagaya-ku (3466 7430, www.loft-prj.co.jp). Shimo-Kitazawa station (Keio Inokashira, Odakyu lines), north exit. **Capacity** 250.
Part of the Loft group, this smallish venue in Shimo-Kitazawa gets booked with up-and-coming or even established local bands that might usually play bigger venues. Overseas acts also perform here on occasion. Shelter is popular, so it's best to arrive early.

Shibuya O-West

2-3 Maruyama-cho, Shibuya-ku (5784 7088 O-West, 3462 4420 O-Nest, 3770 1095 O-Crest, www.shibuya-o.com). Shibuya station (Yamanote, Ginza, Hanzomon lines), Hachiko exit. **Capacity** O-West 500. O-Nest 250. O-Crest 200. **Map** p93.
Across the street from the Shibuya O-East complex (*see p258*), this space usually hosts better-known Japanese indie bands, with a concentration on alt and mainstream rock. There are also two smaller venues within the building: O-Nest presents on-the-way-up

Japanese bands and electronic music creators, and can tend towards the edgy or experimental; while intimate O-Crest holds acoustic and more low-key events.

Shinjuku Loft

Tatehana Bldg B2F, 1-12-9 Kabuki-cho, Shinjuku-ku (5272 0382, www.loft-prj.co.jp). Shinjuku station (Yamanote line), east exit; (Marunouchi line), exit B12; (Oedo, Shinjuku lines), exit 1. **Capacity** Main stage 550. Sub-stage 100. **Map** p101.
Loft has been around for more than 25 years and is a dedicated promoter. Inside are two areas: one is the main space for gigs, the other is a bar with a small stage. Expect loud music of any genre here. At times Loft offers more than just gigs, with all-night events that include DJs. Nearby sister venue Loft Plus One (1-14-7 Kabukicho, 3205 6864) is an unusual place that specialises in live talk events. The entertainment ranges from political discussion to porn stars performing erotic games. *Photo p259.*

Shinjuku Marz

Daiichi Tokiwa B1F, 2-45-1 Kabuki-cho, Shinjuku-ku (3202 8248, www.marz.jp/html/news.html). Shinjuku station (Yamanote line), east exit; (Marunouchi line), exit B13; (Oedo, Shinjuku lines), exit 1. **Capacity** 300.
Funk, rock or J-pop – what the bands here have in common is the ambition to set off on a musical career. Opened in 2001, Shinjuku Marz is doing well despite stiff local competition.

Star Pine's Café

1-20-16 Kichijoji-Honcho, Musashino-shi (0422 23 2251, www.mandala.gr.jp/spc.html). Kichijoji station (Chuo line), central exit. **Capacity** 350.
The biggest of the three Mandala venues. The artists who perform here are mostly experimental, and genres range from jazzy or progressive to avant-garde and dancey. Most of the music is of high quality. It's also the venue du jour for obscure-ish overseas acts. All-night events usually follow weekend gigs.
▶ *For sister venue Mandala 2, see left.*

Studio Jam

2-3-23 Kabuki-cho, Shinjuku-ku (3232 8169, http://jam.rinky.info). Shinjuku station (Yamanote line), east exit; (Marunouchi line), exits B6, B7; (Oedo, Shinjuku lines), exit 1. **Capacity** 200.
In operation since 1980, Studio Jam, located in Shinjuku's red-light district, specialises in 1960s-70s music, with a bit of guitar pop thrown in.

Unit

Za House Bldg, 1-34-17 Ebisu-Nishi, Shibuya-ku (3484 1012, www.unit-tokyo.com). Daikanyama station (Tokyu Toyoko line). **Capacity** 600.
A medium-sized space that hosts Japanese indie-rock bands and a sprinkling of rising international acts such as the XX and the New Mastersounds.

Nightlife

Put on your dancing shoes – Tokyo's club scene is stronger than ever.

Tokyo has the breadth and quality to match any of the major clubbing capitals, but avoids the pretentiousness that plagues many scenes. Thanks to heavy investment, the city has several venues with state-of-the-art sound systems and lighting, and most weekends you can take your pick of international DJs backed up by strong homegrown talent such as the Dexpistols (electro), Goth Trad (dubstep) and Masanori Morita (house).

Tokyo suffered a few losses in the latter half of the last decade, with clubs Maniac Love, Velfarre and the legendary Yellow all closing. But where Yellow once stood, a 'new' club called Eleven has opened, employing the same staff, hosting most of the same resident DJs and giving the city's clubbers another reason to smile.

ARTS & ENTERTAINMENT

WHERE TO DANCE

Clubs are scattered across the capital, but generally match the feel of their locality. So **Shibuya**'s venues are young, cool and cover all the main musical bases. **Aoyama** is more moneyed, less edgy but a good choice if you fancy dressing up or going dancing after dinner. **Daikanyama** is Aoyama's chilled-out younger sister and a good area for those who want a taste of Shibuya cool without the grime. **Shinjuku** offers an eclectic mix of rowdy DJ bars and quirky little dancefloors. And then there's **Roppongi**: seedy, cheesy and drunk 24/7. English is practically the local language – as is tequila – and, while it certainly isn't the snobs' choice, it can be a lot of fun, especially as a warm-up or cool-down to an event in nearby **Azabu** (Eleven is the stand-out choice here).

Other locations include **Harajuku**, which is home to some good smaller clubs, **Ikebukuro** (Shinjuku-lite), and **Shimokitazawa** (mainly live venues, many of which double as clubs). Last, but certainly not least, **Shinkiba** – a warehouse district out in the middle of nowhere – is home to Japan's biggest club, the gargantuan **Ageha** (*see p268*).

One major recent change is that drugs are no longer the taboo they once were, at least among clubbers. Potent ecstasy pills, cocaine (often highly adulterated) and amphetamines of various kinds are regular fixtures in the systems of sweaty clubbers. But don't be deceived by this apparent ubiquity: police periodically search people in the street, with a clear preference for foreign faces, and have been known to operate undercover in clubs. A recent scandal involving the drug abuse of Noriko Sakai, a celebrity once considered squeaky clean, has also put drug abuse in the media spotlight.

Japan's club legislation is technically draconian – no drinking under 20, no dancing after midnight – but the rules are ignored by the police most of the time. The occasional crackdown never seems to affect the scene as a whole, and in the more party-oriented areas (Shinjuku, Shibuya, Roppongi), that messy all-nighter can easily go on until long after sunrise.

INFORMATION & HOURS

For event listings, the user-friendly website **iFlyer** (www.iflyer.jp) offers information on DJs and clubs, and gives promoters the chance

INSIDE TRACK
GOOD MORNINGS

The best place for after-hours clubbing is usually **Rockwest** (*see p267*), especially the Trash party, on the second Sunday of the month, starting from 5.30am.

to advertise their shows free of charge. It also offers a thorough listings service for live dance events in Tokyo.

Meanwhile, internet radio station **Samurai** (www.samurai.fm) highlights its pick of upcoming parties and also has on-demand streaming of sets by Tokyo-based DJs. Japanese DJ Mitomi Tokoto's website **Cyberjapan** (www.cyberjapan.tv) also has a club listings section in English, as well as a photo section highlighting recent fashions at Tokyo clubs.

The **Time Out Tokyo** website (www.timeout.jp) also has a clubs section with listings. **Metropolis** magazine (*see p314*), which is available for free at bars and record stores across the city, offers good insights into the city's nightlife. **Clubberia** (www.clubberia.com) also features listings and occasional interviews with local DJs in Japanese.

Expect to pay ¥1,000-¥2,000 for entry to a DJ bar on the weekend (often free weekdays) and ¥3,000-¥4000 (sometimes more) for one of the big clubs. Many venues include drink tickets with admission.

Bars and small clubs get going early, especially if there's a band on first. The bigger places don't get busy until at least midnight, winding down at around 5am (often much later). For anyone who wants to carry on, there are also parties that will go on until long past midday.

EBISU & DAIKANYAMA

The **Liquid Room** (*see p258*) has shifted its focus to live acts but it still hosts various club events on occasion.

★ Air

Hikawa Bldg B1F-B2F, 2-11 Sarugakucho, Shibuya-ku (5784 3386, www.air-tokyo.com). Daikanyama station (Tokyu Toyoko line). **Open** 10pm-5am Mon, Thur-Sat. **Admission** ¥3,500 (incl 1 drink). **No credit cards**.

Large but intimate, Air is stylish but never flash: it's one of Tokyo's best-designed clubs. Once you are past the notoriously strict bouncers (carry at least two forms of ID), you'll see that the club is run by staff who do not have the snootiness that seems de rigueur for major venues. Air draws big-name international DJs, as well as the best local talent.

▶ *Hungry clubbers can pop upstairs for some decent late-night food in the stylish Frames café.*

Unit

Za House Bldg, 1-34-17 Ebisu-nishi, Shibuya-ku (5459 8630, www.unit-tokyo.com). Daikanyama Station (Tokyu Toyoko line). **Open** 10pm-5am Fri, Sat. **Admission** ¥3,500 (incl 1 drink). **No credit cards**.

Unit has a left-of-centre, eclectic music policy that often attracts a crowd more concerned with the tunes than with partying. The monthly Drum and Bass Sessions vs Dubstep Wars event mixes top UK talent with local DJs and is considered the biggest night of the month for fans of these genres.

HARAJUKU & AOYAMA

Le Baron de Paris

Aoyama Center Bldg B1, 3-8-40 Minami-Aoyama, Minato-ku (3408 3665, www.lebaron.jp). Omotesando station (Chiyoda, Ginza, Hanzomon lines), exit A4. **Open** varies. **Admission** ¥2,000-¥3,500. **Credit** AmEx, DC, JCB, MC, V. **Map** p65.

It's oh so effortlessly hip. Created by product designer Marc Newson and a French graffiti artist, Le Baron's champagne and glitterball aesthetic has made it popular with fashion brands holding events, but it can be empty as often as it's packed. On a good night, this is where you'll find the beautiful people.

▶ *Close by, and with a similar crowd and vibe, is the nightclub Velours (see p264).*

Fai

Hachihonkan Bldg B1F-B2F, 5-10-1 Minami-Aoyama, Minato-ku (3486 4910, www.fai-aoyama.com). Omotesando station (Chiyoda, Ginza, Hanzomon lines), exit B1. **Open** 10pm-5am daily. **Admission** ¥2,500 (incl 1 drink). **No credit cards**.

Air.

Eleven.

Fai specialises in sounds from the '70s and '80s, notably disco, funk, soul and jazz, and often has local big-name house DJs performing on the weekend. This unpretentious spot stays just the right side of cheesy.

Velours

Almost Blue B1, 6-4-6 Minami Aoyama (5778 4777, www.velours.jp). Omotesando station (Chiyoda, Ginza, Hanzomon lines), exit B3. **Open** 10.45pm-4am Wed; varies Fri; 11pm-4am Sat. **Admission** ¥2,000-¥3,500. **Credit** AmEx, DC, MC, V.

It's like the Bubble never burst. Tokyo's extravagant '80s get a rerun at Velours, where crystal chandeliers and antique French furnishings try to disguise the narrow dimensions. The swanky setting has made it a popular venue for unashamedly glitzy events by various fashion brands. The high standard of the DJs often isn't enough to improve the cloying atmosphere.

ROPPONGI & AZABU-JUBAN

328 (San Ni Pa)

B1F, 3-24-20 Nishi-Azabu, Minato-ku (3401 4968, www.3-2-8.jp). Roppongi station (Hibiya, Oedo lines), exit 1. **Open** from 8pm daily. **Admission** ¥2,000 (incl 2 drinks) Mon-Thur, Sun; ¥2,500 (incl 2 drinks) Fri, Sat. **No credit cards**. **Map** p87.

A real veteran of the club scene, the diminutive 328 opened way back in 1979. Expect a mix of genres, from soul to dance classics, and an older crowd. On Saturday, 328 can get packed, so arrive early. It usually stays open past midnight on weekends.

Alife

Enonach Nishi Azabu Bldg, 1-7-2 Nishi-Azabu, Minato-ku (5775 5500, www.e-alife.net). Roppongi station (Hibiya, Oedo lines), exit 2.

Open *Lounge & restaurant* 11pm-5am Mon-Sat. *Club* from 9pm Thur-Sat. **Admission** ¥2,000-¥3,500. **No credit cards**. **Map** p87.

This big club is fairly well appointed, with a spacious party lounge on the second floor, a stylish café on the ground floor and a large dance area in the basement. It has a hedonistic atmosphere and is a haven for younger clubbers.

Bar Matrix

Wind Bldg B1F, 3-13-6 Roppongi, Minato-ku (3405 1066, www.matrixbar.jp). Roppongi station (Hibiya, Oedo lines), exit 3. **Open** 6pm-4am daily. **Admission** free. **Map** p87.

This Roppongi bar/club has a futuristic, metallic interior and a cyber feel. It could be considered emblematic of Tokyo, or at least of what travellers expect Tokyo to be. The music is a mishmash of everything, but tends towards hip hop, R&B and reggae.

Bullet's

Kasumi Bldg B1F, 1-7-11 Nishi-Azabu, Minato-ku (3401 4844, www.bul-lets.com). Roppongi station (Hibiya, Oedo lines), exit 2. **Open** 10pm-5am Fri; 11pm-5am Sat. **Admission** ¥2,000 Fri; ¥1,500 Sat. **No credit cards**. **Map** p87.

If nothing else, this is the cosiest venue in Tokyo. Half the place is carpeted, and guests are asked to remove their shoes. There are also sofas and mattresses to lounge on while you listen to an often experimental line-up of DJs.

Club Jamaica

Nishi-Azabu Ishibashi Bldg B1F, 4-16-14 Nishi-Azabu, Minato-ku (3407 8844, www. club-jamaica. com). Roppongi station (Hibiya, Oedo lines), exit 1. **Open** 10pm-5am Thur-Sat. **Admission** ¥1,500 (incl 1 drink) Thur; ¥2,500 (incl 2 drinks) Fri, Sat. **No credit cards**.

ARTS & ENTERTAINMENT

Opened by a reggae fanatic in 1989, Club Jamaica blasts out roots reggae on Thursday nights, then pulls in a younger crowd at the weekend with dance-hall sounds. It's a small venue with a hard-to-find entrance, but the atmosphere is friendly and the sound system has some serious bass – the back wall is piled high with speakers.

▶ *For more reggae, check out Shinjuku's Garam (see p268) or Open (see p268).*

Colors Studio
Barbizon Bldg B3F, 2-25-23 Nishi-Azabu, Minato-ku (3797 5544, www.colorsstudio. iflyer.jp). Roppongi station (Hibiya, Oedo lines), exit 2. **Open** 10pm-5am Mon-Sat. **Admission** ¥1,000-¥5,000 (incl 1 drink). **No credit cards.**
At Colors Studio, a winding staircase descends three flights to a booming club that contains only the essentials: a bar, a dancefloor and a very loud sound system. Local DJs are often joined by inter-national guests playing house, techno and trance. The Sunday morning after-hours party offers techno from 6am to midday.

★ Eleven
1-10-11 Nishi-Azabu, Minato-ku (5775 6206, www.go-to-eleven.com). Roppongi station (Hibiya, Oedo lines), exit 2. **Open** 10pm-5am; days vary. **Admission** ¥3,000-¥4,000. **No credit cards. Map** p87.
When Eleven opened in early 2010 with a set from house legend Francois K, the queue to get in was still going round the block at 4am. The two-tier basement club has a dark main floor sporting one of the city's best light and sound systems, and a bar/chill-out area above that's often as busy as any-where else in the club. Eleven has a reputation for playing quality US house and is already one of the biggest names on the club scene.

Feria
Feria Bldg, 7-13-7, Roppongi, Minato-ku (5775 0655, www.lounge-feria.jp). Roppongi Station (Hibiya, Oedo lines), exit 7. **Open** 5pm-5am Mon-Sat; 7pm-4am Sun. **Admission** ¥1,000-¥3,500.
In recent years, Feria has become the place to go for the 'Roppongi experience'. Set on five floors, and often with an all-you-can-drink menu, Feria attracts huge numbers of foreigners, and Japanese looking to meet international people. The music is often 'all genre', a mix of hip hop, house and R&B, but the crowd isn't there to listen to the music.

Muse
4-1-1 Nishi-Azabu, Minato-ku (5467 1188, www.muse-web.com). Roppongi station (Hibiya, Oedo lines), exit 1. **Open** from 7pm Mon-Thur, Sun; 7pm-5am Fri, Sat. **Admission** free Mon-Thur, Sun; free for women & ¥3,000 (incl 2 drinks) for men Fri, Sat. **No credit cards. Map** p87.

This three-level club features a stellar bar, cave-like areas, and billiards and ping-pong tables in the base-ment. So it's a shame that it's just a massive meat market. The place is hugely popular with the foreign crowd and is often rammed on weekends. The club sometimes hosts seedy parties, but you'll know by the extortionate price at the door.

★ Warehouse
Fukuo Bldg B1F, 1-4-5 Azabu-Juban, Minato-ku (5775 2905, www.warehouse702. com). Azabu-Juban station (Nanboku, Oedo lines), exits 4, 7. **Open** 10pm-5am Mon, Wed-Sat. **Admission** usually ¥2,500-¥4,000 (incl 1 drink). **No credit cards.**
A spacious venue that has in recent years gained a strong reputation for quality parties. It is a decent alternative to the less salubrious offerings up the hill in Roppongi, and often pulls in international DJs.

SHIBUYA

★ Amate Raxi
3-26-16, Shibuya, Shibuya-ku (3486 6861, www.amrax.jp). Shibuya Station (Yamanote, Ginza lines), south exit. **Open** 10pm-5am Mon-Sat; 6am-noon some Sun. **Admission** ¥2,000-¥3,000. **No credit cards. Map** p93.
Better known as 'Amrax', this club has in recent years gained respect for putting on quality house music events. After the closure of Yellow, Amrax did more than any other venue to fill the void. Large crowds should be expected on the weekend for events that feature respected local DJs and underground international artists.

Club Asia
1-8 Maruyamacho, Shibuya-ku (5458 2551, www.clubasia.co.jp). Shibuya station (Yamanote, Ginza lines), Hachiko exit; (Fukutoshin, Hanzomon lines), exit 3A. **Open** usually from 11pm. **Admission** ¥2,000-¥3,500 (incl 1 drink). **No credit cards. Map** p93.
Club Asia offers three bars and two dancefloors, with a high ceiling that looks spectacular but which doesn't always do the sound any favours. The space is a favourite space with private-party organisers, so check the schedule. The Back to Chill party on the first Thursday of every month is considered the city's best dubstep event.

Club Atom
Dr Jeekahn's Bldg 4F-6F, 2-4 Maruyamacho, Shibuya-ku (5428 5195, www.clubatom.com). Shibuya station (Yamanote, Ginza lines), Hachiko exit; (Fukutoshin, Hanzomon lines), exit 3A. **Open** 9pm-5am Thur-Sat. **Admission** ¥3,000 (incl 2 drinks). **No credit cards. Map** p93.
There are two reasonably open dancefloors at this roomy venue. The one on the fifth floor focuses on mainstream trance or house, while the cave-like

fourth floor offers R&B and hip hop. Atom is wildly popular with the heavily made-up, super-tanned Shibuya 'gals' and, as such, is more interesting from a sociological perspective than a musical one.

Club Bar Family

Shimizu Bldg B1F, 1-10-2 Shibuya, Shibuya-ku (3400 9182, www.club-bar-family.com). Shibuya station (Yamanote line), Miyamasusaka (east) exit; (Ginza line), Inokashira, Tamagawa exits; (Fukutoshin, Hanzomon lines), exit 11. **Open** 10.30pm-4am Mon-Thur; 10.30pm-5am Fri, Sat. **Admission** ¥2,000 (incl 1 drink). **No credit cards. Map** p93.

A tiny space pouring out heavy bass sounds, Family features ground-level hip hop at its best. Perfect if you like thundering rap beats. It's rare to see a non-Japanese face here, but that can mean a warm reception to any visitor who does venture inside. Drinks are a good deal at around ¥600.

Club Camelot

1-18-2 Shibuya, Shibuya-ku (5728 5613, www.clubcamelot.jp). Shibuya station (Yamanote line, Ginza line), west exit; (Fukutoshin, Hanzomon lines), exit 12. **Open** 7pm-5am Thur-Sat. **Admission** ¥2,500-¥3,500 (incl 1 drink). **Credit** AmEx, DC, MC, V. **Map** p93.

While Camelot wants to court the well-heeled and more mature trendsetters, its dress code is never enforced, and the weekend crowd varies from scruffy young Shibuya kids to dressed-up business-people looking to wind down. The place can often descend into a meat market on the weekends. The smaller of the two floors holds 300 and specialises in hip hop, R&B and reggae. Downstairs, in the main area, 700 people can gather on the marble floor or lounge on the white leather sofas.

Club Hachi

Aoyama Bldg 1F-4F, 4-5-9 Shibuya, Shibuya-ku (5766 4887, www.aoyama-hachi.net). Shibuya station (Yamanote line), Miyamasusaka (east) exit; (Ginza line), Inogashira, Tamagawa exits; (Fukutoshin, Hanzomon lines), exit 11. **Open** 10pm-5am Mon-Sat; 5-11pm Sun. **Admission** ¥2,000 (incl 1 drink) Mon-Thur, Sun; ¥2,500 (incl 1 drink) Fri, Sat. **No credit cards. Map** p93.

This dingy but funky club occupies the whole of a run-down, four-storey building on Roppongi Dori, and is hugely popular with students from the nearby Aoyama Gakuin University. The first floor contains a yakitori bar, the second a DJ bar, the third the main dance area, and the fourth a lounge bar. The monthly schedule ranges widely, from drum 'n' bass to R&B, house, techno, hip hop and jazz. Hachi was once the regular haunt of globally fêted DJ Ken Ishii.

La Fabrique

Zero Gate B1F, 16-9 Udagawacho, Shibuya-ku (5428 5100, www.lafabrique.jp). Shibuya station (Yamanote, Ginza lines), Hachiko exit; (Fukutoshin, Hanzomon lines), exit 6. **Open** 11am-2am Mon-Thur; 11am-5am Fri, Sat. **Admission** ¥3,000-¥4,000 (incl 1 drink). **No credit cards. Map** p93.

This branch of a Parisian dining club offers French dining in the daytime and dancing by night. The weekend events draw quality local acts and the odd visiting star, and usually kick off at around 11pm. Downtempo sounds are usually played during the week; but by the weekend the music speeds up to include a mix of house and disco.

Harlem

Dr Jeekahn's Bldg 2F-3F, 2-4 Maruyamacho, Shibuya-ku (3461 8806, www.harlem.co.jp). Shibuya station (Yamanote, Ginza lines), Hachiko exit; (Fukutoshin, Hanzomon lines), exit 3A. **Open** 10pm-5am Tue-Sat. **Admission** ¥2,000 (incl 2 drinks) Tue-Thur; ¥3,000 (incl 2 drinks) Fri, Sat. **No credit cards. Map** p93.

Located in the same building as Club Atom (*see p265*), Harlem has been a centre of hip-hop culture in Japan since the mid '90s. The audience is young and dressed in hip-hop uniforms; the music is straight-up rap with a little R&B.

▶ *Club Bar Family (see left) plays hip hop for a more discerning audience.*

Loop

B1F, 2-1-13 Shibuya, Shibuya-ku (3797 9933, www.club-loop.com). Shibuya station (Yamanote line), Miyamasusaka (east) exit; (Ginza line), Inokashira, Tamagawa exits; (Fukutoshin, Hanzomon lines), exit 11 or Omotesando station (Chiyoda, Ginza, Hanzomon lines), exit B1. **Open** 10pm-5am daily. **Admission** ¥2,000 (incl 1 drink) Mon-Thur; ¥2,500 (incl 1 drink) Fri-Sun. **No credit cards. Map** p93.

Located between Shibuya and Omotesando stations, Loop has a stylish, bare-concrete interior and is an ideal hideout for dance-music aficionados. The dancefloor has moody lighting, an excellent sound system (the music is mainly deep house, tech house and techno) and a friendly vibe.

INSIDE TRACK
OUTSIDE THE WOMB

Womb (*see p268*) has been flexing its brand recently with official events outside of its Shibuya venue. Check its website or local record stores and you may find there's a Womb Cruise, where they take their decks onto a party boat and sail Tokyo Bay, or even a Womb Adventure, where they take over the cavernous Makuhari Messe convention centre in Chiba prefecture.

Womb. *See p268.*

Microcosmos
Fontis Bldg 2F, 2-23-12, Dogenzaka, Shibuya-ku (5784 5496, www.microcosmos-tokyo.com). Shibuya station (Yamanote, Ginza lines), Hachiko exit; (Fukutoshin, Hanzomon lines), exit 3A. **Open** 11.30am-2am Sun-Thur; 11.30am-5am Fri-Sat. **Admission** ¥2,500 (incl 1 drink) Fri-Sat. **Credit** AmEx, DC, MC, V. **Map** p93.
This club has steadily grown in popularity since opening its doors in 2008, and usually focuses on house music. Despite its gaudy decor and below-par sound system, its VIP tables are regularly full, international DJs often play here and the club has seen the numbers through its doors steadily increase.
▶ *On weekdays, it serves inexpensive café meals.*

Module
M&I Bldg B1F-B2F, 34-6 Udagawacho, Shibuya-ku (3464 8432, www.module-tokyo.com). Shibuya station (Yamanote, Ginza lines), Hachiko exit; (Fukutoshin, Hanzomon lines), exits 3, 6. **Open** from 10pm Mon-Sat. **Admission** ¥2,000 (incl 1 drink) Mon-Thur; ¥2,500 (incl 1 drink) Fri, Sat. **No credit cards**. **Map** p93.
There's a relaxing split-level bar on the first floor here, in marked contrast to when you get downstairs to the second level. There, you'll find a loud sound system that causes the foundations to shudder below the small, pitch-black dancefloor, with only a glitter ball for light. Module pulls a much better selection of DJs and a more knowledgeable crowd than many of its peers. It's connections to the former Yellow help.

Organ Bar
Kuretake Bldg 3F, 4-9 Udagawacho, Shibuya-ku (5489 5460, www.organ-b.net). Shibuya station (Yamanote, Ginza lines), Hachiko exit; (Fukutoshin, Hanzomon lines), exit 6. **Open** 9pm-5am daily. **Admission** ¥1,000-¥2,000 (incl 1 drink) Mon-Sat; ¥1,000 Sun. **No credit cards**. **Map** p93.
What the tiny dancefloor at this tiny joint lacks in space, it makes up for in atmosphere. The focus is on soul, jazz and bossa nova, all of which attract a slightly older crowd.

★ Rockwest
Tosen Udagawacho Bldg 7F, 4-7 Udagawacho, Shibuya-ku (5459 7988, www.rockwest.jp). Shibuya station (Yamanote, Ginza lines), Hachiko exit; (Fukutoshin, Hanzomon lines), exit 6. **Open** 10pm-5am daily; 5am-noon Sat, Sun. **Admission** ¥1,000-¥2,500. **No credit cards**. **Map** p93.
Formerly a happy hardcore venue, Rockwest moves to a slower beat these days, with hip hop and soul dominating the schedule. Plus points are the air-conditioning, good sound system, relatively roomy dancefloor and re-entry system. The after hours parties play house or techno.

★ Room
Daihachi Tohto Bldg B1F, 15-19 Sakuragaoka, Shibuya-ku (3461 7167, www.theroom.jp). Shibuya station (Yamanote line), south exit; (Ginza line), central exit; (Fukutoshin, Hanzomon lines), exit 8. **Open** 10pm-5am Mon-Sat. **Admission** ¥1,000-¥2,000 (incl 1 drink) Mon-Thur; ¥2,500 (incl 1 drink) Fri, Sat. **No credit cards**. **Map** p93.
Owned by members of Kyoto Jazz Massive, the Room is a small venue split in two: one half is a concrete-walled bar, the other a pitch-black dancefloor. Put them together and you still have a tiny space, but

it's intimate rather than cramped, and the famous owners help lure talented DJs. Exepct quality funk, club jazz, crossover or breakbeats. Top DJs sometimes come here to try out new sets on their nights off, much to the delight of the clientele.

Ruby Room

Kasumi Bldg, 2-25-17 Dogenzaka, Shibuya-ku (3780 3022, www.rubyroomtokyo.com). Shibuya station (Yamanote, Ginza lines), Hachiko exit; (Fukutoshin, Hanzomon lines), exit 3A. **Open** varies. **Admission** ¥1,000-¥2,500 (incl 1 drink). **No credit cards. Map** p93.
A little box of a venue that used to punch well above its size, the Ruby Room has fallen on tougher times in recent years. Despite a reputation for getting big names to play to a maximum of 150, the club now rarely hosts DJ events, instead focusing on live music and often closing before midnight. Check the online schedule before heading here.

Under Deer Lounge

Jinnan Bldg B1, 1-3-4 Jinnan, Shibuya-ku (5728 2655, www.under-dl.iflyer.jp/venue). Shibuya station (Yamanote, Ginza lines), Hachiko exit; (Fukutoshin, Hanzomon lines), exit 6. **Open** varies. **Admission** ¥2,000-¥2,500 (incl 1 drink). **No credit cards. Map** p93.
The stag's head over the bar does little to soften the sterile atmosphere: this club could easily be converted into a fast food joint. But if it's the music that matters, Under Deer Lounge sometimes comes up trumps with underground but well-attended events. Mani of Primal Scream was one recent DJ.

★ Womb

2-16 Maruyamacho, Shibuya-ku (5459 0039, www.womb.co.jp). Shibuya station (Yamanote, Ginza lines), Hachiko exit; (Fukutoshin, Hanzomon lines), exit 3A. **Open** usually 10pm-5am Thur-Sat; 4-10pm Sun. **Admission** usually ¥3,000-¥4,000. **No credit cards. Map** p93.
Womb is a top-flight club with a vast dancefloor, great lighting, a super-bass sound system and what claims to be 'Asia's largest mirror ball'. House, techno and drum 'n' bass are the usual sounds here. The club consistently features as one of the world's top 10 in magazine polls. Womb's schedule is packed with foreign names, but often with local heroes such as Takkyu Ishino (techno) in support. *Photo p267.*

SHINJUKU

Garam

Dai-Roku Polestar Bldg 7A, 1-16-6 Kabuki-cho, Shinjuku-ku (3205 8668). Shinjuku station (Yamanote, Chuo, Sobu lines), east exit; (Marunouchi line), exit B12; (Oedo, Shinjuku lines), exit 1. **Open** 9pm-6am daily. **Admission** ¥1,000-¥1,500 (incl 1 drink). **No credit cards. Map** p101.

This swinging, foreign-owned Jamaican dancehall and reggae club could double as a walk-in closet. Still, the staff are very friendly, and Garam's become something of an institution, with Japanese MCs, sharp DJs and pounding vibes. To find it, head out of the east exit of Shinjuku station and down the pedestrianised street next to the Studio Alta TV screen. Cross Yasukuni Dori, and it's the third building on the right.

Open

B1F, 2-5-15, Shinjuku, Shinjuku-ku (3226 8855, http://blogs.yahoo.co.jp/club_open). Shinjuku-Gyoenmae station (Marunouchi line), Shinjuku Gate exit. **Open** 5pm-5am Mon-Sat. **Admission** ¥1,000-¥2,000 (incl 1 drink). **No credit cards. Map** p101.
Open is the proud inheritor of the roots reggae tradition in Japan. It was set up by staff who used to work at 69 – the country's very first reggae bar/club – when it closed down about a decade ago.

Rags Room Acid

Kowa Bldg B1F, 2-3-12 Shinjuku, Shinjuku-ku (3352 3338, www.acid.jp). Shinjuku-Gyoenmae station (Marunouchi line), Shinjuku Gate exit. **Open** from 10pm; days vary. **Admission** usually ¥2,000 (incl 2 drinks). **No credit cards. Map** p101.
Finding the entrance to Rags Room Acid (formerly Club Acid) is a challenge in itself – a small sign on Shinjuku Dori provides the only hint of its existence. The best method is to pay attention to the stairways of neighbouring buildings and follow your ears: you can hear anything booming out of here, from ska to rock, hip hop to Latin, R&B to techno to drum 'n' bass.

FURTHER AFIELD

Club Que (*see p259*) in Shimo-Kitazawa becomes a rock-oriented club at weekends.

★ Ageha

2-2-10 Shinkiba, Koto-ku (5534 2525, www.ageha.com). Shinkiba station (Rinkai, Yurakucho lines). **Open** 11pm-5am Thur-Sat. **Admission** usually ¥4,000 (incl 2 drinks). **No credit cards.**
The biggest club in Tokyo, Ageha suffers from a far-flung location and dimensions that can feel a bit too cavernous. It offers three dancefloors, a pool area, numerous bars and chill-out spaces, and the best sound system in town. Women should check out the cubicle nearest to the toilet entrance – it leads to a secret, lockable room. When the club books the biggest DJs, Ageha can be great. When it, often, doesn't, the venue feels a bit barren.
▶ *The club provides a free bus from Shibuya every half hour. Board at the bottom of Roppongi Dori; you'll need photo ID to get on the bus.*

Performing Arts

From gender-bending stage shows to Cirque du Soleil acrobatics.

In 2010, Tokyo lost its most famous performing arts venue, the Kabuki-za – at least for a couple of years, while its mammoth successor is under construction. In the meantime, Japan's most instantly recognisable and accessible traditional performing art can be seen in less famous venues around the city.

Beyond *kabuki*, Tokyo boasts a stage scene to rival any metropolis. Other traditional home-grown forms include ancient *bunraku* puppeteering, which involves a 30-year apprenticeship; stately *Noh* theatre; *takarazuka*, an all-female answer to *kabuki* (with extra camp); and the bizarre avant-garde dance *butoh*. Western shows are also growing in popularity, with musicals and contemporary dance leading the way.

TICKETS & INFORMATION

Weekly listings magazine *Metropolis*, and the daily English-language newspapers (*see p315*) list the most notable performances. Many of the theatre websites listed here have English schedules. You can buy tickets direct from the venue, at convenience and department stores, by telephone from ticket agencies, or online (*see p218* **Tickets**). It's a good idea to book ahead.

TRADITIONAL JAPANESE THEATRE

Fearsome masks, silken costumes, stylised dialogue, intricate choreography and the piquant tones of exotic instruments: these are only a few of the elements that beckon the curious into the mysterious world of traditional Japanese performing arts. Often impenetrable to the outsider, ancient forms such as *Noh*, *bunraku* and *kabuki* employ archaic language and can be difficult even for locals to understand.

However, there is much to appreciate on an aesthetic basis alone, and many of the themes – clan battles, servant-master loyalty, revenge and justice, conflicts between duty and loyalty, unrequited love – are universal. English programmes and simultaneous translations are increasingly available.

As with other traditional theatre forms throughout Asia, Japanese theatre integrates dance, music and lyrical narrative. In contrast to Western theatre's preoccupation with realism, the emphasis is on beauty, the mythic and the ritualistic. Another distinguishing feature is *ma*, perhaps best translated as a 'pregnant pause'. More than just silence, *ma* is the space that interrupts musical notes or words and is used to intensify the power of the dramatic moment.

The Japanese theatre-going experience is also markedly different from that in the West. Cast aside notions of hushed reverence and fur coats: a trip to the theatre is a social outing here, and many people come for an afternoon armed with flasks of hot drinks, packed meals and bags full of goodies, which are noisily chomped throughout the performance. Spectators often comment on the action as it happens, for example calling out the stage name of the performer at significant moments. A particularly fine tableau may well elicit a burst of spontaneous applause.

BUNRAKU

While puppetry in Japan goes back at least to the 11th century, modern *bunraku* takes its name from the Bunraku-za organised in Osaka in the early 19th century, and was developed by city-dwelling commoners of the Edo period (1600-1868). The puppets used in *bunraku* are a half to two-thirds human size and require great skill and strength to operate. Each puppet is operated by two assistants and one chief

Bunraku. *See p269.*

puppeteer. Becoming a master puppeteer is a lengthy process, beginning with ten years' operating the legs, followed by another ten on the left arm before being permitted to manipulate the right arm, head and eyebrows.

Four main elements comprise a *bunraku* performance: the puppets themselves; the movements they make; the vocal delivery of the *tayu*, who chants the narrative and speaks the lines for every character, changing his voice to suit the role; and the solo accompaniment by the three-stringed, lute-like *shamisen*.

KABUKI

Kabuki is said to have originated with Okuni, a female attendant at the Izumo shrine in Kyoto, who first led her mostly female company in performances on the dry bed of the Kamogawa river in 1603. *Kabuki* means 'unusual' or 'shocking', and it quickly became the most popular form of theatre in 17th- and 18th-century Japan. However, concerns over the sexual antics of the entertainers, on and off stage, meant that women performers were banned in 1629; now all *kabuki* actors are male. Women's parts are taken by *onnagata* (specialists in female roles), who portray a stylised feminine beauty. There is no pretence of realism, so the actor's real age is irrelevant – there is no incongruity in a 75-year-old man portraying an 18-year-old maiden.

Of all the traditional performing arts in Japan, *kabuki* is probably the most exciting. The actor is the most important element in *kabuki*, and everything that happens on stage is a vehicle for displaying his prowess. *Koken*, stage hands dressed in black, symbolising their supposed invisibility, hand the actor props, make running adjustments to his heavy costume and wig, and bring him a stool to perch on during long speeches or periods of inactivity.

Most *kabuki* programmes feature one *shosagoto* dance piece, one *jidaimono* and one *sewamono*. *Jidaimono* are dramas set in pre-Edo Japan. They feature gorgeous costumes and colourful make-up called *kumadori*, which is painted along the lines of the actor's face. The actor uses melodramatic elocution, but because *jidaimono* originated in the puppet theatre, the plays also feature accompaniments from a chanter who relates the storyline and emotions of the character, while the actor expresses them in movement, facial expressions or poses. *Sewamono* are stories of everyday life during the Edo period and are closer in style to Western drama.

Every *kabuki* theatre features a *hanamichi*, an elevated pathway for the performers that runs through the audience from the main stage to the back of the theatre. This is used for entrances and exits, and contains a trap door through which supernatural characters emerge.

NOH AND KYOGEN

Japan's oldest professional theatre form, *Noh*, dates back to 14th-century Shinto and Buddhist religious festivals and was used both to educate and entertain. The ritualistic nature of *Noh* plays is emphasised by the masks worn by the principal character. Plays are grouped into categories, which can be likened to five courses of a formal meal, each with a different flavour. Invigorating celebratory dances about gods are followed by battle plays of warrior-ghosts; next are lyrical pieces about women, then themes of insanity, and finally demons. Presentation is mostly sombre, slow and deliberate. Plays explore the transience of this world, the sin of killing and the spiritual comfort to be found in Buddhism.

There are no group rehearsals: there is a pre-performance meeting, but the actors and musicians do not play together until the performance. This spontaneity is one of the appeals of this kind of theatre.

Kyogen are short, humorous interludes that show the foolishness of human nature through understated portrayal. They are interspersed for comic relief with *Noh* pieces, but are intended to produce refined laughter, not boisterous humour.

Cerulean Tower Noh Theatre
Cerulean Tower Tokyu Hotel B2F, 26-1 Sakuragaoka-cho, Shibuya-ku (5728 0168, www.ceruleantower.com). Shibuya station (Yamanote, Ginza, Hanzomon lines), south exit. **Capacity** tickets sold at Cerulean Tower Tokyu Hotel (3476 3000). **Tickets** from ¥5,000. **Credit** AmEx, DC, JCB, MC, V. **Map** p93.
Housed in the basement of the Cerulean Tower hotel, this is the city's newest venue for Japanese theatre. It hosts both professional and amateur *Noh* and *kyogen* performances – without English translation.
▶ *For details about the hotel itself, see p133.*

★ National Noh Theatre
4-18-1 Sendagaya, Shibuya-ku (3230 3000, www.ntj.jac.go.jp/english). Sendagaya station (Chuo, Sobu lines) or Kokuritsu-Kyogijo station (Oedo line), exit A4. **Capacity** 591. **Box office** 10am-6pm daily. **Tickets** ¥2,300-¥6,000; ¥1,700 reductions. **Credit** AmEx, DC, JCB, MC, V.
Noh performances are normally staged here four or five times a month. A one-page explanation of the story in English is available.

National Theatre
4-1 Hayabusa-cho, Chiyoda-ku (3230 3000, www.ntj.jac.go.jp/english). Nagatacho station (Hanzomon, Nanboku, Yurakucho lines), exit 4. **Capacity** *Large Hall* 1,610. *Small Hall* 590. **Box office** 10am-6pm daily. **Tickets** ¥1,500-¥12,000. **Credit** AmEx, DC, JCB, MC, V. **Map** p77.
Kabuki is staged seven months a year in the National Theatre's Large Hall, while *bunraku* is staged in the Small Hall four months a year.

Programmes include the story in English, and English audio guides are available (¥650, plus a refundable ¥1,000 deposit).

★ Shinbashi Embujo
6-18-2 Ginza, Chuo-ku (3541 2600, www.shochiku.co.jp/play). Higashi-Ginza station (Asakusa, Hibiya lines), exit A6. **Capacity** 1,400. **Box office** 10am-6pm daily. **Tickets** ¥2,100-¥15,750. **Credit** AmEx, DC, JCB, MC, V. **Map** p59.
While the Kabuki-za is being rebuilt, most *kabuki* performances are being held here. Ennosuke Ichikawa's 'Super-Kabuki', a jazzed-up, modernised version of the real thing, is also staged here. Samurai dramas are performed during the rest of the year.

MODERN DRAMAS & MUSICALS

Modern theatre productions often portray historical themes, such as *jidai geki* – samurai dramas set in the Edo period. Unlike in *kabuki*, female roles are played by women. No matter how tragic, *jidai geki* must end with a satisfactory resolution, whether it is the

Kabuki Stars
A big-name tradition.

Kabuki actors, like sumo wrestlers, are given honorary stage names at *shumei* (grand naming ceremonies). Among the most prestigious names to look for on a *kabuki* bill are:

Bando Tamasaburo
The current, fifth, Bando Tamasaburo is *kabuki*'s most famous *onnagata* (actor playing female roles).

Nakamura Kanzaburo
The 18th performer to use this, one of *kabuki*'s most prestigious names, has led several *kabuki* tours of the US.

Matsumoto Koshiro
The current Matumoto Koshiro, the fifth to use the name, specialises in male roles. He also appears in movies and musicals.

Ichikawa Danjuro
A dozen people have held this distinguished name. The current Ichikawa Danjuro took a long break to battle leukemia, but is performing again. He is probably the best-known actor outside Japan, having played on four continents.

Noh Future?

Unmasking Japan's oldest theatre form.

Noh is the origin of all forms of traditional Japanese theatre. Both *kabuki* and *bunraku* puppet theatre borrow heavily from the current 240-play repertoire of *Noh* and would likely not exist were it not for the slower-paced, highly dramatised and symbolic performance art.

Noh was the brainchild and life's work of a father and son named Kan-ami and Zeami. When Kan-ami (b. 1333) performed for a shogun in 1374, he so entranced Japan's political leader that his own future as a favoured (and thus financially sponsored) actor was assured. His son Zeami (b. 1363) took on his father's mantle and became far more prolific with the pen, producing around 100 plays that are still performed today.

In 1434, Zeami fell foul of a later shogun and was sent into exile, leaving *Noh* in an uncertain state. For centuries, it remained the preserve of the ruling classes, with the odd show staged at shrines during festivals. The drama almost vanished completely when Japan looked West in the turbulent early years of the Meiji era (1868-1912).

Saved from extinction by imperial patronage, the art form-cum-entertainment nevertheless remained off the radar until the mid 20th century when renowned novelist Mishima Yukio (1925-70) produced his famous *Five Modern Noh Plays*.

Nowadays, interest in *Noh* lags far behind that of *kabuki*, partly due to high ticket prices and the use of archaic language and references. The **National Noh Theatre** (*see p271*) holds only around 600 when full. But things are changing slowly. Increasing numbers of younger Japanese can be seen at performances, numerous universities and private schools now have *Noh* clubs, well-known actors recruit and raise their own entourage of disciples and even kids and women's groups (professional *Noh* actors are all male) are starting to take root. The National Noh Theatre hosts periodical performances by the kids of today, adult actors of tomorrow.

Some 30 theatres across Japan are now used for various *Noh* performances, with a dozen or so of these in Tokyo. Performance lists, schedules and ticket information are all available in English. For the locals or the language-proficient, special 'Guide to *Noh*' performances in modern Japanese are increasing the popularity of this uniquely Japanese form of theatre. Anchored in the past, *Noh* is finally looking to the future.

successful revenge of a murder or the ascent into heaven of the dead heroine aloft a podium. However, influenced by Western drama, plays with happy endings are on the increase.

Famous Western plays and musicals, translated into Japanese, are also common. The **New National Theatre, Tokyo** (*see p250*) provides a forum for the most respected Japanese directors, who take a contemporary approach to Western classics. Artistic director of both **Theatre Cocoon** (*see p275*) and the **Saitama Arts Centre** in suburban Tokyo, Yukio Ninagawa has made a notable splash with his trademark fusions of Japanese and Western aesthetics in productions such as *Hamlet*. **Gekidan Shiki** (Shiki Theatre Company), founded in 1953, currently has seven theatres around the country, where it stages long-running Japanese versions of such well-known favourites as *Cats, Beauty and the Beast* and *A Chorus Line*.

In a city as cosmopolitan as Tokyo, it may come as a surprise to learn that only a smattering of productions in English are available each year, and some of these are thanks to touring troupes from the US or Britain, such as the Royal Shakespeare Company. However, the city has been seeing more avant-garde productions from the likes of Robert Wilson, while the **Festival/Tokyo** (www.festival-tokyo.jp) showcases cutting-edge overseas and domestic work.

There is also a thriving avant-garde theatre subculture in the suburb of Shimo-Kitazawa, which has a number of small venues.

TAKARAZUKA

Featuring an all-women, oft-moustachioed cast, the **Takarazuka Kagekidan** (Takarazuka Opera Company) is another uniquely Japanese creation. Created in 1913 by entertainment tycoon Kobayashi Ichizo to attract people to his Takarazuka resort near Osaka, Takarazuka was to provide 'strictly wholesome entertainment suitable for women and children from good families'. It is another expression of the Japanese fixation with androgynous performers. Its famously disciplined stars perform campy revues combining elements of musicals, opera and Japanese classics in gaudy productions that drive its mostly female audience wild with pleasure. The recent rebuilding and reopening of Hibiya's Tokyo Takarazuka Theater testifies to the continued vigour of this unusual art.

Dentsu Shiki Theatre Umi (SEA)

1-8-2 Higashi-Shinbashi, Minato-ku (0120 48 9944, www.shiki.gr.jp/siteinfo/english). Shiodome station (Oedo line), Shiodome-kaisatsu exit; (Yurikamome line), Dentsu exit. **Capacity** 1,200. **Box office** 10am-8pm daily. **Tickets** ¥3,150-¥11,550. **Credit** DC, JCB, MC, V.
The newest Western-style theatre in Tokyo – part of the Shiki Theatre Company's empire – opened in December 2002 in advertising giant Dentsu's new headquarters in the Shiodome area of Tokyo. Its remit is to provide Western musicals, such as *Phantom of the Opera*, sung in Japanese.

Meiji-za

2-31-1 Nihonbashi-Hamacho, Chuo-ku (3660 3900, www.meijiza.co.jp). Hamacho station (Shinjuku line), exit A2. **Capacity** 1,400. **Box office** 10am-5pm daily. **Tickets** ¥5,000-¥12,000. **Credit** DC, V.
Usually stages samurai dramas, often starring actors who play similar roles on TV. No English.

Tokyo Takarazuka Gekijo

1-1-3 Yurakucho, Chiyoda-ku (5251 2001, http://kageki.hankyu.co.jp/english). Yurakucho station (Yamanote, Yurakucho lines), Hibiya exit or Hibiya station (Chiyoda, Hibiya, Mita lines), exit A13. **Capacity** 2,000. **Box office** 10am-6pm Mon, Tue, Thur-Sun. **Tickets** ¥3,500-¥10,000. **Credit** JCB, MC, V. **Map** p59.
Performances are in Japanese only.

EXPAT THEATRE

With the limited number of English-language performances by companies touring from abroad, Tokyo's expatriate community has stepped up to fill the gap. There is currently a handful of English-language theatre groups in Japan, most of them based in Tokyo.

The most venerable – with over a century of history – is the **Tokyo International Players**, while **Intrigue Theatre** (www.intriguetheatre.com) is a more recent creation. Canadian director Robert Tsonos's **Sometimes Y Theatre** has recently relocated to Japan from Toronto, while **Black Stripe Theatre** (blackstripetheater.com) utilises expat Western actors in modern classics such as *Kiss of the Spider Woman*. Finally, Australian director Dwayne Lawler's **Rising Sun Theatre**, based in Nagoya, has shaken up the Tokyo theatre scene with controversial shows, and he also co-hosts the growing Tokyo Fringe Festival with dancer Shakti.

Tokyo International Players

TIP information 090 6009 4171, www.tokyo players.org. Performances held at the Tokyo American Club, 2-1-2 Azabudai, Minato-ku (3224 3670, www.tokyoamericanclub.org). Kamiyacho station (Hibiya line), exit 2 or Azabu-Juban station (Nanboku, Oedo lines), exit 6. **Box office** 7.30am-11pm daily. **Tickets** ¥4,000; ¥2,500 reductions. **No credit cards. Map** p87.
A keen group of amateur and professional actors, TIP usually stages productions at the long-running Tokyo American Club near Roppongi.

DANCE & PERFORMANCE ART

Tokyo is currently experiencing an explosion of contemporary performing arts. Avant-garde performance troupe **Chelfitsch** (www. chelfitsch.net) and choreographers such as **Un Yamada** (www1.ocn.ne.jp/~yaun/english. htm), who has transformed her joint disease into a source of inspiration, are integrating Eastern and Western aesthetics to create challenging and engaging spectacles.

Festivals in the metropolis, including the **Tokyo Performing Arts Market** (www.tpam.co.jp), and two biennial offerings, **Die Pratze Dance Festival** and **Dance Biennale Tokyo**, are increasingly ambitious, with new works by provocative Japanese and foreign choreographers.

For fans of circus arts, the Blue Man Group rolls into town for extended engagements, and Canada's 'nouveau cirque' juggernaut **Cirque du Soleil** now has a permanent show, *Zed*, in a dedicated theatre near Tokyo Disney Resort.

Classical ballet also has a devoted audience in Japan. The country churns out dancers noted for their technical proficiency, while overseas groups such as the Leningrad State Ballet and the New York City Ballet turn up regularly.

ARTS & ENTERTAINMENT

Tokyo's own companies include the celebrated **New National Theatre Ballet** (www.nntt. jac.go.jp), which recently received an ambitious new Artistic Director in the form of David Bintley. The **Tokyo Ballet** (www.nbs.or.jp) has an outstanding corps and hosts guests such as Sylvie Guillem, while the **Asami Maki Ballet** (www.ambt.jp) stages productions from *Swan Lake* to modern works such as the *Duke Ellington Suite*, which grew out of the company's long-standing relationship with legendary French choreographer Roland Petit. Meanwhile, dancer and heart-throb Tetsuya Kumakawa has been making waves with innovative productions from his **K-Ballet Company** (www.tbs.co.jp/kumakawa).

Anything Western and extroverted is also the rage in Tokyo. Tap dancing seems to be the latest fashion, while Latin dance forms from tango to salsa continue to be trendy. The **Asakusa Samba Carnival** (*see p223*), held in late August, regularly draws crowds of close to half a million.

BUTOH

Japan's greatest contribution to performing arts in the 20th century was the inimitable and enigmatic avant-garde dance form *butoh*. Differing from both classical Japanese and Western modern dance, but utilising aspects of both, *butoh* is immediately recognisable by the (mostly) shaved heads, white body paint and slow, often tortured movements of its performers.

Created by Tatsumi Hijikata and his fellow pioneers, *butoh*, which Hijikata originally named *'ankoku butoh'*, or 'dance of darkness', scandalised Japan in the late 1950s. It is inspired by Japanese folk dance and German Neue Tanz, and is spiritually associated with *Noh* – but looks like none of them. Dancers contort their bodies to express emotions ranging from pain and despair to absurdity and ecstasy. Sometimes they hardly move at all; a *butoh* spectacle can be simultaneously enthralling and exhausting.

Since the 1980s, when *butoh* began to startle overseas audiences, companies such as **Dairakudakan** (www.dairakudakan.com) and **Sankai Juku** (www.sankaijuku.com) have toured abroad on a regular basis. The recent closure of Asbestoskan means Tokyo no longer has a specialist theatre for *butoh*, but the dance form is still widely performed at venues such as the ambitious **Setagaya Public Theatre** or the more intimate **Kagurazaka Die Pratze**.

Meanwhile the **New National Theatre, Tokyo** (*see p250*) also presents modern dance and drama in its two smaller spaces, the Playhouse and the Pit.

Aoyama Round Theatre

*5-53-1 Jingumae, Shibuya-ku (3797 5678, 3797 1400 box office, www.aoyama.org).
Omotesando station (Chiyoda, Ginza, Hanzomon lines), exit B2.* **Capacity** 1,200. **Box office** 10am-6pm daily. **Tickets** vary. **No credit cards. Map** p93.

As its name suggests, this is a theatre that can be used in the round – one of very few in Tokyo. It attracts leading contemporary performers.

★ Cirque du Soleil Theatre Tokyo

2-50 Maihama, Urayasu, Chiba (0570 02 8666, www.zed.co.jp). Maihama station (Keiyo, Musashino lines). **Capacity** 2,170. **Box office** *In person* varies; show days only. *By phone* 7am-4am. **Tickets** ¥7,500-¥16,000. **Credit** AmEx, DC, JCB, MC, V.

Cirque du Soleil is so popular in Japan that the circus troupe got their own permanent home in the grounds of the Tokyo Disney Resort. Everything about the theatre, from the façade to the lighting, was designed with the show, Zed, in mind. Performances take place seven or eight times a week, with reservations accepted online in English.

▶ *For the Tokyo Disney Resort, see p120.*

Galaxy Theatre

2-3-16 Higashi-Shinagawa, Shinagawa-ku (5460 9999, www.gingeki.jp). Tennozu Isle station (Tokyo Monorail), Chuo exit; (Rinkai line), exits A, B. **Capacity** *Art Sphere* 746. *Sphere Mex* 200. **Box office** 10am-6pm daily. **Tickets** vary. **No credit cards.**

This theatre caters to the whims of well-off young fans of contemporary modern dance, booking things that are considered 'in', but not too avant-garde or risqué. The venue's location, on Tennozu Isle, makes it one of the more interesting – and less accessible – of Tokyo's theatrical venues.

Kagurazaka Die Pratze

2-12 Nishi-Gokencho, Shinjuku-ku (3235 7990, www.geocities.jp/kagurara2000). Kagurazaka station (Tozai line), exit 1. **Capacity** 100. **Box office** 6-11pm daily. **Tickets** ¥3,000. **No credit cards.**

This cosy space is a locus for cutting-edge dance, performance and *butoh*, as well as the host of the annual Die Pratze Dance Festival.

Session House

158 Yaraicho, Shinjuku-ku (3266 0461, www.session-house.net). Kagurazaka station (Tozai line), exit 1. **Capacity** 100. **Box office** 10am-10pm daily. **Tickets** ¥2,000-¥2,500. **No credit cards.**

Dancer Naoko Itoh established Session House in order to give solo dancers the opportunity to experiment. The aim is to showcase pure dance without the extensive use of theatrical props and high-tech lighting.

Setagaya Public Theatre

*4-1-1 Taishido, Setagaya-ku (5432 1526,
www.setagaya-ac.or.jp/sept). Sangenjaya station
(Tokyu Denentoshi line), Sancha Patio exit.*
Capacity *Public Theatre* 600. *Theatre Tram* 200.
Box office 10am-6pm daily. **Tickets** vary.
No credit cards.

Like the New National Theatre (*see p250*), this venue
is a favourite with fans and performers. The main
auditorium is modelled on a Greek open-air theatre,
but can be changed to proscenium style. The smaller
Theatre Tram is a popular venue for dance. The
building is the adopted home of the Sankai Juku
butoh troupe, when it's in town.

Theatre Cocoon

*Bunkamura, 2-24-1 Dogenzaka, Shibuya-ku
(3477 9999, www.bunkamura.co.jp). Shibuya
station (Yamanote, Ginza lines), Hachiko exit;
(Hanzomon line), exit 3A.* **Capacity** 750. **Box
office** 10am-7pm daily. *Phone bookings* 10am-
5.30pm daily. **Tickets** vary. **Credit** AmEx, DC,
JCB, MC, V. **Map** p93.

The medium-sized venue of the giant Bunkamura
arts centre in Shibuya is used mainly for musicals,
ballet, concerts and opera.

COMEDY

Japan has a tradition of humorous storytelling
called *rakugo*, which can be seen at a few
venues, including the **Asakusa Engei Hall**
(1-43-12 Asakusa, Taito-ku, 3841 6545) and
the **National Engei Hall** (4-1 Hayabusa-cho,
Chiyoda-ku, 3230 3000, www.ntj.jac.go.jp/
english). You'll need to speak Japanese to
follow the comedy, since there are no venues
with English translation.

For English-language comedy, the **Tokyo
Comedy Store** (www.tokyocomedy.com)
is a group of amateur comics who perform
regularly at various venues in the city.

Suehiro-tei

*3-6-12 Shinjuku, Shinjuku-ku (3351 2974,
www.suehirotei.com). Shinjuku-Sanchome
station (Marunouchi, Shinjuku lines),
exits B2, C4.* **Capacity** 325. **Box office**
noon-8.15pm daily. **Tickets** ¥2,200-¥2,700.
No credit cards. **Map** p101.

A charming old theatre that looks a lot like a bathhouse, Suehiro-tei hosts performances of Japan's
traditional *rakugo* comedy. No English translation.

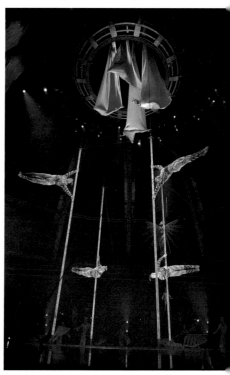

Cirque du Soleil Theatre Tokyo.

Sport & Fitness

From the dojo to the baseball diamond to the hydroplane pool.

If you've come to Japan for sporting reasons, you're probably heading to the dojo for martial arts training. But there's plenty more to this city. Japan is shaking off its inferiority complex in terms of team sports. The national football team still regularly underperforms, as do the capital's league teams, but the baseball stars won the first two World Baseball Classics, and players of both sports have impressed abroad. But while internationalism is celebrated when a local player signs for the Yankees or Red Sox, it's a different story in sumo, where the foreigners are winning, much to the chagrin of the men behind this traditional sport.

Sports facilities abound within the capital but are not always easy to use. Public swimming pools, in particular, have strict, confusing and often amusing rules (such as enforced cool-down periods).

SPECTATOR SPORTS

American football

Gridiron in Japan has a surprisingly large presence. There is a strong university league and even a company league, known as the **X-League** (where firms import top players and give them 'jobs'), which finishes with the **X Bowl** in Kobe in mid December. The climax of the domestic season is the brilliantly named **Rice Bowl**, at the Tokyo Dome (*see right*) in early January, when the college champions take on the winners of the X-League.

Athletics

Japan's real athletics passion has long been the marathon, even more so since Japanese women won the Olympic marathons in Sydney and Athens. The **Tokyo International Marathon** is held in February. It starts and finishes at the **National Stadium** (*see right*) and attracts some of the world's top runners. The IAAF Japan Grand Prix is held every spring in Osaka.

Baseball

Introduced to Japan in 1873, baseball has long held a firm grip here. The first pro side, the **Yomiuri Giants**, was founded in 1934, and

by 1950 a professional competition had been set up. The league eventually split into two divisions (the **Pacific League** and the **Central League**), with six teams in each.

Demand from both players and fans led to inter-league play since 2005, meaning Pacific League sides have been able to milk the cash cow known as the Yomiuri Giants – the New York Yankees of Japanese baseball. Each side plays 140 games a season (late March to October), with the winners of the Central and Pacific leagues meeting in the Japan Series to decide the championship.

Two teams are based in central Tokyo: the Yomiuri Giants at the **Tokyo Dome** (the salaryman's favourite, ergo somewhat dull) and the **Yakult Swallows** at **Jingu Stadium** (open-air, crazy fans and beer on tap – Jingu is the place to go). The **Hokkaido Nippon Ham Fighters** also play some games at the Tokyo Dome, their former home. In the Tokyo area you can also see the **Yokohama Bay Stars**, **Chiba Lotte Marines** and the **Seibu Lions**.

Worryingly for the future of the professional game has been the drain of local superstars to the US major leagues and the growing audience for live broadcasts from the US. Hideki Matsui of the Los Angeles Angels, Daisuke Matsuzaka of the Boston Red Sox and Ichiro Suzuki of the Seattle Mariners are all huge in Japan, and most of their games are broadcast live.

Jingu Stadium
13 Kasumigaoka-cho, Shinjuku-ku (3404 8999). Gaienmae station (Ginza line), exit 2 or Kokuritsu-Kyogijo station (Oedo line), exit A4 or Sendagaya station (Chuo line). **Capacity** 46,000. **Tickets** ¥1,500-¥4,500.
This large open-air stadium is part of the complex that includes the National Stadium and was built for the 1964 Olympics.

Tokyo Dome
1-3-61 Koraku, Bunkyo-ku (5800 9999, www.tokyo-dome.co.jp). Kasuga station (Mita, Oedo line), exit A1 or Korakuen station (Marunouchi, Namboku lines), exit 2 or Suidobashi station (Chuo line), west exit; (Mita line), exits A3, A4, A5. **Capacity** 42,000. **Tickets** ¥1,700-¥5,900.
The Dome, or Big Egg, is home to the Central League's Yomiuri Giants. In the past, the Giants have claimed that every game was sold out, but the growing number of empty seats suggests that tickets are much easier to acquire than before.

Football

The 2002 World Cup saw the eyes of the football universe focused on Japan and co-hosts South Korea, although the closest Tokyo came in terms of venues was suburban Saitama and nearby Yokohama, which hosted the final. Tokyo was also left on the sidelines when the **J.League** was founded in 1993, but the capital now has one top-flight team, **FC Tokyo**, and one that has spent time in the division, Tokyo Verdy 1969. They share a ground in the west of the city. The **Urawa Reds** and **Omiya Ardija** in Saitama to the north, **JEF United Ichihara** to the east, and **Kawasaki Frontale** and **Yokohama F Marinos** to the west are the other major local clubs. The J.League's official website (www.j-league.or.jp/eng) has English-language details of clubs, players and fixtures.

INSIDE TRACK
THE BIG SCREEN

For three years, the **Tokyo Racecourse** (*see p278*) boasted the world's largest high-definition screen. Though it was dethroned in 2009 by the screen at Cowboys Stadium in Texas, Tokyo's 66- by 11-metre (218- by 37-foot) telly is still the world's longest, and generates so much heat that it comes equipped with a gargantuan air-conditioning unit. The screen shows close-ups of the action on the turf, as well as races on other courses.

From 2005, the league expanded to 18 teams and has changed to a single-stage season. The **Emperor's Cup** (Japan's FA Cup) takes place in December, with the final (*see p226*) on New Year's Day. The **Nabisco Cup** (the equivalent of the League Cup) runs throughout the season, with the final in early November. International matches take place year-round and include Asian Cup and World Cup qualifiers, as well as the midsummer Kirin Cup. The **Japan Football Association**'s English website (www.jfa.or.jp/eng) has information on forthcoming matches.

Ajinomoto Stadium
376-3 Nishimachi, Chofu (0424 40 0555, www.ajinomotostadium.com). Tobitakyu station (Keio line). **Capacity** 50,000. **Tickets** *J.League matches* ¥1,200-¥6,000.
The large and impressive home of FC Tokyo and Tokyo Verdy 1969 opened in 2001.

National Stadium
10-25 Kasumigaoka-machi, Shinjuku-ku (3403 4150). Kokuritsu-Kyogijo station (Oedo line), exit A4 or Sendagaya station (Chuo line) or Gaienmae station (Ginza line), exit 2. **Capacity** 60,000.
The 1964 Olympic Stadium still hosts many major events, including the start and finish of marathons, some international and J.League football matches, the Emperor's Cup final, the Nabisco Cup final and major rugby matches.

Nissan Stadium
3300 Kozukue-cho, Kohoku-ku, Yokohama-shi (045 477 5000, www.nissan-stadium.jp/English). Shin-Yokohama station (Tokaido Shinkansen, Yokohama lines), north exit then 15min walk. **Capacity** 70,000. **Tickets** ¥1,900-¥4,500.
Home of Nissan-sponsored Yokohama F Marinos. You can also take a World Cup tour (*see p289*).

Saitama Stadium 2002
500 Nakanoda, Midori-ku, Saitama (048 812 2002, www.stadium2002.com). Urawa-Misono station (Nanboku, Saitama Railway lines). **Capacity** 63,700. **Tickets** *J.League matches* ¥2,000-¥4,500.
This is the country's largest soccer-only stadium and the home of the nation's most popular team, the Urawa Reds. It's a 20-minute walk from Urawa-Misono station, which gets extremely crowded after major events.

Golf

Like much else in Japan, golf suffered when the Bubble burst in the 1990s. At its peak, the **Japan Golf Tour** (JGTO; www.jgto.org) was the richest in the world, lucrative enough to keep

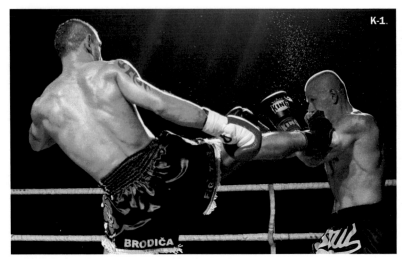

K-1.

local golfers from playing abroad. Reduced sponsorship has seen the tour contract slightly, but it retains very high standards. There are many professional events in the Tokyo area, and many foreign stars visit Japan after the PGA and European tours. The biggest event in the Tokyo area is the **Sumitomo VISA Taiheiyo Masters** in Gotemba, an hour west of Tokyo.

The **Women's Tour** has also produced its fair share of stars, notably Ai Miyazato. In 2003, high-school student Miyazato won a JLPGA tournament, turned pro and caught the imagination of the country, revitalising the waning Women's Tour.

Horse racing

The Japan Racing Association (JRA) manages the ten national tracks and stages the country's big races, while the National Association of Racing (NAR) oversees local courses. Racetracks are one of the few places in the country where gambling is legal. For details in English, visit the Japan Association for International Horse Racing website at www.jair.jrao.ne.jp.

Oi Racecourse
2-1-2 Katsushima, Shinagawa-ku (3763 2151). Oi Keibajomae station (Tokyo Monorail).
Run by the NAR, this course hosts some 120 race days every year. Twinkle Races, evening events that Oi pioneered in the 1990s, have proved very popular with office workers.

Tokyo Racecourse
1-1 Hiyoshi-cho, Fuchu-shi (042 363 3141, www. jra.go.jp/facilities/race/tokyo). Fuchu-Honmachi station (Musashino line) or Fuchukeiba-Seimonmae station (Keio line).
Run by the JRA, Tokyo Racecourse hosts 40 days' racing a year, all at weekends. Many of Japan's most famous races are held here, including November's Japan Cup (*see p225*), an invitational that attracts top riders and horses from around the world.

Hydroplane racing

After horse racing, *kyotei* is the second-most popular focus for betting in Japan (bets start at just ¥100). The race itself involves six motor-driven boats in what is essentially a very large swimming pool; they go round the 600-metre (1,970-foot) course three times, regularly reaching speeds of over 80km/h (50mph). Edogawa Kyotei is the favourite Tokyo venue. The schedule is published in sports newspapers and on the Edogawa Kyotei website.

Edogawa Kyotei
3-1-1 Higashi-Komatsugawa, Edogawa-ku (3656 0641, www.edogawa-kyotei.co.jp). Funabori station (Shinjuku line), south exit. **Admission** ¥50.

Ice hockey

The economic recession has hit the Japan Ice Hockey League hard in recent years. The league came close to folding, but fought back with a novel mode of expansion: importing teams from overseas. So now there is an **Asian League** (www.alhockey.com) consisting of the four remaining Japanese teams (Oji, Tohoku, Nikko Ice Bucks and Nippon Paper Cranes), one team from China, and two from South Korea.

Higashi-Fushimi Ice Arena
3-1-25 Higashi-Fushimi, Hoya-shi
(0424 67 7171). Higashi-Fushimi station
(Seibu Shinjuku line).

National Yoyogi Stadium
1st Gymnasium
2-1-1 Jinnan, Shibuya-ku (3468 1171).
Harajuku station (Yamanote line), Omotesando
exit or Meiji-Jingumae station (Chiyoda line),
exit 2. **Map** p65.

Shin-Yokohama Prince Hotel
Skate Centre
2-11 Shin-Yokohama, Kohoku-ku, Yokohama-shi,
Kanagawa (045 474 1112). Shin-Yokohama
station (Tokaido Shinkansen, Yokohama lines),
north exit then 10mins walk.

K-1

People are often surprised to learn that the record attendance (74,500) for a sports event at Tokyo Dome is held by K-1, a mishmash of martial arts. It's basically a combination of boxing and kick-boxing, with bouts consisting of three three-minute rounds (if there are no knockouts). It has all the appearance of a real sport – bouts take place in a ring with a referee and three judges; doctors are in attendance; rules are enforced; it has a competitive structure – but is not taken completely seriously by all sports fans.

Events are held most months at venues such as the **Nippon Budokan** (*see below*), **Yoyogi Gymnasium** (*see above*) and the **Tokyo Dome** (*see p277*).

Martial arts

Nippon Budokan
2-3 Kitanomaru-koen, Chiyoda-ku (3216 5100,
www.nipponbudokan.or.jp). Kudanshita station
(Hanzomon, Shinjuku, Tozai lines), exit 2.
Map p77.
The Budokan stages the All-Japan Championships or equivalent-level demonstration events in all the martial arts except sumo. Advance tickets are not required, and in many cases admission is free.
▶ *The stadium is also used for concerts; see p257.*

Motor sports

Motor sports have a devoted following in Japan. The **Fuji Speedway** (0550 78 1234, www.fsw.tv), in the foothills of the famous mountain, hosts the annual **Formula 1 Japan Grand Prix**. It's a two-hour train ride from Tokyo. The **Twin Ring Motegi** in Tochigi prefecture, a couple of hours north-east of the capital, has two types of circuit, including

an oval course that's suitable for US-style motor sports. The permanent circuit hosts local **Formula 3** and **Formula Nippon** races, the latter seen as a major stepping stone towards Formula 1.

Motorcycle racing is also a big draw in Japan, and several top riders are home-grown. The **Japanese Grand Prix** is held in September at the Motegi circuit.

Twin Ring Motegi
120-1 Hiyama, Motegi-machi, Haga-gun,
Tochigi-ken (0285 64 0001, www.mobilityland.
co.jp/english). Motegi station (Moka line) then bus.

Pride

Pride competes for attention with K-1 in the mixed martial arts field, and is similar to the Ultimate Fighting Championships in the US. Pride's selling point is that it is 'as close as you can get to street fighting'; everything goes, almost – there's no biting or testicular activity. The sport contains elements of karate, boxing, judo, wrestling and kick-boxing. Fights can include some sporty moments of punching and kicking, and other moments where one fighter sits on the other and beats him to a pulp. It's not for the faint-hearted.

Rugby

Japanese rugby underwent a major upheaval in 2003 with the introduction of a national professional league. Cynics would say Japan already had a professional operation for many years in the form of the corporate league; however, the game was amateurish and in dire need of reform. Now there is a national league, a national championship (which includes the top university teams) and a knockout trophy – and the **Japan Rugby Football Union** (JRFU) has won the nation the right to host the 2019 World Cup.

Tokyo's Waseda University is one of the most popular sports 'franchises' in the country; matches are often held before 60,000 fans at the **National Stadium** (*see p277*). **Prince Chichibu Memorial Stadium** is the official home of rugby and is slap bang in the centre of town, next to Jingu Baseball Stadium. Ticket information is available at the JRFU website: www.jrfu-members.com.

Prince Chichibu Memorial Stadium
2-8-35 Kita Aoyama, Minato-ku (3401 3321).
Gaienmae station (Ginza line), exit 2
or Kokuritsu-Kyogijo station (Oedo line),
exit A4 or Sendagaya station (Chuo line).
Internationals and other big rugby matches not held at the National Stadium are played here.

The Sumo Workout

The big guys show you how to get in shape.

Sumo's incredible hulks might not be obvious role models for a fitness regime, but behind the flab are athletes of awesome strength, stamina and reflexes. Follow their exercises, skip their diets, and you might see some big benefits. The sport's governing body, the Nihon Sumo Kyokai, has created an exercise programme that draws on the sport's signature thrusts, stomps and stretches. Regular practice, they say, will relax your muscles, improve circulation, strengthen the spine, stimulate the nervous system and slow the aging process, among other benefits. The exercises are to be performed barefoot, and the Sumo Kyokai asks that you start and finish the routine with a bow.

SEME-NO-KATA (ATTACKING EXERCISE)
This exercise strengthens the ankles, knees, legs and lower back. It also improves lower-body balance.

One   *Two*

1 Make a fist with both hands, draw your arms into your chest, then shout as you push your arms forward.
2 Bring your arms into your sides again.
3 Shift your weight onto your right foot as you stretch your right arm forward. Focus your eyes on your outstretched hand and keep your other hand tight to your side.
4 Shift your weight to your left foot and repeat the exercise with your left arm.

YOTSUMI-NO-KATA (BELT-GRABBING EXERCISE)
This works your ankles, knees and wrists.

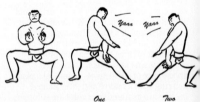

One   *Two*

1 Start as in the Seme-no-kata (above).
2 Shift your weight onto your right leg, raise your right arm, turn your elbow out and thrust your palm toward your forehead.
3 Turn your other outstretched hand inward and thrust it toward your crotch.
4 Repeat for the left side.

Sumo

With a history dating back 2,000 years, Japan's national sport uniquely blends tradition, athleticism and religion. Its rules are simple: each combatant must try to force the other out of the ring (*dohyo*) or make him touch the floor with a part of his anatomy other than his feet. Tournaments take place over 15 days, with wrestlers fighting once a day. Those who achieve regular majorities (winning more than they lose) progress up the rankings, the top of which is *yokozuna* (grand champion). Wrestlers failing to achieve a majority are demoted. *Yokozuna* must achieve a majority in every tournament or will face pressure to retire.

Three of the six annual tournaments take place in Tokyo (in January, May and September)

at the **Ryogoku Kokugikan**, which also hosts one-day tournaments and retirement ceremonies. For ticket information, results and interviews, see the websites of the **Sumo Association** (www.sumo.or.jp/eng).

Ryogoku Kokugikan
1-3-28 Yokoami, Sumida-ku (3623 5111, 5237 9310 balcony seats booking). Ryogoku station (Oedo line), exits A3, A4; (Sobu line), west exit. **Tickets** ¥3,600-¥14,300.
Advance tickets go on sale about a month before each tournament. They're not difficult to get hold of (apart from the most expensive box seats) – though weekends generally sell out. Some unreserved, back-row balcony seats (one per person) are always held back for sale from 8am on the day of the tournament. Many spectators watch bouts between younger

KINSEI-NO-KATA (BALANCE EXERCISE)

The culmination of the sumo routine, these exercises help energy flow around your body.

1 Focus your mind on your abdomen.
2 Turn your heels inward and shuffle forward, scuffing the ground.
3 Return your feet to the start position.
4 Draw a circle with both hands in front of you three times.
5 Press your hands together and slowly raise your upper body while shuffling forward.
6 Keeping your hands pressed together, turn your elbows out.
7 Without raising your hips, raise both hands into the air.
8 Return to the original position.

● *To see the full exercise routine or for information about upcoming tournaments, visit www.sumo.or.jp/eng.*

---

fighters from downstairs box seats until the ticket holders arrive in the mid afternoon. There's also a small museum (closed on tournament days).
▶ *For information on visiting a sumo stable, see pp48-49 Ryogoku.*

Tennis

In professional tennis, it's the women's game that gets the most attention in Japan. A number of female players have won Grand Slam doubles titles, and Japan's most successful player of all time, Kimiko Date, made the semi-finals in the singles at Wimbledon. A more recent favourite was the now-retired Ai Sugiyama.

The biggest event is the **Toray Pan Pacific Open** (*see p223*), a Tier I WTA tournament held in the month following the US Open at the end of September at the **Tokyo Metropolitan Gymnasium**. The biggest men's event is the **Japan Open** (*see p223*) in October, which is held at the **Ariake Tennis Forest** on Odaiba and also features a Tier III WTA event.

Ariake Tennis Forest & Ariake Colosseum

2-2-22 Ariake, Koto-ku (3529 3301, www. tptc.co.jp/park/ariake.htm). Ariake station (Yurikamome line) or Kokusai-Tenjijo station (Rinkai line). **Open** 9am-9pm daily. **Rates** ¥1,500/hr Mon-Fri; ¥1,800/hr Sat, Sun. **Map** p83.

Tokyo Metropolitan Gymnasium

1-17-1 Sendagaya, Shibuya-ku (5474 2112, www. tef.or.jp/tmg). Kokuritsu-Kyogijo station (Oedo line), exit A4 or Sendagaya station (Chuo line).

ACTIVE SPORTS & FITNESS

Aussie Rules football

The **Tokyo Goannas** (www.tokyogoannas. com) satisfy the Australian community's need for sport and drink.

Boxing

There are various gyms around Tokyo, and boxercise fitness training is available at several sports clubs. Also try **Nitta Boxing Gym** (044 932 4639, www.nittagym.com).

Canyoning

Canyoning and white-water rafting, with English-speaking guides, is on offer in the Gunma, Shikoku and Nagano prefectures, each around 90 minutes from Tokyo. See www.canyons.jp for further details.

Cricket

Decent cricket is available in Tokyo, notably among certain expat communities – check out the **Tokyo Wombats** (www.tokyowombats. com) and the **Indian Engineers** (www.iecc japan.com/kantocup.htm). The **Japan Cricket Association** site is www.cricket.or.jp/eng.

Cycling

It's not quite Amsterdam, but Tokyo is a relatively cycle-friendly place. There are no bicycle lanes; technically cyclists are required to ride to the left of vehicles on the roads. In reality, nobody pays any attention to this and all but the couriers use the pavements. The only legal issue to note is that night riders must wear lights and reflectors.

You can carry your bike on a train, as long as you follow the bizarre rule of carrying it in a bag. This rule is enforced with greatly varying degrees of fervour, but if your itinerary requires riding a rail, it's a good idea to take a bin liner to appease any overly eager station staff you might encounter on your journey.

For cycle hire, *see p310.*

Football

There's quite a lot of soccer action in Tokyo, with several competitions for all levels. Major organisations are the **Tokyo Metropolis League** (www.footyjapan.com/tml) and the **International Friendship Football League** (http://home.att.ne.jp/sun/iffl). The British Football Academy (www.footyjapan.com/bfat) also offers English-language coaching sessions for children at locations throughout Tokyo.

Golf

With time and expense posing substantial obstacles to the capital's legion of would-be golfers, driving ranges dot the city. The cost of membership at private golf clubs can easily run to millions of yen, while green fees run from ¥8,000 on weekdays to ¥30,000 at weekends. The least expensive courses are those along built-up riverbanks to the west and north of the capital. There are online reservation sites (try http://gora.golf.rakuten.co.jp), but only in Japanese. The **Tokyo Metropolitan Golf Course** (18 holes at par 63) is the cheapest of the city's public courses; booking is essential at weekends.

Golf in Japan is usually a game of two halves, broken up by an hour-long lunch break.

Tokyo Metropolitan Golf Course

1-15-1 Shinden, Adachi-ku (3919 0111). Oji-Kamiya station (Nanboku line). **Open** dawn-dusk daily. **Rates** ¥5,000 Mon-Fri; ¥6,000 Sat, Sun.

Gyms

Membership of private gyms can be very expensive. Large hotels may have swimming pools or gyms, but sometimes charge extra for using them. If you are in need of some muscle-pumping action, head for one of the following – or, more cheaply, visit one of Tokyo's public sports centres (*see p284*).

Esforta

Shibuya Infoss Tower B1F, 20-1 Sakuragaokacho, Shibuya-ku (3780 5551, www.esforta.com). Shibuya station (Yamanote line), south exit; (Ginza, Hanzomon lines), Hachiko exit.

Open 7am-10.30pm Mon-Fri; 9.30am-7pm Sat, Sun. Closed 1st Sun of mth. **Rates** ¥10,000 membership, then ¥15,000/mth. **Map** p93. Facilities typically include aerobics, sauna, weight machines and sunbeds. The Suidobashi and Akasaka branches have swimming pools.
Other locations throughout the city.

Gold's Gym Harajuku

V28 Building 3F, 6-31-17 Jingumae, Shibuya-ku (5766 3131, www.goldsgym.jp). Harajuku station (Yamanote line), Omotesando exit or Meiji-Jingumae station (Chiyoda line), exit 6. **Open** 24hrs daily; closed 8pm Sun-7am Mon. **Rates** ¥5,250 membership, then from ¥7,350/mth. **Credit** AmEx, DC, JCB, MC, V. **Map** p65. All of the facilities you would expect from this worldwide gym chain.
Other locations throughout the city.

Tipness

Kaleido Bldg 5F-7F, 7-1 Nishi-Shinjuku, Shinjuku-ku (3368 3531, 0120 208 025 freephone, www.tipness.co.jp). Shinjuku station (Yamanote, Chuo, Sobu lines), east or west exit; (Marunouchi line), exit A18 or Shinjuku-Nishi station (Oedo line), exit D5. **Open** 7am-11.15pm Mon-Fri; 9.30am-10pm Sat; 9.30am-8pm Sun. Closed 3rd & 15th of each month. **Rates** ¥3,150 membership, then from ¥5,565/mth. **Credit** AmEx, DC, JCB, MC, V. **Map** p101.
Tipness has more than 25 branches within Tokyo. Most have a pool, aerobics classes and weights gym.
Other locations throughout the city.

Horse riding

Tokyo Horse Riding Club

4-8 Yoyogi Kamizono-cho, Shibuya-ku (3370 0984, www.tokyo-rc.or.jp). Sangubashi station (Odakyu line). **Open** Mar-Nov 9am-5.45pm

---

INSIDE TRACK
THE PALACE RUN

The city's most popular jogging route is the five-kilometre (three mile) circuit of the **Imperial Palace** (*see p78*). It's picturesque, with wide pavements, water fountains and nearby 'ranste' (an abbreviation of 'runner station') offering showers and changing rooms. To keep things orderly, everyone runs anticlockwise around the palace. If you are running in the afternoon or evening, finish with a soak in the **Bain Douche** *sento* (1-5-4 Kojimachi, Chiyoda-ku, 3263 4944, open 3pm-11.30pm Mon-Sat, ¥450), near Hanzomon station.

Tue-Sun. *Dec-Feb* 9am-4.45pm Tue-Sun. **Rates** (¥3,000 surcharge for beginners) ¥6,500 Tue-Fri; ¥7,500 Sat, Sun. **No credit cards.**
Japan's oldest riding club employs some 45 horses and seven instructors. Visitors don't, thankfully, have to pay the annual membership fee of ¥96,000 (to join the Tokyo Horse Riding Club you must be recommended by two members and pay a fee of ¥2 million). Booking is necessary.

Ice skating

Championship events are held at the National Yoyogi Stadium 1st Gymnasium (*see p279*).

Meiji Jingu Ice Skating Rink
Gobanchi, Kasumigaoka, Shinjuku (3403 3458, www.meijijingugaien.jp/sports/ice-skating). Kokuritsu-Kyogijo station (Oedo line), exit A2 or Sendagaya station (Chuo, Sobu lines). **Open** noon-6pm Mon-Fri; 10am-6pm Sat, Sun. **Admission** ¥1,000-¥1,300; ¥500-¥900 children. *Skate rental* ¥500. **No credit cards.**

Takadanobaba Citizen Ice Skating Rink
4-29-27 Takadanobaba, Shinjuku-ku (3371 0910, www.citizen-plaza.co.jp). Takadanobaba station (Yamanote line), east exit; (Tozai line), exit 1. **Open** noon-7.45pm Mon-Sat; 10am-6pm Sun. **Admission** ¥1,000-¥1,300; ¥600-¥800 children. *Skate rental* ¥500. **No credit cards.**

Martial arts

Almost five million people practise martial arts in Japan. There are nine recognised modern forms – aikido, judo, *jukendo*, karate, kendo, *kyudo*, *naginata*, *shorinji kempo* and sumo – and a series of more traditional forms, known as *kobudo*. The national associations of each discipline often have training facilities where you can view sessions. They may also know of dojos that welcome visitors or potential students.

Aikido *Aikikai Federation, 17-18 Wakamatsucho, Shinjuku-ku (3203 9236, www.aikikai.or.jp).*
Also check out the English website www.tokyoseidokan.com – the organisation was established by American teacher Chris Koprowski.
Judo *All-Japan Judo Federation, 1-16-30 Kasuga, Bunkyo-ku (3818 4199, www.judo.or.jp, www.kodokan.org).*
Jukendo *All-Japan Jukendo Federation, 2-3 Kitanomaru Koen, Chiyoda-ku (3201 1020, www.jukendo.or.jp).*
Karate Be warned: there are multiple governing bodies for karate, and they could be reproducing even as you read this. Try www.wpka-kobukan.org (which has a dojo in Nakano, Tokyo); or the Japan Karatedo Federation (3503 6637, www.karatedo.co.jp) in Minato-ku.

Tokyo Marathon.

Kendo *All-Japan Kendo Federation, Yasukuni Kudan Minami Bldg 2F, 2-3-14 Kudan-Minami, Chiyoda-ku (3234 6271, www.kendo.or.jp).*
Wooden-sword fighting, which is held, to some extent, in similar esteem to sumo. Favoured by rightists, politicians, gangsters and the police.
Kobudo *Nippon Kobudo Association, 2-3 Kitanomaru Koen, Chiyoda-ku (3216 5114).*
Kyudo *All-Japan Kyudo Federation, Kishi Kinen Taiikukaikan, 1-1-1 Jinnan, Shibuya-ku (3481 2387, www.kyudo.jp).*
Naginata *All-Japan Naginata Federation (Tokyo Office), Kishi Kinen Taiikukaikan, 1-1-1 Jinnan, Shibuya-ku (3481 2411, http://naginata.jp).*
Wooden spear fighting, popular with girls.
Shorinji Kempo *Shorinji Kempo Federation (Tokyo Office), 2-17-5 Otsuka, Toshima-ku (5961 3950, www.shorinjikempo.or.jp).*
Fascinating karate-type martial art created after the war 'with the aim of educating people with strong senses of compassion, courage and justice'.
Sumo (amateur) *Japan Sumo Federation, 1-15-20 Hyakunincho, Shinjuku-ku (3368 2211, www.sumo.or.jp/eng).*

Running

The big events for hobby runners, held close to the date of the **Tokyo Marathon** (February), are the ten-kilometre (6.2 mile) and 30-kilometre (18.6 mile) road races in Ome in north-west Tokyo prefecture (information on 0428 24 6311).

ARTS & ENTERTAINMENT

Those looking for a little gentle jogging might want to check out the five-kilometre (3.1 mile) route marked out at 100-metre intervals around the Imperial Palace. **Namban Rengo** (www.namban.org) is a hobby runners' club with English-speaking members.

Skiing & snowboarding

Just 90 minutes away by train lies a range of slopes that are snowy in winter. From December to March, JR ticket windows offer all-in-one deals covering ski pass and day-return transport for the destination of your choice, with weekday prices starting from under ¥10,000. Expat-run website www.welovesnow.com has a guide to resorts and can arrange winter sports packages. There are also year-round indoor slopes.

Sayama

2167 Kamiyamaguchi Tokorozawa-shi, Saitama (04 2922 1384, www.sayama-ski.jp). Seibu Kyujomae station (Seibu Ikebukuro line). **Open** 10am-9pm Mon-Fri; also 10pm-6am occasional weekends. **Admission** ¥3,500 Mon-Fri; ¥4,000 Sat, Sun. **Credit** JCB, MC, V.
A 320m (1,050ft) slope for skiers and snowboarders, with clothing, boots, board and ski rental available.

Snova Mizonokuchi-R246

1358-1 Shimo-Sakunobe, Takatsu-ku, Kawasaki-shi, Kanagawa (044 844 1181, www.snova246. com). Tsudayama station (Nanbu line). **Open** 10am-11pm Mon-Fri; 9am-11.30pm Sat; 9am-11pm Sun. **Rates** ¥1,000 membership, then (Mon-Fri) ¥2,500/2hrs, ¥4,000/4hrs; (Sat, Sun) ¥3,000/2hrs, ¥4,000/4hrs. **Credit** JCB, MC, V.
For skiers and snowboarders, though lessons are for snowboarders only. Equipment rental is available.

Sports centres

Each of Tokyo's 23 wards provides sports facilities, with bargain prices for residents and commuters. Most are also open to non-residents and non-commuters, but at higher prices.

Chiyoda Kuritsu Sogo Taiikukan Pool

2-1-8 Uchi-Kanda, Chiyoda-ku (3256 8444, www. city.chiyoda.tokyo.jp/sisetu/sports.htm). Kanda station (Yamanote line), west exit or Otemachi station (Chiyoda, Hanzomon, Marunouchi, Mita, Tozai lines), exit A2. **Open** varies. Closed every 3rd Mon. **Admission** *Pool* ¥600/2hrs. *Gym* ¥500. **No credit cards. Map** p77.
This centre consists of a swimming pool and gym within a weight's throw of Tokyo's business district.

Chuo-ku Sogo Sports Centre

Hamacho Koen Nai, 2-59-1 Nihonbashi-Hamacho, Chuo-ku (3666 1501). Hamacho station (Hibiya, Shinjuku lines), exit A2. **Open** *Pool* 7am-9.10pm daily. *Gym* 8.30am-8.40pm daily. Closed every 3rd Mon. **Admission** *Pool* ¥500. *Gym* ¥400. **No credit cards**.

Ikebukuro Sports Centre

Kenko Plaza Toshima Bldg 9F, 2-5-1 Kami-Ikebukuro, Toshima-ku (5974 7262). Ikebukuro station (Yamanote line), north exit; (Marunouchi, Yurakucho lines), exits C5, C6. **Open** 8.30am- 9.30pm daily. Closed 2nd Mon of mth. **Admission** ¥600; ¥300 reductions. **No credit cards. Map** p69.
A 25m pool on the 11th floor and a well-equipped gym on the tenth floor. Both offer great views.

Minato-ku Sports Centre

3-1-19 Shibaura, Minato-ku (3452 4151, www.city.minato.tokyo.jp/sisetu/sports/center). Tamachi station (Yamanote, Keihin Tohoku lines), Shibaura exit. **Open** 9am-9pm daily. Closed 1st & 3rd Mon of mth. **Admission** ¥700. **No credit cards**.
Pool, sauna, weights gym and aerobics classes.

Shinagawa Sogo Taiikukan Pool

5-6-11 Kita-Shinagawa, Shinagawa-ku (3449 4400, www.ssa.or.jp/modules/contents14). Osaki station (Yamanote line), east exit. **Open** hours vary. **Admission** *Pool* ¥350/2hrs. **No credit cards**.
No-frills pool, as well as tennis and badminton.

Shinjuku-ku Sports Centre

3-5-1 Okubo, Shinjuku-ku (3232 0171, www.shinjuku-spocen.com). Shin-Okubo or Takadanobaba stations (Yamanote line), Waseda exit; (Tozai line), exit 3. **Open** 9am-10pm daily. Closed every 4th Mon. **Admission** *Pool* ¥400 2hrs. *Gym* ¥400/3hrs. **No credit cards**.

Tokyo Metropolitan Gymnasium Pool

1-17-1 Sendagaya, Shibuya-ku (5474 2111, www.tef.or.jp/tmg). Kokuritsu-Kyogijo station (Oedo line), exit A4 or Sendagaya station (Chuo line). **Open** 9am-11pm Mon-Fri; 9am-10pm Sat; 9am-9pm Sun. **Admission** *Pool* ¥600. *Gym* ¥450/2hrs. **No credit cards**.
Run by the Tokyo Metropolitan Government, this centre has both 25m and 50m swimming pools, a weights gym, arena and athletics field. The smaller pool is not open to the public every day and rarely before 1.30pm; phone to check before you go.

Tennis

Municipal courts exist for those who want a game, but applications are often by lottery and sometimes require a minimum of four players. There's also the huge **Ariake Tennis Forest** (*see p281*).

Escapes & Excursions

Shinkyo. *See p300.*

Yokohama	286
Hakone	**292**
Map Hakone	293
Kamakura	**295**
Nikko	**300**
Easy Day Trips	**303**
Kawagoe	303
Jiko-ji Temple	304
Climbing Mt Fuji	304
Oya-machi	306

Escapes & Excursions

Leave Tokyo behind to get a taste of the real Japan.

If your itinerary says 'Tokyo; Kyoto if there's time,' you won't be the first, but you'd be overlooking some major attractions that are within easy reach of the capital.

Japan's second most populous city, **Yokohama**, is just 15 minutes away by *shinkansen* bullet train, and from there it's a quick hop to **Kamakura**, the scenic one-time capital. **Nikko** and **Kawagoe** both offer more photo-fantastic history, while **Hakone** is Tokyoites' favourite weekend getaway destination, offering hot springs and a view of **Mt Fuji**. Pull yourself away from the city and see what the real Japan looks like.

Japan's Second City

YOKOHAMA

With a population of 3.6 million, Yokohama is Japan's second-largest city and yet also one of its newest. Until the mid 19th century, it was a sleepy fishing village on Tokyo Bay, but that all changed after the US-Japanese Treaty of Amity of 1858. Designated one of the first ports open to foreign trade, the village expanded rapidly to become the country's biggest commercial port.

Thanks largely to its waterside location, Yokohama has a spacious feel – especially around the landfill development area known as **Minato Mirai** (literally, 'Port Future'). It also has a cosmopolitan, outward-looking atmosphere and a more relaxed tempo than Tokyo. And although a modern city, it has some historic buildings, traditional gardens and museums to go with its bayside views.

Yokohama is perfect for a day trip from the capital, being less than 30 minutes by train from Shibuya station, and relatively compact to boot. There are five main areas of note in the city, strung along the side of the bay. Skip the commercial district around Yokohama station, unless you need to use the shopping malls, department stores or pick up an airport limousine bus at Yokohama City Air Terminal (YCAT). Minato Mirai offers entertainment and views, and houses some major hotels. **Kannai** and **Bashamichi** form the city's administrative centre. The upmarket **Motomachi** shopping district lies next to **Chinatown**. And the historic **Yamate Bluff** area offers great parks and views.

You can get around the touristy part of the city by boat. **Sea Bass** (045 671 7719, www.yokohama-cruising.jp) has services linking Yokohama station east exit and Yamashita Pier via Minato Mirai every 20 to 30 minutes from 10am until 7.25pm daily. The full trip costs ¥700; ¥350 reductions.

For a more sedate view of the harbour, cruise ships depart from Yamashita Pier and tour the bay. Try **Marine Rouge**, **Marine Shuttle** (both with the same contact details as Sea Bass) or **Royal Wing** (045 662 6125, www.royalwing.co.jp). The 90-minute cruises start from ¥2,400. More pricey dinner cruises are also available.

YOKOHAMA IN A DAY

Minato Mirai, an enormous complex built on landfill reclaimed from old dockland, makes a good place to begin exploring the city.

From Sakuragi-cho station, take the moving walkway outside the Minato Mirai exit and head towards the area's central feature, the aptly named **Landmark Tower** – the second-tallest building in Japan. The lower floors house restaurants and designer boutiques, as does the adjoining **Queen's Square** shopping centre (045 682 1000, ww.qsy.co.jp/english, shops 11am-8pm, restaurants 11am-10pm daily), a giant shopping and dining complex consisting of several separate but linked tower blocks. (If you arrive by the Tokyu Toyoko/ Minato Mirai line, the station is right under the shopping centre.)

This whole area is built on the port's old dry docks, one of which has been preserved for use as a public amphitheatre, adjacent to Queen's Square. Behind the Landmark Tower is the **Yokohama Museum of Art**, with its collection of modern art and photography.

Retracing your steps past the *Nihon Maru*, a preserved pre-war sailing ship once known as the 'Swan of the Pacific', you'll reach the **Kisha-Michi Promenade** (almost directly in front of the tourist centre outside Sakuragi-cho station). Built along the route of an old freight railway track, this will take you towards the giant Ferris wheel in the **Yokohama Cosmoworld** amusement park.

Skirting around **Yokohama World Porters** (045 222 2000, www.yim.co.jp), another giant shopping centre, themed around the concept of international trade and housed in a former dockside warehouse, follow the signs for the 100-year-old **Red Brick Warehouses** (Aka Renga Soko; www.yokohama-akarenga.jp). The smaller Warehouse One is home to an arts centre and exhibition space, and several crafts shops. Warehouse Two houses three floors of shops and restaurants, including Bills (*see p290*) and elegant jazz club **Motion Blue** (045 226 1919, www.motionblue.co.jp).

From a road bridge just behind Warehouse One, take a pedestrian walkway along an old elevated railway line to Yamashita Park. Shortly before the walkway deposits you close to the park, you will see **Osanbashi Pier** on your left. This terminal for international cruise ships was remodelled in 2002 and has become a tourist attraction in its own right for its dramatic architecture and panoramic views of the harbour.

Yamashita Koen itself is a pleasant area of seaside greenery with 1930s cruise ship the *Hikawa Maru* moored alongside. The ship is no longer open to the public, but the park is popular with courting couples. Buildings overlooking the park include the **Silk Museum** (045 641 0841, www.silk museum.or.jp, open 9am-4.30pm Tue-Sun,

¥500), which examines the history of silk production and clothing. There's also the Kenmin Hall concert hall and the graceful old Hotel New Grand, whose main building maintains one room exactly as it was when used by General Douglas MacArthur, the commander of the US occupation forces after World War II. The nearby **Yokohama Archives of History** (045 201 2100, www.kaikou.city.yokohama.jp, open 9.30am-5pm Tue-Sun, ¥200) has an exhibition devoted to the history of the city.

From the far end of the park, the walkway continues past the **Yokohama Doll Museum** in the direction of **Harbour View Park**, which lies at the top of a hill called Furansu (France) Yama. It's quite a steep climb, but well worth it for the lovely view of Yokohama Bay and its bridge.

Leave the park by the gates near British House, cross the road at the traffic lights to the right and continue straight on until you arrive at the **Foreign Cemetery**, established in 1854 to bury sailors who had accompanied Commodore Perry on his mission to open up Japan to foreign trade. It's the final resting place of 4,500 people from 40 countries who

Landmark Tower.

died in the city. Regrettably, the historic graves are off-limits, but you can stroll around the park at the top and look at the small museum.

Looking down the road from the cemetery, you will notice that this area of Yokohama bears a strong resemblance to an English village, complete with its own picture-postcard church. Well above the damp lowlands, this has been considered a desirable address ever since the first British settlers started putting down their roots. An intriguing overview of the history of the area is provided at the **Yamate Museum**, located just before the church, while the young at heart might prefer the 3,000 tin toys from the 1890s to the 1960s on show at the **Tin Toy Museum** (045 621 8710, www.toysclub.co.jp/muse/tintoy.html, 9.30am-6pm Mon-Fri; 9.30am-7pm Sat, Sun, ¥200), to the east of the church.

Dotted around the Bluff area are other houses built by early foreign settlers in Japan, although in many cases the houses have been moved here from elsewhere. A map is available from the museum, and most of the houses are open to visitors. Facing the museum is **Motomachi Koen**; at the top of this park stands the relocated **Ehrismann Residence**, built in 1925 by Antonin Raymond, a Czech assistant of American architect Frank Lloyd Wright.

You can skirt the park and continue south-west toward the Yamate hills and the **Diplomat's House**, one of the most fetching houses in the area. Alternatively, head downhill from the park to the pedestrianised **Motomachi** shopping street (www.motomachi.or.jp), the most upmarket stretch of shops and restaurants in Yokohama. Walk down toward the canal and make for the bridge on your left.

On the other side of the bridge stands the Suzaku-mon, one of the ceremonial gates to Yokohama's **Chinatown** (Chukagai in Japanese). The biggest such community in Japan, it is home to hundreds of Chinese restaurants and shops. You can eat well here after wandering the colourful streets. Leaving Chinatown by the Choyo-mon gate, near the Holiday Inn, turn right to find the entrance to Motomachi-Chukagai station.

If you've got more time to explore, visit **Nissan Stadium**, venue for the 2002 World Cup final, which is a short walk from Shin-Yokohama station; or, further north, the **Kirin Yokohama Beer Village** near Namamugi station (1-17-1 Namamugi, Tsurumi-ku, 045 503 8250, www.kirin.co.jp/about/brewery/factory/yoko, open June-Sept 10am-4.30pm Tue-Sun). There are free tours of the brewery every half hour. Near Negishi station to the south – about 40 minutes by bus from Yokohama station – are the beautiful **Sankeien** garden and the **Negishi Memorial Racetrack** park.

FREE Diplomat's House

16 Yamate-cho, Naka-ku (045 662 8819). Ishikawa-cho station (Negishi line), Motomachi (south) exit. **Open** *July, Aug 9.30am-6pm daily. Sept-June 9.30am-5pm daily. Closed 4th Wed of mth.* **Admission** *free.*

Part of the Italian Garden (a collection of period dwellings), this 1910 house was once the family home of Japanese diplomat Uchida Sadatsuchi.

FREE Harbour View Park
Minato-no-Mieru Oka Koen

114 Yamate-cho, Naka-ku (045 622 8244, 045 623 7812 British House, 045 622 5002 Osaragi Jiro Memorial Museum). Motomachi-Chukagai station (Minato Mirai line). **Open** *Park 24hrs daily. British House 9.30am-5pm daily. Closed 4th Wed of mth. Osaragi Jiro Memorial Museum Apr-Sept 10am-5.30pm daily. Oct-Mar 10am-5pm daily. Closed 4th Mon of mth.* **Admission** *Park & British House free. Osaragi Jiro Memorial Museum* ¥200; ¥100 reductions. **No credit cards.**

One of the city's first attempts at redevelopment, Harbour View Park opened in 1962. The building that housed the first British legation to Japan – now called British House Yokohama – still stands near the rose garden beside one of the park gates. The park also contains a museum dedicated to local novelist Osaragi Jiro (1897-1973).

Landmark Tower

2-2-1 Minato Mirai, Nishi-ku (045 222 5035 Sky Garden, www.yokohama-landmark.jp). Minato Mirai station (Minato Mirai line), exit 5. **Open** *Sky Garden Mid July-Aug 10am-10pm daily. Sept-mid July 10am-9pm Mon-Fri, Sun; 10am-10pm Sat.* **Admission** *Sky Garden* ¥1,000; ¥200-¥800 reductions. **No credit cards.**

Take the world's fastest lift (45km/h, 28mph) to the top of Japan's second-tallest building (296m/972ft) to feast on the spectacular views. On a clear day, you can easily make out Mt Fuji to the west, Tokyo to the north and the Boso Peninsula to the east. The rest of the building is devoted to offices and a hotel.

FREE Negishi Memorial Racetrack & Equine Museum

1-3 Negishi-dai, Naka-ku (045 662 7581, www.bajibunka.jrao.ne.jp). Negishi station (Negishi line) or Sakuragi-cho station (Negishi line) then bus 21 to Takinoue. **Open** *Park 9am-5pm daily. Museum 10am-4.30pm Tue-Sun.* **Admission** *Park free. Museum* ¥100; ¥30 reductions. **No credit cards.**

A wonderful park built on the site of Japan's first Western-style racetrack – having served as a US naval base in the interim (there is still some naval accommodation beside the park). A derelict grandstand survives from its 19th-century glory days, and a museum examines horsey history and man's relationship with the creatures.

Chinatown.

Nissan Stadium – World Cup Stadium Tours

3300 Kozukue-cho, Kohoku-ku (045 477 5000, www.nissan-stadium.jp). Shin-Yokohama station (Tokaido Shinkansen, Yokohama lines), north exit then 15mins walk. **Tours** (except when stadium is in use) 10.30am, noon, 1.30pm, 3pm daily. **Admission** ¥500; ¥250 reductions. **No credit cards.**

The venue that hosted the Germany v Brazil final in 2002 has started to offer tours, taking in the dressing rooms, practice area and pitch. See the Brazilians' tactic-covered whiteboard, take a shot at a silhouette of German goalie Oliver Kahn and gaze in awe at the rubbish the teams left behind. There's also a chance to run out on to the pitch (well, as far as the running track) with the World Cup anthem blazing. The stadium hosts international matches and home games for the Yokohama Marinos.
► *For more about the football scene, see p277.*

Sankeien

58-1 Honmoku-Sannotani, Naka-ku (045 621 0635, www.sankeien.or.jp). Yokohama station, east exit then bus 8 or 148 from bus stop 2 to Honmoku Sankeien-mae. **Open** 9am-5pm daily. **Admission** ¥500; ¥200 reductions. **No credit cards.**

A beautiful, traditional Japanese garden that was laid out by a silk merchant in 1906. When religious relics were being torn down as religion fell from official favour in the Meiji era, the local merchant decided to save the treasures from the bulldozer, importing them from across Japan. The grounds now house a three-storey pagoda from Kyoto, and a feudal lord's residence among many other priceless structures. The park is open in the evening during cherry-blossom season (April) and for Moon Viewing (September).

FREE Yamashita Koen

Yamashita-cho, Naka-ku (Hikawa Maru 045 641 4362, www.nyk.com/rekishi). Motomachi-Chukagai station (Minato Mirai line), exit 1. **Open** 24hrs daily. **Admission** free.

Verdant Yamashita Park is a popular dating spot. The statue in the middle depicts the *Little Girl in Red Shoes*, based on a Japanese song about the real-life story of Iwasaki Kimi. Born in 1902, she was adopted by American missionaries and thought destined for a life of luxury in the US. But, in fact, Kimi never left Japan: abandoned by her foster parents, she died alone, aged nine, of tuberculosis.

Yamate Museum

247 Yamate-cho, Naka-ku (045 622 1188). Motomachi-Chukagai station (Minato Mirai line), exit 5. **Open** 11am-4pm Tue-Sun. **Admission** ¥200; ¥150 reductions. **No credit cards.**

Housed in the last Western-style wooden building still in its original setting, this museum provides a fascinating insight into the early days of Yokohama's development, and the thriving foreign community that grew here.

FREE Yokohama Cosmoworld

2-8-1 Shinkou, Naka-ku (045 641 6591,
www.senyo.co.jp/cosmo). Minato Mirai station
(Minato Mirai line), exit 5. **Open** *Mid Mar-Nov*
11am-9pm Mon-Fri; 11am-10pm Sat, Sun. *Mid*
Nov-mid Mar 11am-8pm Mon-Fri; 11am-9pm
Sat, Sun. **Admission** free.
The Ferris wheel at the centre of this small amusement park, with its giant digital clock, is a
Yokohama landmark. At 112.5m (369ft) high and
with room for 480 passengers, it's one of the largest
in the world. The park has 27 rides in all, including
a water rollercoaster.

Yokohama Doll Museum

18 Yamashita-cho, Naka-ku (045 671 9361,
www.yokohama-doll.museum.or.jp). Motomachi-
Chukagai station (Minato Mirai line), exit 5.
Open 10am-6.30pm daily. Closed 3rd Mon
of mth. **Admission** ¥500; ¥150 reductions.
No credit cards.
Home to nearly 10,000 dolls from 140 countries, this
museum appeals to children and serious collectors.
It also holds occasional puppet shows.

Yokohama Museum of Art

3-4-1 Minato Mirai, Nishi-ku (045 221 0300,
www.yaf.or.jp/yma/english). Minato Mirai station
(Minato Mirai line), exit 3. **Open** 10am-6pm
Mon-Wed, Sat, Sun; 10am-7.30pm Fri. **Admission**
¥500; ¥100-¥300 reductions; additional fee for
special exhibitions. **No credit cards**.
One of the region's major fine art museums, this
Tange Kenzo-designed building is set on a prime,
tree-lined plaza. The permanent collection of
European, American and Japanese modern art and
photography is supplemented by temporary exhibitions ranging from Leonardo da Vinci to contemporary artist Nara Yoshitomo.

Where to eat & drink

Aussie

1-12 Ishikawa-cho, Naka-ku (045 681 3671,
www.juno.dti.ne.jp/~aussie). Ishikawa-cho station
(Negishi line), Motomachi (south) exit. **Open** 5pm-
1am Mon, Wed-Fri; 3pm-1am Sat; 3-11pm Sun.
Average ¥3,500. **Credit** AmEx, JCB, MC, V.
As the name suggests, this restaurant in Motomachi
serves all things Australian, the most popular dishes
being barbecued kangaroo and crocodile.

Bills

Aka Rengo Soko 2, 1-1-2 Shinko, Naka-ku (045
650 1266, www.bills-jp.net). Bashamichi station
(Minato Mirai line). **Open** 9am-11pm daily.
Average ¥2,000. **Credit** AmEx, JCB, MC, V.
This Minato Mirai outpost of Aussie celebrity chef
Bill Grainger's Sydney restaurant is so popular,
you'll need to get there early or line up for hours. If
you make it inside, try Grainger's celebrated pancakes and scrambled eggs with a view of the water.

Kihachi Italian

Queen's East 2F, Minato Mirai 2-3-2, Nishi-ku
(045 222 2861, www.kihachi.co.jp). Minato
Mirai station (Minato Mirai line), Queen's
Square exit. **Open** *Lunch* 11.30am-2.30pm,
tea 2.30-5.30pm, *dinner* 6-11pm Mon-Sat ;
lunch 11.30am-2.30pm, *tea* 2.30-5.30pm,

Yokohama Cosmoworld.

dinner 6-10pm Sun. **Average** lunch ¥2,625; dinner ¥4,200. **Credit** AmEx, DC, JCB, MC, V. This casual modern restaurant looking out towards the Museum of Art is one of the best places to eat in Minato Mirai. The Italian food, popular with a mostly young, female clientele, is produced with aplomb.

Manchinro Honten
153 Yamashita-cho, Naka-ku (045 681 4004, www.manchinro.co.jp). Ishikawa-cho station (Negishi line), Chinatown (north) exit or Motomachi-Chukagai station (Minato Mirai line), exit 2. **Open** 11am-10pm daily. **Average** ¥2,500 lunch; ¥3,500 dinner. **Credit** AmEx, DC, JCB, MC, V. With a history dating back to 1892, this Cantonese restaurant is one of the oldest in Chinatown. It burned down in a fire but reopened in 2002 as the grandest, most lavish restaurant in the area.

Mutekiro
2-96 Motomachi, Naka-ku (045 681 2926, www.mutekiro.com). Motomachi-Chukagai station (Minato Mirai line), exit 5. **Open** noon-3pm, 5-10pm daily. **Average** ¥4,000 lunch; ¥8,000 dinner. **Credit** AmEx, DC, JCB, MC, V. Motomachi's most upmarket French restaurant has the motto '*Mode française, coeur japonais*'. This means that dishes often contain typical Japanese ingredients, especially seafood, but are prepared in a French way. Booking essential.

Peking Hanten (Beijing Fandian)
79-5 Yamashita-cho, Naka-ku (045 681 3535). Motomachi-Chukagai station (Minato Mirai line), exit 2. **Open** 11.30am-1.30am daily. **Average** ¥1,500 lunch; from ¥4,000 dinner (set meals). **Credit** AmEx, DC, JCB, MC, V. This charming restaurant by Choyo-mon – Chinatown's main gate – claims to be the first in Japan to have served Peking duck.

Shin-Yokohama Ramen Museum
2-14-21 Shin-Yokohama, Kohoku-ku (045 471 0503, www.raumen.co.jp). Shin-Yokohama station (Tokaido Shinkansen, Yokohama lines), north exit. **Open** 11am-11pm Mon-Fri; 10.30am-10.15pm Sat, Sun. **Admission** ¥300; ¥100 reductions. **No credit cards.**
A couple of floors are devoted to the history of the variety of noodle that has become a national obsession in Japan, but the main attraction is the eight ramen shops in the basement. Each shop sells a different style of ramen, ranging from Sapporo ramen (miso-based soup) from the north, to Hakata ramen (pork- and chicken-based soup) from the south. Highly recommended is the miso ramen at Sumire.

Thrash Zone
Paseri bldg 2F, 2-19-8 Tsuruyacho, Kanagawa-ku (045 321 0950, www.beer drinkinginternational.com). Yokohama station,

west exit. **Open** 6pm-2am Mon-Sat. **Credit** AmEx, DC, JCB, MC, V. Owner Koichi-san has two passions: craft beers and thrash metal. Luckily, he indulges the former far more than the latter at his compact bar near Yokohama station. He stocks a small but well-chosen selection of brews from Japan and the US.

Tung Fat (Dohatsu Honkan)
148 Yamashita-cho, Naka-ku (045 681 7273, www.douhatsu.co.jp). Ishikawa-cho station (Negishi line), Chinatown (north) exit. **Open** 11am-9.30pm daily. Closed 1st & 3rd Tue of mth. **Average** ¥5,000. **Credit** DC, MC, V. This Chinatown spot is popular for its Hong Kong-style seafood dishes. So popular, that lunchtime is a spectacle, with customers jostling for position while the strict *mama-san* tries to keep everyone in check. While waiting, look at the window display of mouth-watering meats, whole chickens and ducks, sausages and less recognisable animal parts.

Getting there

By train The opening of the Minato Mirai subway extension has made Yokohama even easier to get to from Tokyo. A super-express on the **Tokyu Toyoko line** from Shibuya station takes 25mins to reach Yokohama station (¥260 single) or 33mins to its terminus at Motomachi-Chukagai (¥460).

Those with JR rail passes may prefer to take the **JR Keihin Tohoku line** to Sakuragi-cho from Tokyo, Shinbashi or Shinagawa stations; or take the **Shonan Shinjuku line** from Shinjuku, Shibuya, Ebisu or Osaki, then change at Yokohama on to the **Negishi line** for local stops. Bullet trains on the **JR Tokaido Shinkansen** line take about 15mins from Tokyo station to Shin-Yokohama station.

Tourist information

The **Yokohama Convention & Visitors Bureau** (YCVB) has four information booths, plus an excellent English-language website – www.welcome.city.yokohama.jp/eng/tourism – with downloadable maps and a hotel guide.
YCVB Sakuragi-cho station *1-1-62 Sakuragi-cho, Naka-ku (045 211 0111). Sakuragi-cho station (Negishi line).* **Open** 9am-6pm daily.
YCVB Sangyo Boeki Centre *2 Yamashita-cho, Naka-ku (045 641 4759). Kannai station (Negishi line) then 15mins walk.* **Open** 8.45am-5pm Mon-Fri.
YCVB Shin-Yokohama station *2937 Shinohara-cho, Kohoku-ku (045 473 2895). Shin-Yokohama station, Shinkansen exit.* **Open** 9am-6pm daily.
YCVB Yokohama station *2-16-1 Takashima, Nishi-ku (045 441 7300). Yokohama station, on the east–west walkway.* **Open** 9am-7pm daily.

Hakone Shrine. *See p294.*

Hot Springs

HAKONE

Hakone is where Tokyo comes to relax and get a taste of the countryside. Around 90 minutes from Shinjuku station by the Odakyu line train, this mountainous area offers convenient transportation, beautiful scenery, a host of attractions and, best of all, a natural hot-spring bath, or *onsen*, around virtually every bend of the roads that twist through the mountains.

The best way to see Hakone is to buy the **Hakone Free Pass** (*see p295*), available at all Odakyu railway stations. The pass covers all public transport in Hakone – and what public transport it is. As well as a picturesque railway and a bus service, the Hakone area also has a funicular railway, a cable car and a boat that crosses Lake Ashinoko at its centre.

THE FULL HAKONE

While the 'Hakone Circuit' (*see left* **Inside Track**) will give you your fill of glorious scenery, you'll be missing out on a lot of what Hakone has to offer. Get off the train at either Odawara or Hakone-Yumoto. If you decide to start your journey at Odawara, it's worth making a detour out of the east exit of the station to take the ten-minute walk to **Odawara Castle**, perched on a hill overlooking the town. First built in the early 15th century, and rebuilt in 1960, this picturesque castle was for centuries an important strategic stronghold.

Back at the station, get on the old-fashioned Tozan railway for the next major stop (or the starting point for some), **Hakone-Yumoto** station. 'Yumoto' means 'source of hot water', which should give you some clue as to what this small town is about. First mentioned in eighth-century poetry as a place to bathe, Hakone became a great favourite in the time of the Tokugawa shogunate (1600-1868), with bathers travelling two or three days on foot from Tokyo (then Edo) along the Tokaido Way. The station houses a small tourist office, but the main office is up the hill on the left. Here, you'll find English-speaking assistants, who'll be happy to hand out maps and pamphlets. Restaurants and souvenir shops also line the same street; this is the place to buy the local speciality: small boxes and other objects made using *yosegi-zaiku*, a mosaic-style marquetry technique.

For dedicated modern bathers, the day may end in Hakone-Yumoto. Although the modern town is unremarkable, it is dotted with hot-spring baths: just about every building of any size is a hotel, or *ryokan*, and many allow non-guests to use their facilities. One of the locals'

INSIDE TRACK
THE HAKONE CIRCUIT

Those in a hurry can make the most of their time by trying the 'Hakone Circuit', rather than the 'Full Hakone' (*see right*). Get off the train at either Odawara or Hakone-Yumoto. From there, transfer to the Tozan mountain railway for the 50-minute ride to its terminus at Gora. At Gora, transfer on to the funicular railway up to the end of the line at Sounzan. Here, transfer to the cable car, which takes you down to the banks of Lake Ashinoko at Togendai station. To get across the lake, board one of the pleasure boats and stay on until Hakone-Machi or Moto-Hakone, from where you can take a bus back to where you started. The round-trip should take about three hours, although in the busy summer months it may take longer.

Hakone

1. Hakone Art Museum
2. Hakone Open-Art Museum
3. Hakone Glass Forest
4. Hakone Botanical Gardens of Wetlands
5. Museum of Historical Materials
6. Hakone Toy Museum
7. Old Highway Museum
8. Hakone Ashinoko Narikawa Art Forum
9. Hakone Ashinoku Flower Centre
10. Gora Park
11. Hakone-en Aquarium
12. Pola Museum of Art
13. Hakone Checkpoint Exhibition Hall

© Copyright Time Out Group 2010

favourites is situated on the steep hillside on the other side of the tracks from the station. The **Kappa Tengoku** has segregated open-air baths surrounded by dense woodland, and a steady army of bathers can be seen trooping up the steps to the baths well into the night.

Up the hill from the *onsen* is the delightful **Hakone Kitahara Museum**, crammed with old-fashioned Japanese and foreign tin toys from the 1890s to the 1960s. The souvenir shop sells wind-up robots and charmingly retro goods imported from China and elsewhere.

Back on the train from Hakone-Yumoto, take some time to enjoy the ride itself. It's claimed that this is the world's steepest train line, and so sharp are the bends that at three points the train enters a switchback, going forward and then reversing out of a siding in order to continue its ascent. As you climb the mountain you will see water pouring out of the hillside and cascading under the tracks, some of it still hot.

The next station of any note is Miyanoshita. This is home to one of the highest concentrations of *onsen* baths in the area and is where the first foreigners in Japan came to bathe in the 19th century. To cater for them, the **Fujiya Hotel** was built in 1878, a wooden mix of Japanese and Western styles. Non-residents are free to pop in for a drink or a bite to eat.

Two stops up the line, at Chokokuno-Mori station, is one of the great glories of Hakone.

The **Hakone Open-Air Museum** must be one of the most spectacular in the world. Set on a mountainside overlooking a series of valleys leading to the sea, the museum is dedicated to modern sculpture from all over the globe. Exposed to the elements is a world-class collection of works by Moore, Rodin, Antony Gormley, Alexander Calder, Takamichi Ito and Niki de St Phalle. It's a great place for kids. There's also a display of ceramics by Picasso in a separate pavilion.

From here, it's a ten-minute walk to the next station, Gora, the terminus of the Tozan railway and the start of the funicular that climbs the mountainside. If you're changing from the train, there will be a carriage waiting for you. The first stop on the funicular, Koen Shita, provides a pleasant diversion in the shape of **Gora Park**, a landscaped hillside garden that makes great use of the natural hot water in its hothouses. A walk uphill through the park will bring you to the next stop on the funicular.

This is a good point to visit the **Pola Museum of Art**, deep in the surrounding forest. The museum houses 9,500 works by the likes of Renoir, Picasso and Monet. To avoid damaging the beauty of the countryside, the building is constructed three floors underground, and is only eight metres (27 feet) tall on the surface. To reach the museum, take a bus from Gora station bound for Shisseikaen-mae.

The funicular terminates at Sounzan station, and it's here that many people's favourite part of the Hakone experience begins: the cable car, or **Hakone Ropeway**, as it's known. Riding over the peaks and valleys of Hakone, this four-kilometre (two-and-a-half-mile) ride is Japan's longest – and the world's busiest – cable-car route. Around halfway along its length is **Owakudani** ('big boiling valley'), one of the most breathtaking sights in Hakone. The car passes over, at a height of around 60 metres (200 feet), a smoking hillside streaked with traces of sulphur from the volcanic activity below. The air simply reeks of rotten eggs.

On top of a mountain peak sits Owakudani station, the centre of a large tourist complex of restaurants and gift shops. On a clear day – a rarity, since it's often too cloudy – you can see the peak of Mt Fuji looming over the mountain range in the distance. You can also walk to the source of some of the steam that rises out of the mountain, the ancient crater of **Mt Kamiyama**, the pathway passing over hot streams of bubbling water. The air is thick with hydrogen sulphide, and signs warn of the dangers of standing in one place for too long for fear of being overcome by fumes. If you feel like a snack, try a hard-boiled egg at the top of the path. Sold by the half-dozen for ¥500, the eggs have been cooked in the hot-spring water, the sulphur turning their shells black. According to legend, eating one of these eggs will prolong your life by a year.

From Owakudani, the Hakone Ropeway passes over several more valleys before descending to terminate at Togendai, on the banks of **Lake Ashinoko**. The lake is believed to be in the crater of a volcano that blew its top 400,000 years ago. The volcanic activity that goes on beneath the waters to this day ensures that it never freezes over. From here, a pair of incredibly tacky pleasure boats, one done out as a Mississippi steamer, the other as a Spanish galleon, cross the lake to Hakone-Machi and Moto-Hakone. Only 500 metres (1,600 feet) or so separate the two destinations, but for ease of walking, get off at Hakone-Machi and turn left (with the lake behind you) to head for Moto-Hakone.

On the way is the site of the **Old Hakone Checkpoint**, where travellers to and from Edo would be stopped and often interrogated by border guards. Ruins of the original checkpoint still stand, while other buildings have been reconstructed and opened to the public as a museum. Set back a little from the modern road is what's left of a cedar avenue, planted along the Tokaido Way in the early 17th century. Paved sections of the Tokaido Way are still extant, and keen walkers can

take a short hike from here along one such section, away from the lake towards Hatajuku.

On a promontory into the lake between the two boat stops is **Onshi Hakone Koen Park** (Hakone Detached Palace Garden). The garden of an 1887 villa that once belonged to the imperial family but was destroyed in an earthquake. Further along, past Moto-Hakone and down the side of the lake, is the **Hakone Shrine**, its history going back 1,200 years. The site is clearly marked by a red *torii* (gate) that stands in the lake.

Once you've walked your fill of the area – and there's lots more to see in the Hakone vicinity – head back to Moto-Hakone and take a bus back to Odawara. All buses to Odawara stop in Hakone-Yumoto too.

Gora Park *1300 Gora, Hakone-Machi, Ashigara-Shimogun (0460 82 2825, www.hakone-tozan.co.jp/gorapark).* **Open** 9am-5pm daily. **Admission** ¥500; free reductions. **No credit cards**.
Hakone Kitahara Museum *740 Yumoto, Hakone-Machi, Ashigara-Shimogun (0460 85 6880).* **Open** 9am-5pm daily. **Admission** ¥1,300; ¥600 reductions. **Credit** AmEx, DC, JCB, MC, V.
Hakone Open-Air Museum *1121 Ninotaira, Hakone-Machi, Ashigara-Shimogun (0460 82 1161, www.hakone-oam.or.jp).* **Open** *Mar-Nov* 9am-5pm daily. *Dec-Feb* 9am-4pm daily. **Admission** ¥1,600; ¥800-¥1,100 reductions. **No credit cards**.
Kappa Tengoku *777 Yumoto, Hakone-Machi, Ashigara-Shimogun (0460 85 6121).* **Open** 10am-10pm daily. **Admission** ¥750. *Bath towel* ¥900 (to buy). *Face towel* ¥150 (to buy). **No credit cards**.
Odawara Castle *6-1 Jonai, Odawara-shi (0465 23 1373).* **Open** 9am-5pm daily. Closed 2nd Wed of mth. **Admission** *Park* free. *Castle* ¥400; ¥150 reductions. **No credit cards**.
Old Hakone Checkpoint *1 Hakone, Hakone-Machi, Ashigara-Shimogun (0460 83 6635).* **Open** *Mar-Nov* 9am-4pm daily. *Dec-Feb* 9am-4.30pm daily. **Admission** ¥500; ¥250 reductions. **No credit cards**.
FREE Onshi Hakone Koen Garden *171 Moto-Hakone, Hakone-Machi, Ashigara-Shimogun (0460 83 7484, www.kanagawa-park.or.jp/onsisite).* **Open** 9am-5pm daily. **Admission** free.
Pola Museum of Art *1285 Kozukayama, Sengokuhara, Hakone-Machi, Ashigara-Shimogun (0460 84 2111, www.polamuseum.or.jp).* **Open** 9am-5pm daily. **Admission** ¥1,800; ¥700-¥1,300 reductions. **Credit** AmEx, DC, JCB, MC, V.

Where to eat & drink

Since most of the area's activity centres around the hotels, it's hardly surprising that there are few independent restaurants worth seeking out

INSIDE TRACK
GO WITH THE FLOW

Taking kids to Hakone? When they tire of the tourist trail, take them to **Yunessun** (1297 Ninotaira Hakone-Machi Ashigara-Shimogun, 0460 82 4126, www. yunessun.com/english), a spa resort with waterfalls, three water slides, a hot-spring cave, and baths filled with green tea, coffee, wine or saké.

– though the village of Sengokuhara has more options than most. For the truly hungry, there are snack bars serving curry, noodles and the like at Owakudani and Togendai stations, and on the lake at Hakone-Machi. The **Bella Foresta** restaurant in the Open-Air Museum (*see p294*) serves a decent buffet lunch for ¥1,680, while all the large hotels have at least four restaurants that are open to non-guests. At the **Pola Museum** (*see p294*), there's a café serving snacks and drinks (10am-4.30pm daily) and an upmarket French-style restaurant (11am-4pm daily).

Where to stay

There are hundreds of places to stay in Hakone, ranging from cheap *ryokan* to top-class hotels. Most have their own hot springs. Many have higher rates at weekends, peaking during New Year and Golden Week in May.

If you intend to use Hakone-Yumoto as a base, cheap options include the **Kappa Tengoku** (*see p294*): a double room here costs from ¥6,600 per night on weekdays, although its proximity to the railway tracks might mean an earlier awakening than you'd bargained for. Up in the mountains, the **Fujiya Hotel** (359 Miyanoshita, 0460 82 2211, www.fujiyahotel.co.jp, ¥19,830-¥41,880 double) dates back to 1878 and oozes history – a feature that plays better in the lobby and gardens than in the rooms. In Sengokuhara, the small *ryokan* **Fuji-Hakone Guest House** (912 Sengokuhara, 0460 84 6577, www.fujihakone.com, ¥11,850-¥12,900 double) is a good budget choice. The friendly proprietor, Takahashi Masami, speaks English and is happy to offer sightseeing advice. You can get to the inn by bus direct from Odawara or Hakone-Yumoto stations; alight at the Senkyoro-mae bus stop. Sister outfit **Moto-Hakone Guest House** (0460 83 7880, same website, ¥11,550 double) is on the other side of Lake Ashinoko. Overlooking the lake is the **Palace Hotel** (1245 Sengokuhara, Hakone-Machi, 0460 84 8501, www.hakone.palacehotel.co.jp), where doubles start at ¥18,300 in low season.

For absolute luxury, there's the **Hyatt Regency Hakone** (www.hakone.regency. hyatt.com), where the Mountain View twin rooms (¥23,000-¥45,000) are enormous, as are the scenic terraces. But nothing can rival the ten-room **Kinnotake** boutique hotel (0460 84 3939, www.kinnotake.com), whose rooms come with a private hot spring and a contemporary Japanese-style interior of the kind that design fans dream about (¥36,000-¥54,000 per person).

Getting there

By train There are two types of **Hakone Free Pass**, available at all Odakyu stations and many travel agents. The two-day pass gives you unlimited journeys for ¥5,000, available from Shinjuku station. The three-day pass costs ¥5,500. The ticket price also covers the basic fare on an **Odakyu train** from Shinjuku to Hakone. If you want to travel in comfort on the super-express **Romance Car**, you will need to pay a supplement of ¥870.

If you hold a **JR Pass**, the most cost-effective way of reaching the area is to take a **JR Tokaido shinkansen** to Odawara station, then buy your Hakone Free Pass there. As this pass does not include transport to Tokyo, it costs ¥3,900 (two days) or ¥4,400 (three days). The Free Pass also gives discounts at many local attractions.

Tourist information

Hakone-Yumoto Tourist Information
Kankou Bussankan, 698 Yumoto, Hakone-Machi, Ashigara-Shimogun (0460 85 8911). **Open** 9am-5pm daily.

Odakyu Sightseeing Service Centre
Ground-floor concourse near west exit, Odakyu Shinjuku station (5321 7887, www.odakyu.jp/ english/center). **Open** 8am-6pm daily.
The Odakyu train line's information counter inside the station is aimed at foreign visitors (staff speak English). You can buy the Hakone Free Pass here and make hotel reservations.

Odawara Tourist Information
1-1-9 Sakae-Machi, Odawara-shi (0465 22 2339). Odawara station, in front of the ticket gate. **Open** 9am-5pm daily.

Historic Capital
KAMAKURA

For 150 years, from the 12th to the 14th centuries, Kamakura was Japan's military and administrative capital. The factors that made it a strategic location for the first military government – hills on three sides, Sagami Bay on the other – have also protected it from the encroaching sprawl of Yokohama.

Tsurugaoka Hachiman-gu

It's less than an hour by train from central Tokyo, but the atmosphere is a world away. There are more than 70 active temples and shrines dotted around Kamakura, from the large and eminent to the small and secluded. Few buildings remain intact from the Kamakura period, but many temples and shrines appear unspoilt, giving visitors a rare glimpse of old Japan.

The Minamoto family picked Kamakura for its new base after vanquishing the Taira clan in 1185 and setting up Japan's first military government – marking the start of 700 years of domination by shoguns. The new military rulers encouraged Zen Buddhism, which appealed due to its strict self-discipline, and temples of various sects were established in the area. While traces of the government and

military rule faded quickly after the Minamoto clan and their regents were defeated in 1333, the religious influence endures to this day.

Kamakura is now a major tourist destination, and the temples are well looked after. Most temples require a small entry fee (¥100-¥300). The main attractions are scattered, but most are within walking distance of Kamakura or Kita-Kamakura stations and can be covered in a day trip from Tokyo. You can pick up a free map from the tourist information window at Kamakura station. Most temples are open daily, from 9am until 4pm, but museums and treasure houses are usually closed on Mondays.

GETTING AROUND

Walking is the best way to see the city. Narrow streets take you through quiet residential areas, while hiking routes along the ridges of the hills link different parts of town. After the initial ascent, they are generally fairly easy walks, some leading to picnic areas and parks. The starting points are indicated on the road, as are destinations and estimated durations.

Bikes can be rented from an office (0467 24 2319) behind the police box on the right as you leave the east exit of Kamakura station (open 8.30am-5pm daily; ¥500 first hour, ¥250 extra hour, ¥1,500-¥1,600 full day; bring photo ID). Or you can rent a mountain bike for ¥2,310-¥2,835 a day from **Grove** (0467 23 6667, www.rentalmtb.com), a specialist cycle shop on the left side of the main street (Wakamiya Oji) as you walk down towards the sea.

For a more leisurely mode of transport, take a rickshaw – catch one outside the west exit of Kamakura station or on Wakamiya Oji, by the big *torii* (shrine gate). For half an hour, it costs ¥5,000 for one person, ¥8,000 for two.

Taxis can be caught from either side of the station. There are also regular bus services departing from the east exit. And no visit to Kamakura can be considered complete without a short trip on the venerable tram cars of the Enoden line (Enoshima Electric Railway), which winds from Kamakura station, past Hase station (the stop for Hase Kannon and the Great Buddha), down along the coast to Enoshima island and Fujisawa.

TSURUGAOKA HACHIMAN-GU

Kamakura's main shrine, **Tsurugaoka Hachiman-gu**, is a ten-minute walk from Kamakura station. Hachiman is seen today as the god of war, but in the past he was regarded as the guardian of the whole nation. As one of the most important Shinto shrines in eastern Japan, this is an essential stop for all visitors.

To reach the shrine, head for the red *torii* in the left corner of the square outside the station's east exit. This leads into Komachi Dori, a

---

INSIDE TRACK HANG GLIDER

Kids and trainspotters will enjoy watching the **Shonan monorail**, which is suspended from a track several meters high, giving it the look of an upside-down train or a very slow roller-coaster. It runs between Enoshima and Ofuna station (on the JR network) and stops at Nishi Kamakura station, about four kilometres (2.5 miles) west of Kamakura station.

narrow pedestrian street lined with souvenir and craft shops, boutiques, food stalls and shops. At the far end of this street, turn right to the shrine entrance. Alternatively, walk directly away from the station to Wakamiya Oji. This broad avenue forms a north–south axis from central Kamakura down to the sea. Turning left, make your way along the cherry-lined walkway up the centre of the street; when the trees blossom here in April, it's gorgeous.

The shrine and grounds of Tsurugaoka (Hill of Cranes) were built to subtle and strict specifications. The main shrine at the top is reached through a gate with two guardian figures (Yadaijin and Sadaijin). The steps descending to the right lead to other buildings and the treasure house, where historic, religious artworks from the area are displayed.

WEST OF TSURUGAOKA HACHIMAN-GU

A few minutes' walk from Hachiman-gu is the **Museum of Modern Art, Kamakura** (2-1-53 Yukinoshita, Kamakura, 0467 22 5000, www.moma.pref.kanagawa.jp, closed Mon). In a time of political, economic, social and moral upheaval, local artists and critics thought Japan needed a forum for new art, and, six decades later, Japan's first museum of modern art is still one of its best.

Further west is **Eisho-ji**, the only active Buddhist nunnery in the area. It allows access to parts of its grounds, as does nearby **Jufuku-ji**, reached by a long, maple-lined approach. The quiet ancient cemetery behind, reached by the path to the left of the gate, has many burial caves, some dating from the Kamakura period.

A 20-minute stroll into the hills on this side of the city will bring you to the atmospheric **Zeniarai Benten**, the 'Money-Washing Shrine' dedicated to one of the seven lucky gods. A tunnel going through the mountainside leads into a mysterious area with waterfalls, ponds and small shrines carved into the cliff face, the air filled with incense and ethereal music. Inside the main cave, place your money, notes and all, into bamboo baskets that you then dip in the water. The truly faithful will find their assets have doubled in value.

From here, a 20-minute walk will bring you to Kotokuin temple, home of the **Daibutsu** statue, aka the Great Buddha – the best known of Kamakura's attractions. The temple dates from 741, and the bronze statue of Buddha from 1252. Over 36 feet (11 metres) high and weighing 121 tonnes, the figure appears ungainly and top-heavy from a distance, but from close up the proportions seem perfect. For ¥20 you can go inside the statue.

Hase-dera (also known as **Hase Kannon**) temple is just down the road. The main feature here is the 11-faced statue of Kannon (goddess of mercy and compassion). Over nine metres

Daibutsu.

(30 feet) tall, it was carved in 721 out of a single camphor tree. The temple is also famous for its thousands of small Jizo figurines offered in memory of deceased children and babies (including those who were never carried to full term). Hase-dera also has a revolving library containing Buddhist sutras – worshippers causing the library to rotate receive merit equivalent to reading the entire Buddhist canon – and a small network of caves with statues carved out of the rock. The treasure house contains artefacts excavated from the temple during rebuilding. Hase-dera is also known for its hydrangea that bloom each June. From Hase-dera there's a panoramic view of the town, the beach and Sagami Bay.

EAST OF TSURUGAOKA HACHIMAN-GU

Although none of the main sights are in this area, which thus attracts fewer crowds, there are still many smaller temples worth seeing. The first shrine as you come from Tsurugaoka Hachiman-gu is **Egara Tenjin**, founded in 1104. Tenjin is the patron deity of scholarship and literature, and every 25 January there is a ritualistic burning of writing brushes.

Nearby is the **Kamakura-gu** shrine, founded by the Meiji emperor in 1869. From here, turn left up a lane to **Kakuon-ji**. This small temple offers 45-minute tours by a priest (¥300) on the hour from 10am to 3pm (except noon on weekdays), unless it is raining. The

INSIDE TRACK BEACH PARTIES

Head to Kamakura on a summer weekend and you might find the beach jumping to parties by some of Tokyo's top DJs. Check www.iflyer.jp for dates and further details.

tour is in Japanese only, but the thatched buildings and old wooden statues do not need much explanation.

A 15-minute walk from Kamakura-gu takes you to **Zuisen-ji**, famous for its trees and flowers, especially the plum blossoms in February. This small temple has a Zen garden created in the 14th century by the celebrated priest and landscape gardener Soseki Muso.

From the intersection near Kamakura-gu, head along the main road to reach **Sugimoto-dera**, the oldest temple in Kamakura. It's a beautiful place, with white banners lining either side of the well-worn stone steps. Both the gate and temple have thatched roofs and were originally built in 734. Further along, on the other side of the road, is lovely **Hokoku-ji**, known as the 'bamboo temple' for its extensive grove of giant bamboo, where you can sit and contemplate while sipping whisked green tea. From here it's a short walk to the **Shakado tunnel**. One of the original entrances to the ancient city cut through the hills, this dark (and reputedly haunted) spot is very atmospheric.

Closer to the station is **Hongaku-ji**, a small temple whose ancient gate and guardian statues gaze out towards the entrance to **Myohon-ji**, the oldest and largest of the Nichiren sect temples in Kamakura. Founded in 1260, it nestles deep into a fold in the hills and is surprisingly quiet. Another 15 minutes or so away is **Myoho-ji**, also known as the Moss Temple, where the priest Nichiren once resided. The ancient steps lead up to a hilltop vantage point that remains a favourite spot.

The only major temple close to the sea is **Komyo-ji**, established in 1243, which has a huge wooden *sanmon* gate and an attractive lotus pond with carp and terrapins. A path behind the main prayer hall (on the right next to the playground) leads up the hill, giving views on clear days down the coast to Enoshima island and the Izu Peninsula, with Mt Fuji behind.

At this end of the bay are the remains of **Wakaejima**, the first artificial harbour in Japan. Built in 1232, it went into decline after the capital reverted to Kyoto, and now the stones are only visible at low tide. **Zaimokuza Beach**, the eastern half of the bay, is favoured by dinghy sailors, windsurfers and ever-hopeful weekend surfers (the waves are usually tiny). The western section, **Yuigahama Beach**, is more popular with sunbathers. In summer, temporary huts are built along the sand to provide showers, changing facilities and deckchair rentals, as well as snacks and drinks.

Hokoku-ji.

KITA-KAMAKURA

This area north of the town centre is home to many Rinzai sect temples, among them the famous **Engaku-ji**, the largest Zen temple in Kamakura, situated bang in front of Kita-Kamakura station. The temple was founded in 1282, although the main gate was reconstructed in 1780. The precincts, which extend a long way up into the hills, house more than 15 smaller sub-temples. To the left of the main entrance you can often see people practising Zen archery. On the hill to the right is the famous temple bell – the biggest in Kamakura.

On the narrow road next to the railway tracks is the **Kamakura Old Pottery Museum** (10am-5pm Tue-Sun, ¥300-¥500), housed in a pleasant compound of old and reconstructed half-timbered buildings. Across the tracks is **Tokei-ji**, for a long time a nunnery that offered asylum to women seeking refuge from abusive husbands. It's worth a visit for its lovely garden and grounds, as well as the treasure house (9.30am-3.30pm Tue-Sun, ¥300), which keeps old sutras and scrolls.

Nearby is **Jochi-ji**, a Zen temple noted for the small, ancient bridge and steps at its entrance, its bell tower, the burial caves at the back and a tunnel between the cemeteries. A mountain path leading back to Kamakura station starts from the left of the entrance. On the other side of the main road is a pleasant street winding up to **Meigetsu-in**, a temple noted for its hydrangea gardens.

Heading towards Kamakura brings you to **Kencho-ji**, the oldest Zen temple in Japan. It's an imposing place with large buildings and grounds, although only ten of the 49 original sub-temples survive. Many of the halls have been rebuilt, but their arrangement hasn't changed for over 700 years. The second floor of the majestic *sanmon* gate houses 500 statues of *rakan* (Buddha's disciples), although they are not on view. Behind the last building there's a garden (by Muso Soseki), from which a path leads to steps climbing to **Hanso-bo**, a shrine where the guardian of the temple resides. You will also see statues of *tengu* (goblins) lining the approach. From here you can follow the Ten-en hiking path, which follows the hilltop ridge as far as Zuisen-ji temple in the east of Kamakura.

Back on the main road, a short flight of stairs near the tunnel marks the entrance to **Enno-ji**, a very small temple housing statues representing the ten judges of Hell.

Where to eat

Around Kamakura station, there are many restaurants along Komachi Dori, the narrow shopping street near the east exit. Friendly **T-Side** (2-11-11 Komachi, 0467 24 9572, www.kamakura-t-side.com, lunch sets ¥1,000-¥1,500) serves great Indian food. Around the corner is **Nakamura-an** (1-7-6 Komachi, 0467 25 3500, www.nakamura-an.com, closed Thur, from ¥700), a cosy noodle shop that serves hearty, hand-chopped *soba*.

In Kita-Kamakura, you can try a taste of Zen at **Hachinoki Honten** (7 Yamanouchi, 0467 22 8719, lunch from ¥2,310), which serves elegant *shojin ryori* vegan cuisine close to the main entrance of the Kencho-ji temple. **Sasanoha** (499 Yamanouchi, 0467 23 2068, ¥1,500-¥2,100) offers delicious (but not entirely vegetarian) meals with brown rice.

Facing the ocean in Inamuragasaki (on the Enoden line) is **Taverna Rondino** (2-6-11 Inamuragasaki, 0467 25 4355, set meals ¥1,890-¥3,150), an Italian restaurant as good as most in Tokyo. Reservations are recommended if you want a seat on the outside terrace.

Getting there

By train Kamakura is less than an hour by train from Tokyo. Both Kita-Kamakura and Kamakura stations are on the **JR Yokosuka line** from Tokyo (¥890 single), Shinbashi (¥780) and Shinagawa (¥690) stations; trains run every 10-15mins. There's a more limited service on the **JR Shonan-Shinjuku line** from Shinjuku (¥890), Shibuya (¥890) and Ebisu (¥780). A special two-day return, including unlimited rides on the Enoden line and Shonan Monorail, is the **Kamakura-Enoden Free Ticket** (¥1,970). A cheaper but longer (90mins) option is to take the **Odakyu line** from Shinjuku to Enoshima (¥610; ¥1,210 by express), then transfer on to the Enoden line (¥250 to Kamakura). Day-trip tickets (also with unlimited rides on the Enoden) are available for ¥1,430.

Tourist information

Also check out www.kamakuratoday.com/e.
Kamakura City Tourist Information Service
1-1-1 Komachi, Kamakura Eki Konai, Kanagawa-ken (0467 22 3350, www.city. kamakura.kanagawa.jp). **Open** 9am-5pm daily.

> ### INSIDE TRACK
> ### WISH UPON A TREE
>
> Behind the main building of **Toshogu Shrine** (*see p300*) is a stairway leading to the grave of Ieyasu Tokugawa. Next to the grave is a giant cryptomeria called *kanai sugi* ('wish-fulfilling cypress'). According to legend, if you address a wish to this tree, it is certain to come true.

Shogun Shrines

NIKKO

If you haven't seen Nikko, then you can't say you've really lived – or so says a Japanese adage that's been popular since the Edo period. For over 1,200 years, this area of mountains, lakes, forests and hot springs has been considered a centre of great beauty and spiritual significance. It's still a premier getaway destination for Tokyoites looking for a little respite, culture and scenery. But Nikko's main claim to fame is that it's where the first Tokugawa shogun, Ieyasu, is enshrined and buried. The impressive scale and lavish ornamentation of his mausoleum make Nikko one of the most fascinating sites in the country.

In Japanese, Nikko means 'sunlight', but the name also derives from that of the sacred mountain behind the city, Futara, which is now known as **Mt Nantai**. It was here that the priest Shodo Shonin established a centre for Esoteric Buddhism in 782, and Mt Nantai remains a centre of pilgrimage for religious ascetics.

Ieyasu's mausoleum, the **Toshogu**, is surrounded by numerous temples and shrines, including the equally ornate **Taiyu-in**, the mausoleum of his grandson, Iemitsu, the third Tokugawa shogun. The entire complex, a UNESCO World Heritage site, can be seen in half a day. Most visitors, though, stay overnight so they can also see the area above Nikko, including Lake Chuzenji, the dramatic Kegon Falls, Yumoto Onsen and the vast Oku-Nikko national park.

Nikko lies at the foot of the mountains on the edge of the Kanto plain, about two hours by train due north of Tokyo. It is a small city (population circa 90,000), with souvenir shops, antiques dealers and restaurants lining the main street, which runs from the two train stations up to **Shinkyo**, the sacred bridge that spans the Daiyagawa gorge and marks the entrance to the shrines and temples. The first bridge was built here in 1636; this handsome, red-lacquered third incarnation opened in 2005.

Cross the road in front of the bridge and follow the steps into the forested national park to reach the Toshogu complex, ten minutes away. The road to the left leads to Lake Chuzenji, via the sprawling newer part of Nikko.

The cluster of religious buildings on the far side of Shinkyo bridge includes the Rinno-ji temple, the Toshogu, the Futarasan Shrine and the Taiyu-in Mausoleum. If you want to see them all, it's much cheaper to buy the combined ticket for ¥1,000 as you enter the Rinno-ji or at the Tobu bus counter in the station on arrival. The buildings are generally open daily from 8am to 5pm (until 4pm Dec-Mar).

RINNO-JI

The **Rinno-ji** (admission ¥900), founded in 766, is the largest of the Buddhist temples in the area. Its main hall is called the Sanbutsu-do, after the trinity of Buddhas that are the main attraction. Over five metres (16 feet) high, these gilt-covered wooden statues depict Amida Nyorai, the Thousand-Armed Kannon and the Horse-Headed Kannon – a Buddhist representation of the gods of Nikko's three sacred mountains. Off to one side is a pillar, Sorinto, built in 1643 to repel evil.

In front of the Sanbutsu-do is the temple's treasure house and the **Shoyo-en** (¥300), a beautiful Edo-style strolling garden, with a 200-year-old cherry tree that has been declared a national monument. To the left of the Sanbutsu-do stands a black gate, the Kuremon, and the path that leads to the Toshogu.

TOSHUGO

Even if you forgo the other buildings in the complex, the **Toshogu** (¥1,300) is a must-see. Because of its popularity, it is advisable to arrive early in the morning, before the tour buses converge, or late in the afternoon. It's also very busy during its three annual festivals. On 17 May, horseback archery in medieval hunting attire takes place in front of the shrine, while on 18 May, the Sennin Gyoretsu procession recreates the transfer of the remains of Ieyasu. The 1,000 participants dress as samurai, priests and others in the style of the days of the shogun. A festival on 17 October combines both, but is smaller.

The Toshogu was completed in 1636, during the reign of the third shogun, Iemitsu, according to instructions left by Ieyasu, who had died in 1616. Unusually, the mausoleum blends both Shinto and Buddhist elements, and its flamboyant decorations owe more to Chinese and Korean influences than to native Japanese design. Nearly all the surfaces are brightly painted, with ornate and intricate carvings.

Inside the first gate (*torii*) is a five-storey pagoda built in 1818, and the ticket office. A short flight of stairs leads you through the

INSIDE TRACK CEDAR AVENUE

Nikko is listed in the *Guinness Book of Records* as the home of the world's longest avenue. More than 12,000 cedar trees line 35 kilometres (22 miles) of road, a gift from a feudal lord to shogun Ieyasu Tokugawa almost 400 years ago. There were thought to be around 200,000 trees originally, but they are gradually succumbing to old age and pollution. To reach the avenue, take the Tobu Nikko line to Kami-Imaichi station.

Nikko.

Otemon, also known as the Deva Gate after its fearsome statues, said to scare away evil spirits. The building on the left after the gate is the **Shin-kyusha** (Sacred Stable), where a sacred white horse is housed most of the year. This unpainted building is famous for its monkey carvings, including the renowned San-saru (Three Monkeys) representing the ideal way of life ('hear no evil, see no evil, speak no evil').

Another flight of stairs takes you up to the spectacular **Yomeimon** (Twilight Gate). With its 500 Chinese-style carvings of giraffes, sages, dragons and other imaginary creatures, it is the most elaborate edifice of its kind in Japan. Off to the left before this gate is the Yakushi-do, famous for the large painting of a dragon on the ceiling and for the roaring echo, which the priest regularly demonstrates. There are also 12 ancient statues inside, representing the years of the Chinese zodiac.

Just above the Yomeimon is the similarly ornate **Karamon**, leading to the Oratory and Main Hall. The dragon motif continues in the Oratory, with more carvings at the entrance, and another 100 on the ceiling. To the right of Karamon is the entrance to the **Oku-sha**, the shogun's tomb (an extra ¥520 if you hold the combined ticket). Over the door by the ticket booth is the carving of the **Nemuri-neko** (Sleeping Cat). The stairs lead up the mountain secluded area with two small buildings painted in blue and gold; behind these is the tomb.

The path leading to the left before the entrance *torii* goes to the **Toshogu Treasure Museum** (¥500), where a small selection of the treasures is exhibited on rotation.

The second path to the left (between the pagoda and the Otemon) leads to the **Futarasan Jinja** (¥200). There is little to see inside the shrine, but the sacred spring and other buildings at the back are quite atmospheric.

TAIYU-IN MAUSOLEUM

Further into the hills is the **Taiyu-in Mausoleum** (¥550), where the third shogun, Iemitsu, is buried. Completed in 1653, the gates and buildings are more restrained in scale and style than Toshogu and definitely worth visiting. Many people prefer the black and gold colour scheme and relatively quiet atmosphere.

The first gate has Nio (heavenly kings) guardian figures; soon after comes the Nitenmon, with statues of Komokuten and Jikokuten, two Buddhist guardians. The next gate is the Yashamon, with statues of four demons known as Yashan, and the last is the Karamon, before the main hall of worship. A few artefacts and old treasures are displayed inside. A walk around the main hall leads to the Kokamon gate and towards the shogun's actual burial site, though this is locked at all times.

Back near the Shinkyo bridge, there's a trail leading upstream along the Daiyagawa river to the Ganmangafuchi Abyss, famous for a series of old mossy statues along a stretch of the river filled with large volcanic rocks.

LAKE CHUZENJI & MT NANTAI

To see the area's famed natural beauty, be sure to visit **Lake Chuzenji**, situated high above Nikko. The Iroha-zaka road zigzags to an altitude of 1,300 metres (4,265 feet) – watch

INSIDE TRACK
NIKKO'S THICK SKIN

Nikko is known for *yuba*, or soy-milk skin, thanks to the Buddhist monks that came to run the area's temples. While Kyoto is famed for its fresh, paper-thin *yuba*, Nikko prefers a plump, multi-layered version, often dried, and serves it in everything from ramen to *kaiseki*.

out for the aggressive monkeys alongside the road. The lake offers swimming, fishing and boating, and the surrounding area has many campsites and hiking trails.

Most tourists come to view the **Kegon Falls**, where the lake's waters plunge 100 metres (330 feet) into the Daiyagawa river. The waterfalls, which include 12 minor cascades, are some of the finest in Japan – and especially photogenic in mid winter, when they occasionally freeze over. A lift (¥520) takes you down to an observation platform that's level with the bottom of the falls. The nearby Chanoki-daira ropeway gives views of the lake, Kegon Falls and Mt Nantai. There's also a botanical garden with alpine plants.

North of the lake, **Mt Nantai** rises to almost 2,400 metres (7,877 feet). There is a crater at the top, but most climbers making the five-hour ascent (May to October only) do so for religious reasons, to visit Okumiya Shrine. The side of the mountain gets crowded with worshippers during its festival (31 July-8 August).

Further north from Chuzenji is **Yumoto Onsen**, a hot-spring resort by Lake Yumoto with a good range of accommodation. The road passes through gorgeous sub-alpine meadows and has great views of the mountains.

Where to stay & eat

Although it's possible to see Nikko in a day, there are several good hotels if you want to take things slowly. Prices listed are for double rooms.

One of the oldest hotels in Japan, the **Nikko Kanaya Hotel** (1300 Kami-Hatsuishi, 0288 54 0001, www.kanayahotel.co.jp, ¥17,325-¥63,525) opened in 1873. It's a short ride from either of Nikko's stations on a Tobu bus (¥190) heading for Nishisando, Kiyotaki, Okuhosoo, Chuzenji or Yumoto Onsen; get off at the Shinkyo stop.

The **Turtle Inn Nikko** is a small inn by the river near Shinkyo (2-16 Takumi-cho, 0288 53 3168, www.turtle-nikko.com, ¥6,500). It also has an annex called **Hotori-an** (8-28 Takumi-cho, 0288 53 3663, ¥12,400) a few minutes away. Get off at the Sogo Kaikanmae bus stop for either. Staff speak English.

There are plenty of hotels and pensions in the Lake Chuzenji area, and many of these have natural hot-spring baths (*onsen*). Cream of the crop is the **Chuzenji Kanaya Hotel** (2482 Chugushi, 0288 51 0001, www.kanayahotel. co.jp, from ¥17,325). The bus to Yumoto Onsen stops right in front of the hotel.

It would be a shame to leave Nikko without trying the local speciality, *yuba* (soya milk skin; *see left* **Inside Track**). Gyoushin-Tei (2339-1 Yama-uchi, 0288 53 3751, closed Thur) is set in a 12th-century garden and serves *yuba* in *shojin ryori* or *kaiseki ryori* (¥4,350) courses. There are also numerous noodle shops serving *soba* (including *yuba soba*) along Nikko's main street, and up at Lake Chuzenji. **Enya** (443 Ishiyamachi, 0288 53 5605, www.nikko-enya.co.jp, closed Mon) offers a selection of Japanese and Western meat dishes and over 80 different world beers.

Getting there & around

By train & bus Both Tobu and JR trains go to Nikko, terminating at different but nearby stations in the centre of town. From both stations it's a few minutes by bus (¥190) to Shinkyo bridge and the entrance to the Toshogu, or

Kegon Falls.

a 25-minute walk. Tobu runs buses to Lake Chuzenji (¥1,100, 30mins; a two-day ticket allowing unlimited use of the buses is ¥2,000). There are also occasional buses to Yumoto Onsen.

From Tokyo, the **Tobu** (3481 2871) trains are faster and cheaper, and their bus service to the sights is more regular. From Tobu Asakusa station, limited express trains go directly to Tobu Nikko station (¥2,620 using 1hr 50mins) and should be reserved well in advance. Regular (*kaisoku*) trains cost ¥1,320 and take 20mins longer but don't require reservations.

For **JR** services, take the *shinkansen* (bullet train) from Tokyo station (1hr) or the regular train from Ueno (1hr 30 mins-1hr 50 mins) to Utsunomiya; from there it's 45mins on a local train to JR Nikko station. Single fare: ¥2,520 regular; ¥4,720 by bullet train. There are also some trains from Shinjuku (¥3,900, 2hrs).

Tourist information

Nikko Tourist Information Centre *591 Gokomachi, Nikko-shi, Tochigi-ken (0288 54 2496, www.nikko-jp.org/english).* **Open** 9am-5pm daily. The office is located just off Nikko's main street. **Sightseeing Inquiry Office** *Inside Tobu Nikko station, 4-3 Matsubara-cho, Nikko-shi, Tochigi-ken (0288 53 4511).* **Open** 8.30am-5pm daily.

Easy Day Trips

KAWAGOE

With inner-city rice paddies, wide streets and an overall slower pace of life, **Kawagoe** – less than an hour by train west from central Tokyo – is, in many ways, typical of the suburbs that encompass the city. But the place also has a distinctive side, as hinted at in its nickname, 'Little Edo'. Kawagoe has one of Japan's most extensive collections of intact merchants' houses dating from the 19th century.

The collection isn't huge – fewer than 30 buildings – and they owe their survival (ironically) to the Great Kawagoe Fire of 1893, which destroyed more than a third of the city. As Kawagoe was rebuilt, merchants chose fire-resistant mortar walls and elaborately tiled *onigawara* roofs in the style of the *kura* (the traditional Japanese warehouse) as a safeguard against future disaster. The surviving structures, known as *kurazukuri*, offer a rare glimpse of a Japan long disappeared.

Conveniently for the visitor, most of the remaining *kurazukuri* are situated along one street, Ichiban-gai, a ten-minute walk from Hon-Kawagoe train station. Impressively designed, with carved shutters and supports, some of the buildings are now shops, which are

worth entering as much for their interiors as for the goods on sale. Original furnishings and decorations remain, and shopkeepers won't mind if you choose not to come away with a bamboo flute or a kimono.

Beyond Ichiban-gai is a maze of narrow, streets where a clutch of traditional sweet shops vies for attention with ten or so temples. The generations-old method of preparing the hard candies is on show for all who are curious to get a glimpse of a near-extinct craft.

Back toward the station is **Kita-in** temple (0492 22 0859, open Sept-Feb 9am-4pm daily, Mar-Aug 9am-4.30pm daily, admission ¥400), built in 830 and rebuilt in the 17th century using structures from the original Edo Castle. A side yard contains around 540 *rakan*, stone statues of Buddha's 500 mythical disciples. They're quite a sight; each face is different, representing a host of emotions, from joy to madness.

Looming majestically above all this is the symbol of Kawagoe, the three-storey **Tokino Kane Tower**. Originally constructed in 1624, and rebuilt after the Great Fire, the wooden tower houses a bell that still chimes four times a day, serving to remind all of Kawagoe's place of importance in historical Japan.

Where to eat

Located near Kita-in temple, **Kotobukian** (0492 25 1184, open 11.30am-5pm Mon, Tue, Thur-Sun) specialises in *wariko-soba*, a concoction of green tea buckwheat noodles served with five different toppings, and served in a five-tiered box. For snacks, seek out **Kurazukuri Chaya** (0492 25 5252, open 10am-6pm daily) on Ichiban-gai.

Getting there

By train & bus The **Seibu Shinjuku train** leaves every 15mins from Seibu Shinjuku station to Hon-Kawagoe station (journey time 65mins, ¥480 single; 45 mins, ¥890 express single).

INSIDE TRACK
KAWAGOE FESTIVAL

On the third weekend in October, Kawagoe plays host to a 350-year-old festival. It's ranked as one of the Kanto area's most important fests, and it's also one of the most fun, with dozens of floats resembling a cross between a *Noh* stage and a Punch & Judy tent rolling through the streets, stopping periodically to perform *hikkawase*, a musical 'battle' along the same principle as a breakdancing face-off.

Kawagoe station, slightly further from the city's sights, is on the **Tobu Toju line** from Ikebukuro (fastest route: 30mins, ¥450); an express train departs every 15mins. Kawagoe is also on the **JR Saikyo line** from Shinjuku station (55mins, ¥740); trains run every 20mins. The 'Co Edo Loop Bus', a vintage-style shuttle bus, connects Kawagoe and Hon-Kawagoe stations with the main sights. One-day tickets cost ¥500.

Tourist information

Kawagoe City Tourist Information Bureau
Inside Kawagoe station, 24-9 Wakita-cho,

Kawagoe-shi (0492 22 5556, www.city.kawagoe. saitama.jp). **Open** 9am-4.30pm daily.

JIKO-JI TEMPLE

The oldest temple in the Kanto region outside Tokyo sits on a hilltop in the middle of a green landscape about 70 kilometres (44 miles) north of the capital. Infrequent transport connections mean it takes pretty much all day to get there and back – but the slow journey, followed by a peaceful hour-long walk to the temple itself, is a perfect antidote to the chaos of the capital.

Climbing Mt Fuji

How to ascend Japan's iconic peak.

Japan's most famous and highest mountain (at 3,776 metres/12,388 feet) is renowned for its beauty and spiritual significance. For centuries, pilgrims have made their way to the summit, with shrines on the way up doubling as inns; they would pray and rest at each stage before reaching the top in time for sunrise.

Religious travellers are few and far between these days, but climbing Fuji remains popular. People still go up to see the sunrise, but most use transport to the fifth stage, where the road stops. Since the mountain is covered in snow most of the year, the official climbing season is limited to July and August, although there is

transport to the fifth stage from April until November (out of season the trails are open, but facilities are closed). The best time is the middle four weeks of the climbing season; the most crowded time is Obon Week in mid August. The climb is worthwhile but not easy: a saying goes that there are two kinds of fools, those who never climb Fuji and those who climb it twice.

Choosing which side to tackle Mt Fuji from affects how easy the climb is. Most people follow the Yoshidaguchi Trail from the Kawaguchiko side (north), which offers a 7.5-kilometre (4.7-mile) climb that takes five hours, plus three for the descent. You

From Ikebukuro station, the Tobu Tojo line maps a course through sprawling suburbia to its terminal at **Ogawamachi**, just over an hour away. Surrounded by rolling hills, the town was once noted as a centre for *washi* (Japanese paper) manufacturing, and today families still carry on the gruelling task of turning pulped wood into the uniquely textured material.

From Ogawamachi, the JR Hachiko line has little diesel trains on the hour to the next station, **Myokaku**. From there it's a ten-minute bus ride to the sleepy hamlet of **Nishi-Daira**, where old houses with their adjoining *kura* (warehouses) are the norm, and hens appear to outnumber people. From the bus stop, a two-minute walk into Nishi-Daira will bring you to a crossroads. Here, turn right on to the steep road that disappears into the forested hills above.

The climb is spectacular, with breathtaking views of the opposing hills as they emerge in hazy layers. But the walk is easy and offers an absorbing hour of peace before the tiled roofs of Jiko-ji come into view.

Like most temples throughout Asia, **Jiko-ji** commands a stunning location. Half-hidden between groves of thick blue bamboo, the various temple buildings are connected by a maze of stone steps. At the entrance stands an

---

can also head from the south-west side, starting at one of two new fifth stages, one near Gotemba (6.5 hours up and three down) or another further west (five hours up and 3.5 down).

Some climbers set off at nightfall, timing the ascent to arrive in time for sunrise. More sensible souls climb in daylight and rest in one of the lodges near the peak. With up to 600 people crammed into the huts, arriving and departing constantly, you won't get a sound sleep but you will appreciate the break. Lodges at the eighth stage on the Kawaguchiko side include **Hakuunsou** (0555 24 6514, ¥5,500-¥7,500 per person) and **Honhachigo Tomoekan** (0555 24 6511, ¥7,500-¥9,000). At the seventh stage on the Gotemba side, try **Hinodekan** (0550 89 2867, ¥6,000).

The temperature at the summit can be 20°C (68°F) lower than at the base; the average in July is 4.8°C (40.5°F) and in August 5.8°C (42.5°F). It's often below zero before sunrise. Essential items include good shoes, rainwear, a torch, toilet paper and some bags for your rubbish. Water and food are available at various points along the route, but overpriced.

Once you reach the peak, you might be disappointed to find it no longer a place of solitude and contemplation. Restaurants, souvenir shops, vending machines, portaloos, a shrine and several hundred people will be waiting for you; and the spectacle of the sunrise is not necessarily enhanced by loudspeakers blasting dramatic music. But it is still an amazing feeling to be standing atop Japan's most iconic peak.

GETTING THERE
Details below are for July and August; in other months, transport connections are fewer.

By bus
The fastest and cheapest way to Kawaguchiko is by bus from Nishi-Shinjuku's Keio Shinjuku Expressway Bus Terminal (1hr 45mins, ¥1,700 single). From the Keio bus terminal at Kawaguchiko station to the fifth stage it takes 55mins (¥1,700 single, ¥2,000 return); there are five buses a day. There are also six daily buses from Shinjuku direct to the fifth stage (2hrs 25mins, ¥2,600).

By train
Take the **JR Chuo line** from Shinjuku to Otsuki station (1hr 35mins, ¥1,280). From there, take the **Fuji-Kyuko line** to Kawaguchiko (57mins, ¥1,110) – timetables can be checked with JR in Otsuki (050 2016 1600) or Fuji-Kyuko in Kawaguchiko (0555 72 2911). From Kawaguchiko station to the fifth stage by bus takes another hour.

If you want to start the climb from Gotemba, there are four direct trains (express Asagiri) daily from Shinjuku on the **Odakyu line** (1hr 39mins, ¥2,720). From Gotemba there are three to four buses to the new fifth stage (40mins, ¥1,080 single).

TOURIST INFORMATION

Kawaguchiko Tourist Information
In front of Kawaguchiko station, 3631-5 Funatsu, Kawaguchiko-Machi (0555 72 6700). **Open** 8.30am-5.30pm daily.

old wooden tower supporting a huge bell (dating from 1245) that is rung twice a day. Above are the main structures, many displaying intricately carved designs.

Pre-dating the Late Nara period (710-94), Jiko-ji is believed to have been established in 673 by a priest called Jiko (hence its name). The advent of the Kamakura era saw the temple's rise in prominence, and it quickly became the religious centre for 75 satellite temples that mushroomed across the adjoining hills.

The modern treasure house (open 9am-4pm daily, ¥300) contains a number of valuable items, including the Lotus Sutra, a scroll-like masterpiece of calligraphy painstakingly transcribed by Emperor Gotoba (1183-98), and now a national treasure. **Kannondo**, which stands at the highest point in the compound, also guards a collection of treasures, the principal one being an image of Senju Kannon, the main deity of the area. The image is only open to public viewing on 17 April, the day of the temple's annual festival.

From Jiko-ji, the walk back to Nishi-Daira takes less than half an hour. If time allows, retrace your steps into the village and drop by **Tategu Kaikan** (0493 67 0014, open 9am-4.30pm Tue-Sun), a souvenir shop that stocks an array of locally made food and woodcraft.

Where to eat

There's nowhere to eat near Jiko-ji. Bring a packed lunch or try Myokaku or Ogawamachi, where there are lots of *unagi* (freshwater eel) restaurants. **Futaba Honten** (0493 72 0038, open 11am-2.30pm, 4-8pm daily, closed 1st Mon of mth), five minutes along the shopping street from Ogawamachi station, has belonged to the same family for 250 years and specialises in *chushichi-meshi*, a soup of rice in green tea, and the ubiquitous *unagi*.

Getting there

By train & bus From Ikebukuro station take the **Tobu Tojo special express** to Ogawamachi station (journey 73mins, ¥780 single), then the **JR Hachiko line** to Myokaku (8mins, ¥200), then the **Tokigawa Son'ei bus** to Jiko-ji Iriguchi (10mins). Services are infrequent – this is rural Japan – so it's best to check timings in advance.

OYA-MACHI

The small town of **Oya-machi**, lying 110 kilometres (68 miles) north of Tokyo, in Tochigi prefecture, sits on a mountain of volcanic stone and has been a mining centre for centuries. At its heart is a 27-metre (89-foot) statue carved from a sheer rock face.

Oya-machi is reached by a dusty road that leads to an expansive stone atrium. Huge doorways have been cut into the surrounding cliffs with staggering precision. Within this area is the deceptively small **Oya Stone Museum** (028 652 1232, open 9am-4.30pm Mon-Wed, Fri-Sun (also Thur in Aug), admission ¥600). On display are a number of miners' tools, early photos of the quarrying process, and an exhibit about Frank Lloyd Wright's Imperial Hotel in Tokyo (demolished in 1968), for which he insisted on using Oya stone. Then things get really interesting: you descend a stairwell into a vast underground ex-quarry 60 metres (197 feet) deep and large enough to swallow the Tokyo Dome. The quarry has been used as an aircraft factory in World War II, a mushroom farm and, more recently, a concert hall.

From the museum, it is a short walk back to the bus stop and into Oya-machi proper. There are a handful of shops and houses, many made entirely of stone. At the top of the slope that leads off to the left of the main street are the red gates of **Oya-ji** temple (0286 52 0128, open Apr-Oct 8.30am-5pm daily, Nov-Mar 9am-4.30pm daily, closed 2wks Dec and some Thur, ¥300), a small, ornate structure wedged beneath a cliff.

Founded in 810, the temple has been a tourist destination ever since, largely because of its remarkable reliefs. The first you encounter is the 42-armed Senju Kannon. Carved directly into the rock wall, it dates to the early part of the Heian era (794-1185). On the adjoining wall, are another nine reliefs of varying sizes and quality, created between 600 and 1,000 years ago. A small museum contains little of interest except the remains of an 11,000-year-old skeleton discovered here during restoration.

Across the street, flanked by souvenir shops, stands a massive rectangular entrance cut through the hill. Head through here, and you reach the towering 17-metre (56-foot) **Heiwa Kannon** (Goddess of Peace) statue. Completed in 1954, she hangs from the cliff, gazing benevolently out over the town.

Where to eat

Oya's tourist cafeterias are uninspiring. It's better to bring a packed lunch or eat near Utsunomiya station before boarding the bus.

Getting there

By train & bus From Ueno station take the **JR Tohoku line** to Utsunomiya station; journey times and prices vary from 44mins/¥4,600 by bullet train to 1hr 32mins/¥1,890 by regular train. Take the west exit at Utsunomiya and catch **bus 45** from bus stop 6 to Oya Kannon-mae (25 mins) – pay as you get off.

Directory

Getting Around	**308**
Resources A-Z	**311**
Travel Advice	311
The Local Climate	317
Further Reference	**319**
Vocabulary	**321**
Index	**324**

Getting Around

ARRIVING & LEAVING

By air

Two airports serve Tokyo. Most overseas flights arrive at **Narita International Airport**, which is nearly 70 kilometres (45 miles) from Tokyo and well served by rail and bus links to the city. It's less likely that you'll arrive at **Haneda International Airport**, closer to the city and to the south. Haneda handles mainly internal flights, though a revamp of its international terminal in 2010 saw it expand its routes within Asia.

Narita International Airport
Flight information 0476 34 5000, www.narita-airport.jp/en.
The fastest way to reach Tokyo from Narita is via the **Skyliner** (0476 32 8505 Narita, 3831 0989 Ueno, www.new-skyliner.jp), which launched in summer 2010. It takes 36 minutes to reach Nippori station, and also stops at Ueno. Prices were unavailable at time of writing, though a previous version of this service cost ¥1,920. A cheaper option (¥1,000) is the **Keisei tokkyu** (limited express), a regular train that makes a few stops on its 75-minute route to Ueno station.

For Tokyo station or the west side of the city, the **Narita Express** (NEX; 050 2016 1603, www.jreast.co.jp/e/nex) may be more convenient but is slower, taking around an hour to reach Tokyo station. Run by Japan Railways (JR), all trains go to Tokyo station (¥2,940), with some also serving Shinjuku (¥3,110), Ikebukuro (¥3,110), Omiya (¥3,740) and Yokohama (¥4,180). Trains depart every 30 to 40 minutes, and seats can be reserved up to a month in advance. Foreign passport holders can buy a combination NEX and Suica (*see right* **Tickets & passes**) card for ¥3,500 (or ¥5,000 for first-class 'green car' travel), which comes precharged with ¥1,500 of fares for travel on JR around Japan; it amounts to a 50% discount on the NEX fare. They are sold at the JR East Travel Service Centers in terminals 1 and 2.

Limousine buses (3665 7220, www.limousinebus.co.jp) also run regularly to various key points and certain hotels in the city. There are ticket counters inside the arrivals halls, located near the exits of both terminals 1 and 2; the buses depart from just outside. Fares are ¥3,000.

Taxis are recommended only for those with bottomless wallets: they cost from ¥30,000 and are often slower than the train.

Haneda International Airport
Flight information 5757 8111, www.tokyo-airport-bldg.co.jp.
Haneda is served by the **Tokyo Monorail** (www.tokyo-monorail. co.jp), which leaves every five to ten minutes from 5am to 11.51pm, linking up to Hamamatsucho station (¥470) on the Yamanote line in a little over 20 minutes. The **Keikyu line** (5789 8686, www.keikyu.co.jp) can take you to Shinagawa, also on the Yamanote line, in 19 minutes (¥400). From here you can link up with major JR lines.

Limousine buses to central Tokyo cost in the region of ¥1,000, depending on which part of the city you want to go to. A **taxi** will cost a minimum of ¥6,000.

By rail

Most of Japan's rail network is run by **Japan Railways** (JR). One of the fastest but most expensive ways to travel Japan's elongated countryside is by *shinkansen* (bullet train), which travels at speeds up to 320 kilometres (200 miles) per hour. Tickets can be purchased at JR reservation 'Green Window' areas or travel agents. Call the **JR East Infoline** (*see right*) for information in English.

Trains depart from different stations depending on destination; most leave from Tokyo or Ueno stations. Slower, cheaper trains go to many destinations. Marks on the train platforms show where the numbered carriages will stop. Most carriages have reserved seats only (reservations cost extra), but some carriages are set aside for unreserved seating on each train. Arrive early if you want to sit down.

By coach

Long-distance buses provide one of the cheapest ways to travel through Japan, although anyone over 5ft 6in (1m 68cm) may find the seats small. Most of these buses leave at midnight and arrive early the next morning; all are air-conditioned and have ample space for luggage. Seats can be reserved through a travel agent. Long-distance buses are run by the railway companies; for information, *see below* **JR trains** and *see right* **Private train lines**.

PUBLIC TRANSPORT

Tokyo has one of the most efficient train and subway systems in the world: in the rare event of delays in the morning rush, staff give out apology slips for workers to show their bosses. Services are fast, clean, safe, reliable and – with a little thought and the right map – remarkably easy to use. Almost all stations have signs in English, and signs telling you which exit to take. Subways and train lines are colour-coded.

Subways and trains operate from 5am to around midnight (JR lines slightly later). Rush hours are 7.30-9.30am and 5-7pm, and the last train of the day can be extremely uncomfortable.

Tokyo's rail network is run by several different companies, and changing trains between competing systems can mean paying for two tickets. Transfer tickets are usually available to take you from one line to another, but cost the same as buying two separate tickets and can be tricky to figure out. To simplify things, it's a good idea to get a pair of prepaid travel passes. Armed with a **Suica** or **Pasmo** (*see right* **Tickets & passes**), you can ride on any regular train in Tokyo.

The user-friendly **Jorudan** website (www.jorudan.co.jp/ english) is in English and allows you to type in your starting point and destination to learn routes, times and prices.

JR trains

Overland trains in Tokyo are operated by **Japan Railways East** (www.jreast.co.jp/e), part of the main JR group. It's impossible to stay in Tokyo for more than a few hours without using JR's **Yamanote line**, the loop that defines the city centre – and with which all Tokyo's subway and rail lines link at some point (for connections at each station on the loop, *see p336*). The main stations on the Yamanote line (colour-coded green) are Tokyo, Ueno, Ikebukuro, Shinjuku, Shibuya and Shinagawa. It's very foreigner-friendly, with an infoline in English and information centres at major stations (look for the question mark symbol) that offer help in English.

JR's other major lines in Tokyo are: **Chuo** (orange), **Sobu** (yellow), **Saikyo** (turquoise) and **Keihin Tohoku** (blue). Because of its notoriety for gropers (*chikan*), the insanely crowded Saikyo line offers women-only cars during peak hours.

JR East Infoline

050 2016 1603.
Open 10am-6pm daily.

Subways

There are 13 subway lines in Tokyo. Most are run by **Tokyo Metro** (3941 2004 9am-8pm daily, www.tokyometro.jp/global/en). Its nine colour-coded lines are: **Chiyoda** (dark green), **Fukutoshin** (brown), **Ginza** (orange), **Hanzomon** (purple), **Hibiya** (grey), **Marunouchi** (red), **Nanboku** (light green), **Tozai** (turquoise) and **Yurakucho** (yellow).

Four – slightly pricier – subway lines are run by the metropolitan government, **Toei** (3816 5700, www.kotsu.metro.tokyo.jp/eng). They are: **Asakusa** (pale pink), **Mita** (blue), **Oedo** (bright pink) and **Shinjuku** (green). If you're transferring from Tokyo Metro to Toei trains, buying a transfer ticket is ¥70 cheaper than buying separate tickets.

Subway maps posted in stations are in Japanese. For a subway map in English, *see p334-335*; you can also get one at tourist offices (*see p318* **Tourist information**).

Private train lines

Tokyo's private railway lines mainly ferry commuters to the outlying districts of the city. Because most were founded by companies that also run department stores, they usually terminate inside, or next to, one of their branches.

The major private lines are run by **Keio** (www.keio.co.jp), **Odakyu** (www.odakyu.jp), **Seibu** (www.seibu-group.co.jp/railways), **Tobu** (www.tobu.co.jp), **Tokyu** (www.tokyu.co.jp),

Keisei (www.keisei.co.jp) and **Keikyu** (www.keikyu.co.jp).

You can pick up a full map showing all lines and subways from the airport information counter on arrival. Most private lines offer women-only cars during peak hours: look for the pink window stickers (or the hundreds of grinning faces in the train if you've entered by mistake).

Tickets & passes

Standard tickets

Standard single tickets for adults (under-12s pay half-price, under-6s travel free) can be bought at automatic ticket machines at any station. Many machines feature a symbol saying which notes they accept. Touch-screen ticket machines can display information in English, but should you be unsure of your destination (or unable to read it from the Japanese map), buy a ticket for the minimum fare (¥160) and settle up in a fare adjustment machine (or window) at your destination. These machines, usually bright yellow, are found just before the exit barriers of all stations. Travellers with incorrect tickets do not have to pay punitive fines.

Transferring from one line to another, provided it is run by the same operator, will be covered by the price of your ticket. If your journey involves transferring from one network to another, you will have to buy a transfer ticket (if available) or buy another ticket at the transfer point.

If you're in town for any length of time you're better off buying a travel pass.

Suica & Pasmo

Suica is a prepaid travel pass issued by JR, but also accepted by Tokyo's metro and private rail lines, buses and some taxi companies. It contains an integrated circuit that, when swiped over a Suica panel, automatically deducts the minimum fare from your balance on entry to the station, with the remainder being deducted on exit at your destination. Suica cards can be purchased at JR 'Green Window' areas or at JR ticket machines. A card costs ¥2,000, including a ¥500 deposit. Credit on the card can be topped up at ticket machines (up to ¥10,000).

Pasmo is a similar card, issued by the subway companies, which works in most of the same locations. The only difference is that Suica cards are accepted

by JR lines outside of Tokyo, whereas Pasmo cards are not.

Both cards can also be used for purchases at most station kiosks, some vending machines and the occasional shop.

Frequent travel tickets

There's a huge variety of frequent travel tickets available, from prepaid cards to '11 for the price of ten' trip tickets. There are also combination tickets and one-day passes for one, two or three networks. For more details in English, call the **JR East Infoline** (*see left*).

JRPasses

The **Japan Rail Pass** (www.japanrailpass.net) provides for virtually unlimited travel on the entire national JR network, including *shinkansen* and all JR lines in Tokyo, including the Yamanote line. It cannot, however, be used on the new 'Nozomi' super-express *shinkansen*. It costs from ¥28,300 for seven days, about the same price as a middle-distance *shinkansen* return ticket. It's an essential buy if you're planning to travel much around Japan.

The JRPass is available only to visitors from abroad travelling under the entry status of 'temporary visitor', and must be purchased *before* coming to Japan. You buy an Exchange Order abroad, which is then changed into a pass on arrival in Japan at an exchange office (you'll need to show your passport).

JR East, which runs trains in and around Tokyo, has its own version of the pass (www.jreast. co.jp/e/eastpass), which costs from ¥20,000 for five days. If you are not intending to travel beyond the JREast area (Tokyo and the area to the north and east), this makes a sensible choice. The same conditions apply.

Exchange Orders can be bought at overseas offices of the Japan Travel Bureau International, Nippon Travel Agency, Kinki Nippon Tourist, Tokyu Tourist Corporation and other associated local travel agents, or at an overseas Japan Airlines office if you're travelling by Japan Airlines. Check the Japan Rail Pass website for overseas locations.

Buses

Like the trains, buses in Tokyo are run by several companies. Travelling by bus can be confusing if you're new to Japan, as signs are rarely in English. Toei and Keio bus fares cost ¥200, other buses are ¥210 – no matter what the distance (half-price for kids). Get on the bus at the front and off at the back. Drop the exact fare into the slot in front of the driver. If you don't have it, use the change machine, usually to the right, which will deduct your fare from the money. Fare machines accept ¥50, ¥100 and ¥500 coins and ¥1,000 notes. Stops are usually announced by a pre-recorded voice. A Toei bus route guide in English is available at Toei subway stations and hotels.

Tokyo Bus Association

5360 7111, www.tokyobus.or.jp.
The website and phone line provide information on all bus routes within and leaving Tokyo, in Japanese only.

Water transport

Tokyo's **Suijo river buses** (3457 7830, www.suijobus.co.jp) can't compete with the trains for speed or price, but in good weather they're a much more pleasurable way to cross the city. Boats vary in style from paddle-steamer lookalikes to something that would be more at home in a *Star Trek* movie. All leave from Hinode Pier, a short walk from Hamamatsucho station on the Yamanote line.

TAXIS

Taxi fares begin at ¥710 for the first two kilometres; then ¥100 for every 350 metres or ¥90 per 105 seconds idling. Prices rise by 20% between 10pm and 5am. Stands are located near stations, most hotels, department stores and major intersections. Tipping is not expected.

Hinomaru Limousine

Ark Hills Mori Bldg, 1-12-32 Akasaka, Minato-ku (3212 0505 24hrs, www.hinomaru.co.jp). Roppongi-Itchome station (Chiyoda line), exit 3.
Stretch limos and the like.

DRIVING

Rental costs for garages are equivalent to those for small apartments in Tokyo, so if you rent a car you will have to pay astronomical parking fees (usually around ¥100 for 30 minutes, more in the centre). If you do decide to hire a car, you'll need an international driving licence backed up by at least

six months' driving experience. English-speaking rental assistance is available at many of the large hotels as well as at the airport.

The **Japan Automobile Federation** (www.jaf.or.jp) publishes a 'Rules of the Road' guide (¥1,000) in English. Request one from their Shiba branch office: 2-2-17 Shiba, Minato-ku (6833 9100). A Metropolitan Expressway map in English is available from the **Metropolitan Expressway Public Corporation**, (www.shutoko.jp).

Car hire

If you want to drive outside the capital (which is definitely a much safer option), JR offers rail and car rental packages. Call the **JR East Infoline** (*see p309*) for details.

Toyota Rent-a-lease

Narita International Airport Terminals 1 & 2 (0476 32 1020, http://rent.toyota.co.jp). **Open** 7am-10pm daily. **Other locations** throughout the city.

CYCLING

The bicycle remains the most common form of local transport in Tokyo, but unattended bikes should always be locked as these, along with umbrellas, are the only things that get stolen in Japan. Areas in and around stations are usually no-parking zones for bikes, a rule that locals gleefully ignore, but which can result in your bike being impounded. Some hotels will loan bicycles to guests.

Cycle hire

Cool Bike *3-19 Tsukudo-cho, Shinjuku-ku (3260 6316, www. coolbike.jp/index.php/ems_en.html). Iidabashi station (JR line), east exit; (Nanboku, Oedo, Tozai, Yurakucho lines), exit B4b.* **Open** late Apr-early Sept 9.30am-5.30pm Tue-Sun; mid Sept-mid Apr 9.30am-4.30pm Tue-Sat.
Folding bikes for rent at ¥2,000 per day. For an extra ¥2,000 they will deliver the bike to hotels in the central Tokyo areas. Reserve in English by phone or online.
Mujirushi *3-8-3 Marunouchi, Chiyoda-ku (5208 8241, www. mujiyurakucho.com). Ginza Itchome Station (Yurakucho line), exit A1.* **Open** 10am-9pm daily.
Rent regular or electric bikes in Muji's distinctive minimal

designs. Rental costs are just ¥525 per day (10am-8pm) on weekdays; double at weekends. A ¥3,000 deposit and photo ID are required. Reservations accepted.

WALKING

If you don't mind the congestion, Tokyo is great for walking. The city is 99.9 per cent safe 24 hours a day. The **Tokyo TIC** (*see p318* **Tourist information**) offers information on free walking tours of parts of Tokyo.

When crossing the road, always do so at marked crossings and wait for the green man. If you cross on red, urban legend says that you could be held responsible for the death of those behind you, who may blindly follow you into the traffic.

GUIDED TOURS

Official tour guides in Tokyo have to pass rigorous examinations in the finer points of the city's history and culture. No matter how much you've been reading, you'll learn more from one of these human encyclopaedias.

Hato Bus

3435 6081, www.hatobus.com/en. **Bookings** 9am-7pm daily. **Credit** AmEx, DC, JCB, MC, V.
The nation's largest tour-bus operator offers a wide variety of tours, including half-day, full-day and night trips with English-speaking guides. Prices start at around ¥5,000. Buses depart from a terminal near Hamamatsucho and Daimon stations.

SkyBus Tokyo

3215 0008, www.skybus.jp. **Bookings** 10am-6pm daily. **Credit** AmEx, DC, MC, V.
This open-top double-decker coach offers four routes with English-speaking guides, including an Imperial Palace route and a night-time tour of Odaiba. Tours run several times a day and cost from ¥1,500

Sunrise Tours

5796 5454, www.jtb-sunrisetours.jp. **Bookings** 9am-6pm Mon-Fri. **Credit** AmEx, JCB, DC, MC, V.
Run by the Japan Travel Bureau, Sunrise offers the widest range of English-language tours in Tokyo, as well as trips to further afield locations such as Kyoto, Nikko (*see p300*) or Hakone (*see p292*). The company can arrange pick-ups at most of the city's major hotels. Reservations can be made online.

Resources A-Z

ADDRESSES

Only the largest streets in Tokyo have names, and even they don't appear in addresses. The Japanese system uses numbers in place of names. Central Tokyo is divided into 23 wards, or *ku*. Within each *ku*, there are many smaller districts, or *cho*, which also have their own names. Then come the numbers. The first number is the main area, or *chome*, then a second number signifies which block, and a third number the specific building. Most buildings are named, but this name is used mainly for confirmation. Japan uses the continental system of floor numbering. The abbreviation 1F is the ground floor; 2F means the second floor, or first floor English style. And B1 or B2 refer to the basement levels.

Thus, the address of the Office bar – Yamazaki Bldg 5F, 2-7-18 Kita-Aoyama, Minato-ku – means that it's on the fifth floor of the Yamazaki Building, which is the 18th building of the seventh block of the second area of Kita-Aoyama, in Minato ward.

To track down an address, invest in a detailed bilingual atlas, such as the *Tokyo City Atlas* (Kodansha). Then follow the metal plaques affixed to lamp posts or the front of some buildings.

Alternatively, ask a policeman. It's what the locals do.

In addition, most station exits have detailed street plans of the vicinity posted, with the numbers clearly marked. Maps (usually only in Japanese) can also often be found on the streets themselves.

While the system isn't as tricky as it sounds, few Tokyoites leave home without a map of any new destination. Virtually all websites have maps to print, or if you have access to a fax machine, it's common practice to phone your destination and ask them to fax you a map of how to get there.

AGE RESTRICTIONS

There is no age of consent in Japan. The legal age for smoking and drinking is 20. The minimum voting age is also 20.

ATTITUDE & ETIQUETTE

Japanese people are generally forgiving of visitors' clumsy attempts at correct behaviour, but there are certain rules that must be followed to avoid offending your hosts. For how to behave in a bathhouse, *see p50* **Old Soaks**. For business etiquette, *see below*.

BUSINESS

Etiquette

The Japanese place great emphasis on personal relationships between business partners, and socialising before and after the deal is done is de rigueur. Here are some basic business tips:

● Carry plenty of business cards. You will be spraying them around like confetti.

● Always pass business cards with two hands. Do not write on another person's business card, fold it or put it in your back pocket. When in meetings, read the cards that you have just received carefully and leave them face up on the table throughout, in a neat column according to hierarchy of position.

● If you need an interpreter, hire one of your own and ask them to interpret body language for you.

● When out eating with a group, wait for your comrades to indicate your seat.

● Never offer to split a restaurant bill. Instead, just say thank you ('*Gochiso sama deshita*') if someone else pays.

● If you receive a gift from your host, do not open it in front of them unless you are invited to. If you give a gift, make sure it is professionally wrapped.

● Be prepared to give details of your personal life in a way that would be inappropriate elsewhere.

Conventions & conferences

Many larger hotels have conference and business rooms for hire. For Tokyo's major annual trade fairs, *see pp220-226* **Calendar**.

Makuhari Messe
2-1 Nakase, Mihama-ku, Chiba (043 296 0001, www.m-messe. co.jp). Kaihin-Makuhari station (Keiyo line), south exit.

Tokyo Big Sight
Tokyo International Exhibition Center, 3-21-2 Ariake, Koto-ku (5530 1111, www.bigsight.jp/english). Kokusai-Tenjijo Seimon station (Yurikamome line) or Kokusai-Tenjijo station (Rinkai line) or Ariake terminal (Suijo water bus). **Map** p83.

Tokyo International Forum
3-5-1 Marunouchi, Chiyoda-ku (5221 9000, www.t-i-forum.co.jp/ english). Yurakucho station (Yamanote, Yurakucho lines), Tokyo International Forum exit. **Map** p59.

Couriers & shippers

Federal Express *0120 003 200, www.fedex.com/jp_english.*

DIRECTORY

Hubnet *0120 881 084,*
www.hubnetexp.com/jp/jp.
UPS Yamato Express
0120 271 040, www.ups.com.

Office services

Bell24 System
0120 600 024, www.tas.bell24.co.jp.
Telephone answering services start
from ¥10,500; bilingual costs more.
IRI *Hatchobori Bldg 7F, 2-19-8
Hatchobori, Chuo-ku (5543 1221,
www.iri-japan.co.jp). Hatchobori
station (Hibiya, Keiyo lines), exit A5.*
Public relations company.
Kinko's
0120 001 966, www.kinkos.co.jp.
A complete range of print services,
plus internet access. Check the
website for 24-hour locations.
Kyodo PR
*Dowa Bldg 7F, 7-2-22 Ginza,
Chuo-ku (3571 5171, www.kyodo-
pr.co.jp). Ginza station (Ginza,
Hibiya, Marunouchi lines), exit C3.*
Public relations company.
Servcorp
5789 5800, www.servcorp.net.
Has office space for hire in several
locations in Tokyo with executive
service starting from ¥130,000 per
month plus deposit.
Simul International *T Tsukiji Eto
Bldg 5F, 1-12-6 Tsukiji, Chuo-ku
(3524 3100, www.simul.co.jp).
Tsukiji station (Hibiya line), exit 2.*
Translation services.
Telephone Secretary Centre
5413 7320, www.telese.co.jp.
An answering service starting at
¥18,900 a month, including
bilingual secretaries, word
processing and typing.
Transpacific Enterprises
*COI Uchikanda Bldg 8F,
3-2-8 Uchikanda, Chiyoda-ku
(5297 6131, www.transpacific.jp).
Kanda station (JR line), south exit.*
Translation services.

Useful organisations

American Chamber of Commerce
3433 5381, www.accj.or.jp.
**Australian & New Zealand
Chamber of Commerce**
5312 1988, www.anzccj.jp.
British Chamber of Commerce
3267 1901, www.bccjapan.com.
Canadian Chamber of Commerce
5775 9500, www.cccj.or.jp.
**JETRO (Japan External Trade
Organisation)** *3582 5511
(Japanese-only automated phone
menu), www.jetro.go.jp.*
JETRO Library *Ark Mori Bldg 6F,
1-12-32 Akasaka, Minato-ku (3582
1775, www.jetro.go.jp). Tameike-
Sanno station (Ginza, Nanboku*

lines), exit 13. **Open** 9am-5pm
Mon-Fri. Closed 3rd Tue of mth.
Houses information about trade,
the economy and investment for
just about any country in the world.
Lots of statistics, as well as basic
business directories. Over-18s only.

CUSTOMS

The duty-free allowances for
non-residents coming into Japan are:
200 cigarettes or 50 cigars or 250g
of tobacco for foreign brands, and
the same limits again for Japanese
tobacco; three 750ml bottles
of spirits; 56ml (2oz) of perfume;
gifts or souvenirs up to a value
of ¥200,000. There is no limit on
the amount of Japanese or foreign
currency that can be brought into
the country, though amounts over
$10,000 must be declared.
Penalties are severe for drug
importation: deportation is the
lenient option. Pornography laws
are very strict; anything showing
pubic hair may be confiscated.
For more information, visit **Japan
Customs** at www.customs.go.jp.

DISABLED

Tokyo is not easy for those with
disabilities, particularly when it
comes to public transport. Stations
often have long corridors and
staircases, and only some have
escalators, lifts or wheelchair-
moving facilities, though station
staff will assist those in need. For
the visually impaired, raised dots
on the ground guide the way inside
stations. Trains have 'silver seats'
near carriage exits for use by the
disabled, elderly or pregnant.
The best resource in English
for travellers with disabilities
is an online service, **Accessible
Tokyo**: http://accessible.jp.org.

**Club Tourism Division Barrier-
free Travel** *Centre Kinki Nippon
Tourist Co, Shinjuku Island
Wing 10F, 6-3-1 Nishi-Shinjuku,
Shinjuku-ku (5323 6915, www.
club-t.com). Nishi-Shinjuku station
(Marunouchi line), Island Wing
exit.* **Open** 9.15am-5.30pm daily.
Organises tours that take into
account the needs of disabled
travellers. Make an appointment
to guarantee you deal with an
English-speaking staff member.

DRUGS

Drugs can be found in Tokyo, but
penalties for possession are severe.
Expect deportation or imprisonment.

A spate of high-profile celebrity
drug busts has caused the police
to step up their random searches,
with foreigners a prime target.

ELECTRICITY

Electric current in Japan runs like
the USA's, at 100V AC, rather than
the 220-240V European standard.
Plugs have two flat-sided prongs.
If you bring electrical appliances
from Europe, you'll need an adapter.
Electricity in Tokyo is provided
by **Tokyo Electric Power
Company** (TEPCO, 4477 3099);
gas by **Tokyo Gas** (5722 0111).

EMBASSIES & CONSULATES

Embassies are usually open 9am
to 5pm Monday to Friday; opening
times for visa sections may vary.

Australian Embassy *2-1-14 Mita,
Minato-ku (5232 4111, www.
australia.or.jp). Azabu-Juban station
(Nanboku, Oedo lines), exit 2.*
British Embassy *1 Ichibansho,
Chiyoda-ku (5211 1100, www.
uknow.or.jp). Hanzomon station
(Hanzomon line), exit 4.*
Canadian Embassy *7-3-38
Akasaka, Minato-ku (5412 6200,
www.japan.gc.ca). Aoyama-Itchome
station (Ginza, Hanzomon, Oedo
lines), exit 4.*
Irish Embassy *2-10-7 Kojimachi,
Chiyoda-ku (3263 0695, www.
irishembassy.jp). Hanzomon station
(Hanzomon line), exit 4.*
New Zealand Embassy
*20-40 Kamiyamacho, Shibuya-ku
(3467 2271, www.nzembassy.com/
japan). Yoyogi-Koen station
(Chiyoda line), exit 2.*
South Africa Embassy
*Oriken Hirakawacho Bldg 3-4F,
2-1-1 Hirakawa-cho, Chiyoda-ku
(3265 3366, www.sajapan.org).
Nagatacho station (Hanzomon,
Nanboku, Yurakucho lines), exit 4.*
US Embassy *1-10-5 Akasaka,
Minato-ku (3224 5000, http://
tokyo.usembassy.gov). Tameike-
Sanno station (Ginza, Nanboku
lines), exit 13.*

EMERGENCIES

To contact the police (*keisatsu*)
in an emergency, call **110**; to call
an ambulance (*kyukyu-sha*) or fire
department (*kaji-shoubou*), call
119. From a public phone, press
the red button first. The person
answering should, in theory,
speak English, but if you are with
a Japanese speaker, get them to call.

DIRECTORY

Japan Help Line (*see below* Helplines) offers 24-hour, English-language support but cannot deal with time-sensitive emergencies.

For emergency rooms at Tokyo hospitals, *see below* **Accident & emergency**.

GAY & LESBIAN

For information, *see pp243-249*.

HEALTH

For the Japanese, medical insurance provided by employers or the state covers 70% of the cost of medical treatment; those aged over 70 pay only 10%. Visitors are expected to pay the full amount for treatment received, so should take out medical insurance before travelling. Calls to hospitals – except those to **Tokyo Medical Clinic & Surgical Clinic** (*see right*) – are answered in Japanese; say '*Eigo o hanaseru kata ga imasuka?*' ('Is there an English speaker I can talk to?') and you'll be transferred. Vaccinations are not required to enter Japan.

Tokyo Metropolitan Health & Medical Information Centre *5285 8181 (9am-8pm daily), www.himawari.metro.tokyo.jp*. The *himawari* service provides medical and health information in English and can direct you to the most suitable clinic. An out-of-hours number (5285 8185, 5-8pm Mon-Fri, 9am-8pm Sat, Sun) provides interpretation to help foreign nationals get emergency care. If you get to the hospital and can't communicate with the doctor, call them. But if you're at home bleeding, call 119.

Accident & emergency

The following offer appointments, deal with 24-hour emergencies and have English-speaking staff.
Japan Red Cross Medical Centre *4-1-22 Hiroo, Shibuya-ku (3400 1311, www.med.jrc.or.jp). Hiroo station (Hibiya line), exit 3.* **Open** 8.30-11am Mon-Fri.
St Luke's International Hospital *9-1 Akashicho, Chuo-ku (3541 5151, www.luke.or.jp). Tsukiji station (Hibiya line), exits 3, 4.* **Open** (by appt only) 8.30-11am Mon-Fri.
Seibo International Catholic Hospital *2-5-1 Naka-Ochiai, Shinjuku-ku (3951 1111, www. seibokai.or.jp). Shimo-Ochiai station (Seibu Shinjuku line), north exit.* **Open** 8-11am (or by appt) Mon-Sat. Closed 3rd Sat of mth.

Tokyo Medical Clinic & Surgical Clinic *Mori Bldg 32 2F, 3-4-30 Shiba-koen, Minato-ku (3436 3028, www.tmsc.jp). Shiba-Koen station (Mita line), exit A2 or Akabanebashi station (Oedo line), Tokyo Tower exit.* **Open** 8.30am-5.30pm Mon-Fri; 8.30am-noon Sat. Doctors hail from the UK, America, Germany or Japan, and all speak English. The clinic also has a pharmacy on the first floor.

Contraception & abortion

Condoms reign supreme in terms of contraception in Japan, largely because until 1999 the Pill was available only to women with menstrual problems, and taking it is still generally considered risky. Condoms are sold in most convenience stores and pharmacies. Abortion is legal and not morally controversial. The signature of the 'father' is required. Clinics have different rules regarding how far into the pregnancy they will perform abortions. Medical abortions are not available.

Dentists

The following clinics have English-speaking staff.
Dr JS Wong *1-22-3 Kami-Osaki, Shinagawa-ku (3473 2901). Meguro station (Yamanote, Mita, Nanboku lines), east exit.* **Open** (by appt only) Mon-Wed, Fri, Sat.
Tokyo Clinic Dental Office *Mori Bldg 32 2F, 3-4-30 Shiba-Koen, Minato-ku (3431 4225, www2.gol.com/users/tward/clinic.html). Kamiyacho station (Hibiya line), exit 1 or Akabanebashi station (Oedo line), Tokyo Tower exit.* **Open** (by appt only) 9am-6pm Mon-Fri; 9am-5pm Sat. Japanese insurance accepted.
Tokyo Midtown Dental Clinic *6F Midtown Tower, 9-7-1 Akasaka, Minato-ku (5413 7912, www.tokyo midtown-mc.jp/en/dental). Roppongi station (Hibiya, Oedo lines), exits 4, 8.* **Open** (by appt) Mon-Sat. A state-of-the-art clinic. Japanese insurance accepted.

Doctors

The following clinics have English-speaking staff.
Tokyo Adventist Hospital *3-17-3 Amanuma, Suginami-ku (3392 6151, www.tokyoeisei.com). Ogikubo station (Chuo, Marunouchi lines), north exit.* **Open** 8.30-11am Mon-Fri; by appt afternoons Mon-Thur. No emergencies.

Tokyo British Clinic *Daikanyama Y Bldg 2F, 2-13-7 Ebisu-Nishi, Shibuya-ku (5458 6099, www.tokyobritishclinic. com). Ebisu station (Yamanote, Hibiya lines), west exit.* **Open** 8.30am-5.30pm Mon-Fri; 8.30am-12.30pm Sat. Run by a British doctor, this clinic caters for most aspects of general practice, including paediatrics.
Tokyo Medical Clinic & Surgical Clinic *Mori Bldg 32 2F, 3-4-30 Shiba-koen, Minato-ku (3436 3028, www.tmsc.jp). Shiba-Koen station (Mita line), exit A2 or Akabanebashi station (Oedo line), Tokyo Tower exit.* **Open** 8.30am-5.30pm Mon-Fri; 8.30am-noon Sat. A clinic with friendly, English-speaking doctors, located next to the Tokyo Tower.
Tokyo Midtown Medical Center *6F Midtown Tower, 9-7-1 Akasaka, Minato-ku (5413 0080, www.tokyo midtown-mc.jp/en). Roppongi station (Hibiya, Oedo lines), exits 4, 8.* A clinic affiliated with Johns Hopkins Medicine in the US.

Opticians

See p215.

Pharmacies

See p215.

HELPLINES

The following helplines offer information in English.
Japan HIV Center *5259 0256, www.npo-jhc.com/e_hotline.htm.* **Open** noon-3pm Sat.
Alcoholics Anonymous *3971 1471 (taped message), www.aatokyo.org.*
HELP Asian Women's Shelter *3368 8855.* **Open** 10am-5pm Mon-Fri; in Japanese and English.
Immigration Information Centre *5796 7112.* **Open** 9am-5pm Mon-Fri.
Japan Help Line *0570 000 911, www.jhelp.com.* **Open** 24hrs daily. A non-profit-making worldwide assistance service. Among other services, it produces the Japan Help Line Card, which contains useful telephone numbers and essential information for non-Japanese speakers, as well as a numbered phrase list in English and Japanese for use in emergencies.
Tokyo English Life Line (TELL) *5774 0992, www.telljp.com.* **Open** 9am-11pm daily. Counselling and assistance service run by trained volunteers.

DIRECTORY

Tokyo Foreign Residents' Advisory Centre *5320 7744.* **Open** 9.30am-noon, 1-5pm Mon-Fri. Run by the Tokyo Metropolitan Government, this will help newcomers adjust to Japanese life.

ID

Foreign visitors are required to carry ID (a passport) at all times. Long-term residents should carry their Alien Registration Card.

INTERNET

For local links, *see p320* **Websites**.

Many of Tokyo's 24-hour manga coffee shops (*manga kissa*), such as the **GeraGera** chain, offer cheap internet services. They are often clustered around train stations.

Internet cafés seem to open and close in the blink of an eye, so your best bet is to try a **Kinko's** (www.kinkos.co.jp), which has 24-hour locations all around the city.

Wi-Fi is available in many locations, including **Ben's Café** (*see p190*) and **Respekt Café** (*see p167*). An up-to-date list of wireless hotspots can be found at www.hotspot-locations.com.

LANGUAGE

For information on Japanese language and pronunciation, and a list of useful words and phrases, *see pp321-323* **Vocabulary**.

There are hundreds of schools in Tokyo running courses in Japanese. Most of these offer intensive studies for those who want to learn as quickly as possible. They may offer longer courses too.

Private schools can be expensive, so check out lessons run by your ward office. These cost from as little as ¥100 a month – a bargain compared to the average ¥3,000 an hour for group lessons at schools.

Arc Academy *2-14-7 Shibuya, Shibuya-ku (3409 0391, http:// en.arc-academy.net). Shibuya station (Yamanote, Ginza, Hanzomon lines), east exit.* Offers a wide variety of courses.
Meguro Language Centre *NT Bldg 3F, 1-4-11 Meguro, Meguro-ku (3493 3727, www.mlcjapanese. co.jp). Meguro station (Yamanote, Mita, Nanboku lines), west exit.* A wide range of courses, from private lessons to group lessons.
Temple University *2-8-12 Minami-Azabu, Minato-ku (0120 861 026, www.tuj.ac.jp). Shirokane-Takanawa station (Mita,*

Nanboku lines), exit 2; Azabu-Juban station (Nanboku, Oedo lines), exit 1. Temple University offers fairly cheap evening classes as part of its continuing education programme.

LEGAL HELP

Legal Counselling Centre

Bar Association Bldg, 1-1-3 Kasumigaseki, Chiyoda-ku (3581 2255, www.niben.jp). Kasumigaseki station (Chiyoda line), exit C1; (Hibiya line), exit A1; (Marunouchi line), exit B1. **Open** (by appt) 1-4pm. Consultations in English (¥5,000 for first half hour, ¥2,500 per half hour thereafter). Free for the impoverished on Thursday afternoons. Topics cover a range of issues including crime, immigration and labour problems. Appointments are on a first-come, first-served basis.
Tokyo Legal Affairs Bureau *1-1-15, Kudanminami, Chiyoda-ku (5213 1372). Kudanshita station (Hanzomon, Toei Shinjuku, Tozai lines), exit 6.* **Open** 1.30-4pm Tue, Thur. Free counselling in English by phone.

LIBRARIES

Each ward has a central lending library with a limited number of English-language titles; you need an Alien Registration Card to borrow books. The following reference libraries have a books in English. All close on national holidays. For business libraries, *see p312* **Useful organisations**.

Japan Foundation Library

4-4-1 Yotsuya, Shinjuku-ku (5369 6086, www.jpf.go.jp/e/ about/jfic/lib). Yotsuya San-chome station (Marunouchi line), exit 1. **Open** 10am-7pm Mon-Fri. Closed last Mon of mth.
Books, mags and reference material. Specialises in humanities and social sciences, and also has translations of Japanese novels. Houses about 33,000 books and 300 magazine titles. Lending as well as reference. Under-18s not admitted.
National Diet Library *1-10-1 Nagatacho, Chiyoda-ku (3581 2331, www.ndl.go.jp). Nagatacho station (Hanzomon, Nanboku, Yurakucho lines), exits 2, 3.* **Open** 9.30am-7pm Mon-Fri; 9am-5pm Sat. Closed 3rd Wed of mth. Japan's main library, with the largest number of foreign-language books and materials. Over two million books, 50,000 mags and 1,500 newspapers and periodicals. Under-18s not admitted.

Tokyo Metropolitan Central Library *5-7-13 Minami-Azabu, Minato-ku (3442 8451, www.library. metro.tokyo.jp). Hiroo station (Hibiya line), exit 1.* **Open** 10am-9pm Mon-Fri; 10am-5.30pm Sat, Sun. The main library for the Tokyo government has the largest collection of books about Tokyo and 150,000 titles in foreign languages.

LOST PROPERTY

If you leave a bag or package somewhere, just go back: it will probably still be there. If you left it in a train station or other public area, go to the station-master's office or nearest *koban* (police box) and ask for English-language assistance. Items handed in at the station are logged in a book. You will have to sign in and show ID in order to receive your item. Or ring the general JR/police information numbers below. If you leave something in a taxi on the way to or from a hotel, try the hotel reception – taxi drivers often bring the lost item straight back.

Eidan subway *3941 2004.* Japanese only.
JR (Yamanote line) *3423 0111.* English-speaking service.
Metropolitan Police *3501 0110.* English-speaking service.
Narita Airport *0476 348 000.*
Taxi *3648 0300.* Japanese only.
Toei subway & buses *3816 5700.* Japanese only.

MEDIA

Magazines

If you read Japanese, there's a wealth of what's-on details in weekly publications such as *Pia* and *Tokyo Walker* (both ¥350). If not, there's Tokyo's only paid-for English-language listings monthly, *Tokyo Journal* (www.tokyo.to). The following are all free.

Japanzine *www.seekjapan.jp.* This magazine takes an irreverent look at some of the quirkier aspects of Japan life. It includes both Tokyo and Kansai listings.
Metropolis *www.metropolis.co.jp.* This is Tokyo's biggest and best free weekly magazine, with listings and adverts galore. It's distributed at foreigner-friendly bars, clubs, shops and hotels every Friday.
Tokyo Notice Board *www.tokyonoticeboard.co.jp.* Little more than a collection of classified ads.

Tokyo Weekender
www.weekenderjapan.com.
Can be tricky to find. Contains
expat community gossip and
features of variable quality.

Newspapers

The *Yomiuri Shimbun* is the
world's most-read newspaper, with
a daily circulation of 16 million. For
English readers the choice is limited
to three newspapers: the *Daily
Yomiuri*, the *Japan Times* and
the *International Herald Tribune*,
which incorporates the English
version of the *Asahi Shimbun*. All
cost ¥120-¥180 and are available at
most central Tokyo station kiosks.

Daily Yomiuri
www.yomiuri.co.jp/dy.
Agency reports, features from *The
Times* (Sunday) and the *Washington
Post* (Friday), and some house-
written features. It's the thinnest
newspaper, but the best value.
**International Herald
Tribune/Asahi Shimbun**
www.asahi.com/english.
Launched in 2001 as a joint venture
between the *International Herald
Tribune* and the *Asahi Shimbun*, it
reads like two different newspapers,
with strong international content
but dire coverage of local news.
Japan Times
www.japantimes.co.jp.
The oldest English-language
newspaper in Japan. Consisting
mainly of agency reports, its
motto 'All the news without fear
or favour' could read 'All the news
without flair or flavour'. Reprints
two pages of features from the UK's
Observer each Saturday.
Nikkei Weekly *http://e.nikkei.com.*
The Japanese equivalent of the *FT*
produces this weekly digest from
the world of finance.

Radio

InterFM *www.interfm.co.jp.*
Broadcasting on 76.1MHz, this
is Tokyo's main bilingual station.
Plays rock and pop.
NHK Radio Japan
www.nhk.or.jp/nhkworld.

Television

Japanese state broadcaster NHK
runs two commercial-free terrestrial
channels: NHK General (channel 1)
and NHK Educational (channel 3) –
and two satellite channels: BS1 and
BS2. Tokyo's five other terrestrial
channels – Nihon TV (channel 4),
Tokyo Broadcasting System

(channel 6), Fuji Television (channel
8), Television Asahi (channel 10)
and TV Tokyo (channel 12) – show
a constant stream of unimaginative
pap, relieved occasionally by a good
documentary or drama series.
NHK General news at 7pm
and 9pm daily is broadcast
simultaneously in both English
and Japanese: to access the English
version you'll need a bilingual
TV set (most big hotels have them).
Many non-Japanese TV series and
films are also broadcast bilingually.
NHK also has an English language
news cable channel, NHK World.
Japan's main satellite broadcaster
is Rupert Murdoch's SkyPerfect!
TV, which offers a host of familiar
channels, including CNN, BBC
World and Sky Sports.

MONEY

The yen is not divided into smaller
units and comes in denominations
of ¥1, ¥5, ¥10, ¥50, ¥100 and ¥500
(coins) and ¥1,000, ¥2,000, ¥5,000
and ¥10,000 (notes). The ¥2,000
note is rarely seen.
Prices on display must include
the five per cent sales tax. Some
places list that figure below a much
larger price that doesn't include
the tax. If you see two prices, you'll
be paying the higher one.
Japan is a cash-based society,
and restaurants and bars may
refuse credit cards. Larger shops,
restaurants and hotels accept major
cards, but you should always keep
some cash on you.

Banks & ATMs

Banks are open 9am to 3pm
Monday to Friday. Do not go to
a bank if you're in a hurry – queues
are long, especially on Fridays; you
have to take a number and wait.
ATMs are located inside banks,
and their hours vary greatly. You
can find 24-hour ATMs around
major stations, but elsewhere they
may close anywhere between 6pm
and midnight. Most convenience
stores also have ATMs. All ATMs
have logos showing which cards
are accepted, but most will not take
foreign-issued cards. Among the
banks, **Citibank** is the most useful,
with 24-hour ATMs all over Tokyo
(information 0120 50 4189). Of the
domestic banks, **Shinsei** has the
most customer-friendly reputation,
with 24-hour free ATMs.
Post offices (*see p316*) are also
convenient for cash: their ATMs
allow you to withdraw money with
most foreign cards, and also have

instructions in English. Some
of their ATMs are open 24 hours.
The ATMs at Narita Airport only
work during banking hours. Ensure
you have some Japanese cash if
arriving early morning or at night.

Bureaux de change

You can cash travellers' cheques
or change foreign currency at
any authorised foreign-exchange
bank (look for the signs). Some
large hotels change travellers'
cheques and currency, as do large
department stores, which are open
until about 8pm. Narita Airport has
several bureaux de change staffed
by English speakers, open daily
from around 7am to 10pm.

Lost/stolen credit cards

To report lost or stolen cards, dial
these 24-hour freephone numbers:

American Express *0120 020 120.*
English message follows Japanese.
Diners Club *0120 074 024.*
MasterCard *00531 11 3886.*
Visa *00531 44 0022.*

NATURAL HAZARDS

The Great Kanto Earthquake
of 1923 destroyed much of Tokyo,
and the chances of a future disaster
remain high. Despite precautions,
the 'Big One' could cause terrible
damage. The Kobe Earthquake of
1995 left over 6,000 dead, and the
tremor in Niigata in 2004 killed 30
and left many thousands homeless.
Every year on 1 September,
the anniversary of the 1923 quake,
Tokyo practises how to cope with
a major earthquake. Residents
are advised to keep a small bag
handy, containing essentials such
as a bottle of water, preserved
foodstuffs, some cash and a torch.
If you are caught up, try to shut
off any stoves and gas mains,
secure an exit, and look for a table
or similar to protect you.

OPENING HOURS

Department stores and larger shops
in Tokyo are open daily from 10am
(sometimes earlier, sometimes later)
to around 8pm or 9pm. Smaller
shops are open the same hours
six days a week. Mondays and
Wednesdays are the commonest
closing days; Sunday is a normal
shopping day. Convenience stores
offer 24-hour shopping at slightly
higher prices than supermarkets,
and are found all over the city.

DIRECTORY

DIRECTORY

The major chains are 7-Eleven, AM-PM, Family Mart and Lawson's.

Most restaurants open at around 11am and close around 11pm, though some bars and *izakaya* are open till 5am. Some don't close until the last customer has gone.

Banks are open 9am to 3pm Monday to Friday. Main post offices are open 9am to 7pm weekdays, and often on Saturdays (usually 9am-3pm) or even Sundays; smaller post offices close at 5pm Monday to Friday, and at weekends.

Office hours are 9am to 5pm. On national holidays, many places keep Sunday hours (closing earlier), but most are closed on 1 and 2 January.

POLICE

For a foreign visitor or resident, the most frequent contact with the police is usually through the *koban* – the police boxes dotted around every neighbourhood (marked by two red lights with a gold seal in-between), from which officers patrol the area by car and bicycle. Each major *koban* has officers on duty to deal with enquiries and complaints from the public.

Common causes of friction between Japanese police and foreign nationals are being drunk and aggressive, having noisy parties at home, traffic violations and bicycle theft (if you buy a bike, take careful note of the registration number – you'll need it).

Police officers are only legally entitled to stop people if they are behaving suspiciously, but this can be liberally interpreted. If you are stopped by police officers in Tokyo, present your passport or Alien Registration Card (you're legally required to carry it with you at all times). If detained at a police station, ask to speak to someone from your embassy. Claim you speak no Japanese, even if you do, and don't sign anything you can't read.

To contact the Tokyo police in non-emergencies, call **3501 0110** (English service). Otherwise, *see p312* **Emergencies**.

POSTAL SERVICES

The postal system is run by **Japan Post** (www.jp-network.japanpost. jp/en). Sending a postcard overseas costs ¥70; aerograms cost ¥90; letters under 25g cost ¥90 (Asian countries), ¥110 (Europe, North America, Oceania) or ¥130 (Africa, South America). Post boxes are red; the slot on the left is for domestic mail, the one on the right is for

other mail. When writing addresses, English script is acceptable, as long as it's clearly written. Larger department stores can arrange postage if you buy major items. You can purchase stamps at convenience stores. For couriers, *see p311* **Couriers & shippers**.

Post offices

Post offices – indicated by a red-and-white sign like a letter 'T' with a line over it – are plentiful. Local post offices open from 9am to 5pm Monday to Friday, and are closed at weekends and on public holidays. Larger post offices close at 7pm on weekdays, and may open on Saturdays (usually 9am-5pm) or even Sundays. Post office ATMs accept foreign bank and credit cards.

Poste restante

Poste restante is available at the following post office; mail is held for up to 30 days. You'll need to show your passport to collect mail.

Tokyo Central Post Office
1-5-3 Yaesu, Chuo-ku, Tokyo 100-8994 (3242 7736, www. japanpost.jp/en). Tokyo station (Yamanote, Marunouchi lines), South Marunouchi exit. **Open** 9am-7pm daily.

RELIGION

For information on Japan's two major religions, Shinto and Buddhism, and on visiting religious sites, *see p66* **Gotta Have Faith**.

SAFETY & SECURITY

Japan is one of the safest countries for foreign visitors. Theft is still amazingly rare, so it's not unusual to wander around with the equivalent of hundreds of pounds on you without giving it a second thought. Of course, crime does occur from time to time, and it's best to take the usual precautions to keep money and valuables safe.

There are certain areas of the city, such as Roppongi or Shinjuku's Kabuki-cho, as well as airports and crowded trains, where you should be particularly wary.

SMOKING

Around 40 per cent of the adult population in Japan smokes, more than in any other industrialised nation, and cigarettes are relatively cheap, at around ¥300 per packet

(though this is due to increase in late 2010). Cigarette vending machines are common, but require a 'Taspo' electronic ID card. Cigarettes are also sold in most convenience stores. Smoking is common in restaurants and cafés, although a growing number of venues have started to offer no-smoking areas; very few restaurants are entirely smoke-free. Chiyoda-ku, Shinagawa-ku and Ota-ku have all banned smoking on the streets, and other wards look likely to follow suit. Smoking is banned on the platforms of all private train lines in Tokyo, although JR station platforms still have smoking areas.

TELEPHONES

The virtual monopoly enjoyed by **NTT** (Nippon Telegraph & Telephone) on domestic telephone services was broken in 2001 with the introduction of the Myline system, which allows customers to choose phone-service providers for local and long-distance calls.

Repair Service *113*.
Moving & Relocating *116*.

Dialling & codes

The country code for Japan is 81. The area code for Tokyo is 03. Throughout this guide, we have omitted the 03 from the beginning of Tokyo telephone numbers, as you don't need to dial it when calling from within the city. If you're phoning from outside the city, you need to use the area code. If you're phoning from outside Japan, dial the international access code plus 81 plus 3, followed by the main eight-digit number.

Numbers that start with 0120 are freephone (receiver-paid or toll-free).

International calls

Different companies provide long-distance call services, and charge roughly the same rates. Dial 001 (KDDI), 0033 (NTT Communications) or 0061 (Softbank Telecom), followed by your country code, area code (minus any initial zero) and the phone number. The cheapest time to call is 11pm-8am, when an off-peak discount of 40 per cent applies.

To use a public phone you need to buy a prepaid card or have a lot of change (some old phones refuse all prepaid cards). Find a booth with 'ISDN' or 'International' on the side – usually a green or grey phone. Blue 'credit phones' allow you to make calls using your credit card. Instructions should be given in English as well as Japanese.

If you set up the 'home country direct' service before leaving home, you can dial from most public phones and charge your home bill.

Australia 61
Canada 1
New Zealand 64
Republic of Ireland 353
South Africa 27
UK 44
USA 1

Public phones

NTT still controls nearly all public phones in Tokyo. These are widely available, found in all stations, department stores and on the street, but different varieties will keep most visitors concentrating.

Green phones take flexible phone cards and ¥10 and ¥100 coins, but don't always allow international calls; grey phones are the same, but usually allow international calls; grey and orange phones only take IC cards (snap off the corner before use) and coins, but you can always make international calls; the blue credit phones require a credit card to make international calls and are hard to find. The old pink phones, sometimes the only option even in touristy towns, only take ¥10 coins and cannot make international calls.

Domestic calls cost ¥10 for the first three minutes and ¥10 for every subsequent minute.

Prepaid phone cards

Before the advent of mobile phones, everyone used these cards in the ubiquitous green phones, and they are still useful if you're not getting a mobile. Several kinds of international phone card can be bought in Tokyo, and you can often find promotions in free English magazines such as *Metropolis*.

KDDI (0077 7111, www.kddi.com/ english) produces a 'Super World' prepaid card for international phone calls, sold at most major convenience stores. They come in five values (¥500, ¥1,000, ¥3,000, ¥5,000 and ¥7,000) and can be used with any push-button phone.

NTT East (0120 364 463, www. ntt-east.co.jp/ptd_e) produces two cards, one mainly for the domestic market, the other – an IC card – for both national and international calls. Both cards cost ¥1,000 and are available from vending machines in some phone boxes and convenience stores.

Mobile phones

While it's possible to take a Japanese mobile phone abroad and use it, it's not as simple the other way around. There are three major mobile phone networks in Japan – the biggest, **DoCoMo** (0120 005 250, www.nttdocomo.com; from NTT), plus **Softbank** (0088 21 2000 (press '8' for English), http://mb.softbank.jp.mb) and **Au** (0077 7111, www.au.kddi.com). They all use technologies that are incompatible with each other and with foreign phones.

Residents can buy a phone on a long-term contract, but visitors will have to either buy a prepaid phone or rent one. For both, you'll need to produce your address while staying in Japan (a hotel will be fine). Check in advance whether your phone has bilingual menus and voicemail.

You can purchase a phone for ¥5,000 to ¥10,000 and a prepaid card for ¥3,000 or ¥5,000 from any phone or electronics store. You will need to bring your passport. Smart hotels will often rent phones to guests, or you can do it yourself at a rental outlet or at Narita Airport.

DoCoMo Shop *Shin-Otemachi Bldg 1F, 2-2-21 Otemachi (0120 680 100 freephone, www.mobile rental.jp). Tokyo station (Yamanote, Marunouchi lines), North exit.* **Open** 10am-7pm Mon-Fri; 11am-7pm Sat. **Rates** start at ¥10,500/wk plus ¥60/min for domestic calls.
SoftBank Global Rental *3560 7730, www.softbank-rental.jp.* **Rates** start at ¥250/day, plus ¥105/min for domestic calls, plus insurance.
Has counters (open 7am-9pm daily) in the departure and arrival halls of terminals 1 and 2 at Narita.

Telephone directories

Unless you're fluent, using a local phonebook is out of the question. NTT has an English-language version at http://english.itp.ne.jp.

Useful numbers

Domestic operator **106**; domestic directory enquiries **104**; international directory enquiries **0051**. These numbers are non-English-speaking. The following numbers are for information and maintenance for land lines:

Softbank Telecom *0088 41, http://tm.softbank.jp/english.*
KDDI Information service *0057, www.001.kddi.com/en.*
NTT Communications *0120 506 506, http://506506.ntt.com/english.* Wait for information in English.

TIME

Japan is nine hours ahead of Greenwich Mean Time (GMT). Daylight Saving Time is not used.

TIPPING

Tipping is not expected at all in Japan and people will often be embarrassed if you try. If you leave money at a restaurant, for example, a member of staff may try to return it. At smart establishments, a service charge is often included.

TOILETS

Public toilets can be found in and around most stations.

Some public toilets have no toilet paper, particularly those inside train stations. Buy it from machines or take it (for free) from the marketers handing out tissues printed with advertising on the street.

THE LOCAL CLIMATE

	High (°C/°F)	Rainfall (mm/in)	Sunshine (hrs per day)
Jan	6 / 43	50 / 2.0	6.0
Feb	7 / 45	60 / 2.4	5.7
Mar	9 / 48	100 / 3.9	5.1
Apr	14 / 57	130 / 5.1	5.5
May	18 / 64	135 / 5.3	5.8
June	21 / 70	165 / 6.5	4.0
July	26 / 79	160 / 6.3	4.7
Aug	28 / 82	155 / 6.1	5.7
Sept	23 / 73	200 / 7.9	3.8
Oct	18 / 64	165 / 6.5	4.2
Nov	13 / 55	90 / 3.5	4.7
Dec	7 / 45	40 / 1.6	5.5

DIRECTORY

Western-style toilets are the norm in large shops. In some women's toilets there may be a small box with a button: pushing it produces the sound of flushing. Many Japanese women flush the toilet to cover the sounds they make, so the fake flush was designed to save water.

If you're staying in a Japanese home or good hotel, you may find that your toilet looks like the command seat on the Starship *Enterprise*. Controls operate heating, in-built bidet and sometimes a drying function.

TOURIST INFORMATION

The **Japan National Tourist Organisation (JNTO)** has various offices abroad, plus a **Tourist Information Centre** (TIC) next to Yurakucho station. Its website, **www.jnto.go.jp**, is packed with useful info.

There's also the **Tokyo Tourist Information Centre**, run by the Tokyo Metropolitan Government in its HQ building in Shinjuku.

JNTO *Tokyo Kotsu Kaikan 10F, 2-10-1 Yurakucho, Chiyoda-ku (3201 3331). Yurakucho station (Yamanote line), Kyobashi exit; (Yurakucho line), exit A8.* **Open** 9am-5pm daily.
Friendly, multilingual staff and a wealth of information are on offer here: there are maps, event guides, books on Japanese customs, even NTT English phonebooks, plus a useful budget hotel booking service via the Welcome Inn Reservation Centre. There's nothing on the outside of the building to indicate the tourist office is here – just take the lift to the tenth floor.
Other locations Arrival floor, Terminal 1, Narita Airport (0476 30 3383); Arrival floor, Terminal 2, Narita Airport (0476 34 6251). Open 8am-8pm daily.
Tokyo Tourist Information Centre *Tokyo Metropolitan Government Bldg No.1 1F, 2-8-1 Nishi-Shinjuku, Shinjuku-ku (5321 3077, www.tourism.metro.tokyo.jp). Tochomae station (Oedo line), exit 4.* **Open** 9.30am-6.30pm daily.
If you're visiting the observation deck in the Tokyo Metropolitan Government Building, pop into this ground-floor office.
Other locations 1-60 Ueno-Koen, Taito-ku (3836 3471). In front of the Keisei Ueno station ticket gate 60.
JNTO (UK) *5th Floor, 12/13 Nicholas Lane, London EC4N 7BN (020 7398 5670, www.seejapan. co.uk).* **Open** 9.30am-5.30pm daily.

Contact JNTO for free maps, guides and brochures – but not hotel bookings. Check the website for details of other overseas offices.
Japan Travel Phone *3201 3331.* **Open** 9am-5pm daily.
A free nationwide service for those who are in need of English-language assistance and travel information on places outside Tokyo and Kyoto.
Odakyu Sightseeing Service Centre *Ground-floor concourse, Shinjuku station (5321 7887).* **Open** 8am-6pm daily.
Staff speak English.

VISAS & IMMIGRATION

Japan has general visa-exemption arrangements with the UK, the USA, Canada and the Republic of Ireland, whose citizens may stay in Japan for up to 90 days. Japan also has working holiday visa arrangements with Australia, Canada, New Zealand and the UK for people aged 18 to 30. For information, go to the **Ministry of Foreign Affairs** (www.mofa.go.jp/j_info/visit/visa).

It's illegal to work in Japan without a visa. A 'short-term-stay' tourist visa is good for those not intending to work. Otherwise, your company has to sponsor you for a work visa. You generally must then go abroad to make the application (South Korea is the cheapest option). If you plan to stay in Japan for more than 90 days, you need an Alien Registration Card.

Immigration Information Centre *Tokyo Regional Immigration Bureau, 5-5-30 Konan, Minato-ku (5796 7112, www.moj.go.jp/ ENGLISH/information/iic-01.html). Shinagawa station (Yamanote line), east exit then bus (follow signs).* **Open** 9am-noon, 1-4pm Mon-Fri.

WEIGHTS & MEASURES

Japan uses the metric system – although some room sizes are measured by how many tatami (straw mats) they can hold.

WHEN TO GO

Spring begins with winds and cherry-blossom viewing. The rainy season for Honshu (the main island) begins in June. This is followed by the hot, humid days of summer. Autumn sees the changing of the leaves, while winter brings clear skies, cold days and the occasional snowstorm. Temperatures range from around 3°C (37°F) in January to 35°C (95°F) in July/August.

Summer in Tokyo can be unbearable for those not used to humidity. Carry a fan, some water and a wet cotton cloth with you. Fans are often handed out in the street for advertising campaigns. Spring (March to May) and autumn (September to November) are the nicest times to visit Tokyo.

The two big holiday periods, when much of Tokyo shuts down, are **Golden Week** (29 April-5 May) and the **New Year** (28 Dec-4 Jan).

For annual festivals in Tokyo, *see pp220-226* **Calendar**.

Public holidays

Japan has 14 public holidays. Holidays falling on a Sunday shift to Monday, but Saturday remains an official workday.

New Year's Day 1 Jan
Coming of Age Day 2nd Mon in Jan
National Foundation Day 11 Feb
Vernal Equinox Day around 21 Mar
Showa Day 29 Apr
Constitution Day 3 May
Greenery Day 4 May
Children's Day 5 May
Marine Day 3rd Mon in July
Respect for the Aged Day 3rd Mon in Sept
Autumnal Equinox Day around 23 Sept
Sports Day 2nd Mon in Oct
Culture Day 3 Nov
Labour Thanksgiving Day 23 Nov
Emperor's Birthday 23 Dec

WOMEN

The crime rate in Japan is very low compared to that in many countries.

Women should exercise standard precautions, but the risk of rape or assault is not high, and, in general, women can ride the subways at night or wander the streets with little concern. A lone woman might find she's the subject of harassment by staggering, drunken salarymen, but they are rarely serious; ignoring them generally does the trick.

This said, Tokyo is not totally immune from urban dangers. You should certainly not let fear spoil your holiday, but do exercise caution at night, particularly in busy nightlife areas such as Roppongi and Shinjuku's Kabuki-cho.

A less serious, but still nasty, type of assault occurs on packed rush-hour trains, where women are sometimes rubbed against, groped (or worse). Many Japanese women ignore the offence, hesitant to draw attention to themselves, but shouting in English can be effective.

DIRECTORY

Further Reference

BOOKS

Fiction & literature

Kobe Abe
The Woman in the Dunes
Weird classic about a lost
village of sand.
Alfred Birnbaum (ed)
Monkey Brain Sushi
Decent selection of 'younger'
Japanese writers.
Steve Erickson
The Sea Came in at Midnight
American novel set partly
in a Tokyo 'memory hotel'.
Yasuwari Kawabata
Snow Country
Japan's first Nobel Prize-winner
for literature.
Yukio Mishima
Confessions of a Mask & others
Still Japan's most famous novelist,
decades after his suicide.
David Mitchell
Ghostwritten & Number9Dream
Ambitious novels by UK expat.
Haruki Murakami *1Q84*
Murakami's latest novel sold out
before its release in Japan, despite
its theme being kept secret.
Ryu Murakami
Coin Locker Babies & others
Hip modern novelist, unrelated
to Haruki.
Kenzoburo Oe
A Personal Matter & others
Japan's second winner
of the Nobel Prize.
Banana Yoshimoto
Kitchen & others
Modern writer who's made
a splash in the West.

Non-fiction

Isabella Bird
Unbeaten Tracks in Japan
Amazing memoirs of intrepid
Victorian explorer.
Herbert P Bix *Hirohito and
the Making of Modern Japan*
Post-war Japan.
Nicholas Bornoff
*Pink Samurai: Love, Marriage
and Sex in Contemporary Japan*
All you ever wanted to know
about the subjects.
**Ronald Cavaye, Paul Griffith
& Akihiko Senda**
The World of the Japanese Stage
All you need to know about
traditional Japanese performing arts.

John W Dower
*Embracing Defeat: Japan in
the Wake of World War II*
Account of the American-led post-
war reconstruction of Japan.
Izumi Evers & Patrick Macias
*Japanese Schoolgirl Inferno: Tokyo
Teen Fashion Subculture Handbook*
An illustrated guide to the quirkiest
teen tribes past and present.
Will Ferguson
Hokkaido Highway Blues
One man's manic mission to
hitchhike through Japan following
the progress of the cherry blossom.
Stuart Galbraith *Giant Monsters
Are Attacking Tokyo: Incredible
World of Japanese Fantasy Films*
The ultimate guide to the weird and
wacky world of the city-stomping
giants of Japanese cinema.
Paul Gravett *Manga: Sixty
Years of Japanese Comics*
Beautifully illustrated, large-format
survey of the history of the art form
that's taking over the world.
Philip Harper
The Insider's Guide to Sake
Readable introduction to Japan's
national libation.
David Kaplan & Alec Dubro
*Yakuza: Japan's Criminal
Underworld*
Inside look at the gangs who
control Japan's underworld.
**David Kaplan &
Andrew Marshall**
The Cult at The End of The World
Terrifying story of Aum
and the subway gas attacks.
Rick Kennedy
Little Adventures in Tokyo
Entertaining trips through
the offbeat side of the city.
Alex Kerr
*Dogs and Demons: Tales from
the Dark Side of Modern Japan*
Bestselling account of Japan's
self-destructive streak.
John H & Phyllis G Martin
*Tokyo: A Cultural Guide to Japan's
Capital City*
Enjoyable ramble through Tokyo
with two amiable authors.
Kazuko Okakura *The Book of Tea*
Tea as the answer to life, the
universe and everything. Which,
as every Japanese knows, it is.
Hirotada Ototake
No One's Perfect
True story of a boy who overcame
handicaps and prejudice. A record-
breaking bestseller.

Donald Richie
*Public People, Private People
and Tokyo: A View of the City*
Writer and long-time Japan resident
on the Japanese and their capital.
Mark Robinson *Izakaya*
A cookbook and guide.
Robb Satterwhite *What's What
in Japanese Restaurants*
An invaluable guide to navigating
the menu maze.
Mark Schilling *Encyclopedia
of Japanese Pop Culture*
From karaoke to Hello Kitty,
ramen to Doraemon.
Mark Schilling
*The Yakuza Movie Book: A Guide
to Japanese Gangster Films*
A testament to the enduring appeal
of the gangster in Japanese movies.
Jacob M Schlesinger *Shadow
Shoguns: The Rise and Fall of
Japan's Postwar Political Machine*
Pretty good, non-academic read.
Fredrick L Schodt *Dreamland
Japan: Writings on Modern Manga*
Leading Western authority on
Japan's publishing phenomenon.
Mark Schreiber *Tabloid Tokyo:
101 Tales of Sex, Crime and the
Bizarre from Japan's Wild Weeklies*
Japan laid bare through translated
magazine stories.
Edward Seidensticker *Tokyo
Rising & Low City, High City*
Very readable histories of the city.
Lora Sharnoff *Grand Sumo*
Exhaustive account, if a little
on the dry side.
Noriyuki Tajima
Tokyo: Guide to Recent Architecture
Pocket-sized guide with
outstanding pictures.
**Tadao Takemoto &
Yasuo Ohara** *The Alleged
'Nanking Massacre': Japan's
Rebuttal to China's Forged Claims*
The right-wing Japanese take on the
Imperial Army's actions in China.
Robert Twigger
Angry White Pyjamas
Scrawny Oxford poet trains
with Japanese riot police.
Gary Walters
Day Walks Near Tokyo
No surprises here: detailed routes
for walkers escaping the crowds.
Robert Whiting
*Tokyo Underworld: The Fast Life
and Times of an American
Gangster in Japan*
An enthralling story of underworld
life in the bowels of modern Japan.

Robert Whiting
You Gotta Have Wa
US baseball stars + Japan = culture clash. The template for many sports books written since.

Maps & guides

Shobunsha Tokyo Metropolitan Atlas
Negotiate those tricky addresses with confidence.
Japan As It Is
Eccentric explanations of all things Japanese.
Asahi Shinbun's Japan Almanac
The ultimate book of lists, published annually.

FILM

Akira
dir Katsuhiro Otomo (1988)
The film that started the West's *anime* craze. Freewheeling youth gangs try to stay alive in Neo-Tokyo.
Diary of a Shinjuku Thief
dir Nagisa Oshima (1968)
A picaresque trip through 1960s Tokyo with a master director.
The Eel
dir Shohei Imamura (1996)
Yakusho Koji in a bizarre tale of love in the aftermath of murder.
Fish Story
dir Yoshihiro Nakamura (2009)
Four stories in one, building to an uplifting finale.
Ghost in the Shell
dir Mamoru Oshii (1995)
Complex, animated look at a future society where computers house human minds – and vice versa.
Godzilla, King of the Monsters
dir Inoshiro Honda (1954)
The big green guy makes his debut following an atomic accident, and smashes up Ginza. Subtext: Japan recovers from the blast of Hiroshima.
House of Bamboo
dir Samuel Fuller (1955)
A gang led by an American pulls off raids in Tokyo and Yokohama.
Lost in Translation
dir Sofia Coppola (2003)
Bill Murray and Scarlett Johansson reach across the generations to form an unusual bond. Shot in and around Shinjuku and Shibuya.
**Mononoke Hime
(Princess Mononoke)**
dir Hayao Miyazaki (1997)
Record-breaking animated fable of man's butchery of the environment.
Rashomon
dir Akira Kurosawa (1951)
Influential tale of robbery from Japan's most famous filmmaker.
The Ring
dir Hideo Nakata (1998)

Chilling urban ghost story that has spawned a seemingly endless boom of psycho-horror movies.
Sakuran
dir Mika Ninagawa (2007)
Visually stunning debut feature tells of an Edo-era concubine.
Spirited Away
dir Hayao Miyazaki (2001)
Oscar-winning animated feature from the same studio as *Princess Mononoke*.
Tampopo
dir Juzo Itami (1986)
The idiosyncratic director's trawl through the Japanese obsession for food, particularly ramen noodles.
Tokyo Pop
dir Fran Rubel Kazui (1988)
Aspiring artiste can't make it in New York, so heads off to Tokyo.
Tokyo Story
dir Yasujiro Ozu (1953)
Life in the metropolis and the generation gap it produces are explored in Ozu's masterpiece.
Une avenue à Tokyo
dir Tsunekichi Shibata (1898)
One of the earliest short films showing Meiji-era life in Japan.
The Yakuza
dir Sydney Pollack (1974)
Robert Mitchum stars in writer Paul Schrader's tribute to the Japanese gangster movie.
You Only Live Twice
dir Lewis Gilbert (1967)
Connery's 007 comes to Tokyo. The New Otani Hotel doubles as the HQ of the evil Osato Corporation.

MUSIC

Denki Groove *A*
A multi-faceted band that does pop, dance music and techno.
Hajime Chitose *Konomachi*
Poppy versions of traditional local songs in her unique warble.
Ayumi Hamasaki *A Ballads*
Top-selling female vocalist in Japan.
Misia *Misia Greatest Hits*
The Japanese queen of ballads.
Quruli *The World is Mine*
One of Japan's most talented bands.
Rovo *Flage*
Heavy, progressive rock, with a pronounced jazz influence.
Sheena Ringo *Karuki Zamen Kuri no Hana*
Top female rocker.
Tokyo SKA Paradise Orchestra *A Quick Drunkard*
Innovative music bases on ska beats.
Hikaru Utada *Colors*
Japan's answer to Sade.
Yoshida Brothers *Soulful*
Two young *shamisen* players play traditional music to modern backing tracks.

WEBSITES

www.cnngo.com/tokyo
The latest trends, decent reviews and a little bit of fluff
www.debito.org
Foreigners' rights news from US-born Japanese national Arudou Debito
http://english.itp.ne.jp
NTT's English-language phonebook.
www.gnj.or.jp
GayNet Japan has classifieds, forums and support groups. Good for making short-term friendships.
www.higher-frequency.com
Comprehensive site for clubbers.
www.ima-chan.co.jp/guide
Tokyo Life Navigator is a beginner's guide to surviving Tokyo.
www.japaneseguesthouses.com
Guide to traditional *ryokan* accommodation in Tokyo and other cities, with online booking.
www.japan-guide.com
User-friendly guide to travelling and living in Japan.
www.japanprobe.com
Trends and quirky stories.
www.japantoday.com
Tabloid news about Japan.
www.jnto.go.jp
Site of the Japan National Tourist Organisation (JNTO), featuring useful travel information, tips and an online booking service.
www.jref.com
Extensive database with Japan-related links, plus tourism and culture guides, and forums.
http://nonjatta.blogspot.com
A local journalist blogs about Japanese whisky.
www.ramenadventures.com
www.ramenate.com
English-language blogs on ramen.
www.sake-world.com
A guide to Japan's national tipple by saké columnist John Gauntner.
www.samurai.fm
Tokyo's best online radio station, with local and international DJs.
www.skijapanguide.com
Guide to ski trips from Tokyo.
www.snow-mag.com
Online mag of Japan's design scene.
www.superfuture.com
Hyper-stylish site mapping out shops, bars and restaurants.
www.timeout.jp
Events and reviews from Time Out's Tokyo office.
www.tokyoartbeat.com
Comprehensive gallery listings and visitor reviews.
www.tokyo-subway.net
Interactive subway-route planner.
www.utopia-asia.com/ tipsjapn.htm
Asian gay portal site.

DIRECTORY

Vocabulary

The Japanese writing system is fiendishly complicated. Japanese uses two syllabaries (not alphabets, because the letters represent complete sounds), *hiragana* and *katakana*, in conjunction with *kanji*, characters imported from China many centuries ago. The average Japanese person will be able to read over 6,000 *kanji*. For all but the most determined visitor, learning to read before you go is out of the question. However, learning *katakana* is relatively simple and will yield quick results, since it is used mainly to spell out foreign words (many imported from English).

PRONUNCIATION

Japanese pronunciation presents few problems for native English speakers, the most difficult trick to master being the doubling of vowels or consonants.

Vowels
a as in bad
e as in bed
i as in feet
o as in long
u as in look

Long vowels
aa as in father
ee as in fair
ii as in feet, but longer
oo as in fought
uu as in chute

Consonants
Consonants in Japanese are pronounced the same as in English, but are always hard ('**g**' as in 'girl', rather than 'gyrate', for example). The only exceptions are the '**l/r**' sound, which is one sound in Japanese, and falls halfway between the English pronunciation of the two letters, and '**v**', which is pronounced as a 'b'. When consonants are doubled, they are pronounced as such: a 'tt' as in 'matte' (wait) is pronounced more like the 't' sound in 'get to' than in 'getting'.

Reading the phrases
When reading the phrases below, remember to separate the syllables. Despite the funny way it looks in English, the common name Takeshita is pronounced Ta-ke-shit-ta. Similarly, made (until)

is 'ma-de', not the English 'made', and shite (doing) is 'shi-te', rather than anything else. When a 'u' falls at the end of the word, it is barely spoken: 'desu' is closer to 'dess' than to 'de-su'.

THE BASICS

Yes/no hai/iie
Okay ookee
Please (asking for a favour) onegai shimasu
Please (offering a favour) doozo
Thank you (very much) (doomo) arigatoo
Thank you (for having me) osewa ni narimashita
Hello/hi kon nichi wa
Good morning ohayoo gozaimasu
Good afternoon kon nichi wa
Good evening kon ban wa
Goodnight oyasumi nasai
Goodbye sayoonara
How are you? ogenki desu ka?
Excuse me (getting attention) sumimasen
Excuse me (may I get past?) shitsurei shimasu
Excuse me/sorry gomen nasai
Don't mention it/never mind ki ni shinai de kudasai
It's okay daijoobu desu
My name is... watashi no namae wa… desu
What's your name? o namae wa nan desu ka?
Pleased to meet you doozo yoroshiku
Cheers! kampai!
Do you speak English? eigo o hanashi masu ka?
I don't speak (much) Japanese nihongo o (amari) hanashi masen
Could you speak more slowly? yukkuri itte kudasai?
Could you repeat that? moo ichido itte kudasai?
I understand wakari mashita
I don't understand wakari masen
Do you understand? wakari masu ka?
Where is it? doko desu ka?
When is it? itsu desu ka?
What is it? nan desu ka?

NUMBERS

● 1 ichi; 2 ni; 3 san; 4 yon;
5 go; 6 roku; 7 nana; 8 hachi;
9 kyuu; 10 juu; 11 juu-ichi;
12 juu-ni; 100 hyaku; 1,000 sen;
10,000 man; 100,000 juu-man

DAYS & TIMES

It's at …o'clock …ji desu
Excuse me, do you have the time? sumimasen, ima nan-ji desu ka?
noon/midnight shougo/mayonaka
this morning kesa
this afternoon kyoo no gogo
this evening konban
yesterday/today/tomorrow kinoo/kyoo/ashita
last week/this week/next week sen-shuu/kon-shuu/rai-shuu
the weekend shuumatsu

● **Monday** getsu-yoobi; **Tuesday** ka-yoobi; **Wednesday** sui-yoobi; **Thursday** moku-yoobi; **Friday** kin-yoobi; **Saturday** do-yoobi; **Sunday** nichi-yoobi

● **January** ichi-gatsu; **February** ni-gatsu; **March** san-gatsu; **April** shi-gatsu; **May** go-gatsu; **June** roku-gatsu; **July** shichi-gatsu; **August** hachi-gatsu; **September** ku-gatsu; **October** juu-gatsu; **November** juu-ichi-gatsu; **December** juu-ni-gatsu

EATING OUT

For specific food items, *see p174* **Menu Reader**.

bar izakaya/nomiya
canteen shokudoo
coffee shop kissaten
noodle stall ramen-ya
restaurant (smart) ryotei
May I see the menu? Menyuu onegai shimasu?
Do you have an English menu? eigo no menyuu wa arimasu ka?
I'm a vegetarian watashi wa bejitarian desu
Please can we have the bill? okanjoo onegai shimasu?

ACCOMMODATION

Do you have a room? heya wa arimasu ka?
I'd like a single/double room shinguru/daburu no heya o onegai shimasu
I'd like a room with... …tsuki no heya o onegai shimasu
a bath/shower furo/shawaa
I have a reservation yoyaku shite arimasu

DIRECTORY

Is there... in the room?
heya ni... wa arimasu ka?
air-conditioning eakon
TV/telephone terebi/denwa
We'll be staying...
...tomari masu
one night only ippaku dake
a week isshuu-kan
I don't know yet
mada wakari masen
I'd like to stay an extra night
moo ippaku sasete kudasai
How much is... ?
...ikura desu ka?
including/excluding breakfast
chooshoku komi/nuki de
Does the price include...?
kono nedan wa... komi desu ka?
sales tax (VAT) shoohi zee
breakfast/meal
chooshoku/shokuji
**Is there a reduction
for children?**
kodomo no waribiki
wa arimasu ka?
What time is breakfast served?
chooshoku wa nan-ji desu ka?
Is there room service?
ruumu saabisu wa arimasu ka?
The key to the room..., please
...goo-shitsu no kagi o kudasai
I've lost my key
kagi o nakushi mashita
Could you wake me up at...?
...ji ni okoshite kudasai?
bathtowel/blanket/pillow
basu taoru/moofu/makura
Are there any messages for me?
messeeji wa arimasu ka?
**What time do we have
to check out by?**
chekkuauto wa nan-ji
made desu ka?
Could I have my bill, please?
kaikei o onegai shimasu?
Could I have a receipt, please?
reshiito o onegai shimasu?

MONEY

dollars doru
pounds pondo
yen en
currency exchange ryoogae-jo
**I'd like to change some
pounds into yen**
pondo o en ni kaetain desu ga
**Could I have some small
change, please?**
kozeni o kudasai?

SHOPPING

pharmacy
yakkyoku/doraggu sutoaa
off-licence/liquor store saka-ya
newsstand kiosuku
department store depaato
bookshop hon-ya
supermarket suupaa

camera store kamera-ya
I'd like... ...o kudasai
Do you have...?
...wa arimasu ka?
How much is that? ikura desu ka?
Could you help me?
onegai shimasu?
Can I try this on?
kite mite mo ii desu ka?
I'm looking for...
...o sagashite imasu
larger/smaller ookii/chiisai
I'll take it sore ni shimasu
That's all, thank you
sore de zenbu desu

SIGHTSEEING

Where's the tourist office?
kankoo annai-jo wa doko desu ka?
**Do you have any
information on...?**
...no annai wa arimasu ka?
sightseeing tour kankoo tsuaa
Are there any trips to...?
...e no tsuaa wa arimasu ka?
gallery bijutsukan
hot springs onsen
mountain yama
museum hakubutsukan
palace kyuuden
park kooen
shrine jinja
temple tera
**We'd like to have
a look at the...**
...o mitain desu ga
to take photographs
shashin o toritain desu ga
to buy souvenirs
omiyage o kaitain desu ga
to use the toilets
toire ni ikitain desu ga
Can we stop here?
koko de tomare masu ka?
Could you take a photo of us?
shashin o totte kudasai
Are we allowed to take photos?
shashin o totte mo ii desu ka?

TRANSPORT

**Could you order me a taxi,
please?**
takushii o yonde kudasai?
**Where's the nearest
underground station?**
chikatetsu no eki wa doko desu ka?
**Could I have a map of the
underground?**
chikatetsu no rosenzu o kudasai?
To..., please
...made onegai shimasu
Single/return tickets
katamichi/oofuku kippu
Where can I buy a ticket?
kippu wa doko de kaemasu ka?
I'm going to... ...ni ikimasu
on my own hitori
with my family kazoku to issho

I'm with a group
guruupu de kimashita
I'm here on holiday/business
kankoo/shigoto de kimashita
How much...?
...wa ikura desu ka?
**When does the train for...
leave?**
...iki no densha wa nan-ji
ni demasu ka?
**Can you tell me when
we get to...?**
...ni tsuitara oshiete kudasai?
ticket office kippu-uriba
ticket gate kaisatsu-guchi
ticket vending machines
kenbai-ki
bus basu
train densha
bullet train shinkansen
subway chikatetsu
taxi takushii

HEALTH

**Where can I find a
hospital/dental surgery?**
byooin/hai-sha wa doko desu ka?
I need a doctor
isha ga hitsuyoo desu
**Is there a doctor/dentist
who speaks English?**
eego ga dekiru isha/ha-isha
wa imasu ka?
What are the surgery hours?
shinryoo jikan wa nan-ji desu ka?
**Could the doctor come
to see me here?**
ooshin shite kuremasu ka?
**Could I make an
appointment for...?**
...yoyaku shitain desu ga?
as soon as possible
dekirudake hayaku
It's urgent
shikyuu onegai shimasu
I'm diabetic
watashi wa toonyoobyoo desu
I'm asthmatic
watashi wa zensoku desu
I'm allergic to... ...arerugi desu
contraceptive hinin yoo piru
I feel faint memai ga shimasu
I have a fever netsu ga arimasu
I've been vomiting
modoshi mashita
I've got diarrhoea geri shitemasu
It hurts here koko ga itai desu
I have a headache
zutsuu ga shimasu
I have a sore throat
nodo ga itai desu
I have a stomach ache
onaka ga itai desu
I have a toothache
ha ga itai desu
I've lost a filling/tooth
tsumemono/ha ga toremashita
I don't want it extracted
nukanaide kudasai

SIGNS

General

左 *hidari* left

右 *migi* right

入口 *iriguchi* entrance

出口 *deguchi* exit

トイレ/お手洗い *toire/o-tearai* toilets

男/男性 *otoko/dansei* men

女/女性 *onna/jyosei* women

禁煙 *kin-en* no smoking

危険 *kiken* danger

立ち入り禁止 *tachiiri kinshi* no entry

引く/押す *hiku/osu* pull/push

遺失物取扱所 *ishitsu butsu toriatsukai jo* lost property

水泳禁止 *suiei kinshi* no swimming

飲料水 *inryoosui* drinking water

関係者以外立ち入り禁止 *kankeisha igai tachiiri kinshi* private

地下道 *chikadoo* underpass (subway)

足元注意 *ashimoto chuui* mind the step

ペンキ塗り立て *penki nuritate* wet paint

頭上注意 *zujoo chuui* mind your head

Road signs

止まれ *tomare* stop

徐行 *jokoo* slow

一方通行 *ippoo tsuukoo* one way

駐車禁止 *chuusha kinshi* no parking

高速道路 *koosoku dooro* motorway

料金 *ryookin* toll

信号 *shingoo* traffic lights

交差点 *koosaten* junction

Airport/station

案内 *an-nai* information

免税 *menzee* duty free

入国管理 *nyuukoku kanri* immigration

到着 *touchaku* arrivals

手荷物カート *tenimotsu kaato* trolleys

バス/鉄道 *basu/tetsudoo* bus/train

レンタカー *rentakaa* car rental

地下鉄 *chikatetsu* underground

Hotels/restaurants

フロント *furonto* reception

予約 *yoyaku* reservation

非常口 *hijyo guchi* emergency/fire exit

湯 *yu* hot (water)

冷 *ree* cold (water)

バー *baa* bar

Shops

営業中 *eegyoo chuu* open

閉店 *heeten* closed

階 *kai* floor

地下 *chika* basement

エレベーター *erebeetaa* lift

エスカレーター *esukareetaa* escalator

会計 *kaikee* cashier

Sightseeing

入場無料 *nyuujoo muryoo* free admission

大人/子供 小人 *otona/kodomo* adults/children

割引 (学生/高齢者) *waribiki (gakusei/koureisha)* reduction (students/senior citizens)

お土産 *o-miyage* souvenirs

手を触れないでください *te o furenai de kudasai* do not touch

撮影禁止 *satsuei kinshi* no photography

Public buildings

病院 *byooin* hospital

交番 *kouban* police box

銀行 *ginkoo* bank

郵便局 *yuubin kyoku* post office

プール *puuru* swimming pool

博物館 *hakubutsu-kan* museum

DIRECTORY

Index

Note: Page numbers
in **bold** indicate section(s)
giving key information
on a topic; *italics*
indicate photos.

A

Abe, Shinzo 28
abortion 313
accident & emergency 313
**accommodation
125-142**
the best 131
by price
budget 123, 127, 130,
133, 137, 139, 140
deluxe 125, 127, 131,
133, 135, 138
expensive 122, 126, 129,
132, 134, 136, 138, 140
moderate 123, 125,
126, 133, 134,
136, 137, 139
capsule hotels 122, **140**
long term 142
love hotels 140,
141, *249*
Minshuku 122, **140**
Ryokans 134
Adams, Will 21
ADMT Advertising
Museum Tokyo 60
Afurilampo 252
age restrictions 311
Ageha 262, **268**
Aikido 283
air, arriving by 308
Ajimoto Stadium 277
Akasaka
accommodation 131
coffee shops 187
Akasaka Detached Palace
36, **103**
Akasaka Prince Hotel 37
Akihabara 42, **75**
cafés 40
Akihito, Emperor 28
American football 276
Americans in Japan 22
Ameyoko 108, **199**
Ameyoko Market *106*, 108
Amlux Toyota Auto Salon
70, **71**
amusement parks 227
Ando, Tadao 38
Anglo-Japanese alliance
(1902) 29
Animate 70
anime 39, 41, 42
Aoyama 62-64
art galleries 239
bars 179
coffee shops 188
nightlife 262
restaurants 154

Aoyama Cemetery 63
Aoyama Round Theatre
274
Aqua City 82
aquariums 228
Arakawa Streetcar Line
49, **70**
architecture 34-38
art
festivals 223
galleries 237-242
iPhone apps 242
Art Fair Tokyo 221
Art-Link Ueno-Yanaka 223
Art Theatre Guild (ATG)
233
Asagaya 118
Asahi Building 46
Asakura Choso Museum
112, *113*
Asakusa 44-51
accommodation 122
art galleries 237
bars 176
restaurants 147
Asakusa Engei Hall
46, **275**
Asakusa Kannon temple
19, 44, **49**
Asakusa Samba Carnival
46, **223**, *274*
Asami Maki Ballet 274
Asano, Naganori 24
Ashikaga, Takauji 20
Asukayama Park 70, **71**
Athénée Français Cultural
Center 233
Athletics 276
ATMs 315
Aum Shinrikyo 118
Aussie Rules Football 281
Autumn Leaves (Koyo) 225
Awa Odori 223, *225*
awamori 181
Azabu-Japan Noryo
Festival 223
Azabu-Juban 88
nightlife 262, **264**
Noryo Festival 88, **223**
Azabu, restaurants 161

B

Bakurocho 237
Bank of Japan 36, **76**
banks 315
barbers 215
bars 176-186
gay & lesbian 243
baseball 276
season, start of the 221
Bassey, Shirley 251
Battledore Market
(Hagoita Ichi) 225
bed & breakfast
see Minshuku

beer 186
Beer Museum Ebisu 52
Benshi 232
Bentendo 106
Bic Camera 70
Black Rain 118
'black ships' **22**, 29
books 200
further reference 319
Bosaikan 70, **71**
Boshin Wars 24
boxing 281
Bridgestone Museum
of Art 74, **76**, 80
Buddhism 19, 29, 67
bullet trains 27
Bunka-Bunsei period 29
Bunka Gakuen Costume
Museum 103
Bunkamura The Museum
92, **96**
bunraku 269, *270*
bureaux de change 315
bus 309
buses 309
bushido 20
business etiquette 311
butoh 269, **274**

C

cafés *see* coffee shops
canyoning 281
capsule hotels 122, **140**
car hire 310
Caretta Shiodome 60, **197**
CEATEC Japan 223
Center Gai 91, *94*
Cerulean Tower Noh
Theatre 271
Chelfitsch 273
Cherry-Blossom Viewing
(Hanami) 220
children 227-231
babysitting & nurseries
231
cafés 227
cinema 235
equipment rental 231
fashion shops 202
halls 229
playgrounds 230
toy shops 202
Chinese New Year 220,
226
Choan-ji temple 112
Christmas Day 225
Christmas Eve 225
Chrysanthemum Festival
224
Chuo Line 114, **117**
Chushingura 24
Ciné Pathos 234
Ciné Quinto 234
Ciné Saison Shibuya 234
Ciné Switch Ginza 234

cinema *see* film
Cinema, Le 92, **233**
Cinem@rt 234
Cinema Rise *233*, 234
Cinema Square Tokyo 234
Cirque du Soleil 273
Cirque du Soleil Theatre
Tokyo 274, *275*
classical music 250
climate 317
clubs *see also* nightlife
gay & lesbian 243
coach, arriving by 308
coffee shops 187-191
brand name coffee 190
Coltrane, John 251
comedy 275
Coming of Age Day
(Seijin no Hi) 224
Communications Museum
74, **76**
Conder, Josiah 35, 76, 109
confectionary shops 210
conferences 311
consulates 312
contraception 313
conventions 311
Corbusier, Le 109
couriers 311
Crafts Gallery 36
credit cards, lost/stolen 315
cricket 281
Currency Museum 75, **76**
customs 312
cycle hire 310
cycling 281, 310

D

Daien-ji temple 112
Daikanyama 54
bars 177
nightlife 262, **263**
restaurants 148
Daimaru 74, **192**
daimyo 22
Daimyo Clock Museum
112, **113**
Daiichi Insurance Building
36
dance 273
festivals 223, 273
Dance Biennale Tokyo 273
Danjuro, Ichikaway 271
Daruma Fair 226
De De Mouse 252
Decks 82
Dejima 21
dentists 313
department stores 192
Design Festa 221
Diary of a Shinjuku Thief
100
Die Pratze Dance Festivals
273
Diet Building 36

disabled visitors 312
doctors 313
Dokan Ota 20
driving 310
drugs 312
Drum Museum 46, **49**

E
Earth Day Tokyo 221
earthquakes 71
Ebisu 52-55
  accommodation 125
  art galleries 237
  bars 176, **177**
  coffee shops 187
  nightlife 263
  restaurants 148
Ebisu Garden Cinema 234
Ebisu Garden Place 52
Edo 18, **20**, 29
Edo Castle 21, 35
Edo Era (1600-1868) 20
Edo-Shitamachi
  Traditional Crafts
  Museum 46
Edo-Tokyo Museum 49, **50**
Edo-Tokyo Open-Air
  Architecture Museum
  115, 117, **120**
Eishoji 105
EKD 252
electricity 312
electronics shops 202
embassies 312
emergencies 312
Emperor's Birthday
  (Tenno Tanjobi) 225
Emperor's Cup 277
Emperor's Cup Final 226
Ende & Bockman 36
etiquette 311
Eurospace 235

F
fashion shops 204
Festival Brasil 221
Festival of the Steel Phallus
  221
festivals 221-226
FIFA Club World Cup 225
film 232-236
  festivals 222, 224
  further reference 320
  love seats 232
  multiplexes 236
  private screenings 236
  venues 233
Fire Museum **103**, 229
Fire-Walking Ceremony
  (Hi-watari) 220
First National Bank 35
fitness *see* sport & fitness
food shops 210
Football 277, 282
47 Ronin Memorial Service
  (Ako Gishi-sai) 225
47 *ronin* vendetta
  22, **24**, 29
Fuji Kindergarten 32
Fuji Rock Festival 256
Fuji TV Building 37, 81,
  82, *82*

Fuji, Mt 286, **304**, *304*
Fujiwara family 19
Fujiwara Opera Company
  250
Furukawa Mansion 35
Futako Tamagawa 114

G
GA Gallery 66
Galaxy Theatre 274
galleries 237-242 *see also*
  museums & galleries
gay & lesbian 243-249
  bars & clubs 243
  host clubs 248
  love hotels 249
  marriage & adoption 244
  sex clubs 248
  transgender 243
Geisha no Teodori 232
Genroku period 29
Ghibli Museum 119
gift shops 211, **213**
Gins, Arakawa and
  Madeline 32
Ginza 56-61
  accommodation 125
  art galleries 237, **238**
  bars 176, **177**
  coffee shops 188
  restaurants 150
Ginza Honeybee Project 58
Ginza Théâtre Cinema 235
Glass Hall Building 74
Godzilla 29
Go-Hojo family 20
Gokoku-ji 35
Golden Gai 98, **185**
Golden Week 220
golf 277, 282
Goro-Goro Taiken Theatre
  46
Great Kanto Earthquake
  (1923) **25**, 29
Ground-Cherry Market
  (Hozuchi-ichi) 222
guided tours 310
gyms 282
Gyokushin Mitsuin temple
  114

H
Hachiko 91
hairdressers 215
Hajime, Mori 116
Hakone 286, **292-295**
Hakone Circuit, the 292
Halyu-za 235
Hamaguchi, Osachi 26
Hama-Rikyu Detached
  Garden 60, *60*
Hanae Mori Building 37
Hanayashiki Park 45, 46,
  49, **50**, 227
Hanazono Shrine 98
Haneda International
  Airport 308
Hara, Takashi 25
Harajuku *63*, **64-67**
  art galleries 239
  bars 179, **180**
  coffee shops 188

nightlife 262
  restaurants 154
Harris, Townsend 22
hat shops 208
Hatayama 29
Hato Bus 310
Hatoyama, Yukio 28, 32
Hattori Building 36
hazards, natural 315
health 313
Hearn, Lafacadio 72
Heian (Kyoto) 19, 29
Heisei Era (1989-) 28
helplines 313
Herzog and de Meuron 31
Hibiya Koen 58
Hibuya Park 79
Hijikata, Tatsumi 274
Hirohito, Emperor **25-26**,
  26, 29
Hiroo 88
Hiroshima, atomic bomb
  dropped on 27, 29
history 18-29
Hongan-ji 35, *36*
Hopkins, Michael 75
Horoshige 22
horse racing 278
horse riding 282
Horseback Archery
  (Yabusame) 221
hot springs 292-295
hotels *see* accommodation
Hoterukan 35
house & homeware shops
  216
hydroplane racing 278
Hyokeikan building 36

I
Ibuse, Masuji 118
ice hockey 278
ice skating 283
ID 314
Idemitsu Museum of Arts
  74, **78**, 80
Ieyasu 75
Ieyasu Tokugawa **20**, 21,
  21, 29, 75, 105, 300
Iidabashi Ginrei Hall 235
Ikebukuro 68-73
  accommodation 127
  art galleries 239
  nightlife 262
  restaurants 158
Ikebukuro Sports Centre
  68, **284**
immigration 318
Imperial Hotel 36
Imperial Museum 35
Imperial Palace 23, *23*, 58,
  74, *78*, 282
Imperial Palace East
  Gardens **74**, 79
Imperial Residence 30
Inokashira Nature &
  Culture Park 228
Inokashira Park 118, *119*,
  119
Institut Franco-Japonais
  235
internet 314

Inukai, Tsuyoshi 26
Iris Viewing 222
Ishihara, Shintaro 28
Isozaki, Arata 37
Ito, Chuta 35, 36
Iwanami Hall 235

J
Japan Cup 225
Japan Folk Crafts Museum
  94, **96**
Japan Open Tennis 223
Japan Railways 308
Japan Science Foundation
  Science Museum 74, **78**,
  79, 229
Japan Stationery Museum
  48, **51**
Japan Traditional Craft
  Centre 70, **212**
jazz 118, 254
jewellery shops 208
jidohanbaiki 201
Jiko-ji Temple 304
Jingu Baseball Stadium
  63, **277**
Jingu Stadium 277
Jiyu Gakuen Myonichikan
  70, **71**, 72
Jokan-ji temple 49
Jomon period 29
Jomon shell mounds 19
Joypolis 227
JR Passes 309
JR trains 308
Judo 105, 283
Jukendo 283

K
K-1 279
kabuki 22, 269, **270**
Kabuki-cho 98
Kagurazaka Die Pratze 274
Kamakura 29, 286,
  295-299
Kamikawa, Aya 243
Kaminarimon 44, **46**
Kanagawa (1854), Treaty of
  22
Kanda Festival 221, *222*
Kanei-ji 21, 105
Kannon-ji temple 111
Kano, Jigoro 105
Kansei reforms 29
Kanto 19
Kanzaburo, Nakamura 271
Kappabashi Dori 48, **199**
karate 283
Kasal Seaside Park 228
Katayama, Tokuma 36
katsuobushi 110
Kawagoe 286, **303**
Kawagoe Festival 303
K-Ballet Company 274
Kegon Falls 302, *302*
Keisei tokkyu 308
Ken, Takaseki 250
kendo 283
Kenzo, Tange 28, 250
Kichijoji 118
Kichijoji Baus Theatre 235
Kidzania 228

Kineca Omori 235
Kira, Yoshinaka 24
Kita City Asukayama
    Museum 71
Kitano, 'Beat' Takeshi 233
Kitanomaru Koen **74**, 79
Kite Museum 75, **78**
Kiyomizu Kannondo
    temple 106
Kiyosumi Complex 237
Kobudo 283
Koenji 118
Koganel Park 230
Koishikawa Korakuen 72
Koizumi, Junichiro **28**, 29
Koshiro, Matsumoto 271
Kumakaway, Tetsuya 274
Kume Art Museum 54
Kurokawa, Kisho 32, 38
Kurosawa, Akira 232
kyogen 270
Kyoto **19**, 29
Kyu Iwasaki-tei House
    & Gardens 109
Kyudo 283

L

Lake Chuzenji 301
language 314
Laos Festival 221
Laputa Asagaya 235
Last Samuri, The 108
LDP (Liberal Democratic
    Party) **27**, 29
legal help 314
lesbian *see* gay & lesbian
libraries 314
Limosine buses 308
Live in Japan 251
'Long Sleeves Fire' (1657)
    22, 111
lost property 314
love hotels 140, **141**, **249**

M

MacArthur, Douglas **27**, 36
Maekawa, Kunio 37
Maga Web 81, **84**
magazines 200, 314
maid cafés **40**, 41
Makuhari Messe 257
malls 197
Managa 99
Manchuria 26, 29
Mandarake *116*, 117, **212**
manga 39, **200**
Manjiro, John 72
Mark City 94, **197**
martial arts 279, 283
Marui 70
Marunouchi 25, **74-80**
    accommodation 127
    art galleries 239
    coffee shops 189
    restaurants 158
Marunouchi Building 38,
    75, 143, **197**
Masakado, Taira no 19
mascots 96
MCAS helicopter shuttle
    138
media 314

Meguro 54
Meiji, Emperor 18, **23**, 29
Meiji Jingu Grand Autumn
    Festival 224
Meiji Jingu Shrine 62, 66,
    67, 103
Meiji Jingu Spring Festival
    (Haru no Taisai) 221
Meiji Restoration **23**, 29
Meiji Shrine 35, **67**
Meiji Shrine Gardens
    63, **67**
Mejiro Teien 70, **72**
Metropolitan Police
    Department Museum
    57, **58**
Minamoto clan 19, 20
Ministry of Justice 35
Minshuku 122, **140**
Mishima, Yukio 24, 28
Mitsubishi Ichigokan
    Museum 32, **78**, 80
Mitsui Memorial Museum
    80
Mitsukoshi 57, **195**
Miyashita Nike Park 92
Miyazaki, Hayao 233
Mizuma Art Gallery
    115, **242**
mobile phones 317
money 315
Mongol invasions 20, 29
Moon Viewing (Tsukimi)
    223
Mori, Minoru 31, 85
Mori Art Museum 86, **88**,
    89, 237
motor sports 279
Mt Fuji *see* Fuji, Mt
Mukogaoka shell mound 19
Murasaki, Shikibu 19, 29
Museum of Contemporary
    Art, Tokyo (MoT) 120
Museum of Contemporary
    Sculpture 115
Museum of Emerging
    Science & Innovation
    82, **84**
Museum of Imperial
    Collections 79
Museum of Maritime
    Science 82, **84**
museums & galleries
    child friendly 229
    galleries 237-242
    by type
    advertising: ADMT
        Advertising Museum
        Tokyo 60
    animation: Ghibli
        Museum 119
    archaeology: Kita City
        Asukayama Museum
        71
    architecture: Edo-Tokyo
        Open-Air Architecture
        Museum *115*, 117, **120**
    art: Bridgestone Museum
        of Art 74, **76**, 80;
        Bunkamura The
        Museum 92, **96**; GA
        Gallery 66; Kume Art
        Museum 54; Mitsubishi

Ichigokan Museum
    32, **78**, 80; Mitsui
    Memorial Museum **80**;
    Mizuma Art Gallery
    115, **242**; Mori Art
    Museum 86, **88**, *89*,
    237; Museum of
    Contemporary Art,
    Tokyo (MoT) 120;
    National Art Center
    Tokyo 38, *38*, **88** 237;
    National Museum of
    Modern Art 74, 79, **80**;
    National Museum of
    Western Art 106, **109**;
    New Otani Museum 89;
    Nezu Museum 63;
    Okura Shukokan
    Museum of Fine Art
    90; Shoto Museum of
    Art 94, **97**; Sompo
    Japan Museum 100,
    104; Suntory Museum
    of Art 90; Tachihara
    Michizo Memorial
    Museum 113;
    Takeshisa Yumeji
    Museum of Art 113;
    Tokyo Metropolitan
    Art Museum 37; Tokyo
    Metropolitan Teien Art
    Museum 36, 54, **55**;
    Tokyo National
    Museum 36, 106, **110**;
    Ueno Royal Museum
    106, **110**; Ukiyo-e Ota
    Memorial Museum of
    Art 64, **67**; University
    Art Museum 106, **110**;
    Watari-Um Museum of
    Contemporary Art 63,
    64; Yayoi Museum of
    Art 113
art & crafts, traditional:
    Edo-Shitamachi
    Traditional Crafts
    Museum 46; Idemitsu
    Museum of Arts 74,
    78, 80; Japan Folk
    Crafts Museum 94,
    96; Toguri Museum
    of Art 94, **97**; *see also*
    Japan Traditional
    Craft Centre
beer: Beer Museum Ebisu
    52
clocks: Daimyo Clock
    Museum 112, **113**
communications:
    Communications
    Museum 74, **76**; NHK
    Broadcast Museum 89
costume: Bunka Gakuen
    Costume Museum 103
culture: Parco Museum of
    Art & Beyond 94
design: 21_21 Design
    Sight 88
drums: Drum Museum
    46, **49**
electricity: TEPCO
    Electric Energy
    Museum 94, **97**

film: National Film
    Centre 57, **58**
firefighting: Fire Museum
    103, 229
history: Edo-Tokyo
    Museum 49, **50**;
    Shitamachi Museum
    108, *108*, **110**
kites: Kite Museum
    75, **78**
maritime science:
    Museum of Maritime
    Science 82, **84**
miscellaneous: Asakura
    Choso Museum 112,
    113; Okamoto Taro
    Memorial Museum 63,
    64; Shibusawa
    Memorial Museum 71
missionaries: Zoshigaya
    Missionary Museum
    70, **72**
money: Currency
    Museum 75, **76**
photography: Tokyo
    Metropolitan Museum
    of Photography 52, **54**
paper: Paper Museum 71
parasites: Parasite
    Museum 54, **55**
police: Metropolitan
    Police Department
    Museum 57, **58**
railways: Old Shinbashi
    Station 60, **61**
science: Japan Science
    Foundation Science
    Museum 74, **78**, 79,
    229; Museum of
    Emerging Science &
    Innovation 82, **84**;
    National Science
    Museum 106, 230;
    Tokyo Metropolitan
    Waterworks Science
    Museum 82, **84**;
    Tama Rokuto
    Kagakukan 230
sculpture: Museum
    of Contemporary
    Sculpture 115
stationery: Japan
    Stationery Museum
    48, **51**
swords: Sword Museum
    103, **104**
tobacco & salt: Tobacco
    & Salt Museum 94, **97**
war: Tokyo Metropolitan
    Memorial & Tokyo
    Reconstruction
    Museum 49, **51**;
    Yushukan War-Dead
    Memorial Museum
    80

music 250-261
    classical & opera 250
    festivals 254, 256, 257
    further reference 320
    jazz 254
    rock & pop 257
music & entertainment
    shops 217

musicals 271
Myth of Tomorrow 241

N

Nabisco Cup 277
Nagasaki, atomic bomb
  dropped on 27, 29
Naginata 283
Naka-Meguro 114
Nakamise Dori 46, **200**
Nakano 117
Nakano Broadway
  42, 117, **200**
Nakano Sun Plaza Hall
  251, **258**
Nanking (1937), Rape of
  27, 29
Nantai, Mt 301, **302**
Naosuke Ii **23**, 29
Naoto Kan 29
Nara 29
Narita Express 308
Narita International
  Airport 308
National Art Center Tokyo
  32, 38, *38*, **88**, 237
National Children's Castle
  (Kokomo no Shiro)
  63, **229**, *231*
National Engei Hall 275
National Film Centre
  57, **58**, 235
'National Learning' 23
National Museum of
  Modern Art 74, 79, **80**
National Museum of
  Western Art 106, **109**
National Noh Theatre
  271, 272
National Science Museum
  106, 230
national seclusion policy
  (1639) **21**, 29
National Stadium 63, 276,
  277, 279
National Theatre 271
National Yoyogi Stadium
  257
Natsume, Soseki 111
Nature Study Institute
  & Park 55, *55*
New Meiji constitution 29
New National Theatre,
  Tokyo (NNTT) 103, **250**,
  272, 274
New National Theatre
  Ballet 274
New Otani Museum 89
New Year Congratulatory
  Visit (Ippan Sanga) 226
New Year Grand Sumo
  Tournament (Ozumo
  Hatsu Basho) 226
New Year Hakon Ekiden
  222
New Year's Day 225
newspapers 315
Nezu 111, *112*
Nezu Museum 63
Nezu Shrine 113
NHK Broadcast Museum
  89

NHK Hall 250
NHK Symphony Orchestra
  250
Ni-chome 100
nightlife 262-268
Nihon Opera Kyokai 250
Nihonbashi 21, 75, *75*
nihonshu (sake) 181
Nikko 286, **300**, *301*
Nikolai Cathedral 35, **76**
Nippon Budokan **74**, 79,
  257, 279
Nishi-Azabu 88
Nishi-Ogikubo 118
Nissan Gallery 57
Nissan Stadium 277
Nogawa Park 230
Nogi, Maresuke 32
Nogi Jinja 85, **89**
Noh theatre 269, **270**, **272**
NTT Inter Communication
  Centre 104
'nuberu bagu' 232, 233

O

Oazo 75, **197**
Obon 223
Ochanomizu 76
Ochanomizu Square
  Building 37
Oda, Nobunaga 20
Odaiba 81-84
  accommodation 131
Odaiba Seaside Park 82
Oedo Onsen Monogatari
  81, 82, **84**
office services 312
Ogikubo 118
Okamoto, Taro 241
Okamoto Taro Memorial
  Museum 63, **64**, 241
Okura Shukokan Museum
  of Fine Art 90
Ol Racecourse 278
Old Shinbashi Station
  60, **61**
Olympic Games (1964)
  27, 29
Omoide Yokocho 103
Omotesando Hills 38, 62,
  143, *197*, **197**
One Love Jamaica Festival
  221
Onin War (1467-77) 20
onsen 50, 292-295
opening hours 315
opera 250
opticians 215
Orchard Hall 92, **251**
Osamu, Tezuka 99
Oshima, Nagisa 100
Ota, Dokan 75
Ota Sekenaga 20
Otaku 39-42
Otoko Machi Map 243
Otume Road 42
Oya-Machi 206
Ozu, Yasujiro 232

P

P' Parco 70
pachinko 73

*A Page of Madness
  (Kurutta Ippeiji)* 232
Palette Town 81, 82
Panda Buss 44
Paper Museum 71
Parasite Museum 54, **55**
Parco 70, 94
Parco Museum of Art
  & Beyond 94, **96**
**parks, gardens &
  open spaces**
  Hama-Rikyu Detached
    Garden 60, *60*
  Hibiya Koen 58
  Inokashira Park 118,
    119, **119**
  Kasal Seaside Park 120
  Koganei Park 230
  Meiji Shrine Gardens
    63, **67**
  Nature Study Institute
    & Park 55, *55*
  Nogawa Park 230
  Rikugien 120
  Shinjuku Chuo Park 103
  Shinjuku Gyoen 100,
    104, 230
  Showa Kinen Park 230
  Sumida Koen 46
  Tetsugakudo Park 117
  Ueno Koen 105
  Yoyogi Park 62, 66, **68**,
    221, 230
Pasmo 309
Pearl Harbor attack (1941)
  27, 29
Pecha Kucha 177
**performing arts
  269-275**
  comedy 275
  dance & performance art
    273
  expat theatre 273
  modern drama &
    musicals 271
  traditional Japanese
    theatre 269
Perry, Commodore
  Matthew 22
pharmacies 215
photography shops 202
Plum Blossoms 226
police 315
post offices 316
postal services 316
poste restante 316
Prada 31, *33*
pride 279
Primal Scream 251
Prince Chichibu Memorial
  Stadium 279
public holidays 318
public transport 308
pubs *see* bars

R

radio 315
rail, arriving by 308
Rainbow Bridge 81
Rampo, Edogawa 68
Rapin, Henri 36
religion 316

resources A-Z 311-318
restaurants 31, **143-175**
  cuisine 144-145
  etiquette 143
  solo dining 154
  by type
  African 171
  American 165, 173
  Asian 168
  Australian 167
  bistro 155, 164
  café 167
  Cambodian 167
  Chinese 149, 156, 158,
    161, 164, 168
  crêperie 155
  French 148, 154, 155,
    156, 161, 163, 165
  Fusion 148, 150, 161, 166
  grill 147, 166, 168
  Hawaiian 173
  Indian 156, 158, 161
  International 149, 156
  Italian 159, 166, 167, 171
  Japanese: casual 151
  Japanese: confectionery
    173
  Japanese: grill
    152, 162, 173
  Japanese: Gyoza 158
  Japanese: Hotpot 147,
    159, 171
  Japanese: Izakaya 148,
    152, 153, 155, 158, 159,
    161, 165, 167, 170, 171
  Japanese: Kaiseki
    144, 165
  Japanese: Kushi-age
    144, 169
  Japanese: modern
    154, 155, 161, 162,
    163, 165, 169
  Japanese: Monjayaki 170
  Japanese: Nabemono 144
  Japanese: Oden **144**, 147
  Japanese: Okinawan 151
  Japanese: Okonomiyaki
    145, 147, 148
  Japanese: oyster bar 162
  Japanese: Ramen **144**,
    148, 154, **157**
  Japanese: Sashimi **144**,
    173
  Japanese: Shabu-Shabu
    145
  Japanese: Shojin ryori
    144, 162, 170, 171, **172**
  Japanese: Soba
    144, 159, 169
  Japanese: Sukiyaki
    145, 150, 158
  Japanese: Sushi **145**,
    153, 161, 162, 166
  Japanese: Tempura
    145, 151, 153, 167
  Japanese: Teppanyaki
    145
  Japanese: Tofu **145**,
    162, 166, 169, 170
  Japanese: Tonkatsu
    145, 154
  Japanese: Traditional
    147, 152, 170

Japanese: Udon **144**, 171
Japanese: Unagi **145**,
147, 159, 162
Japanese: Yakitori
145, 150, 158, 171
Korean 168
macrobiotic 165, 166
Mediterranean 155
Mexican 149, 155, 173
Mongolian 158
Nepalese 149
pizzeria 173
Portuguese 171
Spanish 164, 173
steak 165
tapas 150, 159, 166
Thai 153, 159, 163, 164
Tunisian 156
Turkish 156
vegetarian 149, 156, 173
Vietnamese 168
Reversible Destiny Lofts 32
Rice Bowl 276
Rikkyo University 70
Rikugien 120
Ring, The 118
Rinno-ji 300
rock & pop music 256
Rokku 46
Rokumeikan reception hall
35
Roppongi 85-90
accommodation 131
art galleries 240
bars 181
nightlife 262, **264**
restaurants 161
Roppongi Art Triangle 80
Roppongi Hills 38, 85, 143,
197, **198**
rugby 279
running 282, **283**
Russo-Japanese War
(1904-05) **25**, 29
Ryogoku Kokugikan
48, **280**
ryokan 122, **134**
Ryusen-ji temple 112

S

safety 316
Saigo, Takamori 108
St Mary's Cathedral 37
St Patrick's Day Parade
220
Saitama Stadium 2002 277
sake **181**, 211
Samurai 263
San-ai Building 57
Sangenjaya Chuo Gekijo
235
Sanja Festival 46, **222**
Sanrio 70
sarin gas attack (1995)
28, 29
Sato, Sogokeikau 38
security 316
Seibu 68, **195**
Sejima, Kazuyo 33
Sekigahara (1600), Battle of
20
Sendagi 111

Sengaku-ji Temple 24, **120**
Senso-ji *see* Asakusa
Kannon temple
Sento 51
seppuku 24
Session House 274
Seta Onsen **50**, 114
Setaya Public Theatre 275
Setsubun 226
Seve-Five-Three Festival
(Shichi Go San) 224
Shibusa Shirazu 253, *253*
Shibusa Shirazu Orchestra
254
Shibusawa Memorial
Museum 71
Shibuya 91-97
accommodation 133
art galleries 241
bars 176, **183**
coffee shops 189
nightlife 262, **265**
restaurants 165
Shibuya O-East 251, **258**
Shigenaga Edo 19
Shimizu, Kisuke 35
Shimo-Kitazawa 114, **116**
nightlife 262
Shimo-Takaido Cinema 236
Shin Marunouchi Building
75, **198**
Shinagawa Aquarium 228
Shinbashi 57, **58**
Shinbashi Embuju 271
Shin-Bungeiza 236
Shinjuku 98-104
accommodation 135
art galleries 241
bars 176, **184**
coffee shops 190
nightlife 262, **268**
restaurants 167
Shinjuku Chuo Park 103
Shinjuku Dori 98, *103*
Shinjuku Gyoen
100, **104**, 230
Shinjuku Ni-chome 243
Shinjuku Piccadilly 232
shinkansen 27
Shinkiba, nightlife 262
Shinto 66
Shiodome 31, 58
shippers 311
Shirokane 237
shitamachi 22, 32
Shitamachi Museum
108, *108*, **110**
shochu 181
shoe shops 209
Shogun shrines 300
Shonagon, Sei 19
Shonan monorail 296
Shonen Jump 99
**shops & services
192-218**
markets 199
streets 199
vending machines 201
Shorinji Kempo 283
Shoto Museum of Art
94, **97**
Showa Era (1926-89) 26
Showa Kinen Park 230

Shrines *see* temples
& shrines
Sino-Japanese War
(1894-95) 29
skiing 284
SkyBus Tokyo 310
smoking 316
snowboarding 284
Sompo Japan Museum
100, **104**
Sony Building 57, *57*, **203**
Soseki, Natsume 72
souvenir shops 211, **213**
Spa at Mandarin Oriental
Tokyo 50
spas **50**, 216
Spiral Building 37
Spirited Away 233
**sport & fitness
276-284**
active sports & fitness
281
festivals 222, 223,
225, 226
shops 218
spectator sports 276
sports centres 284
**springs, hot 50,
292-295**
stadiums 257
Starck, Philippe 37
Studio Alta 98
subways 309
Suehiro-tel 275
Suica 309
suicide 24
Suijo river buses 310
Sumida Koen 46
Sumida river 48
Sumida River Fireworks
46, **223**
Sumida Triphony Hall 251
Summer Sonic 257
Sumo 48, **270**, 283
Sunrise Tours 310
Sunshine City 68, 70,
72, 198
Sunshine 60 Building 70, **72**
Sunshine 60 Dori 70
Suntory Hall 251
Suntory Museum of Art 90
Super Dry Hall 37
superstitions 224
Sword Museum 103, **104**

T

Tachihara Michizo
Memorial Museum 113
Taika Reform 19
Taira clan 19, 20
Taisho Era (1912-26) **25**, 29
Taiyu-in Mausoleum 301
takarazuka 57, 269, **273**
Takeshita Yumeji Museum
of Art 113
Takeshita Dori 64, **200**
Takigi Noh 223
Tales of Genji 29
Tama Rokuto Kagakukan
230
Tama Zoo 229
Tamasaburo, Bando 271

Tange, Kenzo 37, 100
Tatsuno, Kingo 36
taxis 308, 310
teashops **191**, 211
Telecome Center 82
telephones 316
television 315
temples & shrines
Asakusa Kannon temple
44, **49**
Bentendo 106
Choan-ji temple 112
Daien-ji temple 112
Eishoji 105
Gyokushin Mitsuin
temple 114
Hanazono Shrine 98
Jokan-ji temple 49
Kaminarimon 46
Kanei-ji 105
Kannon-ji temple 111
Kiyomizu Kannondo
temple 106
Meiji Jingu Shrine
62, 66, **67**, 103
Nezu Shrine 113
Ryusen-ji temple 112
Sengaku-ji Temple 120
Tenno-ji temple 111
Tokokawa Inari Shrine
90
Toshogu Shrine
106, *109*, **110**
Zojo-ji Temple 90
tennis 284
Tenno-ji temple 111
TEPCO Electric Energy
Museum 94, **97**
Tetsugakudo Park 117
Tezuka, Takaharu and Yui
32
Thai Festival 221, **222**
theatre, Japanese
traditional 269
Theatre Cocoon 92, **275**
Theatre Image Forum 236
Theatre N Shibuya 236
ticket agencies 218
tipping 317
Tobacco & Salt Museum
94, **97**
Tobu 68, **195**
Tobu Spice 70
Tocho 100
Toguri Museum of Art
94, **97**
Toho Cinemas 86, 232,
235, **236**
toilets 317
Tojo, Hideki **27**, 72
Tokokawa Inari Shrine 90
Tokoto, Mitomi 263
Tokugawa shogunate
20, 21, 22, 29
Tokugawa, Ieyasu *see*
Ieyesu Tokugawa
Tokyo Anime Center 42
Tokyo Ballet 274
Tokyo Big Sight 38, 82, *84*
Tokyo Bunka Kaikan 251
Tokyo Bus Association 310
Tokyo Central Post Office
36

INDEX

Tokyo City View 86, **88**, *89*
Tokyo Comedy Store 275
Tokyo Disney Resort
120, 227
Tokyo Dome 257, 276, **277**
Tokyo Dome City 228
Tokyo Filmex 233
Tokyo Game Show 223
Tokyo International Film
Festival **224**, 233
Tokyo International Forum
37, *37*, 74, 250, **253**
Tokyo International
Lesbian & Gay Film
Festival 222
Tokyo International
Marathon 276, 283, *283*
Tokyo International
Players 273
Tokyo Jazz Festival 254
Tokyo Metro 309
Tokyo Metropolitan
Art Museum 37
Tokyo Metropolitan
Art Space 70, **253**
Tokyo Metropolitan
Children's Hall 229
Tokyo Metropolitan
Festival Hall 37
Tokyo Metropolitan
Fire Brigade Parade
(Dezome-shiki) 226
Tokyo Metropolitan
Golf Course 282
Tokyo Metropolitan
Government Building
No.1 28, 37, *100*, 102,
103, **104**
Tokyo Metropolitan
Gymnasium 37
Tokyo Metropolitan
Memorial & Tokyo
Reconstruction Museum
49, **51**
Tokyo Metropolitan
Museum of Photography
52, **54**
Tokyo Metropolitan Teien
Art Museum 36, 54, **55**
Tokyo Metropolitan
Waterworks Science
Museum 82, **84**
Tokyo Midtown 38, 85, 86,
143, 197, **198**, *198*
Tokyo Midtown Tower
31, 86, **90**
Tokyo Monorail 308
Tokyo Motorcycle Show
220, *221*
Tokyo Motor Show 224
Tokyo National Museum
36, 106, **110**
Tokyo Opera City
103, 250, **251**
Tokyo Performing Arts
Market 273
Tokyo Racecourse
277, **278**
Tokyo Sea Life Park 229
Tokyo Sky Tree 32, **38**
Tokyo Station 36, 75
Tokyo Stock Exchange
75, **80**

Tokyo Story 57, 232
Tokyo Symphony
Orchestra 250
Tollywood 236
Tora no Ana 41, **201**
Toray Pan Pacific Open
Tennis Tournament 223
Tori no Ichi Fair 224
Toshimaen **72**, 227
Toshogu, Nikko 300
Toshogu Shrine
106, *109*, **109**
Toto Tokyo Center
Showroom 100, **104**
tourist information 318
Toyotomi, Hideyoshi 20
train lines 309
Treaty of Kanagawa (1854)
29
Trim Sports Centre (Jingu
Gaien 'Jido Yuen') 230
Tripartite pact (1940) 29
Tsukiji Fish Market 57, **61**
Tsurugaoka Hachman-gu
296, *296*
24 (Niju-Yon) Kaikan 249
21_21 Design Sight 38, **88**

U
Ueno 105-110
accommodation 137
coffee shops 190
restaurants 169
Ueno Koen 105
Ueno Royal Museum
106, **110**
Ueno Zoo 106, 229
Ukiyo-e Ota Memorial
Museum of Art 64, **67**
UN University 37
Un Yamada 273
United Nations University
Centre 63, **64**
University Art Museum
106, **110**
Uplink Factory *234*, 236
Uraga 29
Urban Dock LaLaport
Toyosu 199

V
Valentine's Day 226
Vaughan, Sarah 251
Venus Fort 199
Vinoly, Rafael 37, 74, 250
visas 318
vocabulary 321-323

W
Wako 57
walks & walking 310
Old Tokyo 79
Yanaka 111
War-End Anniversary 223
Watanabe, Hitoshi 36
Watanabe, Ken 108
Watanabe, Sei 38
Watari-Um Museum of
Contemporary Art 63, **64**
Water transport 310
Waters, Thomas 35

websites 319
whisky 182
White Day 220
Womb 266, **268**
women 318
World Cup (2002) 28
World War II 27
Wright, Frank Lloyd
25, 27, 36, 72

Y
Yamato court 19
Yanaka 111-113
accommodation 137
art galleries 241
restaurants 169
Yanaka Cemetery 111
Yasukuni Shrine 79, **80**
Yayoi Museum of Art 113
Yayoi period **19**, 29
Yebisu Garden Place 199
Yokohama 286-291
Yokohama Arena 257
Yokoyama Taikan
Memorial Hall 109, **110**
Yomiuri Giants 276
Yoritomo, Minamoto 20
Yoshida, Tetsuro 36
Yoshinobu 111
Yoshiwara 22, 49
Yoshizumi, Miura 19
Yotsuya 103
Yoyogi 103
Yoyogi National Stadium
37, 66, **279**
Yoyogi Park 62, 66, **68**,
221, 230
yuba 302
Yukio, Ninagawa 116
Yushukan War-Dead
Memorial Museum **80**

Z
Zepp Tokyo 81, 251, **258**
0123 Kichijoji 229
Zojo-ji Temple 21, 35, **90**
zoos 228
Zoshigaya Cemetery 70
Zoshigaya Missionary
Museum 70, **72**

BARS INDEX
A971 181
African Bar Esogle 184
Agave 181
Albatross 184, *184*
Albatross G 185
Bar High Five 177
Bauhaus 181
Bello Visto 183
Bobby's Bar 180
Buri 177
Cask 181
Cavern Club 182
Chandelier Bar/Red Bar 184
Combine 186
Dagashi 177
Dalmasu Sake Bar 176
Dubliners 70, **185**
Harajuku Taproom 179,
180

Heaven's Door 116, **186**
Hibiki 179
Kamiya Bar 46, **176**, *177*
King Rum 180
Kissa Ginza 177
L Garden 183
La Jetée 185
Lion Beer Hall 179
Mado Lounge 183
Malt Bar Whisky Voice 81
Mandarin Bar 180
Meninas, Las 118, **186**
Mother 186
Office 179
Peter 179
Pink Cow 184
Popeye 49, **186**
Quons 179
Rockfish 179
S University of Tokyo 186
Shirokuma 184
Shot Bar Shadow 185
Sign 180
Super-deluxe 177, **183**,
183
These 183
Tokyo Sports Café 183
Two Rooms 180
What the Dickens 52, **177**
Zoetrope 186

**COFFEE-SHOPS,
CAFES & TEASHOPS
INDEX**
A to Z Café 188
@Home Café 40
Angelus 187
Bear Pond Espresso 190
Ben's Café *188*, 190
Benisca 188
Bon 190
Café de L'Ambre 188
Café Bach 190
Café Fontana 188
Café Fouquet 188
Café Mai:lish 40
Café Paulista 188
Café Russia 119
Cha Ginza (Uogashi-
Meicha) 191, *191*
Daibo 189
Deva Deva 119
Ef 187
Harimaya café 187
Jinenjyo 112
Ki No Hana 188
Lion 189
Marunouchi Café 189
Miro 190
Mironga 189
Mononopu Café & Bar 41
Nakajima no Ochaya
(Hamarikyu Onshi Telen)
191
Saryo Tsujirl 191
Satel Hotel 190
Swallowtail 41
Tajimaya 190
Time Out Café & Diner
52, **187**
Tokyo Baby Café 227
Volontaire 189

INDEX

HOTELS INDEX

Akihabara Washington Hotel 139
ANA InterContinental Tokyo 132
Asakusa View Hotel 122
Asia Center of Japan 133
Bron Mode 141
Business Hotel S 249
Central Land Shibuya 140
Cerulean Tower Tokyu Hotel 94, **133**
Citadines Tokyo Shinjuku 136
Claska 140
Conrad Tokyo 125
Excel Hotel Tokyo 94, **134**
Four Seasons Hotel Tokyo at Chinzan-so 138
Four Seasons Hotel Tokyo at Marunouchi 74, **127**
Ginza Mercure 126
Granbell Hotel 134, *135*
Grand Hyatt Tokyo 86, **131**
Hilltop Hotel 129, *129*
Hilton Tokyo 135
Homelkan Honkan/Daimachibekkan 137
Hotel Arca Torre Roppongi 133
Hotel Avanshell 132
Hotel Bellegrande 139
Hotel Com's Ginza 126
Hotel Excellent 125
Hotel Ibis 133
Hotel Kazusaya 129
Hotel Listo 141
Hotel Monterey Hanzomon 139
Hotel New Koyo 140
Hotel New Otani Tokyo 131
Hotel Nihonbasi Salbo 130
Hotel Nuts 249
Hotel Okura Tokyo 132
Hotel Selyo Ginza **125**, 131
Hotel Unizo 134
Hotel Villa Fontaine Shlodome *125*, 126
Imperial Hotel 57, **126**
Intercontinental Tokyo Bay 138
Japan Minshuku Centre 140
Juyoh Hotel 140
Kayabacho Pearl Hotel 129
Keio Plaza Hotel 131, **136**, *136*
Kimi Ryokan *126*, 127
Mandarin Oriental Tokyo 127, *127*
Marunouchi Hotel 129, *130*
Maguro Emperor 141
Meridien Grand Pacific Tokyo, Le 131
Meridien Hotel Pacific Tokyo, Le 138
Minshuku Association of Japan 140
P&A Plaza 94, *139*, **141**
Park Hotel Tokyo **126**, 131

Park Hyatt Tokyo 98, 122, 131, **135**
Ritz-Carlton Tokyo 102, *102*, **132**, *133*
Ryokan Katsutaro 112, **137**
Ryokan Ryumelkan Honten 129
Ryokan Sawanoya 113, **137**
Ryokan Shigetsu 123
Sakura Hotel 130
Sakura Ryokan 123, *123*
Shangri-La 127
Shinjuku Kuyakusyo-Mae Capsule Hotel 140
Shinjuku Washington Hotel 136
Star Hotel Tokyo 136
Strings Hotel Tokyo 138
Sukeroku No Yado Sadachiyo 123
Takanawa Prince Hotel, New Takanawa Prince Hotel & Sakura Tower 139
Tokyo International Youth Hostel 139
Tokyo Prince Hotel Park Tower 132
Ueno First City Hotel 137
Ueno Tsukuba Hotel 137
Villa Giulia 142
Westin Tokyo 52, **125**
YMCA Asia Youth Centre 130

RESTAURANTS INDEX

A Raj 158
A16 159
Adding:blue 155
Aguri 115, **171**
Angkor Wat 167
Aroyna Tabeta 159
Artémis, L' 155
Atelier de Joël Robuchon, L' 154, **163**
Azumitel 150
Bangoko 163
Bangkok Kitchen 153
Banrekiryukodo 161
Bar de España Muy 159
Basanova 157
Beacon *164*, 166
Benoit 155
Bird Land 150
Bistrot des Arts 148
Bon **171**, *171*, 172
Botan 158
Brasserie aux Amis 161
Brasserie Paul Bocuse le Musée 163
Bretagne, La 155
Buchi 166
Buri 170
Café Eight 173
Cardenas Charcoal Grill 148
Casita, La 149
Chibo 148
China Café Eight 164
China Grill – Xenion 167

Chion Shokudo 158
Cicada 164
Coriander 165
Crayon House Hiroba 154
Créations des Narisaway, Les 143, **155**
Daigo **170**, 172
Dhaba India 161
Don Ciccio 166
Fonda de la Madrugada 155
Fukuzushi 161
Fumin 156
Garçon de la Vigne 164
Gaya 166, *169*
Ghungroo 156
Goemon 169
Gonpachi *149*, 161
Gordon Ramsay at Conrad Tokyo 154
Hannibal Deux 156
Hantel 169
Harem 156
Harmonie 164
Hatsuogawa 147
Higashiyama 171
Hyakunincho Yataimura 168
Ieyasu Hon-jin 158
Ikebukuro Gyoza Stadium 158
Ikenohata Yabu Soba 169
Inakaya 154, **162**
Ippudo 148
Isegen 158
Itosho **162**, 172
Izumo Soba Honke 159
J's Kitchen 165
Jidaiya 170
Jinroku 158
Junkadelic 173
Kagaya 151
Kaikatel 156
Kaikaya 165
Kanda Yabu Soba 159
Kandagawa Honten 159
Kanetanaka-so 165
Komagata Dojo 147
Kondo 151
Kookaï 148
Kunbila 149
Kurkku Kitchen 156
Kururi 157
Kyushu Jangara Ramen 154
Lauburu 156
Legato 164
Little Okinawa 151
Lohotol 149
Maimon 162
Makani & Lanai 173
Malsen 154
Manpuku 157
Manuel Churrascaria 171
Matsuya 168
Meat Shop Sato 150
Mugitoro 147
Nagi 157
Natural Harmony Angolo 154
Negiya Heikichi 165
New York Grill 168
Nezu Club 169

Nihonryori Ryugin *153*, 162
Ninja 170
Ninniku-ya 149
Nodaiwa 162
Oak Door 165
Ohmatsuya 152
Oshima 152
Osteria La Luna Rossa 173
Otafuku 147
Ozasa 150
Pierre Gagnaire Tokyo *163*, 165
Pintokona 162
Pure Café 156
Respekt Café 167
Restaurant-I 154
Robata 152
Roti 165
Ryugin 143, **162**
Saisons, Les 154
Sakura Sakura 170
Sanko-in **171**, 172
Sasanoyuki 170
Seigetsu 170
Seirinkan 31, 115, **173**
Shilingol 158
Shin-Hinomoto 152
Shisen Hanten 161
Shunju Tsugihagi 152
Sometaro 147
Soranoniwa 166
Stefano 171
Sushi 151
Sushi Bun 153
Sushi no Midori 153
Sushi Ouchi 166
T 162
Tableaux 150
Tachimichiya 148
Taillevent Robuchon 52
Takara 159
Tama 155
Tamahide **151**, 171
Tapas Molecular Bar 154, **161**
Ten-ichi 153
Tetsu 157
Thien Phuoc 168
Tio Danjo 150
Toaun 119
Tokachiya 153
Torigoya 115
Torijaya 171
Tribes 171
Tsunahachi 167
TY Harbor Brewery 173
Ukai Tofuya *160*, 162
Ukai Toriyama 171
Underground Mr Zoogunzoo 167
Uogashi Nippon-Ichi 166
Vin Chou 147
Yamada Chikara 143, **163**
Yangiya **151**, 173
Yoshiba 48, **147**
Yozakura Bijin 158
Yukun-tel 167
Zakuro 112

Maps

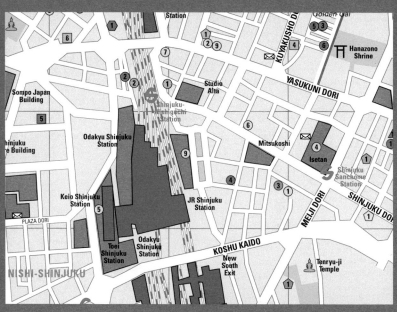

Place of interest	▨
Park	▨
Hospital/university	▨
Post office	⊠
Temple	⛩
Shrine	开
Railway station	▨
Subway station	⑤
District . . . . **GINZA**
Ward . . . . **SHIBUYA-KU**
Hotel	▨
Sightseeing	▨
Restaurant	●
Bar	●
Coffee shop	○
Shops & services	○
Children	⬠

Regional Maps   **332**
Japan   332
Trips Out of Town   333

Transport Maps   **334**
Tokyo Subway   334
Yamanote Line
   Connections   336

Street Maps
*See individual chapters in the
Sights section. These maps are
indexed on the Central Tokyo
overview map on pp12-13.*

Clubs	⬠
Film	⬠
Galleries	⬠
Gay & Lesbian	▲
Music	⬠
Performing Arts	⬠
Sport	⬡

Japan

Wakkanai

Abashiri

Asahikawa

Hokkaido

Kushiro

Otaru   Sapporo   Obihiro

Muroran

Hakodate

Aomori

Hachinohe

Hirosaki

Miyako

Akita   Kamaishi

Sakata

Yamagata   Sendai

Niigata   Fukushima

Koriyama

Aizuwakamatsu

Nagaoka

Utsunomiya   Mito

Toyama   Maebashi

TOKYO   Choshi

Kanazawa   **JAPAN**

Yokohama

Honshu   Kamakura

See p333

Oki-Shoto

Nagoya

Matsue   Kyoto

Toyohashi

Okayama   Kobe   Osaka   Hamamatsu

Takamatsu

Hiroshima   Wakayama

Kure   Tokushima

Shimonoseki   Matsuyama   Kochi

SOUTH KOREA

Kitakyushu   *Shikoku*

Korea Strait

Fukuoka

Sasebo   Omuta

Kumamoto

Nagasaki

Kyushu

Miyazaki

Kagoshima

SEA OF JAPAN

PACIFIC OCEAN

0   300 km

0   150 miles

© Copyright Time Out Group 2010

Osumi-shoto

Nikko
(p300)
Imaichi
Kanuma
Oya-machi
(p306)
Moko
Shibukawa
Kiryu
Tochigi
Takasaki
Maebashi
Ashikaga
Mito
Isesaki
Ota
Shimodate
Fujioka
Tatebayashi
Oyama
Ishioka
Kumagaya
Kago
Chichibu
Ageo
Kasukabe
Tsukuba
Lake
Kasumigaura
Kawagoe
(p303)
Omiya
Nado
Sarawa
Sayama
Saitama
Abiko
Tachikawa
Kawaguchi
Sakura
Ome
See pp12-13
Funabashi
Narita
Airport
Hachioji
TOKYO
Yotsukaido
Otsuki
Mt Takao
Chiba
Sagamihara
Tokyo
Bay
Ichihara
Atsugi
Kawasaki
Mt Fuji
(p304)
Hadano
Chigasaki
Yokohama
(p286)
Mobara
Gotemba
Fujisawa
Kisarazu
jinomiya
Kamakura
(p295)
Hakone
(p292)
Odawara
Yokosuka
Boso
Peninsula
ji
Mishima
Numazu
Sagami Bay
Ito
Tateyama
Izu
Peninsula
Oshima
Island
PACIFIC OCEAN
Shimoda
Izu
Islands

0   40 km

0   20 miles

© Copyright Time Out Group 2010

Trips Out of Town

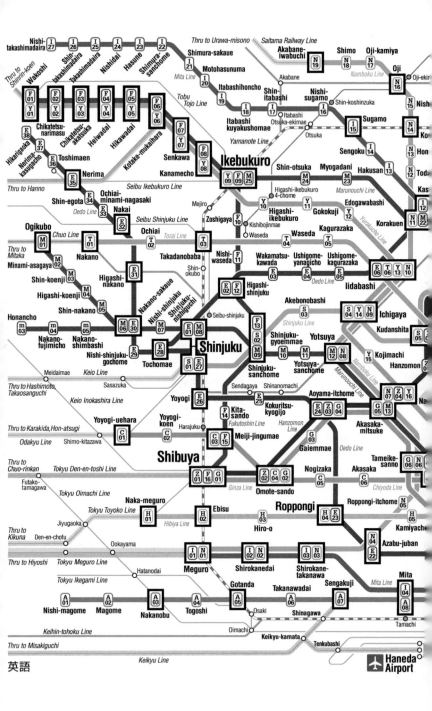

英語

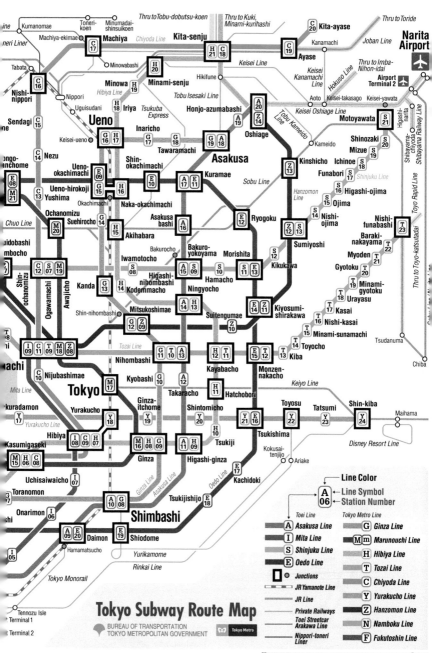

Tokyo Subway Route Map

BUREAU OF TRANSPORTATION
TOKYO METROPOLITAN GOVERNMENT

Line Color

A 06 — Line Symbol / Station Number

Toei Line	Tokyo Metro Line
A Asakusa Line	G Ginza Line
I Mita Line	M m Marunouchi Line
S Shinjuku Line	H Hibiya Line
E Oedo Line	T Tozai Line
☐ ● Junctions	C Chiyoda Line
JR Yamanote Line	Y Yurakucho Line
JR Line	Z Hanzomon Line
Private Railways	N Namboku Line
Toei Streetcar Arakawa Line	F Fukutoshin Line
Nippori-toneri Liner	

M BUREAU OF TRANSPORTATION TOKYO METROPOLITAN GOVERNMENT   Tokyo Metro Co. Ltd. © 2008.6

Yamanote Line Connections

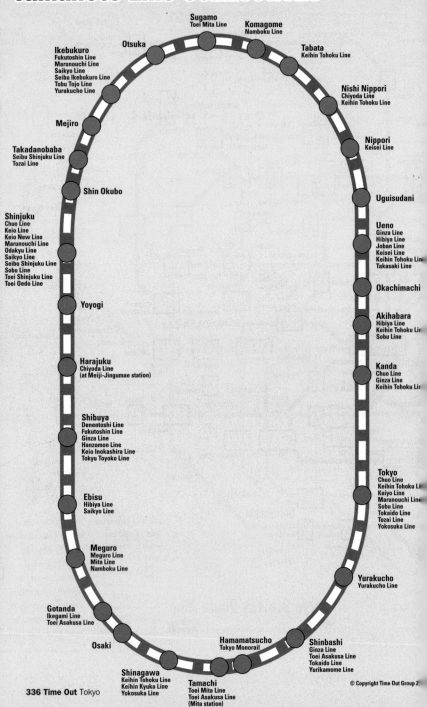

Sugamo
Toei Mita Line

Komagome
Namboku Line

Otsuka

Tabata
Keihin Tohoku Line

Ikebukuro
Fukutoshin Line
Marunouchi Line
Saikyo Line
Seibu Ikebukuro Line
Tobu Tojo Line
Yurakucho Line

Nishi Nippori
Chiyoda Line
Keihin Tohoku Line

Mejiro

Nippori
Keisei Line

Takadanobaba
Seibu Shinjuku Line
Tozai Line

Uguisudani

Shin Okubo

Ueno
Ginza Line
Hibiya Line
Joban Line
Keisei Line
Keihin Tohoku Line
Takasaki Line

Shinjuku
Chuo Line
Keio Line
Keio New Line
Marunouchi Line
Odakyu Line
Saikyo Line
Seibu Shinjuku Line
Sobu Line
Toei Shinjuku Line
Toei Oedo Line

Okachimachi

Yoyogi

Akihabara
Hibiya Line
Keihin Tohoku Line
Sobu Line

Harajuku
Chiyoda Line
(at Meiji-Jingumae station)

Kanda
Chuo Line
Ginza Line
Keihin Tohoku Line

Shibuya
Denentoshi Line
Fukutoshin Line
Ginza Line
Hanzomon Line
Keio Inokashira Line
Tokyu Toyoko Line

Tokyo
Chuo Line
Keihin Tohoku Line
Keiyo Line
Marunouchi Line
Sobu Line
Tokaido Line
Tozai Line
Yokosuka Line

Ebisu
Hibiya Line
Saikyo Line

Meguro
Meguro Line
Mita Line
Namboku Line

Yurakucho
Yurakucho Line

Gotanda
Ikegami Line
Toei Asakusa Line

Osaki

Hamamatsucho
Tokyo Monorail

Shinbashi
Ginza Line
Toei Asakusa Line
Tokaido Line
Yurikamome Line

Shinagawa
Keihin Tohoku Line
Keihin Kyuko Line
Yokosuka Line

Tamachi
Toei Mita Line
Toei Asakusa Line
(Mita station)

© Copyright Time Out Group 2